FROM CONDITIONING TO
CONSCIOUS RECOLLECTION

OXFORD PSYCHOLOGY SERIES

Editors

FROM CONDITIONING TO CONSCIOUS RECOLLECTION

Memory Systems of the Brain

Howard Eichenbaum

Neal J. Cohen

OXFORD
UNIVERSITY PRESS

OXFORD
UNIVERSITY PRESS

Oxford   New York
Auckland   Bangkok   Buenos Aires   Cape Town   Chennai
Dar es Salaam   Delhi   Hong Kong   Istanbul   Karachi   Kolkata
Kuala Lumpur   Madrid   Melbourne   Mexico City   Mumbai   Nairobi
São Paulo   Shanghai   Taipei   Tokyo   Toronto

Copyright © 2001 by Oxford University Press

Published by Oxford University Press, Inc.
198 Madison Avenue, New York, New York 10016

www.oup.com

First issued as an Oxford University Press paperback, 2004

Oxford is a registered trademark of Oxford University Press

Library of Congress Cataloging-in-Publication Data
Eichenbaum, Howard.
From conditioning to conscious recollection: memory systems of the brain /
Howard Eichenbaum, Neal J. Cohen.
p. cm. — (Oxford psychology series ; no. 35)
Includes bibliographical references and index.
ISBN 0-19-508590-6; 0-19-517804-1 (pbk.)
1. Memory.   2. Cognitive neuroscience.
I. Cohen, Neal J.   II. Title.   III. Series.
QP406.E336   2000
612.8'2—dc21   00-037516

1   3   5   7   9   8   6   4   2

Printed in the United States of America
on acid-free, recycled paper

This book is dedicated to our fathers, who live on in our memories. In doing so, they remind us of why it is that we have chosen to spend so much of our lives trying to understand the mysteries of memory.

Contents

11 Dissociating Multiple Memory Systems in the Brain   371

12 Emotional Memory and Memory Modulation   394

13 Habits, Skills, and Procedural Memory   435

14 Working Memory and the Prefrontal Cortex   471

15 Multiple Memory Systems in the Brain:
       Where Do We Stand?   507

       References   515

       Index   573

Acknowledgments

We are indebted to many people for the ideas articulated in this book. The number of colleagues who have taught us, stimulated our thinking, and encouraged or challenged us over the years about our ideas is very large—too large to acknowledge fully here. Those whose work is described below are cited in the text itself. In addition, we take this opportunity to express our gratitude to a smaller, though nonetheless considerable number of people who, through various personal interactions with one or the other of the authors in the last several years, have contributed much to this latest version of our views about the memory systems of the brain.

We wish to thank our various colleagues who have in one way or another most directly challenged us during the writing of this book to think hard(er) about the complex issues in memory research, whether in agreement with our ideas or, at least as often, in taking opposing views. This set of people includes David Amaral, Jocelyn Bachevalier, Marie Banich, Randy Buckner, Jack Byrne, Larry Cahill, Tom Carew, Sue Corkin, Joel Davis, Mike Davis, Sam Deadwyler, John Disterhoft, Yadin Dudai, Norbert Fortin, Joaquin Fuster, John Gabrieli, David Gaffan, Michela Gallagher, Ann Graybiel, Kristen Harris, Michael Hasselmo, Len Jarrard, Eric Kandel, Ray Kesner, Jeff Kogan, Joe LeDoux, Chip Levy, John Lisman, Earl Miller, Mort Mishkin, Morris Moscovitch, Richard Morris, Bob Muller, Betsey Murray, Lynn Nadel, John O'Keefe, Steve Petersen, Peter Rapp, Dan Schacter, Geoff Schoenbaum, Matt Shapiro, Alcino Silva, Larry Squire, Chantal Stern, Wendy Suzuki, Endel Tulving, Norm White, and Stuart Zola. Special thanks are due to Jim McGaugh and Matt Shapiro, who read parts of the book, "test drove" a preliminary version in their courses, and offered many very helpful suggestions and comments.

We wish also to thank the very substantive contributions of many talented people who have passed through one or another of our laboratories during the past few years. They have been subjected to our ideas (and vice versa) on a daily basis and have helped to shape our presentation of them in this book and in various papers; they have also been the prime movers of much research reported in this book. They include, from HBE's lab, Anna Allen, Pablo Alvarez, Joshua Berke, Michael Bunsey, Rebecca Burwell, Yoon Cho, Paul Dudchencko, Jeff Dusek, James Goebel, Megan Libby, Paul Lipton, Sean Montgomery, Aras Petrulis, Seth Ramus, Jonathan Robitsek, Heikki Tanila, Emma Wood; and from NJC's lab, Rob Althoff, Russ Poldrack, Jennifer Ryan (who also doubled as consulting personal terrorist [trainer]), Scott Selco, and Tracey Wszalek.

Our gratitude also goes to Anna Allen, Michelle Barberra, Linda May, and Sean Montgomery, who provided critical assistance with technical aspects of the book production.

Finally, our everlasting gratitude to our wives, Karen and Maureen, for tolerating another of our monstrously time-consuming writing collaborations.

The jacket illustration provides a schematic view of a horizontal section through the human brain, and indicates some of the main pathways of the memory systems discussed in the book. On the left hemisphere the declarative memory system is sketched. The main pathways involve widespread areas of the cerebral cortex, bidirectionally connected to the parahippocampal region plus surrounding hippocampus (both in orange). On the right hemisphere the highlighted areas include the prefrontal coretex (purple) that mediates working memory, the striatum (gold) and cerebellum (green) that mediate different aspects of habit and procedural memory, and the amygdala (pink) that mediates emotional memory and memory modulation. The striatum and the amygdala each receive inputs from widespread areas of the cortex, whereas the cerebellum receives a more restricted input. The amygdala sends outputs that modulate memory processing in the striatum and hippocampus.

FROM CONDITIONING TO CONSCIOUS RECOLLECTION

1

How Is Memory Organized in the Brain?

The nature and organization of memory has been a puzzle to writers, philosophers, and scientists for hundreds of years. Particularly during the last several decades it has been the subject of an enormous amount of scientific research and controversy. With the rise of modern neuroscience it became possible to address issues of memory in new ways, permitting us to look to the brain for new insights about the nature and organization of memory. A clearer picture about memory and brain function has emerged in recent years, which is revolutionizing how we think about not only the organization of memories but also the organization of higher brain functions more generally. This view is leading us away from some current and common conceptualizations of memory and the brain.

The new view emerges from two basic insights: (1) Memory is a fundamental property of the brain, and its storage is intimately tied to ongoing information processing in the brain, and (2) memory is manifested in multiple ways by multiple functionally and anatomically distinct brain systems. These two insights are at the heart of the issues that will be presented at length in this book. But before getting too far ahead of ourselves in supporting these assertions, it seems appropriate to first give some perspective from the background of prominent views on memory storage, and to try to indicate why the currently prominent views have proven limited in the understanding they offer. Then we return to our two major themes about memory.

Localization and Specification of Memory in the Brain

Two fundamental questions addressed by neuroscientific inquiries into memory concern memory localization (Can we identify memory with particular areas or

3

parts of the brain or with specific brain events?) and memory specification (How are memories encoded by the brain?). Localization would seem to be a straightforward question, capable of being answered by identifying areas of the brain critical for memory, or by identifying areas that change in some way associated with memory. Specification would also seem to be a straightforward question. To the extent that memory is mediated by lasting changes in the brain, it should be possible to characterize the nature of such *traces* of experience amidst the ongoing processing activities of the brain. But the history of research on both these problems has proven to be complicated and controversial. A crucial reason for this state of affairs, in our view, is that the question of localization, although ostensibly only about *where* memory resides in the brain, is directly complicated by the issue of *what* memory is (i.e., about how we should conceive of the traces that experience leaves in the brain).

In our view, the more basic question, underlying the issues of localization and specification, is this: Is memory made of some special "stuff"? It could be that memory is fundamentally different in some way from the substrates of the brain's ongoing processing activities so that it could be detected, wherever in the brain it is located, allowing us in principle to answer both the localization and specification questions at the same time. The view that a given memory might be represented in the brain as one or another specific molecule would be an example of this idea. The view that memories are otherwise distinguished as material *entities* that are *warehoused* in the brain, or that particular memories are handled by dedicated memory circuits, as in a digital computer, are other variants of this idea.

Or, alternatively, is memory a fundamental property of brain, made of precisely the same stuff as the rest of the brain's functional repertoire? In this view, memory should be seen as a natural outcome, and fundamental part, of the brain in operation and should reside throughout the brain. If this is fully the case, the localization and specification questions meld with investigations about the circuitry and coding mechanisms of the functional systems of the brain. These alternative views are considered in turn.

Memories Encoded as Specific Molecules

In the 1960s the notion that specific memories could be encoded in particular molecules was taken quite seriously (e.g., see treatments in John, 1967; Adam, 1971). The idea was spawned by demonstrations of "transfer" of memory through cannibalism in planaria. In these experiments "donor" worms were trained to avoid shock by turning in one direction in a T maze. Then the donors were fed to naive subjects, which subsequently showed a preference for the trained direction of the donors. Could there be a specific molecule that had been created through training in the donors? Could this molecule then successfully be incorporated into a memory representation in brains of naive animals? These intriguing findings generated numerous attempts to "transfer" memories in rats. Donor animals were trained in any of a variety of learning paradigms, including simple bar-pressing, maze-learning, or avoidance tasks. Soluble materials were extracted from their brains and injected into the brain or peritoneal space of naive animals, which were subsequently trained or tested in the same task. Many reports claimed successful memory transfer in several learning protocols.

Other experimenters failed to replicate the transfer phenomenon. The efforts included a famous report on unsuccessful attempts by 23 coauthors (Byrne et al., 1966). Numerous objections were raised about the control procedures, and about the specificity of the behavioral effects induced by the transferred material. These issues were addressed, sometimes with substantial success. But the transfer phenomenon remained inconsistent and its basis was unclear. At the end of this era of research, its pinnacle of success was achieved in the discovery and synthesis of a short peptide, named *scotophobin,* claimed to underlie the transfer of trained dark avoidance (Ungar et al., 1972). Was this the first identified memory molecule? Or was it a hormonelike substance that modulated visual sensitivity in some way that altered light-dark preference? We don't know, because this line of research ended with a combination of concerns about the reliability of the transfer phenomenon and the death of its most avid proponent.

More important than the technical details of this controversy was that some of the most fundamental questions about the idea of memory molecules were never formally debated. How could transferred molecules find their way to the specific neural circuitry that mediated the relevant learned behavior? Why would specificity of molecules be needed when the specificity of behavior is so well accomplished through the known specificities of neural circuitry in functional pathways of the brain? How could there be enough molecules to represent the infinite variety of our possible memories? The possibility of discovering a memory molecule, more than these questions about the rationale of the approach, drove pursuits of the elusive transfer effect. But this line of research failed to find a lasting constituency and simply disappeared.

Memory as a Warehouse

Perhaps the most commonly held view about memory, one that many memory researchers share with the lay public and that is captured in various metaphors for memory, is that memory works like a *warehouse* of information. This view sees specific memories as items of knowledge warehoused in the brain. Some memory researchers think the items might be stored at different locations during successive stages of short-term and long-term storage. At nearly every conference on memory one can hear researchers talk about how a memory is "stored" in a particular brain area during one period of processing and then "transferred" to some other area at another stage.

Such a metaphor entails at least two suggestions about the nature of memory. It suggests that memory is a rather static or passive affair. Memories are items to be stored away, each in its own place according to some organizational scheme, until such time as they are needed, whereupon some search is undertaken to retrieve those items. Our *external* memories are certainly stored in this way–the information in books (and libraries), in diaries, in our appointment calendars, and on the hard drives of our computers. The view that our internal (biological) memories are also stored in this way is captured nicely in James's (1890/1918) characterization of recollection:

An object which is recollected, in the proper sense of that term, is one which has been absent from consciousness altogether, and now revives anew. It is brought back, recalled, fished up, so to speak, from a reservoir in which, with countless other objects, it lay buried and lost from view. (p. 646)

The warehouse metaphor of memory also suggests the existence of one or more brain region(s) that are dedicated to the storage of memory–the "warehouses" themselves. In the early days of brain research, efforts to characterize the role of different cortical regions led to identification of sensory and motor areas, with other portions of cortex designated *association areas,* which were thought to be the repository of memories or "ideas." Such regions were thought to be memory storage areas *rather than* (sensory or motor) processing areas.

But it turns out this is not at all how memory is organized in the brain. No one has found regions that serve as dedicated warehouse(s) of memories in the brain. Those cortical regions once thought to be set aside exclusively for accumulating new information over the course of experience are now seen as multimodality or supramodality processing areas responsible for very sophisticated processing abilities. They also seem to support particular aspects of memory storage, as we shall see, but in concert with their information-processing functions. Patients with damage to one or another of these association areas will have deficits in comprehending aspects of language or in identifying faces that were previously well learned, for example, while also being unable to learn new materials in that domain, an effect suggesting a merger of the information-processing and memory roles of these regions. Accordingly, we must conclude that memories are not items warehoused in individual, memory-dedicated brain regions, nor are memories transferred among areas.

Memory as a Switchboard

Another common metaphor for memory is the *switchboard* notion–that memory is a set of associations between neural representations interconnected by a switchboard. The switchboard metaphor became most popular in the early half of this century, when psychologists attempted to reduce memory to the fundamental mechanism of association. Earlier, physiologists had divided the cerebral cortex into sensory processing areas, identified with the posterior cortex, and motor processing areas, mainly in the anterior cortex. Pavlov had just succeeded famously in identifying a conditioned reflex, showing that a very simple kind of memory could indeed be reduced to the apparent connection between an arbitrary stimulus and a similarly arbitrary response. Combining these findings, a prevalent view was that associations were instantiated within specific circuits that connected sensory and/or motor representations in the cortex.

Guided by this view, Lashley (1929, 1950) pioneered the effort to localize the stimulus-response associations thought to underlie maze learning in rats. He surveyed the entire cerebral cortex, attempting quite directly to disconnect the relevant sensory-to-motor connections by knife cuts between posterior sensory and anterior motor cortical areas (Figure 1.1), as well as by removing portions of the cortex from virtually all areas and to a differing extent in different animals. He then trained rats on a set of maze problems that were progressively more difficult

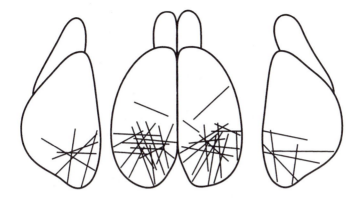

Figure 1.1. Composite diagram showing top and lateral views of the rat brain indicating long axes of lesions that separated cortical areas. None of these lesions produced a substantial effect on learning ability. (Reproduced, with permission, from Lashley, 1963; Copyright Dover Press.)

(Figure 1.2a) and compared the severity of subsequent learning deficits with the location and extent of cortical damage. In other experiments he also examined the effects on retention of the maze problems following selective damage performed after initial learning. His results were a dramatic refutation of the switchboard metaphor, as well as of the warehouse metaphor: Maze performance could not be compromised, and hence maze memories were not stored in any single location or in any particular pathway within or between sensory and motor areas. Contrary to many popularizations of his work, Lashley did not deny the functional specialization of cortical areas. But he did vehemently argue against any notion that complex memories, of the kind that would support maze performance, were stored in specific brain areas or in particular neural connections.

Rather than viewing complex memories as being localized within dedicated storage areas or in particular brain circuits, Lashley viewed memories as being diffusely distributed in the brain. He adduced support for this view from what has become the best known of his findings from his series of maze-learning studies, namely, that the severity of impairment in maze performance was closely related to the amount of cortical damage regardless of the location of the damage (Figure 1.2b).

A closely corresponding view about diffusely distributed memory storage emerged from later pioneering electrophysiological studies by John (1967, 1972) and his colleagues. In those experiments cats were trained to perform distinct approach or avoidance responses to different repetitive stimuli (different frequencies of flickering lights). John and his colleagues found specific evoked-response patterns of gross electrical potentials that were widespread in the brain and that corresponded to each of the conditioned stimuli. In addition, when the animal omitted an appropriate response or gave an inappropriate one, the form of the evoked field response followed the incipient behavior and not the stimulus evoking the neural pattern. In other experiments animals were trained on discrimination problems in which they had to make a specific response to one particular

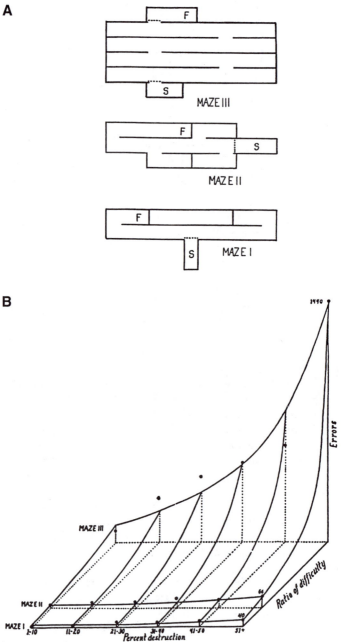

Figure 1.2. A. Schematic diagrams of "Lashley" mazes used to test learning capacity following cortical damage in rats. S = start department. F = food compartment. B. Relationships between the difficulty of learning the mazes shown in A,
the amount of cortical destruction, and errors made during learning. (Reproduced, with permission, from Lashley, 1963; Copyright Dover Press.)

stimulus and another response to a different stimulus. When a novel neutral stimulus was presented, the neural pattern evoked by that stimulus duplicated that customarily seen for either one or the other of the familiar stimuli, depending on which response the animal made (Figure 1.3).

John concluded from these findings that the evoked neural response reflected the "readout" of memory that would guide the appropriate response, rather than the processing of a specific stimulus. Moreover, these observed evoked responses were grossly similar across many brain areas, reflecting in John's view a common mode of memory processing across various functionally specialized areas. Finally, from results showing marked variability in the responses of individual cells to each stimulus, contrasting with the remarkable consistency of multiple neuron ensembles, John argued that memories are encoded as a "statistical configuration" of neural activity that coordinates activity of circuits throughout the brain to read out memories.

Taken together, the work and views of Lashley and John seriously challenged the warehouse or switchboard ideas by showing that complex memories cannot

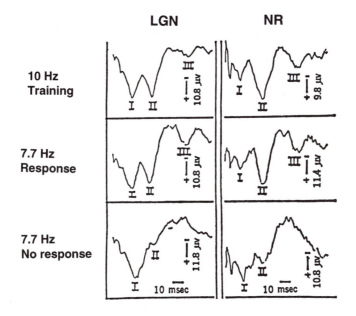

Figure 1.3. Averaged visually evoked responses recorded in the lateral geniculate nucleus (LGN) and nucleus reticularis (NR) of the cat. A 10 Hz flickering visual stimulus was used in training the animals and behavioral responses were executed on all these trials. A 7.7 Hz flickering visual stimulus was used as a probe during repeated testing for behavioral generalization; data are separated according to whether the animal exhibited the generalized behavioral response or withheld the response. (Reproduced, with permission, from John, 1972; Copyright American Association for the Advancement of Science.)

be localized within specific memory-dedicated brain areas or within a specific circuitry between discrete brain areas. Rather, they viewed memory as diffuse yet coordinated and organized by an undesignated spatial and temporal synchronization. Current research, to be presented in the subsequent chapters of this text, permits us to confirm the fundamental conclusion that memory is distributed broadly and permits us to go well beyond those initial views to offer a concrete framework for understanding the coordination and organization of distributed memory.

Memory as a Cellular, Synaptic, or Molecular Event

If memory storage cannot be localized to specific memory-dedicated regions of the brain, can memory be identified with particular brain *events?* In part because of the failure to localize the memory trace at the anatomical level, and in part because of the tremendous explosion of and successes in molecular biology, much current memory research has turned to a different level of analysis that involves identifying the molecular and cellular substrates of changes in neuronal activity underlying memory. Here, instead of localizing the memory trace anatomically, the engram is specified in terms of critical molecules or synaptic or other cellular structures rather than brain areas or brain circuits.

Has any cellular or molecular mechanism surfaced that might be identified with learning and memory? The answer is not only a strong yes, but many yesses. Mechanisms for which there is at least suggestive evidence include, at the cellular level, changes in membrane properties that affect ion flow and changes in synaptic efficacy through the growth of synapses and, at the molecular level, changes in the pool of transmitter-related functions at the presynaptic or postsynaptic site. Indeed, there may be an embarrassment of riches here: There are many plausible candidate mechanisms. This is illustrated particularly clearly in work on the molecular mechanisms that might underlie a form of neural plasticity called long-term potentiation (LTP). Some investigators discovered evidence suggesting that LTP depends on increased transmitter release at the presynaptic site, whereas others uncovered evidence for changes in receptor sensitivity at the postsynaptic site. This discrepancy led to bitter debate, each side pointing to the limitations of the other while increasing the strength of the evidence in favor of its own view. This debate seemed to be guided, although implicitly, by the assumption that the mechanism of LTP had to be one or the other (i.e., that there is or should be a single memory mechanism). But why not *many* mechanisms? On what grounds should we assume any unitary mechanism? If memory is a fundamental property of brain and a natural outcome of the brain in action (a possibility we raised at the outset of this chapter), then there is no reason to expect any single brain event to be *the* memory mechanism. Rather, there could be as many memory mechanisms as there are cellular and molecular events that contribute to neural activity and information processing. Our best guess is that the use of neural pathways results in alterations of the homeostasis of many cellular and molecular processes, and that each contributes—and indeed might be sufficient—to support the resulting behavioral changes that reflect memory (for a related discussion, see Sanes & Lichtman, 1999).

Memory as a Fundamental Property of the Brain's Information-Processing Activities

This book rejects any notion that memory exists as distinct "items" that are stored in place in specific memory-dedicated brain regions, or that memory reflects simple switchboardlike connections between stored representations, or that memory can be identified with a single set of brain events. It's not that these metaphors are totally wrong or useless, but that they are misleading in treating memory as a special category of brain events or brain activities. Instead, we would suggest that memory be conceived of as a fundamental *property* of brain systems and a natural *outcome* of the brain's various processing activities, rather than an *entity* stored in the brain. In this view, memory is an integral part of those ongoing information-processing activities and is tied to those very brain activities.

The brain systems that support perceptual recognition, sensorimotor integration, motor coordination, and more purely cognitive operations such as language production and comprehension, logical reasoning, and the like are enormously complex, invoking the coordinated activity of many brain areas and brain events. Brain events related to retrieving and using memory are a critical element of any of these examples of brain activity or information processing, as is memory for the processing activities performed. That is, memory is integrally tied to these various processing systems and is both a part and a product of the ongoing processing activities of these systems. Experience is reflected in, and causes changes in, the operation of these systems in one manner or another; in our view, that *is* memory and is the purpose or function of memory.

Levels of Analysis and the Organization of Memory Systems

Given the above view of memory as being a part and a product of the brain's various processing systems, it is entirely reasonable to expect that a variety of different (rather than any single kind of) brain events will be identified with memory as a function of the different processing systems that are shaped by experience. This view raises a pair of very important questions: To the extent that there are different brain events that underlie memory (i.e., different memory mechanisms), is it the case that memory can then take different forms and have different properties? And if so, are the different forms and different properties that behavioral memory can take caused by there being different memory mechanisms, at the cellular or molecular level, or by there being different brain processing systems exhibiting memory, at a more macro, systems level?

These questions take us to the second major theme of this book: Memory is manifested in multiple ways by multiple functionally and anatomically distinct brain systems. In the remainder of this chapter we anticipate the evidence, to be discussed in detail subsequently, of multiple forms of memory, and then we explain why this evidence is best understood at the level of brain systems rather than at the level of cellular and molecular mechanisms.

To introduce the multiple-memory-system idea we will preview the central idea of one of the earliest theorists of memory, the French philosopher Maine de

Biran. He suggested that there are different forms of memory for what we would now call *habitual behaviors, emotional reactions,* and *conscious recollection* of ideas and events. He argued that each of these types of memory has different properties and can be distinguished in the performance and experiences of individuals. Does this categorization exist only at the level of phenomenological experience? Or do these distinctions emerge from differences in the properties of separate brain systems that mediate behavioral, emotional, and ideational functions? As will be made clear in subsequent chapters, there is now evidence that these forms of memory experience (and others) arise from different brain systems. Note that this perspective is consistent with the evidence indicating that memory is distributed and is a fundamental property of the brain's information-processing activities, and it provides the initial framework for how memory is organized.

A more modern approach to the idea of multiple memory systems comes from Cohen and Squire (1980) and has been extended and elaborated by the current authors (e.g., see Eichenbaum, Otto, & Cohen, 1992; Cohen & Eichenbaum, 1993). This view distinguishes between declarative and procedural memory and ties them to different brain systems. Declarative memory is seen as dependent upon the hippocampal system and related structures, whereas procedural memory is seen as dependent upon on-line tuning and modification of a variety of cortical and subcortical processors. Other multiple-memory-system views have emerged, all attempting to identify different forms of memory with the operation of different brain systems.

Although considerable current research remains focused on the critical cellular mechanisms of neural plasticity that underlie memory, it is important to place this research in the context of the problem of memory organization. Although it is surely the case that some of the discoveries forthcoming from studies on cellular mechanisms will be key to a full understanding of memory, and that some of these will be fundamental to addressing diseases of learning and memory, knowledge about the details of the cellular mechanism may matter rather little for clarification of distinctions between types of memory that emerge at the systems and cognitive level. This view may upset reductionists who seek to understand memory through its cellular basis. It is certainly possible that one cellular mechanism will turn out to be the one that the declarative memory system uses, while another mechanism might turn out to be the one that mediates plasticity in some other (e.g., procedural) memory system, such that a dissociation of types of memory can be observed based on selective manipulations of different cellular plasticity mechanisms. But unless and until it becomes clear that a particular cellular mechanism *had to be* the substrate for a particular form of memory, it will not shed light on the distinction made at the higher level of analysis (see Cohen, 1985, for discussion). We already know, for example, that one mechanism (NMDA-receptor-dependent LTP) is found not only in the hippocampus but also in other brain areas that, we will see, are components of different memory systems. And even within the hippocampus itself, there are at least two distinct mechanisms of cellular plasticity (one dependent on NMDA receptors and one or more not). Thus the search for cellular plasticity mechanisms that support memory should be thought of as largely orthogonal to the search for the brain pathways and circuit-level mechanisms that support different types of memory.

One final question must be posed in this introductory chapter: How many memory systems are there, and how are they organized? In a recent compilation Schacter and Tulving (1994) addressed this question and began by considering how one should go about classifying memory systems. They argued that memory systems should be distinguished primarily by their psychological characteristics: (1) A memory system would perform tasks for a very large class of tasks that have the same functional features, for example, short-term memory for information from a variety of modalities; (2) each memory system would exhibit unique functional properties—for example, short-term memory is typically in the superficial details of the representation of information; and (3) there would be convergent dissociations that distinguish each memory system from others. Among the latter are neuropsychological dissociations by which different types of memory are associated with the functions of particular brain structures. Based on these considerations, Schacter and Tulving outlined a framework of 5 "major" systems containing 11 "subsystems" for distinct forms of memory, and this classification does not include a system for emotional memory (Table 1.1). Squire & Zola-Morgan (1991; Figure 1.4) proposed a different classification that includes six kinds of memory, and this one only partially overlaps with Schacter and Tulving's. The specifics of these proposals will be covered in some detail below. For now, we want to make two points about these classifications. First, each involves defining memory systems according to cognitive or psychological criteria, and each considers the role of particular brain structures as just one line of confirming evidence. Second, there is at this time no consensus on just how many memory systems there are or on how to categorize them according to cognitive dimensions.

With regard to the first point, concerning how to define memory systems, the approach we advocate here is somewhat different from the others. Based on the

Table 1.1 The tentative memory taxonomy offered by Schacter & Tulving (1994).

System	Other terms	Subsystems	Retrieval
Procedural	Nondeclarative	Motor skills Cognitive skills Simple conditioning Simple associative learning	Implicit
Perceptual Representation	Nondeclarative	Visual word from Auditory word from Structural description	Implicit
Semantic	Generic Factual Knowledge	Spatial Relational	Implicit
Primary	Working	Visual Auditory	Explicit
Episodic	Personal Autobiographical Event		Explicit

Note. From *Memory Systems* (p. 26), by D. L. Schacter & E. Tulving, 1994, Cambridge, MA: MIT Press.

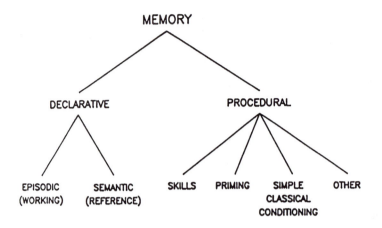

Figure 1.4. The tentative memory taxonomy offered by Squire and Zola-Morgan (1991). (Reproduced, with permission, from Squire & Zola-Morgan, 1991; Copyright American Association for the Advancement of Science.)

theme that has recurred in this chapter that memory is a fundamental property and natural outcome of the brain's ongoing processing activities, we would suggest asking how the properties of different forms of memory conform with and arise from the operating characteristics of the brain systems that support them. Accordingly, the emphasis here is as much on the nature of processing performed by the candidate brain systems as it is on the properties of the candidate forms of memory.

With regard to the second point, concerning the "correct" number of memory systems, a perhaps radical extension of the above theme is the possibility that there are as many memory systems as there are functional brain systems. We will explore this idea in subsequent chapters.

The Structure of This Book

The remainder of this book is devoted to a comprehensive analysis of the notion of multiple memory systems, and to our attempt to identify and characterize at least the major ones. Chapter 2 offers a review of the history of ideas about multiple memory systems. This chapter is a preview of all that follows and discusses at length the evolution of thoughts and the central observations leading to current views on multiple memory systems. This overview focuses on the conceptual issues more than on the neurobiological details and puts each of the following chapters in the context of our recurring themes.

The subsequent chapters are organized into three parts. Part I addresses issues common to all memory systems, providing background before we move on to considering the individual candidate memory systems of the brain. Chapter 3 provides the fundamentals of cellular plasticity and thereby provides a way to understand how cellular mechanisms might mediate memory storage in the brain's various processing systems. Chapter 4 reviews the research on the critical role of the cerebral cortex in memory. As will become apparent, the cortex is a major component of all (or nearly all) memory systems. Accordingly, understanding of its role is a good place to start the focus on neurobiological studies of memory systems.

Parts II and III detail a set of specific candidate memory systems and the brain systems that support them. Part II focuses entirely on one memory system: the hippocampal memory system. This story receives the greatest attention in this book for two reasons. First, it is the system about which the most is known, by far. Accordingly, this story, more than the story of any other brain system, serves as an introduction to the functions of all the memory systems. Second, it turns out that the hippocampal memory system is the one that mediates what most of us commonly think of as "memory," our ability to consciously recollect everyday facts and experiences.

Within Part II, chapter 5 considers the evidence from the study of amnesia in humans, which offered the initial insights into the role of the hippocampal system. In chapters 6 and 7, we review attempts to model amnesia in experimental animals, and then in chapter 8, we outline the efforts to understand how information is encoded within the hippocampal system by looking at the physiological activity of elements of the system. In chapter 9, we indicate the critical relationship between the hippocampus and the cortical processors thought to be the site of long-term memory storage, and we show how these areas might interact as a memory system. Finally, chapter 10 reviews evidence concerning the special role of the hippocampal system in memory consolidation, the process by which transient memories become permanent and become independent of hippocampal mediation.

Part III introduces other memory systems of the brain. After a general review of dissociations among the functions of memory systems (chapter 11), we present evidence about a brain system that mediates emotional memories and modulates other kinds of memory in an emotional context (chapter 12), and systems that mediate the acquisition of behavioral habits (procedural memories; chapter 13). In chapter 14 we review a special form of memory known as *working memory,* which mediates a short-term form of representation. In the final chapter we return to the two basic insights introduced at the outset of this chapter and consider how well they characterize our understanding of memory systems in the brain.

2

Multiple Memory Systems

A Historical Perspective

This chapter provides a historical review and analysis of systematic attempts to characterize different forms of memory and of the central observations that commit us to the idea of multiple memory systems. The review focuses more on conceptual issues about the properties of different forms of memory than on the details of their neurobiological implementation. By the end of the chapter, we introduce some of the most recent discoveries and modern ideas about different forms of memory, leading up to the current conceptual and experimental framework for understanding multiple memory systems in the brain. This review will provide an overall framework for viewing memory systems that we will use throughout the subsequent chapters of this book, when we delve into the instantiation in the brain of these different memory systems.

Consideration of the history of these ideas offers perspectives about the properties of multiple memory systems that, in some respects at least, are remarkably current, and it also offers a sense of the enormous progress made in recent years. There have been several other efforts to trace the history of notions about different forms of memory to which we can commend the reader and that offer intriguing reading as well as useful insights about the evolution of thinking on this issue (see Herrmann & Chaffin, 1988; Schacter, 1987a; Schacter & Tulving, 1994). It is our hope that appreciation of the current framework will be enhanced by the attempt to connect it to the early conceptual views, and to connect the ideas about the properties of various forms of memory to the details (to be presented in subsequent chapters) of the brain systems that mediate them.

In reading the following historical overview, it would be useful to keep in mind a number of general observations about the commonalities and the differences among the various views. First, each of the views of different forms of memory includes description of a complex form that, in humans, supports "conscious" memory, as opposed to other forms of memory that characteristically do not reach consciousness or involve conscious awareness. The framework for multiple memory systems adopted in this book continues this tradition and indeed is captured in our separation between Part II (chapters 5–10) and Part III (chapters 11–13), in which we consider separately the memory system whose operation supports conscious recollection and the other memory systems that operate outside conscious awareness, respectively.

Second, whereas the earlier notions viewed different forms of memory as organized hierarchically, with more complex forms building on the simpler mechanisms, the more modern accounts make a claim of functional independence, emphasizing the parallel operation of multiple memory systems.

Third, whereas the earliest views distinguished among forms of memory in terms of their functional properties or characteristics, later views gradually became more neurobiologically based as more became understood about brain function. The landmark studies on the patient H.M. and other examples of amnesia marked the beginning of the era in which forms of memory became tied to distinct brain structures. Notions of multiple memory systems formally appeared as a brain systems concept only in the mid-1970s.

Early Views

The starting point for this review of proposals about multiple forms of memory is the philosopher Maine de Biran (1804/1929; see also an account of his work by Schacter & Tulving, 1994), whose ideas were mentioned briefly in chapter 1. In his book *The Influence of Habit on the Faculty of Thinking*, he argued that "habit" is a fundamental mechanism that underlies much of cognition, much as we assume today that the formation of "associations" is the fundamental mechanism of learning. He proposed that habits were simple and automatic mechanisms not only mediating acquired behaviors that operate independently of conscious control and conscious recollection but also underlying more complex, conscious aspects of memory. Maine de Biran proposed that habits were expressed in three distinct forms of memory differing in their mechanisms and properties. One, the most complex of these, he called *representative memory,* expressed in the form of conscious recollection of a well circumscribed "idea." The second, designated *mechanical memory,* refers to when the habit mechanism generates not a recalled idea but a repetition of a movement. Finally, *sensitive memory* refers to when the habit mechanism generates a feeling, or "fantastic," albeit vague or obscure, image, that is, without recall of the ideas behind it. Thus, mechanical memory was seen as expressing habits in elemental form and sensitive memory as the addition of an affective or "feeling" component; they were considered similar in that they could operate without conscious recall and could be the source of the most inflexible and obstinate behaviors.

Although Schacter and Tulving (1994) concluded, and we must concur, that Maine de Biran's writings had little influence on modern theories about multiple forms of memory, there are striking parallels between his views and those to be elaborated here.

Another early figure whose views on memory will turn out to have important parallels to the ideas we develop in this book is Gall (1835), who, unlike Maine de Biran, was a very well-known figure in psychology. Gall's reputation came from his association with the pseudoscience of phrenology, and also with the scientifically respectable notion that specific psychological functions can be localized within the cerebral cortex (for discussion of Gall's contributions, see Zola-Morgan, 1995). In his efforts to develop an "organology" of the brain, Gall collected and examined differences in hundreds of skulls and casts of heads of humans and animals. Through detailed comparisons he correlated prominent morphological aspects of skulls—and, by inference, of the underlying cortex— with distinctive aspects of behavior, cognitive capacity, and personality. Gall's attempt to characterize and anatomically compartmentalize a broad range of mental "faculties" did not fare well historically. Although a few of his faculties are currently successful subjects of neuropsychological and neuroscientific research (e.g., "language" or "melody"), most of the faculties he attempted to identify were far too undifferentiated to be assigned to discrete brain processors (e.g., "marvelousness," "secretiveness," or, for that matter, "language"), and the idea that faculties could be correlated with bumps on the skull proved to be unfortunately naive. However, Gall's views on memory are very instructive. He assumed that each mental faculty had its own specialized memory, an attribute of each of the cortically localized mental faculties rather than a faculty itself. Thus Gall was very much opposed to the idea that memory was a unitary capacity. If this were so, he argued, an individual's ability to remember different types of material would strongly intercorrelate. His observations, by contrast, indicated strong differences in memory capacities across cognitive domains. Accordingly, Gall's position ends up anticipating one of our major themes here, that memory is a fundamental aspect of the distinct processing functions of cortical processors (also see the account of Gall's work by Fodor, 1984).

Systematic Psychology at the Turn of the Century:
William James

Before the turn of the century the notions about the distinctions and connections between "habit" and a more recollective or consciously mediated form of "memory" had taken sufficient hold that James (1890/1918) wrote of them in widely separated chapters in his treatise *Principles of Psychology*. Like Maine de Biran, James considered habit a very primitive mechanism that is common among biological systems: "The phenomena of habit in living beings are due to plasticity of the organic materials of which their bodies are composed" (p. 105). Within the nervous system, though, he viewed the mechanism of habit in terms of its known electrical activity: "Nothing is easier to imagine than how, when a current once has traversed a path, it should traverse it more readily still a second time" (p. 109). Thus, James felt that a simple habit was nothing more than the discharge of a well-worn reflex path.

Having reinforced the simplicity and ubiquity of the habit mechanism, James attributed to it great importance in more complicated behavioral repertoires. He suggested that well-practiced behaviors and skills, including walking, writing, fencing, and singing, are mediated by "concatenated discharges in the nerve-centres due to the presence of systems there of reflex paths, so organized as to wake each other up successively" (p. 108). Thus complex habits involve the serial production of movements and unconscious sensations leading to other movements and sensations. In practical terms (upon which he often focused), James argued that "habit simplifies the movements required to achieve a result, makes them more accurate and diminishes fatigue" (p. 112), and that "habit diminishes the conscious attention with which our acts are performed" (p. 114). So, not only are habits the building blocks for complex behaviors, but they can also serve to eliminate the need for conscious supervision once the behavior becomes routine. Expanding further along this line, James even suggested the critical importance of habits in mediating social phenomena: "Habit is thus the fly-wheel of society, its most precious conservative agent" (p. 121). He recommended early and often reinforcement of good habits as a key exercise in ethical and cognitive development.

James recognized "memory" as being something altogether different from habit, albeit based on it, and as being a very complicated phenomenon with many facets. James is perhaps best known for having originated the distinction between *primary memory* and *secondary memory*. Primary memory is what we today call *short-term* or *working memory.* It is a short-lived state where new information has achieved consciousness and belongs to our stream of thought. James viewed primary memory as the gateway by which material would "enter" secondary memory, or what we now call *long-term memory,* but emphasized that the "intellectual value (of the experience) lies in the after-memory" (p. 645). His separation of primary from secondary memory was highly influential, and many of his speculations about secondary memory will provide a critical foundation for our claims about the nature of different forms of (long-term) memory. Accordingly, his descriptions of secondary memory will be considered at some length here.

James defined secondary memory as "the knowledge of an event, or fact, of which meantime we have not been thinking, with the additional consciousness that we have thought or experienced it before" (p. 648). In addition to its personal and temporal aspects, the full characterization of memory was framed in terms of two other properties, its structure as an elaborate network of associations and its basis in habit mechanisms:

> It follows that what we began by calling the "image," or "copy," of the fact in mind, is really not there at all in that simple shape, as a separate "idea." Or at least, if it be there as a separate idea, no memory will go with it. What memory goes with is, on the contrary, a very complex representation, that of the fact to be recalled *plus* its associates, the whole forming one "object" ... known in one integral pulse of consciousness ... and demanding probably a vastly more intricate brain-process than that on which any simple sensorial image depends. (pp. 650–651)

This theme is continued in his characterization of memory retrieval:

> We make a search in our memory for a forgotten idea, just as we rummage our house for a lost object. In both cases we visit what seems to us the probable *neighborhood* of that which we miss. We turn over things under which, or within which, or along side of which, it may possibly be; and if

it lies near them, it soon comes into view. But these matters, in the case of a mental object sought, are nothing but its *associates*. The machinery of recall is thus the same as the machinery of association, and the machinery of association, as we know, is nothing but the elementary law of habit in the nerve centres. (p. 654)

So, like Maine de Biran, James attributed the underlying basis of association and memory to habit. But James extended his theorizing in a way that will prove critical for more modern views of memory, emphasizing that the "habit" had to be elaborated in a particular way for the formation of associations to support the richness of memory. Thus the underlying foundation of recall was a complex, yet systematic, set of associations between any particular item and anything co-occurring in one's previous experiences with the item.

In his elaboration on the "conditions of goodness in memory," that is, on individual differences in memory ability and on how to improve one's memory, James offered further elaboration: "Memory being thus altogether conditioned on brain paths, its excellence in a given individual will depend partly on the *number* and partly on the *persistence* of these paths" (p. 659, italics added). He viewed the persistence of memory as innately determined, albeit variable with age and across individuals. Because persistence is a physiological property James characterized as "native tenacity or physiological retentiveness" (p. 659), he concluded it was not modifiable by experience or training ("No amount of culture would seem capable of modifying a man's general retentiveness, p. 663). So James focused more on the *number* of brain paths as the main determinant of memory, and he was emphatic about its importance:

In mental terms, the more other facts a fact is associated with in the mind, the better possession of it our memory retains. Each of its associates becomes a hook to which it hangs, a means by which to fish it up by when sunk beneath the surface. Together they form a *network of attachments by which it is woven into the entire tissue of our thought.* The "secret of a good memory" is thus the secret of forming diverse and multiple associations with every fact we care to retain. But this forming of associations with a fact, what is it but thinking about the fact as much as possible? Briefly, then, of two men with the same outward experiences and the same amount of innate tenacity, the one who THINKS over his experiences most, and *weaves them into systematic relations with each other,* will be the one with the best memory. (p. 662, italics added)

Some of James's comments were directed at the study habits of his pupils, admonishing them not to cram for exams: "Things thus learned in a few hours, on one occasion, for one purpose, cannot possibly have formed many associations with other things in mind" (p. 663). Cramming thus would lead merely to a concatenation of habits that could be expressed only by specific repetition of the material learned. Such "regurgitation" of readings or lecture material lacks the creativity and insights that can result from a memory search.

Finally, James emphasized the role of associative elaboration of memory, by appealing to the brain:

The brain tracts excited by the event proper, and those excited in its recall, are in a part different from each other. If we could revive the past event without any associates we should exclude the possibility of memory, and simply dream that we were undergoing the same experience as if for the first time. (p. 657)

To summarize, James distinguished between regeneration of the to-be-remembered item itself and the set of associations made in memory during the learning episode (and in subsequent retrieval episodes). James suggested a habit mechanism could support an elaborate and systematic network of associations within which one could search for the to-be-remembered items using the associates and vice versa. This search engine, operating on the network associations, was held to be the basis of conscious recollection. Finally, the ability to regenerate the items and the ability to search for their associations might be mediated by different neural systems.

James never contrasted "habit" and "memory" as distinct forms of memory, although he did anticipate the idea that their expression could be dissociated, even for the very same learned material. A more direct recognition of two forms of memory can be attributed to the philosopher Henri Bergson (1911):

The past survives under two distinct forms: first in motor mechanisms; secondly in independent recollections. . . . The utilizing of past experience for present action—recognition in short—must take place in two different ways. Sometimes it lies in the action itself, and in the automatic setting in motion of a mechanism adapted to the circumstances; at other times it implies an effort of the mind which seeks in the past, in order to apply them to the present, those representations which are best able to enter into the present situation. (p.87)

The Rise of Behaviorism, at the Expense of Progress on Multiple Forms of Memory

The history of the development of ideas about multiple forms of memory suffered a detour in the early part of this century. As James was completing his text, contemporaneous experimentalists were building the foundations of behaviorism, the view that all learning and behavior is based on conditioned reflexes. This work led away from consideration of the complex form(s) of memory that supports conscious recollection and of how that form differs from simpler forms of memory. However, to the extent that "habits" refer to the same phenomena and/or rely upon the same mechanisms as conditioned reflexes, it is important for us to consider this chapter in the history of thought in psychology for the insights it might provide about simple forms of memory. Accordingly, in the next sections of the current review we delve into conditioned reflexes and habit, and we then turn to the challenges to that whole line of work.

The origins of behaviorism began separately in the United States and Russia. At the turn of the century, Thorndike (1898) had invented his puzzle box, with which he observed cats learning to manipulate a door latch to allow escape from a holding chamber. Around the same time, Small (1901) introduced the maze to studies of animal learning, inspired by the famous garden maze at Hampton Court in London. In 1907 Watson published his accounts on maze learning by rats, and in 1913 he published his behaviorist "manifesto," formalizing the notion that learning can be fully understood by careful observation of behavior, and claiming we need never return to terms such as *consciousness.*

Independently in the early 1900s, Pavlov (1927) and Bechterev (1907), physiologists in Russia, had been experimenting on autonomic nervous system reflexes in dogs. Pavlov was studying the physiology of digestion and observed that dogs would secrete saliva not only when given food but also when presented with an arbitrary stimulus following repeated pairings of the arbitrary stimulus and food delivery. He called this phenomenon the *conditioned reflex.* Also, Bechterev studied the respiratory motor reflex by which cold applied to the skin produces a reflexive "catching" of the breath (as we have all experienced when jumping into a cold bath). He discovered that an arbitrary stimulus applied repeatedly at the same time as the cold would eventually set off the same reflex by itself. Bechterev called this learning an *associated reflex* and successfully demonstrated other associated reflexes, for example, in defensive paw movements. A new terminology for describing conditioned reflexes, as well as key assumptions about their operational properties, took hold instantly: Any neutral stimulus, called the *conditioned stimulus,* or CS, repeatedly paired with any *unconditioned stimulus* (US) that produces a *reflexive unconditioned response* (UR), comes to elicit a *conditioned response* (CR) that is more or less identical in form to the UR.

The neurology of the conditioned reflex, especially as elaborated by Sherrington in his classic 1906 text, gave biological validity to what behaviorists saw as the elemental mechanism of learned behavior. Sherrington also introduced the idea that reflex modification was likely based on alterations in the synaptic connections between neurons. Before long the conditioned reflex and the theoretical force of behaviorism combined neatly, although there were, and still are, debates about the distinctions between the fundamental association in Pavlovian conditioning and that in Thorndike's instrumental learning. Pavlov's principle of reinforcement held that an association between the conditioned and unconditioned stimulus was sufficient to account for the emergence of the conditioned reflex. By contrast, Thorndike's law of effect focused on the notion that behaviors followed by positive reinforcement are more likely to be repeated. Put in contrasting terms by the behaviorists, when a rat learns to press a bar for food, Pavlov's law could explain why the rats might salivate at the sight of the bar, but Thorndike's law would have to be added to explain why the rat presses the bar (see Mackintosh, 1994, for further discussion). Despite this difference in views about what is the fundamental association, these viewpoints came to be referred to collectively as *stimulus-response,* or S-R, *learning,* and we can think of them as offering a physiological instantiation of the habit mechanism. To the thinkers of this time, having a full accounting of S-R learning would solve the problem of memory. We now have a more ambitious goal: to understand each of the various forms of memory.

The Challenge of Cognitivism: Tolman and Cognitive Maps

The current treatment of the early years of experimental psychology and learning has largely ignored many of the influential achievements of noted behaviorists, including such prominent figures as Hull and Skinner. The reader is referred to the many texts on animal learning theory which offer detailed accounts of this work. However, because this perspective did not contribute to the elaboration of the notion of multiple forms of memory—and, indeed, kept the focus largely away from such an idea—we will instead move on to major early challenges to the simplicity of behaviorism.

This challenge to behaviorism came from psychologists such as Yerkes (1916) and Kohler (1924), who argued that animals did not learn complex problems by a combination of random trial and error and eventual reinforcement of a correct solution, but that at least the higher animals had insights into relationships between means and ends. This approach clearly affronted the behaviorists' desire never to return to notions like *insight.* And they succeeded in rebuffing this challenge because Yerkes's and Kohler's ideas did not provide clear operational criteria (see Macintosh, 1983). On other hand, Tolman (1932, 1948, 1949) was more successful in challenging behaviorism precisely because he developed operational definitions for mentalistic processes including *purposive behavior* and *expectancy.* Moreover, he rigorously tested these ideas using the same species (rats) and maze-learning paradigms that were a major focus of the prominent S-R theorists.

Tolman's view differed diametrically from those of the contemporary behaviorists. Yet he considered himself very much a "behaviorist"—indeed, more so than Watson, Hull, and their colleagues—because his own focus was at the "molar" (whole animal) level, which he argued was more true to behaviorism than others' focus on the "molecular" (specific muscular and glandular) level emphasized in the efforts to reduce behavior to specific stimuli and responses. But this does not mean that Tolman wanted only an overt behavioral level of description (as did Skinner). Clearly Tolman's goal was to get behind the behavior not by specifying particular elements of muscular action, but by identifying the complex cognitive mechanisms, purposes, expectations, and insights that guided behavior. Tolman (1932) wrote about the evolution of his own thinking:

> [I began to have] a growing belief that a really useful Behaviorism would not be a mere "muscle twitchism" such as Watson's. It soon appeared to me that "responses," as significant for psychology, are defined not by their physiological details, but rather by the sort of rearrangements between organism and environment. (p. xiii).

Tolman claimed to dislike the terms *purpose* and *cognition,* but he felt compelled to confront them as essential ingredients of an explanation of behavior. His contribution was to define cognition, purpose, and insight operationally, and to demonstrate their existence and importance in learning and memory. In his classic 1948 paper entitled "Cognitive Maps in Rats and Men," he contrasted the two schools of thinking about learning:

> First, there is a school of animal psychologists which believes that the maze behavior of rats is a matter of mere simple stimulus-response connections. Learning, according to them, consists in the strengthening of some of these connections and in the weakening of others. The rat's central nervous system, according to this view, may be likened to a complicated telephone switchboard . . . those connections which result in the animal's going down

the true path become relatively more open to passage of nerve impulses, whereas those which lead him into the blinds become relatively less open. (pp. 189–190)

Let us now turn to the second main school. This group (I belong to them) may be called the field theorists. We believe that in the course of learning something like a field map of the environment gets established in the rat's brain. . . . The stimuli, which are allowed in, are not connected by just simple one-to-one switches to the outgoing responses. Rather, the incoming impulses are usually worked over and elaborated into a tentative, cognitive-like map of the environment. And it is this tentative map, indicating routes and paths and environmental relationships, which finally determines what responses, if any, the animal will finally release. (p. 192)

Thus, Tolman's basic premise was that learning generally involved the acquisition of *knowledge* about the world, and in particular about relationships among stimuli and between stimuli and their consequences, and that this knowledge led to expectancies when the animal was put in testing situations. Contrasts between his view and that of the "molecular" behaviorists can be most strikingly distinguished on three key features of learning: the contents of the memory representation, the role of reinforcement, and the expression of memory in performance.

With regard to the contents of the memory representation, the behaviorists argued that the contents of memory involve habits that can be characterized as acquired stimulus-response reflex sequences. Their guiding ambition was to describe learning in terms of habits in sufficient detail and elaboration to eliminate the need for considering fuzzy terms like *cognition*. But for Tolman (1948) learning involved the creation of a "cognitive map" that organized the relations among stimuli and consequences based on "interconnections or field relationships between such groups of stimuli" (p. 145). This discussion of the relationships among stored aspects of knowledge is much closer to the view of James than to that of the behaviorists of Tolman's day. Knowledge of such relations would lead to a "field expectancy" that would guide behavioral solutions to obtain desired consequences.

With regard to reinforcement, for the S-R theorists reinforcement was the driving force of learning. Thus Thorndike's (1911) "law of effect" attributes all learning to the principle that behaviors that lead to a positive reinforcement are more likely to be repeated. For S-R theorists from Hull to Skinner, reinforcers were viewed as the force that strengthened stimulus-response connections. Notably, Pavlov (1927) himself was not so strongly bound to the role of reinforcers as strengthening connection; to him the contents of learning involved the association of conditioned and unconditioned stimuli through temporal contiguity. In Pavlov's paradigm, that key association was between the bell, as conditioned stimulus, and the taste of food, as unconditioned stimulus; through the learned association the food comes to substitute for the food taste in evoking salivation. For Tolman, however, reinforcers served simply as more information on which to confirm one's expectancies about when, where, and how rewards were to be obtained. Thus Tolman felt learning was driven not by reinforcement but by curiosity about the environment and seeking of knowledge for expectancies about its predictive structure. Reinforcers would certainly determine what behavior might eventually be emitted but were not necessary for establishment of the cognitive map itself.

With regard to how memories are expressed, for the S-R theorists the responses emitted are precisely the motor commands that are the end point of stimulus-response reflexes. The range of behavioral responses, then, is fully determined as the motor patterns that were elicited and reinforced during learning itself. To molecular behaviorists learning and performance were ideally identical. But to Tolman learning and performance were fundamentally independent events. That is, what an animal knew about the world and what it was going to do about it were surely related (through expectancies) but were not the same thing, as the behaviorists held. Thus, Tolman argued, animals could use their cognitive maps and field expectancies to guide the expression of learned behavior in a variety of ways not limited to repetition of the behavioral patterns exhibited and reinforced during learning. This kind of flexibility will prove to be an important aspect of modern views of memory.

These differences in perspective might have simply been shrugged off by the behaviorists if what they were doing was all just theorizing. One noted S-R theorist asserted in frustration about the impreciseness of Tolman's accounts, "In his concern with what goes on in the rat's mind, Tolman has neglected to predict what the rat will do. So far as the theory is concerned the rat is left buried in thought" (Guthrie, 1952, p. 143). Indeed, Tolman's descriptions of the particular structure of cognitive maps were vague compared to the exquisite level of mechanistic detail provided by some of the behaviorists. For example, Hull (1943, 1952) sought a mathematical characterization of learning in terms of stimulus-response habit elements and indeed could be considered among the first computational modelers to build an account of learning performance with equations on habit strength. But the strength of Tolman's theorizing was that it did *not* leave the rat "buried in thought." Quite the contrary, he operationalized the role of reinforcement and behavioral expression in substantial experimental findings that challenged the prevailing behaviorist doctrine.

Two lines of Tolman's investigations most strongly addressed the central issues of whether reinforcement was required for learning and what was the range of responses for which memory could be expressed. With regard to reinforcement, Tolman's experiments focused on the phenomenon of latent learning. In these studies rats were allowed to run through a complex maze without receiving any food rewards in the goal box. After several trials of such experience a reward was introduced, and then performance in terms of errors at choice points was compared with that of other subjects that had been rewarded on each of the initial trials. Tolman and his colleagues found that following the single rewarding event, rats' performance became as good as that of the rats that had been rewarded all along (Figure 2.1). Tolman interpreted these results as showing that the learning accrued during the unrewarded trials was as strong as that for animals rewarded on many trials, calling into question in a very direct way any critical role of reinforcers in the initial establishment of the memory trace. But to the behaviorists these results were more a challenge to create additional subtle variables that linked stimuli and responses, awaiting a reinforcer to potentiate behavior through incentives and motivations.

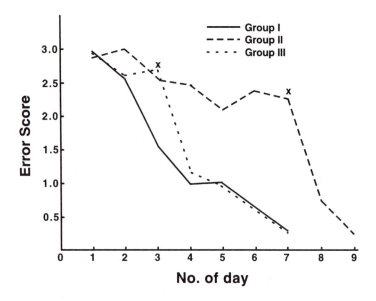

Figure 2.1. Data from Tolman's latent learning experiment. Rats in Group 1 were provided a food reward at the goal box of a maze on each training day. Rats in Group 2 were not rewarded on the first 6 days, but received rewards beginning on day 7 (see x). Rats in Group 3 were not rewarded on the first 2 days, but received rewards from day 3 onward (see x). Rats in both Groups 2 and 3 showed very little sign of learning until the day after rewards were provided, but then immediately and thereafter performed as well as the rats who had been rewarded from the outset of training. (Reproduced, with permission, from Tolman, 1951; Copyright University of California Press.)

With regard to the range of behavioral expression available as a consequence of learning, Tolman's studies on the routes taken in maze learning were particularly impressive. Tolman viewed these studies in terms of two types of neural representation used to solve maze problems. One, the view favored by S-R theorists, was a "striplike" representation consisting of the strengthening of specific sequence of connections that linked stimuli and responses. The other view, preferred by Tolman, held that the representation was more complicated and "more like a map control room than it is like an old-fashioned telephone exchange" (Tolman, 1948, p. 192), involving a "tentative cognitive-like map of the environment," a "comprehensive" map that drew a wider arc than the striplike map. The difference between these alternative models, Tolman argued, would emerge not during training, but only when there was a change in the environment not allowing repetition of the original route.

Tolman and his students performed several experiments pitting these views against one another in analyses of maze learning by rats. Their studies focused on whether rats could demonstrate "insight" by taking a roundabout route or a shortcut in a maze when such strategies were warranted and were inconsistent with a previous reward history that favored a different route. In an experiment that demonstrated detour taking in rats, Tolman and Honzik (1930) used an elevated maze that involved three diverging and then converging routes from a starting place to a goal box (Figure 2.2). During preliminary training the rat could take any route and came to prefer the shortest. When this route was blocked (at Block A) most rats would prefer to switch to the next shortest route. Only when this route was also blocked would they take the longest path. In the critical test phase, a new block was introduced at a point where the two shorter paths converged (Block B). Rats began by running down the shortest path (Path 1) as usual. But instead of immediately selecting the next shortest path (Path 2), as they had done during the preliminary phase when the shortest route (Path 1) was blocked, most rats immediately selected Path 3.

In addition to this "detour" ability, Tolman also provided evidence that rats could take shortcuts. Such a capacity had been noted anecdotally in earlier stud-

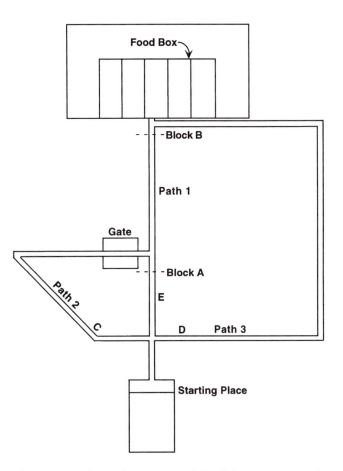

Figure 2.2. The maze used in Tolman's test of the ability of rats to infer a required detour. See text for explanation. (Reproduced, with permission, from Tolman, 1951; Copyright University of California Press.)

ies. For example, Tolman noted Lashley's report of rats that, having learned to solve a maze, escaped the usual covered tunnel apparatus and ran directly across the top of it where they climbed down into the goal box (Tolman, 1948). Even earlier, Small (1901) had observed that within a trial or two rats preferred a short-cut over the response route that had been reinforced on many previous trials. The systematic investigation of detour ability came with an experiment of Tol-man's where rats were trained to approach a goal via a single circuitous route; then the maze was substituted with many direct paths, some leading toward and others away from the goal locus (see Figure 2.3; Tolman, 1949). Most rats ran to the path that took them directly to where the entrance of the food box had origi-nally been located. These studies provided compelling operational evidence of Tolman's assertions that rats had inferential capacities revealed in the flexibility of the behavioral repertoire that could be brought to bear in solving problems for which behavioral theory had no explanation.

Nevertheless this evidence did not end the debate. Rather, it simply inspired more sophisticated additions to the S-R theorists' construction of the internal representation of habit. The debate became focused on the central issue of whether rats acquire maze problems by learning specific turning "responses" or by developing an expectancy of the "place" of reward. The issue was addressed with a simple T-maze apparatus where "response" versus "place" strategies could be directly compared by operational definitions (Figure 2.4, top). The basic task involves the rat's beginning each trial at the base of the T and being rewarded at the end of only one arm (e.g., the one reached by a right turn). The accountings of what was learned in this situation differ strongly in the two theoretical ap-proaches. In this situation, then, according to S-R theory, learning involves acqui-sition of the reinforced (e.g., right-turn) response. By contrast, according to Tol-man's account, learning involves the acquisition of a cognitive map of the environment and the expectancy that food was to be found at a particular loca-tion in the test room. The critical test involved effectively rotating the T by ex-actly 180 degrees, so that the choice arms still ended in the same two loci (albeit which arms reached those loci was now exchanged), and the start point was now at the opposite end of the room. The S-R theorist would predict that a rat would continue to make the previously reinforced right-turn response at the choice point, leading it to a different goal location than that where the food was pro-vided during training. By contrast, the prediction of Tolman's account was that the rat would switch to a left turn in order to arrive at the expected location of food in the same place in the room where it was originally rewarded.

Tolman et al. (1946) provided initial evidence in favor of his prediction, but subsequent efforts to replicate this result were mixed. In a comprehensive review of a decade of these experiments, Restle (1957) concluded that place learning was more often favored but that there were conditions under which response learning was preferred. His analysis indicated that the nature of the available cues was the primary determining factor for the differences in the results. In general, whenever there was salient extramaze visual stimulation that differentiated one goal location from the other, a place representation predominated, and whenever such differential extramaze cues were absent the response strategy predominated. Such a pattern of results did not, of course, declare a "winner" in the place-versus-response debate. Instead these results suggested that both types of repre-

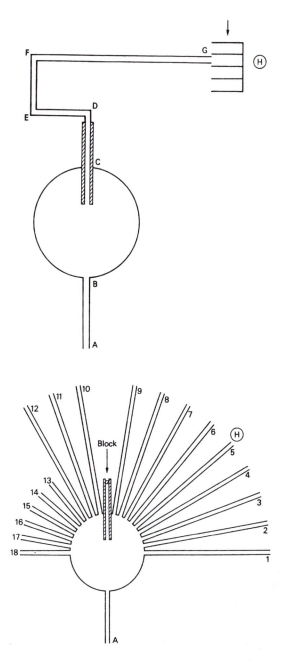

Figure 2.3. The mazes used in a test of rats' ability to infer a shortcut. Top: A was the starting location and G was a set of goal compartments. A-B and D-G were open pathways whereas C was enclosed by high walls. H was a lamp that shown on the goal site. Bottom: After training in the maze shown above, rats' ability to take a shortcut was tested in this apparatus. The rats began at A and then could select any of the arms 1-18. The largest number of rats chose arm 6, which led most directly toward the trained goal site. (Reproduced, with permission, from Tolman, 1984; Copyright American Psychological Association.)

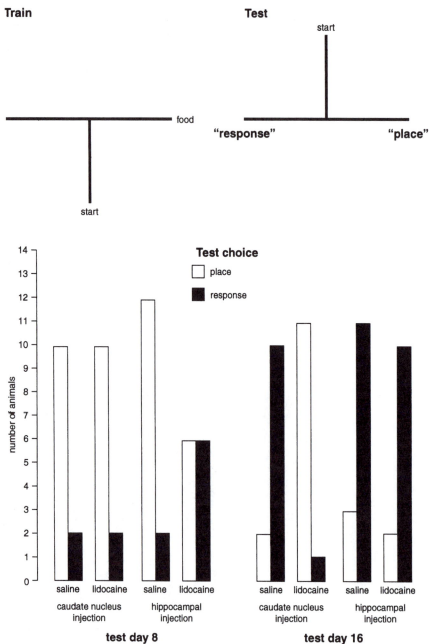

Train

food

start

Test

start

"response"   "place"

Test choice
☐ place
■ response

number of animals

saline   lidocaine   saline   lidocaine

caudate nucleus
injection

hippocampal
injection

test day 8

saline   lidocaine   saline   lidocaine

caudate nucleus
injection

hippocampal
injection

test day 16

sentation are available to the rat, and that it might use either one under conditions of different salient cues or response demands.

Tolman himself (1949) was conciliatory in his explicit suggestion that "there is more than one kind of learning" (p. 144). He offered the idea that different theories and laws might all have some validity for some types of learning. Tolman suggested the possibility of both S-R and cognitive map representations, as well as elaborations of each. He also suggested a distinct form of learning for emotional dispositions for stimuli (calling these *cathexes*) similar to Maine de Biran's sensitive memory. As a true "behaviorist" Tolman did not consider whether these different types of learning were mediated by different brain pathways. But it turns out that different types of learning do exist, that they follow different rules, and that they are supported by different brain mechanisms.

A most elegant demonstration of such a conclusion was provided by Packard and McGaugh (1996), 50 years after the classic Tolman et al. (1946) study. In Packard and McGaugh's experiment, rats were trained for a week on the T-maze task, then given the rotated-maze probe trial. Then they were trained for another week with the maze in its original orientation, and then finally presented with an additional probe trial. Packard and McGaugh found that normal rats initially adopted a place representation, as reflected in their strong preference for the place of the previous goal during the first probe trial. However, after the additional week of overtraining, normal rats switched, now adopting a response strategy on the final probe test. So, under these training circumstances, rats developed both strategies successively. Their initial acquisition was guided by the development of a cognitive map, but subsequent overtraining led to development of the response "habit."

But Packard and McGaugh's experiment went beyond merely showing that the same rats can use both learning strategies. In addition to the pure behavioral testing, Packard and McGaugh also examined whether different brain systems supported these different types of representation. Prior to training, all animals had been implanted with indwelling needles that allowed injection on the probe tests of a local anesthetic or saline placebo directly and locally into one of two brain structures, the hippocampus or the caudate nucleus. The choice of these particular brain structures follows from work conducted in the 50 years intervening between Tolman's and Packard and McGaugh's work, particularly the work

---

Figure 2.4. Place versus response learning. Top: Diagrams of the T-maze apparatus used in training rats to make a particular response (turn right) to obtain a food reward in a particular place, and then testing to determine whether they had learned a particular (turn right) response or the place of the reward. See text for further explanation. Bottom: Data from a test trial presented the day after 7 days of training trials and again the day after 14 days of training. Each panel indicates the number of rats whose choice is consistent with the place or response strategy. Different groups of rats were injected with a local anesthetic or saline bilaterally into the hippocampus or striatum (caudate nucleus) on the corresponding test day only. (Reproduced, with permission, from Packard & McGaugh, 1996; Copyright Academic Press.)

on human amnesia that so conclusively ties the hippocampus to certain aspects of memory (this work will be described in later sections of this chapter). Injection of minuscule quantities of the anesthetic silenced local neural activity for several minutes. The results in normal animals described above were from those subjects that were injected with placebo on both probe tests (Figure 2.4, bottom). However, the effects of the anesthetic were striking. On the first probe trial, animals that were injected with anesthetic into the caudate nucleus behaved just as control subjects had: They were predominantly "place" learners, a result indicating the place representation did not depend on the caudate nucleus. But the animals that had been injected with anesthetic into the hippocampus showed no preference at all, a result indicating they relied on their hippocampus for the place representation, and that this was the only representation normally available at that stage of learning. On the second probe test a different pattern emerged. Whereas control subjects had by now acquired the response strategy, animals given an anesthetic in the caudate nucleus lost the turning response and instead showed a striking opposite preference for the place strategy. Animals given an injection of anesthetic into the hippocampus maintained their response strategy.

When these data are combined, a clear picture of the evolution of multiple memory representations emerges. Animals normally develop an initial place representation that is mediated by the hippocampus, and no turning-response representation has developed in this initial period. With overtraining, a response representation that is mediated by the caudate nucleus is acquired and, indeed, predominates over the hippocampal place representation. The latter is not, however, lost; it can be "uncovered" by inactivation of the caudate nucleus and suppression of the turning-response strategy. Why in particular the hippocampus and caudate nucleus might serve these particular roles in memory will be discussed extensively later. For now, these findings offer compelling evidence that elements of both the S-R and the cognitive map views were right: There are distinct types of memory for place and response, and they are distinguished by their performance characteristics as well as by the brain pathways that support them.

Cognitive Maps in Humans, Too: Barlett's *Remembering*

Around the same time that Tolman was describing his classic studies on maze learning in rats, the British psychologist Bartlett (1932) published *Remembering,* his treatise on human memory. And just as Tolman's theory challenged S-R behaviorism, Barlett's work stands in stark contrast to the then-established and better known rigorous methods that guided the pursuits of most of his contemporary psychologists. Moreover, the insights it provided into the structure and richness of memory proved to be critical for modern views of memory. His work was central in bringing the field of memory research—and this review—back to issues about the nature of the more complex form(s) of memory that supports conscious recollection. Accordingly, Bartlett's work is considered here at some length.

The tradition of rigorous methodology had begun with Herman Ebbinghaus (1885), who admired the mathematical analyses that had been brought to the psychophysics of perception, and who sought to develop similarly precise and quantitative methods for the study of memory. Ebbinghaus had rejected the use of introspection as capable of providing evidence on memory. He developed objective assessments of memory in "savings" scores that measured retention in terms of the reduction in trials required to relearn material, and he used statistical analyses to test the reliability of his findings. Furthermore, to create learning materials that were both simple and homogeneous in content Ebbinghaus invented the "nonsense syllable," a meaningless letter string composed of two consonants with a vowel between. With this invention he avoided the confounding influences of "interest," "beauty," and other features that he felt might affect the memorability of real words, and he simultaneously equalized the length and meaningfulness of the items, albeit by minimizing the former and eliminating the latter. Ebbinghaus was and still is hailed as a pioneer of systematic scientific methodology in the study of human verbal memory.

Bartlett differed in two major ways. First, his interest was in the mental processes used to recover memories, that is, in *remembering* more than in *learning*. He was not so much interested in the probability of recall, which dominated Ebbinghaus's approach, as in what he called "effort after meaning," the mental processing taken to search out and ultimately reconstruct memories. Second, Bartlett shuddered at the notion of using nonsense syllables as learning materials. By avoidance of meaningful items, he argued, the resulting memories would necessarily lack the rich background of knowledge in which new information is stored. Indeed, the subtitle of Bartlett's book is *A Study in Experimental and Social Psychology,* highlighting his view that "real" memory is embedded in the full fabric of a lifetime of experience, prominently including one's culture.

Barlett's main strategy was called the *method of repeated reproduction.* His most famous material was a short folktale titled "The War of the Ghosts," which was adapted from an original translation by the explorer Franz Boaz. He selected this story for several reasons: The syntax and prose were derived from a culture quite different from that of his British experimental subjects, the story contents lacked explicit connections between some of the events described, and the tale contained dramatic and supernatural events that would evoke vivid visual imagery in his subjects. These qualities were, of course, exactly the sort of thing Ebbinghaus worked so hard to avoid with his nonsense syllables. But Bartlett (1932) focused on these features because he was interested primarily in the content and structure of the memory obtained, and less in the probability of recall of specific items. It is worth reading that folktale here:

The War of the Ghosts

One night two young men from Egulac went down to the river to hunt seals, and while they were there it became foggy and calm. Then they heard war-cries and they thought: "Maybe this is a war party." They escaped to the shore, and hid behind a log. Now canoes came up, and they heard the noise of paddles, and saw one canoe coming up to them. There were five men in the canoe, and they said: "What do you think? We wish to take you along. We are going up the river to make war on the people."

One of the young men said: "I have no arrows."

"Arrows are in the canoe," they said.

"I will not go along. I might be killed. My relatives do not know where I have gone. But you," he said, turning to the other, "may go with them."

So one of the young men went, but the other returned home.

And the warriors went up the river to a town on the other side of Ka-lama. The people came down to the water, and they began to fight, and many were killed. But presently one of the young men heard the warriors say: "Quick, let us go home: that Indian has been hit." Now he thought: "Oh, they are ghosts." He did not feel sick, but they said he had been shot.

So the canoes went back to Egulac, and the young man went ashore to his house, and made a fire. And he told everybody and said: "Behold I accompanied the ghosts, and we went to fight. Many of our fellows were killed. They said I was hit, and I did not feel sick."

He told it all, and then he became quiet. When the sun rose he fell down. Something black came out of his mouth. His face became contorted. The people jumped up and cried.

He was dead. (p. 65)

Each subject read the story twice, then was instructed to reproduce it exactly 15 minutes later, and again at successively longer retention intervals. Here is the second reproduction given by one subject 20 hours after learning:

The War of the Ghosts

Two men from Edulac went fishing. While thus occupied by the river they heard a noise in the distance.

"It sounds like a cry," said one, and presently there appeared some men in canoes who invited them to join the party on their adventure. One of the young men refused to go, on the grounds of family ties, but the other offered to go.

"But there are no arrows," he said.

"The arrows are in the boat," was the reply.

He thereupon took his place, while his friend returned home. The party paddled up the river to Kaloma, and began to land on the banks of the river. The enemy came rushing upon them, and some sharp fighting ensued. Presently someone was injured, and the cry was raised that the enemy were ghosts.

The party returned down the stream, and the young man arrived home feeling none the worse for his experience. The next morning at dawn he endeavored to recount his adventures. While he was talking something black issued from his mouth. Suddenly he uttered a cry and fell down. His friends gathered around him.

But he was dead. (p. 66)

Bartlett did not use rigorous operational definitions or statistical measures, but his analyses were compelling nonetheless. He made three general observations on this and other reproductions of the story: First, the story was considerably shortened, mainly by omissions. Second, the syntax became more modern and taken from the subject's culture (e.g., "refused on the grounds of family ties," "endeavored to recount his adventures"). Third, the story became more coherent and consequential. From these observations Bartlett concluded that remembering was not simply a process of the recovery or forgetting of items, but that memory seemed to evolve over time. Items were not lost or recovered at random. Rather, material that was more foreign to the subject, or that lacked sequence, or that was stated in unfamiliar terms, was more likely to be lost or changed substantially in both syntax and meaning, becoming more consistent with the subject's experiences. For example, in the original segment of the story the young man heard the warriors say, "Quick, let us go home: that Indian has been hit," and concluded, seemingly without sufficient reason, "Oh, they are ghosts." This was converted to a more familiar statement that did not imply a logical connection: "Presently someone was injured, and the cry was raised that the enemy were ghosts." Similarly, the first appearance of a somewhat irrational statement—"He did not feel sick, but they said he had been shot"—was omitted in the reproduction. The second reference was converted to the more logical and common statement that the young man was "feeling none the worse for his experience."

These and many other examples led Bartlett to develop an account of remembering known as *schema theory.* He attributed the origin of schema theory to the neurologist Sir Henry Head (1920), who had proposed that new perceptual experiences were represented in the cerebral cortex only in the context of previous experiences:

> The sensory cortex is the storehouse of past impressions. They may rise into consciousness as images, or more often, as in the case of spacial impressions, remain outside central consciousness. Here they form organized models of ourselves which may be called schemata. Such schemata modify the impressions produced by incoming sensory impulses in such a way that the final sensations of position or locality rise into consciousness charged with relations to something that has gone before. (p. 607)

Bartlett (1932) wrote that he strongly disliked the term *schema,* because it was at once too definite and too sketchy, and he could define a schema only in general terms as "an active organization of past reactions, or of past experiences" (p. 201). Nevertheless he found this term useful in his struggle to distinguish the rote learning of a sequence of items or movements from the creative process of remembering. Following Head, he granted that the simplest schemata were habit-like traces of items in sequential order of experience. But he elaborated this "low-level" mechanism, arguing that our experience of particular sequences builds up en masse, so that "in remembering, we appear to be dominated by particular past events which are more or less dated, or placed, in relation to other associated particular events. Thus the actively organized setting looks as if it has somehow undergone a change, making it possible for parts of it which are remote in time to have a leading role in the play," and thus allowing the organism "to construct or to infer from what is present the probable constituents and their order which went to build them up" (p. 202).

It appears that Bartlett viewed mere repetition as a "low-level" form of memory by which a series of reactions can be reproduced in order. But to explain his observations on remembering he also saw the need for the organism to "break up this chronological order and rove more or less at will in any order over the events which have built up its present momentary 'schemata'" (p. 203). He proposed that remembering is therefore a *(re)constructive* process and not one of mere *reproduction,* as Ebbinghaus preferred and as would guide low-level rote memory. He offered one possible mechanism that could perform this (re)constructive process. Remembering required, in Barlett's terms, the ability to "turn round" on one's own schemata, using consciousness to search within the simpler learned sequences for rational and consistent order and to reconstruct them anew consistent with one's whole life of experience. In this way Bartlett gave consciousness a function beyond merely being aware. It played a central role in the reconstructive act of remembering, so that it was consciously mediated, running contrary to the "active school in current psychological controversy which would banish all reference to consciousness" (p. 214).

Later Challenges to S-R Theory From Studies on the Psychology of Animal Learning

We now return to the psychology of animal learning, and to developments in that discipline that followed Tolman's era. Despite the best efforts of Tolman and the other field theorists, the search for a unitary set of rules of learning was never really slowed. Indeed, it might be said that the obvious success of the simple behavioral approach of Skinner, in his zealous and focused application of Thorndike's law of effect, held sway over most of the field for several years. And the simple logic of Pavlov's law of contiguity found strong substantiation in neurophysiological model systems and in thinking about basic learning mechanisms both then and currently (Rescorla, 1988a; 1988b; Holland, 1990). There continued to be arguments about whether the basis of associations was the contiguity of an action and a reward (Thorndike's and Skinner's instrumental or operant learning) or an arbitrary stimulus and a stimulus that generates a reflexive response (Pavlovian conditioning). But regardless of one's preference, the guiding theme of research into the 1950s and 1960s remained the simple notion of the repeated close temporal contiguity of any set of items as necessary and sufficient conditions for learning.

However, as new and different behavioral paradigms were explored, "exceptions" to the law of contiguity appeared. It may not be too simplistic to say that much of the progress in animal learning theory since the late 1960s can be characterized as the discovery and reconciliation of the exceptions to the rule of contiguity. Among the first and most powerful challenges to simple contiguity were Garcia and Koelling's (1966) studies on flavor aversion learning. In this paradigm animals are typically exposed to a novel-flavored food or drink, and are later made ill by means of a toxin or X-radiation (for a review see Rozin & Kalat, 1971). Upon later testing the animals avoid the novel food or drink. There are three features of this kind of Pavlovian conditioning that violate the customary rules of contiguity. First, striking right at the heart of the notion of close temporal contiguity, flavor aversion learning is robust even if the delay between the novel taste and the illness is several hours. Second, violating the notion that S-R learning requires the repeated wearing in of a pathway between S and R, flavor aversion conditioning can be strong even after a single training trial. Third, whereas rats immediately learned an aversive association between a flavor and illness, associations between flavor and shock are not easily acquired. Conversely, rats readily learn to avoid a fluid food marked by distinctive visual cues when they are shocked for licking a drinking tube; but, they do not easily associate a visual cue with illness (Garcia & Ervin, 1968; see Rozin & Kalat, 1971). These findings called into question the key Pavlovian doctrine that learning can occur between any arbitrary neutral stimulus and any unconditioned stimulus. Rescorla and Holland (1982; Rescorla, 1988a) have retrospectively summarized the literature beginning at that time, categorizing exceptions to the rule of contiguity in terms of controversial issues regarding the conditions of learning, the contents of learning, and the influence of learning on behavior.

With regard to the conditions of learning, several studies have called into question whether close temporal contiguity is necessary or sufficient for the formation of associations. In addition to the findings on flavor aversion learning that challenge the necessity of contiguity, there are also data that call into question its sufficiency. The most common example is the so-called blocking phenomenon of Kamin (1968, 1969), in which effectiveness of a given stimulus in entering into associations is dependent on parameters other than the contiguity of an unconditioned stimulus. Animals are initially given pairings of a stimulus A and a unconditioned stimulus, followed by pairings of A plus another stimulus X with the unconditioned stimulus, and are then tested for conditioned responses to A and X. Typically animals trained in this sequence showed poorer responses to X than other animals that had not been pretrained on A alone. Thus, A → US followed by AX → US results in good responding to A but not to X. By contrast, training at the outset with AX → US produces good responding to both A and X. The pretraining with A → US had "blocked" the associability of X when presented only in combination with A (AX → US), even though X had as many contiguous presentations with the reinforcer in both situations.

With regard to the contents of learning as originally formulated, Pavlovian conditioning could occur between any designated neutral stimulus and any arbitrarily selected unconditioned stimulus. Clearly the findings on flavor aversion conditioning showed that there are severe constraints on what stimuli can enter into associations with one another. In addition it is now also clear that associations can be formed with much more than the specified conditioning stimulus. Perhaps the most prominent example here is the phenomenon of contextual conditioning, in which animals learn not only about the designated CS but also about the situation in which the CS-US pairing occurs (Balsam & Tomie, 1985). A typical example is the contextual-fear-conditioning paradigm, in which rats or mice are initially familiarized with a novel test chamber, then presented with a tone CS followed by a brief shock. Just one or a few pairings of tone and shock result in the animal's adopting a rigid freezing posture, as well as several other behavioral and physiological responses associated with fear, on subsequent presentations of the tone. However, even before the tone is presented again—that is, as soon as the animal is placed back in the test apparatus—it begins to express the fear responses substantially (and then expresses these responses even more when the tone is presented). Thus the animal has learned an association not only between the designated tone CS and shock, but also between the context and the tone-shock pairings. Therefore the formal structure of a learning paradigm from the perspective of the experimenter may be only a part of what the animal learns from the overall experience.

With regard to the influence of learning on behavior, the original Pavlovian formulation held that the CS comes to substitute for the unconditioned stimulus in producing the same reflexive behavior elicited by the US. However, considerable research on conditioned responses has provided strong evidence against this simple notion. For example many studies have now shown that the form of the conditioned response is often very different from that of the unconditioned response. Even in the case of Pavlov's salivary conditioning the CR typically lacked components of the UR. For example, swallowing was a typical component of the unconditioned response, but not of the conditioned response (Rescorla & Holland, 1982).

More profound examples of unexpected patterns of conditioned responses came from efforts by Breland and Breland (1961, 1966) to use Skinner's operant conditioning regimens to train unusual experimental subjects on typical laboratory tasks. They found, for example, that pigs trained to drop a coin into a box adapted their natural rooting behavior to flip the coin into the air toward the container, rather than adopt the seemingly more straightforward and "efficient" behavior of carrying the coin in their mouths and dropping it into the box. When they attempted to train raccoons to perform a similar task, they were stymied by the animal's preoccupation with rubbing coins against one another and dipping them repeatedly into the container without dropping them. It rapidly became clear to these investigators that the scope of possible conditioned responses was limited by the range of the subject's natural repertoire of innate behaviors.

Another example of limits on the scope of possible conditioned responses comes from fear-conditioning paradigms where conditioned stimuli are associated with shock. In all variants of this task the US (shock) always produces frantic movement by the animal. Yet, depending upon the responses available to the animal, following training the CS can elicit either running or the opposite movement pattern: freezing. These and many other examples have shown that there are considerable constraints on the form of conditioned responses that can be produced, or that can be produced readily. In addition it turns out that the nature of the CR depends very much on the characteristics of the CS. For example, when a tone is the CS, conditioning to food can be primarily expressed as crouching. But, when a light is the CS, conditioning to food can be primarily expressed as rearing (Holland, 1977).

These and many other findings led many investigators to conclude that, contrary to a set of simple and general laws of learning, there are many "constraints" on the conditions in which those laws hold. In his classic review of the literature on fear and avoidance learning, Bolles (1970) concluded that punishments can produce only a restricted set of "species-specific defense reactions (SSDRs)" (p. 33). He showed that learning SSDRs such as freezing or escape in a chamber where shocks are presented occurs exceedingly rapidly. Conversely, contingencies that interfere with SSDRs and ones that call for conditioned responses other than SSDRs result in poor learning. The most common example given was the poor conditionability of bar pressing to avoid shocks. As Timberlake and Lucas (1989) later concluded more generally, Pavlovian conditioning might be better seen as a process by which a stimulus engages a whole behavioral system that is relevant in the particular learning situation.

In the same year that Bolles's analysis appeared, Seligman (1970) proposed a more sweeping view in which learning is severely constrained by the "preparedness" of particular associations. Thus some stimuli are prepared within the nervous system to associate and some are not, and some responses are prepared to be conditioned to some CSs and some are not. Shettleworth (1972) expanded on this analysis, exploring several examples of "adaptive specializations" of learning in natural situations to make her argument that there are constraints on the kinds of stimuli animals can learn about, and on the kinds of responses they can learn, as well as constraints on the learnability of relationships between responses and reinforcers, stimuli and responses, and stimuli and reinforcers. Perhaps Rozin and Kalat (1971, 1972) articulated this perspective most forcefully, arguing that all learning involves situation-specific adaptations, each with its own set of learning rules.

Parallel Discoveries From Ethological Studies on Learning and Memory

During the early part of this century another school of behaviorists were examining learning, along with other aspects of behavior that can be observed in natural situations. These were the ethologists. It is probably fair to say that learning and memory were not their primary concern. Rather, they sought to apply evolutionary principles to explain adaptive behaviors, and their techniques were largely observational, although some of the most stunning findings, including those by the noted ethologists Tinbergen (1951) and Lorenz (1965), were based on experimental studies where critical stimuli were simplified or manipulated. In general, the ethological and psychological studies of memory went on in parallel. Whenever there was a connection it was more often couched in an antagonistic debate on the relative importance of "nature" versus "nurture" as the basis for complex behaviors. The ethologists argued that the psychologists were not studying "real" (natural) behavior, whereas the psychologists argued that the ethologists failed to simplify and control behavior sufficiently for detailed analysis.

Nevertheless, the findings by the psychologists showing "constraints on learning" began the rapprochement of these perspectives. Clearly the selection of the stimulus exemplified in the flavor aversion paradigm and the notions of "preparedness" and "adaptive specializations" of learning brought about this realignment in thinking by psychologists. It is worth noting that this really is a realignment because some of the original investigators held the same view. For example, in introducing the maze to studies on rodent learning Small (1901) acknowledged that "the experiments must conform to the pyscho-biological character of the animal if sane results are to be obtained" (p. 206).

Perhaps Shettleworth (1993) best characterized both the differences and the progress toward reconciliation of psychological and ethological viewpoints by contrasting the ethologists' approach as "top-down" to the psychologists' "bottom-up" approach. The top-down approach begins with the assumption that learning is an evolved adaptation, like other anatomical and physiological characteristics. From this perspective, learning is analyzed in terms of the functions that information storage serves for survival. The notion that there are multiple memory systems is then a direct consequence of the different adaptive problems animals and their brain systems must solve. The multiple memory system view would naturally lead to a consideration of different conditions, contents, and forms of expression of memory mediated by different neural systems within any particular animal and across species.

Sherry and Schacter (1987) took the similar position that memory involves adaptive specializations and they explicitly connected this idea to the notion of multiple memory systems. They proposed that new memory systems might have evolved whenever there existed a functional incompatibility between different memory demands. As an example they compared song learning and food caching in birds. Song learning requires a period early in life during which one's local dialect must be adapted to a basic species prototype for song and then used across multiple breeding seasons in adulthood. It seems the requirements were addressed by the evolution of an innate species-specific template, a developmental sensitive period, and very long-term retention of song memory without decay. By contrast, food caching requires relatively continuous (nonseasonal) memory of many arbitrary locations, a capacity for "erasure" of caches recovered, and then new learning of more caches with interference from previous memories. This kind of memory would not benefit by a template, a developmental sensitivity period, or a permanent memory store. Instead food caching requires fundamentally different characteristics, including a large storage capacity and flexible addition and deletion from the stored listing.

Sherry and Schacter also described the incompatibilities of the acquisition of habits and skills and the memory of specific events in human learning and memory. They pointed out that a fundamental feature of habit and skill learning is the gradual detection and preservation of the *invariances* of the perceptual cues and execution of movements across episodes of their acquisition and use. By contrast, memory of specific events fundamentally requires preservation of the *variances* in the contextual details of different episodes. Thus, in both birds and humans, two different kinds of memory were deemed *functionally incompatible* and thus required the evolution of distinct memory systems to accomplish them.

Summing up the modern evolution of animal learning theory, we conclude that what began as searches by psychologists for general learning principles ultimately converged with the findings from the ethological approach. The combined discoveries of these different disciplines indicate that there are multiple adaptive systems of the brain, each governed by its own distinct set of operating principles (see Holland, 1990; Shettleworth, 1993).

The Emergence of a Cognitive Neuroscience of Memory: Hebb

Even at the peak of the successes guided by the S-R approach, there were disconcerting findings from the early neuroscientists attempting to identify the brain locus of conditioned reflexes. In particular, Lashley's exhaustive search for the pathway and locus of the conditioned reflex circuit had been nothing short of a disaster. As described above, despite his initial belief in the conditioned-reflex mechanisms as a basis of learning, Lashley failed totally in finding a specific S-R path. Maintaining this view in the face of the data could only lead to the conclusion that learning is just not possible (Lashley, 1950).

However, at the same time that Lashley left the field with the issue of localization unresolved, the Canadian psychologist Hebb provided a possible reconciliation of the S-R and field theory views in his 1949 treatise *The Organization of Behavior.* Furthermore, Hebb proposed a rapprochement of these views by introducing neurobiological reality into the concepts of cognitive maps and schemas. At the outset of his book Hebb recognized both the "switchboard" (S-R) and "field" (cognitive map) theories and argued that the eventual explanation of mentalistic phenomena would have to incorporate neural transmission mechanisms that lead from sensory excitation to motor responses. He viewed his theory as

> a kind of connectionism, one of the switchboard variety, though it does not deal in direct connections between afferent and efferent pathways: not an "S-R" psychology, if R means *muscular* response. The connections serve rather to establish autonomous central activities, which then are the basis of further learning. (p. xix)

Thus Hebb validated the "field" phenomena indicated by Tolman's and Lashley's research and argued for the need for conceptions that are "molar" enough to be useful as an explanation of behavior. Indeed, he ended up offering ideas about the neural instantiation of much more complex a form of memory than the earlier researchers would have envisioned.

Hebb's (1949) writing focused on the notion of "cell assemblies," diffuse circuits of connected neurons that develop to represent specific percepts and concepts. Considering how cell assemblies might develop Hebb, wrote, "The first step in this neural schematizing is a bald assumption about the structural changes that make lasting memory possible" (p. 60). His proposal was similar to its predecessors in focusing on the synapse as the likely locus of structural change; but it was original in diverging from previous foci on single specific sensory-to-motor synapses exercised during learning, instead emphasizing reverberatory activity among a set of many cells outlasting the learning event and leading to a stabilization of the cooperative activity of cells in that "cell assembly."

Hebb's most famous postulate involves a mechanism of how this reverberatory activity would result in permanent structural change:

> When an axon of cell A is near enough to excite a cell B and repeatedly or persistently takes part in firing it, some growth process or metabolic change takes place in one or both cells such that A's efficiency, as one of the cells firing B, is increased. (p. 62)

In the growth of such a cell assembly, initial presentations of a stimulus might set off firing patterns in a particular sequence and, through circuits that feed back onto the initially activated cells, would continue the overall pattern of activation (Figure 2.5A). If each cycle of activity follows Hebb's synaptic postulate, the synaptic resistance between each consecutive cell in the circuit becomes lower. Thus when reexcited by a similar input the entire assembly tends to reestablish itself (today we call this pattern *completion*). This postulate, of course, has become the guiding theme of research on a model of use-dependent synaptic efficacy known as long-term potentiation (LTP) and, more generally, is embodied in the learning mechanism used in a variety of computational modeling efforts.

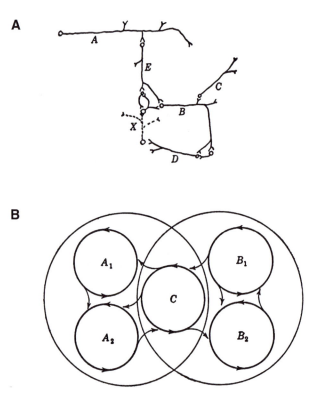

Figure 2.5. Hebb's model of cell assemblies. A. This diagram illustrates a set of cortical cells that might be involved in processing visual information. The recurrency of the connections between cells B, X, and D could mediate the establishment of a cell assembly that includes all of the cells pictured. In particular the enhancement of an initially weak set of synaptic connections for cell X could provide a critical link between cells in the assembly. B. An illustration of set of cell assemblies that could interact to mediate indirect associations between conceptual representations A-C. Subsystem C could act as a link between two systems, one composed of A_1, A_2 and C and the other composed of B_1, B_2 and C. (Reproduced, with permission, from Hebb, 1949; Copyright John Wiley & Sons, Inc.)

It is important to note that the particular set of cells involved in a cell assembly could be quite arbitrary. The "coding" of the learned stimulus is in the coincident activity of the cells in the cell assembly and not in any particular cell or switchboardlike path through it. Hebb also noted that as long as the cell assembly is moderately large and the interconnections are sufficiently rich, the loss of any particular connection or subset of the cells might not compromise the overall coding of the larger assembly, a phenomenon that in connectionist or artificial neural network modeling is called *graceful degradation*. Furthermore, Hebb pressed the cell assembly concept into use to explain the perception of complex stimuli composed of multiple distinct elements (Figure 2.5B). He proposed that cell assemblies for a set of related perceptual elements must overlap sufficiently to excite one another in a "phase sequence" that would embody the whole complex and indeed could alternate among perceptions of the whole and the elements determined by the pattern of those activations among cell assemblies.

There are three levels of organization and consequent mechanism in Hebb's full theory: First, interconnected cells previously active together tend ever after to re-create the same conjoint firing patterns. Second, large sets of these cells that involve reentrant loops onto one another develop reverberatory activity that organizes the circuit into distributed and potentially widespread cortical cell assemblies that encode perceptual units within their cooperative activity. Third, overlapping cell assemblies can encode complex percepts or behavioral actions by a phase sequence of their activity.

Hebb quite explicitly outlined how the establishment of cell assemblies and phase sequences during conceptual development would provide the context and basis for later learning, consistent with Bartlett's views of new learning as guided by and imposed on schemata developed through enculturation. To Hebb this meant that adult learning is not associations of unrelated processes but has to be built upon the cell assemblies and phase sequences in novel combinations. Consistent with Barlett's observation that unfamiliar or illogical events are the first forgotten, Hebb (1949) stated that

> prompt learning is only possible when the stimulation sets off well-organized phase sequences, but not otherwise.... Adult learning is thus a changed relationship between the central effects of separate stimulations, and does not directly concern the precipitating stimulus or, primarily, the motor response whose control is embedded in the central activity. (p. 128)

In accounting for Bartlett's studies, the way in which information that is lost or altered to fit subjectively meaningful representations is determined by one's preexisting phase sequences.

Hebb felt these mechanisms could be extended even further. If two sets of phase sequences each partially activated a common set of "fringe" sequences, then a connection between them could develop without any direct overlap. By such a mechanism Hebb (1949) proposed that "two concepts could acquire a latent 'association' without ever having occurred together" (p. 132). Such representations might subserve conceptual leaps in the form of "insights" into the connection between two experiences or ideas. Hebb also proposed this mechanism might underlie the inferential behavior of Tolman's rats in solving maze problems and conscious purposeful behavior more generally. As should be clear, the brain mechanisms that Hebb was after were *not* those underlying the simple forms of memory discussed by earlier researchers but those supporting more complex, cognitively mediated and consciously aware memory.

Breakthroughs From the Study of Human Amnesia

The modern era of cognitive neuroscience studies of memory can perhaps be dated to two major breakthroughs that came from the study of patients with pervasive "global" amnesia. This research and the animal studies that followed will be surveyed in detail in succeeding chapters. Here we will provide only an introduction that relates the major findings to the historical considerations presented above.

The first of these breakthroughs came with the report by Scoville and Milner (1957) of what has become probably the most famous neurological patient in the literature, the man known by his initials, H.M. As described more fully in chapter 5, this patient had the medial temporal lobe area removed to alleviate his severe epileptic attacks. H.M. consequently suffered what appeared to be a nearly complete loss of the ability to form new long-term memories: His impairment, tested since the late 1950s, has been shown to extend to "words, digits, paragraphs, faces, names, maze routes, spatial layouts, geometric shapes, nonsense patterns, nonsense syllables, clicks, tunes, tones, public and personal events, and more" (Cohen, 1984). Coming just a few years after Lashley failed to find evidence that the memory "engram" could be localized, this report served notice to the field that the brain mechanisms of human memory could be studied.

The selectivity of the impairment in this case—H.M.'s impairment occurs in the context of normal perceptual, motor, and intellectual capacities—showed unequivocally that memory could be dissociated from other psychological capacities. Furthermore, the pattern of memory loss in H.M. showed selectivity even within the domain of memory. Although H.M. appeared to have virtually no capacity for retaining new everyday memories across any extended delay, he could briefly retain information over short delays, if he wasn't interrupted (i.e., as long as he was working with that information). Thus, he showed sparing of *immediate memory* or *primary memory,* as James called it, or *working memory,* as we will refer to it. Moreover, H.M. retained the ability to retrieve remote memories, including childhood experiences as well as information about the world overlearned early in life (e.g., about language, objects, and social skills). Thus the learning and memory deficit he suffered was both profound in its severity and circumscribed to the retention of new everyday memories once they left conscious attention. This pattern of findings was interpreted as a success in the identification of a brain area critical to the formation of new long-term memories, but not of working memory or of retrieval or storage of long-ago learned information.

These findings brought renewed interest to the writings of Ribot (1882), who described several cases of retrograde amnesia in which recollection was lost of both the events of the accident precipitating the amnesia and sometimes a period of the patient's life before the accident, but in indirect relation to how long ago the information was acquired: Recent memory was most susceptible, with more remote memories more resistant to amnesia. He concluded that a certain amount of time is necessary for memory to "organize" and "fix" itself in order to become insensitive to trauma. Müller and Pilzecker (1900) first used the term *consolidation* to describe this phenomenon and studied how material interpolated between learning and testing could affect memory performance. They suggested the existence of persisting physiological activity that was necessary for several minutes to fix the memory of new material. Burnham (1903) provided a more detailed examination of consolidation in cases of retrograde amnesia, describing his conclusions in physiological and cognitive terms:

In normal memory a process of organization is continually going on, a physical process of organization and a psychological process of repetition and association. In order that ideas may become a part of permanent memory, time must elapse for these processes of organization to be completed. (p. 132)

This organization process could be instantiated by Hebb's reverberating cell assemblies, described above. Indeed, several studies beginning in the era following Hebb's proposal showed that several brain treatments, given early but not late after learning, could block or facilitate subsequent retention, consistent with a lasting, labile, neurally mediated consolidation process (for reviews see Glickman, 1961; McGaugh, 1966; McGaugh & Herz, 1972).

Returning to the status of H.M.'s recently acquired long-term memory, Milner (1962) reported an exception to H.M.'s global amnesia, showing that he was able to learn new motor skills. Another hint of an exception to the otherwise pervasive scope of amnesia in H.M. (Milner, Corkin, & Teuber, 1968) and in other amnesic patients (Warrington & Weiskrantz, 1968) came from findings of an ability of prior exposure to objects or words to influence subsequent perceptual identification of these items, an effect that only much later came to be understood as reflective of a preserved "repetition priming" (or "priming"). But it was a considerable time before most investigators came to view these "exceptions" to amnesia as indicative of a large domain of preserved learning capacities in amnesia.

The second breakthrough came in 1980 when Cohen and Squire reported the complete preservation of the acquisition, retention over 3 months, and expression of perceptual skill (of reading mirror-reversed words) in amnesic patients. These patients showed fully intact skilled performance, yet were markedly impaired both in recognizing the particular words on which they trained and in recollecting their training experiences. These investigators were struck by the dissociation of the ability to benefit or otherwise have performance shaped by a series of training experiences, an ability that appeared fully normal in the amnesic patients, from the capacity to explicitly remember or consciously recollect those training experiences or their contents, which was markedly impaired in the patients. They, and others, were reminded of Claparede's (1911/1951) report of an amnesic woman who, although not explicitly remembering an earlier meeting with Claparede during which he pricked her hand with a hidden pin while greeting her with a handshake, subsequently refused to shake hands with him again.

Cohen and Squire (1980) attributed their observed dissociation, together with the earlier hints about aspects of possibly spared memory in amnesia, to the operation of distinct forms of memory, which they called *procedural memory* and *declarative memory,* respectively, adopting the terms from a similar distinction in artificial intelligence. These forms of memory were seen as functionally distinct memory systems, one dedicated to the tuning and modification of networks that support skilled performance, and the other to the encoding, storage, and retrieval on demand of new data about facts and events. These functionally distinct memory systems were tied to separate brain systems, with declarative memory—but not procedural memory—seen as critically dependent on the medial temporal lobe and midline diencephalic structures damaged in various amnesias. This particular multiple-memory-system view and its subsequent extension and elaboration by the current authors (e.g., Eichenbaum, Otto, & Cohen, 1992; Cohen & Eichenbaum, 1993) are discussed more fully starting in chapter 5.

In succeeding years the full scope of preserved learning capacity in amnesia has become better appreciated, although various investigators have emphasized different aspects thought to be central to the dissociation between spared and impaired aspects of memory. Graf and Schacter (1985; Schacter, 1987a) have emphasized the inability of amnesic patients to show forms of memory expression requiring conscious recollection *(explicit memory)* while retaining the ability to express memory implicitly in performances that do not entail gaining conscious access to a prior learning experience *(implicit memory)*. Others have also emphasized the limitation of spared memory performance in amnesic patients to examples of memory without awareness (see Moscovitch, 1984). Tulving (1993) has preferred to speak of impaired memory in amnesia as focusing on episodic memory, leaving semantic memory intact. Both of these views are discussed in more detail below.

While there are several different terminologies offered in the literature as a description of the forms of memory spared and impaired in amnesia, there is strong consensus on much of the phenomenology of hippocampal-dependent and hippocampal-independent memory in humans, as will be discussed in detail below. One way to frame the distinction between these two domains of memory is in terms of the task variables that provide sufficient conditions for demonstrating preserved versus impaired memory in amnesics, as Moscovitch (1984) has done. He argued that amnesics show learning on tasks that satisfy the following conditions:

(1) The tasks are so highly structured that the goal of the task and the means to achieve it are apparent; (2) the means to achieve the goal are available to the subject (i.e., the response and strategies used to arrive at the goal are already in the subject's repertoire); and (3) success in achieving the goal can be had without reference to any particular postmorbid event or episode. (p. 106)

We return to the issue of how exactly to characterize the nature of amnesia following hippocampal damage in humans in chapter 5, advocating an extension and elaboration of the declarative-procedural distinction that we have been exploring for many years. Next we review two other lines of study that have supported the distinction between declarative and procedural memory and have provided insights into its mechanisms. One of these involves studies on the cognitive processes that underlie memory performance in normal human subjects. The other involves efforts to develop animal models of amnesia following damage to the same brain region removed in H.M.

Contributions From Modern Considerations of Normal Memory Processing in Humans

Considerable evidence for the existence of multiple memory systems has come from recent studies on normal human learning and memory. The major evidence focuses on the distinction between conscious or explicit memory and unconscious or implicit memory that has its roots in the descriptions of William James and of Henri Bergson, alluded to earlier.

Ebbinghaus (1885) noted that some memory performances in which savings were shown lacked a conscious awareness that the items had been seen before. This observation raised for him the question of the connections between recollection and consciousness. Schacter (1987a) described this and other early demonstrations of memory without consciousness, characterizing conceptions during that period as not fundamentally separating unconscious from conscious memory, but differentiating them by strength in that the unconscious trace was considered just too weak to reach a threshold required for conscious experience. Furthermore, Schacter described several studies since 1950 that have provided compelling evidence for robust unconscious memories. These include demonstrations of "memory" for material that is neither recalled nor recognized. In these situations memory is expressed in lasting effects of subliminally encoded information, learning of reinforcement response or classical contingencies and language rules without conscious awareness, and repetition priming, a phenomenon by which exposure to a word or object facilitates its re-identification upon subsequent presentation with a degraded form of the item.

The phenomenon of repetition priming has been the most studied of these approaches and has yielded the most data on the characteristics and independence of unconscious memory. In his comprehensive reviews of this data, Schacter (1987a; Schacter et al., 1993) argued that there are five lines of evidence indicating that priming effects can be dissociated from conscious, explicit memory. First, variations in the type of study have differential effects on later priming or remembering. For example, focusing study on the meaning of word items (e.g., by judging their semantic category) but not the word's physical features (e.g., judging whether it has more consonants or vowels) improves explicit remembering. Both methods of study improve priming and recall. Second, unlike explicit remembering, priming is highly sensitive to shifts in the superficial qualities of items on the retention test. Thus shifts in the font or typecase of words or changes in the modality (auditory or visual) of presentation between initial exposure and testing substantially diminish the level of priming observed. Conversely, explicit remembering is classically insensitive to such shifts in superficial qualities. Third, priming and explicit remembering can have substantial differences in the retention intervals over which information can be recovered. Some priming phenomena are relatively transient compared to remembering, whereas others outlast one's recall. Fourth, unlike priming, explicit remembering is very sensitive to interference by the learning of related items. Finally, and perhaps most compelling, performance on priming and explicit remembering of specific items has been shown to be statistically independent, that is, uncorrelated. This last dissociation is particularly powerful when compared to the finding that free recall and recognition of items are closely correlated, a finding suggesting they reflect the same source of stored information (see Tulving, 1984).

Tulving (1972, 1983, 1984, 1985) expanded on distinctions between conscious and unconscious memory in humans, suggesting the existence of three separate memory systems with different operating characteristics and different levels of associated consciousness. He maintained the distinction between implicit, nonconscious memory and adopted Cohen and Squire's (1980; Cohen,

1981, 1984) designation *procedural memory*. In addition he divided conscious memory into two distinct forms called *semantic memory* and *episodic memory*. These forms of memory were conceived of as hierarchically organized, with the two higher forms being built upon the lower one(s):

> Procedural memory enables organisms to retain learned connections be-tween stimuli and responses, including those involving complex stimulus patterns and response chains, and to respond adaptively to the environment. Semantic memory is characterized by the additional capability of internally representing states of the world that are not perceptually present. It permits the organism to construct mental models of the world, models that can be manipulated and operated on covertly, independently of any overt behavior. Episodic memory affords the additional capability of acquisition and retention of knowledge about personally experienced events and their temporal relations in subjective time and the ability to mentally "travel back" in time. (Tulving, 1985, p. 387)

Tulving viewed each system as differing in its methods of acquisition, representation and expression of knowledge, and level of conscious experience. He viewed the mode of information acquisition in the procedural system as requiring overt action resulting in a representation in the form of a retuning of the system itself, through changes in the probabilities of specific responses to specific stimuli. In this system memory expression is rigidly determined during learning itself. By contrast, the mode of acquisition in the semantic and episodic systems can be covert observation, not requiring action and resulting in representations of relations among items that constitute our conscious knowledge of the world. Memory expression in the semantic and episodic systems is flexible in that it can occur in various conditions, including formats far removed from that of the original learning. In the case of episodic memory the representation includes additional personal information about the context in which learning occurred, and expression includes a consciousness of where and when events happened from a personal perspective. In addition, Tulving considered procedural learning nonconscious, as contrasted with semantic memory, which is "knowledge of the world" in that it involves introspective awareness of internal and external events. He reserved for episodic memory a capacity for "self-knowing" consciousness, the awareness of one's existence in subjective time from past to future—characterizing memories as being in one's personal past as opposed to knowledge structures that lack a conception of what is in the past. These characterizations share much with many of the earlier views described above, with the additional division of semantic and episodic memory. Tulving attributed to animals the procedural and semantic levels of memory but reserved for humans the capacity for episodic memory experience.

We shall return to this view of memory systems in chapter 5 when we consider theories of amnesia and give a more extensive and formal accounting of hippocampus-dependent and hippocampus-independent memory systems in humans.

Animal Models of Amnesia

Work on understanding the role of the hippocampal system in animals has been strongly influenced by the human amnesia work, but its progress has been somewhat mixed. Indeed, the animal research intended to clarify the anatomical and physiological bases of declarative memory is characterized by controversy about the fundamental memory-processing functions of the medial temporal lobe structures damaged in H.M. Here we will provide a brief overview of the first attempts to model amnesia in animals, and we introduce three prominent proposals about the function of the hippocampal system derived from these efforts, relating each to its historical background. We return to these issues in Part II of this book, where we attempt some final closure.

After the initial descriptions of H.M. there were several attempts to create an animal model of the severe and global anterograde amnesia associated with hippocampal damage. These initial efforts were disappointing in that the range of the learning deficit observed in animals with hippocampal system damage was quite limited compared to the disorder observed in humans. After complete bilateral hippocampal removal animals could learn many of the simple conditioning, maze-learning, and perceptual discrimination tasks developed earlier by animal learning theorists. Conversely they were impaired in other maze or discrimination tasks. This mixture of findings indicated that there was a learning impairment, but the nature of the deficit was certainly not as "global" as that observed in H.M. The different interpretations of the pattern of findings by separate investigators led at first to proposals about hippocampal function in animals that were not specifically tied to memory, but more to attention (Kimble, 1968) or response inhibition (Douglas, 1967). Nevertheless, many experiments were aimed at discovering the fundamental nature of amnesia in animals after hippocampal damage.

In the mid and late 1970s three separate theoretical themes developed, each espousing a multiple-memory-systems approach and each suggesting a selective role for the hippocampus in a distinct higher-order form of memory versus hippocampus-independent mechanisms for simpler forms of learning (Hirsh, 1974, 1980; O'Keefe & Nadel, 1978; Olton et al., 1979). We will refer to these as hypotheses that suggest the hippocampal system mediates *cognitive mapping* (O'Keefe & Nadel, 1978; Nadel, 1991, 1992), *conditional associations* (including contextual learning; Hirsh, 1974, 1980; Winocur & Olds, 1978; Sutherland & Rudy, 1989), and *working memory* (Olton et al., 1979). Each account will be described in terms of the fundamental properties of memory and in terms of its origins in the history of learning theory.

Cognitive Mapping

O'Keefe and Nadel's central contribution was to assign Tolman's cognitive mapping system to the hippocampus and to interpret the accumulated voluminous literature on the behavioral effects of hippocampal damage in animals and on emerging data on the functional correlates of hippocampal neural activity in terms of this hypothesis. In their analysis of the effects of hippocampal damage on different behavioral tasks O'Keefe and Nadel (1978) concluded that animals with hippocampal system damage are severely impaired in many forms of spatial exploration and learning and, conversely, are impaired in a relatively small number of nonspatial learning tasks.

In addition, in 1971, O'Keefe and Dostrovsky reported the discovery of hippo-campal "place cells," principal neurons that fire when an animal is in a particular location in its environment. The existence of cells with these functional qualities was interpreted as direct physiological evidence of the existence of Tolman's cognitive map. The combination of their synthesis of the findings from hippo-campal ablation studies and the discovery of hippocampal place cells led O'Keefe and Nadel to conclude that the hippocampus mediates spatial memory.

O'Keefe and Nadel's analysis went well beyond making a simple distinction between "spatial" and "nonspatial" learning modalities. Their proposal about spatial learning involved the acquisition of cognitive maps that corresponded roughly, if not topographically, to the salient features of physical environment. They referred to the domain of memory supported by the hippocampus as a *locale system* that maintains a molar model of spatial relations among objects in the environment, which is driven by curiosity rather than reinforcement of specific behaviors, and which is capable of very rapid learning. By contrast hippocampus-independent learning was viewed as being supported by a *taxon system* that mediates dispositions of specific stimuli into categories, is driven by the reinforcement of approach and avoidance behaviors, and involves slow and incremental behavioral adaptations.

Each of the properties of O'Keefe and Nadel's locale and taxon systems can be traced directly to Tolman's conceptions about cognitive maps and habits. Thus the form of representation in O'Keefe and Nadel's locale system is identical to Tolman's characterization of cognitive maps as guiding the acquisition of knowl-edge about an environment defined in terms of the interconnections among vari-ous distal stimuli, even to the extent that O'Keefe and Nadel referred to this as a system for "cognitive maps." O'Keefe and Nadel's conception of taxon learning, in which reinforcement mediates category inclusion, shares much with Tolman's (1949) characterization of *cathexes*, in which reinforcement serves to attach posi-tive and negative valences to categories of items; it seems that what cathexes were to the psychoanalytic theory prominent in Tolman's period taxons were to O'Keefe and Nadel's more contemporary ethological perspective. O'Keefe and Nadel explicitly contrasted the rapid acquisition of information into cognitive maps with incremental learning of taxons; this property was implicit in Tolman's conception of reinforcement as "confirming" knowledge about the world, rather than strengthening habits. Tolman made the capacity for flexibility and inferen-tial expression of knowledge central among the properties of field expectancies, and of his evidence for the existence of cognitive maps. In O'Keefe and Nadel's account flexible memory expression appears variously as an implicit aspect of mapping as opposed to route taking and, in Nadel's 1992 description of cognitive maps, as permitting "multiple access routes."

Conditional and Contextual Associations

At about the same time as O'Keefe and Nadel developed their theory, Hirsh (1974) proposed that the hippocampus supports a capacity for contextual re-trieval, the ability to utilize the context in which conditioned cues occur to re-trieve the appropriate association. He initially employed this model to explain the deficit following hippocampal damage in learning to turn in one direction or the other in a T maze depending on an imposed motivational context (hunger or thirst). The ambiguity in turn direction was, according to this account, resolved by a hippocampus-dependent mechanism that employed motivational state as a contextual cue for retrieving one of the possible responses. Conversely, Hirsh (1974) characterized the behavior of animals with hippocampal damage as "habit prone," in that they investigate fewer hypotheses and rigidly adopt behaviors associated with reinforcement very early, consistent with "everything for which early S-R theorists would have wished" (p. 439). Contrary to the present characterization of this account as an addendum to conditioning theory, Hirsh considered his proposal about hippocampus-dependent representations "neo-Tolmanian," although he did not make clear how cue-context interactions are maplike. Hirsh later (1980) extended the account to all forms of conditional operations and specifically compared his views with those of O'Keefe and Nadel, arguing that the two accounts differ only in that "O'Keefe and Nadel hold that logical operations occurring within the hippocampus are applied only to information about space in the literal sense," whereas Hirsh (1980) held that "they are applied to problem spaces in the sense of analytical geometry, of all kinds" (p. 180).

The historical descendant of Hirsh's proposal regarding hippocampal function in contextual and conditional associations is Sutherland and Rudy's (1989; Rudy & Sutherland, 1995) configural association theory. According to this account the hippocampus is critical for learning associations of configural stimuli, and the learning of elemental associations occurs independently of the hippocampal system. These investigators were rather explicitly driven by a motivation to preserve an S-R account of learning in situations that exceed the conventional boundaries of conditioning mechanisms. Their theory can be construed as an attempt to resolve paradoxes in conditioning that occur when cues have ambiguous reinforcement assignments depending upon their juxtaposition or context, and the hippocampus is viewed as the critical structure mediating the resolution.

To make their case, Sutherland and Rudy quite rightly selected the negative patterning problem for fundamental consideration. In this paradigm, two different stimuli are assigned a positive associative value when presented alone, but negative associative value when presented conjointly. This situation presents a serious challenge to conditioning theory because, according to an S-R account, it is not possible for the combination of two stimuli independently associated with reward to have a net negative association. To resolve the dilemma, Sutherland and Rudy proposed that the hippocampus supports the creation of a configural stimulus, acting as a "nand-gate" in digital logic, that receives input from the individual cues and yielding a negated output when both cues are present. This output can then be employed as a *unique CS,* a "configural cue" that is distinct from its constituent elements, used thereafter to support associations with reinforcers in the conventional way. From this perspective, the configural association account calls not for a wholly new form of memory organization, but only for a special mechanism that can convert combinations of ambiguous stimulus presentations into unique representations that can subsequently be employed within the traditional conditioning framework.

"Working" (Episodic) Memory

Also in the 1970s Olton and his colleagues (1979) originated yet a different formulation of hippocampal function that distinguished *working memory* and *reference memory*. Notably, Olton's use of the term *working memory* differs in meaning from the same term used in today's characterizations of a form of short-term memory in humans and animals (see chapter 14). The memory process Olton conceived of would today be viewed as more similar to "episodic memory," memory for a particular experience involving one's own actions, than our current conception of "working memory" as the contents of current consciousness (see chapter 14). Nevertheless, according to Olton's distinction, working memory refers to a representation that is critical for performance on one trial but is "not useful" on subsequent trials of an experimental session. The last part of this characterization is, importantly, an understatement: In all working memory tests the memory cues are reused frequently, so a representation based on cumulative reinforcement history is explicitly *counterproductive*. By contrast, *reference memory* refers to learned performance based on representations that are useful across all trials.

To investigate this distinction, Olton invented the radial maze, a maze composed of a central start platform with multiple arms radiating in all directions like the spokes of a wheel. In their classic studies, Olton and colleagues (1979) initially placed a bait at the end of each of 8 arms and then allowed the rat to forage for the food. After several such trials, rats learn to forage efficiently, running down each arm only once without repetition. Good performance requires the animal to remember each arm progressively visited and then before the next trial to "erase" those memories. Olton distinguished working memory from reference memory operationally, using a 17-arm maze in which many of the arms were never baited. Thus, to be maximally efficient in foraging, animals had to simultaneously demonstrate their capacity for working memory, by visiting each of the baited arms only once, and for reference memory, by not visiting the never-baited arms at all.

Using this task Olton showed that rats with hippocampal damage were severely impaired in the working-memory component of the task, but unimpaired in the reference memory component. He extended these findings in two ways. In several conventional tests for working memory that reused spatial cues, including delayed response and alternation tasks, it was shown that animals with hippocampal system damage were severely impaired. Conversely animals with hippocampal damage were not impaired on a variety of simple conditioning and discrimination tasks that require only reference memory. In addition Olton and colleagues found that the working and reference memory distinction applied to nonspatial as well as spatial memory. Rats with hippocampal system damage were impaired in performing the same basic working-memory task altered so that performance had to be guided by specific nonspatial visual and tactile cues that distinguished each arm, and not by the spatial locations of maze arms.

In interpreting these findings it is important to focus on what must be remembered during the relevant within-trial retention period, which is the animal's own immediately previous interaction with maze arms, that is, the most recent personal behavioral "episode." In the literature on animals, this kind of working memory has been described as a form of episodic memory (Olton, 1984), and indeed this is perhaps a better designation. Although it is not clear whether this kind of memory is fully consistent with the personal nature of human episodic memory (cf. Tulving, 1985), the critical memories in working memory tasks share much with human episodic memory, defined as a record of the events surrounding a particular temporally defined experience in which the subject was an active participant. Viewed this way, the working-memory hypothesis, like the other themes in theories of hippocampal function, can be traced to earlier theoretical accounts based on properties of normal memory (Tulving, 1972; James, 1890/1918). Moreover, interpreting the deficits on these tasks associated with hippocampal system damage as a loss of episodic memory capacity aligns the findings on animals with the observation of severe impairment of episodic memory in human amnesia (Schacter & Tulving, 1982) and with the accounting of episodic memory as one subdivision of the domain of declarative memory (Squire, 1992; Cohen, 1984).

The three accounts considered above are alternative formulations to the declarative-procedural view, which has been formally extended to animal models of amnesia in our writings (e.g., Eichenbaum et al., 1992; Cohen & Eichenbaum, 1993). Our discussion of these accounts here has been limited to showing their historical roots. In a later section of this chapter, and in Part II of this book, we consider their fit with the voluminous data on human and animal amnesia, and we show why the declarative-procedural framework accommodates more of the full scope of the extant data.

Two Central Areas of Current Research

The findings on H.M. and the efforts to model amnesia in animals have led to current emphases in two major areas of research. One of the central issues forced by the divergent theoretical proposals about hippocampus-dependent memory is the nature of the cognitive mechanisms that are mediated by the hippocampal system. We are faced with the possibility that declarative memory in humans evolved separately from some other hippocampus-mediated memory function in animals, and we are faced with reconciling the disparate accounts from the work on animals. Is there a fundamental set of cognitive mechanisms that could tie all these views together?

The other central issue generated by the discoveries about spared memory capacities in amnesia is a full accounting of the nonhippocampal memory systems. How are these systems characterized and divided by the kinds of memory they support. How many of them are there? What are their anatomical pathways and cognitive mechanisms?

These two central issues are considered separately in Parts II and III of this book. The remainder of this chapter is a preview of both issues, as related to the historical considerations presented above.

Cognitive Mechanisms That Underlie Declarative Memory: Relational Representation and Flexible Memory Expression

Each of the three accounts of hippocampal memory function in animals models presented above contains some of the features of declarative memory in humans.

The cognitive mapping account captures the "molar" view of memory character-ized by Bartlett and Tulving but restricts the role of the hippocampus to spatial memory. The conditional/contextual and working-memory accounts can be re-lated to other specifics about declarative memory, but each of these is also lim-ited in explanatory power to the particular behavioral paradigms in which they are studied. In efforts to identify more fundamental features of memory depen-dent on the hippocampus—and, by inference, reflecting fundamental processes that underlie declarative memory—other investigators have proposed more gen-eral and fundamental functional properties of hippocampal information process-ing. One view, proposed by Kesner (1990), is that the hippocampus encodes both spatial and temporal attributes of stimuli. This view quite straightforwardly goes far to encompass the spatial component of cognitive mapping, the temporal com-ponent of working memory, and spatiotemporal features that define contexts. In-deed, Kesner's attribute theory might properly be viewed as a more comprehen-sive approach to Hirsh's notion of the role of the hippocampus in retrieving memories in terms of these broadly defined contextual features.

Attempting to combine the key features of all of these views and identify the psychological mechanisms that underlie declarative memory expression, we have (Eichenbaum et al., 1992a, 1992b; Cohen & Eichenbaum, 1993) developed the hypothesis that declarative memory supports a *relational representation,* that is, an encoding of memories according to relevant relationships among the items. Furthermore, a central property of this type of memory is its support of *flexible expression* of memory, a quality that permits inferential use of memories in novel situations. Conversely, nondeclarative forms of memory, such as procedural memory, involve *individual representations;* such memories are isolated in that they are encoded only within the brain modules in which perceptual or motor processing is engaged during learning. These individual representations are *in-flexible* in that they can be revealed only through reactivation of those modules within the restrictive range of stimuli and situations in which the original learn-ing occurred.

These characterizations of the different forms of memory have been tested within the general framework that damage to the same structures known to be critical for declarative memory in H.M. should be essential for these particular properties of memory representation in animals. Most of these investigations ex-ploited the excellent learning and memory capacities of rats in spatially guided and odor-guided learning. In these studies, rats with hippocampal damage were found to be selectively impaired in tasks that encourage the learning of relation-ships among stimuli (Eichenbaum et al., 1988, 1989; see also Alvarado & Rudy, 1995; Sutherland et al., 1989). Conversely, intact learning was observed in tasks that encouraged separate representations for the items to be remembered. In addi-tion, even when learned performance was indistinguishable from normal, ani-mals with hippocampal system damage were impaired when challenged to choose between familiar stimuli presented in novel configurations, that is, to use their memories flexibly (Bunsey & Eichenbaum, 1996; Dusek & Eichenbaum, 1997).

These findings provide an extension to animals of classic views on human memory, including James's (1890) description of "memory" as involving an elab-orated network of associations that can be applied across a broad range of situations, Tolman's characterization of inference in cognitive mapping, and Hebb's proposal that conscious memory supports inferences about indirect relations between stimuli not previously experienced together. The proposed cognitive mechanisms also provide a bridge to present-day characterizations of human declarative memory, such as Cohen's (1984; Cohen & Eichenbaum, 1993) description of declarative memory as "promiscuous" in its accessibility by novel routes of expression, as well as Dickinson's (1980) views about inferential capacities as evidence for "declarative" processing in animal memory. Precisely how these cognitive mechanisms are mediated by hippocampal function within the larger brain system that mediates declarative memory is the substance of Part II of this book.

Characterizing the Nonhippocampal Memory Systems

The above studies indicate that one particular form of memory, declarative memory, depends on the hippocampal region. At the same time, the observations on spared memory in the absence of normal hippocampal function provides a preliminary characterization of what the other types of memory are. However, this work by itself does not designate what brain systems and structures support these other forms of memory, nor does it tell us whether or how the other forms are subdivided. Nevertheless, many studies over the years have provided relevant evidence on memory processing by other brain structures, and there has been intense research outlining the nonhippocampal memory systems of the brain in the last decade. This work will be discussed in detail in Part III of this book.

As a preview, we will introduce here one recent study by McDonald and White (1993) showing a "triple dissociation" between memory systems involving the hippocampus, the amygdala, and the striatum. Rats were trained on Olton's radial maze according to one of three protocols. One version was Olton's standard working-memory task, and replicating Olton's results, performance on this task was disrupted by lesions of the hippocampus. Damage to the amygdala or dorsal striatum had no effect. In another version of the task, the rats were merely confined in one maze arm with food rewards, were then separately confined in another arm without reward, and then were finally tested for a preference between those arms. Choice performance was disrupted by lesions of the amygdala but not of the hippocampus or dorsal striatum. In yet another version of the task, rats were rewarded for approaching arms that were illuminated, but not non-illuminated arms, and the locations of the illuminated arms changed across trials. Performance on this task was disrupted by lesions of the dorsal striatum but not of the hippocampus or amygdala.

These results suggest that three different forms of memory representation can guide radial maze learning, and that these types of memory can be differentiated by altering the task demands so that performance falls under the primary control of one particular system. Within this general framework, McDonald and White (1993) suggested the hippocampus is a critical part of a memory system for the acquisition and flexible expression of (spatial) relationships among stimuli, that the amygdala is a critical part of a memory system for associating stimuli with reinforcers, and that the striatum is a critical part of a memory system for associating specific stimuli with motor responses.

McDonald and White's characterizations strongly parallel the three forms of memory proposed by Maine de Biran, as discussed at the outset of this chapter. His defining properties of representative, sensitive, and mechanical memory, proposed on philosophical grounds, may now be understood to reflect the memory functions of distinct anatomical pathways associated with the hippocampus, the amygdala, and the striatum. Moreover, the distinct properties of these memory systems can be fully attributed to the parallel pathways for processing sensory information through different brain systems.

This experiment merely illustrates a large body of data that implicate the hippocampus, amygdala, and striatum, as well as other brain structures, as components of different memory systems in the brain. At this point, an outline of the memory systems of the brain is provided (Figure 2.6). The outline contains an elaboration of the anatomical structures that make up the hippocampal memory system and the other pathways for the forms of emotional (amygdala) and procedural (or habit; striatum) memory systems introduced above. In addition, the outline contains other pathways not discussed in any detail here. In particular, this outline shows that there are multiple pathways for the emotional and procedural/habit memory systems; these will be elaborated in chapters 12 and 13, respectively. In this outline, we also indicate interactions among cortical areas as supporting working memory; this topic will be discussed in chapter 14.

The framework outlined in Figure 2.6 is based on two major considerations. First, it follows the known anatomical pathways that mediate different forms of memory. Note that the cerebral cortex plays a critical role in each pathway, indicating that it is a common source of information for all (or most) forms of memory

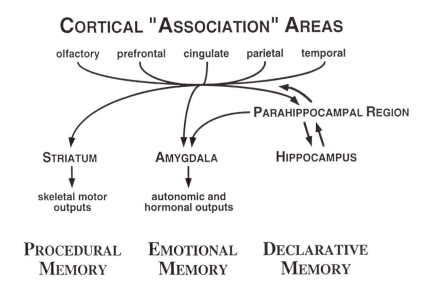

Figure 2.6. Our tentative taxonomy of brain systems that mediate different forms of memory.

and is also a major target structure influenced within the processing of memory. Its role in memory representation will be discussed at length in chapter 4. Second, this outline indicates that each memory system is instantiated not by a single brain structure but by an entire brain system. Within this larger anatomical context, dissociations of the type shown in McDonald and White's experiment are possible only because the hippocampus, amygdala, and striatum are parts of different systems. Nevertheless this diagram makes it clear it would be wrong to identify a particular form of memory with each of these structures alone. Rather we must consider the functional roles of all of the brain structures involved in each of these systems, as well as the nature of neural coding and neural plasticity that mediates memory at each stage. This book will take at least some initial steps in this direction. Considerations of neural plasticity mechanisms as a general issue will be emphasized in chapter 3.

How Many Memory Systems Are There?

Behind all these considerations there remains the general issue of whether there is a relatively short list of distinct "memory systems" defined by their functional characteristics (e.g., habit learning, emotional learning, semantic memory, episodic memory, and so forth), or whether this approach necessarily becomes an endless dissection of major and minor subdivisions of memory. The alternative conclusion is that memory systems are best viewed not as entities but as characterizations of the plasticity properties of different functional systems of the brain. These two alternative views of memory also have a long history: Accounts of a short list of memory systems began with Maine de Biran, whereas Gall proposed early the idea of distinct faculties, each with its own memory. We raised the theme at the outset of this book that memory is a fundamental property and natural outcome of the information-processing activities of the brain's various processors. Does this view rule out multiple memory systems?

A reconciliation may be a found in a consideration of cortical systems versus cortical-subcortical interactions. Perhaps there are strong commonalities in the forms of plasticity that exist in the various cortical processors, each cortical system maintaining its own memory capacities in a way that shares fundamental properties with all the others. But in the interaction of these cortical systems with various deep structures of the brain, such as the pathways that lead to the hippocampus, the striatum, and the amygdala, we may see very different forms of memory expression that we would want to characterize as separate memory systems. This idea will be explored in detail in subsequent chapters. For now let it be said that this review has only raised some of the critical questions about different forms of memory. How each works and how they may sometimes work together is the subject of the remainder of this book.

PART I

FUNDAMENTALS

3

Cellular Plasticity Mechanisms

Virtually all notions about memory have considered, at least conceptually, the existence of some elemental mechanism that mediates the formation of associations and thereby supports one or another form of memory. Early proposals, such as those of Maine de Biran and William James, talked about a simple "habit" mechanism as the fundamental substrate of all forms of adaptive behavior, although they understandably didn't get very far in elucidating its neural mechanisms. Pavlov and Sherrington, from differing behavioral and physiological perspectives, recognized the modification of synaptic function—synaptic plasticity—as the basic substrate of the conditioned-reflex mechanism. Hebb broadened this notion beyond that of stimulus-and-response associations, outlining a cascade of events beginning with synaptic plasticity as the fundamental associative mechanism that underlies the development of cell assemblies representing specific percepts, thoughts, and actions. Modern neuroscience has made tremendous advances since Hebb's time in our understanding of cellular mechanisms and their possible role in memory.

This chapter reviews some of the recent progress toward an understanding of synaptic plasticity as the main candidate for a cellular mechanism of memory. Synaptic plasticity seems to take various forms, as indicated in the Introduction, and we will not be able to consider all of them. Instead, we focus largely on one particular example, that seen in long-term potentiation (LTP), in order to provide the fundamentals of cellular plasticity. This particular form of plasticity is of particular importance in the context of the present book because LTP has been studied extensively in the hippocampus, a brain structure that will feature very prominently here.

The goal of this chapter is to offer a way to understand how cellular mechanisms might mediate storage in the brain's various processing systems. To some extent, this chapter may be seen as a sidebar, off the main path of this book's treatment of multiple memory systems, given the absence of any evidence linking different forms of memory or memory systems to different synaptic plasticity mechanisms. Some readers may wish to skip ahead to chapter 4. However, knowledge about the rules of synaptic modifications and their cellular substrates provides constraints on models of various brain systems and the forms of memory supported by the operation of such systems. As will become apparent in later chapters, some of the details about the synaptic mechanisms of hippocampal LTP does indeed inform our thinking about the nature of the memory supported by the hippocampal system.

Hippocampal Long-Term Potentiation as a Model Memory Mechanism

This chapter focuses on the form of synaptic plasticity known as LTP, together with some of the related synaptic plasticity mechanisms that have received considerable attention in experimental analyses in recent years. The phenomenon of LTP was first discovered by Terje Lomo, a PhD student working in Oslo under the guidance of Per Anderson. Lomo was exploring the physiology of hippocampal circuitry, and in particular the phenomenon of frequency potentiation, an increase in the magnitude of responsiveness elicited by multiple, rapidly applied stimulations (see Figure 3.1 for an introductory view of the hippocampus and its circuitry. He observed that repetitive high-frequency electrical stimulation (called *tetanus*) of the pathway from the entorhinal cortex to the dentate gyrus resulted in a steeper rise time (slope) of the excitatory synaptic potential to a subsequent single pulse, as well as recruitment of spike activity from a greater number of dentate cells (that is, an increase in the so-called population spike; see Bliss & Lynch, 1988, for review of these two components of LTP). These changes in the synaptic and cellular responses to single pulses, based on the presence of a previous tetanus, lasted for several hours, leading Lomo to name the phenomenon "long-term potentiation" (Figure 3.2). In subsequent years, Bliss, Lomo, and Garder-Medwin (Bliss & Lomo, 1973; Bliss & Gardner-Medwin, 1973) characterized the basic properties of the synaptic and cellular components of LTP, creating considerable excitement about this phenomenon as a model for lasting history-dependent synaptic change. The finding of LTP spawned a veritable cottage industry within the field of neuroscience. Readers interested in a more complete history of the discoveries and debates on many issues about LTP are referred to the well-documented volumes edited by Baudry and Davis (1991, 1994, 1996).

What fascinated researchers at the outset were the remarkable parallels between properties of LTP and memory. Morris (1989), for example, noted five fundamental properties that make LTP such an attractive model of memory. First, LTP is a prominent feature of the physiology of the hippocampus, a brain structure universally identified with memory. Subsequent work has made clear that the hippocampus is not the only site of LTP, but its functional role as a component of one of the brain's major memory systems would seem to demand that it possess a memory mechanism.

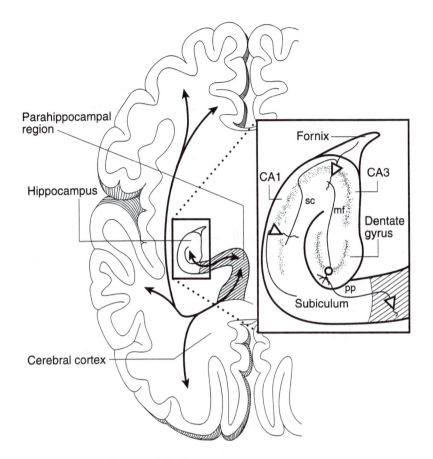

Figure 3.1. Major pathways of the hippocampus. Left: Illustration of a horizontal section through the human brain showing major pathways by which the hippocampus is connected with cortical areas. Inset: Schematic diagram of major intrahippocampal connections.

The second and third properties have to do with temporal characteristics. LTP develops very rapidly, as one would require of a plausible memory mechanism, typically within 1 minute after a single stimulus train delivered with the proper parameters. Moreover, like a good memory, LTP can be quite long-lasting. In *in vivo* preparations it can be observed for hours after a single stimulation train, or for weeks or more after repetitive stimulations ("reminders"?).

Fourth, LTP has the sort of *specificity* one would require of a memory mechanism: Only those synapses activated during the stimulation train are potentiated. Other, neighboring synapses, even on the same neurons, are not altered. This phenomenon parallels the natural specificity of our memories, in which we are able to remember many different specific episodes with the same person (e.g., one particular date you had, out of many, with a given individual) or object (e.g., where you parked your car today rather than last week), and thus would be a key

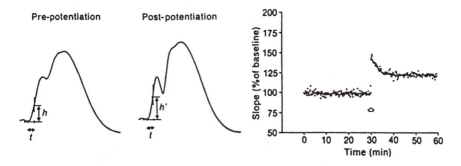

Figure 3.2. Long term potentiation. Extracellularly recorded field potentials obtained in the dentate gyrus after single pulse stimulations of the perforant path. A typical measure of potentiation is a change in the slope of the field potential ($h' > h$ over time t). (Reproduced, with permission, from Morris, 1989; Copyright Oxford University Press.)

requirement of any useful cellular memory mechanism. In addition, the property of specificity may be key to the magnitude of the storage capacity of brain structures. The idea here is that each cell can participate in the representation of multiple memories, each composed of distinct subsets of its many synaptic inputs. Perhaps this is also related to the phenomenon, to be discussed subsequently, that hippocampal cells can have quite different representations across changing learning situations (see below).

Fifth, and perhaps most definitively important for memory, LTP is *associative* in that potentiation occurs best when multiple inputs are stimulated simultaneously during the tetanus. This phenomenon has been demonstrated most elegantly in studies that employ activation of separate pathways that synapse on the same hippocampal neurons (Levy & Steward, 1979). In these studies the two pathways involve the combination of a "weak" input, designated as one that does not produce potentiation at any stimulation level, plus a "strong" input for which a threshold level of stimulation suffices to produce LTP. Associativity is observed when the weak input is activated at the same time as the strong input, resulting in LTP of the weak as well as the strong pathway. The time window for this sort of association was initially thought to be quite brief, on the order of a few milliseconds, and thus quite limited in the extent to which it could support Pavlovian conditioning, which usually involves a separation of hundreds of milliseconds between the CS and the US. However, there is new evidence that a form of associativity may be possible within a broader, and more behaviorally meaningful, time window. A recent study by Frey and Morris (1997, 1998) indicated that activity at hippocampal synapses that produces only a short-lived potentiation can nonetheless create a synaptic "tag" that lasts a few hours. Subsequent strong activation of a neighboring pathway within that period leads to lasting potentiation of both the "strong" pathway and the previously "tagged" synapses. Thus LTP could serve to associate or integrate patterns of activity over a time window that has obvious behavioral significance.

The property of associativity is especially appealing because it offers a cellular model of Hebb's (1949) postulate regarding the mechanism for structural change in neural connections. Recall from the discussion in chapter 2 Hebb's suggestion that the essential trigger for changing synaptic efficacy involved the repeated activation of a presynaptic element *and* its participation in the success in firing the postsynaptic cell ("when an axon of cell A is near enough to excite cell B and repeatedly takes part in firing it . . ."). This view would allow that Cell A could, if connected near enough to the activation zone of Cell B, fire Cell B on its own, and that this would be sufficient to trigger the structural change. But we know that at least 100 synapses would have to be active nearly simultaneously to fire a hippocampal neuron (Andersen & Trommald, 1995), so only the simultaneous activation of many inputs is likely to accomplish the co-occurrence of presynaptic and postsynaptic activity. The property of associativity, by permitting the ability to associate or integrate patterns of activity, simultaneously satisfies the induction requirement of LTP that there be a combination of presynaptic and postsynaptic activation and offers a fundamental mechanism for encoding associations between functionally meaningful activation patterns (Brown & Chattarji, 1994).

Molecular and Cellular Bases for the Induction and Maintenance of Hippocampal LTP

There is substantial understanding and agreement about the initial steps in the molecular and synaptic basis of LTP, particularly as seen in the hippocampus. This story will be reviewed here only briefly; full accountings of this work are provided in several reviews (Bliss & Lynch, 1988; Bliss & Collingridge, 1993; Nicoll et al., 1988; Collingridge & Bliss, 1987; Madison et al., 1991).

The elucidation of cellular and molecular mechanisms of LTP have been facilitated greatly by the development of the in vitro hippocampal "slice" preparation in which thick transverse sections of the hippocampus are taken from the brain and kept alive in a Petri dish. This preparation lacks the complex influences of the normal inputs and outputs of the hippocampus, but it provides an especially clear access to cells and intrinsic connections of the hippocampal circuit. Most of these studies have focused on area CA1 of the hippocampus, where the in vitro preparation allows multiple input and output pathways to be preserved intact and to be manipulated independently.

Many studies have shown that the induction of LTP in area CA1, both in the hippocampal slice and in the intact preparation, requires two fundamental synaptic events: activation of presynaptic inputs and depolarization of the postsynaptic cell. Both are ordinarily accomplished within a single high-frequency stimulus train: The initial stimulation depolarizes the cell for a relatively prolonged period during which the following stimulations provide simultaneus postsynaptic activations. However, high-frequency stimulation is not required per se. Instead, for example, direct depolarization of the postsynaptic cell by injection of current through an intracellular electrode, combined with low-frequency presynaptic input, will suffice. Conversely LTP induction can be blocked by preventing depolarization, or by hyperpolarization of the postsynaptic cell.

The molecular mechanism that underlies LTP induction in CA1 appears to involve special properties of a combination of synaptic receptors (Figure 3.3). Considerable evidence points to the amino acid glutamate as the primary excitatory transmitter in the hippocampus and elsewhere where LTP is found. There are several types of glutamate receptors, most prominently divided into those that are excited by N-methyl-D-aspartate (NMDA receptors) and those that are activated by α-amino-3-hydroxy-5-methyl-4-isoxazolepropionate (AMPA receptors; also called *quisqualate/kainate receptors*). These two types of receptors can be dissociated functionally by pharmacological manipulations. In particular, the NMDA receptors are selectively and competitively blocked by the antagonist D-2-amino-5-phosphonovalerate (AP5). A major discovery in revealing the mechanism of LTP was that AP5 has little effect on excitatory postsynaptic potentials (EPSPs) elicited by low-frequency stimulation, indicating that AMPA receptors, and not NMDA receptors, mediate normal synaptic transmission in the hippocampus. In contrast, AP5 completely blocks LTP following high-frequency stimulation trains, indicating that glutamate activation of NMDA receptors is critical to this form of synaptic plasticity.

Discoveries about two major differences between NMDA and AMPA receptors in their regulation of postsynaptic ion permeability in CA1 offer an explanation of the role of these receptors in LTP (Figure 3.3). First, activation of AMPA receptors increases the permeability of the postsynaptic membrane to both sodium (Na+) and potassium (K+) ions but does not alter cell permeability to calcium (Ca++). By contrast, activation of NMDA receptors increases permeability to Ca++ as well as to Na+ and K+ ions. Second, unlike for AMPA receptors, ion flow through NMDA receptors is highly dependent on the voltage state of the postsynaptic cell at the time of NMDA receptor activation. In the resting state, NMDA receptor channels are blocked by another divalent ion, magnesium (Mg++), which prevents the flow of the other ions even in the presence of glutamate at the receptor (Figure 3.3a). However, when the membrane of the postsynaptic cell is depolarized, Mg++ is expelled from the receptor channel, allowing glutamate to bind and the ions including Ca++ to flow (Figure 3.3b). Thus the effect of the initial activations in the high-frequency stimulus train is to activate the AMPA receptors, depolarizing the postsynaptic cell membrane. This unblocks the NMDA receptor channels so that succeeding stimuli activate the NMDA receptor, allowing Ca++ to enter the postsynaptic cell.

The entry of Ca++ into the intracellular space is a key step in the induction of LTP. This is shown in at least three lines of work: First, LTP is prevented when CA++ is bound by intracellular injection of a calcium chelator (a molecule that binds up calcium). Second, LTP is triggered by intracellular injection of a caged Ca++ compound that releases calcium molecules. Third, the entry of Ca++ into the postsynaptic cell following stimulation trains has been directly imaged with confocal fluorescence microscopy. There is evidence, however, that Ca++ entry does not, by itself, lead to lasting synaptic potentiation; rather, some sort of NMDA receptor activation seems to be required. One possibility under scrutiny is that glutamate also activates metabotropic (that is, nonsynaptic) receptors coupled to phosphoinositide-mediated release of intracellular stores of Ca++ as an amplification mechanism.

A. Normal synaptic transmission

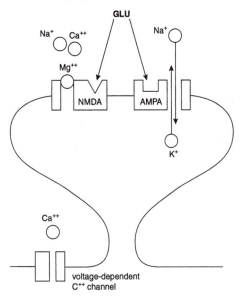

B. During depolarization

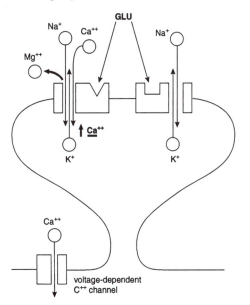

Figure 3.3. Molecular mechanism of the induction of LTP. GLU = glutamate; See text for explanation. (Adapted with permission from Nicoll, Kauer, & Malenka, 1988; Copyright Cell Press.)

The succeeding steps in the establishment and maintenance of LTP are less well understood and can be provided only in outline form at this time (Figure 3.4). The leading view is that the role of Ca++ is to activate kinases, enzymes that phosphorylate proteins, transforming them into their active configuration. Specific candidates of the critical kinases include Type II Ca++/calmodulin-dependent kinase (CaMKII), Ca++/phospholipid-dependent protein kinase C (PKC), and tyrosine kinase *fyn*. CaMKII is a very attractive candidate. It is present in large quantities in the postsynaptic area; although its initial activation depends on Ca++, it undergoes an autophosphorylation by which it becomes independent of the transient Ca++ influx, tetanus stimulates its production, and pharmacological antagonism or genetic elimination of CaMKII blocks LTP. Thus CaMKII is well positioned to be influenced by Ca++ concentrations and a brief activation. This prolonged activation mediates long-lasting consequences, one of which might be the conversion of inactive AMPA receptors into active ones, "waking up" previously "silent" synapses (Malinow, 1994; Malenka & Nicoll, 1997). PKC is also strongly implicated by experiments showing that its activation results in marked potentiation of the EPSP that occludes further potentiation by stimulation trains. Furthermore, intracellular injection of PKC enhances synaptic trans-

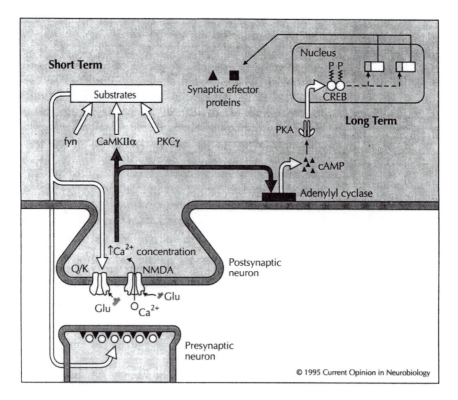

Figure 3.4. Model of the molecular mechanisms of short term and long term processes following LTP induction. (Reproduced, with permission, from Mayford, Abel, & Kandel, 1995; Copyright Elsevier Science.)

mission, and application of PKC antagonists blocks LTP. PKC could regulate a number of phosphoproteins (see Benowitz & Routtenberg, 1987). Finally *fyn* is a candidate kinase based on evidence that genetic elimination of it results in attenuation of LTP.

In addition to modifying existing proteins, there is evidence that the maintenance of LTP also depends on new protein synthesis. Experiments using protein synthesis inhibitors indicate that proteins synthesized from preexisting mRNA are required for lasting LTP. In addition, there is also evidence that maintaining LTP depends upon the cAMP-responsive transcription factor CREB. One possible mechanism for CREB involves the Ca++ influx activating adenyl cyclase, which in turn activates cyclic AMP. This could in turn activate PKC, leading to the phosphorylation of many proteins, including CREB. The phosphorylated form of CREB is known to modulate the transcription of genes so as to increase the expression of several proteins. There is some evidence that genetically altered mice who lack a form of CREB have deficient LTP maintenance.

One possible target of new protein synthesis is the production of neurotrophins, molecules long known to be regulated by neural activity and having the capacity to promote morphological change and increased connectivity (Lo, 1995; Finkbeiner et al., 1997). Candidate neurotrophic factors include nerve growth factor (NGF), brain-derived neurotrophic factor (BDNF), and neurotophin-3 (NT-3) and its relatives NT-4/5, and NT-6. Stimulation trains capable of inducing LTP increase BDNF and NT-3 mRNAs in the hippocampus. In turn, BDNF and NT-3 (but not NGF) potentiate glutaminergic transmission in CA1, and these effects occur within minutes and last hours. Finally, genetically altered mice that lack BDNF have impaired hippocampal LTP.

Where Is the Synaptic Alteration?

A major unresolved question is whether the locus of lasting synaptic alteration following LTP is presynaptic or postsynaptic. Of course, changes at both sites are entirely possible (e.g., Colley & Routtenberg, 1993). The evidence on both sides of this issue is considerable, and it may not be possible to fully resolve the issue with current methods available to study the hippocampal preparation. Recent attempts to resolve the question have focused on quantal analysis, a protocol that involves reducing presynaptic release to a statistical phenomenon, allowing estimation of the magnitude of the postsynaptic response to a single quantum of transmitter. During LTP there is a decrease in the percentage of failures of postsynaptic response and a decreased variability of responses to presynaptic stimulation, both consistent with an increase in the probability of presynaptic release. However, there is also observed an increase in quantal amplitude of the response, which is consistent with an increase in postsynaptic receptor efficacy. Thus the current evidence from quantal analyses is consistent with both loci as being involved in plastic change.

There are also conceptual issues to consider in this controversy. Possible cellular mechanisms for postsynaptic modification are straightforward to envision, as discussed just above. By contrast, because the initial effects of combined pre- and postsynaptic activity evoke cellular mechanisms localized in the postsynaptic cell, an ultimate change in presynaptic physiology would require production and transport of some sort of retrograde messenger that travels from the activated postsynaptic site to the presynaptic site. Several candidates for the retrograde messenger have been proposed (e.g., arachidonic acid, nitrous oxide [NO], carbon dioxide [CO]), but so far, none has received more than fragmentary support.

Hippocampal Long-Term Depression (LTD)

If there was only a form of plasticity that *increased* synaptic efficacy, eventually all synapses would become "saturated" (i.e., raised to a ceiling level of efficacy), and no further learning could occur. So most think that, in addition to the potentiation of synapses, there must be a mechanism of depotentiation, or *long-term depression* (LTD) of synaptic efficacy. LTD can also enhance the relative effect of LTP at neighboring synapses, improving center-to-surround or signal-to-noise contrasts, as well as increasing the range of synaptic coding patterns by a population of synapses inputting onto a single postsynaptic cell. The phenomenon of LTD has been reviewed in detail elsewhere (Christie et al., 1994; Malenka, 1994; Bear & Malenka, 1994) and will be outlined only briefly here.

Several variants of LTD have been observed, even within the hippocampal preparation (Figure 3.5). In general, the learning rule for LTD involves activity-dependent plasticity with a direct violation of the Hebb rule for LTP. Thus LTD has been reported at synapses where there is either presynaptic activity or postsynaptic activity, but not both (said another way, when presynaptic activity occurs without concomitant postsynaptic activity, and vice versa). The protocols for LTD fall into three basic categories: (a) Heterosynaptic LTD involves depression of inactive synapses following activation of the postsynaptic neuron, without activation of the presynaptic element, either by stimulation of separate converging synapses on the postsynaptic cell or by antidromic activation; (b) conversely, associative LTD involves depression of synapses where presynaptic activity is induced in the absence of postsynaptic firing, so that the presynaptic

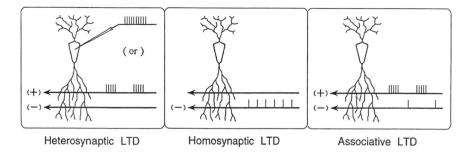

Heterosynaptic LTD   Homosynaptic LTD   Associative LTD

Figure 3.5. Conceptual models of paradigms for the induction of long term depression. (Reproduced, with permission, from Christie, Kerr, & Abraham, 1994; Copyright John Wiley & Sons, Inc.)

elements are activated weakly and out of phase with strong stimulation to converging synapses; and (c) like associative LTD, homosynaptic LTD also involves depression of synapses where presynaptic activity occurs in the absence of postsynaptic firing. However, in this case the uncorrelated presynaptic-postsynaptic activity involves activation of presynaptic elements in a pattern that produces no activation or only weak activation of the postsynaptic cell, typically by very low-frequency stimulation of the presynaptic fibers. All of these forms of LTD have been observed at one pathway or another in the hippocampus, but it remains to be seen if they obey the same induction and maintenance rules and are available at all sites in the hippocampus.

Heterosynaptic LTD has been produced at a variety of frequencies of stimulation, is saturable, and can last over several days in vivo. It can be induced in previously potentiated pathways and can be reversed by LTP-inducing stimulation protocols. Blocking cellular inhibition with GABA antagonists does not prevent LTD, indicating that LTD does not simply reflect enhancement of the primary pathway for inhibition in the hippocampus. Postsynaptic depolarization is sufficient to produce LTD and seems to involve Ca++ influx into the postsynaptic cell. It is not entirely clear that heterosynaptic LTD involves no presynaptic activity, as spontaneous uncorrelated activation in the presynaptic pathway cannot be fully eliminated. This leaves the possibility that heterosynaptic LTD shares induction properties with homosynaptic LTD or associative potentiation.

By contrast, homosynaptic LTD involves an explicitly or implicitly anti-Hebbian procedure. The *explicitly* anti-Hebbian form involves the stimulation of different pathways out of phase with one another. This procedure has been used successfully in several different preparations but has not been studied extensively. Several variants of the *implicitly* anti-Hebbian procedure involve stimulation of only one pathway, most elegantly in protocols that involve presynaptic excitation during postsynaptic cell inhibition (Thiels et al., 1994; Huerta & Lisman, 1995). The paradigm of Thiels and colleagues uses a paired-pulse stimulation protocol so that the second pulse is delivered during the wave of GABA-mediated inhibition that is maximal 25 ms after the first pulse. Heurta and Lisman's (1995) paradigm involves a single short burst of activation of the presynaptic terminals during the inhibitory phase of the naturally occurring 7–12 Hz hippocampal rhythm known as theta (Figure 3.6). These protocols are especially interesting because the temporal pattern of activation duplicates natural bursting activity of hippocampal neurons (see below). In addition Heurta and Lisman's LTD protocol contrasts with a parallel protocol for the production of LTP. Thus, when the same pattern of stimulation is presented on the opposite phase of the theta rhythm, the result is a local LTP, combined with heterosynaptic LTD on neighboring inactive synapses. These forms of LTP and LTD are NMDA-receptor-dependent.

The form of lasting hippocampal synaptic depression that has received the most recent attention is a homosynaptic LTD protocol that involves prolonged low-frequency stimulation of a single pathway. In this protocol, the same pathways used for study of LTP in CA1 can be depressed by a long series of continuous 1-Hz stimulation (Figure 3.7). Surprisingly, it turns out that this form of synaptic plasticity shares several features with LTP. This form of synaptic depression is saturable and reversible by LTP-inducing stimulation. It is also in-

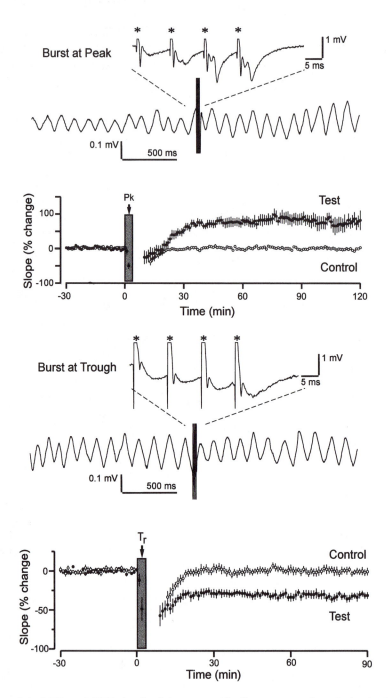

Figure 3.6. LTP and LTD in the hippocampal slice preparation. Left: A single burst of 4 shocks at the positive peak of theta (Pk) produces LTP. Right: A single burst of 4 shocks at the trough of theta (Tr) produces LTD. (Reproduced, with permission, from Huerta & Lisman, 1995; Copyright Cell Press.)

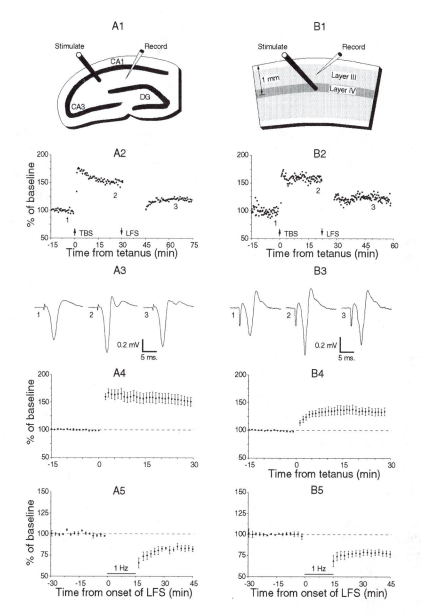

Figure 3.7. LTP in hippocampal (left) and cortical (right) slices. In both preparations LTP is produced by theta-burst stimulation (TBS) and in both, depotentiation is produced by low frequency stimulation (LFS). The second and third rows show depotentiation from an initially potentiated state. The fifth row shows LTD from an unpotentiated state. (Reproduced, with permission, from Bear, 1996; Copyright National Academy of Sciences, U.S.A.)

put-specific and requires activation of NMDA receptors as well as a rise in Ca++ concentration in the postsynaptic cell. Lisman (1989) proposed a model for the signaling cascades that might mediate LTP versus LTD, depending on the timing of activations and consequent levels of the rise in intracellular Ca++. According to this model, large rises in Ca++ level that would accompany rapid trains of stimulation activate CaMKII or other protein kinases, whereas smaller rises in Ca++ would activate a protein phosphatase, such as calcineurin. The kinase and phosphatase mediators could act on a common pathway that alters synaptic proteins by regulating the phosphorylation of synaptic proteins. Bear (1996) proposed that the regulation of potentiation and depression of synaptic efficacy by a common learning rule may be possible. According to his model, there is a "modification threshold" so that active synapses are potentiated when the total synaptic response exceeds a particular threshold and depressed when the total synaptic response falls below that threshold. Bear and his colleagues (1996) showed that levels of LTP and LTD, and the switchover between these events, followed model-predicted parameters in CA1, as well as in the cerebral cortex.

A Different Mechanism for LTP Within the CA3 Region of the Hippocampus

Most of the discussion above about the mechanisms of LTP is from studies of the excitatory synapses in two regions of the hippocampus, the connection between CA3 and CA1, and between the entorhinal cortex and dentate gyrus. However, another major pathway in the hippocampus, the mossy fiber projection from the dentate gyrus to CA3, also shows LTP. However, this form of potentiation appears to be mediated by a quite different cellular and molecular mechanism (Zalutsky & Nicoll, 1990; Nicoll & Makenka, 1995). The mossy fiber termination zone is devoid of NMDA receptors, and correspondingly LTP in CA3 is not affected by NMDA receptor antagonists, even though such drugs prevent LTP in adjacent associational synapses that have NMDA receptors. Mossy fiber LTP does require the influx of Ca++ into the presynaptic but not the postsynaptic cell. Moreover, paired-pulse facilitation, a phenomenon by which presynaptic release of transmitter is enhanced for a short period by activations spaced at 50 ms, is reduced during mossy fiber LTP. These findings strongly indicate that mossy fiber LTP is entirely mediated by a facilitation in presynaptic release of transmitter. In addition, the mossy fiber synapse is capable of both heterosynaptic and homosynaptic LTD when conditions are insufficient to produce LTP (Derrick & Martinez, 1996). The finding of two strikingly different mechanisms of synaptic plasticity, just within the hippocampus, serves to emphasize the importance of considering multiple plasticity mechanisms.

Anatomical Modifications Consequent to LTP

Most researchers believe that lasting changes in neural connectivity ultimately require altered morphology of synapses. Although this research area has been plagued by technical issues of the proper means of preserving tissue for examination with the electron microscope, there is now substantial evidence that LTP does result in structural alterations in synaptic connections consistent with increases in synaptic efficacy (for detailed reviews see Harris et al., 1989; Wallace et al., 1990). Most of these data focus on the protruding heads of dendritic spines that are the excitatory synapses of the dentate granule or CA1 pyramidal cells, the same sites that involve NMDA-receptor-dependent LTP.

We'll consider first the studies of dentate gyrus. Fifkova and colleagues (1977) first reported structural changes in the perforant pathway indicating a swelling of granule cell spines. Desmond and Levy (1988) described several changes in dentate granule cell synapses following LTP, particularly a striking increase in the number of "concave" heads of dendritic spines (Figure 3.8). This finding is consistent with Fifkova's earlier observations of increased spine head surface area and area of the apposed pre- and postsynaptic membranes. The increase in concave spines occurred without any appreciable increase in the number of synapses, and indeed there was a small decrease in synapse number attributed to concurrent heterosynaptic LTD. The combination of increased concave spines without decrease in spine number suggested that LTP in the dentate gyrus results in an "interconversion" of nonconcave spines into the concave morphology. Among the types of concave synapses that both Desmond and Levy (1988) and Fifkova and colleagues (1977) observed were "spinule" synapses, characterized as having an evagination of the postsynaptic element into the presynaptic element, increasing the area and proximity of contact. Geinisman and colleagues (1993; Geinisman, 1993) reported that the major change in granule cell spine morphology following LTP is a marked and selective increase in "perforated" axospinous synapses, characterized as spines that are horseshoe-shaped and/or fenestrated and partitioned into separate zones of postsynaptic density (Figure

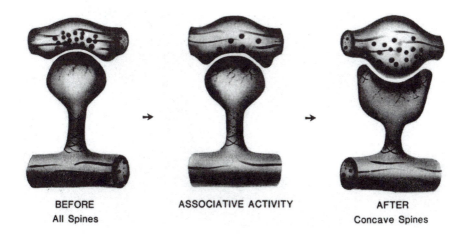

BEFORE
All Spines

ASSOCIATIVE ACTIVITY

AFTER
Concave Spines

Figure 3.8. Desmond and Levy's (1988) model of interconversion of activated spines from convex to concave states as a result of LTP. (Reproduced, with permission, from Desmond & Levy, 1988; Copyright John Wiley & Sons, Inc.)

3.9). These perforated synapses bear striking similarities to increased concave and spinule morphologies, supporting the "interconversion" account by which LTP results in increases in synaptic contact area by expansions of the pre- and postsynaptic cell membranes in surrounding one another.

Studies on CA1 have provided strikingly parallel results. Two laboratories have described changes in spine dimensions consistent with the overall rounding (concavity) of spines, although these changes may be transient (Lee et al., 1980; Chang & Greenough, 1984; Sorra and Harris 1998; see Klintsova & Greenough, 1999). Recent studies using newly available high-resolution optical methods have detected growth of new spines on postsynaptic dendrites in CA1 shortly after induction of LTP (Engert & Bonhoeffer, 1999; Maletic-Savatic et al., 1999). In addition, lasting changes in spine number have been reported in CA1, and these changes have been characterized as reflecting the transformation of synapses into types with protracted necks as well as sessile types. Overall the coordination of increased presynaptic and postsynaptic active contact, as observed in studies on

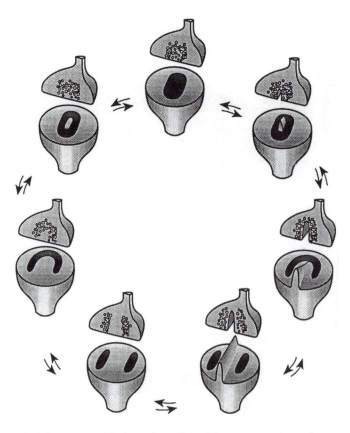

Figure 3.9. Geinisman et al.'s (1993) model of interconversion of nonperforated (top) to perforated (bottom) spines as a result of LTP. (Reproduced, with permission, from Geinisman, deToledo-Morrell, Morrell, Heller, Rossi, & Parshall, 1993; Copyright John Wiley & Sons, Inc.)

both the dentate granule and CA1 pyramidal cells, seems to obviate the question of whether the fundamental basis of LTP is pre- or postsynaptic in origin (Lisman & Harris, 1989).

LTP Beyond the Hippocampus

Although LTP was first discovered in the hippocampus, and it is easily studied there because of the laminar separation of synaptic inputs and outputs, potentiation of synaptic efficacy is widespread in the brain and is rapidly becoming viewed as universal plasticity mechanism. Among the areas where LTP, and/or LTD, have been demonstrated are several areas of the neocortex, piriform cortex, amygdala, neostriatum, cerebellum, and even spinal cord.

Perhaps best studied of the nonhippocampal areas is the visual cortex (Bear, 1996; Singer, 1995). In the rat visual cortex, Artola et al. (1990) demonstrated bidirectional activity-dependent modification of synapses in which low levels of activity result in synaptic depression, whereas high levels of activity produce potentiation, just as in the hippocampus. Bear and colleagues (1996) developed the in vitro slice preparation of rat visual cortex and found that stimulation of the input Layer IV results in LTP and LTD in principal cells of Layer III with the same protocols effective for producing these phenomena in the hippocampus (Figure 3.7). Low-frequency stimulation resulted in LTD and high-frequency stimulation produced LTP. Both forms of synaptic modification are synapse-specific and depend on NMDA receptors. Intracellular injections of current that produce postsynaptic depolarization or hyperpolarization paired with low-frequency synaptic activation produce synaptic enhancements and decrements, respectively (Fregnac et al., 1994). Furthermore, similar findings have now been made in rat somatosensory cortex (Castro-Alamancos et al., 1995) and in human inferotemporal cortex (Chen et al., 1996). LTP in other brain areas will be discussed in greater detail below, in the context of the relationship of LTP to behavioral memory.

LTP and Memory: Is There a Strong Connection? Can We Enhance It?

We hope that the above review of LTP captures at least some of the sense that this is an exciting phenomenon, one that is seen, deservedly, as the most prominent model of synaptic plasticity that might underlie memory. As Stevens (1998) put it, this mechanism is so attractive that it would be a shame if the mechanism underlying LTP turned out not to be a memory mechanism. But there should be no doubt about the fact that LTP is not memory: It is a laboratory phenomenon never observed in nature. The best we can hope is that LTP and memory have a common mechanism. In recent years disappointing evidence has emerged, amid the more positive findings, regarding all main lines of evidence that have been offered to connect LTP and memory. Issues and concerns about the linkage between LTP and memory have been raised in several papers (e.g., Andersen &

Trommald, 1994; Andersen & Moser, 1995; Bliss and Richter-Levin, 1993; Cain et al., 1996; Diamond & Rose, 1994; Eichenbaum & Otto, 1993; Eichenbaum, 1995, 1996; Hargreaves, et al., 1990; Keith & Rudy, 1990; Stevens, 1998), including some by one of the current authors (HE).

Here we attempt just to summarize the history of the research on the possible linkage between LTP and memory. Several relatively direct approaches have been pursued in attempting to demonstrate that LTP and memory have common physiological and molecular bases. Each of these complementary approaches will be briefly presented and discussed in light of the observed (and inherent) limitations they have in convincingly connecting LTP and memory. These efforts can be categorized into three general strategies: demonstrations of changes in synaptic efficacy consequent to a learning experience ("behavioral LTP"), attempts to draw associations between natural neural activity patterns and activation parameters for inducing LTP, and attempts to prevent learning either by "saturation" of LTP in a hippocampal pathway or by pharmacological or genetic manipulation of the molecular mechanisms of LTP induction. After considering these three approaches, this chapter concludes by introducing other recent approaches, aimed at showing a continuity of plasticity from molecular to synaptic to circuit and systems levels of analysis.

"Behavioral LTP"

Do conventional learning experiences produce changes in synaptic physiology similar to the increases in EPSP and cellular responses that occur after LTP? Seeking changes in synaptic physiology consequent to learning is an ambitious and optimistic approach because one might well expect the magnitude of synaptic change observed in gross field potentials to be vanishingly small following any normal learning experience—a virtual needle in a haystack. In addition, most computational neuroscientists believe that learning involves changes in synaptic efficacy in both the positive and negative directions, that is, both LTP and LTD. Thus learning would likely result in changes in the distribution of potentiated and depressed synapses with little or no overall shift expected, and consequently no expected change, or even an overall negative change (Xu et al., 1998), in the averaged evoked field potentials commonly used to measure LTP.

Addressing the first of these concerns by using powerful and extended experience as the learning event, the initial reports showed enhancement of excitatory synaptic potentials and population spikes after different types of learning experience. The early studies include ones in which several aspects of synaptic physiology were observed to change in the perforant pathway response in rats who had been exposed for prolonged periods to an "enriched" as compared to an "impoverished" environment. The "enriched" rats lived in a large housing area with litter mates, with continuous social stimulation and various forms of environmental stimulation through their opportunity to investigate and interact with many objects placed in their shared cages, whereas the "impoverished" rats had solitary housing, the absence of stimulating objects, and a small living space. In a particularly illustrative study of this type by Green and Greenough (1986), hippocampal slices were taken from these rats and were tested for various aspects of synaptic and cellular responsiveness. It was found that rats who had lived in the enriched environment, compared to those restricted to the impoverished environment, had an increased slope of the synaptic potential and larger population action potentials, but no change in the presynaptic fiber volley or the amplitude of the antidromic population spike. These changes are entirely consistent with the pattern of increased synaptic efficacy observed following LTP. These changes were not permanent; they disappeared if the enriched-condition animals were subsequently isolated for 3–4 weeks prior to the analyses. In another study that involved prolonged exposure to an enriched environment, recordings were taken from behaving animals with chronic electrode implants (Sharp et al., 1985, 1987). Increases in the dentate population spike were observed to grow gradually over several days of exposure, and to dissipate after several weeks.

Similar increases in the dentate population spike have been observed in behaving animals following more specific learning experiences, including a shock-motivated brightness discrimination (Ruthrich et al., 1982), appetitively motivated operant conditioning (Skelton et al., 1987), and Pavlovian eye blink conditioning (Weisz et al., 1984), each of these changes lasting at least several hours. This combination of findings suggests that a variety of learning experiences can result in increases in the efficacy of hippocampal synapses. The series of studies on behavioral LTP that received the greatest attention involved reports of short-lived changes in synaptic physiology following brief exploration of a novel environment, called *short-term exploratory modulation* (STEM; Sharp et al., 1989; Green et al., 1990). These investigators induced rats to explore a novel or familiar environment and observed a gradual growth in synaptic field potential that outlasted the exploratory experience by several minutes.

These studies generated considerable excitement, although even from the outset there were a number of unsettling features of the observations. It was not clear how closely related the synaptic changes were to real learning, and the changes did not last longer than 30 minutes. Of more concern was that, unlike LTP, the synaptic field potential and population spike changed in opposite directions: The EPSP was enhanced whereas the population spike was diminished, although the onset latency of the population spike was paradoxically reduced. This discrepancy was interpreted as a reflection of widespread strengthening of synapses including mostly those on inhibitory interneurons, leading to the overall diminished population spike. However, the difference in the direction of the population spike change was in striking contrast to the observations from the earlier described studies. Control studies dissociated known influences of attention, EEG state, and motor activity (Hargreaves et al., 1990) from those that appeared to follow the exploratory behavior itself (Green et al., 1990). Thus, for example, medial septal lesions that eliminated theta patterns in the EEG did not block the STEM effects. And walking on a treadmill by highly experienced rats only produced very transient changes. So it seemed the changes could be attributed to the lasting effects of the exploratory experience itself.

However, contrary to the conclusions of these studies, subsequent studies by Moser and colleagues (1993) showed conclusively that the observed EPSP and population spike changes were not mainly due to a learning experience. They attempted to study the STEM phenomenon during real learning, and they selected the Morris water maze as a behavioral task that is particularly good for assessing hippocampal function. Animals were implanted with chronic stimulation and recording electrodes, and field potentials were collected before and after spatial memory training in the water maze. To their surprise, Moser et al. found precisely the opposite effects of STEM, a substantial decrease in the field synaptic potential combined with increases in population spike amplitude and onset latency. Noting that they had used the conventional procedure of training rats in water below body temperature (to motivate them to escape), Moser et al. tested the possibility that body temperature plays a role. In a systematic study they found that indeed manipulations of body temperature could reproduce the main effects of STEM (Figure 3.10). Thus, by raising the water maze temperature, or by simply heating the animals with a lamp, they found both the enhancement of the field synaptic potential and the reduction in the population spike amplitude and onset latency. Furthermore, these measures closely correlated with local temperature changes in the hippocampus, and both effects could be reproduced or inverted by heating or cooling the animal, respectively. In addition, the effects of brain temperature could be seen either in or out of training situations, both in the hippocampus and elsewhere in the brain.

Moser et al. attributed each property of STEM to the well-known effects of temperature on cellular physiology: Higher temperatures facilitate transmitter release and hyperpolarize cell membranes, thus increasing synaptic potentials and decreasing the number of cells contributing to the population spike. In a further dissociation of these physiological changes from memory, Moser and Andersen (1994) showed that the brain cooling did not affect spatial learning, suggesting that fluctuations in synaptic efficacy frequently occur and present a major form of "noise" that must be overcome by some sort of normalization during information processing.

In a follow-up study of the synaptic field potentials and population spikes, Moser et al. (1994) tightly controlled for the effects of temperature per se and independently assessed the effects of the theta rhythm, arousal, and locomotor activity (Figure 3.11). They found that theta activity prominent during REM sleep without movement or arousal resulted in elevation of the population spike and reduction of spike onset latency with no observable effect on the synaptic potential. Arousal, produced by an intense high-frequency tone, resulted in a decrease in spike amplitude, no change in spike latency, and a decrease in field synaptic potential. Locomotor activity on a treadmill, or higher locomotor activity during exploration, resulted in modest increases in the population spike, a more substantial decrease in the synaptic potential, and no effect on spike latency. Thus much of the change that was observed could be explained by variations in temperature, motor activity, and EEG state. However, using a subtraction procedure to eliminate each of these effects, Moser et al. estimated that there was still a modest residual change in potentials occurring during exploration that could reflect learning. Moreover, this residual effect took the form of increases in both the synaptic potential and the population spike, just as in LTP and in other examples of "behavioral LTP" discussed previously. In sum, the finding of a small residual increase in synaptic efficacy similar in pattern to LTP is precisely the needle in the haystack anticipated at the outset of these studies!

Other approaches to identifying behavioral LTP have examined whether transmission of sensory evoked responses is facilitated when the sensory stimuli are the cues for learning. Deadwyler and colleagues (1988) first examined this issue

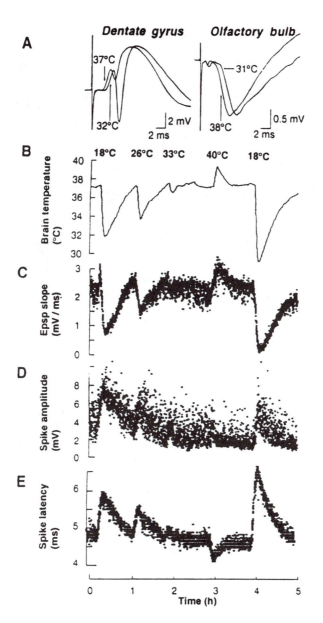

Figure 3.10. Alterations in dentate field potentials resulting from swimming in a Morris water maze with the water at different temperatures. A. Superimposed field potentials showing similar changes in the dentate gyrus and olfactory bulb—in both cases cooling resulted in delayed EPSPs. B-E. Changes in brain temperature, EPSP, and spike potential properties in the dentate field potentials. (Reproduced, with permission, from Moser, Mathiesen, & Andersen, 1993; Copyright American Association for the Advancement of Science.)

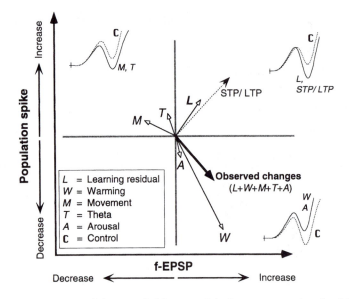

Figure 3.11. Summary of dentate field potential changes associated with behavior, temperature, and other factors. (Reproduced, with permission, from Moser, Moser, & Andersen, 1994; Copyright Cold Spring Harbor Laboratory Press.)

using a discrimination task where rats were required to distinguish between two pure tone stimuli. They found that auditory evoked field potentials in the dentate gyrus varied with the trial sequence so that the N1 component of the evoked potential was greatest following consecutive S– trials and was smallest following consecutive S+ trials (Figure 3.12). Indeed the size of the N1 accurately predicted the recent history across many trial sequences. In addition, these variations corresponded to trial sequence fluctuations in the magnitude of the dentate field EPSP to perforant path stimulation, showing a close parallel with the variations in the natural evoked potentials.

Recent observations offer confirming evidence for a connection between the phenomena of LTP and enhanced sensory transmission in a different neural circuit. In this case the circuit under study was the pathway from the medial geniculate nucleus of the thalamus to the lateral amygdala nucleus that is part of the critical circuit for auditory fear conditioning (see chapter 12). Rogan and LeDoux (1995) first used high-frequency electrical stimulation of the thalamic inputs to induce LTP within the lateral nucleus of the amygdala. Consequently they found an enhancement of synaptic responses within the same area of the amygdala to natural auditory stimulation. In a follow-up study, Quirk et al. (1995) found the converse. That is, they showed that fear conditioning enhances short-latency sensory evoked responses of neurons in the amygdala.

These findings are illuminating in two ways. First, they support the view that there is nothing special about the hippocampus or spatial memory when it comes to LTP, consistent with the above picture of multiple memory systems and loci for critical plasticity. Second, the approach taken in these experiments points

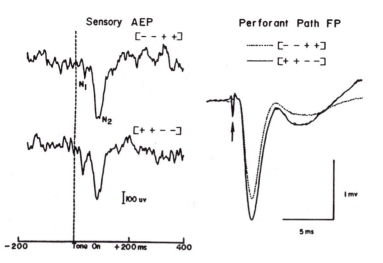

Figure 3.12. Changes in the auditory field potential (AEP) and stimulation pro-duced field potential (FP) in the dentate produced by different sequences of trials in which the negative (–) and positive (+) tone stimulus is presented. (Repro-duced, with permission, from Deadwyler, Hampson, Fisher, & Marlow, 1988; Copyright John Wiley & Sons, Inc.)

toward a potentially more decisive and therefore possibly more fruitful way to link LTP and memory. The magnitude, direction, and longevity of increases in auditory evoked synaptic potentials paralleled those parameters for electrically induced synaptic potential, showing us that natural information processing can make use of the very cellular and molecular mechanisms set in place by conven-tional, artificially induced LTP. Correspondingly, the observation of increased neuronal sensory responses following conditioning shows us that, like LTP, real learning can enhance information processing relevant to the task.

In addition, Rogan et al. (1997) have now shown that repeated pairings of auditory stimuli and foot shocks that train rats to fear the tones alter evoked sensory responses to the tones in the same way as LTP in that pathway (Figure 3.13). Thus, in rats with properly timed pairings, tones produce evoked poten-tials of greater slope and amplitude, just as do electrical stimulus trains applied to this pathway. No enhancement of field potentials is observed with unpaired tone and foot shock presentations, even though this conditioning control leads to as much of a behavioral response (freezing) as paired presentations (even the unpaired control rats learn to freeze to the environmental context where shocks are received). Furthermore, this behavioral LTP is enduring, lasting at least a few days, as long as the behavioral response during extinction trials. This approach takes us beyond mere similarities between LTP and memory, bringing into conti-guity the identical neural pathways and experimental procedures that define LTP and sensory processing in memory.

Finally, an approach recently pioneered by Wilson and McNaughton (1994) focuses on another likely consequence of enhanced functional connectivity in the

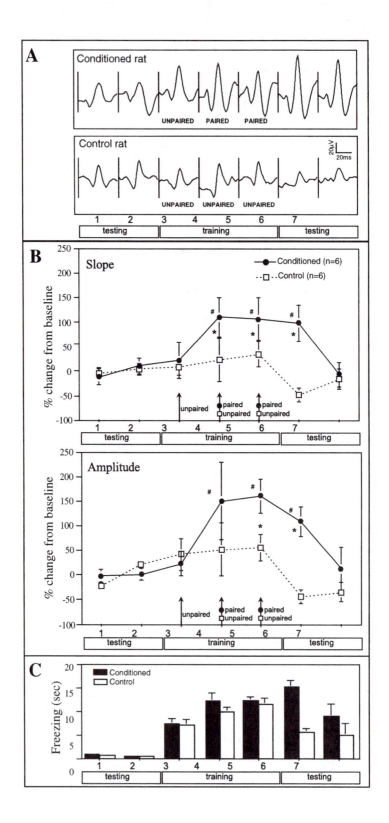

hippocampal population following learning experiences. They found persistently increased cross-correlations among hippocampal neurons that were coactive during exploration of a novel environment. In addition, other recent work described below indicates that correlated hippocampal spatial firing patterns predict spatial learning performance, and both learning performance and correlated hippocampal neural activity are compromised in mice lacking NMDA receptors. A great advantage of measuring hippocampal plasticity in terms of increases in correlated firing patterns is that both the learning situation and the physiological correlate are fully natural.

Natural Hippocampal Firing Patterns and LTP Induction: Shared Patterns of Neural Activation

One of the strengths and limitations of laboratory LTP is that the patterns of afferent activation used to induce LTP are highly unnatural. The typical stimulation pattern involves 100–400 Hz stimulation for several seconds, a pattern that virtually never occurs in hippocampal pathways in normal animals. And the typical stimulation used in LTP induction involves simultaneous coactivation of hundreds if not thousands of afferent fibers, another aspect of hippocampal physiology never seen in nature. The latter aspect of stimulation is difficult to eliminate. One needs to stimulate many fibers in order to observe the responses of distant cells that are only broadly connected with the specific inputs stimulated. However, some have questioned whether the pattern of tetanus needs to be so unnatural. In fact, there is now evidence that patterns of afferent activation mimicking naturally occurring hippocampal neural activity are sufficient, and much more efficient in producing LTP than the typical bombardment.

A prominent rhythm of activity within the hippocampus and elsewhere is the aforementioned "theta" rhythm, a near-sinusoidal EEG pattern that occurs at 4–12 Hz and is most prominent during exploratory and locomotory behavior (Vanderwolf, 1969). This rhythm reflects a cycle of excitability of hippocampal neurons, so that both CA1 pyramidal cells and dentate granule cells are at maximal excitability after the positive peak of the theta cycle (Rudell et al., 1980). In addition, hippocampal neurons preferentially fire in bursts of activity, 2–5 spikes at 3–10 ms interspike intervals, associated with the theta rhythm (Ranck, 1973; Fox & Ranck, 1975; see Figure 3.14). Furthermore, hippocampal pyramidal cells preferentially coactivate in association with the theta rhythm, providing for the possibility of associative inputs that might induce LTP (Kuperstein et al., 1986).

Figure 3.13. Changes in auditory field potentials in the amygdala following fear conditioning. A. Raw field potentials in with consistently paired tone-shock combinations versus control conditions where tones and shocks were not consistently paired. B-C. Changes from baseline in the field potential characteristics and acquired behavioral response of freezing after tone presentations in testing prior to tone-shock pairs, during training, and in extinction testing following training. (Reproduced, with permission, from Rogan, Staubli, & LeDoux, 1997; Copyright Macmillan Magazines Ltd.)

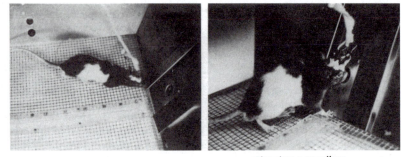

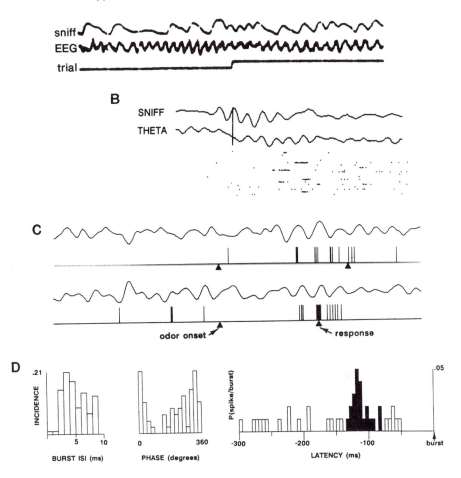

Figure 3.14. Hippocampal neural activity associated with performance in odor discrimination. A. Rat approaching and subsequently sniffing at the odor stimulus port. Note synchronization of sniff cycles and theta cycles in EEG at the time of trial onset. B. Averaged sniff and theta signals, and activity of a hippocampal neuron time-locked to trial onset. C. Hippocampal spike burst activity time-locked to the average theta rhythm. D. Averages of activity of a hippocampal neuron showing characteristics of bursts and latency of spike activity preceding bursts (natural prime burst-like activity). (Reproduced, with permission, from Eichenbaum, Otto, & Cohen, 1992; Copyright Academic Press.)

Following these findings, several investigators sought to determine if short bouts of electrical stimulation timed appropriately to activate hippocampal cells in patterns associated with the theta rhythm would be sufficient to produce LTP. Indeed these studies have shown that lasting potentiation is induced preferentially by electrical stimulation that involves aspects of hippocampal neural activity associated with the theta rhythm. LTP in CA1 slices was preferentially induced by short but high-frequency bursts of stimulation (4 pulses at 100 Hz) presented in pairs of stimulus bouts so that 4 pulses from one set of synapses preceded a similar bout from another set of synapses on the same CA1 cells, a stimulation pattern called *theta burst* (Larson et al., 1986; see also Winson & Dahl, 1986, for description of a similar protocol used in whole animals). Under conditions where theta burst pairings were presented every 2 s, lasting potentiation was observed. The authors concluded that the first of each burst pair acted as a "priming" effect that facilitated synaptic modifications resulting from the second. In subsequent studies, Larson and Lynch (1986) showed that potentiation can be induced by a single theta burst pattern, that is, by a single sequence of bursts from converging pathways. Rose and Dunwiddie (1986; see also Diamond et al., 1988) showed that potentiation occurs even if a single pulse precedes a burst by 130–200 ms presented within the same pathway, a pattern called a *prime burst* pattern, in waking animals (Figure 3.15). The LTP produced in both "theta burst" and "prime burst" protocols is blocked by AP5 and is therefore

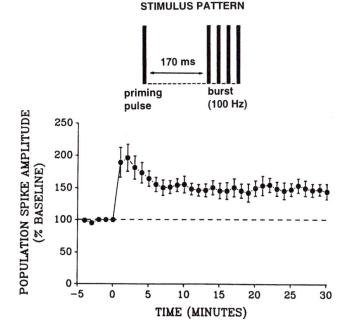

Figure 3.15. Prime-burst pattern of stimulations and resulting CA1 field spike potential changes in vitro. (Reproduced, with permission, from Diamond, Dunwiddie, & Rose, 1988; Copyright Society for Neuroscience.)

considered dependent on NMDA receptors. Patterned stimulation of this type is most effective in inducing LTP in dentate gyrus when delivered at the peak of the dentate theta rhythm (Pavlides et al., 1988; Greenstein et al., 1988), and as described above, a single burst well timed within the theta cycle can produce significant synaptic potentiation or depression (Huerta & Lisman, 1995). Together, these data suggest that theta burst stimulation (i.e., one or a few brief episodes of high-frequency stimulation applied in the appropriate temporal relationship to prior activity and to the ongoing theta rhythm) can reliably enhance synaptic efficacy in a brain area critical to the formation of certain types of memory. These observations suggest that theta bursts should be observable in real neural activity patterns associated with learning performance.

A study by Otto et al. (1991) found that all the characteristics of theta burst patterned activation occur simultaneously and selectively during episodes of memory processing. In rats performing spatial and olfactory tasks, the firing patterns of putative CA1 pyramidal cells indeed discharged in high-frequency bursts, phase-locked to the positive peak of the dentate theta rhythm. Furthermore, these bursts were preceded by neural activity preferentially at intervals corresponding to the theta rhythm. Importantly, the theta burst patterns emerged only during significant behavioral events associated with likely periods of stimulus analysis, selection, or storage. Thus the optimal conditions for hippocampal LTP induction indeed are present when animals actively engage hippocampal processing for putative mnemonic functions. Moreover, as predicted by Lisman (1997), these brief bursts provide an improvement in the signal-to-noise ratio of the coding of behavioral events, as observed in both spatial and olfactory-stimulus-related firing patterns. While these brief events may lead to only small and temporary adjustments of synaptic strengths across the network during learning, a lasting "consolidation" of them may be mediated by coincident bursts that occur across the hippocampal population during "off-line" activities (Buzsaki & Chrobak, 1995). In addition, whereas the theta rhythm has been studied primarily in the rodent hippocampus, there is now evidence of a prominent theta rhythm associated with memory processing in widespread areas of the cerebral cortex in humans (Kahana et al., 1999).

It is encouraging that these characteristics of natural activity patterns are so similar to those optimal for induction of LTP. But what remains unclear is whether the observed natural patterns actually produce changes in synaptic efficacy. To address this question, one can employ these "natural" stimulation patterns as learning cues. Studies using such an approach have demonstrated clear relationships between learning performance and synaptic responses to electrical stimulation used as the conditioning stimulus in learning situations. Roman and colleagues (1987, 1993) found that theta-burst-patterned stimulation to the lateral olfactory tract (LOT) potentiates population EPSPs in the piriform cortex when the stimulation was employed as a discriminative cue substituting for an odor stimulus. Doyere and Laroche (1992) used high-frequency stimulation bursts in the perforant path as the CS in a conditioned-emotional-response paradigm, finding that the decay of burst-potentiated responses in the dentate gyrus predicted forgetting of the conditioned response. Given the recent Moser et al. (1993) findings, though, it is clear these observations now need to be confirmed with appropriate controls for the possibility that the effects are secondary to temperature changes and behavioral influences over hippocampal evoked potentials that could be selectively associated with the learned behaviors. However, if this approach is validated, it should be possible to examine whether depotentiation protocols would result in loss of memory performance ("forgetting") for electrical conditioning stimuli.

Blocking LTP and Memory

The major limitation of the above-described approaches is that the experiments only provide correlations between aspects of LTP and memory. The converse approach is to draw cause-and-effect links between the phenomenology of LTP and of memory by blocking LTP and determining if memory is prevented. Three particular approaches are described here that differ in how the LTP block is accomplished. The first involves using electrical stimulation to drive LTP to saturation; the second involves pharmacological manipulations of neurochemical steps in the induction of LTP; and the third involves genetic manipulations that interfere with LTP.

"Saturation" of LTP.   One approach to causally linking LTP and memory that generated initial excitement was the effort to block learning by "saturating" (i.e., driving to asymptote) all of the excitatory synapses in the dentate gyrus before training. Although a very interesting approach, it raises several obvious concerns, even before considering the data. Is it really possible to saturate *all* the synapses in the hippocampus, even in a single stage of the hippocampal circuit? Is information processing (as contrasted with plasticity) within the hippocampal network fully normal following the intense stimulation protocol required, which involves 10-fold repeated 400-Hz bombardment each day for 2 weeks (see McNamara et al., 1993)? Wouldn't such a powerful manipulation of synaptic weights also influence memory codes currently stored in the hippocampus as well as its target structures? Nonetheless, early studies indicated that saturation of the perforant path synapses did result in severe impairment in learning a new spatial location for escape from bright lights in a open field, whereas memory of an original escape location accomplished in the normal state was largely spared (McNaughton et al., 1986). In addition, succeeding experiments demonstrated a generalization to a different spatial learning task, the Morris water maze, and found that learning capacity returned after a month-long recovery period when synaptic efficacy levels dropped back to baseline (Castro et al., 1990).

These findings stimulated subsequent efforts by several investigators to replicate the saturation effect. A series of five studies found no effect of saturation on water maze learning across a variety of experimental protocols, including a direct replication by the original investigators (Korol et al., 1993) and replications by other groups (Jeffery & Morris, 1993; Sutherland et al., 1993), and by yet other groups that attempted even seizure-producing-level stimulation (McNamara et al., 1993; Cain et al., 1993).

In a follow-up study using this approach, the original investigators addressed two predominant issues: the likelihood that the original saturation did not block synapses throughout the hippocampus, and differences between the originally used open-field spatial "reversal" task and the subsequent water-maze-learning task. They showed that the standard saturation protocol did not actually saturate synapses in any hippocampal region, but that such stimulation was sufficient to replicate the learning impairment in the original open-field spatial-reversal learning task. Unfortunately, they failed to find any deficit in the water maze, unless the stimulation pattern involved maximal seizures (Barnes et al., 1994). However, Moser et al. (1998) revisited this approach, with greater success. They developed a stimulating array that cross-activated the major bundle of afferents reached the dorsal part of the hippocampus. This more thorough form of stimulation in one hemisphere was combined with removal of the contralateral hippocampus and testing of the residual capacity for potentiation after "saturation." These elaborations of the protocol revealed that stimulation of the hippocampus produced a reliable spatial learning deficit when the residual capacity for potentiation was less than 10%. Thus the mixture of the earlier results may have been due to inadequate saturation.

Pharmacological and Genetic Blockade of LTP. Perhaps the most compelling and straightforward data on a potential connection between the molecular basis of LTP and memory has come from experiments where a drug or genetic manipulation is used to block LTP and, correspondingly, prevent learning. Here again there was the need for optimistic assumptions. It had to be assumed that the drugs were selective to plasticity and not normal information processing in the brain, and that they would knock out a critical kind of plasticity. These assumptions were accepted based on the observation that drugs, such as AP5, that selectively block the NMDA receptor prevent hippocampal LTP while sparing normal synaptic transmission (e.g., Bliss & Lynch, 1988). Thus, to the extent that the role of the NMDA receptor is fully selective to plasticity, one might predict these drugs would indeed block new learning without affecting nonlearning performance or retention of learning normally accomplished prior to drug treatment.

Consistent with these predictions, some of the earliest and strongest evidence supporting a connection between LTP and memory came from demonstrations that drug-induced blockade of NMDA receptors prevents new learning (Figure 3.16; Morris et al, 1986). Additional experiments showed no effect of AP5 on retention of the same kind of water maze spatial learning when training was accomplished prior to drug treatment. This would be fully predicted because NMDA receptors are viewed as required only for the induction of LTP and not for its maintenance. Furthermore, the deficit was limited to spatial learning, known from other work to be dependent on the hippocampus, and not to a simple visual discrimination, known not to be dependent on hippocampal function. Other evidence provided largely consistent findings from several learning paradigms (see review by Staubli & Lynch, 1991) and extended these findings to other brain pathways mediating a different type of memory (Kim et al., 1991). In addition, complementary reports indicated that drugs that enhance the induction of LTP also facilitate learning (e.g., Staubli et al., 1994; Hampson et al., 1998).

More recent work with targeted genetic manipulations have shown that blocking the cascade of molecular triggers for LTP also results in severe memory impairments (e.g., Silva et al., 1992a, 1992b; Grant et al., 1992; reviewed in Mayford et al., 1995; Silva et al., 1997; Silva & Giese, 1998). In one of the early studies of this type, mice with a mutation in the alpha isoform of CaMKII had deficient LTP

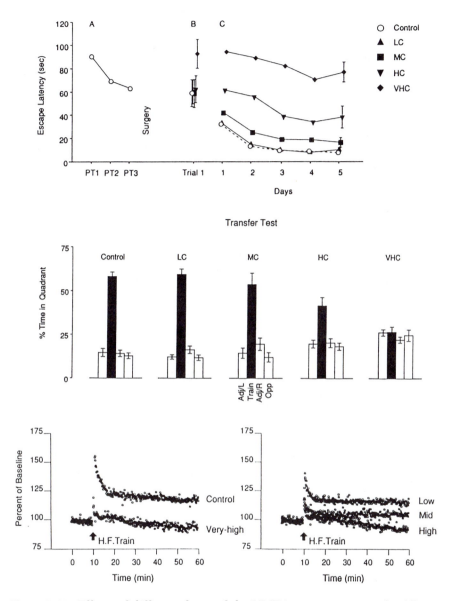

Figure 3.16. Effects of different doses of the NMDA receptor antagonist AP5 on water maze performance. Top: Escape latencies during pretraining days (PT1-3), on the first trial of training and on subsequent training days in control rats infused with vehicle and in rats with infusions that resulted in low (LC), middle (MC), high (HC), or very high (VHC) concentrations of AP5 in the hippocampus. Middle. Performance on transfer tests where the escape platform was removed. Memory of the location of previous escapes is indicated by high dwell times in the training quadrant. Bottom: Relationship between AP5 concentration and amount of LTP measured in post-training evaluations. (Reproduced, with permission, from Davis, Butcher, & Morris, 1992; Copyright Society for Neuroscience.)

(see above) and were selectively impaired in learning the Morris water maze. Despite the fact that the genetic manipulation was effective throughout development, the hippocampus appeared normal in architecture and was normal in its basic physiological responsiveness. Since that time, similar learning-specific impairments have been reported in several different types of knockout mice with deficiencies in LTP, with a special emphasis on knockouts of CREB (Bourtchuladze et al., 1994; Kogan et al., 1997; reviewed in Eichenbaum, 1997b; Frank & Greenberg, 1994; Silva et al., 1997; Stevens, 1994).

The manipulation of biochemical mechanisms by interference with specific genes allows investigators to identify the critical molecular events at a very high level of specificity. For example, a study by Giese et al. (1998) showed that substitution of a single amino acid in CaMKII that prevents its autophosphorylation results in severe learning and memory deficits. In addition, other new genetic approaches are providing greater temporal as well as region-specific blockade of gene activation (Mayford et al., 1996). In one study (Tsien et al., 1996a, 1996b), the genetic block was limited to postdevelopment activation of the genes for the NMDA receptor specifically in the CA1 subfield of the hippocampus, which selectively blocked LTP in that region. Despite these highly selective temporal and anatomical restrictions, the mice with this mutation were severely deficient in spatial learning.

These pharmacological studies, though impressive, have not provided unambiguous support for the hypothesis that LTP is necessary for memory. Some of the earlier experiments showed that a fraction of hippocampus-dependent learning survived even a total block of the capacity for LTP. In a careful and detailed replication of their original study, Morris and colleagues measured intrahippocampal AP5 concentrations and found that a dose of AP5 sufficient to fully prevont any signs of LTP still shows some degree of water maze learning, albeit not as good as that of control subjects (Figure 3.16; Davis et al., 1992). Other studies also showed some degree of preserved hippocampus-dependent learning, even with doses sufficient to prevent LTP (Staubli et al., 1989).

Newer experiments provide converging evidence of intact hippocampus-dependent learning even when the capacity for hippocampal LTP is fully blocked (Bannerman et al., 1995; Saucier & Cain, 1995). These studies showed that blocking NMDA-dependent LTP does not necessarily prevent the central component of water maze learning, that is, the encoding of a new spatial map. This demonstration was accomplished by isolating new spatial learning from the acquisition of more general task knowledge when animals were provided in advance with background swimming skills and experience in a water maze. Such "pretraining" was found to protect against the otherwise detrimental effects of an NMDA receptor blocker on new spatial learning. By one interpretation hippocampal NMDA receptors may thus be critical for learning a spatial strategy, but not for encoding particular maps (Bannerman et al., 1995). Alternatively, pretraining may merely overcome the motor side effects of NMDA receptor blockers by providing preliminary acquisition of swimming skills (Saucier & Cain, 1995; for review see Cain, 1997). Bannerman and colleagues' study showed this could not be the full explanation, because pretraining animals to use a nonspatial strategy—that is, to search randomly for a trial-specific escape site—should have been sufficient to override motor side effects but in fact did not protect fully against the effects of AP5 on subsequent spatial learning. Nevertheless, these observations have led Morris (see Morris & Frey, 1997) to conclude that NMDA-receptor-dependent LTP is not required for learning new spatial locations per se.

More recent work sheds further light on a more specific role that NMDA-receptor-dependent LTP might play. Steele and Morris (1999) have developed a new version of the water maze task in which the location of the escape platform is moved every day, and animals are given four trials to learn the new location (Figure 3.17). Across a series of training days the rats became skilled at the task so that they consistently found the platform very rapidly the second time it was presented. Subsequent to initial drug-free training, AP5 treatment resulted in a deficit on Trial 2 performance. Moreover this deficit was dependent on the time interval between Trial 1 and Trial 2, so that no impairment was observed with a 15-s intertrial interval, but significant deficits ensued if the intertrial interval was extended to 20 min or longer. These data suggest that memory for specific episodes of spatial learning remains dependent on NMDA receptors and LTP, even after the animals have learned the environment and the general rules of the spatial task. This finding is consistent with previous results indicating the importance of NMDA receptors in other trial-specific memory tasks (e.g., Tonkiss et al., 1988). However, by contrast, Shapiro and O'Conner (1992) argued that doses of NMDA receptor antagonists that impair new learning without affecting motor performance do not result in event-specific memory held over many minutes. These data, as well as the mixture of findings reviewed above, provide strong provisional evidence for the necessity of NMDA-receptor-mediated plasticity in some types of learning. At the same time, it is clear that some forms of learning performance can be intact even in the absence of this form of plasticity.

A series of studies suggests that the cascade of molecular events that are invoked by LTP may also mediate cortical plasticity that underlies memory. A particularly good example of this work involves a set of studies focused on taste learning mediated by the gustatory cortex of rats (Rosenblum et al., 1993, 1997; Berman et al., 1998). When rats are exposed to a novel taste and subsequently become ill, they develop a conditioned aversion specifically to that taste, and this learning is known to depend on the gustatory area of the insular cortex. Blockade of NMDA receptors by infusion of the antagonist AP5 produces an impairment in taste aversion learning, whereas the same injections given prior to retention testing, or into an adjacent cortical area, had no effect. Thus it is likely that modifications in cortical taste representations depend on LTP. Furthermore, blockade of protein synthesis in the gustatory cortex by infusion of an inhibitor prior to learning also prevents development of the conditioned taste aversion. By contrast, the same injection given into a neighboring cortical area, or given to the gustatory cortex hours after learning has no effect. Consistent with this finding, MAP kinase as well as a downstream kinase protein were activated selectively in gustatory cortex within 10 minutes of exposure to a novel taste and activation peaked at 30 minutes, whereas exposure to a familiar taste had no effect. Conversely, a MAP kinase inhibitor retarded conditioned taste aversion. This combination of findings provides complementary lines of evidence that strongly implicate the NMDA mediated plasticity and subsequent specific protein syn-

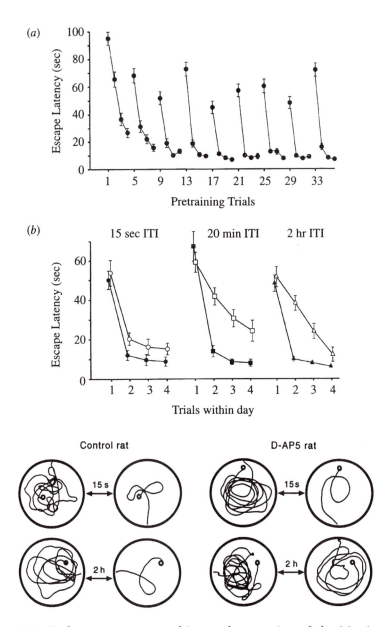

Figure 3.17. Performance on a matching-to-place version of the Morris water maze task and effects of infusion of AP5. Top: a. Performance in learning the task. Rats are trained on a series of 4 trials per day with the escape platform in a novel location. Note the reduction in the latency between trials 1 and 2 within each day after the first few training sessions. b. Escape latency on trial 2 presented at different delays after the first trial (filled circles = controls; open circles = AP5). (Reproduced, with permission, from Morris & Frey, 1997; Copyright The Royal Society of London.) Bottom: Examples of swimming patterns of control and AP5 rats on the first two trials at different delays. Note relatively direct swim paths on trial 2, except with a 2 hr delay on AP5 rat. (Reproduced, with permission, from Steele & Morris, 1999; Copyright John Wiley & Sons, Inc.)

thesis as playing a critical role in cortical modifications that mediate this type of learning.

The Future of Studies on LTP and Memory

The findings from each of the above-described approaches do not prove LTP and memory do *not* share the same bases, and indeed these studies leave substantial room for continued optimism. In the studies on changes in synaptic efficacy, the experiments that controlled for temperature and other general effects showed the expected changes after extended experience (Green & Greenough, 1986), and small changes in both the field EPSP and population spike were observed in the same direction as LTP after brief experiences (Moser et al., 1994). LTP saturation may have the expected effect in limited circumstances (Barnes et al., 1994; Moser et al., 1998). Even the recent studies that showed learning despite LTP blockade can be given an optimistic interpretation that hippocampal LTP is critical for learning something about space, the extent of which may depend on previous experience and demand for episodic memory (Morris & Frey, 1997; Steele & Morris, 1999).

Nevertheless, we cannot take the pattern of somewhat equivocal results lightly, and with the benefit of hindsight, we can see some reasons why they might have failed. First, there have now been demonstrated multiple forms of LTP, some of which are not dependent on the NMDA mechanism, suggesting there may be a variety of parallel mechanisms that can support increased efficacy in a pathway that represents associations and therefore parallel ways to mediate memory performance. If this is indeed the case, then, to the extent that some experimental manipulations are fully selective to only one plasticity mechanism, experiments aimed to show a critical role seem doomed to fail. For example, the CA3 mossy fiber synapse demonstrates a form of LTP that is not NMDA-dependent, and the CA3 cell population is thought by some to be the best example of an associative memory network. Drugs that selectively block NMDA-dependent LTP would not prevent information from getting into or out of the CA3 network. So it is entirely possible that changes in the CA3 network could support substantial hippocampus-dependent learning capacity, even in the absence of functional NMDA receptors in the hippocampus.

Second, when an experiment reports that memory is or is not blocked by a manipulation of LTP, the results are only meaningful in the context of where in the brain the LTP manipulation is effective and which brain system supports that kind of memory. This consideration may go far to explain why saturation-like hippocampal stimulation (Berger, 1984) and pharmacological treatments that block hippocampal LTP (Mondadori et al., 1989; Weiskrantz & Mondadori, 1991) can result in the facilitation of learning mediated mainly by nonhippocampal circuits and indeed where hippocampal representations may only interfere (McDonald & White, 1993). Considerations of different forms of plasticity and multiple memory systems indicate we have to be much more sophisticated when assessing the role of LTP in memory performance. Studies that focus on comparing neural activity or the effects of drugs and genetic manipulations on normal (non-learning) information processing versus changes associated with learning will be the most successful. Studies on the amygdala (Rogan et al., 1997) and other studies showing LTP in other areas, including the cerebral cortex (see Bear, 1996), are guiding this direction.

Third, even in the majority of experiments that limit consideration to hippocampus-dependent learning and LTP in the hippocampus, there is the general difficulty in distinguishing the effects of a manipulation that results in hippocampal malfunction from one that selectively blocks hippocampal plasticity. Thus, even in principle, blocking hippocampal plasticity and blocking overall hippocampal function are expected to have more-or-less identical selective consequences: Both are expected to interfere selectively with long-term retention of a particular kind of memory, and neither is expected to interfere with normal perception, motivation, motor performance, memory for some types of information, or short-term memory of any type. Consistent with these expectations, in nearly every experiment to date (e.g., Lyford et al., 1993), blocking hippocampal LTP results in the same pattern of deficit and spared function as observed after explicit hippocampal damage although, as might also be expected, physiological or pharmacological blockade of hippocampal LTP is temporary and may be less effective than an overt lesion. This consideration calls into question the premise that drugs or genetic manipulations that block LTP spare normal hippocampal information processing.

Some recent studies suggest, however, that progress is being made in distinguishing the effects of blocking hippocampal plasticity versus those of eliminating hippocampal function. Steele and Morris (1999) have provided evidence that blockade of NMDA receptors selectively prevents delayed but not immediate place recognition, whereas hippocampal lesions result in impairments at all times. Also, Good and Bannerman (1997) showed that blockade of NMDA receptors does not result in a deficient memory for the context in which a conditioned response was learned, whereas hippocampal lesions prevent context-dependent learning. These studies open up ways in which we may yet be able to differentiate hippocampal information processing and hippocampal memory. On the other hand, an alternative explanation of these dissociations is that, even in the absence of NMDA receptor function, other forms of synaptic function and plasticity still available in the hippocampus could have been sufficient to mediate these types of learning; the lesser effects of NMDA receptor blockade may be attributable to the partial blocking of molecular synaptic events and plasticity by pharmacological means.

Our acceptance of the view that these manipulations are selective for hippocampal plasticity does not rely on any functional dissociation, but rather solely on the observation that the drugs or genetic manipulations do not affect synaptic transmission as revealed in evoked-potential protocols. It is important to remember that large-scale evoked field potentials never actually occur during normal information processing. So the data available from these studies do not allow us to conclude that other more relevant patterns of hippocampal information processing are fully normal under the influence of drugs such as AP5. A newer generation of combined electrophysiological and pharmacological-genetic studies is providing evidence critical to this question. Several studies have how examined the nature and persistence of spatial representations of single hippocampal neurons and neuronal populations in animals with compromised capacity for LTP.

These studies involve genetically altered mice or rats with pharmacologically blocked LTP and recordings of so-called place cells, hippocampal neurons that fire when the animal is in a particular location in its environment (see chapter 8 for a detailed explanation of place cells). Rotenberg et al. (1996) found that mutant mice expressing an active form of CaMKII that impairs one form of LTP and spatial learning have impoverished and unstable hippocampal spatial representations. Hippocampal cells of these mice initially develop spatially specific firing patterns, albeit in fewer cells, and the spatial specificity of these patterns is reduced. Perhaps most important, unlike normal mice, which have very stable hippocampal spatial representations, the spatial firing patterns in mutant mice are lost or changed if the animal is removed from the environment and later replaced even within a few minutes. Acute pharmacological blockade of NMDA receptors in rats also resulted in instability of the spatial firing patterns of hippocampal neurons, without affecting the incidence or spatial specificity of previously acquired spatial firing patterns (Kentros et al., 1998). The drug did not prevent the initial establishment of hippocampal spatial firing patterns or their short-term retention between repeated recording sessions separated by brief intervals. By contrast, the maintenance of a newly developed spatial representation across days was severely compromised.

The consequence of LTP blockade for the network processing of hippocampal spatial representations has also been examined. McHugh et al. (1996) examined the spatial firing patterns of groups of neighboring hippocampal neurons in mice with the CA1 specific knockout of NMDA receptors. They also reported that these cells had diminished spatial specificity and characterized a reduction in the coordinated activity of neurons tuned to overlapping spatial locations. Furthermore, they tied these findings to the spatial memory impairment by showing how the loss of cross-correlation in mutant hippocampal place cells leads to an impoverished network prediction of sequential locations during navigation behavior. In a different study, Cho et al. (1998) characterized hippocampal spatial representations in mice with knockouts of CaMKII or CREB. As in the other studies, they observed diminished spatial selectivity in both mutants, as well as diminished stability of the spatial representations when some of the environmental cues were altered. CaMKII mutant mice could not recover their spatial representations when the environmental cues were returned to their original configuration. However, the CREB-knockout mice, in which spatial learning and LTP are partially preserved (Giese et al., 1998), recovered their spatial representations in the original environment. These results suggest that the network processes that bind together single neuron representations of spatial cues are particularly dependent on LTP. Further investigations of the coding of space by hippocampal networks offer a particularly promising direction for relating synaptic plasticity processes to memory functions.

4

—

The Cerebral Cortex and Memory

Before turning to discussion of the various memory systems of the brain, starting in the next chapter, we consider here the central role that the cerebral cortex plays in all memory systems. The bulk of memory is stored in the cerebral cortex, it turns out, *not* within specific memory-dedicated regions, but rather within each of the many distinct processing systems in cortex that support perceptual, motor, and cognitive functions.

As indicated in chapter 1, although Gall's phrenology was justifiably discredited, the notion that cerebral cortex is made up of multiple, functionally distinct processing regions has proven correct. Also correct is the idea that memory is integrally tied to these various processing systems. What should become apparent as we consider some of those processing systems here is that memory is both a necessary part and an obligatory product of their ongoing processing activities.

This chapter will begin with a brief summary of the evidence regarding functional specialization of the cortex. Then the role of experience in shaping the responses of neurons in various cortical areas will be reviewed. There are striking commonalities in the forms of plasticity observed across cortical areas and among different types of experiential modifications. These commonalities will provide the basis for the subsequent outline of general rules for how memories are represented in the cortex and, more specifically, how memory is embedded in the various networks, as a fundamental part of these networks in operation.

Information Processing and Memory Storage in Cerebral Cortex

Gall's early attempts to make functional assignments of cortical areas were considerably off-base. This has been attributed rightly to his methodology, which was largely based on anecdotal observations of individual correlations between certain "abilities" and gross structural features of the skull or head. For example, the organ of "amativeness" was localized in the cerebellum because Gall noted a warm spot on the neck of a passionate widow. Gall was sometimes close in his calls, albeit often for the wrong reasons. He assigned language to the frontal lobes because of a medical student with a prodigious verbal memory and bulging eyes, and he supported the claim with case studies of frontal lobe damage and aphasia. Indeed Broca's demonstrations in the 1860s of cases of aphasia with very localized prefrontal damage were viewed as support for both Gall's specific identification of a language area and his general views on cortical localization.

Although most of Gall's specific functional assignments turned out to be quite wrong, modern scientific approaches showed that the general idea of localization was quite right. Shortly after Broca used case studies to localize speech to the prefrontal cortex, Wernicke provided a complementary demonstration showing selective loss of verbal comprehension following a localized temporoparietal lesion. Many subsequent case studies have, over the years, shown that injury to one or another local cortical area resulted in specific perceptual, motor, or cognitive impairments. Taken collectively, such case studies basically form a catalog of neuropsychological data on humans with specific brain damage. These data demonstrate unequivocally the localization of function in cerebral cortex, from the initially coarse dissociations between, say, language and nonlinguistic cognitive functions, to more modern dissociations between, for example, visual recognition of faces versus other objects (Moscovitch et al., 1995, 1997; Farah, 1996; Farah et al., 1998). In addition, experimental studies on animals where specific cortical lesions could be produced with great accuracy showed equally specific functional deficits. Progressing from the earliest pioneering studies of Flourens (1824), who showed that sensory and motor functions could be dissociated by selective anterior or posterior cortical lesions, and Ferrier (1890), who showed that localized motor cortical damage in monkeys could produce specific hand paralysis or deficits in conjugate eye movements, to many modern studies that have characterized highly specific behavioral deficits following localized cortical damage, we can see the functional specializations of different cortical areas.

The same conclusion arises from parallel anatomical studies and, more recently, functional neuroimaging studies. Neuroanatomical work has made it clear that the cortex could be subdivided into areas that were distinct in their local architecture, and in connectional pathways. Brodmann (1909) provided the first architectonic map of the cerebral cortex, where areas were subdivided based on cell types and their laminar organization (Figure 4.1). Several subsequent mappings of the human and animal cortex followed. Among these, Brodmann's and another by Von Bonin and Bailey (1947; Figure 4.1) are most often remembered today because their labeling systems are in current use. There was (and still is) disagreement about the number and types of areas, and about their evolutionary origins. Nevertheless, even from the outset, it was expected that the microanatomical differences among these areas would provide the substrate for, and therefore would be seen as reflecting, functional differences. These original observations have been extensively supplemented by further anatomical techniques, including histochemistry and connectional studies, as well as by physiological techniques, including recording and stimulation studies. The latter have pro-

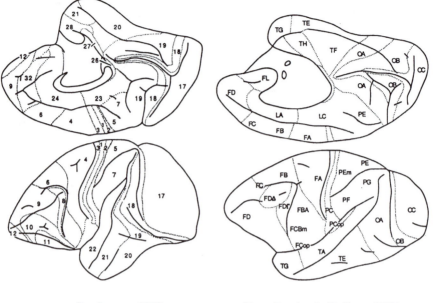

Brodmann, 1909   **Von Bonin & Bailey, 1947**

Figure 4.1. Cytoarchitectonic maps of the macaque monkey cortex. (Reproduced, with permission, from Fuster, 1995; Copyright MIT Press.)

vided substantially greater resolution of the anatomical divisions and, perhaps more important, given us a greater understanding of the functional distinctions among these areas in a number of species.

Functional neuroimaging work, using positron emission tomography (PET) and, more recently, functional magnetic resonance imaging (fMRI), has provided strong confirmation of the functional specialization of different cortical regions. These techniques have permitted detailed mapping of the functionally distinct cortical visual areas in posterior portions of cerebral cortex, including identification of very specialized areas that seem to process complex stimuli such as faces ("fusiform face area"; Kanwisher et al., 1997), places ("parahippocampal place area"; Epstein & Kanwisher, 1998), and different categories of objects (Martin et al., 1995, 1996).

Summarizing the functional specializations of cortex, as demonstrated by neuropsychological, neuroanatomical, and neuroimaging studies, is well beyond the scope of this chapter. Indeed, it is the subject of various books or texts in cognitive neuroscience and cognitive neuropsychology (e.g., see Banich, 1997; Kolb & Wishaw, 1996; Gazzaniga, Ivry, & Mangun, 1998). However, a few very general principles should be committed to mind for the present purposes (Kaas et al. 1990; Pandya & Yeterian, 1985). First, the cortex can roughly be divided into posterior fields that are involved in perceptual processing and anterior areas that are involved in motor processing (Figure 4.2). Second, in the posterior cortex, most of the fields are divided by sensory modality. Third, the fields in both the

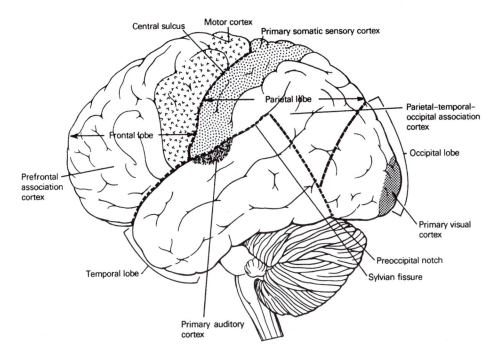

Figure 4.2. Major divisions and functional areas of the human cerebal cortex (left hemisphere). (Reproduced, with permission, from Kandel & Schwartz, 1985.)

anterior and posterior cortex involve processing hierarchies. In the anterior cortex, there is the primary motor area just in front of the central sulcus, where the muscles of the body are mapped out in a topographic organization, with adjacent areas of cortex representing muscle groups in adjacent areas of the body (Figure 4.3). The primary motor cortex is the origin of a progression of projections to higher-order processing areas that are involved in the sequencing and organization of response output and, more generally, in the planning, executing, and withholding of goal-directed behaviors.

In the posterior cortex there are distinct primary areas for each sensory modality. Each of these is characterized by cells that respond to stimulation within a small circumscribed spatial region of the sensory field, known as a *receptive field,* and respond preferentially to other specific trigger features of the stimulus. The receptive fields and other trigger features are organized in a topographic map of the sensory field and of other relevant sensory dimensions, so that adjacent neurons represent contiguous parts of the field and closely related dimensions of the trigger features (Figure 4.4). In each sensory modality these primary areas are the origins of a hierarchy of specialized processing regions leading to more and more complex perceptual areas. Eventually some of these streams of sensory processing are combined in multimodal cortical areas, which in turn project to the supramodal processing areas in frontal, temporal, and parietal cortices.

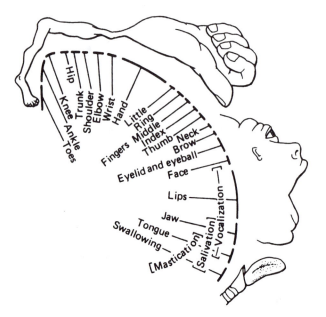

Figure 4.3. Map of the human motor cortex. (Reproduced, with permission, from Kandel & Schwartz, 1985.)

Information Processing and Memory Storage in Cortical Visual Areas

In order to appreciate how memory is integrally related to specific cortical processors, at this point we turn to an extended, specific example of functional specialization and memory representation in cortex. The obvious choice for this example is vision, because its functional properties and its cortical substrates have been so extensively studied. Van Essen and colleagues (1992) have championed the notion that there exist more than 30 functionally distinct visual fields that encompass a large proportion of the primate brain. They have argued that the different visual areas follow a complicated combination of parallel and sequential pathways that are organized hierarchically into at least 10 stages of processing (Figure 4.5). These stages involve, at the earliest levels, distinct areas involved in identification of basic properties of stimuli, such as their orientation, spatial frequency, speed, color, and binocular disparity.

The early visual cortical areas are particularly well characterized, involving topographically organized representations composed of small columns of cells with systematically organized receptive fields. The best understood of these areas is primary visual cortex (V1), where cells of the input layer respond to small spots of light in highly restricted receptive fields. Neighboring principal cells in other layers respond to stable or moving contrast edges with similarly small receptive fields. Cells with these response properties are organized along two dimensions, one corresponding to a preference for activation by the ipsilateral or

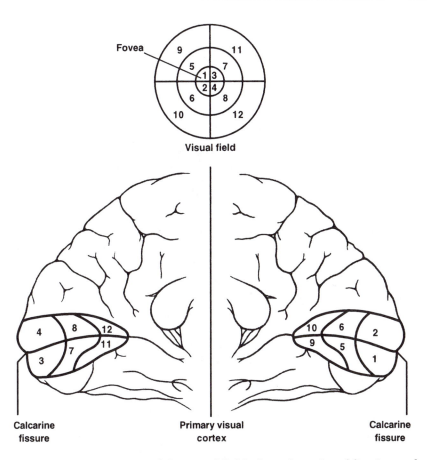

Figure 4.4. Top: Designation of the visual fields from the point of fixation at the fovea. Bottom: Corresponding map of parts of the visual field onto the primary visual area (V1) in the human cortex. Views are on the medial surface of the posterior part of the hemispheres. (Reproduced, with permission, from Kandel & Schwartz, 1985.)

contralateral eye (called *ocular dominance*), and the other corresponding to preferences for an optimal orientation of the contrast edge (Figure 4.6). The cells are arranged in columns, so that through the depths of the cortical layers neurons have very similar properties in ocular dominance and orientation selectivity. Ipsilateral and contralateral ocular dominance columns alternate, and orientation columns are arranged in a systematic sequence. The combination of a full set of ocular dominance and orientation columns that represent the same small receptive field area is known as a *hypercolumn*. Sets of such modules are organized systematically to provide a full representation of the contralateral visual field for each hemisphere.

Higher levels of visual processing involve emergent properties, functions that appear to arise from combinations of inputs from the lower levels, such as optic

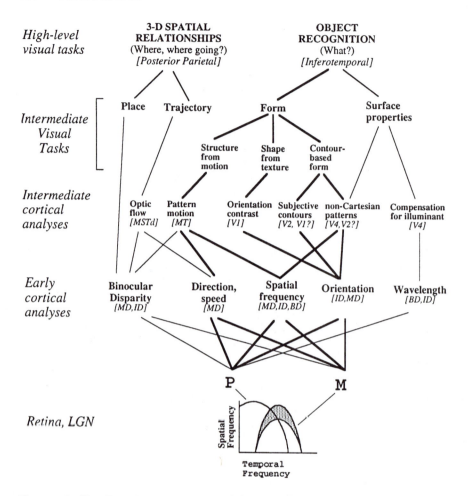

Figure 4.5. Van Essen's organization of functional stages of visual processing. (Reproduced, with permission, from Van Essen & Deyoe, 1995; Copyright MIT Press.)

flow and complex contour identification. Although aspects of their organization scheme have been the subject of debate (Merigan & Maunsell, 1993; Hilgetag et al., 1996), there is general agreement that vision appears to be organized into distinct processing streams, including most prominently a dorsal pathway for visuospatial processing and a ventral pathway for object identification (Figure 4.7). These two processing pathways are very complicated, with much integration between the two streams among modules for processing of contour, spatial, and motion information.

Of these processing streams, the focus here is on the ventral-going stream, where the connection between the perceptual processing functions of this system and the memory functions of this system has been explicitly studied. The major player in this work is the inferotemporal cortex (Von Bonin and Bailey's area TE,

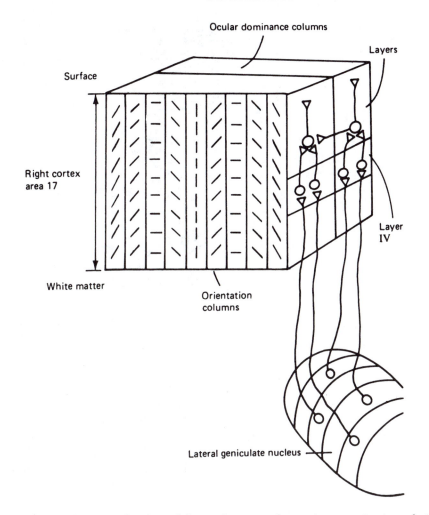

Figure 4.6. Schematic diagram of the pathways and putative organization of visual feature detection in the primary visual cortex. (Reproduced, with permission, from Churchland & Sejnowksi, 1992; Copyright MIT Press.)

also sometimes called IT), the final exclusively visual stage of processing in the ventral pathway (see Figure 4.7). In addition to being the highest-order visual processor for identification of objects, it is thought to be the site of long-term storage of memory about visual objects.

The evidence for this claim comes from multiple converging lines of work. Inferotemporal cortex receives information from earlier stages in the ventral visual stream that, combined, permits it to compute the three-dimensional form of objects and, then in turn, projects to the hippocampal system—the brain system that, as we will see, is thought to help mediate the storage of long-term (declarative) memory in various cortical areas. Neurons in inferotemporal cortex respond exclusively to visual stimuli and are responsive to whole objects, positioned any-

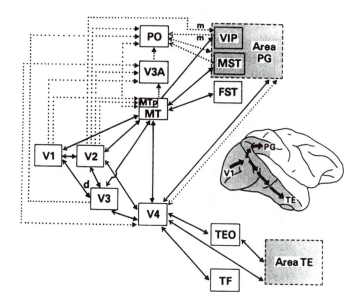

Figure 4.7. Pathways of higher visual processing divided into dorsal and ventral streams. (Reproduced, with permission, from Churchland & Sejnowski, 1992; Copyright MIT Press.)

where within their large receptive fields (their receptive fields always include the fovea, corresponding to the critical role of foveal vision in form perception, and typically extend into both the left and the right visual fields). These cells respond similarly in waking and anesthetized animals (Gross et al., 1979) and show the same selectivity to objects, or to some aspect of visual color or form, across changes in size, contrast, form, or location, as well as luminance, texture, and relative motion (Sary et al., 1993).

To elaborate on the firing properties of inferotemporal neurons, in the very first studies of inferotemporal cells by Gross and colleagues (1969, 1972) some cells were noted to have highly selective response properties. A particularly frequently cited example is a cell that responded best to the silhouette of a monkey's hand (Figure 4.8, top). Other cells responded to the shape of a banana or a toilet brush (used to clean monkey cages). Often these responses to complex stimuli can be reduced to more elemental, albeit still somewhat complicated, forms. Tanaka and colleagues (1993) first identified cells with highly complex optimal stimuli, then reduced the featural components systematically in an effort to identify simplified versions of the stimulus that would drive the cells equally well. In many cases they discovered effective but simpler stimulus features (Figure 4.8 middle), and in most inferotemporal cells they could identify a moderately complex combination of shape, color, and texture that was adequate to produce as robust a response as the original stimulus. Furthermore, cells near one another tended to have similar response properties suggesting a columnar or clustered organization of cell properties (see also Wang et al., 1996).

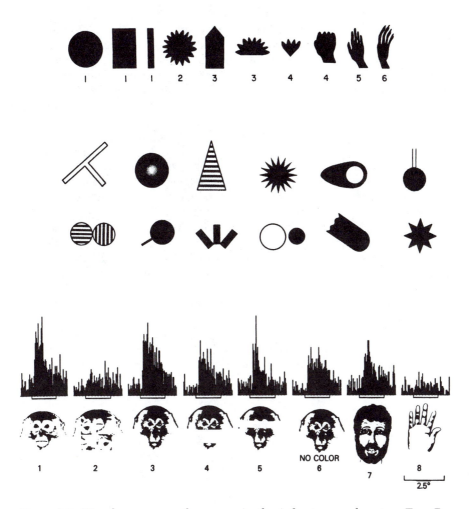

Figure 4.8. Visual responses of neurons in the inferotemporal cortex. Top: Responses of a cell to a series of silhouette patterns, ranked in order of the magnitude of neural response. (Reproduced, with permission, from Gross, Miranda-Rocha, & Bender, 1972; Copyright American Physiological Society.) Middle: Examples of trigger features of IT cells. (Reproduced, with permission, from Tanaka, 1993. Copyright American Association for the Advancement of Science.) Bottom: Responses of an IT cell to a monkey face (1), with different alterations of that face (2-6), and to a human face (7) and hand (8). (Reproduced, with permission, from Desimone, Albright, Gross, & Bruce, 1984; Copyright Society for Neuroscience.)

Perhaps most widely cited are cells that respond best to faces, a finding that has been replicated and studied extensively in a number of laboratories. The responses of these cells are relatively invariant to size, color, contrast, and position (Desimone et al., 1984; Perrett et al., 1982, 1987). Some cells respond to particular featural components of faces (Yamane et al., 1988), but others respond selectively to a particular face orientation or decrease firing rate when parts of the face are eliminated or scrambled (Figure 4.8 bottom). Some of these cells have selective responses to face identity, and the selectivity of these responses is maintained across a variety of stimulus transformations. Analyses of the responses of many cells to a set of monkey faces (Hasselmo et al., 1989) or human faces (Young & Yamane, 1992) show that populations of inferotemporal cells encode complex facial dimensions, including overall shape similarity, identity, expression, and familiarity.

Damage to this area or to its inputs in humans results in visual agnosia, a selective deficit in visual object recognition (e.g., Damasio et al., 1990). Moreover, this area is activated in various PET or fMRI studies of neurologically intact individuals performing tasks requiring visual object recognition (e.g., Grady et al., 1995; Haxby et al., 1996; Sergent, 1992).

Correspondingly, damage to inferotemporal cortex in monkeys produces a complex visual impairment (Gross, 1973). Unlike damage to early visual areas, visual fields are intact, as are thresholds and acuity of visual detection. However, visual discrimination is impaired whether the discriminative stimuli involve color, brightness, two-dimensional patterns, or three-dimensional objects. The degree of impairment is dependent on the difficulty of the task as measured by the number of trials required for normal animals to learn the discrimination. Problems acquired by normal animals in 30 trials are learned as rapidly in animals with inferotemporal lesions. By contrast, problems that are acquired by normal animals in 300–500 trials are not learned by animals with inferotemporal lesions even in 1,000 or more trials, although, once learned, retention of problems learned with difficulty is normal.

A similar pattern of higher order perceptual and learning impairment compared with spared elemental perceptual functions is observed in tactile processing after damage to the posterior parietal cortex, and in auditory processing after damage to the superior temporal gyrus. These findings suggest that end points in each sensory pathway provide the same general processing function.

The deficit in monkeys with damage to inferotemporal cortex may result from the loss of "perceptual constancy" (i.e., loss of the ability to recognize a target stimulus across changes in many perceptual qualities, including retinal location, rotation, size, color, and contrast). One line of evidence in favor of this view comes from an exception to the rule that the degree of learning impairment is proportional to task difficulty. This exception is observed in discriminations between mirror-image or inverted stimuli. These problems are quite difficult for normal monkeys, even when they involve stimuli that are not difficult to discriminate when paired with qualitatively distinct cues. By the level-of-difficulty criterion, monkeys with inferotemporal lesions would be expected to do exceptionally poorly on mirror-image or inverted-stimulus problems. However, they perform no worse than, and sometimes outperform, normal animals on such problems (Gross, 1978; Holmes & Gross, 1984a; 1984b). Furthermore, monkeys with inferotemporal damage do no worse at these problems than at discriminations among qualitatively different cues of similar complexity. One interpretation of this pattern of findings is that the difficulty encountered by normal monkeys is due to a challenge not in distinguishing cues, but in learning that the "same" cue has different significance when presented in different orientations. Perhaps monkeys with inferotemporal damage have relatively less difficulty in learning these discriminations because they do not suffer from recognizing the cues as the "same" objects but treat them like two distinct cues with a moderate discrimination difficulty. These conclusions suggest that inferotemporal cortex is critical in conserving perceptual categorization across the many translations familiar stimuli typically can have when we see them across many presentations.

The ability of this processing system to support the identification of a vast array of objects, and to do so in a way that is invariant across a wide array of transformations of those objects (in terms of position, orientation, lighting, and the like), requires a large, experience-dependent store of memories about the visual form of objects from various positions, orientations, and so on. Where is that store of knowledge about visual objects? The data indicating (1) visual agnosia following damage to TE, and not elsewhere, (2) the same perceptual constancy in the responses of TE neurons that is seen in object perception, and (3) the anatomical placement of TE at the end of the line of ventral visual stream processors, with the next stage the hippocampal system, suggest that TE is the site of storage of knowledge about visual objects. Finally, on logical (design) grounds it makes sense to store such knowledge within the system that provides the ability to identify and attach meaning to visual objects.

Plasticity of Cortex in Development and Adulthood

In the previous section, the link between processing and memory functions of inferotemporal cortex involved the central role played by stored knowledge of objects, acquired through experience, in the perceptual processing and identification of objects. Memory is a necessary part of the operation and, simultaneously, a product of this system. In this section, the linkage between memory and processing involves the tuning and modification of the processing networks (i.e., of the wiring of the network and of the maps they form) by experience. We start with the visual system, as in the previous section and then move to consideration of various other cortical systems.

The tuning and modification of cortical processing networks by experience is seen most notably during development, particularly in the "critical period" of the first several weeks of life. The classic studies by Hubel and Wiesel (1970) showed that response properties of primary visual cortex neurons are plastic (modifiable by experience) during the critical period. Monocular eye closure in kittens during the first 4 weeks of life resulted in a shift in ocular dominance of all cells toward a preference for the active eye. In similar fashion, Blakemore (1974) showed that restricting exposure in kittens to stimuli with only certain orientations (e.g., only vertical or only horizontal) during the critical period resulted in a shift of all cells toward selectivity for the trained orientation. Such manipulations are not nearly so effective in producing tuning of visual cortex after this early critical period ends, a finding that led most investigators to conclude that cortical organization becomes fixed in adulthood.

Do other kinds of sensory deprivation, administered outside the critical period, cause plastic reorganization of sensory maps in any processing domain? Early attempts to demonstrate cortical plasticity in adulthood were viewed with skepticism, but there is now considerable evidence that the adult cerebral cortex is capable of reorganization following deprivation of inputs in several systems, across a range of species (Kaas, 1991, 1995). In the early 1980s several parallel efforts employed the systematic topographical mappings of primary sensory and motor areas in various species, using nerve cuts or amputations as the best parallel to eye closure. For example, in the owl and squirrel monkey primary somatosensory cortex, the normal representation of the hand is extremely orderly, involving a systematic map of sequential digits (Figure 4.9, top left). When the nerve innervating the glabrous surfaces of digits 1, 2, and part of 3 was cut, the cortical region normally representing these areas was initially unresponsive. However, after several months this cortical area became responsive to stimulation of neighboring regions of the palm and to intact portions of digit 3. In subsequent studies where digit 3 was amputated, the area that had been deafferented became responsive to stimulation of the neighboring digits 2 and 4 and the palm pads. The same pattern of results has been observed in other mammals. For example, removal of a digit in the raccoon results in a similar reorganization, so that the representation of neighboring digits expands into the deafferented zone of cortex.

A parallel pattern of reorganization follows selective deafferentation of other primary cortical areas as well. In the visual system, reorganizations of the visual field map have been observed following small lesions of the retina in cats (Kaas et al., 1990) and monkeys (Gilbert & Wiesel, 1992). In the latter experiments, a laser light was used to produce a very small lesion of the retina that deprives animals of a 5-degree area of the visual field. This lesion initially produces a 10-mm diameter area of silent primary visual cortex, but after a 2-month recovery period, the topography of the cortex is reorganized so that the formerly deafferented zone becomes responsive to neighboring parts of the visual field (Figure 4.9, top right). Note, however, that whereas *complete* recovery requires a prolonged period, some cells at the border of the deafferented area become responsive to stimulations in intact visual field areas within hours of the lesion.

Similar results have been obtained in studies on the primary auditory cortex of the guinea pig (Robertson & Irvine, 1989), as well as in the monkey (Schwaber et al., 1993). Auditory cortex is topographically organized in a sequence of isofrequency bands (Figure 4.9, bottom left). In these studies a restricted area of the tonotopically organized cochlea was lesioned, so that a single isofrequency band of the auditory cortex representation was deprived of input. Initially, cells in this band became silent to normal levels of stimulation, although they were responsive to louder stimuli. After a month of recovery, these cells became fully responsive to tones in the frequencies neighboring that lost after the lesion.

This pattern of recovery from deafferentation can be observed not only for primary sensory areas but also for primary motor cortex. In mammals, the primary motor area, like primary sensory areas, is organized as a topographic map that parallels the adjacent somatosensory representation in posterior cortex (Figures 4.9, bottom right). After section of the motor nerve that innervates the mus-

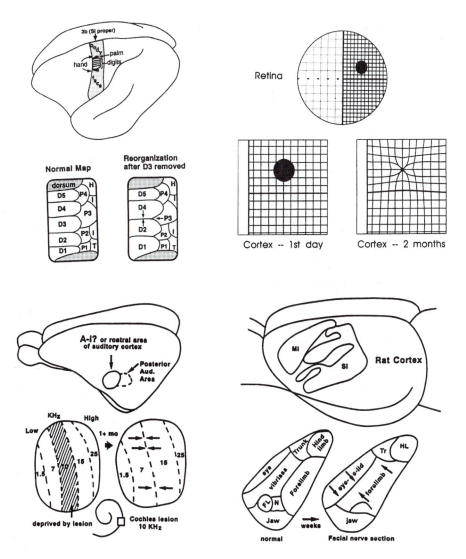

Figure 4.9. Reorganization of cortical areas after denervation. For each panel, the relevant mapping area is shown at the top, and normal representations with initially silent areas, and reorganized representations below. Top-left: Response of somatosensory cortex to digit removal in the monkey. (Reproduced, with permission, from Kaas, 1995; Copyright MIT Press.) Top-right: Response of the visual cortex to a retinal lesion in the cat. (Reproduced, with permission, from Gilbert, 1992; Copyright Cell Press.) Bottom-left: Response of auditory cortex to cochlear lesion in guinea pig. Bottom-right: Response of motor cortex to vibrissae removal in the rat. (Reproduced, with permission, from Kaas, 1991; Copyright Annual Reviews.)

cles of the facial vibrissae, the specific representation of those muscles is initially unresponsive to local microstimulation. However, after a week of recovery, stimulation in this area results in contractions of neighboring muscle groups (Sanes et al., 1990). These reorganizations have been observed at all levels of cortical hierarchies and appear to originate within the cortex itself (Diamond et al., 1994).

Finally, although the anatomical extent of reorganization in the above examples is fairly limited, massive reorganization has now been observed following prolonged recovery periods. In monkeys 12 years after section of the dorsal spinal roots of the arm, the deafferented arm area in the primary somesthetic cortex became responsive to tactile stimulation of the face and trunk, body areas corresponding to the adjacent parts of the somatotopic map (Pons et al., 1991). A similar pattern of innervation by neighboring somatotopic regions appears to occur in humans following amputation of the arm. Thus in a patient with arm amputation, tactile stimulation of neighboring parts of the face produced very specific feelings of touch in adjacent parts of the phantom hand (Ramachandron et al., 1992).

All of these phenomena speak to the integral role of memory in the basic processing functions of these various cortical systems. Experience shapes the operation of these systems, altering the mapping of the sensory and motor world by primary sensory and motor cortices. Thus memory is embedded in these networks, a fundamental part of these networks in operation.

Investigation of the possible mechanisms of such examples of tuning and modification of cortical networks serves to further emphasize the linkage between memory and processing. There are indications that the reorganization of sensory maps, as well as the normal initial organizing of sensory maps, arises from competition among inputs. Some of the earliest and most impressive evidence for competitive mechanisms underlying cortical organization, and reorganization, came from studies of the optic tectum in frogs (Constantine-Paton & Law, 1978). This approach exploited the regenerative capacities of the frog nervous system to examine the effects of increased input, rather than deprived inputs as in the studies described above. In frogs, the major projection of the retina arrives in the part of the midbrain known as the *optic tectum,* the highest visual area of the frog brain. This projection is entirely crossed so that all of the fibers from the left eye arrive in the right tectum and vice versa (Figure 4.10, top). This pattern of connections can be visualized by injecting a radioactively labeled amino acid into one eye and then observing its transport into the synapses of the optic tectum. Constantine-Paton and Law's (1978) manipulation was to add a third eye to the head of the frog embryo. At this time the protoeyes are only flattened evaginations from the optic vesicles. But as the animals mature, the retinal elements develop optic nerves that innervate one or the other optic tectum along with the hosts' eyes. In each of these animals, the topographic pattern of retinotectal synapses was dramatically altered, so that the normally continuous pattern of monocular input was replaced with periodic bands of input from the two eyes innervating that half of the tectum (Figure 4.10, bottom); that is, the additional eye mapped onto one or the other tectum along with the natural eye. Thus a competition of inputs from two eyes is produced in frogs, eliciting a pattern of ocular dominance stripes essentially the same as that observed in mammals with naturally occurring binocular inputs to each side of the cortex.

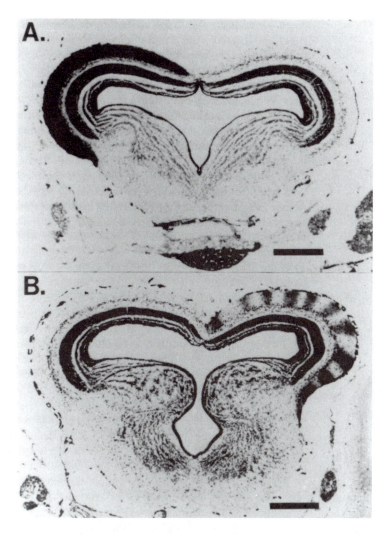

Figure 4.10. Reorganization of the frog optic tectum (top layers in frontal section of the frog brain) A. Black area on left side (right hemisphere) indicates deposition of radioactive amino acids transported following an injection into the right eye. This shows that the normal projection is entirely contralateral. B. Pattern of transport in a frog with a third eye transplanted near the normal right eye. The left optic tectum (on right) receives alternating zones of input from both eyes. (Reproduced, with permission, from Constantine-Paton, 1981; Copyright MIT Press.)

Is this peculiar phenomenon restricted to the lowly frog? It seems not. In new-born ferrets, Roe et al. (1990) deprived the retina of one eye from sending inputs to its major targets in the superior colliculus and visual thalamus, and they concurrently sectioned the normal auditory afferents going to the medial geniculate nucleus of the thalamus. Subsequently, the retinal projections innervated the deafferented medial geniculate nucleus, resulting in visual responses being observed in auditory thalamus and auditory cortex. The visual map in auditory cortex involved an organized topographic map in which the two-dimensional visual fields were precisely mapped onto the axis of cortex that normally serves the one-dimensional representation of auditory frequencies. These findings indicate that the competitive activities of inputs are sufficient to determine the general aspects of cortical organization; that is, the mechanism by which such a processing system reorganizes after deprivation is no different from the mechanism by which the processing system becomes organized in the first place.

Cortical Reorganization During Learning

Do these dramatic changes in cortical organization come about only after the drastic alterations of deafferentation or by aberrant inputs? What we really wish to know is whether similar changes occur during "real" learning and, if so, whether such changes are of sufficient magnitude to be observable after typically limited real-learning experiences. It is now clear that reorganizations of primary cortical areas can indeed occur as a consequence of conventional learning experiences and are indeed observable with standard recording methods.

For example, a number of studies have now shown changes in cortical responses following Pavlovian conditioning. Among the most elegant of these demonstrations come from experiments by Weinberger and his colleagues (Weinberger, 1995a, 1995b) showing shifts in the tuning curves of auditory cortical cells following training in tone-cued classical conditioning. Initially, recordings were taken from a single auditory cortex neuron of an anesthetized guinea pig, and its frequency tuning curve was fully characterized (Figure 4.11). Then a non-optimal frequency was selected as the conditioning stimulus (CS), and its presentation was paired repeatedly with foot shocks, so that eventually presentation of the tone alone produced a pupillary conditioned response that reflected an expectancy of the shock. After this training the frequency tuning curve of the cell was again characterized. The typical finding was that auditory cortex neurons showed enhanced responses to the CS frequency and reduced responses to other frequencies including the former best frequency of the cell. When the training involved a discrimination between one tone associated with shock and another not paired with shock, responses to the CS+ were increased, whereas those to the CS– were decreased, as were the responses to other frequencies, including the cell's former best frequency. These effects developed in just a few conditioning trials and were long-lasting. Indeed the magnitude of the novel response grew over the hour after training and was maintained at least 24 hr, for as long as observations could be made. Overall, these changes in the response distribution across the population of auditory cells indicates a general shift in the topographic map, strongly toward greater representation of the task-relevant frequency at the

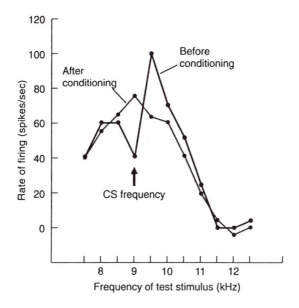

Figure 4.11. Tuning curve for an auditory cortex neuron before and after classical conditioning with a 9 kHz tone as the conditioning stimulus (CS). (Reproduced, with permission, from Weinberger, 1993; Copyright Elsevier Science.)

expense of other frequencies in the audible spectrum—a pattern of results markedly similar to results from the sensory deprivation experiments in kittens.

Similar enhancements of tuning toward conditioning frequencies have also been observed in monkeys. Recanzone et al. (1993) trained monkeys to discriminate small frequency differences and found that the monkeys' performance improved progressively over a period of several weeks. In subsequent recordings they found changes in the size of the auditory cortex representation of the task-relevant frequencies, the sharpness of tuning to these frequencies, and the latencies of cellular responses—all were greater than those of untrained frequencies or of all frequencies in untrained animals (Figure 4.12). Furthermore, the changes in area of the cortical representation were correlated with the improvement in task performance.

Changes in response patterns of sensory cells following training are not limited to auditory cortex. In parallel studies on tactile discrimination learning, Recanzone and colleagues (1992a, 1992b, 1992c) trained monkeys to hold a joystick while a 20-Hz flutter vibration was applied to a small area of a single finger. To obtain rewards the monkey had to release the stick whenever the stimulations were presented at any of several higher flutter frequencies. After months of training, Recanzone et al. recorded cellular responses in the primary somatosentory cortex and found that the hand representation in the stimulated finger area was more complex, increased in size several-fold, and receptive fields were substantially increased in overlap (Figure 4.13). These expansions of the stimulated area occurred at the expense of other parts of the finger representation, similar to

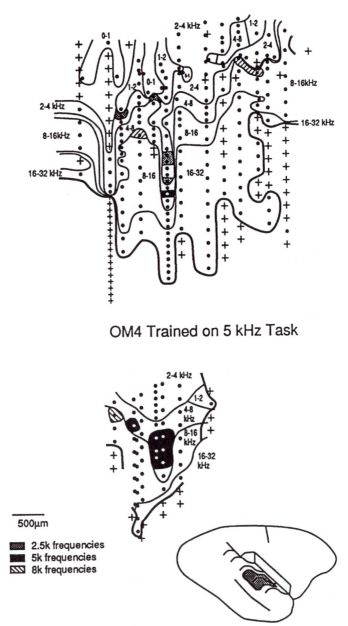

Figure 4.12. Auditory cortex maps for monkeys presented with passive stimulation (top) or discrimination training (bottom) with a 5 kHz tone. Inset: location of auditory area. (Reproduced, with permission, from Recanzone, Schreiner, & Merzenich, 1993; Copyright Society for Neuroscience.)

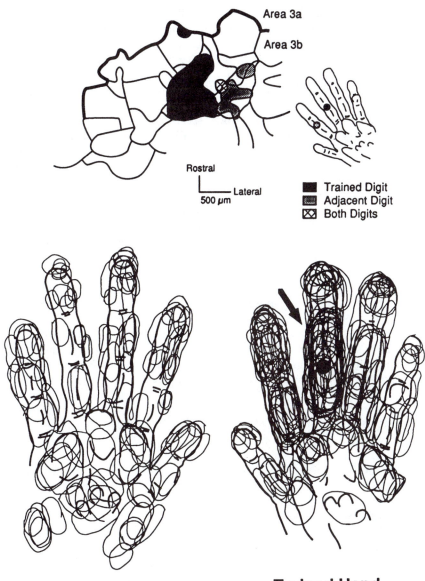

Untrained Hand **Trained Hand**

Figure 4.13. Somatosensory maps of the hand area of a monkey trained on a tactile frequency task. Top: Size of area of representation of trained and untrained digits. Bottom: Receptive fields in trained and untrained hands. Black circle indicates area of stimulation. Note large number of overlapping receptive fields (arrow). (Reproduced, with permission, from Recanzone & Merzenich, 1991; Copyright Oxford University Press.)

Weinberger's and Recanzone's findings on auditory responses after training. In a different task that required monkeys to discriminate the roughness of tactile stimuli presented to varying loci on the finger, the receptive fields in the somatosensory cortex were *reduced*, unlike in the above described findings, although the overall area of the finger representation was, as in the above study, increased greatly to take over regions previously unresponsive to these stimuli (Jenkins et al., 1990).

Finally, similar reorganization has now also been observed in the primary motor cortex as a result of training (Nudo et al., 1996). In this study, monkeys were trained on one of two different tasks that involved different arm and hand movements, and the motor cortex was mapped with microstimulation before and after each type of training. Training on a small-object retrieval task that required skilled use of the digits resulted in expansions of digit representations and complementary contraction of the wrist and forearm representations. Conversely, training on a key-turning task that required use of the forearm resulted in expansion of forearm representation at the expense of contraction of the digit representations.

Functional neuroimaging data provide evidence of similar effects in humans. The learning of specific finger-movement sequences has been shown to result in changes in the distribution (the spatial extent) of activation in motor cortex (Karni et al., 1995) and the cerebellum (Flament et al., 1996).

Taken together, these and the above mentioned results document that well-controlled training procedures can produce profound shifts in the organization of responses in several, and perhaps all, primary cortical areas. Memory is indeed an integral part of the operation of cortical processing areas.

Cellular Mechanisms That Mediate Cortical Reorganization Following Training Experiences

What are the fundamental circuitry and synaptic bases of cortical organization? Observations at the level of cell assemblies and at the level of cellular plasticity rules provide strong evidence that the LTP mechanisms outlined in chapter 3 underlie the effects of training experiences.

Hebb (1949) proposed that cortical representations of memories would be found in the establishment of cell assemblies, potentially widespread collections of neurons that fired as a group to represent the elements of a percept. Merzenich and colleagues (1990; Merzenich & Sameshima, 1993; DeCharms & Merzenich, 1996) and Singer (1990, 1995) are among many investigators (see Palm, 1990; Laurent, 1997) who have supported this view by providing evidence that experience reshapes the cortex by increasing the correlation of firing patterns of neurons so as to create coherent cell assemblies. Several lines of evidence converge on this view. For example, the Recanzone et al. (1992a, 1992b) studies showing enlarged representations of digit areas would seem to reflect greater numbers of cells firing together during activation of the relevant tactile stimuli. Further analyses of these data indeed confirmed increased coherence of the cell population activity with the 20-Hz training stimulus, and the extent of coherence was well correlated with behavioral performance (Recanzone et al., 1992c). These data provide strong, albeit indirect, evidence of an enlarged cell assembly that represents a learned stimulus.

Forced coherence of activity inputs can also produce this type of reorganization. Allard et al. (1991) created an artificial syndactyly (a "webbed-finger" condition) by sewing together the skin of digits 3 and 4 of owl monkeys. After several months of artificially induced synchronous movement and stimulation, the representations of those fingers in the primary somatosensory area were greatly reorganized. The normal discontinuity between the finger representations was abolished and replaced with a wide zone in which the progression of receptive fields extended across the normal discontinuity as if the two fingers had a single representation (Figure 4.14), and this representation persisted after finger separation. These observations indicate that a forced temporal coincidence of stimulation is sufficient to reorganize cortical representations into new groupings based on coincident activation.

More impressive evidence of cell assembly coding comes from studies showing increased cross correlation among cells even when neuronal firing rates do not provide information about stimulus quality. Stimulus-specific changes in cross-correlation have been observed in the auditory cortex, and these correlation-based responses can be used to create a frequency map of the primary audi-

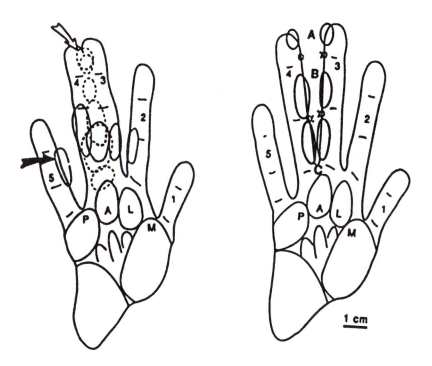

Figure 4.14. Receptive fields in the digits of a monkey hand after fusion of the fingers (left), and after their separation (right). Note overlapping receptive fields in both situations. (Reproduced, with permission, from Clark, Allard, Jenkins, & Merzenich, 1988; Copyright Macmillan Magazines Ltd.)

tory cortex (deCharms & Merzenich, 1996). These findings are consistent with other observations of the coupling in prefrontal cortex cells during specific learned movements even when their overall firing rates did not change (Vaadia et al., 1995). Cross-correlation among neighboring cells is a common finding, and may well be related to the clustering of stimulus properties within local areas (Gochin et al., 1991). Conversely, forcing neighboring cells to fire together may be sufficient to result in correlated firing. In one study cells in the auditory cortex were forced to fire closely timed to one another by first identifying a tone that would drive one cell, then presenting the driving tone immediately after each spontaneous spike of another cell while the monkey attended to the tones. This initially forced correlation between two cells outlasted the experimental manipulation, resulting in increased spontaneous cross-correlation between those cells for several minutes after the training had ceased (Ahissar et al., 1992).

Singer (1995) elaborated this notion, suggesting that feed-forward projections from the retina to the cortex are responsible for the generation of feature-selective receptive fields during development, and that these synaptic strengths become relatively fixed after the critical period. In order to account for training-induced plasticity after the critical period, Singer suggested that reciprocal connections between neighboring cells mediate dynamical associations among neurons into cell assemblies that represent combinations of stimulus features. At the appropriate developmental stage the feed-forward connections are highly susceptible to experience-dependent modifications, and they appear to obey a correlation rule of coherent activity.

In support of this account, Fregnac et al. (1992) showed that orientation preferences of primary visual neurons could be altered by pairing visual stimulation with an intracellular level of polarization. They depolarized cells during stimulation with a nonoptimal contrast orientation and hyperpolarized cells during stimulation with the initially optimal stimulus orientation. This treatment resulted in alterations in the optimal orientation in favor of the stimulus paired with depolarization and against that of hyperpolarization (Figure 4.15). This plasticity depends on the same NMDA mechanisms discussed earlier with regard to hippocampal LTP, and it follows the synaptic modification rules by which LTD and LTP are induced differentially at different levels of Ca^{++} influx (Bear et al., 1987).

Additional supporting evidence indicates that the extent to which changes in visual response properties are observed closely parallels the critical period for plasticity. Furthermore, the decline in NMDA-dependent plasticity is associated with a reduction in the number of NMDA receptors, an increase in postsynaptic inhibition that prevents lifting of the Mg^{++} block, and changes in the gating characteristics of the remaining NMDA receptors. Finally, rearing animals in the dark retards the decline in LTP and correspondingly extends the critical period.

Singer (1995) argued that plasticity in the adult cortex is likely mediated by associative connections. This view is consistent with the pattern of long horizontal connections in the primary visual cortex and with the rapidity of some of the receptive field changes that occur after highly localized retinal damage (Gilbert et al., 1996). In one study Pettet and Gilbert (1992) produced "artificial scotomas" by masking the visual receptive field of a recorded cell in primary visual cortex. This manipulation led to a dramatic increase in the size of that cell's receptive field. The extent of these receptive field changes corresponded to the lateral

BEFORE PAIRING

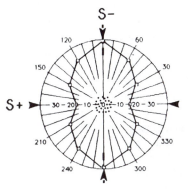

AFTER PAIRING

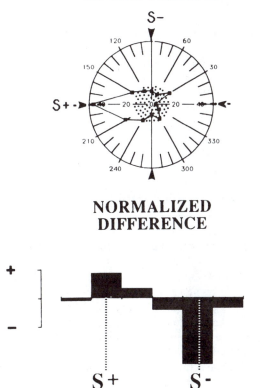

NORMALIZED DIFFERENCE

Figure 4.15. Alteration in the orientation selectivity of a neuron in the primary visual cortex of a kitten before and after following pairing of a bar-stimulus at S+ orientation with depolarization and another bar at S– orientation with hyper-polarization. (Reproduced, with permission, from Fregnac, Shulz, Thorpe, & Bienenstock, 1992; Copyright Society for Neuroscience.)

range of associative connections, occurred within minutes of occlusion, and could be reversed repeatedly. All these aspects of plasticity suggest that the modification of existing associative connections could support much of the adult plasticity of receptive fields associated with training.

With regard to the role of the plasticity in adulthood, Singer (1995) cited a wealth of data showing strong synchronous cross-correlations of neighboring cells in various cortical areas and argued that flexible participation in such assemblies resolves the combinatorial problem of representing an infinite number of percepts. In one demonstration Kreiter and Singer (1996) showed that pairs of visual neurons that have overlapping receptive fields exhibit synchronized firing when responding to a single contrast edge stimulus that could suboptimally activate both cells at once. They did not fire synchronously when two different stimuli that were optimal for each cell were presented simultaneously. This finding showed that synchronization bound together the responses of the two cells to encode the single stimulus.

These changes in responsiveness during adulthood seem to be dependent on a Hebbian mechanism. Cruikshank and Weinberger (1996) demonstrated that forced covariance of depolarization or hyperpolarization, similar to that used by Fregnac and colleagues (1992), results in changes in tone-produced responses of auditory neurons. In anesthetized guinea pigs, they applied an excitatory current during auditory stimulation with one nonoptimal tone on half the trials and, on the other trials, an inhibitory current during stimulation with another nonoptimal tone. As a result, responsiveness to the tone paired with the excitatory current was enhanced, whereas responses to the tone paired with the inhibitory current were reduced.

A Short-Term Form of Cortical Plasticity

A different aspect of memory can be seen in the operation of various cortical processors, this one involving a short-term form of plasticity. Various neurons in inferotemporal cortex have been found to be sensitive to (i.e., change firing in accordance with) their recent history. The initial evidence came from studies of short-term or working memory. In the standard delayed match-to-sample task typically used to study short-term memory, an animal is presented with a sample cue, followed by a memory delay during which that sample has to be remembered. Then, one or more choice stimuli are presented and the animal is required to respond, depending on whether the choice cue is the same as the sample (a match) or not (a nonmatch) (Figure 4.16). Fuster and Jervey (1981) performed the first studies in which cortical neurons were recorded in monkeys performing this task. They characterized the responses of cells in the inferotemporal cortex following presentations of the sample and choice cues, and during the delay period. In one version of their task the monkey was presented with a color cue and required to retain it for up to 20 s prior to the choice. They identified cells that fired differentially to specific colors of the sample and choice. Some of these cells maintained high levels of activity during the memory delay, and this activity was specific to the sample cue (Figure 4.16).

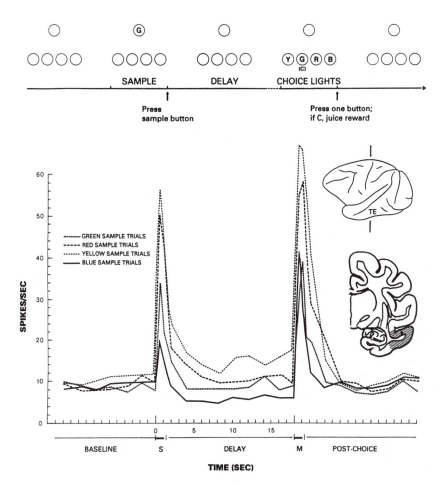

Figure 4.16. Top: A trial in the delayed matching to sample task. The green stimulus (G) was presented as sample, then after a memory delay reappeared along with other cues (Y,R,B) as the correct choice. Bottom: Responses of a cell in inferotemporal cortex through trials with each of the four possible color sample cues. Insets at the right indicate the locus of recording sites. (Reproduced, with permission, from Fuster, 1995; Copyright MIT Press. Reproduced, with permission, from Fuster & Jervey, 1982; Copyright Society for Neuroscience.)

In another version of the task, compound stimuli with both color and pattern information were presented as samples. When one particular pattern was presented, the color dimension had to be remembered. When other patterns were presented, the pattern information had to be remembered. Some inferotemporal cells responded selectively to a color or pattern, and the activity of many of these responses was strongly modulated by the relevant memory dimension. In a subsequent study Fuster (1990) found that the magnitude of the enhancing effect was correlated with the animal's response latency.

Following these initial observations, several other studies showed that infero-temporal neurons sometimes show enhanced responses to matching choice cues (Mikami & Kubota, 1980), as well as cue-selective activities during the delay period (Miyashita & Chang, 1988). In an analysis of neural responses to a set of complex visual patterns, Eskandar et al. (1992a, 1992b) found that responses to nonmatch stimuli carried significant information about the sample cue, and that much of this information was contained in the temporal pattern of the spike train rather than in the firing rate. They proposed that the inferotemporal cortex performs a comparison between temporal patterns of responses to the stored sample representation and the current choice cue and computes a cross-correlation by effectively multiplying these patterns. A similar pattern of stimulus-selective delay responses has now also been observed for tactile stimuli (Koch & Fuster, 1989), and delay activity for spatial and object cues has been studied extensively in the prefrontal cortex (see chapter 14).

Other studies have revealed yet other correlates of short-term memory in inferotemporal cells (see Brown, 1996; Desimone, 1996). These studies have found that many inferotemporal cells show suppressed responses to repeated stimuli (Brown et al., 1987; Baylis & Rolls, 1987; Miller et al., 1991b), a finding that is strikingly similar to the unusually rapid habituation of visual responses observed in inferotemporal cells in both anesthetized and waking animals (Miller et al., 1991a). In the earliest observations of this phenomenon, Brown and colleagues (1987) found that inferotemporal cells showed suppressed stimulus-selective responses to stimulus repetition in monkeys performing a delayed matching task where stimuli were reused repeatedly across trials. Baylis and Rolls (1987) used trial unique cues and also found suppressed responses when the sample reappeared as the choice (Figure 4.17). The response suppression was, however, very sensitive to disruption so that presentation of a single intervening stimulus was sufficient to eliminate the effect. In a subsequent study these authors observed similar suppressed responses to repeated face stimuli (Rolls et al., 1989).

More recently Miller and colleagues (1991b; Miller & Desimone, 1994; Miller, Li, & Desimone, 1993; Li et al., 1993) have reported multiple correlates of short-term memory in the inferotemporal cortex. They elaborated the delayed match-to-sample task to include multiple-choice cues, and the monkey was required to refrain from making a behavioral response until the matching choice appeared (Figure 4.18, top). The initial main finding was that inferotemporal cells showed suppressed responses on repetition of the sample cue as choice. These responses were maintained across intervening items but were reset between trials, except for a general decrement in responses across the entire session. A few cells showed the opposite response: an enhancement of responses to matching choice stimuli. In addition, delay firing was observed in some cells, but this activity ceased upon presentation of any subsequent stimulus.

In subsequent studies, the task was changed so that the intervening nonmatch choice stimuli repeated prior to re-presentation of the sample as choice (the "ABBA" paradigm). In this situation the proportions of inferotemporal responses changed so that many cells showed suppression for any repeated stimulus, whether it was a repetition of the sample or of a nonmatching intervening stimulus. However, now a much larger proportion of cells showed match enhancement responses, and these were observed only for repetition of the sample cue (Figure

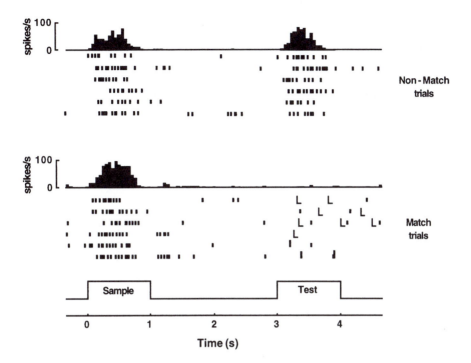

Figure 4.17. Responses of an inferotemporal cortex neuron to presentations of sample and test (choice) stimuli. Note suppression of responses to match tests. L = lever press behavioral response. (Reproduced, with permission, from Baylis & Rolls, 1987; Copyright Springer-Verlag.)

4.18, bottom). This pattern of findings was interpreted as evidence for a combination of memory mechanisms within the inferotemporal cortex. Match suppression was viewed as a passive consequence of stimulus repetition so that it occurs whether or not the stimulus has to be remembered. On the other hand, match enhancement was viewed as reflecting the continued processing of a stimulus to maintain a memory. Delay firing could also be used to bridge a delay, but it appears this mechanism cannot be sustained through interfering stimuli by the inferotemporal cortex. It can, however, be sustained by neurons in dorsolateral prefrontal cortex, which is thought to mediate at least some forms of working memory (see chapter 14).

An Associative Form of Cortical Plasticity

One final form of cortical plasticity to be discussed here permits associations between stimuli to be learned. Thus, in addition to the acquisition of knowledge about the objects processed by a particular network, the tuning and modification of cortical networks, and the short-term form of plasticity discussed thus far, various cortical neurons also show an associative form of plasticity.

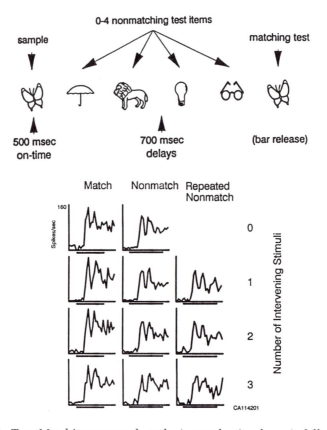

Figure 4.18. Top: Matching to sample task. A sample visual cue is followed by 0 to 4 nonmatching test items and then a matching choice cue. Bottom: Responses of a cell in inferotemporal cortex in monkeys performing a variant of this task where some nonmatching test stimuli were presented repeatedly. Note enhanced response to matching stimuli over both types of nonmatching stimuli. (Reproduced, with permission, from Miller, Li, & Desimone, 1993; Copyright Society for Neuroscience. Reproduced, with permission, from Desimone, Miller, Chelazzi, & Lueschow, 1995; Copyright MIT Press.)

The first report of an associative memory correlate came from an experiment where young kittens were trained to avoid a forearm shock by moving the arm to a particular position when signaled by an oriented visual grating presented to one eye (Spinelli & Jensen, 1979). An orthogonal visual grating was presented to the other eye as the CS– and its presentation was not associated with shock. Following several weeks of training, recordings were made in the forearm area of the somatosensory cortex, and cells were examined for both tactile and visual responsiveness. In trained animals a large number of cells showed selective visual responses to the training cues. Presentations of the CS+ and CS– in the correspondingly stimulated eyes produced robust responses in the forelimb area of the somatosensory cortex that represented the shocked arm, whereas presentation of other line orientations was relatively ineffective. In addition, presentations of oriented visual gratings were relatively ineffective in the hemisphere ipsilateral to the shocked arm.

Other associative neural responses have been observed, inadvertently, in the cortex of animals performing discrimination or delayed matching to sample tasks. In an experiment designed to characterize inferotemporal neuron responses to visual cues during discrimination performance, Iwai et al. (1987) observed many cells that showed stimulus-selective activation prior to the presentation of the visual cues. The monkeys were trained to discriminate four different visual patterns: a plus sign, a triangle, a square, and a circle. Before presentation of each of those stimuli, a brief tone signaled the monkey to fix its eyes on the central position of the visual display in anticipation of the visual stimulus onset (Figure 4.19). To the surprise of these investigators, a third of the visually responsive

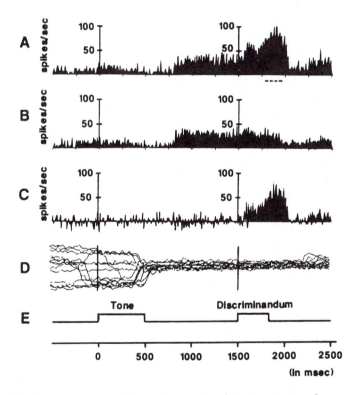

Figure 4.19. Responses of cell in inferotemporal cortex to visual cues and to a tone that signaled the later presentation of those cues. A. Response on trials with a "plus sign" visual cue. B. Responses on trials with three other visual cues. C. Response on plus-sign trials minus that on other trial types. D. EOGs indicating fixation of the eyes on the screen where the visual cues were presented. Note that the anticipatory response of the neuron is the same on all trial types, but firing wanes when the plus-sign is not presented. (Reproduced, with permission, from Iwai, Aihara, & Hikosaka, 1987; Copyright Elsevier Science.)

inferotemporal neurons fired after the onset of the tone at long latencies and continued to fire after the onset of the visual stimulus. At that point the cells either increased their firing rate if the optimal cue was presented or ceased firing if a different stimulus was presented.

Koch and Fuster (1989) made a similar serendipitous finding while characterizing responses of somatosensory cortex neurons to tactile cues in monkeys performing a tactile delayed match-to-sample task. In this task the tactile cues were presented behind a screen, and an auditory click signaled the monkeys that the sample cue was available for manual manipulation. The surprising finding was that 22% of the cells in this somatosensory area were activated by the auditory cue, and all of these cells continued to be active during the arm movement that acquired the sample tactile stimulus (Figure 4.20).

In a study explicitly designed to evaluate associative responses, Sakai and Miyashita (1991) examined responses of inferotemporal neurons to 24 fractal stimulus patterns. These stimuli were arbitrarily paired so that on each trial one stimulus of a pair was presented as a sample cue and, after a delay period, was

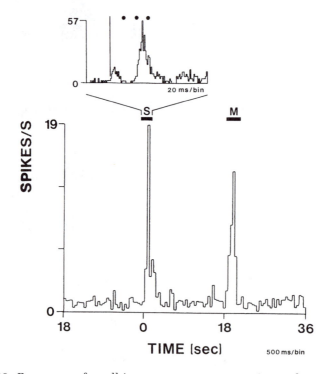

Figure 4.20. Responses of a cell in somatosensory cortex in monkeys performing a tactile delayed matching task. Top: At the outset of the sample phase, the cell fired at the onset of an auditory click that signaled the availability of the tactile sample (indicated by the vertical line), and then fired again during sample manipulation (between the 2nd and 3rd dots). Bottom: On a broader time scale, the cell fired both during sample and match presentations. (Reproduced, with permission, from Koch & Fuster, 1989; Copyright Springer-Verlag.)

followed by a choice between the assigned paired cue and one of the other stimuli. After acquisition of this paired-associate task over a series of training sessions, two different associative correlates were observed in the firing of these
neurons. "Pair-coding" neurons fired maximally for the two cues that were paired
associates, more than for any other cues (Figure 4.21, top). "Pair-recall" neurons
increased firing rate during the delay period following presentation of the associate of the optimal cue (Figure 4.21, bottom). This study made clear that the preferences of specific inferotemporal neurons for specific objects could be modified
in a long-term way to include a preference for the objects paired with them during learning. More recently, Erickson and Desimone (1999) trained monkeys in a
task where pairs of visual patterns were presented sequentially such that a "predictor" stimulus was followed by a delay, then by go or no-go "choice" stimulus.
Early in training the responses of perirhinal cortex neurons during the delay was
correlated with the responses to the predictor stimuli, and not to the choice stimuli, suggesting that at this stage of learning these cells were merely maintaining
representations of the predictors. However, after substantial training, the responses of perirhinal neurons to repeatedly paired predictor and choice stimuli
became more similar, compared to responses to unfamiliar stimulus pairings.
Furthermore, the magnitude of activity during the delay period became correlated
with the magnitude of the responses to the repeatedly paired stimuli. These results confirm the findings of Sakai and Miyashita, and reveal the course of ac-
quistition of the stimulus associations.

Finally, Schoenbaum and Eichenbaum (1995a) designed a test to characterize
the odor responsiveness of cells in the orbitofrontal cortical region that receives
olfactory inputs in rats. On each trial animals were presented with one of eight
odors, half of which were associated with reward for a discriminative response
and half of which were not rewarded regardless of response. They found a substantial proportion of cells that were driven by odors. Moreover, many of these
neurons also fired in association with the reward values of the odors, so that half
fired more vigorously to all odors associated with reward, and the other half had
greater responses to all nonrewarded odors—and within these odor sets, they
showed differential firing across the odor series (Figure 4.22). In general the sequence of odor presentations was random. However, there were specific exceptions to the sequence so that some odors reliably predicted presentation of another specific odor on the subsequent trial. Thus, like the task described above,
this protocol involved a predictive relationship between some pairs of odors.
Because the second of these pairs also occurred without prediction on some trials, differential responsiveness to the odors with regard to their predictability
could be evaluated. Two forms of associative firing correlates were observed.
Some cells had different odor-specific responses depending on whether an odor
was predicted. Some of these cells showed greater responses when they were
predicted, whereas others showed greater responses to an odor when it was unexpected (Figure 4.23, top). Other cells fired in anticipation of the predicted stimulus, and even more when that particular stimulus was presented (Figure 4.23,
bottom).

Taken together, these findings suggest that in the course of processing, cortical
neurons are sensitive to both short-term and long-term contingencies of the items
they are called upon to handle. Here, too, then, memory becomes an integral

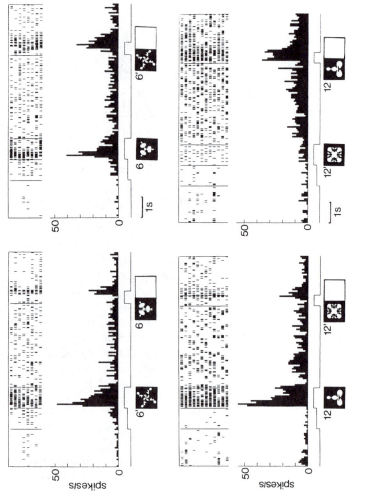

Figure 4.21. Two types of firing patterns that reflected the paired association. Top: A "pair-coding" neuron that fired for both associated stimuli. Bottom: A "pair-recall neuron" that fired when one of the cues was presented, or in anticipation of that cue predicted by its associated stimulus. (Reproduced, with permission, from Sakai, Naya, & Miyashita, 1994; Copyright Cold Spring Harbor Laboratory Press.)

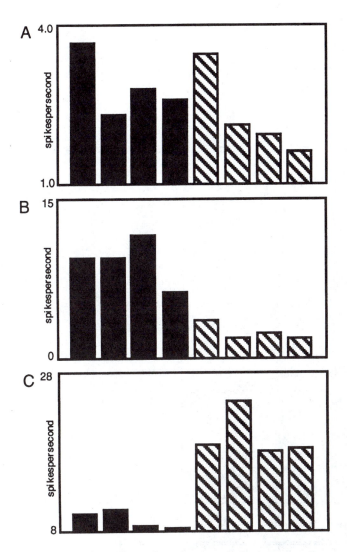

Figure 4.22. Responses of 3 cells in the orbital prefrontal cortex of rats trained to discriminate odors. The first 4 bars represent responses to four different rewarded odors and the second 4 bars represent responses to four different nonrewarded odors.

part of the normal operation of these cortical processing systems, as experience continues to shape the nature of the processing that is performed.

Common Properties Within a Diversity of Cortical Memory Correlates

The list of cellular memory correlates seems almost as large as the number of studies that report them. However, these diverse findings can be consolidated by

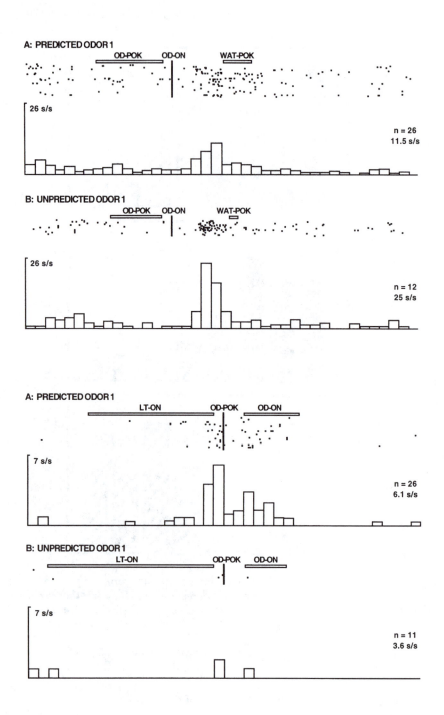

thinking about memory as encoded in two general ways. *First,* memory is reflected in the capacity of cortical cells to *bias* or *modulate* their stimulus-evoked responses. These codings occur as incremental (enhanced) and decremental (suppressed) responsiveness. A combination of incremental and decremental changes could be employed to shift a tuning curve, and many coordinated tuning-curve shifts could account for the expansion or shrinkage of parts of the overall sensory representation within a cortical area. These response biases can be held briefly, as observed in the working memory tasks, or permanently, as observed in the increased resolution in the cortical maps for relevant stimuli. In working memory tasks, enhanced responses could selectively pass an attentional "filter" (Desimone, 1992). Suppressed responses could reflect subthreshold sustained activation, that is, "primed" neural activity that subsequently requires less processing to identify the familiar stimulus.

Second, memory is reflected in the capacity of cortical cells to *sustain* or *reactivate* responses in the absence of the stimulus ordinarily required to evoke the representation. This type of coding can be observed in firing patterns maintained during the delay in working-memory tasks, providing a confirmation of Hebb's (1949) "reverberating-circuit" notion. In addition, the capacity of cortical cells to regenerate item-specific firing patterns when cued by an associated event seems to confirm Hebb's model of complex memories as "phase sequences" involving replays of linked stimulus representations.

These observations serve to emphasize one of our fundamental themes, that memory should be conceived of as intimately intertwined with information processing in the cortex, indeed so much so that the "memory" and "processing" are inherently indistinguishable. By one construal of this view, memory is nothing more nor less than the plastic properties of specific cortical information processings. By another equally valid construal, all cortical information processing inherently involves adaptations to stimulus regularities and contingencies and/or storage of the information processed. In either view, in the cerebral cortex, information processing and memory combine to constitute the structure of our knowledge about the world. The memory code is thus both constrained by and revealed in acquired biases in evoked activity patterns and in the ability to re-create those knowledge representations.

Figure 4.23. Responses of 2 cells in the orbitofrontal cortex of rats when a particular odor was sometimes predicted by the previous presentation of another particular odor. Top: A cell that suppressed firing to an odor that was predicted. Bottom: A cell that was activated just before presentation of a predicted odor, and had an enhanced response to the odor when it was predicted. OD-POK = nose poke to the odor sampling port that initiated the trial; OD-ON = odor onset; WAT-POK = nose poke to the water reward port; LT-On = light onset that indicate trial could be initiated. (Reproduced, with permission, from Schoenbaum & Eichenbaum, 1995; Copyright American Physiological Society.

PART II

THE BRAIN SYSTEM THAT MEDIATES DECLARATIVE MEMORY

As outlined in chapter 2, there is substantial evidence of several memory systems in the brain. However, this is not a democratic organization of memory systems in which all types of memory are "separate and equal." That is, they do not involve entirely parallel brain systems and are not involved to the same extent in controlling every aspect of our behavior. Most important, these systems are not equivalently involved in "everyday memory," the memory that is invoked when we are asked about facts and events from our recent or remote past. That kind of memory depends on one particular brain system, and that system will receive correspondingly extensive attention in this part of the book.

You have now been prepared for this endeavor by a historical introduction to ideas about "conscious memory." And you should feel bolstered by reviews of the cellular basis of plasticity that is prevalent in this system, as well as of the cortical representations on which this system depends. The first stage of our examination of the declarative memory system (chapter 5) involves a review of neuropsychological findings from the study of amnesic patients, humans who suffer deficits in declarative memory as a result of damage to the hippocampal region. This chapter serves to introduce the reader to many of the learning and memory tests that are used to explore declarative memory and, in examining the results of these tests, to further characterize the nature of declarative memory in humans. This chapter will also review complementary evidence indicating that the hippocampal region is activated in normal human subjects during memory performance, as revealed in functional brain-imaging studies. These considerations will be followed by two reviews of the attempts to model the phenomena of amnesia in animals. One of these covers studies on nonhuman primates (chapter 6), and the other reviews efforts with other species, especially rodents (chapter 7). These chapters will cover both the successes and the failures in modeling human amnesia and will emphasize how they have led to a greater understanding of the fundamental properties of declarative memory.

These reviews will be followed by an analysis of the information-coding properties of neurons in the hippocampus (chapter 8). The findings provide a complementary view of hippocampal memory processing: Studies on amnesia inform us about what capacities are lost after elimination of the hippocampus, whereas recording studies characterize what kind of information is captured by cellular activity in the same structure. The combination offers a particularly powerful view into the contribution of the hippocampus to memory function.

Whereas all of the previous chapters of this section focus on the hippocampus (or generally on the "hippocampal region"), chapter 9 expands the considerations to the larger system in which the hippocampus operates, in particular the parahippocampal cortical region surrounding the hippocampus and the cerebral cortex. Each of these areas plays a distinct role within the declarative memory system. Finally, chapter 10 focuses on memory consolidation, a particularly important aspect of this system so far not considered in detail. This chapter relates all the elements previously described to characterize how components of the hippocampal system work together to mediate the long-term organization and retention of declarative memories.

5

Hippocampal Function in Humans

Insights From Amnesia and
Functional Brain Imaging

In 1933, a 7-year-old boy was knocked down by a bicycle, hit his head, and was unconscious for 5 minutes. This mundane injury is suspected to have been the precipitating event that ultimately led to some of our greatest insights into memory processing by the brain. The following description of this patient, taken largely from writings by Scoville and Milner (1957), Milner et al. (1968), Ogden and Corkin (1991), and Corkin (1984), is an overview of a unique case study that has guided memory research since the late 1950s. Three years after that accident the boy began to have minor epileptic seizures, followed by his first major seizure while riding in his parents' car on his 16th birthday. Because of the epileptic attacks his high school education was erratic, but eventually he graduated in 1947 at age 21 with a "practical" course focus. Subsequently he worked on an assembly line as a motor winder. However, the seizures became more frequent, on average 10 minor attacks each day and a major attack each week, and he eventually could not perform his job. The attempts to control the seizures with large doses of anticonvulsant drugs were unsuccessful and led to consideration of a brain operation. There was no evidence of localization from electroencephalographic (EEG) studies. Nevertheless, because of the known epileptogenic qualities of the medial temporal lobe areas, a frankly experimental operation was considered justified as an effort to ameliorate his devastating seizure disorder. In 1953, when H.M. was 27, William Scoville performed a bilateral medial temporal lobe resection.

The surgical approach to this area is difficult, because the relevant tissue lies inside the part of the temporal lobe near the midline, almost in the center of the brain. The surgical procedure involved making a hole above the orbits of the eyes and lifting the frontal lobes. From this approach the anterior tip of the temporal lobe could be visualized, and the medial part resected. Suction was used to remove all of the tissue bordering the lateral ventricle for 8 cm back, including cortical areas surrounding the deep structure, specifically the piriform gyrus, uncus, and parahippocampal cortex, and then the amygdala and hippocampus. A recent MRI analysis confirmed that the surgeon's notes were largely accurate (Corkin et al., 1997). The removal included the rostral two thirds of the hippocampus, as well as the amygdala and surrounding cortex very selectively (Figure 5.1).

The operation reduced the frequency of seizures to a point where they were now largely prevented by medication, although minor attacks persisted. However, one striking and totally unexpected consequence of the surgery was a grave loss of memory capacity. This person, known by his initials, H.M., is probably the most examined and best known neurological patient ever studied, largely because of the combination of the unusual purity of the ensuing memory disorder, the static nature of his condition, his cooperative nature, and the skill of the researchers who protected and worked with him.

After recovery from his operation, H.M. returned home and lived with his parents. There he did household chores, watched TV, and solved crossword puzzles. Following his father's death he attended a rehabilitation workshop and became somewhat of a handyman, doing simple and repetitive jobs. Eventually his mother and then another relative could no longer care for him, so he was moved to a nursing home, where he still resides, participating in daily social activities of the home, as well as watching TV and solving difficult crossword puzzles. He is characterized as a highly amiable and cooperative individual. He rarely complains about anything and has to be quizzed to identify minor problems such as headaches. He never spontaneously asks for food or beverage, or to go to bed, but he readily follows directions for all of his daily activities. His temper is generally very placid, although one of the author's recalls one day when H.M. was depressed about "having not done anything with his life." However, when H.M. was assured that he was indeed a very important person, his mood returned to its normal rather upbeat state, and he told one of his famous stories about once considering a career in neurosurgery. He is aware of his memory disorder but is not consistently concerned about it. Sometimes, when given a rather difficult memory question, H.M. reminds the tester, "You know I have a memory problem."

The severe magnitude of H.M.'s memory disorder has continued unabated since the time of the surgery. Immediately after his operation he no longer recognized the hospital or staff and recalled nothing of the daily events during his recovery. Upon returning home he never learned the locations of commonly used objects, such as the whereabouts of a lawn mower he had used just the day before. He did the same jigsaw puzzles and read the same magazines day after day, without becoming familiar with them.

Some of the most compelling examples of the severity of H.M.'s amnesia come from anecdotes of those who have worked with him. One of the present authors (H.E.) recalls his first encounter with H.M., while transporting him from the nursing home to MIT for a testing period in 1980. On the way to the nursing home H.E. had stopped at a nearby McDonald's fast-food restaurant for lunch and had left a coffee cup on the dashboard of the car. When H.E. retrieved H.M., he sat him comfortably in the back seat and they began the trip to Boston. After just a

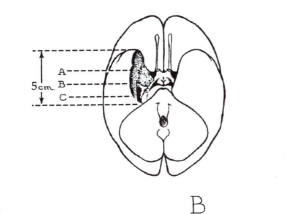

A
Entorhinal cortex   Amygdala

B
Collateral sulcus   Hippocampus
                     Entorhinal cortex

C
Small lesion   Hippocampus

D

Figure 5.1. A reconstruction of the area of medial temporal lobe removal in case H.M., based on MRI scans. (Reproduced, with permission, from Corkin, Amaral, González, Johnson, & Hyman, 1997; Copyright Society for Neuroscience.)

few minutes H.M. noticed the cup and said, "Hey, I knew a fellow named John McDonald when I was a boy!" He proceeded to tell some of his adventures with the friend, and so H.E. asked a few questions and was impressed with the elaborate memories H.M. had of that childhood period. Eventually the story ended and H.M. turned to watch the scenery passing by. After just a few more minutes, he looked up at the dashboard and remarked, "Hey, I knew a fellow named John McDonald when I was a boy!" and proceeded to relate virtually the identical story. H.E. asked probing questions in an effort to continue the interaction and to determine if the facts of the story would be the same. H.M. never noticed he had just told this elaborate tale and repeated the story almost exactly as before. A few minutes later the conversation ended, and he turned to view the scenery again. However, just minutes later, once more H.M. looked up to the dashboard and exclaimed, "Hey, I knew a fellow named John McDonald when I was a boy!" H.E. helped him reproduce, as well as he could, the same conversation yet again and then quickly disposed of the cup under the car seat.

Those who examine H.M. typically remark that, within a moment's break in their interactions, H.M. will forget their names, having ever met them, and any details about the testing that has just ended. These authors' experiences were no different. H.E. tested H.M. for several hours each day for 2 weeks on painfully tedious olfactory psychophysical assessments. H.M. never remembered having met him or what kind of testing had been done. Having found, like many others before, that H.M. could not recall his name, H.E. tried to determine if H.M. might perform better on a recognition test. "Eichenbaum or Axelrod?" H.E. inquired, forcing H.M. to choose between H.E.'s name and a foil carefully matched for ethnic association, number of syllables, and also beginning with a vowel. When H.M. correctly recognized "Eichenbaum" the first time, H.E. was pleased but understood the odds of guessing correct once were 50%. So H.E. tested him repeatedly, appropriately counterbalancing for name order. H.M. consistently guessed right. Had H.E. broken the streak of his failure to remember the names of so many more accomplished investigators? Finally H.E. brought in the other author of this book (N.J.C.), who looks a bit like H.E. "Eichenbaum or Axelrod?" H.E. demanded. "Eichenbaum," H.M. said with confidence. He just seemed to prefer that name.

H.M. has retained some information that has been introduced since his operation. However, those items he remembers typically involve material to which he has been exposed excessively. For example, he knows his parents are now dead. He has learned the meaning of the word *astronaut* and a few other very common words that have come into usage since his operation (see Gabrieli, Cohen, & Corkin, 1988). He knows who Elvis Presley and John Kennedy were, although they came into fame after his operation. However, his memories of these and other facts are fragmentary and confused at best, as illustrated by the following reproduction of an interview with the neuropsychologist Jenni Ogden (Ogden & Corkin, 1991):

J.O.: Do you know who Elvis Presley is?
H.M.: He was a recording star, and he used to sing a lot.
J.O.: Do you think he is still alive, Elvis Presley?
H.M.: No, I don't think so.

J.O.: Have you any idea what happened to him?

H.M.: Well I believe he got the first bullet I think was for Kennedy, I think it was.

J.O.: You remember Kennedy?

H.M.: Yes, Robert.

J.O.: What was he?

H.M.: Well, he was President. I think about three times. He was appointed President too.

J.O.: He got a bullet. What was that all about?

H.M.: Well, they were trying to assassinate him.

J.O.: And did they? Did they kill him or not?

H.M.: No they didn't.

J.O.: So, is he still alive?

H.M.: Yes, he is alive, but he got out of politics in a way.

J.O.: I don't blame him.

H.M.: No, guess not.

J.O.: How long ago was he the President do you think?

H.M.: He became President after Roosevelt. 'Course there was Teddy Roosevelt. That was a long time before that.

J.O.: What is Franklin Roosevelt's wife's name?

H.M.: I can't think of it.

J.O.: It starts with "E" I think. —Eleanor. You were going to say that?

H.M.: No I wasn't. I was going to say "Ethel."

Notably, Ethel is the name of Robert Kennedy's widow. Clearly H.M. has learned and retained a few of the most famous names of the 1960s. But his knowledge about the details of their notoriety is minimal compared to contemporaries who were saturated with information about them. Furthermore, the information that is retained is disorganized, so that he confuses the individuals and the facts about them. Also, his islands of spared memory contrast with equally impressive failures. For example, despite watching the television news every night in the summer of 1973, he could not identify Watergate or John Dean, although he could guess who the president was (Nixon) when prompted by the letter N. In 1980, he remembered correctly that a very popular TV situation comedy character Archie Bunker called his son-in-law "meathead" but incorrectly stated that Howard Cosell did news on television (he was a sportscaster), and that Barbara Walters was a singer (she is a television journalist).

The Selective Nature of H.M.'s Memory Disorder

H.M.'s disorder is highly selective, in two important ways. First, his impairment is almost entirely isolated to a disorder of memory, as distinguished from other higher-order perceptual, motor, and cognitive functions. Second, even within his memory functions, the disorder is limited to particular domains of learning and memory capacity. The following sections will review the evidence concerning these two aspects of his preserved and impaired capacities.

Intact Perceptual, Motor, and Cognitive Functions,
Contrasted with Severe Memory Disorder

H.M. has normal visual fields, visual adaptation, and other commonly tested vi-sual-perceptual functions. He can recognize and name common objects. With re-gard to somatosensory functions, H.M. has some peripheral neuropathies and some loss of fine motor coordination, although the staff at his rehabilitation workshop said the quality of his work was excellent. He does have a curious olfactory perceptual deficit. Although his odor thresholds, intensity discrimina-tion, and adaptation are normal, he cannot identify or discriminate odors at all, an impairment likely related to the ancillary piriform cortex damage (Eichen-baum et al., 1983).

H.M.'s intelligence as measured by the Wechler-Bellevue Scales was above average on both the Verbal and Performance tests just before the operation. After the surgery his IQ actually rose somewhat, perhaps because of the alleviation of his seizures. H.M.'s language capacities are largely intact, although he exhibits slight deficits in verbal fluency, and his spelling is poor. He appreciates puns and linguistic ambiguities and communicates well and freely. His spatial perceptual capacities that do not depend on memory are mixed. For example he has some difficulty copying a complex line drawing and cannot use a floor plan to walk a route from one room to another in the MIT testing facility. On the other hand, he does well on other complex spatial perceptual tasks and can draw and recognize an accurate floor plan of his former house.

His intact higher cognitive capacities are contrasted with impairments typi-cally observed after prefrontal cortex damage. These differences are particularly important because other patients who have become amnesic due to Korsakoff's disease or communicating artery aneurysm have prefrontal damage thought to contribute to their memory disorder. The classic test for prefrontal damage is the Wisconsin card-sorting test, a task where subjects are asked to sort a deck of cards that differ along dimensions of symbol, number, and color. They are not told the rule of sorting in advance but must discover it using experimenter-provided feedback after each decision. Initially, one sorting rule (e.g., color) is arbitrarily selected. When the subject has figured this out, the sorting rule is switched and the subject must discover the change. Patients with prefrontal damage character-istically perseverate a discovered sorting rule, maintaining performance consis-tent with an old rule long after normal subjects have discovered the new rule. H.M. shows no perseveration and performs the task as well as normal subjects (Figure 5.2).

By contrast, H.M. has almost no capacity for new learning, as measured by a large variety of conventional tests. He was not given standard memory tests prior to the operation. After the surgery his score on the Wechsler Memory Quotient has been consistently 35 points or more below his Full Scale IQ, indicating a severe memory disorder. He scores zero on components of the test that assess memory for logical facts from a story, verbal paired associates, and picture recall.

The composite results on a broad variety of specific tests have shown that H.M.'s memory deficit is "global" in that he is impaired in every conventional stimulus modality. His delayed recall is impaired whether the items are stories,

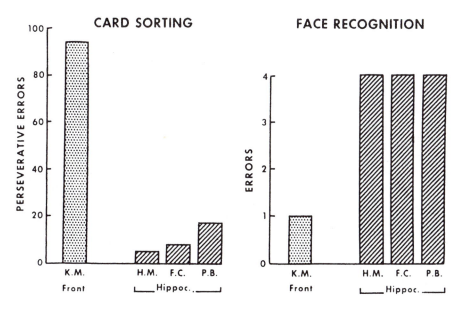

Figure 5.2. Comparison of performances of case H.M. and that of other amnesic subjects with that of a case of frontal lobe damage. The card sorting test is a standard assay of frontal function, in which subjects must rapidly shift rules for categorizing playing cards. The face recognition test is a conventional assay of memory for pictures of people. (Reproduced, with permission, from Milner, Corkin, & Teuber, 1968; Copyright Elsevier Science.)

verbal paired associates, digit strings, new vocabulary words, drawings, nonverbal paired associates, block diagrams, songs, common objects, or object locations. He is unable to learn simple mazes and fails at delayed recognition of words, nonsense syllables, numbers, geometric drawings, faces, and tonal sequences.

Intact and Spared Domains of Memory Capacity

H.M. can remember material learned remotely prior to his operation. His memory for the English language seems fully intact. He also retains many childhood memories. By contrast, all memory for events for some period preceding the operation is lost. One story that reinforces the contrast between his intact remote memory and impaired recent memory involves another car trip when investigators were bringing H.M. home after a period of testing. Upon leaving the highway in his hometown they asked H.M for directions to his house. He promptly and courteously led them through several turns until they arrived at a street familiar to him. Yet he thought they were not at the correct address. When the investigators called his mother, it was revealed they had come to the street he used to live on prior to his operation, and not the area to which he had subsequently moved.

The extent of H.M.'s retrograde amnesia was first estimated as the 2 years preceding the surgery, based on postoperative interviews. Later objective tests revealed a longer period of lost recent memory. These include a set of tests for recall of tunes, public events, and famous faces that became familiar in specific decades. Although the scores were somewhat mixed, in general he performed well on items from the 1940s and before but borderline or poorly on the items from 1950 onward. He tended to attribute most tunes to the 1940s, systematically altering the dates from other decades to converge on this period. He recognized public events into the 1950s but not beyond. He could recognize and describe famous pictures of scenes from the 1940s but not beyond. In a test of personal remote memory, he was given a set of nouns and asked to relate each to a personal event from any period in life, and to state when the event took place. All of H.M.'s personal memories were from age 16 and younger. Consistent with these results, H.M does not remember the end of World War II or his high school graduation. These findings indicate that H.M.'s remote memory impairment dates back at least until 1942 (Sagar, Cohen, Corkin, & Growdon, 1985).

In addition, H.M.'s immediate or short-term memory is intact. He can immediately reproduce a list of numbers as long as that of control subjects. His decay of short-term memory is normal on both recognition and recall tests. His initial acquisition of pictorial material is also fully intact. The memory deficit becomes evident as soon as his immediate memory span is exceeded or after a delay with some distraction.

The early studies on H.M. also revealed two "exceptions" to his otherwise profound defect in lasting memory. One of these, called *mirror drawing*, involves the acquisition of sensorimotor skill. In this task the subject sits at a table viewing a line drawing and his or her hand only in a mirror (Figure 5.3). The line drawing contains two concentric outlines of a star, and the task was to draw a pencil line within the outlines. Errors are scored each time an outline border is contacted. This test may seem simple, but in fact normal subjects require several trials before they can successfully draw the line without committing crossover errors. H.M. showed strikingly good improvement over several attempts within the initial session and considerable savings across sessions, to the extent that he consistently made very few errors on the third test day. This success in learning this sensorimotor skill contrasted with his inability to recall ever having taken the test.

In addition, H.M. also showed strikingly good performance in perceptual learning in a task called the *Gollins partial pictures task,* which involves the recognition of fragmented line drawings of common objects. For each of 20 items subjects are presented with a series of five cards containing fragments of a realistic line drawing of the same object. The first card of each series contains the fewest fragments of the drawing, and the last card contains the complete drawing. Subjects are initially shown all 20 of the most difficult items and asked to identify the object drawn on each one. Then the second, slightly more complete version of each item is presented, with the ordering of the 20 cards randomized, so it is impossible to anticipate an item based on its predecessor. The procedure is continued with successively more complete versions of each item until all are identified. Then, after an hour of intervening activity, the entire test is repeated, and the number of errors (unidentified drawings) is scored. H.M.'s scores on the retest were not as good as those of age-matched controls, but he showed a surpris-

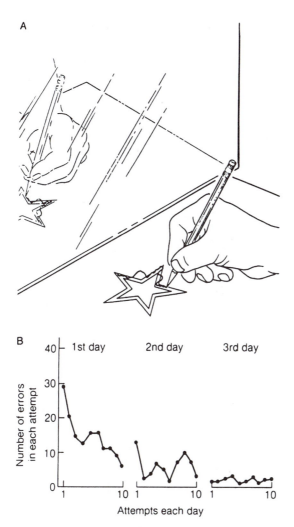

Figure 5.3. The mirror drawing test, and H.M.'s performance across 10 attempts on three successive days. (Reproduced, with permission, from Milner, Corkin, & Teuber, 1968; Copyright Elsevier Science.)

ing degree of savings, especially considering he could not remember having taken the initial test (Figure 5.4).

Summary of the Early Findings

H.M. was important as much for the selectivity of his deficit he was for its severity. Subsequent to the discovery of his amnesia Scoville publicized the findings,

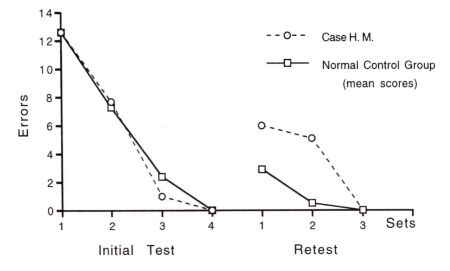

Figure 5.4. Examples of items from the Gollin's partial pictures test, and H.M.'s performance measured by the number of errors on the entire series. (Reproduced, with permission, from Milner, Corkin, & Teuber, 1968; Copyright Elsevier Science.)

and supported Milner, Corkin, and others in their research on H.M., in great part to ensure that the operation would not be performed again. H.M. was among a group of patients who underwent the experimental operation for bilateral medial temporal lobe resection. However, all the other patients were severely psychotic, muddling the interpretation of the memory tests. The resection in some of the patients involved only the uncus and amygdala, and these patients' memory was intact. Also, the severity of the amnesic deficit in other patients was related to the amount of hippocampal damage, so it was concluded that the hippocampus and immediately adjacent cortex were the likely critical area for memory.

H.M.'s amnesia is characterized by several cardinal features: (a) intact perceptual, motor, and cognitive functions; (b) intact immediate memory; (c) severe and global anterograde amnesia; (d) temporally graded retrograde amnesia; and (e) spared remote memory. At that time views about memory were most influenced by the notion that different cortical areas contained specific perceptual and memory functions together, so that perception, cognition, and memory were considered inseparable and, by Lashley's (1929) proposal, widely distributed in the brain. The case study of H.M. was a breakthrough because it showed that a general memory function could be dissociated from other functions. In addition, the findings of exceptions to severe global amnesia, in successful sensorimotor and perceptual learning, foreshadowed a second major breakthrough that promises to further clarify the nature of hippocampal processing in memory.

Spared Learning Ability in Amnesia:
Implications for the Nature of Memory Processing
Mediated by the Medial Temporal Lobe

That second major breakthrough came when Cohen and Squire (1980) first presented data suggesting that the instances of intact memory in H.M. and other amnesic patients were not "exceptions" to their amnesia, but representative of a large domain of spared learning ability in amnesia. Cohen and Squire demonstrated a striking dissociation in amnesic patients between an intact ability for "knowing how" to accomplish a task and impairment in "knowing that" specific items had been experienced before. Their subjects included a group of amnesic patients of different etiologies. Some suffered from Korsakoff's syndrome as a consequence of chronic alcoholism. Other patients had been given a course of electroconvulsive shock treatments for relief of major depression. One patient had sustained a stab wound that damaged the diencephalon. All of these subjects were severely amnesic as indicated by poor scores on conventional tests of memory, as well as by their inability to remember day-to-day events. These subjects, and groups of normal controls, were trained on a mirror-reading-skill task. On each trial three words were presented in mirror-reversed text (Figure 5.5, top), and subjects were asked to read them aloud as quickly as possible and to press a button when finished. Subjects practiced this skill for several blocks of trials each day for several days and then were retested 13 weeks later. Half of each block of trials involved new words, and the other half involved the same words repeated on all blocks. Performance on nonrepeated and repeated items was compared to evaluate the ability to acquire the general skill of mirror reading as distinguished from memory for particular items read repeatedly.

Both normal subjects and amnesics became proficient at mirror reading, and there was no difference in the rate of acquisition for this perceptual skill (Figure 5.5, bottom). In addition, all groups showed a steeper learning curve for the repeated items than for the nonrepeated items, indicating some level of specific learning even by the amnesics. However, this facilitation was smaller for the amnesic subjects than for the controls, indicating they had a selective impairment on remembering specific words. Overall there was hardly any forgetting of the skill component between sessions by amnesics or controls. By contrast, amnesics showed substantial forgetting of specific items, unlike controls. Thus the amnesics had a selective deficit in memory for specific words but intact learning ability in the pattern-analyzing perceptual skill.

These observations were properly heralded as a revelation about memory-processing functions accomplished by the medial temporal lobe. Subsequently, several laboratories uncovered a variety of examples of spared learning ability in amnesia. The range of these will be explored here, classified into four tentative categories based on the phenomenology of learning: general skills, specific habits, conditioning, and repetition priming.

General Skill Learning

Skill learning involves a broad collection of motor, perceptual, or cognitive operations or procedures that are typically acquired through an incremental and slow

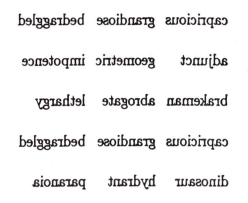

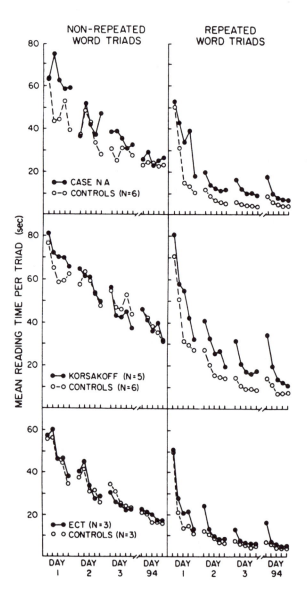

process of repetition. The acquisition of a general skill involves improvement in performance or adoption of a general rule applied across many exemplars, none of which need to be remembered individually.

An excellent example of a general skill is the mirror-reading task described above, for which completely spared learning ability was observed only on the general skill of reading mirror-reversed words. However, there are several other examples that involve some degree of general improvement. The earliest evidence of preserved skill learning in amnesia is the improvement in mirror drawing observed in H.M., described above, although the generality of learning was not specifically tested. Other early examples also came from the studies on H.M. He increased the speed with which he could navigate through a 10-choice tactual maze, although he did not learn to execute the correct sequence of maze choices (Corkin, 1965). H.M. also showed substantial learning on a rotary pursuit task that required him to manually track a position on a slowly revolving disk, although his rate of acquisition was not fully normal (Corkin, 1968). Later came several examples of fully intact perceptual-motor learning in rotary pursuit by amnesic patients (Figure 5.6; see Brooks & Baddeley, 1976; for review, see Cohen & Eichenbaum, 1993).

There have been several other demonstrations of skill-learning abilities that are intact in amnesia, and these extend the range of intact skill learning to cognitive rules. Knowlton et al. (1992) presented subjects with nonword letter strings that were generated by an artificial "grammar" that determined general rules for sequencing and length of the letter strings (Figure 5.7). The subjects studied these strings by reproducing each item immediately after its presentation. Then they were informed that the letter strings were formed by complex rules. Subsequently they were shown novel letter strings one at a time and asked to classify them as "grammatical" or "nongrammatical" according to whether they conformed with the rules. Finally subjects were tested to determine if they could recognize grammatical letter strings after a brief study phase. Both amnesic and normal subjects were able to correctly *classify* the letter strings on about two thirds of the trials. By contrast, the amnesic patients were impaired in a test that required explicit *recognition* of the studied grammatical items.

Knowlton and Squire (1993) tested subjects on a perceptual classification task in which they learned to categorize dot patterns presented on a computer monitor. The stimuli were composed as low- or high-distortion variations on a prototype pattern of dot positions (Figure 5.8). Subjects initially studied a set of dot patterns on a computer monitor and were instructed that these constituted exemplars of a single category. Five minutes later they were asked to judge whether each of a large set of novel patterns was in the same category as the training

Figure 5.5. The mirror reading test. Top: Mirror-reversed word triads. Note that one triad repeats. Bottom: Performance of amnesic patients of three different etiologies and controls on the general skill of mirror reading (left) and on that skill plus memory for repeated items (right). (Reproduced, with permission, from Cohen & Squire, 1980; Copyright American Association for the Advancement of Science.)

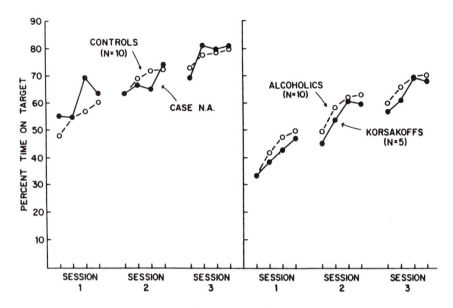

Figure 5.6. Rotary pursuit task. This test involves learning to keep a stylus "on track" within a wavering line drawn on a rotating disk. (Reproduced, with permission, from Cohen & Eichenbaum, 1993; Copyright MIT Press.)

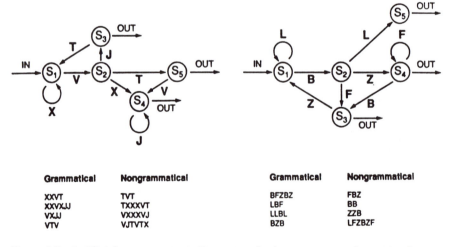

Figure 5.7. Artificial grammar test. Two sets of rule systems used to string letters into "grammatical" and "nongrammatical" series. (Reproduced, with permission, from Knowlton, Ramus, & Squire, 1992; Copyright Blackwell Publishers.)

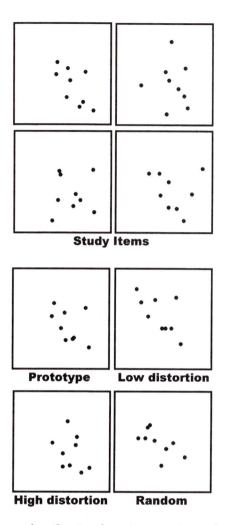

Study Items

Prototype   **Low distortion**

High distortion   **Random**

Figure 5.8. Dot pattern classification learning test. Examples of items subjects studied, the prototypes from which these were derived, and examples of low and high distortion items, plus an example of a random foil. (Reproduced, with permission, from Knowlton & Squire, 1993; Copyright American Association for the Advancement of Science.)

patterns. Normal subjects and amnesic patients produced similar patterns of category judgments and performed with similar accuracy overall. By contrast, on a separate recognition test amnesics were impaired in remembering a set of dot patterns they had seen 5 minutes earlier. This experiment demonstrates intact acquisition of the specifically defining aspects of the prototype, as well as acquisition of the general capacity for categorization.

Perhaps the most impressive example of preserved cognitive skill learning in amnesia was the success in training H.M. on a set of cognitive rules that mediate solution of a complex, multistep puzzle. This experiment involved the Tower of Hanoi puzzle, a game in which the subject is confronted with a stack of five blocks placed in order of decreasing size on one of three pegs on a board (Figure 5.9). The task is to move and restack the blocks onto another peg, following two rules: Only one block can be moved at a time, and one can never place a larger block on top of a smaller one. To solve the problem subjects have to shuffle blocks among the three pegs, repetitively building smaller then larger subsets of the entire stack. The minimal number of moves to solution is 31, and reaching this goal requires learning a recursive stacking rule that can be applied repetitively to solve the problem from any configuration of the blocks. H.M. and other amnesics have succeeded at learning this task, under conditions where they were continuously refocused on the recursive subset strategy (Cohen et al., 1985).

Habit Learning

Habit learning also typically occurs incrementally and involves gradual improvement in speed and biases in performance following specific regularities in stimu-

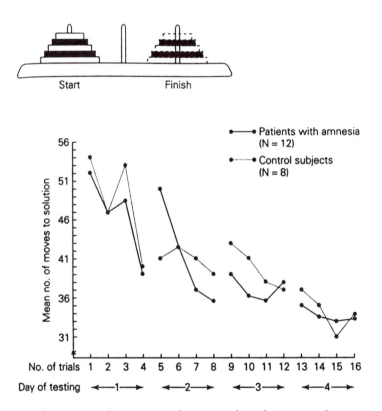

Figure 5.9. The Tower of Hanoi puzzle test, and performance of amnesics and controls over a series of training sessions. (Reproduced, with permission, from Banich, 1997; Copyright Houghton Mifflin Company.)

lus-response sequences. A compelling example of intact learning of a specific perceptual-motor habit came from Nissen and Bullemer's (1987) examination of manual sequence learning in a task called the *serial reaction time test*. On each trial subjects were shown a light at one of four locations on a computer monitor and had to press one of four keys that corresponded to that light location. On each trial the lights were presented in a consistent pattern, and the entire pattern was presented repetitively in each training session so that subjects could antici- pate the position of the next light. As a control, in separate testing blocks the sequence of light positions was randomized. Normal subjects and amnesics de- creased their reaction times to press the keys and did so at an equal rate (Figure 5.10). Both groups showed minimal improvement when the light position se- quence was random, indicating that the improvement on regular sequences in- volved acquisition of a specific habit and not a general ability to coordinate the pressing of keys for appropriate lights. Notably, a similar dissociation has been observed in rats with hippocampal damage. They show normal gradual learning of appropriate spontaneous orienting responses anticipating items in a repetitive sequence of maze arm presentations, even though they fail to recognize specific arm presentations within each test session (Kesner & Beers, 1988).

Another example of spared learning of a specific habit in human amnesic pa- tients comes from studies of speed reading. Several experiments have shown that amnesics improved their reading times over the course of repeating a story aloud (Moscovitsh et al., 1986; Musen et al., 1990). Comparison of performance across the two stories shown in the example in Figure 5.11A indicate that there was no general facilitation between stories, indicating that the habit was text-specific. Moreover, this intact capacity does not seem to rely on memory for the content of the story, as demonstrated in an experiment showing the phenomenon extends to nonwords as well as text. The nonwords were composed of low-frequency

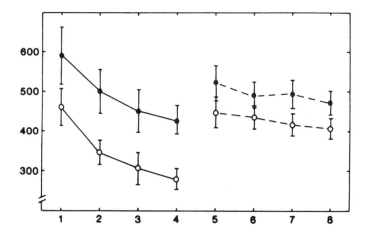

Figure 5.10. Performance (latencies to complete the series) of normal control sub- jects (open circles) and Korsakoff's amnesics (filled circles) across training trials in the serial reaction time test. (Reproduced, with permission, from Cohen & Eichenbaum, 1993; Copyright MIT Press.)

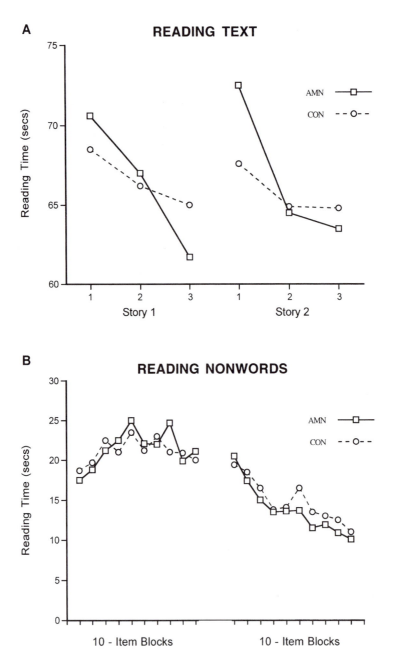

Figure 5.11. Enhancement in reading time for repeated stories (A), and nonword strings (B), nonrepeating on left, repeating on right. (Reproduced, with permission, from Squire, 1992; Copyright American Psychological Association.)

words with single-letter substitutions in each syllable to make them pronounceable (e.g., locapic, ganisper). Musen and Squire (1991) showed a similar improvement in reading speed in both normal controls and amnesics reading 100-item
lists of repeating nonwords (Figure 5.11B, right), as compared to control nonrepeating nonwords (Figure 5.11B, left). Improvement was observed only with the
repeated nonwords in both groups. This comparison again shows that the facilitation is specific to the sequence of repeated nonwords and is not a reflection of a
general learning to read new nonwords.

A final example of intact habit learning in amnesics involves the acquisition
of probabilistic classifications (Knowlton et al., 1994, 1996). In this task subjects
are presented repeatedly with a number of cues that predict one of two arbitrary
outcomes, but the prediction is probabilistic in that each stimulus configuration
determines the outcome on only a specific percentage of trials. Learning is measured as increasing performance in matching the predicted outcome based on
any set of cues. For example, in one task, Knowlton et al. (1994) presented subjects with one to three playing card cues on a computer monitor and asked them,
based on these cues, to predict whether the "outcome" would be rain or shine
(Figure 5.12). Each cue was associated with a different predictive value. For example one card predicted "sun" on 75% of the trials, another on 60%, and another on 25% of the trials. Card combinations predicted the weather according
to their joint probabilities. Because it is very difficult to remember the many
specific combinations of cards presented, and because memory for specific trials
can be contradicted in repetitions because of the probabilistic nature of the regularities, the benefit of remembering specific trials is minimized. Nevertheless,
after 50 training trials both normal subjects and amnesic patients had improved
gradually, reaching a level of well over that predicted by chance. It should be
kept in mind that ideal performance on this task is not 100%, because the cards
only probabilistically predict the outcomes. In subsequent debriefing the same
amnesics were impaired in remembering specific facts about the testing sessions.

Conditioning

Conditioning refers to the acquisition of reflexive responses to stimuli that are
repeatedly paired with an unconditioned stimulus that elicits the reflex, following the Pavlovian protocol described in chapter 2. The earliest report of intact
simple conditioning by an amnesic patient dates back to an anecdotal observation
made by the Swiss psychologist Claparde (1911/1951), who hid a needle between
his fingers and pricked the hand of a Korsakoff's amnesic patient while greeting
her with a handshake. Subsequently the patient refused to again shake hands,
although she could not recall the specific incident. She pulled her hand back
reflexively and would say only, "Perhaps there is a pin hidden in your hand."

In a formal study of classical eyelid conditioning, Weiskrantz and Warrington
(1979) repeatedly paired a compound tone-light conditioning stimulus (CS) with
an air puff unconditioned stimulus (US) to the eye and measured conditioning
as the occurrence of eye blinks during the CS period prior to the US. In this study
they demonstrated intact conditioning by two amnesic patients. More recently,
intact eyelid conditioning has been shown in amnesic patients and patients with
unilateral temporal lobectomies (Daum et al., 1989, 1991). H.M. is impaired in

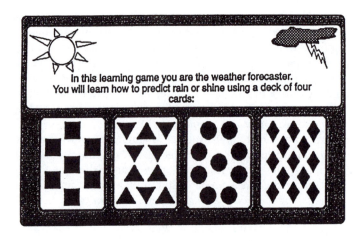

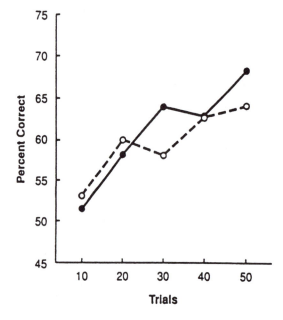

Figure 5.12. "Weather forecasting" probabilistic learning test. Example of stimulus presentation with all four cards, and overall performance of normal control subjects (CON), amnesics (AMN), and Parkinson's patients with modest (PD) or severe (PD*) symptoms. (Reproduced, with permission, from Knowlton, Mangels, & Squire, 1996; Copyright American Association for the Advancement of Science.)

eyelid conditioning (Woodruff-Pak, 1993), but this may be due to cerebellar atrophy consequent to chronic antiepileptic medication. In the first systematic study comparing amnesics and control subjects, the amnesics demonstrated normal classical eyelid conditioning and extinguished the conditioned responses when the CS was presented repeatedly without the US (Figure 5.13; Gabrieli et al., 1995b).

These examples of intact eyelid conditioning all involve a procedure known as *delay conditioning,* in which the presentation of the US overlaps with the last part of the CS. Another procedure, known as *trace conditioning,* involves a brief CS followed by a trace interval during which no stimulus is presented, followed by the US alone. The distinction between these two types of classical conditioning is important because it has been shown that rabbits with hippocampal damage normally acquire the eyelid response with the delay conditioning procedure but cannot learn under the trace conditioning procedure. Just like rabbits with hippocampal damage, human amnesics are impaired in trace eyelid conditioning (McGlinchey-Berroth et al., 1997). Moreover, this deficit has been related to the conscious awareness of the stimulus contingencies (Clark & Squire, 1998).

Repetition Priming

Perhaps the most intensively studied form of memory that can be accomplished fully normally in amnesic patients is the phenomenon known as *repetition prim-*

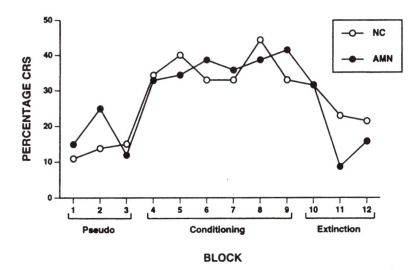

Figure 5.13. Classical conditioning of the eyeblink response. Performance of normal control subjects (NC) and amnesics (AMN) on pseudoconditioning (pseudo— unpaired tones and air puffs), conditioning trials (paired tones and air puffs), and in extinction (tones alone). (Reproduced, with permission, from Gabrieli, Carrillo, Cermak, McGlinchey-Berroth, Gluck, & Disterhoft, 1995; Copyright American Psychological Association.)

ing. Several comprehensive reviews are available on the topic of repetition priming in normal subjects as well as in amnesic patients (Richardson-Klavehn &
Bjork 1988; Shimamura, 1986; Schacter, 1990; Schacter et al., 1993; Schacter &
Buckner, 1998b; Tulving & Schacter, 1990). Priming involves initial presentation
of a list of words, pictures of objects, or nonverbal materials, and then subsequent
reexposure to fragments or very brief presentation of the whole item. In the reexposure phase, learning is measured by increased ability to reproduce the whole
item from a fragment or by increased speed in making a decision about the item.
Although the format of their test is not that typically used today, the first study
showing intact priming in amnesia was Warrington and Weiskrantz's (1968) demonstration of success by amnesic patients on the Gollins partial picture task described above. As was also later the case with H.M., the amnesics did not show
as rapid learning as controls, but they did improve substantially and showed
considerable retention across days. In this test, however, normal subjects may
have benefited by remembering the set of object names between tests.

A more recent study, by Graf et al. (1984), illustrates particularly well a striking dissociation between intact priming and impaired declarative memory performance by amnesic subjects. This experiment used the word stem completion
task, a test of verbal repetition priming in which subjects initially study a list of
words, then are presented with the first three letters of each word and asked to
complete it. The stimulus words are selected as ones for which the stem can be
completed more than one way to compose a high-frequency word. For example,
the word *motel* is used because its stem, *MOT* can be completed to form either
the stimulus word or *mother* (see other examples in Figure 5.14, top). Priming is
measured by the increased likelihood that the subject will complete the stimulus
word presented during the study phase. In this experiment, subjects initially
studied a list of such words and, to make sure they attended to them, had to
identify shared vowels among sets of words or rate the words according to how
much they liked them. Then, in the test phase, they were presented with the
three-letter word stems and tested for their memory in one of three ways. In the
free recall condition, subjects were not presented with stems but just asked to
recall the studied words. In the *cued recall* condition, subjects were presented
with the word stems and told to use them as cues to remember words that were
on the list. In the *completion* condition, they were presented with word stems
and asked simply to "write the first word that comes to mind." The amnesics
were impaired in recall as tested either with cuing or without (Figure 5.14, bottom). By contrast they were not impaired on the completion test. A particularly
revealing comparison can be made between the performance of amnesics across
the different test conditions. They did much better in the cued-recall than in
the free recall condition, but no better in cued recall than in completion. One
interpretation of these findings is that performance in cued recall might be entirely supported by priming. By contrast the controls did much better in cued
recall than in priming, suggesting they used the stems to aid an active search in
recalling the words.

Intact priming in amnesia is not restricted to nameable objects and verbal material. Gabrieli and colleagues (1990) showed intact priming by H.M. in a task
explicitly designed to be refractory to verbalization. In this test H.M. and normal
control subjects were presented with a set of stimuli each of which consisted of

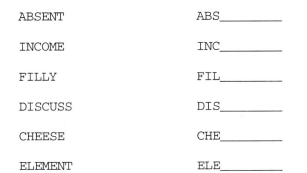

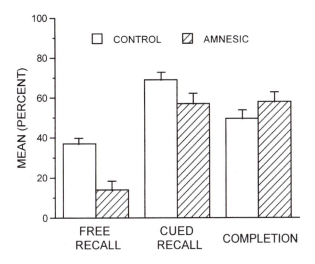

Figure 5.14. Word stem completion test of verbal priming. Top: On the left are examples of study words, and on the right, examples of the word stems used for cueing. Bottom: Performance of normal control subjects and amnesics on three versions of the test. (Reproduced, with permission, from Graf, Squire, & Mandler, 1994; Copyright American Psychological Association.)

five dots arranged in a unique pattern (Figure 5.15, top). To establish baseline performance subjects were asked to draw on the dots any line pattern they wished. Substantially later they were presented with a set of predetermined target patterns and asked to replicate them on a corresponding dot pattern. After exposure to the entire list plus a distracter task, they were provided with the dot pattern again and asked to complete it any way they wished. Priming scores were calculated based on the incidence of baseline patterns. As shown in Figure 5.15 (bottom), H.M. showed significant above-chance priming for dot patterns, indicating as much memory as the normal control subjects. This intact performance is contrasted with his very poor performance on a forced-choice recognition task for the same dot patterns. Subsequent studies by Musen and Squire (1992) confirmed the observation of intact dot pattern priming in a larger set of amnesics.

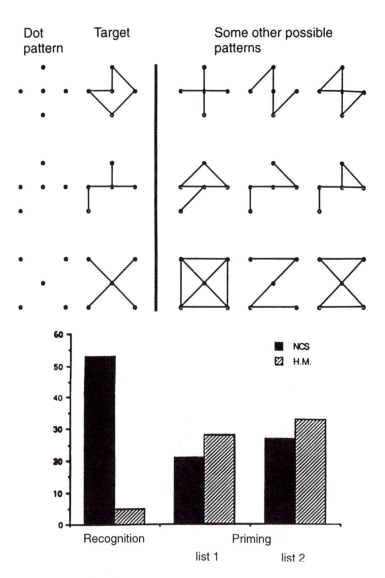

Figure 5.15. Priming for dot patterns test. Top: Examples of dot patterns and target completion pattern, plus some possible alternatives. Bottom: Performance (percent correct) as measured by recognition of the target and by correct completion in normal control subjects (NCS) and case H.M. (Reproduced, with permission, from Gabrieli, Milberg, Keane, & Corkin, 1990; Copyright Elsevier Science.)

Another key issue in repetition priming is whether new associations can be learned by this mechanism. The typical test for associative repetition priming involves the initial study of word pairs followed by the testing with the same pairings versus different pairings of the same words. Associative priming is measured by a facilitation of priming of the second word when it is preceded by the first. For example, if the initial study involved the pair *window-reason,* subjects would be tested for priming by being asked to complete the stem *window-rea.* Associative priming would be revealed by a facilitation in this test over that for *officer-rea,* where *officer* had previously been paired with a different word during study. An alternative test method involves presenting entire word pairs and measuring reading time, with the expectancy that reading time would be faster for repeated pairs than recombined pairs of the same words.

Graf and Schacter (1985) and Moscovitch et al. (1986) initially presented data showing associative priming in amnesic subjects. However, subsequent studies found that amnesics were impaired in this sort of priming task (see Squire, 1992). Using the reading-speed measure, Musen and Squire (1993) did not observe associative priming in either normal control subjects or amnesics after a single exposure to word pairs. However, if the study phase involved 10 repeated pairings of words, substantial and equivalent associative priming was observed (Figure 5.16). More recently, Moscovitch (1994) explored this matter further. As in the other experiments, he had the subjects study arbitrary pairings of words. Then, in the test phase, he had them indicate simply whether both items in a test pair were words. On negative trials at least one member of a pair was a pronounceable but meaningless string. He found that normal subjects could perform the lexical decision task more quickly for repeated word pairs than recombined pairs, and amnesic subjects also showed the significant associative priming effect.

Another form of associative priming that is apparently successful after a single exposure involves a variant of the Stroop paradigm (Musen & Squire, 1993). In the Stroop task subjects are presented with color names printed in incongruent colors (e.g., the word *red* printed in green) and asked to identify the color of the print (ignoring the content of the word). Normal subjects are initially slow in saying the incongruent color as compared with saying the same word in the congruent color. However, they improve in identification speed on subsequent repetitions, demonstrating an effect that could be attributed to acquisition of a new color-word association. Finally, demonstrating that this association is specific, the identification time for the same color is again raised when the word is printed in a different incongruent color. Equivalent improved color identification speeds were observed in the control and amnesic subjects (Figure 5.17), and this learning was specific for the repeated color-word associations. Thus, implicit learning of new associations is intact in amnesia.

Characterizing Impaired and Spared Memory Domains in Human Amnesics

There have been numerous attempts to identify the common properties among the variety of types of learning and memory spared in amnesia, and to distinguish them from the common aspects of learning and memory on which amnesics fail.

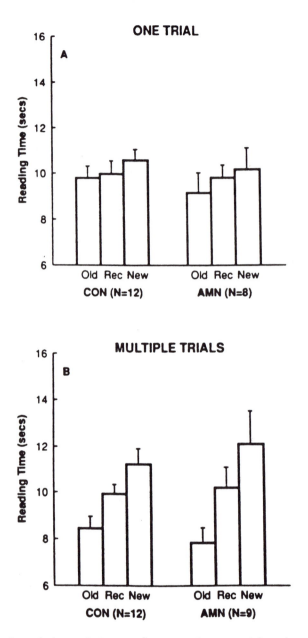

Figure 5.16. Associative priming performance in one trial and multiple trial learning tests. CON = normal control subjects; AMN = amnesics. (Reproduced, with permission, from Musen & Squire, 1993; Copyright American Psychological Association.)

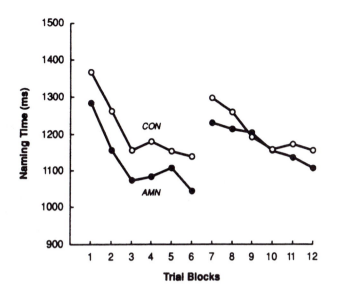

Figure 5.17. Stroop test of implicit learning of color-word associations. CON = normal control subjects; AMN = amnesics. (Reproduced, with permission, from Musen & Squire, 1993; Copyright American Psychological Assocation.)

We can begin here by listing some limitations that do *not* apply to the domain of spared memory in amnesia. Intact learning in amnesia is not limited to general skills, such as motor or perceptual skills, but includes a variety of forms of highly specific new learning. This is evident in several of the tasks described above, including the speed-reading tasks, light-key sequencing, verbal associative priming, color-word association (Stroop) task, and weather prediction task, all of which involve learning specific stimulus combinations or sequences. Also, intact learning in amnesia is not limited to simple or easy tasks, as clearly shown by the improvements in very difficult tasks such as weather prediction. Conversely, under some conditions, intact learning can be so robust as to influence memory in amnesics more than in normal subjects (Squire & McKee, 1992). In addition, spared learning in amnesia is not limited to types of learning that involve slow incremental improvement but includes a variety of forms of one trial learning, such as observed in numerous repetition priming tests. Indeed, priming for single exposures to pictures both can be robust and last at least a week in amnesic subjects (Cave & Squire, 1992). Finally preserved learning in amnesia is not limited to any particular category of learning materials, as one can see in the broad range of examples given above, including intact learning for words, nonwords, common objects, tones, nonverbalizable pictures, motor patterns, spatial patterns, and more. In sum the domain of intact learning ability is global, and it can be either fast or slow and includes both general skills and highly specific information content. In other words, the common properties among examples of intact memory in amnesia are not to be found in relatively objective parameters such as the modality of information, or the speed or specificity of memory. Instead, views on the critical features that are common to intact learning in amnesia focus on more complex and higher order properties and, in particular, the form of memory expression, the extent of conscious access to memories, and the structure of the memory representation. Theories about amnesia focusing on each of these will be reviewed next.

Implicit and Explicit Memory

One of the most objective attempts to formalize the general learning abilities of amnesics was Moscovitch's (1984) proposal of a list of sufficient conditions for demonstrating preserved memory. This list, introduced in chapter 2, focused on task demands, and suggested that amnesics show savings on tests that are highly structured, involve response strategies already in the subjects repertoire, and in which success can be achieved without reference to any particular event or episode. In short, Moscovitch argued that amnesics will succeed whenever they simply have to perform a task guided by the conditions and strategies at hand. The new memory is revealed in *implicit* changes during the performance of the task, by a change in either the speed or the bias in choices that are readily available.

Moscovitch's characterization focuses on the conditions for expression of memory and reflects the distinction made by Graf and Schacter (1985; see also Richardson-Klaven & Bjork, 1988; Schacter, 1987a) between "explicit" and "implicit" memory. Explicit memory involves conscious recollection generated by direct efforts to access memories. Explicit tests of memory involve direct inquiries that ask the subject to refer to a specific event of learning or a specific fact in their knowledge. Examples of explicit tests of memory include "What were the words on the list you studied?" and "Which of these two items did you see before?" The full range of explicit memory tests includes a large variety of direct measures of recall or recognition of word or picture lists, paired associates, story recall, and indeed most of the common tests of memory that are performed so poorly by amnesic patients. Explicit memory expression also includes most everyday instances of memory, such as recalling what one had for breakfast this morning or what the capital of France is. Both examples involve conscious efforts to search for a specific event or fact.

By contrast, implicit memory involves unconscious changes in performance of a task as influenced by some previous experience. Implicit tests of memory involve indirect measures such as changes in the speed of performance or in biases in choices made during performance of a task that can be solved with the information at hand. Examples of implicit memory tests include the full variety of assessments of motor, perceptual, and cognitive skills, habits, conditioning, and repetition priming described above at which amnesic patients usually succeed. Notably none of these tests require the subject to be aware of her or his memory, or to "remember" a specific event or fact.

Whereas implicit and explicit memory tests provide powerful tools for distinguishing the performance domains in which amnesic patients succeed and fail, there is reason to believe that the capability for conscious versus unconscious recall that defines the implicit-explicit distinction does not adequately describe amnesia. With regard to consciousness per se, it is clear that amnesic patients have an intact capacity for conscious experience and indeed can consciously retrieve remote memories and can consciously search for new memories, albeit with less success than normal. Moscovitch (1994) has, however, more recently suggested that amnesia involves an impairment in storing the consciousness of an experience along with new factual material, consequently preventing the ability to retrieve the awareness of having experienced it before.

To test whether the implicit-explicit distinction itself can account for differences in performance by amnesics, Cohen and his colleagues assessed different aspects of memory for pictures using eye movement monitoring to provide an implicit measure of retention (Ryan et al., 2000; Whitlow et al., 1995). Subjects were initially shown images of real-world scenes twice, then were subsequently shown either the same scene a third time or a manipulated scene in which the relations among some of the elements of the scene changed by moving, adding, or eliminating objects. Subjects were directed to answer questions about the relationships in the scenes, but did *not* make explicit judgments about their previous experience with the scenes, and their eye movements had nothing to do with their response requirements. Implicit memory for the scenes was seen in two dissociable aspects of their eye movement behavior. All subjects, normals and amnesics alike, showed a *repetition effect*, manifested as a decrease in sampling of previously viewed scenes compared to new scenes. In addition, normal subjects showed a *relational manipulation effect*, exhibited as increased viewing of the regions where manipulations of relations among scene elements had occurred in the manipulated scenes. For example, eye movements were drawn to regions that were now, after the manipulations, empty of objects. Accordingly, the relational manipulation effect revealed memory for relations among the constituent elements of the originally studied scenes. Amnesic patients failed to show this effect. If implicit memory was generally preserved in amnesia, one would have expected both types of eye movement effects, both offering implicit measures of memory, to be manifested normally in amnesia. Instead, whereas the eye movements of patients showed normal implicit memory for repetition of whole scenes, the eye movements of patients showed *impaired* implicit memory for relations among the constituent objects of scenes.

In a more recent study, Chun and Phelps (1999) also challenged the conclusion that hippocampus-dependent learning necessarily involves conscious recollection. Guided by the view that the hippocampus processes relationships among items stored in memory, they examined amnesic patients' ability to show implicit learning of complex relationships, specifically relationships between visual cues and the context in which they are presented. Subjects were trained to locate a target stimulus (the letter 'T' in various orientations) among a background of many 'L' (also in various orientations) distractors. On most trials, the background context was a novel configuration of distractors and the location of the T could not be predicted by previous experiences. However, on other trials, one of a set of background configurations was repeated and consistently predicted a particular location of the target stimulus. In normal subjects, the time required to find the T decreased with practice in both types of trials, consistent with many other examples of perceptual skill learning discussed in this chapter. In addition, their search times were decreased by a greater amount in those trials with repeated configurations of target cues and background contexts. Moreover, the latter effect was not associated with the subjects' conscious awareness that the context had been repeated. Normal subjects could not discriminate novel from repeated backgrounds, and even subjects who were aware that repetitions had occurred could not identify the repeated contexts, nor did they show greater facilitation for repeated contexts than other subjects who were unaware. Thus this protocol assessed the capacity for learning specific cue-context relationships without conscious awareness. Chun and Phelps found that amnesic subjects with hippocampal damage, like normal subjects, decreased their search times with practice on the novel context trials, in accordance with other findings that perceptual skill learning is preserved in amnesia. However, in contrast to the normal subjects, amnesic patients failed to show the added facilitation on repeated cue-context trials. These results of this study are entirely consistent with the findings of Whitlow et al. (1995) and Ryan et al. (in press), and provide compelling evidence that the hippocampus plays a role in a particular type of memory representation, specifically in representing stimulus relations, and not specifically in the capacity for conscious recollection (Eichenbaum, 1999a).

Episodic and Semantic Memory

A related proposal is Tulving's (1972, 1993) distinction between "episodic memory" and "semantic memory." Episodic memory contains autobiographic records of specific events, personal experiences that occur in a unique spatial and temporal context. Tulving refers to this kind of memory as "time traveling," the capacity to re-experience particular events in one's life. Semantic memory is one's world knowledge, a body of memories not dependent on or tied to any specific event when the information was obtained. In recent years several authors have suggested that the pattern of impaired and spared memory capacities in amnesia can be explained as an impaired episodic memory capacity and intact semantic memory (Parkin, 1987). This view readily accounts for the impairment in day-to-day episodic memory ("What did you have for breakfast?"). In addition, to the extent that performance on conventional free recall and recognition tests is stronger in normal subjects, who can refer to a specific learning experience, their superior episodic memory can account for the broad range of memory deficits observed in amnesia. Furthermore, according to this view, amnesic subjects perform well on implicit memory tasks because the memory demands are truly context-free in that there is no requirement to refer to the learning experience directly, and no advantage is conferred on normal subjects in remembering the items. The episodic-semantic distinction shares much with Moscovitch's (1984) characterization of successful memory performance whenever amnesics do not have to "conjure up, that is, 'remember,' any previous experience or a newly learned fact" (p. 106). Indeed the episodic-semantic and implicit-explicit views are fully compatible, to the extent that implicit memory tests always and only require semantic memory.

In support of this view, Tulving et al. (1988) described a patient, K.C., with normal intelligence, preserved general knowledge, and fragmentary general knowledge of his past. He also has expert knowledge from work done 3 years before a closed-head injury. By contrast, K.C. does not remember a single personal event from his previous life and does not remember new events. He has some capacity to gradually acquire new knowledge, as demonstrated in studies aimed at very gradual accumulation of semantic knowledge by teaching methods that reduce interference associated with making errors (Tulving et al., 1991; see also Hamann & Squire, 1995). In addition, there are now several cases of child-hood brain injury that have resulted in amnesia for everyday life events, but near-normal general world knowledge (e.g., Vargha-Khadem et al., 1997). Some of the latter cases appear to have relatively circumscribed damage to the hippocampus, suggesting specific involvement of this structure in episodic memory.

Disentangling episodic and semantic memory is a difficult problem. Surely these patients forget "facts," such as a list of words, just as rapidly as they forget daily events, such as what they had for breakfast. Gabrieli et al. (1988) addressed the issue of semantic learning in amnesia by attempting to train H.M. on new vocabulary. H.M. and normal subjects were trained on eight little known words in a series of phases, receiving implicit test instructions that directed them away from using conscious recollection of the training experiences. They first studied definitions for the words and then were tested by having them choose the correct definition for each word from a list. Then they studied synonyms for these words and were tested by having them choose the correct synonym from a list. Finally, they saw sentence frames and had to complete each one with the correct word from a list. Normal subjects learned the new words readily, completing each phase within a few trials. Despite this exhaustive regimen, H.M. showed virtually no acquisition of new semantic knowledge.

This is not to say that amnesics cannot acquire any semantic knowledge. Glisky et al. (1986) and Tulving et al. (1991) succeeded in prolonged training of subjects in computer commands and related terminology using painstaking, grad-ual, "error-free," training methods. These subjects did subsequently show apti-tude for learning new computer terms. But the range with which they could use this new learning was stunningly constrained. Their learning could only be ex-pressed in a replication of the training conditions. This "hyperspecificity" (Schacter, 1985) of preserved learning capacity is not characteristic of our com-mon use of semantic memory in guiding everyday performance on a broad range of one's jobs in daily life.

Declarative and Procedural Memory

Cohen and Squire (Cohen, 1984; Squire & Cohen, 1984) distinguished between an impaired capacity in amnesia for "declarative memory," the memory for facts and events that can be brought to conscious recollection and can be expressed explicitly, and "procedural memory," which involves the acquisition of skills and preferences that can be expressed unconsciously by implicit changes in the speed or biasing of performance. Notably, the terms *declarative* and *procedural,* like the explicit-implicit distinction, focus on different types of memory expres-sion. However, the declarative-procedural distinction also posits fundamental differences in the nature of memory representations that underlie performance. Specifically, Cohen (1984) argued that declarative representations permit the pro-cessing and storage of comparisons among learning events and among the items within learning events. Elaborating on this idea, the critical property of declara-tive memory that permits this ability is the encoding of memories in terms of the relations among multiple items and events. Thus the nature of declarative representation is fundamentally *relational* and can be envisioned as a multidimensional network of memories—a memory "space"—entailing a highly inter-connected network with connections among informational elements characteriz-ing possible relations (Cohen & Eichenbaum, 1993; Eichenbaum et al., 1992a, 1992c).

A consequence of the relational nature of declarative representation, and a second defining property of declarative memory, is that the stored representa-tions are broadly accessible, and they can be expressed independently of the cir-cumstances in which the information was initially acquired (Cohen, 1984). A central property of relational networks is that activation of a subset of informa-tional nodes leads to activation of other informational elements, including both those previously activated at the same time during the learning experience and those only indirectly connected with the activated node, revealing all manner of relations among the stored items. In this way, declarative memories can be acti-vated by all manner of external sensory or even purely internal inputs, regardless of the current context. This in turn gives rise to the final critical property of declarative memory, namely, *representational flexibility*—the ability of declara-tive memories to be manipulated and used flexibly to guide performance under an enormous range of testing conditions, including those differing significantly from the circumstances of original learning. Thus, declarative memory is to be considered inherently generative, conferring the ability to construct novel re-sponses in new situations.

Both the impaired memory abilities and the spared performance of amnesic patients can be explained within this account. Typical recall and recognition tests demand that subjects search their memory of words, pictures, or ideas for precisely the ones learned in a previous study phase. What distinguishes the items to be recalled or recognized is the events surrounding the learning, for example, in remembering precisely the words that were on the list or in retrieving a learned word by the one it was related to in the study phase. By this view conscious recollection is an act of accessing the relational network for a set of memories, and using the network to guide the search and choice of items for explicit expression.

The characteristics of declarative memory can be illustrated in the simple ex-ample of remembering what one had for breakfast this morning. In this situation declarative memory is invoked as we search back to the experience of breakfast, which is a complex combination of acts and experiences, and we retrieve just the names of the items we had to eat. Declaring one's memory is a prototypical illustration of accessing a set of experiences and expressing them by talking about items from the network of memories that define that experience. By way of con-trast, implicit expression of what one had for breakfast would involve something like the repetition of the breakfast event, with changes in the choice of breakfast items or changes in the speed of eating the same items as one had already eaten that day.

Some of the examples of formal memory tests described above also provide strong illustrations of the relational nature and representational flexibility of de-clarative memory. For example, in the Whitlow et al. (1995) and Ryan et al. (in press) eye-movement work, and in the Chun and Phelps (1999) visual search experiment, amnesics were impaired in measures of implicit memory for spatial relations among the objects in the displays. Notably, they showed intact implicit memory for the familiarity with the objects and, within the same test, loss of memory for relations among those same items. In the experiments that show intact semantic learning by amnesic patients, it is notable that successful learning was accompanied by a "hyperspecificity" of acquired knowledge. Amnesics who could reevoke learned terms in repetitions of trained situations could not use the same information to solve new computer problems. Repetition priming, a kind of learning intact in amnesia, has also been characterized as "hyperspecific" in its expression. For example, stem completion for printed words relies on repetition of the exact font used during initial exposure.

In the next section of this chapter we will provide evidence from functional brain-imaging studies in normal human subjects. This evidence converges with our conclusion from studies of amnesia that the hippocampal region is selectively involved in declarative memory.

Functional Neuroimaging Studies of the Human Hippocampal System

Until very recently, data on the role of the hippocampal system in memory have been acquired predominantly through neuropsychological studies of amnesia. However, it is now possible to monitor the ongoing operation of the human hippocampal system during various memory performances by using functional neuroimaging methods (positron emission tomography [PET] and functional magnetic resonance imaging [fMRI]). Functional neuroimaging studies in humans can inform us about the aspects or kinds of memory in which the hippocampal system is and is not involved, providing a way to assess its functional role that is more like that of electrophysiological studies of the activity of single neurons in hippocampus in animals. In this section, we summarize the literature on functional imaging studies of the hippocampal system, discuss its concordance with results from neuropsychological studies, and consider the fit of the imaging data to a number of the major theories of hippocampal function. This summary of the rapidly burgeoning imaging literature cannot be fully inclusive, being necessarily limited by space constraints. A more extended treatment is offered in Cohen et al. (1999).

Early attempts to observe hippocampal activation in PET or fMRI during one or another memory performances were largely disappointing. As recently as 1996, it was noted that "the hippocampus has been a recalcitrant target of functional neuroimaging studies" (Aguirre et al., 1996). The failure of the early studies to find hippocampal activation even on memory tasks that neuropsychological studies suggested were critically hippocampus-dependent raised concerns that functional imaging data would fail to converge with neuropsychological data, bringing those literatures into conflict on the role of the hippocampal system in memory.

However, a growing number of studies in recent years have shown that the human hippocampal system can be seen in action during various memory performances after all, and as we shall see, the results of these studies correspond well to those of the earlier (and still ongoing) neuropsychological studies. For example, consider the range of to-be-remembered materials over which the hippocampal system operates. Studies of patients with bilateral damage to the hippocampal system have shown that amnesia is a *global* memory deficit. As discussed earlier, such patients have a material- and modality-general impairment, encompassing verbal and nonverbal, spatial and nonspatial materials, regardless of whether they are presented visually, auditorily, and so on, indicating that the hippocampal system's role in memory is, likewise, *non*specific with regard to material and modality. At the same time, studies of patients with unilateral damage to the left or right medial temporal lobe region have shown clear material-specific memory impairments: Verbal and nonverbal memory performances are selectively compromised after medial temporal lobe damage in the left and the right hemisphere, respectively (e.g., see Milner, 1971, 1972). Thus, there is a laterality to the hippocampal contribution to memory, corresponding to the kinds of processing for which the hemispheres are specialized. How well do the findings from functional imaging studies of memory correspond to this picture from neuropsychological studies?

Across a variety of functional imaging studies we can see both the globalness of hippocampal processing, when considered bilaterally, and also the material-specificity of left versus right hippocampal system processing. Looking across the range of studies successfully observing hippocampal system activation, we see how broad a range of stimulus materials can engage this system. Ignoring the hemisphere in which activation occurs, hippocampal activation has been reported for words (Martin et al., 1997; Kelley et al., 1998; Wagner et al., 1998), objects (Schacter et al., 1995, 1997; Kanwisher et al., 1997; Martin et al., 1997; Kelley et al., 1998), scenes (Tulving et al., 1994b; Stern et al., 1996; Gabrieli et al., 1997; Montaldi et al., 1998; Brewer et al., 1998), faces (Sergent et al., 1992; Grady et al., 1995; Kapur et al., 1995; Haxby et al., 1996; Kelley et al., 1998), spatial routes (Maguire et al., 1997), and landmarks or locations (Maguire et al., 1997; Aguirre & D'Esposito, 1997). In addition, in studies that compared different classes of materials, clear hemispheric specializations have been seen. The results of an fMRI study by Kelley et al. (1998) and a PET study by Martin et al. (1997) showed greater left than right hippocampal activation for words, and greater right than left hippocampal activation for nonfamous faces or objects. Accordingly, with regard to materials, there is good concordance of the functional imaging and the neuropsychological data.

Functional Neuroimaging and the Role of the Hippocampal System in Memory

What do the functional imaging results tell us about the aspects or kinds of memory for which the hippocampal system is and is not engaged? After many failures to observe hippocampal activation, the earliest successes led to some new ideas about the functional role of the hippocampal system, ideas that made little contact with those from the neuropsychological work. We shall discuss these ideas and consider how well they do or do not account for the rapidly growing set of successful hippocampal findings. We shall then turn to several of the theories of memory and the hippocampal system that derive from the amnesia literature, and we shall consider their fit to the functional imaging data. In all, five different ideas about hippocampal system function will be considered, in turn.

Novelty

Based on the finding in a PET study of (right) limbic system activation for novel items compared to previously studied items, Tulving et al. (1994b) proposed that there are novelty-encoding networks in the brain responsible for detecting novel stimuli and encoding that information in memory, and that the limbic system, including especially the hippocampal system, is a critical part of that network.

In the Tulving et al. (1994b) study, subjects viewed scenes (taken from old *National Geographic* magazines) twice prior to scanning, and then 24 hours later, they viewed these "old" scenes and "new" ones while being scanned. In each block, the scan window consisted of either old or new scenes exclusively (although the beginning and end of each block contained both old and new scenes). Subjects were informed before each scan whether the majority of the items they were about to see would be old or new and were instructed to count the oddballs. Greater activation in the new-old subtraction was observed in various right-hemisphere limbic structures, including particularly the hippocampal system. A few subsequent studies have reported results consistent with greater engagement of the hippocampal system for the processing of novel as compared to already familiar materials. One example comes from an fMRI study by Stern et al. (1996) using color scenes (magazine photos) as the stimuli. Subjects viewed the scenes in alternating experimental and control blocks, in which either a series of different scenes was presented once (experimental) or just one scene was presented repeatedly (control). They were instructed to study the scenes so that they might be able to recognize them later, and they were scanned during this study phase. Greater activation was seen in (posterior) hippocampal regions for the novel scenes in the experimental condition compared to the single repeated scene in the control condition. In perhaps the most striking example of a novelty detection effect, Martin et al. (1997) simply presented visual noise patterns repeatedly and demonstrated a selective activation of the right hippocampus by the presentation of novel visual noise patterns, compared to the second presentation of the same patterns.

Despite these impressive observations, looking at the larger functional imaging literature, there are three classes of findings that provide difficulty for the view that novelty per se is driving these activations. First, there are reports in which greater hippocampal activation was found for old versus new items, a pattern opposite to what was predicted in the novelty account of hippocampal system function. Second, there are reports in which differences in hippocampal activation were found across conditions that were equal in novelty. Third, there are reports in which varying novelty systematically across conditions produced no differences in hippocampal activation. One example of each of these three classes of negative findings is offered below to illustrate the problem; various other negative findings along these same lines could have been included that would make the same points. In addition, two further considerations also give us pause in considering the novelty idea of hippocampal function. They will be discussed at the end of this section.

Greater Activation for Old Versus New Items

For example, Schacter et al. (1995, 1997) explored memory for possible and impossible (line drawings of) objects in two PET studies. Subjects were scanned while they made either possible/impossible or old/new recognition judgments on previously studied versus novel objects. Both of these conditions produced hippocampal activation bilaterally compared to a no-decision baseline condition, for both old and new possible objects, showing more activation for repeated than for novel possible objects.

Differences in Hippocampal Activation Across Conditions in Which There Was No Difference in Novelty

For example, Montaldi et al. (1998) showed subjects old *National Geographic* magazine photos in their study and had them perform either an associative encoding task (in which they were to focus on what the picture was about, how the features related to each other within the picture, and the spatial locations of items) or a perceptual matching task (in which three photos were shown and subjects were to match the top with one of the other two, being warned that there was a high degree of similarity in the theme of the choices and any attention paid to the theme would not help). Greater (left) hippocampal activation was found for the associative encoding condition compared to the perceptual matching condition, even though they involved the same photos and hence did not differ in degree of novelty.

No Differential Hippocampal Activation Across Conditions That Systematically Vary Novelty

Buckner et al.'s (1995) series of PET studies involved comparing conditions in which subjects were presented word stems (the initial few letters of words) of which half could be completed to words that had been on a prescanning study list versus conditions in which subjects were presented with stems that completed only novel (nonstudied) words. No hippocampal activation was reported.

Novelty and Priming Effects?

There is one final concern regarding the novelty idea that we have not seen discussed elsewhere in the literature. A variety of previous studies have shown that cortical visual processing regions show diminished activation levels for materials that have been repeated (for a review, see Buckner et al., 1998), that is, more activation for novel than for repeated stimuli. To the extent that the parahippocampal region may be closely tied to the sensory processing streams that provide input to it and hence related to high-level stimulus analysis or manipulation rather than to memory processes (see Cohen et al., 1999), at least some of the "hippocampal system" activation reported for novel versus repeated items may be the same sensory system *priming* that is seen in extrastriate cortex and other cortical processing areas.

Contact with Neuropsychological and Other Findings?

Studies of amnesia show that although hippocampal damage does impair the ability to distinguish novel from repeated items (as evidenced, say, in impaired recognition memory or delayed match-to-sample task performance), and hence that the hippocampal system may be considered a necessary element in detection of novelty, the memory impairment extends well beyond novelty detection. As we have seen, amnesic patients are profoundly impaired at learning arbitrary relations among items even when they are repeated over and over, showing deficits in paired-associate learning (of arbitrary pairings of words), learning face-name pairings, or learning vocabulary (i.e., word-meaning pairings) (see Cohen, Poldrack, & Eichenbaum, 1997). Findings from recordings of hippocampal neurons are also outside the scope of the novelty account. Just consider the well-known findings of "place fields" in which particular hippocampal neurons fire reliably whenever the animal is in one or another particular "place" in its environment (e.g., O'Keefe, 1979; McNaughton, 1989). The place fields develop with exposure to the environment and then remain constant as the animal navigates through the familiar space, long after that environment has lost whatever novelty it may have possessed. Accordingly, the novelty idea has little explanatory power outside the functional imaging data, thereby providing an independent reason to argue against it as a full account of hippocampal function.

Retrieval Success

Nyberg et al. (1996) proposed that the hippocampal system is involved in the successful retrieval of previously stored information (i.e., in the reactivation of stored representations). This idea was prompted by the results of their PET study, in which subjects listened to two lists of words prior to being in the scanner. For one list, subjects were to decide whether each word was said by a male or female speaker (perceptual encoding); for the other list, they had to decide whether each word referred to a living or a nonliving thing (semantic encoding). Subjects were subsequently tested for recognition memory while being scanned, in a series of test blocks that assessed memory separately for perceptually encoded and semantically encoded words. Greater (left) medial temporal lobe activation was observed for blocks that tested words from the semantically encoded list compared to the perceptually encoded list. The fact that there was a higher rate of successful recall of semantically encoded words compared to perceptually encoded words suggested to Nyberg et al. (1996) that increased hippocampal activation for semantically encoded words was a consequence of the role of this region in successful recall (i.e., in successfully gaining access to some memory representation). This connection was seen more formally as a strong positive correlation across subjects and conditions between test performance and medial temporal lobe activation.

Some support for this idea can be drawn from a PET study of face processing and memory by Kapur et al. (1995), in which greater hippocampal system activation was found in conditions in which subjects were to distinguish repeated from novel nonfamous faces, or to identify which famous faces were of politicians, compared to a condition in which they were to identify the gender of each face. The two conditions that showed hippocampal activation thus were those in which performance required subjects to successfully retrieve stored information about (the identity or the prior occurrence of) a face, as distinguished from the condition in which they just needed to make a perceptual judgment about a face.

However, there are four classes of findings in the larger functional imaging literature that would seem to present problems for the retrieval success idea. One illustrative example is provided for each. In addition, problems with relating this idea to the amnesia data are noted. First, there are findings in which differential hippocampal system activation is observed across conditions that all entail successful retrieval. Second, there are studies in which no hippocampal system activation occurs in conditions with successful retrieval. Third, there are studies in which hippocampal system activation is observed for new items and may even be greater for new items than for previously studied items. Fourth, there are encoding-time studies, in which hippocampal system activation was observed during study or passive viewing conditions.

Differential Hippocampal System Activation Across Conditions That All Entail Successful Retrieval

For example, in Maguire et al.'s (1997) PET study, London taxicab drivers were asked to do four "recall" tasks: (1) recall a route from one place in the familiar city of London to another, (2) recall the location of a famous landmark to which they had never been, (3) recall the plot of a familiar movie, and (4) recall a particular scene from a familiar movie. Greater (right) hippocampal system activation was seen during recall of routes than during any other condition, even though successful performance in *any* of the conditions required successful retrieval of information, and the performance levels were shown to be comparable across conditions.

No Hippocampal System Activation in Conditions Where There Is Successful Retrieval

One example is the PET study by Sergent et al. (1992), using a procedure very similar to that of the Kapur et al. (1995) study cited above as support for the retrieval success account. Subjects were shown a set of faces and objects (some of which were repeated) and were asked either to recognize/identify the repeated objects/faces or indicate the gender of the face. Despite the fact that successful performance on the recognition/identification tasks required successful retrieval of previously stored memory, no hippocampal system activation was observed here.

Greater Hippocampal System Activation For New Items Than For Previously Studied Items

Successful reactivation of previously stored memory must be greater for materials that were actually studied previously than for novel materials. Yet the imaging findings used to support the novelty account in the previous section, such as the Tulving et al. (1994b) study, show exactly the opposite pattern—more hippocampal activation for novel materials—and thus necessarily go against the retrieval success account. The retrieval success idea and the novelty idea (and the data that might support one versus the other) are in direct conflict, and hence neither one will be able to accommodate the full range of imaging data.

Hippocampal System Activation During Encoding-Time Study or Passive Viewing Conditions

An increasing number of studies have reported hippocampal activation at encoding time. For example, in Kelley et al.'s (1998) fMRI study, hippocampal system activation was observed when subjects actively or passively encoded words, non-famous faces, or line drawings of objects. Unless it is argued that encoding, and even passive viewing, of all of these various kinds of stimuli involves successful reactivation of previously stored memory (which seems particularly unlikely for unfamiliar faces, which have no prior representations in memory) and that this reactivation is what is driving the hippocampal activity observed at encoding time, such results represent a serious problem for the retrieval success account of hippocampal function.

Contact with Neuropsychological and Other Findings?

There was much discussion in the 1970s and 1980s about whether amnesia was fundamentally a deficit—and hence whether the hippocampal system played a critical role—in retrieval processes, encoding processes, or storage and/or consolidation processes. Although Warrington and Weiskrantz (1968, 1970) staked out an early position in support of a retrieval deficit hypothesis of amnesia, we believe that the currently prevailing views either are agnostic about which is the critical stage of processing or have a hybrid theory of hippocampal involvement that cuts across the stages of processing. Certainly there is no compelling evidence from neuropsychological work suggesting that the hippocampal system is uniquely involved in retrieval processes. A similar conclusion seems to arise from consideration of the functional imaging literature. We have noted that neither the retrieval success account nor the novelty account is capable of accommodating the full range of imaging data on the role of the hippocampal system in memory. Rather than just dismissing these two accounts, however, it might be more useful to generalize these two ideas somewhat, treating them as being more generally about the role of the hippocampal system in two different stages of memory processing—encoding and retrieval. In that case, the question being addressed by these accounts concerns the *stage* of memory processing rather than the *domain* of memory processing in which the hippocampal system is involved. Recent discussions in the literature suggest that various portions of the hippocampal system may be involved differentially in these two stages of memory processing (see Lepage et al., 1998; Schacter & Wagner, 1999).

We turn now to three major views of the domain of memory processing supported by the hippocampal system and consider their fit to the functional imaging data.

Explicit (Versus Implicit) Memory

We turn first to Graf and Schacter's (1985) widely noted distinction between explicit memory, involving conscious recollection of some prior study episode, and implicit memory, in which the effects of previous experience can be manifested without requiring the gaining of conscious access to any specific experience, and we consider whether the hippocampal system is disproportionately engaged in explicit memory.

The first application of this account to functional imaging appeared in a PET study by Squire et al. (1992). Subjects studied word lists outside the scanner. Their memory was subsequently tested in a number of different conditions while being scanned. At test they were given word stems and asked to complete the stems either with the first word that came to mind (priming condition), with a word from the study list (memory condition), or with the first word that came to mind that was *not* on the study list (baseline condition). In the memory and priming conditions, the stems were constructed so that half could be completed to words from the study list. Hippocampal system activation was found bilaterally for the memory condition, which involved explicit memory instructions, as compared to either the priming condition, which involved implicit memory instructions, or the baseline condition. The finding that hippocampal activation was greatest under explicit memory instructions supports the explicit memory account.

Other support for the explicit memory account comes from a pair of PET studies by Schacter et al. (1995, 1997) in which subjects studied possible and impossible objects and were tested in the scanner while making either possible/impossible object decisions or (explicit) recognition memory judgments. Hippocampal system activation was observed when subjects made (explicit) recognition judgments for either new or previously studied possible or impossible objects. Hippocampal activation was greatest for recognition of studied possible objects compared to new possible objects, consistent with when explicit remembering would be most needed. No hippocampal activation was found in the comparison of the studied-impossible objects versus new-impossible objects comparison, presumably because subjects had no representations of impossible objects to explicitly remember. And no hippocampal activation was observed when making possible/impossible judgments about the possible objects, presumably because explicit remembering of previous exposures to real objects is not necessary in order to determine that a given object is indeed possible.

There are, however, three classes of findings that present difficulties for the explicit memory account of hippocampal function. First are findings of hippocampal system activation in encoding-time tasks. Second are findings of differences in hippocampal activation across conditions that all involve explicit remembering. Third are findings of no hippocampal activation for the critical explicit memory condition.

Hippocampal System Activation in Encoding-Time Tasks

There are many reports of hippocampal activation during encoding for various materials: words (Kelley et al., 1998; Martin et al., 1997; Wagner et al., 1998), objects (Kelley et al., 1998; Martin et al., 1997), faces (Kelley et al., 1998), non-sense words (Martin et al., 1997), or scenes (Stern et al., 1996; Brewer et al., 1998). Yet, at encoding time, particularly in the passive viewing conditions included in some of these studies, there is not likely to be much, if any, explicit remembering of specific prior learning episodes. The explicit memory account is fundamentally a retrieval time theory (although not the same as the retrieval *success* idea), concerned with a particular kind of remembering. Accordingly, this account will necessarily be consistent only with the retrieval time data and in conflict with the encoding-time data.

Differences in Hippocampal Activation Across Conditions That All Involve Explicit Remembering

One example is the Maguire et al. (1997) study of London taxicab drivers. As we saw earlier, greater hippocampal system activation was obtained during recall of routes than during any of the other three recall conditions (famous landmarks, movie scenes, or movie plots), even though successful performance in *any* of the conditions required explicit remembering. Unless one wanted to argue that the explicit remembering demand differed across these various conditions (i.e., that for whatever reason more explicit remembering is entailed in recalling routes), the explicit memory account fails to offer an explanation for the variance in hippocampal activation across the conditions.

No Hippocampal Activation for the Critical Explicit Memory Condition

The Buckner et al. (1995) PET study, discussed earlier, failed to find hippocampal activation in any of its series of experiments on cued recall versus completion of word stems, despite using the same methods as in Squire et al. (1992)—the study that had provided the original application of the explicit memory account to functional imaging. It is entirely possible that subjects in the latter study were using explicit remembering in both experimental and control conditions, regardless of instructions, and thus failed to show (differential) hippocampal activation because this system was active in *both* conditions. But taken together with the other two classes of findings that go against the predictions of the explicit memory account, the explicit memory account fails to handle the full range of imaging data.

Spatial (Cognitive) Mapping

Although O'Keefe and Nadel's (1978) well-known view that the hippocampal system plays a crucial role in spatial memory, permitting the ability to construct, maintain, and make use of spatial maps of the environment, cannot provide a full accounting of human amnesia, as we discussed earlier, it has been applied to functional imaging literature. We will consider it here.

This view of hippocampal function was first and, thus far, most successfully applied to functional imaging studies in the report by Maguire et al. (1997), in which they used PET to image the hippocampal system of experienced London taxi drivers as they retrieved information about routes (i.e., engaged in route finding) around London. As we have already discussed, greater activation of (right) hippocampal system structures was seen during recall of route information than during recall of famous landmarks, movie plot lines, or movie scenes. Other support can be derived from a PET study by Aguirre and D'Esposito (1997), in which subjects learned to navigate in a virtual reality (VR) environment. Subjects were then scanned while they made judgments about the appearance or relative position of particular places in the VR environment compared to a control condition involving scrambled versions of the same stimuli. Hippocampal system activation was observed bilaterally for both conditions that tested memory of the learned VR places compared to the control condition.

However, there are three sets of findings that would seem to provide problems for the spatial mapping account of hippocampal function. First are findings that spatial processing activates the parahippocampal region rather than the hippocampus itself. Second are findings that hippocampal system activation is produced in a variety of tasks that have little or nothing to do with spatial mapping as defined in the spatial theory of hippocampal function. Third are findings of differential hippocampal activation across conditions that are equally (non)spatial. Illustrative examples of each will be considered.

Spatial Processing Activates the Parahippocampal Region but Not the Hippocampus

In neither the Maguire et al. (1997) nor the Aguirre and D'Esposito (1997) studies cited above in support of the spatial account of hippocampal function was activation found in the hippocampus itself; both of these studies noted that their activations were from parahippocampal cortex. This is troubling because the spatial account has made clear that the hippocampus itself should be the focal point of spatial (cognitive) mapping ability, and the neurons with the best place fields in rats are in hippocampus proper. In addition, it has become clear that the parahippocampal region includes an area (recently termed the *parahippocampal place area*) that is activated by houses or other scenes (Epstein & Kanwisher, 1998) and which may be the source of the activations seen by Maguire et al. (1997) and Aguirre and D'Esposito (1997).

Hippocampal System Activation in Nonspatial Tasks

There are now numerous reports of hippocampal activation in various tasks that have little or nothing to do with spatial mapping as defined in the spatial theory of hippocampal function. This is illustrated well by the large number of studies showing hippocampal activation in encoding-time tasks, including study or even passive viewing of single words (Kelley et al., 1998; Martin et al., 1997; Wagner et al., 1998), objects (Kelley et al., 1998; Martin et al., 1997), letter strings (Martin et al., 1997), faces (Kelley et al., 1998), or scenes (Stern et al., 1996; Brewer et al., 1998), in which it is difficult to see how the basic processing entailed would depend in any significant way upon spatial mapping processes. In a more recent study Maguire and Mummery (1999) found activation within the left hippocampus associated with the retrieval of memories that had strong personal relevance and strong temporal specificity, as compared to weak relevance and temporal specificity. Thus the specificity for right hippocampal activation associated with spatial processing may reflect the general differences between the left and right hemispheres, more than a specific role for the hippocampal region in navigation.

Differential Hippocampal Activation Across Conditions that Are Equally (Non)spatial

For example, Tulving et al.'s (1994b) report of greater hippocampal activation for novel than for repeated scenes and Stern et al.'s (1996) report of more hippocampal activation for a set of different scenes than for one scene presented repeatedly—both constitute findings in which it is difficult to see how the conditions differed in their dependence on spatial mapping processing in any way. The spatial view cannot account for the variance in results across conditions that are equally (non)spatial.

Relational Memory Processing (Declarative Versus Procedural Memory)

In the preceding sections we have shown some limitations of various competing theories of hippocampal function in accounting for all findings from functional imaging studies, just as these same views had certain limitations in accommodating all of the neuropsychological findings. Here we consider the fit of the functional imaging data to the idea from the declarative-procedural memory framework that the hippocampal system is critically involved in memory binding or relational memory processing.

This idea was first tested in the neuroimaging literature by Cohen et al. (1994) in an fMRI study in which subjects were presented with stimuli composed of faces, names, and icons and were either to study and recognize the previously presented face-name-icon triplets from among repairings of the same stimuli or to make gender discriminations. Greater hippocampal activation was found for learning and remembering the triplets than for making gender judgments on the same stimuli (see Cohen et al., 1997, for further discussion of these results). These findings are consistent with Maguire and Mummery's (1999) report of hippocampal activation for retrieval of memories that involved combinations of specific materials, their personal relevance, and their temporal relationship to other events.

Perhaps the strongest support for the relational memory account from the functional imaging work comes from a PET study by Henke et al. (1997). In that experiment, subjects were shown a series of pictures of a person and of a house (either the interior or the exterior) simultaneously. The task instructions required subjects to decide if the person was either an inhabitant of or a visitor to the house and thus encouraged them to make an association between (i.e., bind) the person and the house, or to make separate decisions about the person (is it male or female?) and the house (is it an exterior or interior view?), thus encouraging them to encode the house and the person separately. Henke et al. found greater (right) hippocampal system activation when the materials were encoded relationally than when they were encoded separately, supporting the claim that the hippocampal system is involved in memory binding.

In assessing how other imaging findings might be handled, or not handled, by this account, it seemed that each of the various studies that earlier were considered the best data in support of the other accounts also provided clear support for the relational memory idea. Consider first the Tulving et al. (1994b) and Stern et al. (1996) studies cited in support of the novelty account, in which greater hippocampal activation was found for novel scenes than for previously viewed scenes. More encoding and relational binding of the various elements in these scenes would be expected for never-seen versus already-seen items, and hence greater hippocampal activation would be predicted by the relational account. This would be expected to be particularly evident in the Stern et al. (1996) study, in which the experimental condition entailed presenting a brand-new scene every 3 s, whereas the control condition had the same single scene presented every 3 s. The experimental condition would necessarily invoke more relational processing of the many new relationships appearing within and across the constantly changing scenes than would be the case for the control condition with the single unchanging scene. More generally, an effect of stimulus novelty on hippocampal activation makes good sense within the relational account of hippocampal function. Interestingly, in attempting to explain why they observed hippocampal activation in their task at a time, several years ago, when many other imaging studies (most of them using verbal stimuli) had been less successful, Stern et al. (1996) stated:

> The key difference between imaging studies that do or do not show the hippocampal activity is probably not specifically related to the use of verbal versus visual information, but more likely relates to the complexity and relational characteristics of the information being presented. Simple verbal stimuli, unlike complex visual pictures and faces, do not require the formation of new representations or relationships. (p. 8664)

Turning to the various encoding-time data discussed above, the success of these studies in eliciting greater hippocampal activation in experimental conditions involving a series of changing scenes, faces, words, and so on compared to control conditions that presented subjects with just a fixation point (e.g., Kelley et al., 1998; Wagner et al., 1998; Brewer et al., 1998) or noise patterns (e.g., Martin et al., 1997) seems to provide good support for the relational memory account. These control conditions place absolutely minimal demands on a relational memory or memory-binding system of the kind we have proposed and hence make it possible to generate experimental conditions capable of eliciting much more relational memory processing and thereby permit hippocampal activation to be observed.

The studies cited in support of the retrieval success account, such as Nyberg et al. (1996), would seem to provide equally strong support for the relational account. Nyberg et al. (1996) reported more hippocampal system activation for words that had been encoded semantically than for words encoded perceptually. Good semantic encoding, involving relating the item to its various semantic associates, would certainly invoke the relational memory processing we attribute to the hippocampal system and thus would be expected to produce greater hippocampal activation.

The hippocampal system activation observed in the Schacter et al. (1995, 1997) studies, cited as providing strong support for the explicit memory account, provides just as strong support for the relational memory account. The recognition judgment task is a relational memory task in which subjects must attempt to relate the object presented to a previously established representation made at the time of encoding. More generally, it is the relational nature of all explicit memory tasks (the requirement of making contact with some specific study episode related to the test item) that causes hippocampal system damage to impair explicit memory test performance (see Cohen & Eichenbaum, 1993; Cohen et al., 1997) and that causes explicit memory tests to have a chance of activating the hippocampal system.

Finally, the data cited as providing strong support for the spatial mapping account would also provide good support for the relational account and help to illustrate an important point about the relational account. Maguire et al. (1997) found greater hippocampal activation for recalling routes than for recalling landmarks, film plots, or film frames. All these conditions involve relational processing, but they differ considerably in the amount and nature of relational processing required. As intentionally designed by Maguire et al. (1997), route recall involved both topographical and sequential relations; film plot recall depended largely on sequential relations, and landmark recall depended just on topographical relations; and film frame recall depended on neither topographical nor sequential relations. Viewed in terms of a general relational demand, one can see that route recall requires the greatest amount of relational processing and thus would be expected to produce the most hippocampal activation. This is exactly the result obtained by Maguire et al. More generally, the kinds of spatial processing that are required for navigating successfully through the environment and that would be seen by the likes of O'Keefe and Nadel as spatial mapping functions are seen by us as a subset of relational memory processing. Finding hippocampal activation in conditions that invoke the processing of spatial relations, therefore, would provide support for both accounts equally. However, findings such as those considered earlier, in which hippocampal activation is observed in conditions invoking *non*spatial relational processing, support only the relational account.

In contrast to all of the other accounts we have considered earlier in this section, there are no examples of findings, of which we are aware, in which hippocampal activation occurred in the *wrong* conditions for the relational memory theory. Rather, the relational memory account seems to accommodate more nearly the full range of imaging data than any other explanatory account of hippocampal function that we have considered, thereby converging with the neuropsychological findings.

An additional advantage of the declarative-procedural account is that, unlike the explicit-implicit and episodic-semantic distinctions, its properties can make contact with the experimental literature on studies of memory in animals. Efforts to model the characteristics of human amnesia in animals will be considered in the next two chapters. Then, in chapter 8, we will consider the evidence from the animal analogue of functional brain imaging, recordings of hippocampal neural activity in animals performing memory tasks.

6

Animal Models of Amnesia

The Nonhuman Primate

Question: Why model amnesia in animals? Answer: Because the limitations of research on human subjects are significant and the potential advantages of studying memory in animals are numerous. In studies on humans fundamental memory processes cannot be examined separately from potentially overwhelming influences of linguistic competence that can overshadow capacities for memory per se, because language plays so important a role in all of human cognition including memory. In addition, the experience the animal subject brings to a memory test can be manipulated at a level of selectivity and resolution that is just not possible in human subjects. We can control virtually the entirety of an animal's life experiences that can contribute to new learning. And in particular, studies of retrograde memory loss in humans cannot sufficiently control the nature or amount of learning that occurs prior to brain damage. In animals, of course, one can perform the critical prospective consolidation studies in which specific information is learned to a controlled and measured degree before a specific experimental brain lesion is made at a later date.

In addition, a fundamental goal of neuroscientific studies of memory is to identify the specific contributions of anatomically defined brain areas. In examinations of human clinical cases, the extent and selectivity of brain areas damaged suffers at the whim of Mother Nature, whose tools of disease, stroke, or ischemia are most often not very selective. Even in cases where brain tissue is removed by a surgeon for medical reasons, critical issues of anatomical specificity for the sake of research questions are appropriately secondary to clinical priorities and so are often compromised. In creating an animal model of amnesia the specificity of experimental lesions is limited only by the tools for making selective brain damage or disconnection. The ability to make considerably more selective brain damage opens up the possibility of identifying specific contributions of closely neighboring brain structures.

Furthermore, studies on animal amnesia can contribute to levels of analysis below that of neuropsychological investigations. That is, by identifying cognitive operations that are critically mediated by specific brain structures, experiments on animal amnesia provide behavioral tools for direct exploration of neural coding mechanisms and measures of neural plasticity. The current state of the art in physiological investigations of the human brain involve impressive new techniques for imaging functional activation of brain areas in behaving human subjects. But the spatial and temporal resolution of these techniques is far more coarse than that provided in studies of single-cell activity that are commonly pursued in animal models, and most believe an understanding of the neural code lies at the level of single cells and their ensemble activity.

Finally, explorations of animal memory can provide insights about how particular memory mechanisms evolved. To the extent that specific cognitive operations that depend on particular brain systems are common between humans and animals, we can conclude these operations are fundamental to a particular kind of memory processing by that system. Correspondingly, to the extent that specific cognitive operations that depend on particular brain systems differ between humans and animals, or among animal species, we derive clues about the particular adaptive significance of specific cognitive operations and about the potential evolutionary advances some species might exhibit over others.

At the same time, and particularly with regard to investigations of declarative memory, there are special challenges associated with animal models of amnesia. Obviously animals do not express their memories by verbal declaration. Whether or not any animal species has a capacity for conscious recollection is a matter of scientific and philosophical debate. Furthermore, it is not clear what "explicit" expression means in the context of the common animal testing paradigms you will read about in this and succeeding chapters. These issues are major bottlenecks for research on animal memory in general, and for understanding declarative memory specifically. In this chapter and others that follow we will address how these challenges have been ignored, to the detriment of progress, and how they are currently being met with greater success.

Early Efforts

Almost immediately after the early reports on H.M. and other patients suffering the consequences of medial temporal lobe excision, efforts began to reproduce elements of the amnesic syndrome in monkeys. The major aim of these early efforts was to gain improved anatomical specificity, and to control for experience gained remotely prior to the brain damage. More generally, the properties of a valid animal model of the human amnesic syndrome were clearly outlined: (a) Sensory, motor, motivational, and cognitive processes should be intact; (b) in addition, short-term memory should be intact; (c) following preserved short-term performance, memory should decline with abnormal rapidity, that is, exceeding the rate of natural forgetting in intact control subjects; (d) the deficit should be global in scope for the to-be-learned materials; that is, the impairment should span sensory and conceptual modalities of new learning; and (e) there should be a graded retrograde impairment, so that learning accomplished recently prior to brain damage would be lost, whereas learning accomplished remotely long before the damage should be spared.

The early studies on monkeys, pursued initially by Scoville and Milner, began appropriately by reproducing the same pervasive medial temporal damage that was removed in H.M. Their behavioral assays focused on visual discrimination and matching-to-sample tasks that were already being used in comparative studies on the cognitive functions in monkeys. Testing typically involved the use of the Wisconsin General Testing Apparatus (WGTA), a telephone-booth-sized box composed of three chambers. Two outer chambers contained the experimenter and the monkey facing each other from opposite ends. A smaller stimulus display chamber separated the experimenter and monkey chambers, preventing the monkey from seeing the experimenter, who could raise and lower a series of guillotine doors to present stimuli and rewards on a horizontal board in the middle chamber. The board contained multiple inch-deep wells in which small food rewards (raisins, peanuts) could be hidden. The rewards in the wells were covered by discriminative stimuli the animal would use to guide its performance.

In visual discrimination training, typically there would be two stimuli for each problem, usually flat plaques painted with different colors or patterns, or easily discriminable three-dimensional objects. One stimulus would be arbitrarily assigned the "positive" and rewarded on each trial, and the other the "negative" value and never rewarded. The two stimuli would appear horizontally displaced covering two different food wells, and their left-right positions was carefully randomized across trials. The animal could obtain the reward by displacing a preassigned positive stimulus, uncovering the baited well. If the negative stimulus was displaced, uncovering the unbaited well, a door was quickly lowered to prevent the subject from correcting choice. The usual measure of learning was the number of trials required or errors made prior to reaching a criterion of accuracy, typically 90% correct performance over 20–30 trials. A simple variation of this task, called *spatial discrimination*, was to use two identical plain plaques as stimuli, and to reinforce choices to one place, the left or the right. Other variations involved alternation in consecutive trials between two different places or two different objects regardless of their locations.

Delayed matching to sample often employed the same WGTA and most of the same kind of stimuli and general procedures. However, each trial was composed of three distinct phases (Figure 6.1). In the first phase, called the *sample phase*, a single stimulus was presented covering a baited central well. After the sample was displaced and the reward secured, an opaque door was lowered for a variable delay phase during which the monkey had to remember the stimulus. In the third phase, called the *choice phase*, two stimuli were presented, each covering a lateral well. One stimulus was identical to the sample and was baited. The other stimulus was different and not baited. Typically in these early studies, the same two stimuli were reused on every trial, with the sample selected randomly across trials. As will be described later, there are several important variations on this task, employing different kinds of stimuli, a different "nonmatching" rule by which the subject must select the alternative to the sample item in the choice phase, and different testing chambers and stimulus presentation methods. The

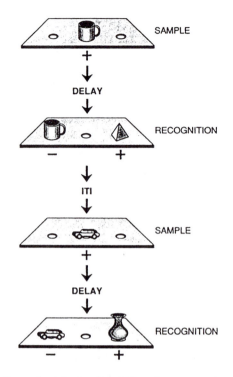

Figure 6.1. Illustration of trials in the delayed non-match to sample test with trial-unique objects as memory cues. (Reproduced, with permission, from Rapp & Amaral, 1989; Copyright Society for Neuroscience.)

variations in stimuli included the use of two identical plain plaques, and the requirement was for the subject to select the same location it had seen on the sample trial. This is called the *classic delayed-spatial-response task.*

So, how did the early efforts to model amnesia fare? Not impressively well. It was true that the general pattern of results was mostly consistent with the above-enumerated properties of amnesia. And some of those properties, such as preserved nonmemory and short-term memory capacities, as well as the global scope of the deficit, were very well modeled. But the *magnitude* of both the anterograde and the retrograde components of the memory deficit was quite modest compared to the apparent almost total loss of memory observed in H.M. Monkeys with substantial removals of all of the medial temporal lobe structures were only mildly impaired on learning new visual pattern, color, object, or auditory discrimination problems (Orbach et al., 1960; Kimble and Pribram, 1963; Correll and Scoville, 1965, 1967; Cordeau and Mahut, 1964). Furthermore, in these studies the investigators expected the critical variable in new learning to be the time interval between repeated stimulus presentations, with the specific expectation that because of rapid forgetting the monkeys with medial temporal damage would be more impaired when the interval was longer. Indeed the greatest deficit was observed when the monkeys were required to learn six discrimination problems intermixed, such that repetitions for each problem were separated by 5 min (Correll and Scoville, 1965), a subsequent study showed that the increased interference associated with learning multiple problems concurrently was the critical factor, and not the increased interval between trials associated with this situation (Correll and Scoville, 1970). Other studies concurred on the absence of a specific effect of memory delay, finding that the length of the intertrial interval had little influence on the modest deficit in discrimination learning by monkeys with medial temporal damage (Orbach et al., 1960; Kimble and Pribram, 1963; Correll and Scoville, 1970). In relearning visual pattern or object discriminations monkeys had acquired a few weeks prior to the surgery, significant deficits were observed compared to intact subjects (Orbach et al., 1960; Correll and Scoville, 1965). However, the *magnitude* of this retrograde impairment was also disappointing: Monkeys with medial temporal lobe damage merely showed less savings from the previous learning and not a complete loss of recently acquired information.

Furthermore, monkeys with medial temporal lobe lesions performed surprisingly well on matching to sample and other delayed-response tests (Correll and Scoville, 1965, 1967; Drachman and Ommaya, 1964). The task was trained preoperatively, and there was a retrograde impairment in reacquisition of the task with short delays. This loss of recent memory was consistent with the characteristics of human amnesia. However, having reacquired the task after the surgery, the monkeys performed rather well even at memory delay intervals of several seconds.

Some of the earliest studies also reported several other mixed findings, including deficits following medial temporal damage on spatial discrimination reversal, but not on delayed spatial response or spatial alternation with delays between trials, or on object reversal (Correll and Scoville, 1967; Mahut, 1971), although, on more difficult pattern discrimination tasks, deficits in discrimination reversal learning were observed (Spevak and Pribram, 1973). The deficit on spatial reversal was apparent for both visual and tactile presentation of stimuli (Mahut & Zola, 1973), and there was observed a complementary striking and paradoxical *facilitation* of object reversal learning (Zola & Mahut, 1973).

This pattern of results was becoming ever less consistent with the characteristics of human amnesia. Medial temporal lesions did succeed in producing retrograde loss of previous learning. But some of the findings pointed strongly to a specific deficit in the spatial modality, although even within spatial learning there were mixed results. And the magnitude of both the retrograde and anterograde impairments was very unimpressive compared to the findings from studies on amnesia in humans following the same brain damage. It was a state of affairs that led many to suggest that there might be a true species difference in the role of the medial temporal lobe in memory, so that memory relied much more on hippocampal function in humans than in animals.

Breakthrough

A breakthrough came with the combination of a novel twist in the procedures used for the delayed-matching-to-sample task combined with a modification in the approach to removing medial temporal lobe structures. The key aspects of the task variant, first reported by Gaffan (1974) and shortly after characterized in detail by Mishkin and Delacour (1975), involved the use of new sets of stimulus objects on each trial (the *trial-unique stimulus procedure*) plus a nonmatching reward contingency. Thus, on each trial, the sample was a novel three-dimensional "junk" object. Then, to obtain a reward during the choice phase, the subject was required to select a different novel junk object over the now-familiar sample object. Because an entirely novel sample is used on each trial, it is appropriate to think of this task as a test of recognition for the newly familiar object. Notably this characterization of the task is quite different from that of the task where the same stimuli are used repeatedly; in such a situation both stimuli are highly familiar, so their potential for recognition would hardly differentiate them.

The distinction between the trial-unique and repetitive stimulus procedures could not have had a more profound effect on monkeys' performance in the delayed matching (or nonmatching) task. In a detailed analysis Mishkin and Delacour (1975) compared performance when the same stimuli were used repetitively on all trials versus trial-unique stimuli, and they compared performance under the matching versus nonmatching rules. The results were clear-cut in showing that prolonged training of nearly 1,000 trials was required for subjects to learn either the matching or the nonmatching rule with repetitive stimuli, whereas much less training was required with trial-unique stimuli. In addition, the nonmatching rule was easier to acquire than the matching rule, with the former requiring only about 100 training trials and the latter about 400 trials. The finding that delayed-nonmatching-to-sample (DNMS) with trial-unique cues is optimal was attributed to monkeys' innate attraction to manipulating novel objects. The use of trial-unique stimuli and the nonmatching rule both emphasized and exploited this natural aspect of monkey behavior.

Gaffan (1974) was the first to report that monkeys with damage to the hippocampal region were impaired in performance on a delayed-matching-to-sample task with trial-unique stimuli. In this study the damage involved a transection of the fornix, the major fiber bundle connecting the hippocampus with subcortical structures (see below). In initial training following the fornix transection, there was no deficit in acquiring the task using a short 10-s memory delay. In addition monkeys with fornix transections performed as well as intact subjects (over 90% correct) at the shortest memory delays, demonstrating that they could perceive the objects, encode them into very-short-term memory, and perform the matching rule to obtain rewards (Figure 6.2). However, a substantial deficit appeared if the delay was increased to above 1 min. In addition, Gaffan examined performance in another variant of the task where multiple sample objects were presented in sequence, and then memory for them was tested with a subsequent series of choice tests. In this assessment, monkeys with fornix transections also performed well with the minimal one-item list but were substantially impaired when multiple samples had to be held in memory concurrently.

Mishkin (1978) used a different surgical approach and the nonmatching variant of the task but came to the same conclusions about the selective role of the hippocampal region in this type of recognition memory. Initially a set of monkeys was trained on the DNMS task using a short 10-s memory delay. Then Mishkin employed a novel two-component surgical procedure by which he first elevated

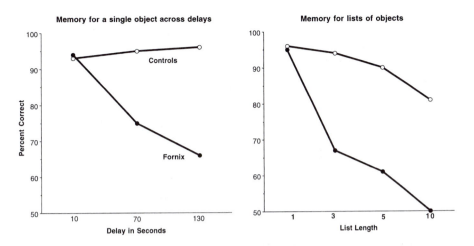

Figure 6.2. Performance of intact monkeys and monkeys with fornix transection on delayed non-match to sample. (Reproduced, with permission, from Gaffan, 1974; Copyright American Psychological Association.)

the frontal lobes and removed the amygdala as well as cortex surrounding it and then elevated the temporo-occipital cortex and removed the hippocampus and cortex surrounding it. This combination hippocampus-amygdala ablation resulted in a substantial deficit in relearning DNMS, requiring about 10 times the number of trials required for preoperative learning. In addition, when the memory delay was increased to 30–120 s or a list of 3–10 objects was used, substantial drops in performance were observed in monkeys with the combined hippocampus-amygdala lesions, compared to continued superb performance by intact controls. In addition, Mishkin also tested subjects with either hippocampus or amygdala ablation alone and found the impairments to be mild at most. Thus he concluded that the full duplication of structures removed from the medial temporal lobe area in H.M. was required to obtain a substantial memory impairment.

It is worth emphasizing, once again, how important was the development of the trial-unique stimulus presentation procedure. In a later study Owen and Butler (1981) directly compared the effects of fornix transection on delayed non-matching to sample with trial-unique and trial-repeated stimuli. Like Gaffan (1974) they found that monkeys with fornix transection acquired the trial-unique stimulus version of the task at a normal rate, performed well at short delays, but were impaired at long delays. Acquisition of the trial-repeated stimulus version of the task was difficult for all subjects, and performance declined very rapidly at increasing delays even in normal subjects. However, by contrast with the impairment in the trial-unique stimulus version of DNMS, there was no impairment associated with fornix transection when the same stimuli were used on each trial. These findings indicate that impairment on DNMS is not seen under all conditions where the performance demands challenge normal animals, such as with long delays or sample lists on trial-unique DNMS. There was no deficit even though the trial-repeated version of the task is quite difficult for normal monkeys.

Rather, the different pattern of results on the two task variants seems to emphasize the special nature of the trial-unique stimuli in depending on recognition for newly familiar items.

In sum the Gaffan and Mishkin studies, both involving the invention of the trial-unique delayed-matching and nonmatching tasks, constituted a major breakthrough for the development of the nonhuman primate model of amnesia. They led to two directions of research progress that depended on the animal model, one focused on the scope of memory processing that depends on medial temporal lobe structures, and the other focused on which components of the medial temporal lobe region are critical.

The Pattern of Impaired and Spared Memory Following Hippocampal Damage in Monkeys

The introduction of a new benchmark assessment of amnesia monkeys based on the DNMS task opened up the opportunity to readdress whether this approach would indeed provide a valid model of the fundamental characteristics of human amnesia. Recall that these characteristics include spared nonmemory functions and short-term memory in the face of rapid forgetting, global scope of amnesia across learning materials, and graded retrograde amnesia.

A central issue is the selectivity of the deficit to memory and the sparing of perceptual, motor, motivational, and attentional or other cognitive functions. The DNMS task provides an automatic and ideal control in that all of those nonmemory functions are fully required even when in the absence of a memory delay. Thus, if monkeys with medial temporal lobe damage perform normally at the shortest delay, it must be that they can attend to, perceive, and encode the object cues; that they can execute the choice responses; that they are motivated to participate in the task; and that they can acquire and retain the nonmatching rule.

Producing a DNMS task with no memory delay at all is problematic because, quite simply, the manually operated WGTA apparatus requires 8–10 s to exchange sample and choice objects. Nevertheless, in the original Gaffan (1974) study, as well as in the replication by Owen and Butler (1981), monkeys with fornix transections indeed acquired the task with the shortest delays at a fully normal rate. However, in his initial study Mishkin (1978) found that monkeys with complete medial temporal ablations were deficient in the postoperative reacquisition of DNMS at short delays, requiring on average almost 1,000 trials to relearn the task compared to full retention in intact control subjects. Subsequent studies have confirmed this finding (e.g., Zola-Morgan & Squire, 1985; Malamut et al., 1984), leaving it unclear whether the minimal 8 to10-s delay is a sufficient memory demand to benefit by a contribution from medial temporal lobe structures, or whether medial temporal lobe damage results in a nonmemory impairment that is eventually overcome with extended training.

To address this issue directly, Alvarez et al. (1994) developed an automated version of the DNMS task that employed complex visual patterns presented on a "touch screen" of a video display. This computerized task allowed them to use 0.5-s delays during acquisition of the DNMS task. The task was much more difficult than the conventional version of DNMS, probably because the stimuli were now two-dimensional patterns instead of three-dimensional objects, so that intact subjects required approximately 2,000 trials to learn the task at the brief delay. Nevertheless, following an ablation that included the hippocampus and surrounding cortex, the rate of learning was fully normal. Furthermore, in subsequent testing with delays up to 10 min, normal monkeys showed a gradual decline in performance (forgetting), and at delays exceeding 1 s, a deficit in monkeys with hippocampal damage emerged. Notably the magnitude of the impairment was modest: less than a 10% difference in accuracy at a 10-min delay. Nevertheless the rapid forgetting effect was highly reliable, demonstrating a selective deficit in the memory component of this delayed-nonmatching-to-sample task.

Another characteristic of human amnesia is that the deficit is apparent regardless of the nature of the learning materials. That is, the impairment is global with regard to the stimulus modality of items to be remembered. Shortly after Mishkin's (1978) initial report, this issue was addressed by Murray and Mishkin (1984). They developed a variant of the DNMS task in which monkeys were initially trained on the conventional version of the DNMS task and then retrained with the room lights dimmed to complete darkness. The position of the sample and choice objects was indicated by light-emitting diodes, but these did not provide sufficient illumination to see the objects. Thus the animals had to perceive and encode the objects entirely by tactual cues. Normal monkeys required about twice as many trials to relearn the task in the dark, but performance was over 90% correct in the final preoperative stage of tactual DNMS testing even over long delays (Figure 6.3). In subsequent testing after surgeries, normal animals immediately reacquired the task and performed well at all delays. After removal of the hippocampus, amygdala, and surrounding cortex, relearning at a short de-

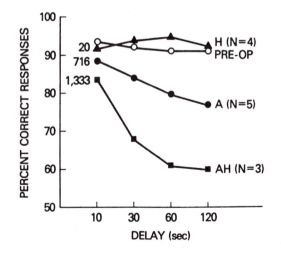

Figure 6.3. Performance on tactual delayed non-match to sample by monkeys before surgery (PRE-OP) and after surgical removal of the hippocampus (H), amygdala (A) or both structures (AH). (Reproduced, with permission, from Murray & Mishkin, 1984; Copyright Society for Neuroscience.)

lay was substantially impaired, and the deficit grew as the delay was elongated to 2 min. Thus the pattern of sparing of ultimate performance at a short delay and increasing impairment at longer delays was identical to that observed for the visually guided version of the same task, demonstrating the multimodal scope of the amnesic deficit.

In addition, the scope of the amnesic deficit has also been extended to several variants on delayed matching to sample and object learning. Mishkin and colleagues found that the scope of the impairment following damage to the hippo-campus-amygdala and surrounding cortex includes a similar deficit on delayed matching (instead of nonmatching) to sample using trial-unique objects as stimuli (Murray & Mishkin, 1984; Malamut et al., 1984). In addition, they also found that medial temporal lobe ablation results in the same pattern of spared short-term memory and rapid forgetting in a reward association version of the task where displacements of separate sample objects are either rewarded or not rewarded, and then the subject is forced to select a previously rewarded object over a nonre-warded object in the choice phase. This task differs in that the choice items are equally familiar and the monkey has to remember their previous reward status to guide choice performance.

In an effort to create a battery of tasks for memory assessment, Zola-Morgan and Squire (1985) confirmed the findings of Mishkin (1978) on the DNMS task and demonstrated parallel impairments on other tasks in monkeys with complete medial temporal lobe ablations (Figure 6.4). They found that these monkeys demonstrate a similar pattern of performance on the classic spatial delayed-response task in which the stimuli consist of two identical black plaques and the left-right location of the sample must be remembered over a variable delay. Monkeys with medial temporal ablations learned the delayed-response task at the same rate as normal subjects and performed equally well at short delays. However, their performance fell off abnormally rapidly when the delay was increased to 15–30 s. They also examined the performance of these monkeys on two different versions of simple object discrimination tasks. In one of these tasks, monkeys learned novel two-object discriminations. On each problem one object was consistently associated with reward and the other not rewarded on successive 20 trials. Monkeys with medial temporal damage were impaired in accuracy on the initial training day, and impairments were observed on retesting at 24-hr and 48-hr intervals. Finally, these monkeys were also trained on a concurrent object discrimination task in which eight different discrimination problems were presented for five trials each intermingled in each training session. This was a difficult problem in that normal monkeys required on average over 500 trials to reach near-perfect performance on all the pairs. Animals with medial temporal lobe damage required even more trials, on average over 1,000, to reach the same criterion. Combining the findings among these tasks, the scope of the amnesic deficit is observed across a variety of stimuli and response demands and different levels of difficulty of the various problems. Importantly, human amnesics tested on a similar set of tasks showed a similar pattern of deficits across the same memory demands (Squire et al., 1988; Aggleton et al., 1988).

Another central characteristic of the amnesic syndrome is the phenomenon of graded retrograde memory loss. As described in chapter 5, H.M. and other amnesic patients display a loss of memories backward in time from the moment of

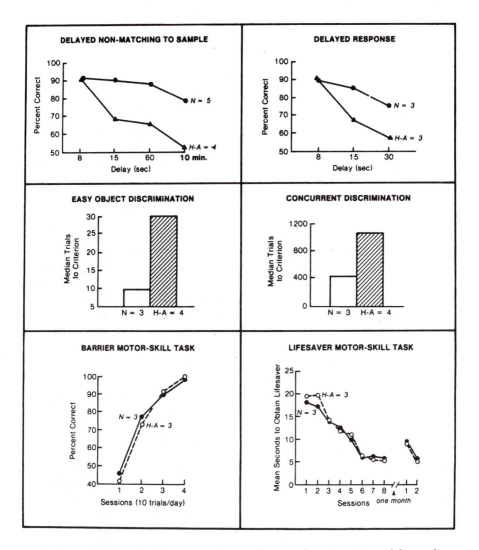

Figure 6.4. A battery of memory tests for monkeys, and comparisons of the performance of normal animals (N) and animals with combined hippocampus-amygdala (and surrounding cortical) removals. (Reproduced, with permission, from Zola-Morgan & Squire, 1984; Copyright Society for Neuroscience.)

brain damage, with the most severe loss in the period just prior to the damage and total sparing of remotely acquired memories, including childhood recollections and general knowledge acquired early in life. However, a major problem in the interpretation of retrograde memory loss in human patients is that the amount and timing of prior learning experiences can only be estimated roughly. Conversely, one of the major advantages of an animal model of amnesia is that one can examine the retrograde loss of memories with a prospective design. That is, one can provide measured amounts of learning at specific times prior to brain damage that occurs suddenly. In so doing, one can directly compare the strength of memories acquired at different times in intact animals, and one can more accurately measure the period and magnitude of retrograde loss.

Unfortunately, the DNMS task is unsuitable for this kind of study because single exposures to objects do not provide sufficiently strong memories to endure testing weeks or months after learning. To address this issue and develop a task that would be suitable for a study of retrograde memory, Zola-Morgan and Squire (1990) developed an object discrimination task where subjects were presented with pairs of novel objects like those used in DNMS testing, and they repeatedly reinforced the choice of one object over the other (see chapter 10 for procedural details). Normal monkeys scored about 80% correct on last acquired problems, and their performance declined to as low as 60% for more remotely learned problems, showing some forgetting for problems learned more than 2 months before. By contrast, monkeys with hippocampal damage were substantially impaired, performing at just above 60% on problems presented within 2 weeks of the surgery. They performed significantly better on remotely learned discriminations, those acquired 4 months prior to the surgery. This pattern of recent retrograde memory loss and spared remote memory, emphasized most strikingly by worse performance on recent than on remote memory within the hippocampal group, provides compelling evidence that damage to the hippocampal region results in a graded retrograde amnesia (see chapter 10 for an extended discussion).

In addition to the above-discussed aspects of *impaired* learning and memory following hippocampal damage, there is the critical characterization of a *spared* domain of new learning capacity in H.M. and other amnesic patients. Toward the goal of modeling this phenomenon, there are specific examples that represent a domain of spared learning in monkeys following ablation of the entire medial temporal lobe. One spared domain that closely parallels intact motor skill learning in human amnesics is the acquisition of manual skills in monkeys. Zola-Morgan and Squire (1984) devised two manual skill tests on which monkeys could be trained in the WGTA. One of these involved training the monkeys to reach around a clear barrier to obtain a reward. Another involved challenging the monkeys to obtain a doughnut-shaped candy ('Lifesaver') reward that was presented in the middle of an irregularly bent stiff wire (a coat hanger). To rapidly retrieve the reward the monkey had to improve its manual manipulation of the candy around the turns of the coat hanger. In both tasks Zola-Mogan and Squire found that monkeys with medial temporal damage improved in performance at the same rate as normal subjects, demonstrating preserved motor skill learning in amnesia (Figure 6.4).

Another domain of learning that appears to be spared following medial temporal lobe damage is the acquisition and retention of single visual discrimination problems that are acquired gradually. This spared learning capacity was described in some of the early studies on medial temporal lobe ablations in monkeys (Orbach et al., 1960) and was reexamined by Malamut et al. (1984) using the same junk object stimuli employed in DNMS. In this study monkeys were presented with one trial per day on each of 20 different object discriminations, and this was repeated for each monkey until it reached a criterion of 90 correct responses out of 100 consecutive trials. Monkeys were trained on two sets of such problems preoperatively. Following the surgery, they were retrained on the same problems, then trained on a new set of 20 problems. Overall the results were that intact monkeys showed good retention of the previously acquired problems and learned a new set in an average of eight training sessions.

Monkeys with complete medial temporal lobe ablations, and no damage to the adjacent visual cortical areas, also showed good retention and no impairment in new learning. These results were contrasted with a replication of the impairment on a variant of the DNMS task in which the matching (rather than nonmatching) rule applied. Thus, even with the same learning rule that required subjects to choose objects that had been previously rewarded, the findings across the two tasks strongly contrasted. When repeated presentations of stimuli were separated by 24 hrs in the concurrent discrimination task, monkeys with medial temporal ablations performed well. However, when repeated presentations occurred in periods longer than 1 sec but within 1 min, the same monkeys were severely impaired.

These findings may seem confusing: If monkeys with medial temporal damage forget abnormally rapidly, why would they be impaired when the requirement is to remember objects for a minute, but not impaired in a task that requires accumulated learning across trials that span a day? An intriguing interpretation of these data is that medial temporal structures sustain the representation for single presentations of an object for a relatively short period spanning no more than several minutes (Eichenbaum et al., 1994). Under this view, medial temporal lobe structures do not participate in 24-hr retention of single trial presentations, and therefore having a functional medial temporal lobe provides no advantage in solving this version of the concurrent discrimination problem. To the extent that is the case, removal of the medial temporal lobe would not be expected to result in a deficit in learning, as observed. However, this does not address the issue of how even the intact monkeys solve this problem. The view proposed here is that the learning of biases toward or away from specific stimuli can be accomplished entirely with the intact cortical areas responsible for visual processing necessary to performance in this task (see chapter 4). Supporting this view, Malamut et al. (1984) found that when their medial temporal lesions encroached upon the inferotemporal visual area, deficits in relearning these concurrent discriminations emerged. Importantly, this particular finding is not consistent with assessments of 24-hr concurrent learning that have been employed on human amnesics (Squire et al., 1988). Whereas normal humans subjects improve gradually on a version of this task created for humans, amnesics show very little learning in this situation. This discrepancy does limit the animal model to some extent and suggests that humans and monkeys may solve the problem in different ways.

Combining the findings from across all of these tasks, the nonhuman primate model of amnesia is largely validated. Monkeys with complete medial temporal lobe ablations similar to the surgery performed on H.M. show intact nonmemory capacities. They also show spared short-term memory as well as intact memory for information acquired remotely prior to the surgery. The scope of the deficit is global across spatial, visual, and tactile stimulus modalities and extends to reward association as well as simple recognition. Finally, there is a spared domain of new learning capacity, reflected in normal acquisition of motor skills and gradually acquired sensory discriminations.

Delineating the Role of Anatomical Components of the Medial Temporal Lobe

Having succeeded in the development of a set of behavioral assessments that characterize amnesia in monkeys with medial temporal lobe ablations, highest among the next goals was to determine which temporal lobe structures are critical. In H.M. the entire medial temporal lobe region was removed, including the amygdala, the hippocampus, and the immediately surrounding cortex. Furthermore, each of these major areas is composed of several subdivisions. The amygdala is a composite of several interconnected nuclei. The hippocampus has several serially connected subdivisions. And the surrounding cortex is composed of at least three cytoarchitecturally distinct areas, including the entorhinal, perirhinal, and parahippocampal cortex. Which of these areas is critical to memory?

Milner's (1974) survey of the early neuropsychological studies on human amnesia suggested that it is the hippocampus, because the magnitude of amnesia seemed to correlate with the extent of hippocampal damage across several cases; indeed, there was a patient in whom the amygdala was damaged but the hippocampus spared and no memory deficit was observed. As discussed above, Mishkin (1978) argued from his initial findings that damage to both the amygdala and hippocampus was required to produce a severe memory deficit. Milner's and Mishkin's conclusions are generally consistent with one another, but both overlooked the potential contribution of the surrounding cortical areas. The following discussion will outline the course of research using the behavioral model described above to provide a preliminary answer to this question. A central technical issue in this story concerns the surgical approach used in the early studies, as well as the strategies taken to address problems with that approach. As mentioned above, in most of the studies so far discussed, as in H.M., the surgery involved a direct visually guided approach to removing the amygdala and hippocampus (Figure 6.5). Because both of these structures are buried under the temporal cortex, this approach required removing at least part of the surrounding perirhinal, entorhinal, and parahippocampal cortex to reach either the amygdala or the hippocampus. So, in those studies, a hippocampal or an amygdala ablation always included part of this cortex, confounding the interpretation of the data and not allowing the investigators to conclude with confidence that either of those buried structures was itself critical. As it turns out, this was a problem that led to some false conclusions, as you will see below. Readers interested in more details on this story should also read reviews by Zola-Morgan and Squire (1992) and Murray (1996).

One part of the story about which there is general agreement is that the amygdala is not critical to the kind of memory modeled by these tasks. Zola-Morgan and colleagues (1989b, 1991) most directly addressed this issue by developing a stereotaxic surgical method that allowed them to selectively ablate the amygdala, including virtually all of its nuclei, without damaging the surrounding cortical areas. Circumscribed lesions of the amygdala had no effect on performance on tasks for which larger medial temporal ablation produces a deficit—specifically DNMS (Figure 6.6), retention of object discriminations—and concurrent object discrimination. And amygdala lesions did not affect performance on tasks for

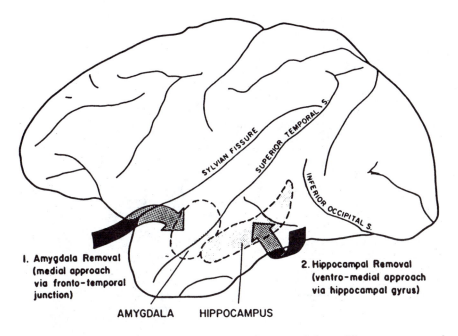

Figure 6.5. Surgical approach for removing the amygdala or hippocampus, and both of these were used to remove both structures. Note that each approach requires a removal of some of the surrounding cortex. (Reproduced, with permission, from Squire & Zola-Morgan, 1983; Copyright Academic Press.)

which performance is impaired by larger medial temporal ablations, including visual pattern discrimination and the Lifesaver motor skill task.These lesions were not entirely benign, in that the same monkeys showed alterations in emotional responsiveness. When shown either neutral objects, such as a rubber boot or a set of keys, or potentially threatening objects, such as a rubber snake or a mirror, normal monkeys simply visually inspect the stimulus, evoke no response, or avoid it. By contrast, monkeys with amygdala lesions manually or orally contact these stimuli. The increased reactivity and manipulation of stimuli by monkeys with amygdala lesions was distinctly dissociated from the memory deficits observed in other subjects with hippocampal damage but no amygdala damage. Damage to both the hippocampal region and the amygdala resulted in abnormalities in both emotional reactivity and memory. Amygdala lesions do result in deficits on other memory tasks, and these will be characterized later. For now, the bottom line is that the deficits in DNMS and related tasks following large medial temporal lobe ablations can not be attributed to damage to the amygdala per se.

The other obvious structure that was implicated in the early neuropsychological studies of human amnesia was the hippocampus. Its specific role, independent of the surrounding cortex, has been examined in two general ways.One approach, used from the outset by Gaffan and colleagues (e.g., Gaffan, 1974), has been to transect the fornix, the major fiber bundle connecting the hippocampus

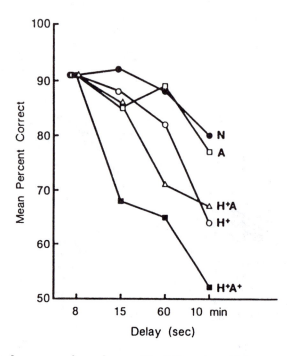

Figure 6.6. Performance of monkeys with different medial temporal lesions on DNMS. N = normal controls; A = amygdala (stereotaxic); H+ = hippocampus (surgical); others are combinations of these lesions. (Reproduced from Zola-Morgan, Squire, & Amaral, 1989; Copyright Society for Neuroscience.)

with subcortical areas. Using this lesion as a substitute for direct hippocampal ablation has been, and continues to be, controversial. Transection of the fornix cuts off substantial inputs and outputs of the hippocampus, and so it seems likely that the hippocampus could not process information fully normally after this lesion. And unlike direct hippocampal ablation, fornix transection does not cut off substantial fibers of the cortex surrounding the hippocampus. So, as Gaffan has argued (e.g., Rupniak & Gaffan, 1987), fornix transection may be the most selective way to disrupt the functions of the hippocampus. However, others view fornix transection as at the same time too extensive and too limited to substitute for a hippocampal ablation. Fornix transection can be viewed as too extensive because it eliminates connections of all hippocampal subdivisions, including those of the subiculum (see chapter 9), which some do not consider a part of the hippocampus proper. Also, a fornix transection can be viewed as too limited because it does not interrupt connections between hippocampal subdivisions and the cortex, which are thought of by most as the main information-bearing conduits for hippocampal memory processing. That is, even after a fornix transection, cortical information can reach the hippocampus, and the hippocampus can send the outcomes of its processing back to cortex. So one might not expect a fornix transection to eliminate the main contributions of the hippocampus to cortical memory processing.

Despite these concerns, as described above, Gaffan (1974; see also Owen & Butler, 1981) described a severe deficit in delayed matching to sample with trial-unique object stimuli following fornix transection. However, subsequent efforts by Mishkin and colleagues (Bachevalier et al., 1985), Zola-Morgan and colleagues (1989a), and Gaffan himself (1994) found that the deficit following fornix transection was modest compared to that of medial temporal lobe ablation. In addition, damage to the mammillary bodies, a major subcortical target of fornix fibers, also had relatively little effect (Zola-Morgan et al., 1989a; Aggleton & Mishkin, 1985). Nevertheless, we recommend you reserve a final conclusion about this approach to producing hippocampal dysfunction until after consideration of the results from other methods.

The other approaches involve direct and selective damage to the hippocampus itself in one of three ways (Figure 6.7). One method involves the production of a transient ischemic event, cutting off circulation to the cerebral cortex for a few minutes. This procedure, when appropriately limited in time, results in a severe but seemingly selective loss of hippocampal cells. Following this procedure monkeys show a pattern of performance that reflects the essential impairment on long-delay DNMS and spared pattern discrimination (Zola-Morgan et al., 1992). The DNMS deficit was equivalent to that following lesions of the hippocampus

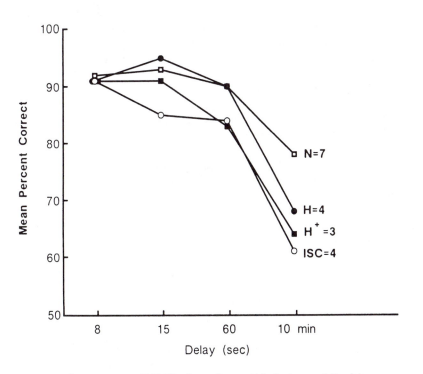

Figure 6.7. Performance on DNMS of monkeys with lesions of the hippocampus produced in three different ways. N = normal controls; H = stereotaxic lesion with radiofrequency current; H+ = surgical removal of hippocampus and surrounding cortex; ISC = transient ischemia.

plus immediately surrounding cortex, suggesting the cortical damage added little to the deficit. However, the deficit was also less severe in other ways, including no impairment in learning DNMS at a minimal delay, no impairment on concurrent object discrimination, and a smaller impairment on retention of object discriminations. Furthermore, the method of producing selective hippocampal damage by ischemia has been criticized because of the possibility that there may be occult damage to other brain areas not revealed by conventional histological analyses (Bachevalier & Meunier, 1996). Although there are arguments on both sides of this issue (Squire & Zola, 1996), the criticisms of this method prevent it from providing compelling evidence on the issue of specific hippocampal involvement.

The other methods for producing selective hippocampal ablations involve the development of stereotaxic operation procedures that permit direct damage to the hippocampus without ancillary cortical damage. Accomplishing this was somewhat of a technical feat, because the exact location of the hippocampus in the temporal lobe is highly variable in monkeys. To attain the required selectivity and completeness of a lesion, a special atlas is created for each monkey, first by initially implanting radio-opaque beads on the skull surface, then by making a series of MRI images that show both the hippocampus and the beads. Subsequently the damage is produced by positioning special electrodes at measured loci relative to the observable skull beads. The damage to the hippocampal tissue has been accomplished by two different methods: by passing radiofrequency current that heats a local area of tissue (Alvarez et al., 1991) and by microinjection of the neurotoxin ibotenic acid (O'Boyle et al., 1995; Murray & Mishkin, 1998).

In the initial reports of these lesions by Alvarez et al. (1995), monkeys with selective hippocampal damage, like those with the larger lesions that included cortical damage, were impaired at long-delay performance on the DNMS task, although the deficit was modest (Figure 6.7). And the monkeys with the selective hippocampal lesions were not impaired at the pattern discrimination task or the Lifesaver retrieval task. However, the magnitude of the memory impairment was modest, appearing only at the 10- and 40-min delays in DNMS, and there was no deficit on retention of object discriminations or on the concurrent object discrimination. Most important, the magnitude of the deficit was quite modest, no more than a 10% decline in performance at the long delays. Furthermore, the findings on fornix transection become more interesting in light of these data, in that the research from the same laboratory showed that the effects of a fornix lesion also produced a decline of about 10% in long-delay performance (Zola-Morgan et al., 1989a). So, it appears after all that transection of the fornix may indeed disrupt the hippocampal contribution to DNMS performance. The surprise is that the magnitude of the hippocampal contribution is quite small. A recent compilation of data from a large group of monkeys with selective hippocampal damage produced by ischemia, radiofrequency lesions, or ibotenic acid infusions revealed a statistically reliable deficit that appears as early as with a 15-s delay (Zola et al., 2000). This finding is consistent with the finding on rapid memory loss in human amnesia, but the magnitude of the deficit observed in monkeys was quite small.

Furthermore, in parallel studies where monkeys were trained on the DNMS task preoperatively, and injections of ibotenic acid were used to ablate both the hippocampus and the amygdala selectively without damaging the underlying cortex, no impairment was observed. These monkeys performed fully normally on the conventional DNMS task with delays as long as 2 min or sample lists as long as 10 items (O'Boyle et al., 1995). In addition, to test whether an impairment would emerge with even longer delays and lists, Murray and Mishkin (1998) developed a variant of the DNMS task where a list of 40 sample objects was presented at 30-s intervals. Subsequently choice tests were presented in the reverse order at 30-s intervals, so that the effective memory delays spanned from 30 s to 40 min, and the longest delay was filled with all of the other testing. Under these difficult conditions normal monkeys showed very good performance up to 5-min delays, with a smooth dropping in performance to about 60% correct at delays over 20 min (Figure 6.8). Monkeys with ablations of the hippocampus and amygdala showed a virtually identical pattern of performance.

These findings of modest or no effect of selective hippocampal damage contrasted sharply with data from contemporaneous studies that examined the role of the cortical areas immediately surrounding the hippocampus and amygdala. Parallel experiments by Murray and Mishkin and colleagues (Murray & Mishkin, 1986; Meunier et al., 1993) and by Zola-Morgan and Squire and colleagues (1989c; Suzuki et al., 1993) provided compelling evidence that damage to the combined perirhinal, parahippocampal, and entorhinal cortex produces a very

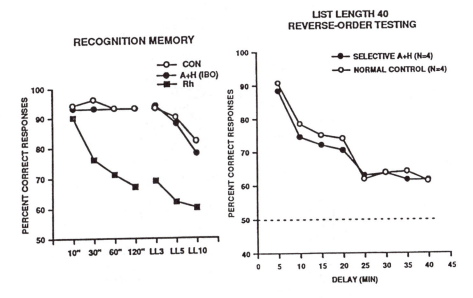

Figure 6.8. Performance of monkeys with different medial temporal lesions on single object DNMS (left) and on a variant in which a list of 40 items is tested in the reverse order of their presentation (right). CON = normal controls; A+H (IBO) = ibotenic acid lesions of the amygdala and hippocampus; Rh = lesion of rhinal cortex (perirhinal plus entorhinal areas). (Reproduced, with permission, from Murray & Mishkin, 1998; Copyright Society for Neuroscience.)

severe deficit on the acquisition, long-delay, and sample-list performance of DNMS, as well as on retention of object discriminations and concurrent object discrimination, and on the acquisition and long delay performance of the tactual version of DNMS (Figures 6.8, left; Figure 6.9). Furthermore there was no impairment on pattern discrimination. The severity of the impairment was at least as great as that of the original combined medial temporal lobe ablation that involved the hippocampus, amygdala, and surrounding cortex. Indeed, to achieve the learning criterion with short delays on DNMS, monkeys with damage to the perirhinal and entorhinal cortex required remedial training with repetition of the sample trial. Finally, there appears to be a hierarchy of importance of distinct areas within this region. Perirhinal damage produces the greatest deficit, parahippocampal lesions less effect, and entorhinal lesions a significant, yet lesser, effect.

One possible explanation of the results of the cortical lesions is that this ablation completely disconnects the hippocampus. Because a direct hippocampal lesion is never complete, the cortical ablation might disrupt hippocampal processing even more than the direct method. And on theoretical grounds, it is precisely the cortical-hippocampal interactions that are viewed as critical to memory (see chapter 9). However, other studies by both these groups showed that extensive damage to this cortical region exacerbates the effects of complete removal of hippocampus itself by the direct surgical approach, showing that the effect of the cortical damage cannot be accounted for as simply a complete hippocampal disconnection (Zola-Morgan et al., 1993; Meunier et al., 1993). One other study might have been of relevance here: Bachevalier et al. (1985) found a severe mem-

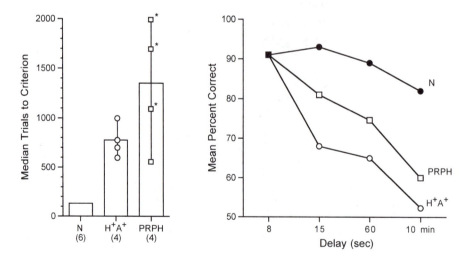

Figure 6.9. Performance of normal monkeys (N) and monkeys with large lesions of the medial temporal area (H+A+) or selective removal of the perirhinal and parahippocampal cortex (PRPH) on DNMS. LEFT: Trials to acquire the task at the shortest memory delay. RIGHT: Performance across delays. (Reproduced, with permission, from Zola-Morgan, Squire, Amaral, & Suzuki, 1989; Copyright Society for Neuroscience.)

ory impairment in monkeys following the combination of a fornix transection and severing of amygdalofugal pathways. This finding was originally interpreted as supporting Mishkin's argument that combined hippocampal and amygdala disruption were necessary and sufficient to produce the memory deficit. But it has become clear that these lesions undercut fibers of the cortical areas surrounding the hippocampus and amygdala.

In quantitative comparisons of the effects of different versions of hippocampal damage, Zola-Morgan et al. (1994) argued that the magnitude of the deficit on DNMS and other tasks is significant with selective hippocampal damage alone and becomes increasingly severe with added damage to the surrounding cortex (Figure 6.10). However, another way to view this same data set is an account that asserts that the magnitude of the deficit is directly proportional to the amount of damage to the cortical areas of the medial temporal lobe. According to this view, the selective hippocampal lesion may produce an effect only to the extent that the radiofrequency lesions in the hippocampus results in cell loss in the afferent

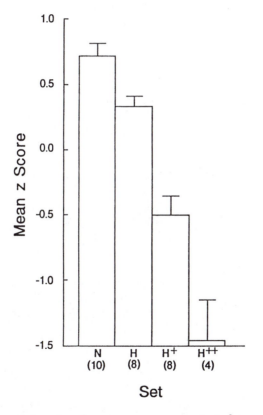

Figure 6.10. Comparison of performance on memory tests by monkeys with different types of hippocampal lesions. Z-scores were based on a combination of performances on DNMS and easy object discrimination. (Reproduced, with permission, from Zola-Morgan, Squire, & Ramus, 1994; Copyright John Wiley & Sons, Inc.)

areas of the surrounding cortex, as noted in the histological analyses of the brains (Alvarez et al., 1995).

What Does the Hippocampus Itself Do?

The findings described above do not bode well for the original view that the hippocampus itself is the critical brain area for memory. Alternatively, it is possible that the DNMS task, as well as its relatives used in that test battery, are more sensitive to memory-processing functions of the cortical areas surrounding the hippocampus than to the contribution of the hippocampus itself. The functional role of those cortical areas will be discussed in detail in chapter 9. The remainder of this chapter will focus on other experimental protocols that suggest there is a role for the hippocampus itself in memory in monkeys. Indeed there have been several studies that have shown deficits in learning and memory following damage to the hippocampus itself or indirectly by way of fornix transection. These two approaches will be treated equivalently here, even though some have criticized the applicability of fornix transections to studies of hippocampal function (see above). Keep in mind that the effects of fornix transection and of direct hippocampal lesions were equivalent on the DNMS task; at least in that sense, these lesions are equivalent.

The early findings indicated hippocampal or fornix damage disrupts spatial discrimination and reversal learning in the WGTA (e.g., Mahut & Zola, 1973), and a more recent study has confirmed that fornix transection causes an impairment in some types of simple spatial learning and reversal (Gaffan, 1994a; 1994b). In addition, Murray et al. (1989) trained monkeys on a DNMS task using a T-maze, similar to the kind of task that has received widespread use in testing memory in rats (see next chapter). Monkeys with fornix transections were severely impaired in this task. However, the overall pattern of data on fornix lesions and learning guided by spatial cues is mixed. Gaffan and colleagues (Gaffan & Harrison 1989; Rupniak & Gaffan, 1987) have shown that learning guided by spatial as well as object cues can be either impaired or spared following fornix lesions, depending on whether or not successful performance demands processing complex configurations of objects and background cues. Monkeys with hippocampal system damage performed as well as normal subjects when the reward assignment of objects was contingent on the place in the test room where the cues were presented but were severely impaired when object-reward assignments depended on the configuration of the cues within backgrounds composed of the same stimuli.

Gaffan (1985) also argued that the critical requirement that involves hippocampal function is that the animals must remember spatial or other cues to guide movements, rather than the use of spatial cues in general. In one study, Rupniak and Gaffan (1987) reported that monkeys with fornix lesions are also impaired in using visual patterns to select go or no-go touching movements, indicating that the deficit may be in associating movements with any type of external stimulus. Other studies have presented mixed results on the effects of fornix lesions on go, no-go visual discrimination learning (e.g., Mahut, 1972), leaving it unclear what aspects of simple discrimination learning are sensitive to fornix lesions. A recent study by Wise and Murray (1999; see also Murray & Wise, 1996) offers a possible resolution to the mixed results from the previous studies on stimulus response associations. Monkeys were trained to repeatedly learn sets of new arbitrary associations between specific visual patterns presented on a video screen and directional movements of a joy stick. For example, pattern A might be associated with upward movement of the joystick, whereas pattern B was associated with a rightward movement and pattern C with a downward movement. Normal monkeys developed a strong learning set, such that they could learn new sets of associations within a few trials each. By contrast, following damage to the hippocampus and adjacent parahippocampal cortex, these monkeys showed a persistent impairment, making many more errors than prior to surgery. These findings indicate that hippocampal damage does result in an impairment in stimulus response learning, under conditions where multiple problems are learned rapidly by normal subjects.

In addition, Gaffan (1994b) reported a persistent impairment in concurrent learning of complex visual pattern discrimination problems where objects (colored alphabetic symbols) are presented against backgrounds of random ellipses and other symbols on a video monitor. Monkeys with fornix transections were impaired (a) in learning to discriminate objects that could appear in one of two places on the same background, (b) in learning to discriminate places (without accompanying objects) in unique backgrounds, and (c) in learning to discriminate objects that appeared in one place on a unique background. They were unimpaired in learning to discriminate objects that appeared at various locations in many different backgrounds across trials. So, when animals with fornix transection had to find a particular object independent of a varying background, they performed well. But whenever the configuration of objects and background elements in the scene were predominant cues, they were slower in learning than intact animals. More recently, Doré et al. (1998) showed that monkeys with selective hippocampal damage produced by ibotenic acid infusions are also impaired in using contextual cues to solve visual discrimination problems. In their study, monkeys were presented with sets of four concurrent discrimination problems, each involving five visual patterns presented in different spatial configurations across trials. For each problem the monkey was required to find the assigned stimulus within the array, and touch it to obtain a reward. Monkeys with hippocampal lesions were not deficient in learning the initial set of problems, but showed an impairment in acquisition of a second set. This impairment was largely a consequence of the normal animals demonstrating significantly more rapid learning on the second set, whereas monkeys with hippocampal damage showed no improvement over the rate of learning on the first set. The common factor in the Gaffan (1994b) study and the Doré et al. (1998) study was that monkeys with hippocampal damage did not benefit from the use of contextual cues that usually facilitate rapid visual discrimination learning.

In a study that involved selective neurotoxic lesions of the hippocampus itself, Ridley and colleagues (1995) reported that monkeys with direct and localized damage within hippocampal area CA1 were impaired on a variety of conditional discrimination tasks that involved spatial cues predicting which of two visual objects was rewarded, visual object cues predicting which of two spatial locations was rewarded, and visual cues indicating which of two visual objects was rewarded. The same monkeys were not impaired at learning a variety of simpler spatial or object discriminations that did not involve conditional reward assignments. These authors concluded that the central feature of hippocampal involvement was the conditional relationship between the cues and, conversely, that no impairment is observed when a task can be solved by learning a direct reward or response association of a stimulus (see also Ridley & Baker, 1991).

Other studies indicate that some forms of learning that require associations between stimuli depend critically on hippocampal function. Saunders and Weiskrantz (1989) developed a "paired-associate" task in which monkeys learned to choose two object stimuli when presented in specifically assigned pairs (e.g., AB and CD), but not when the same objects were presented "mispaired" (AC or BD). Learning in this task was gradual and required several phases of training, but monkeys with fornix transections performed as well as normal subjects throughout all the training phases. When all subjects were performing above 90% correct, a probe test was given to determine whether the subject could appropriately pair objects that were presented separately. Initially one of the objects was presented as a "sample" in the center of the display (e.g., A), and then two other objects were also presented at either side. One of those choice objects was the assigned pair with the sample (B), and the other object came from a different pair (e.g., C). All the normal monkeys selected the paired choice items at above chance levels, whereas monkeys with fornix transections performed randomly. These data are consistent with the results of Gaffan and colleagues' showing that monkeys with hippocampal damage can learn reward associations of stimulus configurations, but this experiment indicates that normal monkeys and monkeys with hippocampal damage learn this task differently, so that they are unable to identify the stimulus elements when they are separated in a novel probe test. Below more will be made of the distinction between the ability to acquire conditional and configurational discrimination tasks and expressing knowledge about the separate stimulus elements.

In addition to these rather complicated tasks, there is also emerging evidence that the hippocampus itself plays a role in variations on simple visual recognition memory tasks that differ from the standard DNMS task. In the Alvarez et al. (1995) study of monkeys with selective radiofrequency lesions of the hippocampus, these animals showed a substantial impairment during the initial phase of learning the DNMS task, which effectively became more modest later in training. Understanding this impairment requires consideration of the course of learning in this task by normal animals. In the very first few trials of learning DNMS, normal monkeys showed a strong tendency—nearly 90%—to select the novel object in the choice phase. Thereafter performance deteriorated but later returned as the animals permanently acquired the task after approximately 150 trials. Within those first few trials, it was found that monkeys with selective hippocampal lesions had almost no preference for the novel choice object. These results suggest that, even though the delay was very short, a memory impairment was evident when performance was based on the natural tendency to manipulate novel objects.

Furthermore, in a recent study by Beason-Held et al. (1999) selective partial damage was produced within the hippocampus by ibotenic acid injections. Subsequently these monkeys, unlike those of Alvarez et al. (1995), required many more trials than normal monkeys to acquire the DNMS task at a short delay. Afterward these animals showed an impairment at delays of 2 and 10 min, and the magnitude of the persistent long-delay deficit was comparable to that observed in the Alvarez et al. study. Beason-Held et al. also subsequently trained their monkeys on a novel variant of the task in which multiple object or spatial cues had to be remembered. In one version of this task, aimed to measure the "span" of memory for objects or colors, the monkey was initially presented with a single three-dimensional object or colored disk covering one of 18 wells (arranged in three rows of 6) on a large testing board. After the monkey obtained the reward hidden under that object, a 10-s delay ensued, and then the monkey was presented with two objects or disks, one the same as the initial sample and the other a new stimulus, and both covering new positions on the board. To obtain another reward the monkey had to displace the new stimulus. Subsequently the "list" was lengthened by then presenting an additional new object along with all the previously presented stimuli. By this method the object span was measured as the number of objects that could be remembered before an error was made (i.e., when a familiar one was selected). A similar test of spatial span involved presenting an increasing number of plain brown plaques covering an elongating sequence of familiar well locations. In all three tasks monkeys with selective hippocampal damage were impaired, and indeed the greatest impairment was observed on the object span test. Thus, this more elaborate version of the DNMS task, requiring memory for multiple familiar objects, may provide a more sensitive test of the contribution of the hippocampus itself to the memory of single experiences with novel items.

In addition, a recently developed variant on simple visual recognition memory appears to provide a substantially more sensitive test of the contribution of the hippocampus (Zola et al., 2000; see also Pascalis & Bachevalier, 1999). In this test, called visual paired comparison, monkeys are presented with one or two novel pictures on a video screen. Then, following a variable delay, they are presented a novel picture and one of the now familiar pictures in two successive tests, with the test pictures in different left-right arrangements. The monkey's eye movements are rated to measure the fixation time on each of the two test pictures. Normal monkeys typically show approximately a 2:1 preference in viewing time for the novel over the familiar picture. Monkeys with surgical ablations of the hippocampus and subjacent parahippocampal cortex or selective radiofrequency or ibotenate lesions of the hippocampus show the normal preference if the delay is very brief, but almost no preference if the delay is extended beyond a few seconds. It is not fully clear why this impairment in visual recognition is more profound and fully apparent in short delays compared to that observed in the DNMS task. However, Pascalis and Bachevalier (1999) have suggested that monkeys may use different strategies to solve the two problems. In the DNMS task monkeys are trained to displace objects of food rewards and learn the nonmatching rule. Because of these demands, they may rely on a working memory strategy, somehow "rehearsing" the recently viewed sample object during the delay. By contrast, in the visual paired comparison task, there is no explicit demand for remembering the sample stimuli; rather the monkeys simply look at the stimuli as a consequence of their natural curiosity, and so may not attempt to rehearse the sample pictures. Thus, an intact working memory capacity may mediate the spared performance of animals with hippocampal damage on DNMS, whereas the absence of such a strategy reveals the recognition impairment in the paired comparison task.

Combining all of these data, it is clear that the phenomena of human amnesia can be modeled in monkeys. Large medial temporal damage, including all of the structures removed in H.M., produces the full scope of the anterograde and retrograde impairment. Perceptual, motor, motivational, and cognitive functions appear to be intact, as is immediate memory for different types of stimulus materials. In addition, a graded retrograde memory impairment has been described. This model has been successfully advanced to delineate the critical structures within the temporal lobe. This effort has shown that the amygdala is not critical for the types of memory tested in these studies and has shown that the perirhinal, parahippocampal, and entorhinal cortex play a critical role. The hippocampus itself makes little if any contribution to standard DNMS performance but appears to be involved in variations of recognition and conditional discrimination for the same stimulus materials. As will be discussed in the next chapter, studies on rodents have been even more forthcoming on what aspects of learning and memory depend on the hippocampus itself.

7

Animal Models of Amnesia

Nonprimates

Efforts to understand the functional role of the hippocampus in behavior of any sort in nonprimates predated the first description of human amnesia following medial temporal damage (see Douglas, 1967; Isaacson et al., 1961). Perhaps the very earliest proposal about hippocampal function was based on anatomical observations suggesting the hippocampus might be a higher olfactory center. Tests of this idea by Swann (1934) and Allen (1940) showed, however, that damage to the hippocampus in rats or dogs did not result in an impairment in their capacity for odor discrimination. Subsequently, further pioneering anatomical investigations of Papez (1937) led to the view that the hippocampus participated in a brain circuit for emotional processing. Supporting this notion, the classic neuropsychological studies by Kluver and Bucy (1939) showed that large temporal lobe ablations, including hippocampus, indeed caused abnormalities in emotional behavior. However, subsequent studies indicated that removal of the hippocampus was not an essential component of the temporal lobe damage responsible for the abnormal emotional expression. Then came the stunning findings on H.M., whereupon work with rodents turned to reproducing the amnesic impairment, understanding its nature, and examining in detail the functional properties and functional role in memory of the medial temporal lobe structures.

Shortly after Scoville and Milner's (1957) report, several laboratories developed procedures for ablation of the hippocampus in rats, cats, and rabbits. There was at that time a large variety of behavioral tests under study by learning theorists, and most of these were employed in the numerous experiments that followed. But for each task the pattern of results was puzzling at best, and certainly *not* consistent with the findings of severe and global amnesia observed in H.M.

Here we will begin with a brief synopsis of this very large literature, constituting literally hundreds of papers. Our initial focus will be on a few behavioral paradigms that received the most attention, particularly simple approach and avoidance conditioning and various forms of discrimination learning. We cannot be fully comprehensive because even this restricted portion of the literature is voluminous. More comprehensive reviews can be found in Cohen and Eichenbaum (1993), O'Keefe and Nadel (1978), Olton et al. (1979), Gray (1982), Gray and McNaughton (1983), and Rawlins (1985).

Approach and Avoidance Conditioning

The earliest assessments of learning and hippocampal function in rodents included two different tests of avoidance conditioning. One of these, called *shuttle-box avoidance,* involved training rats to alternate (shuttle) between two adjacent compartments of an alleyway. In Isaacson and colleagues' (1961) version of this task, each trial began with a buzzer that signaled the rat to shuttle to the alternate chamber before the floor in the currently occupied side was electrified by a mild current. The surprising result was that rats with large ablations of the hippocampus and overlying parietal cortex learned the task in *fewer* trials than normal rats or rats with cortical damage only, and they retained this learning solidly across testing days. Of course, these results are just the opposite of what one would expect of an impairment in new learning ability, and hardly a cause for celebration in the effort to model human amnesia.

Shortly after, and contrasting with the first results, Isaacson and Wickelgren (1962) found that rats with hippocampal ablations were *unable* to learn a different sort of avoidance task called *passive avoidance.* Initially, hungry rats were trained to approach a chamber that had food. They began each trial in a large compartment and were then signaled by a door opening to leave that compartment and to approach and enter the small food-containing chamber. After learning to execute the approach behavior immediately upon opening of the door, one day they were shocked while eating and driven out of the reward chamber. Normal rats and rats with hippocampal ablations rapidly learned the initial approach response, and consistent with the earlier experiment, rats with hippocampal ablations had shorter approach latencies and less variability in learning. However, the two groups responded quite differently in the avoidance component of training. After having been shocked just once in the reward chamber, none of the normal rats reentered. By contrast each of the rats with hippocampal damage did return to the chamber in which they were shocked. Although there was a learning impairment here following hippocampal damage, the overall pattern of findings did not offer compelling support for a simple amnesic disorder: After outperforming normal rats on the initial learning phase, rats with hippocampal damage showed a deficit in passive avoidance that seemed to reflect an inability to give up the previously acquired response, rather than a failure to learn per se.

Spared acquisition of simple conditioned responses after hippocampal damage was also evident in experiments that focused on standard Skinnerian operant conditioning for food rewards. Rats with hippocampal ablations learned more rapidly than normal rats to press a bar in order to obtain rewards (Schmaltz & Isaacson, 1967). There were noted several subtle abnormalities in the timing of their bar pressing during more elaborate operant reinforcement schedules, but these patterns of operant responding could not be interpreted as a deficit in memory. Several more recent examples of rats with hippocampal damage outperforming normal animals in learning simple approach behaviors have been reported (see Packard et al., 1989), confirming that hippocampal damage actually *facilitates,* rather than retards, some forms of learning and memory. Taken together, these results put the rodent work in opposition to the neuropsychological findings with H.M. and other amnesic patients.

Discrimination Learning

The pattern of early findings on the acquisition of simple sensory or spatial discriminations was no easier to reconcile with the deficit in human amnesia than were those findings on approach and avoidance learning considered above. In one of the first of these studies, Kimble (1963) found that rats with large hippocampal ablations acquired a simultaneous visual discrimination normally. This task employed a Y maze where one choice arm was black and the other white, and their left-right positions were randomly changed across trials. Rats with hippocampal ablations learned the task just as rapidly as normal rats even though the interval between trials was 8 min, surely long enough to result in forgetting between trials if the animals had a long-term memory impairment.

More puzzling, a different result was obtained in the successive discrimination version of the same task. On each trial of this test, the rats were presented with one of two mazes, either a maze with two black goal arms or a maze with two white goal arms. The right arm contained food when the goal arms were white, whereas the left arm contained the food when the goal arms were black. In this variant of visual discrimination, rats with hippocampal damage required over twice as many trials as normal rats to reach a learning criterion. However, after a 2-week period, rats with hippocampal ablations showed as good retention as normal rats. As was the case with passive avoidance, although a discrimination-learning impairment was observed following hippocampal damage, the overall pattern of results could not be interpreted as supporting a rodent model of amnesia. Rats with hippocampal damage were not consistently impaired in learning new visual stimulus-reward associations, and there was no impairment in long-term retention in either version of the task.

Many subsequent efforts continued to provide mixed results on the effects of hippocampal damage on simple discrimination learning in rats and other species (for a tabulation, see O'Keefe & Nadel, 1978). There were some more-or-less consistent findings: Simple discrimination learning was intact in three times as many experiments as not. Whether learning was cued by nonspatial stimuli (that is, by specific visual, auditory, tactile or olfactory cues) or by spatial cues (such as left and right arms of a T or Y maze), the performance of rats with hippocampal damage on initial acquisition was more often intact, although there were also many examples of deficient learning. However, when animals were required to reverse reward assignments for the same stimuli used in a previous discrimination, animals with hippocampal damage more often showed impairments, although again there were many exceptions.

Hypotheses About Hippocampal Function in Attention, Evaluation, and Behavioral Inhibition

These results, along with many other mixed results on other tasks, led to several early proposals about the function of the hippocampus in rats (for a survey, see Schmajuk, 1984). Most prominent among these were variations on the notion that the hippocampus plays a role in attention, stimulus evaluation, and associated behavioral inhibition (for details, see Douglas, 1967; Douglas & Pribram, 1966; Kimble, 1968; Vinogradova, 1975; Altman et al., 1973; Gray, 1982; Gabriel et al., 1986; Gray & Rawlins, 1986). Notably, each of these hypotheses rejected the view that the hippocampus is necessary for memory formation in a direct or simple way and so clearly diverged from the conclusions about hippocampus forthcoming from the study of human amnesia. Instead, the hippocampus was envisioned as mediating the detection of novel or unexpected stimulus events and then halting ongoing behavior during evaluation of the event and of its potential for changing otherwise prepotent or ongoing behavioral activity.

These hypotheses accounted for many of the findings from the studies on the effects of hippocampal ablations in rodents. The initial acquisition of a stimulus-response association was viewed as not relying strongly on attentional processes but rather could be mediated by gradual establishment of habitual behavior, as long as the choice of stimuli provoked little or no conflict between competing response associations. Indeed one could even envision how *not* having a hippocampus might facilitate acquisition of the simplest conditioned responses and discriminations by eliminating any "hesitancy" an animal might have during initial learning. Normal animals might stop and evaluate each stimulus, consider whether it was the same as the one on the previous trial, and even test out response alternatives. To the extent that such uncertainties and behavioral variability lead to occasional erroneous choices, initial learning might progress a bit more slowly than in amnesic rats with damage to the hippocampus. By contrast, animals with hippocampal damage would have no such "hesitancy" and would instead be expected to respond immediately and without variability to salient stimuli.

In our own studies with rodents, we have found variants of odor discrimination learning in which rats with hippocampal damage learn more rapidly than do intact rats (Eichenbaum et al., 1988). Furthermore, in parallel electrophysiological studies on normal rats, hippocampal principal neurons fired differentially depending on whether a current odor stimulus was the same as or different from the stimulus on the previous trial (Eichenbaum et al., 1989). Thus, in a task where having a hippocampus actually retards learning, the hippocampus seems to process the relation between previous and current stimuli, providing a possible mechanism for the evaluation and comparison of successive stimuli, and for the selection and confirmation of responses to those stimuli.

By contrast, according to these views, hippocampally mediated evaluative processing becomes quite essential in learning situations where the nature of stimuli or their consequences change. The most straightforward example is a discrimination reversal, where animals must switch responses they make to previously acquired associations because of an experimenter-imposed reversal of the reward value of the to-be-discriminated objects. In such tasks, animals with hippocampal lesions are often impaired. Passive avoidance tasks also require animals to inhibit their prepotent approach response, and this kind of learning, too, is usually deficient after hippocampal damage. Other findings not introduced above also can be explained by the same account. For example, following hippocampal ablation rats are often severely impaired in learning complex mazes with many turns and blind alleys (see O'Keefe & Nadel, 1978). In these situations, hippocampal processing is viewed as necessary to sort out the conflicting information in deciding whether a left or right turn is appropriate at each choice point. And this account could explain why rats show relative insensitivity to subtle changes in reinforcement probability, such as when partial reinforcement schedules are enforced in operant conditioning, as well as the frequent finding of impairments in the extinction of conditioned responses, which involve inhibiting behaviors that are no longer reinforced.

Other evidence consistent with accounts of hippocampal evaluative processing come from studies by Devenport and colleagues (1988; Devenport & Holloway, 1980; see also Osborne & Black, 1978), and by Amsel (1993), that examined the details of behavior in rats during learning, performance, and extinction in both operant and maze-learning situations. They observed that rats with hippocampal damage had reduced variability of behaviors during learning and conversely were abnormally inclined to retain superstitious behaviors during continued performance and extinction. For example, during bar press operant conditioning, rats with hippocampal damage persisted in arbitrary superstitious behaviors that occasionally coincided with reward, whereas normal animals dropped superstitious behaviors quickly. Furthermore, rats with hippocampal damage became stereotyped in the rhythm of their bar pressing.

In maze-learning situations rats with hippocampal damage sampled fewer arm choices than normal rats and again exhibited stereotyped behavior in their stimulus sampling compared to intact animals, whose behavior reflected a never-ending testing and examining of the maze in a variety of ways. Amsel (1993) argued that the deficiency in behavioral variability after hippocampal damage was due to the loss of the vicarious trial-and-error behavior characteristic of normal rats exploring new environments.

Taken together, we get a picture of rats with hippocampal damage being driven by direct and simple stimulus-reward associations, and being overly resistant to exploring options and changing their behavior. This picture seems to have little correspondence with the human amnesic disorder. There is little evidence from the early work on rodents that points to the hippocampus as an essential mediator of new memory formation.

Breakthroughs

In the mid-1970s, new progress was made in the establishment of a rodent model of amnesia, one that made closer contact with the human neuropsychological literature by emphasizing the participation of hippocampus in some aspect of memory or of representation, through theoretical breakthroughs that developed along three separate themes that were introduced in chapter 2: (a) O'Keefe and Nadel (1978, 1979; see also Nadel, 1991, 1992) proposed that the hippocampus mediates a "cognitive map," precisely the kind of cognitive processing suggested by Tolman (1948) to account for rats' maze-learning abilities; (b) Hirsh (1974, 1980) suggested that the hippocampus mediates conditional operations in memory (i.e., the ability to access an appropriate association through the use of another stimulus or context in which the association was learned); and (c) Olton and colleagues (1979) postulated that the hippocampus mediates "working" (episodic) memory, the ability to retain information acquired in a single instance for a single subsequent use.

Despite major differences in the fundamental processing function assigned to the hippocampus, all these views shared two general aspects of their formulations that are very important. First, each proposal espoused a multiple-memory-systems approach in which the hippocampus plays a selective role in a distinct, higher order form of memory whereas hippocampus-independent mechanisms are sufficient to mediate simpler forms of learning and memory. The recognition of multiple forms of memory, only one of which depends on the hippocampus, constituted a major breakthrough of research on rodent memory in that period.

Second, there was substantial agreement on the characteristics of hippocampus-independent learning, so that all three proposals described the capacities of animals with hippocampal damage in a manner consistent with characterizations of "habit" learning described in chapter 2. O'Keefe and Nadel (1978, 1979) characterized learning without the hippocampus as involving dispositions of specific stimuli into approach and avoidance categories, and as involving slow and incremental behavioral adaptation. Hirsh (1974) characterized the behavior of animals with hippocampal damage as "habit-prone," in that they investigate fewer hypotheses and rigidly adopt behaviors associated with reinforcement very early, consistent with "everything for which early S-R theorists would have wished" (p. 439). Olton and colleagues (1979) characterized hippocampus-independent learning as based on permanent assignments of cues to appropriate responses (see also Thomas & Gash, 1988). The combination of these qualities remains undisputed in accounting for the success of rats with hippocampal damage in simple approach and avoidance conditioning and in discrimination learning.

Furthermore, in all of these accounts, interference among remembered items loomed large as a challenge to the habit process. When an animal is required to respond one way to a stimulus under some circumstances and another way under other circumstances, processes that mediate habitual behavior fall short and the animal must adopt a single, partially effective response strategy. This is not to say that a habit mechanism cannot adapt to fine distinctions between two similar circumstances, but rather that it does so only very slowly. So, according to each of these views, animals with hippocampal damage are impaired at learning that involves interference because the habit mechanism is much slower to accommodate. More recently Shapiro and Olton (1994) argued that virtually all kinds of memory problems in which animals with hippocampal damage are impaired can be characterized as containing interference of one sort or another.

Beyond general agreement on what the hippocampus does *not* do, the three theories differed substantially. The following sections will discuss each of these accounts in some detail. Each proposal has received support from a particular key line of experimentation, different for each of the theories. Because the three theories draw their support from different empirical findings, each theory necessarily fails to account for other results and hence cannot provide a complete accounting for hippocampal function. Nevertheless each theory contains an essential contribution to our understanding of the overall processing function of the hippocampus.

Cognitive Mapping

O'Keefe and Nadel's (1978) central contribution was to see the hippocampus as providing a mechanism for implementing in the brain the cognitive maps of Tolman (1948). In a monumental achievement, they surveyed the extensive literature on the anatomy and physiology of the hippocampus, and on the neuropsychological studies of the effects of hippocampal damage in animals and humans. Each of these areas of knowledge was interpreted as supporting their overall hypothesis that the hippocampus specifically mediates the construction and use of spatial maps of the environment. With regard to the studies on animals, they emphasized that hippocampal system damage typically results in severe impairment in most forms of spatial exploration and learning. Conversely, they noted that impairment in nonspatial learning is less commonly reported. These conclusions were combined with evidence of hippocampal "place cells" (i.e., of the relationship of hippocampal neuron activity to the location of the animal in space while exploring its environment; see chapter 9), leading them to suggest that hippocampal processing is a critical element of spatial memory.

It is important to emphasize that O'Keefe and Nadel's (1978) analysis went well beyond making a simple distinction between "spatial" and "nonspatial" learning. They proposed that the acquisition of cognitive maps involves a wholly distinct form of cognition from that of habit formation. Cognitive maps involve the representation of places in terms of distances and directions among items in the environment and are composed as a rough topological map of the physical environment that the animal uses to navigate among salient locations and other important cues. They envisioned cognitive maps as enabling animals to act at a distance, that is, to *navigate* to locations beyond their immediate perception. In addition, cognitive mapping was characterized by a rapid, all-or-none assignment of cues to places within the spatial map. This kind of learning was envisioned as driven by curiosity, rather than reinforcement of specific behavioral responses, and as involving relatively little interference between items because they would be represented separately in a map or in different maps for distinct situations.

It is clear that animals with hippocampal damage have abnormal exploratory activity patterns and severe impairments on many spatial learning tasks, most profoundly on complex maze tasks involving a sequence of many turns and tasks that require remembering lists of locations. In addition, some careful examinations of spatial learning have strongly supported O'Keefe and Nadel's (1978) characterization of hippocampus-dependent memory as involving the encoding of spatial relations among environmental cues. Among the most powerful results supporting the cognitive mapping view are the findings from an experiment by O'Keefe and Conway (1980), showing that whether or not animals with hippocampal damage could learn normally depended on the spatial arrangement of the same cues (Figure 7.1). Rats were trained to find a food reward in one arm of a plus-shaped maze, beginning each trial from the far end of any of the other three arms. The maze was surrounded by a dark curtain, so that the available salient cues were a small set of stimuli the experimenter located within the curtain. These stimuli were arranged in one of two ways for different sets of rats. One set of rats was tested on a version of the test, called the "distributed-cues task," in which the cues were dispersed around the maze, distant from the ends of any of the arms. The other set of rats was tested on the "clustered-cues version" of the task, in which the same cues were grouped together just off the end of the goal arm. It is notable that the behavioral performance of *normal* rats was different in these two tests. Intact rats found the clustered-cue task more difficult than the distributed-cue version, suggesting that normal animals treated the cues as distinct items and solved the maze problem depending on the configuration of those items with respect to the arms.

All the animals were initially trained to solve these problems; then half of each group received a fornix transection. In retraining, the results with the two versions of the task were strikingly different. Normal rats and rats with fornix transections showed perfect retention of the clustered-cue task. Normal rats also showed perfect retention of the distributed-cue task. But animals with fornix lesions were severely impaired on the distributed-cues task. Thus, when rats with a fornix transection could learn simply to approach a large combination of cues, they succeeded. But when they had to use the spatial arrangement among the cues to guide their performance from different starting points, and none of these cues could be approached directly to obtain the reward, they performed very poorly.

Another spatial memory task that has received widespread use in studies of learning and memory is the water maze. Originally developed by Morris (1981), this task involves a large swimming pool filled with tepid water made murky by the addition of milk powder. An escape platform is hidden just beneath the surface of the water at an arbitrary location. Rats are very good swimmers and rapidly learn to locomote around the pool, but they prefer not to swim and will seek the platform so that they can climb onto it. Animals cannot see the platform directly, but instead must use distant spatial cues that are visible above the walls of the pool around the room. On each training trial, the rat begins swimming from one of multiple locations at the periphery of the maze, so that they cannot consistently use a specific swimming course to reach the escape platform. Rats learn to use a spatial navigation strategy to find the platform even after training from a consistent starting point, as evidenced in their ability after training to locate it efficiently from novel starting points (Morris, 1981).

Morris and colleagues (1982) showed that hippocampal ablation results in severe impairments in the water maze task (Figure 7.2). In the initial trials, all animals typically required 1–2 min to find the platform. During the course of repeated trials, normal animals rapidly reduced their escape latency, so that they eventually reached it within 10 s from every starting point. Rats with hippocampal ablations also reduced their escape latencies, showing some extent of learning. However, they reached asymptotic performance at approximately 35-s latencies, largely due to a reduction of completely ineffective strategies such as trying

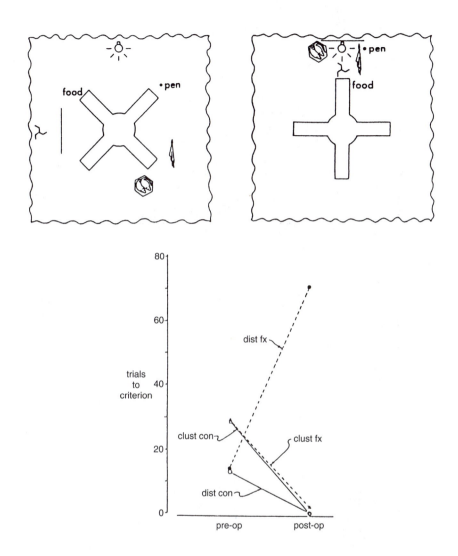

Figure 7.1. Place learning task. Top: Schematic diagram of arrangement of maze with cues distributed (left) or clustered (right). Bottom: Performance in learning prior to surgery (pre-op) and after surgery (post-op) in control rats (con) and rats with fornix transection (fx). Dist = distributed cues; clust = clustered cues. (Reproduced, with permission, from O'Keefe & Conway, 1980; Copyright Psychonomic Society.)

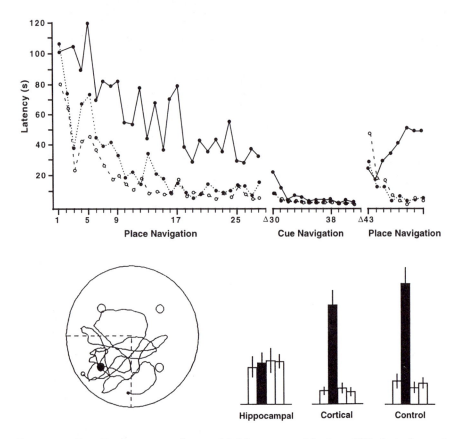

Figure 7.2. Top: Performance of rats with hippocampal lesions (filled circles and lines), cortical lesions (filled circles—dashed lines), and normal controls (open circles) in acquiring the water maze task. Place navigation = hidden platform; Cue navigation = visible platform. Bottom: Swim path of a control subject on the transfer test (dashed lines indicate quadrant of the maze in which the platform had been located), and swim times of rats in different maze quadrants; black bar corresponds to the training quadrant. (Reproduced, with permission, from Morris, Garrud, Rawlins, & O'Keefe, 1982; Copyright Macmillan Magazines Ltd.) Right: Illustration of swim paths of control rat and rat with hippocampal lesion performing a transfer test.

to climb the walls; however, they never learned to swim directly to the platform location in the manner that normal rats do.

In a subsequent "transfer test" the escape platform was removed, and rats were allowed to swim for 1 min with no opportunity for escape. In this transfer condition, normal rats circled in the close vicinity of the former location of the platform, as measured by a strong tendency to swim within the quadrant of the pool in which it had been located (Figure 7.2). Rats with hippocampal ablations showed no preference for the quadrant of the platform, highlighting the severity of their spatial memory deficit. In a different version of the water maze task,

Morris maze transfer test

control

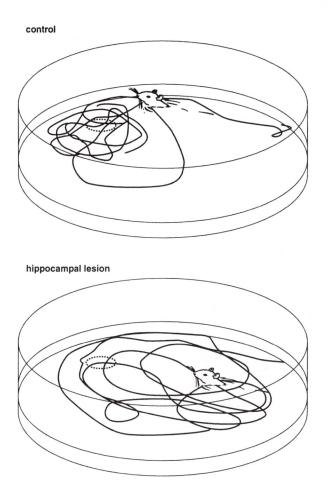

hippocampal lesion

Figure 7.2. Continued.

when the escape platform could be seen above the surface of the water (cue navigation), both normal rats and rats with hippocampal ablations rapidly learned to swim directly to it. This protocol emphasized the distinction between intact learning to approach the platform guided by a specific local cue, and no capacity for learning guided by the relation among distant spatial cues. Since Morris and colleagues' original experiment, several studies have confirmed the selective impairment on the spatial version of the Morris water maze task following hippocampal damage, and this task has become a benchmark test of hippocampal function in rodents.

Spatial memory has been an important element of efforts to develop a rodent model of human amnesia. Kesner and Novak (1982) tested short- and long-term memory for spatial locations in a task that allowed an examination of the serial position curve for spatial items (Figure 7.3). They found that normal rats showed the same pattern of serial position effects in spatial memory that humans show for verbal memory (see chapter 5). Normal rats' memory performance was better for items early or late in a list than for items in the middle. Furthermore, when a delay was inserted before retention testing, memory for items at the end of the list (the recency effect) dropped off, but memory for the initial list items (the primacy effect) was unaffected. Rats with hippocampal lesions showed selective loss of the primacy component, indicating a deficit in long-term memory but preserved short-term memory. In addition, recent efforts by Cho and colleagues (1993, 1995; Cho & Kesner, 1996) have demonstrated a graded retrograde impairment in memory for discriminations among maze arms following hippocampal region damage. Thus, similar to the pattern of findings in human amnesia, amnesic rats with hippocampal ablations have intact short-term retention but a delay-dependent deficit in retention of new spatial information and graded retrograde amnesia for spatial memories.

"Working" (Episodic) Memory

Olton and his colleagues (1979) proposed an alternative view of the role the hippocampus plays in learning and memory. Their work revolved around a novel test apparatus called the *radial-arm maze.* This maze is composed of several (typically four, eight, or more) runway arms radiating outward like spokes of a wheel from a central platform (Figure 7.4), and there are many variants in the number of arms and reward contingencies involved in this task. In the standard, "working-memory" version, at the outset of each trial a food reward is placed at the end of each of the arms of the maze. During the course of a trial, the rat is free to enter each arm to retrieve the food rewards. Once retrieved, the food rewards are not replaced during that trial. Rats rapidly learn to approach each arm just once on a given trial. On subsequent trials, all of the arms are baited again just once. The number of arms entered during a trial provides a measure of the ability of the rat to remember which arms it has visited on that particular trial. Memory for information needed on a given trial, which changes from trial to trial—in this case the specific arms visited on that trial—was called "working memory," as distinguished from "reference memory," which was characterized as memory for information that is constant across trials (that there is a food reward at the end of each arm, that the rewards are not replaced during a trial but are replaced between trials, etc.). Olton and colleagues reported that rats with hippocampal system damage were impaired in working memory, differing from normal rats by repeatedly visiting the same arms. Note, however, that the term *working memory* has a different meaning in the current cognitive and neuroscience literatures, referring to the ability to temporarily hold information *on-line* while the subject is working on that information; this memory capacity has been tied to the function of prefrontal cortex rather than hippocampus (see chapter 14). The memory of the specific arms visited on a given trial, necessary to perform Olton's radial arm maze, required information to be held for a period that often far outlasted the limits of working memory, as cognitive neuroscientists currently understand that capacity. Accordingly, we consider it more appropriate to characterize the

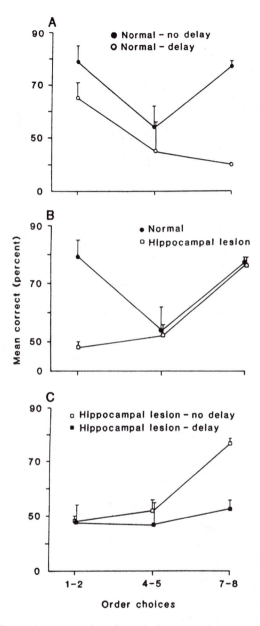

Figure 7.3. Serial position curve for a list of places. Performance on early, middle or late items in a series of radial maze arms visited. (Reproduced, with permission, from Kesner & Novak, 1982; Copyright American Association for the Advancement of Science.)

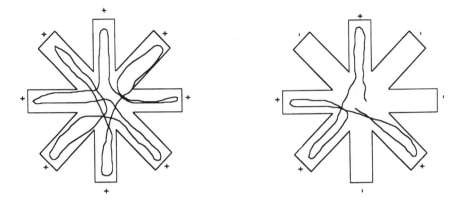

Figure 7.4. Two variations of the radial maze task. Left: All maze arms are baited once, and the rat must visit each without a repetition. Right: Only half the arms are baited. Rats learn never to visit the unbaited arms and visit each baited one once per trial.

type of memory necessary for successful performance in the radial arm maze as memory for unique episodes on maze arms.

In a classic experiment demonstrating the working-memory impairment after hippocampal system damage, Olton and Papas (1979) added a variation on the reward contingencies. Some arms of the maze were baited once each trial, following the working-memory contingency. In addition, other arms were never baited, and rats were to learn across trials not to enter these arms at all. The latter capacity is another example of "reference memory" emphasizing the fixed nature of the stimulus-response associations for these arms. In this study, a 17-arm radial maze was employed with 8 once-baited and 9 nonbaited arms. After initial preoperative training of all animals to high levels of performance on both components of the task, half the animals received a fornix transection. Subsequently, normal animals continued to perform at very high levels on both the working- and reference-memory components of the task. By contrast, rats with fornix transections performed less well than normals from the outset of postoperative testing on both components of the task but improved rapidly on their reference memory choices. However, they never performed at better than chance even with extended training on the working-memory component of the task.

Olton and his colleagues argued that the hippocampal system was selectively involved in working memory, or in processing that reduces the interference inherent in working-memory procedures. On a conceptual level Olton viewed working memory as capturing the distinction raised by Tulving (1972) between "episodic memory" events tied to specific time and place and "semantic memory" for knowledge that is time- and event-independent (see chapter 5).

Olton's proposal was seen as in direct conflict with the cognitive mapping notion, and a host of experiments were soon forthcoming providing support for one or the other proposal. The working-memory hypothesis provided the better explanation of one of the early and persistent complexities of data on spatial discrimination, reversal learning, and alternation. Early studies found that hippocampal damage generally does not prevent learning of a simple spatial discrimination on a Y or T maze. O'Keefe and Nadel (1978, 1979) were quick to point out that this maze problem can be solved in two ways, by orienting for a left or right turn or by going to the place of reward (see chapter 2). In their view, the hippocampus mediates the place strategy but not the orientation strategy, so that when deprived of hippocampal function the rats have an alternative solution and hence are unimpaired. However, an equally frequent result in the early studies is that rats with hippocampal damage are impaired at spatial reversal learning and are unable to learn to alternate left and right arm selections in Y or T mazes (for references, see O'Keefe & Nadel, 1978; Olton et al., 1979) and can show the clear dissociation between intact spatial discrimination and impaired alternation in the same T-maze apparatus outfitted with different types of choice points (Figure 7.5; see also Thomas & Gash, 1988). It might well be that rats find it easy to adopt an orientation strategy in spatial discrimination but strongly favor a place strategy in reversal learning and have to use a place strategy in delayed alternation. But it is not the nature of the spatial cues that differentiates these alternatives among these tasks. Rather, it is the demand to use the same cues in different ways for each task that is the critical factor. The working-memory–reference-memory dichotomy accounts for these results more directly, in that only reference memory is required for the spatial choice never rewarded, but working memory is required for the alternation of choices.

A line of evidence strongly favoring the working-memory account involved Olton and Feustle's (1981) success in extending the role of the hippocampus to working memory in the radial maze guided by nonspatial stimuli. The structure of the task was generally the same as in the previous tests of spatial working memory. Each of multiple maze arms was baited just once, and perfect performance was measured as the ability of the rat to obtain all the rewards by entering each arm only one time. For the nonspatial version of this task, however, they created a four-arm maze in which the walls and floor of each arm were covered by a distinct set of tactile and visual cues, and distant cues were eliminated by covering the arms with a translucent gauze (Figure 7.6). Furthermore, after each arm entry the rat was briefly confined to the central platform while the arms were rearranged to eliminate any consistent arm positions or their configuration. Thus the rats had to remember entered arms by their distinctive internal (intramaze) cues and ignore any spatial cues about the locations of the arms. After initial preoperative acquisition, normal rats continued to perform the task well, but rats with fornix transections failed to reacquire the task even with extended retraining, despite the nonspatial nature of this variant of the task.

Conditional Operations

Hirsh (1974, 1980) proposed that the hippocampus plays a critical role in tasks where the significance of discriminative stimuli is contingent or conditional on other stimuli, and he characterized this sort of learning as involving hippocampally mediated conditional operations or contextual retrieval. He argued that hippocampal processing of the conditional selection among response alternatives

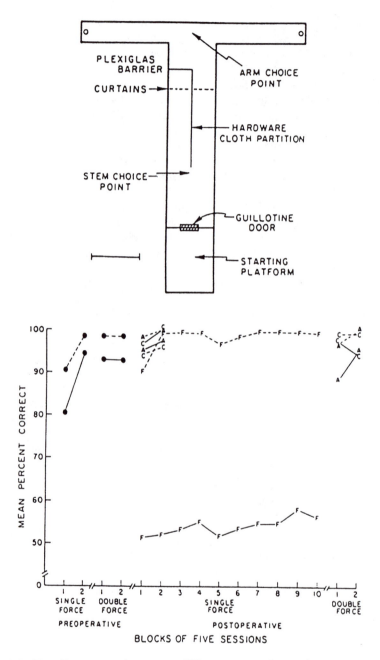

Figure 7.5. Top: T-maze used to assess different types of spatial memory. Bottom: Performance of controls rats (C), rats with amygdala lesions (A), and rats with fornix lesions (F) in acquiring the task before surgery (preoperative) and in postoperative testing with one (single force) or two (double force) sample trials. (Reproduced, with permission, from Olton, 1986; Copyright Plenum Press.)

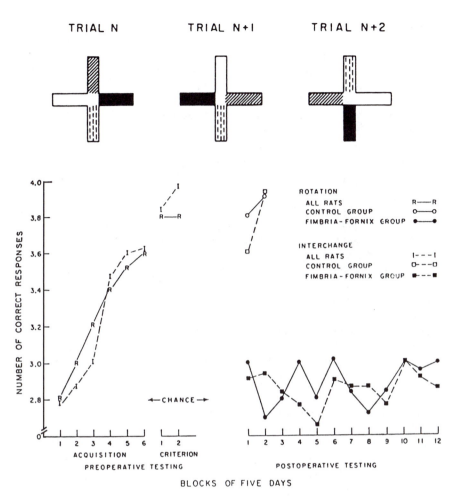

Figure 7.6. Nonspatial radial maze task. Top: Illustration of rearrangments of maze surfaces on a succession of arm interchange trials. Bottom: Performance on the interchange procedure, and with rotation of all the arms. (Reproduced, with permission, from Olton & Feustle, 1981; Copyright Springer-Verlag.)

comes into play whenever there is significant interference between competing responses across highly similar situations.

In support of this view of conditional operations, Hirsh et al. (1979) showed that rats with hippocampal damage failed to learn to behave in one of two ways in a T maze dependent on a conditional cue. He placed food at one goal in the maze and water at the other. On alternate days animals were either food- or water-deprived. Normal animals learned to approach each motivationally appropriate goal independently, typically learning both response contingencies more-or-less simultaneously. By contrast, animals with hippocampal damage acted as if confronted by a single problem. On some blocks of trials they would do well on one component of the problem, for example, but correspondingly would perform below chance on the other component by approaching the same goal across the entire series of trials.

Hirsh (1974) also considered other problems on which rats with hippocampal damage failed as being consistent with a critical demand for conditional operations. For example, he explained Kimble's (1963) mixture of findings on simultaneous and successive versions of visual discrimination learning in terms of differential demands for conditional operations. In his view, the successive discrimination constituted a conditional task in which whether the rat should turn left or right was dependent on the color of both maze arms. However, in the simultaneous discrimination, learning to select the black or white arm was not conditioned on any other cue.

Hirsh (1974, 1980) also considered the findings on reversal learning consistent with a conditional operations view. He emphasized the common finding that animals with hippocampal damage acquired a discrimination reversal in about as many trials as it would take if learning proceeded first by gradual unlearning of the initial response, and then an equivalent period for learning the new response contingency. He interpreted this as precisely what one would expect if learning was driven by a simple habit mechanism in animals whose hippocampal system was damaged. By contrast, normal rats typically required more trials to learn a reversal than they did the initial discrimination, but fewer than the total number trials expected if they had to extinguish and relearn. Hirsh suggested that normal rats make use of a capacity to condition ongoing learning according to the most recent contingencies.

Contributions and Limitations of Hypotheses on Selective Memory Functions of the Hippocampus

Research directed at tests of each of these views has provided mixed support and refutation of each. The sum of this work, in our view, indicates that each notion has identified a critical—but nonetheless limited—aspect of the fundamental role of the hippocampus. As with the early literature, the quantity of research directed at evaluating these proposals is enormous, far too great to describe in detail here. Instead, what follows are descriptions of some of the experiments that extend our understanding of each of the previous characterizations of hippocampal function and that lead the way to a synthesis.

The major limitation of Olton's working-memory proposal is the many demonstrations of impaired spatial reference memory. The examples given above are sufficient to make this point; we'll mention just two here. The data from Morris's water maze, which is clearly a (spatial) reference memory task, are in direct contradiction to the working-memory theory. Performance on both versions of O'Keefe and Conway's plus maze involved (spatial) reference memory, yet learning impairment was observed in one version but not the other.

Exceptions to the Rule of Space

This is not to say that spatial memory has unambiguously won out. There have now been many reports confirming the finding of severe impairments in spatial learning, leading to the widespread adoption of the view that the hippocampus is critical for spatial memory processing. More problematic is the widespread adoption of the stronger conclusion that the hippocampus is *dedicated* to spatial memory processing, at least in rodents. This is problematic because there are several lines of evidence indicating that this view is at once both too broad and too narrow. The spatial memory view of hippocampal function is too broad because there are multiple examples of intact performance after hippocampal damage in tasks guided by the same spatial cues as other task variants associated with severe impairment. This hypothesis is also too narrow, because there are multiple examples of impaired learning in tasks that do not involve cognitive or spatial mapping. Some of these tasks involve a particular kind of place learning that does not involve spatial mapping, and other tasks have no critical spatial component at all. Some of these examples will be discussed next.

Although perhaps the clearest demonstration of the critical role the hippocampus plays in place learning comes from experiments using the Morris water maze (Morris et al., 1982), several experiments have now demonstrated successful learning of this task in animals with hippocampal damage, and the results reveal greater insights into the nature of hippocampal processing of spatial information. In the standard version of this task, rats are released into the water at different starting points on successive trials, a manipulation that strongly encourages rats to compare the views among the positions of extramaze stimuli and the rat's own position across trials. Indeed, it is difficult to imagine how the task could be solved without a representation of spatial relations among cues that disentangles otherwise conflicting associations of the separate views seen from each starting point.

Eichenbaum et al. (1990) assessed the importance of this demand by training rats on a version of the task where rats were released into the maze from a constant start position on each trial. Initially, animals were trained to approach a visible black-and-white-striped platform. Then the visibility of the platform was gradually diminished in a series of training stages that involved a large, visible white platform, then smaller platforms, and finally sinking the platform below the water surface. With this gradual training procedure, rats with fornix transections learned to approach the platform directly, although they were slower to acquire the response at each phase of training (Figure 7.7). In addition, their final escape latencies were slightly higher than those of intact rats, due to an increased tendency for "near misses," trials on which they passed near the platform without touching it and were forced to circle back. But in contrast to the standard version of this task, animals with fornix transection were able to learn the location of the escape platform.

To confirm that both sets of rats were using the same extramaze cues to guide performance, Eichenbaum et al. (1989) applied the standard "transfer" test developed by Morris (1984) in which the escape platform is removed and the swimming pattern of the rats is observed for a fixed period. Both normal rats and rats with fornix transections swam near the former location of the platform, indicating that they could identify the place of escape by the same set of available extramaze cues rather than solely by the approach trajectory. After several probe tests, these rats were to learn a novel escape location using multiple starting points. Rats with fornix transection failed completely. The success of rats with fornix

PLACE LEARNING

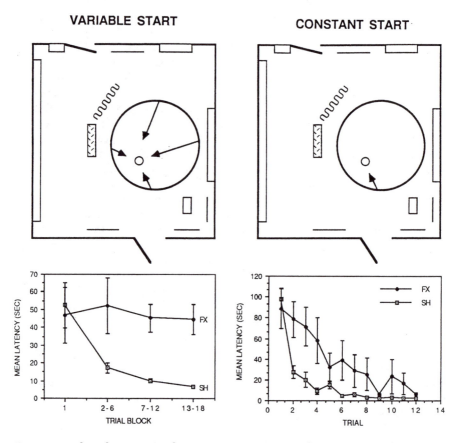

Figure 7.7. Place learning in the water maze. Top: In the conventional, variable start, version of the task rats begin each trial from one of four locations in random order (see arrows). In the constant start version, they always begin from the same location. Bottom: Performance of normal controls (SH) and rats with fornix transection (FX) in acquiring these tests. (Reproduced, with permission, from Eichenbaum, Stewart, & Morris, 1990; Copyright Society for Neuroscience.)

transection on the constant-start version of the task, contrasted with their failure on the standard variable-start version, indicated that it was not the use of distal spatial cues per se, but rather other factors governing how these cues were used, that determined the critical involvement of the hippocampus.

Eichenbaum et al. (1989) were now in a position to ask the critical question: Were there differences in the way in which fornix rats and the normal rats learned and represented the task? This was addressed by using a series of probe tests, each involving an alteration of the cues or starting points, intermixed within a series of repetitions of the instruction trial. One of the probe tests demonstrated a particularly striking dissociation between the two groups of rats. In this test, the platform was left in its normal place, but the start position was moved to various novel locations. When the start position was the same as that used during instruction trials, both normal rats and rats with fornix lesions had short escape latencies (Figure 7.8). On the critical probe trials with novel starting positions, normal rats also swam directly to the platform regardless of the starting position. By contrast, rats with fornix lesions rarely swam directly to the escape platform, sometimes went far astray, and subsequently had abnormally long aver-

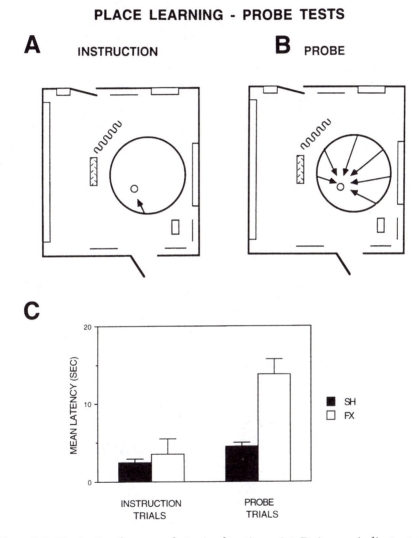

Figure 7.8. Navigation from novel starting locations. A & B. Arrows indicate starting locations in training and probe testing trials. C. Performance of normal control rats (SH) and rats with fornix transection (FX). (Reproduced, with permission, from Eichenbaum, Stewart, & Morris, 1990; Copyright Society for Neuroscience.)

age escape latencies on these probe trials. This striking deficit in rats with fornix lesions is demonstrated by a close examination of their individual swim trajectories (Figure 7.9). All the normal rats nearly always swam directly to the platform regardless of their starting point. But rats with fornix transections swam in various directions, occasionally leading them straight to the platform, but more often in the wrong direction, and they sometimes never found the platform in this highly familiar environment.

In another probe test, Eichenbaum et al. (1989) rotated by 180 degrees a few of the most prominent cues that the rats would see while swimming from the constant start locus toward the escape platform. Intact rats were generally not influenced by the rotation of just a few of the salient cues in the environment, but most rats with fornix transections headed initially toward these rotated cues (Figure 7.10). This pattern of data suggests that rats with fornix transections were abnormally influenced by cues in the direct path of their swims, and that their representation could not support locating the escape platform from novel views in a highly familiar environment (see also Compton et al., 1997).

In related experiments Whishaw and colleagues (1995; Whishaw & Tomie, 1997) have extended the finding of intact water maze learning in rats with fornix transections. They trained rats initially using a visible platform, placing them on the platform, then in the water farther from the platform in each of the variable start directions. By this method of gradual training using a visible platform, rats

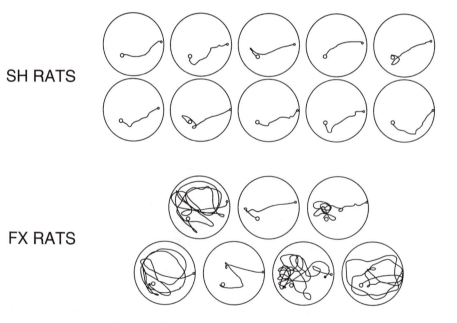

SH RATS

FX RATS

Figure 7.9. Swim paths of each normal control rat (SH) and each rat with fornix transection (FX) on the probe trial that began from the "east" start location. (Reproduced, with permission, from Eichenbaum, Stewart, & Morris, 1990; Copyright Society for Neuroscience.)

CUE-ROTATION

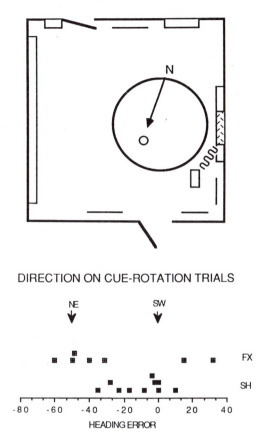

Figure 7.10. Cue rotation probe trial. Top: Starting location and re-arrangement of cues. Bottom: Initial heading directions of normal control rats (SH) and rats with fornix transection (FX). (Reproduced, with permission, from Eichenbaum, Stewart, & Morris, 1990; Copyright Society for Neuroscience.)

with fornix transections learned the task as well as normal rats and showed normal patterns of swimming trajectories throughout. Then a hidden platform was substituted at the same location and training continued. During this phase, the escape latencies of rats with fornix transections were initially much higher than those of normal rats, and they continued to show more near misses throughout training. However, their escape latencies converged on those of normal rats after several sessions, and they showed a strong bias for the former platform quadrant when the platform was subsequently removed. These findings show that even the variable-start version of the water maze can be learned by animals with hippocampal damage, under highly regimented conditions.

Whishaw and colleagues (1995) have also further analyzed the limitations of rats with fornix transections. After successful hidden-platform training, the same rats were tested on a variant of the task in which the platform location was moved each day and training proceeded for four trials from different starting points. Normal rats showed shorter escape latencies across the four trials within each day and generally improved on the task across test sessions. By contrast rats with fornix transections were impaired and showed no general improvement across days. In a follow-up study, Whishaw and Tomie (1997) replicated the success on initial place learning by rats with fornix transection, and the poor performance on reversal. In addition, they found that the deficit during reversal was related to the tendency by rats with fornix transections to return to the originally learned platform location (Figure 7.11). This perseveration of an initially learned escape location was taken as further evidence for successful place learning, albeit clearly

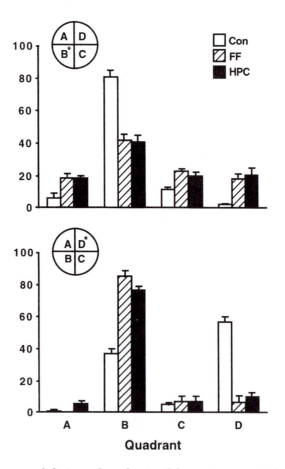

Figure 7.11. Percent of choices of quadrants of the water maze in the first 20 trials in which the platform was hidden in quadrant B (top), and then during reversal learning when the platform was hidden in quadrant D (bottom). Con = normal controls; FF = fimbria fornix transection; HPC = hippocampal lesion. (Reproduced, with permission, from Whishaw & Tomie, 1997; Copyright John Wiley & Sons, Inc.)

mediated by a different strategy than that used by normals, one that did not support rapid reversal learning (see also Day et al., 1999).

When Is a Place Not a Space?

Another line of evidence ultimately limiting the utility of describing hippocampal function as being "dedicated" to spatial processing involves a set of behavioral tasks that emphasize learning about spatial contexts. The involvement of the hippocampus in learning about an important spatial context is readily demonstrated within an experiment performed by Phillips and LeDoux (1992). In this study, rats were initially adapted repeatedly to a Skinner-box-sized conditioning chamber. On two subsequent daily training sessions they were returned to the chamber, and on each of two training trials per day, a 20-s tone was presented and terminated with 0.5-s foot shock. The rats acquired two kinds of conditioned fear. First, within the second training session, when the tone was presented on the first trial, the rats displayed several indices of fear, including the adoption of a striking freezing posture. Second, by the beginning of the second training day, the rats also froze when placed in the chamber prior to any tone presentations, showing they were also conditioned to the environmental context in which the previous tones and shocks had occurred. Ablation of the hippocampus blocked the acquisition of the context-elicited freezing but spared the conditioned response to the tone (Figure 7.12; Phillips & LeDoux, 1991; Selden et al., 1991; Kim & Fanselow, 1992; see Holland & Bouton, 1999, for review). This is a remarkable dissociation of learning functions of the hippocampus. The results clearly show that the hippocampus is not necessary for conditioned fear to a specific phasic cue that is temporally associated with the shock reinforcer. However, in exactly the same training circumstances, the hippocampus *is* necessary to acquire a conditioned fear response to the background context where tones and shocks occur.

Nadel and Willner (1980) have argued that animals with hippocampal damage fail at contextual learning because they cannot remember the "place" where the shock occurred. However, in a variant of Phillips and LeDoux's task where no tone is presented prior to the shock, both normal animals and those with hippocampal damage condition strongly to the context (Phillips & LeDoux, 1992). Because the available spatial cues were identical in the two versions of the task, the observation of spared versus severely impaired learning after hippocampal system damage cannot be attributed simply to the availability of spatial cues that compose the environment. Rather, one must take into consideration how the animal was encouraged to use those cues in the two versions of the task. A likely explanation is that, in the standard version of the task, the animal was attending to the tone when the shock was delivered, leaving the environment to serve only as a "background" context. However, in the version of the task where no tone was presented, the animal may have been attending to some other specific but unidentified cue (e.g., a wall of the chamber or the grid floor) when the shock was delivered. In this situation that particular cue can be regarded as having been brought out of the background and as serving the same role as the tone in the other version of the task. When the animal was reintroduced into the environ-

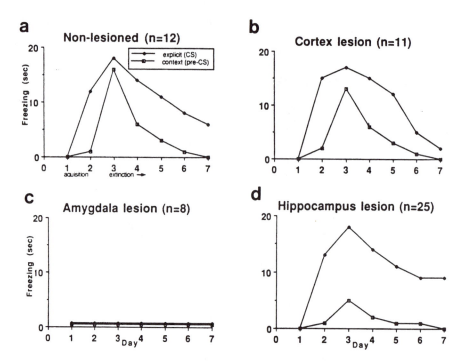

Figure 7.12. Performance in cued and contextual fear conditioning. In the acquisition sessions the explicit CS (a tone) predicts the shock. During subsequent extinction trials only tones are presented. Contextual learning was measured as the time freezing prior to presentation of the CS. (Reproduced, with permission, from Phillips & LeDoux, 1992; Copyright The American Psychological Association.)

ment, that particular cue would have been immediately present and would have been expected to elicit freezing. So, in the version without the tone, rats appear to freeze in the context immediately only because the functional "cue" is present at the outset. This interpretation is entirely consistent with Nadel and Willner's proposal that contexts are places where other things happen. However, what is not addressed by this account is how the chamber in this situation is necessarily used as a "cognitive map" that the rat employs to navigate among important locations. In contextual fear conditioning, the entire environment composes the contextual cue. The task does not require subjects to navigate from one location to another based on computations of spatial metrics. Rather, the subject's mere presence within the set of cues that compose the environment is the critical cue.

In our view, it is important to distinguish between cognitive mapping, requiring computations of spatial metrics based on cue locations, and place recognition, which only requires sufficient cues to identify a familiar environment. This point can be better elaborated by a reconsideration of Olton and Feustle's (1981) experiment on nonspatial working memory, and some of the experiments that followed. When Olton and Feustle observed the impairment in working memory for maze arms that could be differentiated by nonspatial cues, they interpreted the result as supporting a general working-memory function of the hippocampus. However, the generality of this deficit in nonspatial memory was initially brought into question by Aggleton et al. (1986), who used similar cues to study delayed nonmatching-to-sample performance in rats with hippocampal damage. In their study the memory cues, like those in the Olton and Feustle study, were maze arms, but here they were small and elaborately decorated trial-unique enclosed boxes. The task also had a memory demand like that of Olton and Feustle's task, in that animals were initially presented with one cue and then rewarded for selecting against it in a choice test. However, contrary to the results of Olton and Feustle, Aggleton and colleagues observed no deficit in rats with hippocampal damage in remembering these cues. Subsequent studies on several variations of these nonspatial memory tasks have either confirmed substantial and enduring deficits after hippocampal damage (Jagielo et al., 1990; Raffaelle & Olton, 1988) or found little or no effect (Aggleton et al., 1989; Mumby et al., 1992; Rothblat & Kromer, 1991; Shaw & Aggleton, 1993). These experiments have differed along several methodological parameters, most prominently differences in the use of a matching or a nonmatching rule, differences in the use of trial-unique cues or repeated use of cues across trials, and differences in whether the cues were discrete objects or distinctive boxes. How can we understand such different outcomes?

Rawlins and his colleagues have sought to disentangle these variables with a series of studies on rats with fornix transections performing several variations of the task (Cassaday & Rawlins, 1995; Rawlins et al., 1993; Yee & Rawlins, 1994). They examined the importance of the match versus nonmatch rule and the use of trial-repeated and trial-unique cues, and they explored a variety of memory cues including small and large boxes with simple or complex designs, with their boxes sometimes containing objects as redundant or as critical cues. These studies showed that the matching and nonmatching rule was not a critical variable. However, the unexpected key parameters were the size, complexity, and uniqueness of the memory cues. No impairment was observed on variants of the task that employed objects or small boxes as stimuli. However, when the stimuli were large boxes that differed only in the patterns on their walls, a severe impairment was observed, confirming Olton and Feustle's (1981) results. The complexity and uniqueness of cues with the large boxes were important factors, so that the performance of rats with fornix damage substantially improved with the addition of different objects and with use of trial-unique stimuli. Indeed no deficit was observed when the cues were large boxes that contained multiple trial-unique objects (Cassaday & Rawlins, 1995). Combining the data across these studies, they concluded that the hippocampus is not required for working memory when the cues are three-dimensional objects, and that small boxes are treated as if they were objects. However, the hippocampus is critical when the boxes contain fewer distinctive cues and are large enough to contain the entirety of the rat's body. This suggests that when the boxes are large enough to be considered "places," hippocampal processing becomes important.

So, are we back where we started with regard to the spatial memory or cognitive mapping hypothesis? Nadel and Willner, and others who espouse the spatial view of hippocampal function, may take comfort in this "place" interpretation of the deficit in what were otherwise considered nonspatial working-memory tasks.

However, in these tasks there is no demand to remember the spatial locations of the boxes (i.e., no requirement to navigate among the boxes and remember their locations). Based on these considerations, Rawlins and colleagues concluded that the large boxes are processed not within a spatial map but as "contexts"—whole environments that can occupy different locations in the larger world. To conceive of this distinction, think of your favorite fast-food restaurant, one that belongs to a chain of identical restaurants located throughout the city and the country. Surely we think of these as "places" where we eat, but we don't concern ourselves with navigational issues as part of this thought (i.e., not while thinking of the place right now; we do so only when we are actually headed there to eat). Rather, in this situation we use the term *place* to mean a context—the place where we can get such-and-such food item and that has a drive-through window—and this conception of a place falls outside O'Keefe and Nadel's cognitive mapping account.

Further Explorations of Conditional and Context-Dependent Learning

Reinterpreting some of the early results to emphasize not spatial memory processing but context-dependent learning permits us to also bring to bear a good portion of the newer literature on the role of hippocampus in nonspatial memory tasks. A particularly interesting portion of that newer literature concerns tasks involving both a memory delay and conditional or contextual operations. One very simple example is tasks that require the animal to alternate between two choices on successive trials when there is a substantial delay between trials. Winocur (1985) found that normal rats and rats with hippocampal damage rapidly learned to press a bar each time it was inserted into the test chamber. Subsequently, only every other trial was rewarded. Normal rats learned to inhibit responses on alternate trials, and their performance was better when the delay between trials was short rather than longer (Figure 7.13). Rats with hippocampal damage also could perform the task, but only when the delay was short; their performance deteriorated abnormally fast when the memory demand was increased. These findings suggest that rats with hippocampal damage could perform the critical conditional operation but could not remember the conditional cue. Of course, the common observation of deficits following hippocampal damage on alternation in two-choice maze performance as well as on working memory in the radial maze (see above) is consistent with the same interpretation.

Further evidence concerning conditional operations per se have centered on Sutherland and Rudy's (1989) proposal that the hippocampus is critical for learning associations of configural stimuli (i.e., combinations of otherwise ambiguous stimulus elements). In their view, the learning of reward associations of *un*ambiguous stimuli occurs independently of the hippocampal system. These investigators, more explicitly than Hirsh, focused on configural association as a resolution to the paradox of ambiguous reinforcement history. They argued that configural association circumvents the need for a conditional operation by creating a unique cue for the association, in addition to elemental associations, rather than ambiguous elemental associations on another cue. As discussed in greater detail in chapter 2, Sutherland and Rudy initially selected the negative patterning problem as

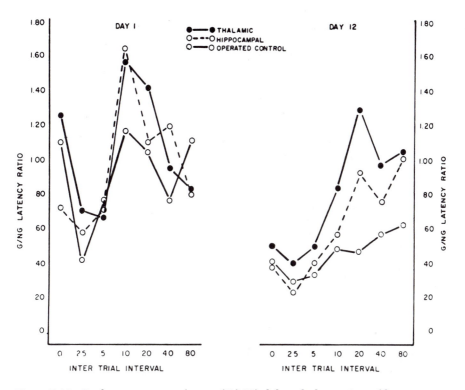

Figure 7.13. Performance on go/no go (G/NG) delayed alternation of bar presses. (Reproduced, with permission, from Winocur, 1985; Copyright Elsevier Science.)

a critical test of their hypothesis. In this paradigm, animals learned to associate two different stimuli with reward when each was presented alone, but with non-reward when they were presented together, a set of contingencies that cannot be supported by a simple accumulation of reward value for each stimulus element. Sutherland and Rudy proposed that the hippocampus solves this problem by the creation of a configural representation that can be employed as a *unique CS*—a "configural cue" that can be associated with its own reward value, independent from the values of its constituent elements (Figure 7.14, top). Also offered in support of their hypothesis was Sutherland and Rudy's (1989) finding that rats with hippocampal damage failed to learn a task that required them to bar-press in the presence of either a light or a sound but to inhibit bar pressing to the combination of a light and a sound (Figure 7.14, bottom). They also mustered supporting evidence from other experiments in which rats were required to learn different responses to specific cues, depending on a conditional cue. In one study, they found that rats with hippocampal damage failed at a Y-maze problem in which they had to choose between a black and a white goal box contingent on whether the starting chamber was illuminated (Sutherland et al., 1989). In another study, they found that rats with hippocampal damage failed to learn a transverse patterning task. This test was composed of a set of three visual discrimina-

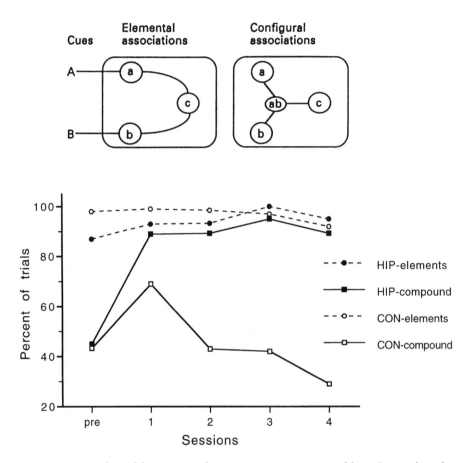

Figure 7.14. Configural learning in the negative patterning problem. (Reproduced, with permission, from Rudy & Sutherland, 1995; Copyright John Wiley & Sons, Inc.)

tion problems that contained overlapping elements, each of which was the rewarded stimulus in one problem and the nonrewarded stimulus in another (Figures 7.15, 7.16; Alvarado & Rudy, 1995). The deficit on transverse patterning has since been replicated using olfactory cues (Dusek & Eichenbaum, 1998). Notably these data support either Hirsh's account or Sutherland and Rudy's account, because we cannot tell whether normal animals solved the problems by conditional operations (response to one stimulus contingent upon whether it is paired with another) or configural associations (response to the stimulus configuration with a response to one of the cues).

Additional evidence for the view that animals with hippocampal damage fail in conditional operations comes from studies on context-dependent retrieval. These experiments involve behavioral paradigms in which learned performance of a "simple" association depends on testing within the context of original learning. In a particularly striking example of this kind of learning, Penick and Solo-

SETS OF SIMULTANEOUS VISUAL DISCRIMINANDA

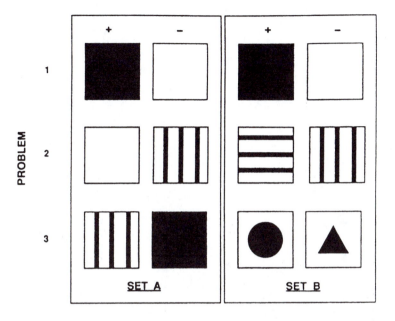

Figure 7.15. Stimuli for the two sets of discrimination problems. Simultaneous solution of set A (transverse patterning) requires a resolution of the ambiguous reward assignments for each cue. Solution of set B (elemental stimuli) does not. (Reproduced, with permission, from Alvarado & Rudy, 1995; Copyright American Psychological Association.)

mon (1991) trained rabbits for several days in the standard classical eyelid-conditioning paradigm (see chapter 13). On the next day, they were retrained using the identical procedures except that for half the animals the sound-proof chamber in which training occurred was altered in visual, olfactory, and tactile dimensions. For normal animals, the switch in context was highly disruptive, causing an immediate drop in conditioned responses. By contrast, animals with hippocampal damage were not disrupted in the altered-context condition, showing as much savings in this condition as normal animals did with continued training in the original context (Figure 7.17). Another study, by Good and Honey (1991), showed that rats with hippocampal ablations also failed to show context-dependent operant conditioning. In this study, rats were trained to bar-press to a light cue in one context and to bar-press to a sound cue in another context. Subsequently, normal rats responded more to each cue in its training context, but rats with hippocampal damage responded equally to both cues in either context. Finally, Olton (1986) extended the notion of context-dependent retrieval to explain why rats with hippocampal damage are impaired in learning to withhold bar press responses for a fixed temporal period after a rewarded bar press, a procedure known as *differential responding at low rates* (DRL; see Sinden et al., 1986).

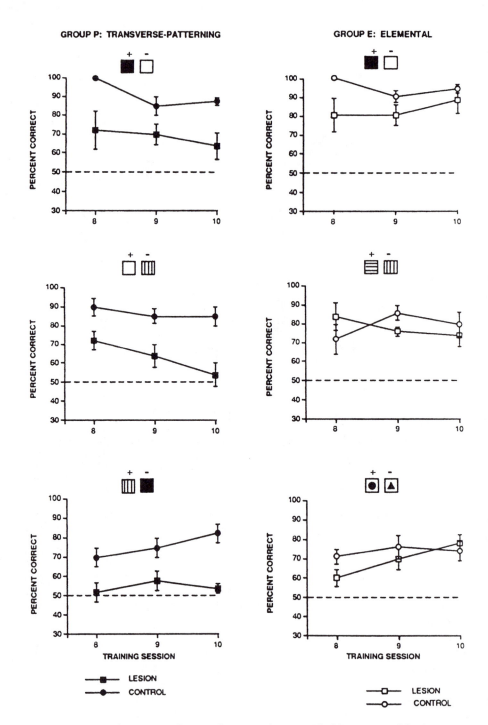

Figure 7.16. Performance of normal rats and rats with hippocampal lesions on the two sets of problems described in Figure 7.15. (Reproduced, with permission, from Alvarado & Rudy, 1995; Copyright American Psychological Association.)

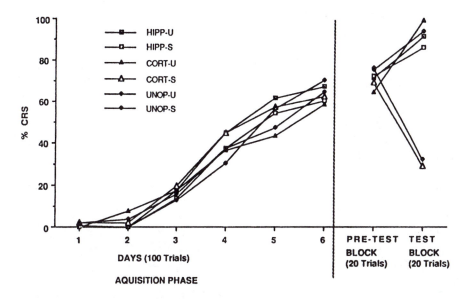

Figure 7.17. Performance measured as percent conditioned eyeblinks during initial acquisition and subsequent pre-testing in the same conditions and then testing in the unswitched condition (U) or in the switched condition (S). HIPP = hippocampal lesion CORT = cortical lesions; UNOP = normal subjects. (Reproduced, with permission, from Penick & Solomon, 1991; Copyright American Psychological Association.)

Each of these findings strongly demonstrates a critical hippocampal involvement in nonspatial learning and memory and points to conditional operations being dependent on hippocampal processing. However, just as place learning can sometimes be accomplished despite hippocampal damage, so, too, can some conditional and configural learning tasks be performed by amnesic animals. Several studies have failed to find impairments after hippocampal damage on variants of the same conditional and configural learning tasks discussed above (Whishaw & Tomie, 1995; Gallagher & Holland, 1992; Davidson & Jarrard, 1989; Jarrard & Davidson, 1991; Davidson et al., 1993; see Alvarado & Rudy 1995) or can even facilitate this kind of learning (Han et al., 1998; Bussey et al., 1998), leading to a reappraisal of configural theory by Rudy and Sutherland (1995) in which they contended that subtle procedural variables can alter the demands to make successful performance dependent or independent of hippocampal processing (see McDonald et al., 1997; Holland & Bouton, 1999).

With regard to context-dependent learning, Winocur and colleagues (1978, 1987) have shown that, under some conditions, rats with hippocampal damage are abnormally strongly dependent on contextual cues for discriminative performance. In one study, Winocur and Olds (1978) reported that rats with hippocampal system damage showed abnormally poor retention of a pattern discrimination when their retention was tested in a different environmental context. Conversely, although rats with hippocampal damage showed the usual deficit in learning to reverse a visual discrimination trained in the same context as the discrimination was originally acquired, they showed abnormally good reversal learning performance when that training was presented in a context different from the original discrimination. Winocur and colleagues (1987) also found that whereas normal rats acquired an aversion to an environment with a strength proportional to the probability of a CS predicting shock, rats with hippocampal system damage conditioned strongly to the same environment at all levels of shock predictability.

A recent experiment by Good et al. (1998) offers a possible reconciliation of the findings on different forms of conditional and contextual learning. They directly compared the effects of hippocampal damage on context-dependent learning and on conditional discriminations where the conditional cues were contexts. Rats were trained to perform approach responses to specific visual or auditory cues, wherein each conditioned response was initially trained in one of two chambers that differed in visual and olfactory cues. Then they tested for context dependency by evaluating the conditioned approach responses in switched contexts. Subsequently they *required* a discrimination between the contexts by differentially reinforcing each cue in only one context. Rats with hippocampal damage had a striking deficit in the initial test of context dependency, but no impairment in the ability to acquire the context-guided conditional discrimination. Furthermore, the intact contextual discrimination performance was shown to rely on a combination of the visual and olfactory contextual cues, indicating that hippocampus-damaged rats could form a representation of the configuration of cues that defined the context. Good and colleagues concluded that the hippocampus is critical only in situations where contextual learning is "incidental" within the demands of the task, but not when the solution of the problem is "contingent" on context processing.

Convergence on the Relational Account of Hippocampal Function in Memory

Even as each of the proposals discussed above can account for some of the important data on preserved versus impaired learning and memory in rodents with hippocampal damage, the above review should make clear that there is little in common between those characterizations of hippocampus-dependent memory in rodents and the characterization of hippocampus-dependent memory in humans. Indeed, superficially the above-described proposals seem to have little in common even with each other. Each view has accumulated substantial support and, at the same time, can be seen as limited in its explanatory power. This dilemma has inspired us to identify the common threads among these views on the function of the hippocampus in animals, a search guided also by the findings on human amnesia.

As originally applied to the study of amnesia, Cohen and Squire (1980; Cohen, 1984; Squire, 1987) characterized declarative memory as the record of everyday facts and events that can be explicitly remembered (i.e., brought to conscious recollection) and, typically, as subject to verbal reflection or other explicit means of expression (see Graf & Schacter, 1985; Schacter, 1987). By contrast, procedural memory has been characterized as the nonconscious acquisition of a bias or adaptation that is typically revealed only by implicit or indirect measures of memory. These descriptions indeed present a formidable challenge for the study of declarative memory in animals. We do not have the means for monitoring conscious recollection in animals; the very existence of consciousness in animals is a matter of debate (see Eichenbaum et al., 1992a, for an extended discussion of this point with regard to hippocampal function). An assessment of verbal reflection is, of course, out of the question, and it is not otherwise obvious how to assess "explicit" memory expression in animals. However, the latter may in fact be possible if we consider further characterizations that have been offered to distinguish declarative and procedural memory. To the extent that these descriptions do not rely on consciousness or verbal expression, they might be operationalized for experimental analysis in animals.

To this end, Cohen (1984) offered descriptions that could be helpful toward the goal of operationalizing fundamental properties of declarative memory. He suggested that

> a declarative code permits the ability to *compare and contrast* information from different processes or processing systems; and it enables the ability to *make inferences* from and generalizations across facts derived from multiple processing sources. Such a common declarative code thereby provides the basis for access to facts acquired during the course of experiences and for conscious recollection of the learning experiences themselves. (p. 97, italics added)

Conversely, procedural learning was characterized as the acquisition of specific skills, adaptations, and biases; such "procedural knowledge is tied to and expressible only through activation of the particular processing structures or procedures engaged by the learning tasks" (p. 96).

The present authors have exploited two distinctions revealed in these characterizations during our development of assessments of declarative and procedural memory that may be applicable to animal studies. First, declarative memory is distinguished by its role in comparing and contrasting items in memory, whereas procedural memory involves the facilitation of particular routines for which no such comparisons are executed. Second, declarative memory is distinguished by its capacity to support inferential use of memories in novel situations, whereas procedural memory only supports alterations in performance that can be characterized as rerunning more smoothly the neural processes by which they were initially acquired.

We have extended these distinctions to make contact with the broad literature on hippocampal function in animals, resulting in a proposal for the representational mechanisms that might underlie declarative memory. Based on this general aspect of hippocampus-dependent memory, our hypothesis is that the hippocampal system supports a *relational representation* of items in memory (Eichenbaum et al., 1992a, 1992b; Cohen & Eichenbaum, 1993). Furthermore, we have suggested that a critical property of the hippocampus-dependent memory system is its *representational flexibility,* a quality that permits inferential use of memories in novel situations. According to this view, the hippocampal system mediates the organization of memories into what may be thought of as a multidimensional memory "space" with particular items in memory as informational "nodes" in the space and the relevant relations between the items as "connectives" between informational nodes. In such a memory space, activation of one node would result in activation of all connectives that are sufficiently strongly associated and, consequently, other informational nodes including ones never directly associated with the originally activated element. Such a process would support the recovery of memories in a variety of contexts outside the learning situation and would permit the expression of memories via various pathways of behavioral output. The combination of relational representation (a consequence of processing comparisons among items in memory) and representational flexibility (a quality of relational representation that permits inferential expression of memories) suggests an information-processing scheme that might underlie declarative memory in humans and animals as well. Most important, this description of the nature of declarative memory is testable in animals.

A deeper analysis suggests that the relational memory account combines the common threads that run through all of the earlier-described hypotheses about hippocampal function in animal memory, as we will try to show. Some of the proposals emphasize the encoding of relations among simultaneously presented cues, particularly those proposals that highlight the role of hippocampus in cognitive mapping or conditional operations. Other proposals suggest that the hippocampal system supports the representation of temporal relations among cues presented sequentially, as required for working memory or for comparisons of present information with representations of past events (Gray & Rawlins, 1986; Gabriel et al., 1986). All of these proposals implicate the hippocampal system in processing comparisons among items in memory, and in the encoding of critical relations among items presented either simultaneously or sequentially, and most are explicit about critical hippocampal mediation of "flexible" memory expression.

Conversely, according to our view, hippocampus-*in*dependent memories involve *individual representations;* such memories are isolated in that they are encoded only within the brain modules in which perceptual or motor processing is engaged during learning. These individual representations are *inflexible* in that they can be revealed only through reactivation of those modules within the restrictive range of stimuli and situations in which the original learning occurred. One might expect individual representations to support the acquisition of task procedures that are performed habitually across training trials; individual representations should also support the acquisition of specific information that does not require comparison and consequent relational representation.

In the remainder of this section we will elaborate on evidence supporting the relational account of hippocampal memory function (see Cohen & Eichenbaum, 1993, for an earlier and more extensive accounting). The evidence we will emphasize to illustrate the relational nature of hippocampus-dependent memory processing comes from studies that exploit the excellent learning and memory capacities of rats in odor-guided tasks. The first set of experiments examines discrimination and reversal learning, showing once more that learning performance may be severely impaired or completely intact depending on performance demands; we will examine in some detail the nature of the critical demands and how they lead to different behavioral outcomes. The second set of experiments examines directly the role of the hippocampus in flexible memory representations and the expression of memory through indirect tests of acquired knowledge.

Odor Discrimination Learning

The learning ability of intact rats was compared with that of rats with transection of the fornix on variations of discrimination learning and reversal paradigms using odors as cues. In a simultaneous discrimination task, two odor cues were presented at the same time and in close spatial juxtaposition, and the discriminative response required a selection between equivalent left and right choices (Eichenbaum et al., 1988). Under these training conditions, rats with fornix lesions were severely and persistently impaired on a series of different odor discrimination problems (Figure 7.18, left). Alternatively, in a successive discrimination task, odors were presented separately across trials, and the response required only completing or discontinuing the stimulus-sampling behavior, thus eliminating an explicit response choice. In striking contrast to the preceding results, under these training conditions rats with fornix lesions performed *at least as well as* normal rats in acquiring the same series of discrimination problems that they had failed to learn under other task demands (Figure 7.18, right; see also Eichenbaum et al., 1986a; Otto et al., 1991; Staubli et al., 1984). It would

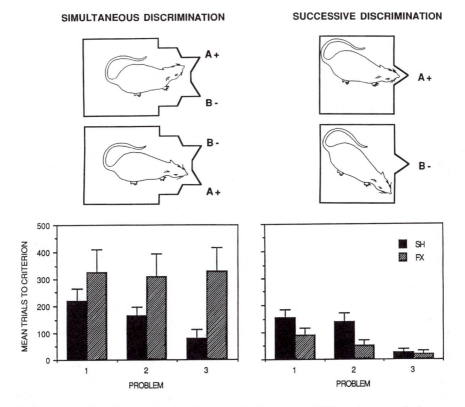

Figure 7.18. Odor discrimination learning by intact rats (SH) and rats with fornix transection (FX). (Reproduced, with permission, from Eichenbaum, Fagan, Mathews, & Cohen, 1988; Copyright American Psychological Association.)

seem that severe impairment, transient impairment, or even facilitation may be observed under different task demands, even with the identical stimulus materials, depending upon the demand for stimulus and response comparison.

Note that these results stand in striking contrast with Kimble's findings on the simultaneous and successive black-white discrimination tasks described above. The combination of these data shows that formal task descriptors such as discrimination learning, simultaneous and successive stimulus presentation, and different modalities of stimuli do not adequately capture the critical variables in hippocampal memory processing. At the same time these data do show that the hippocampus is involved in nonspatial learning and memory, and that other aspects of how the information is processed are critical. The critical differences in performance by rats with hippocampal system damage can be related, we believe, to the demand for stimulus and response comparison.

In our initial efforts to assess the capacity for representational flexibility in normal rats and rats with hippocampal system damage, we pursued a follow-up experiment based on the simultaneous discrimination task (Eichenbaum et al., 1989). Our investigation exploited a surprising finding in the results from that training condition; although rats were generally impaired on this task and failed to learn some of the discriminations altogether, they succeeded in learning some of the discrimination problems as rapidly as normal animals (Figure 7.19). To understand why they occasionally succeeded and to explore the nature of memory representation when they did succeed, we trained yoked pairs of normal rats and rats with fornix lesions on a series of simultaneous odor discrimination problems until the rat with the fornix lesion in each pair had acquired two problems within the normal range of scores. Then we assessed the flexibility of their representations by challenging them with probe trials composed of familiar odors "mispaired" in combinations not previously experienced. Thus, in occasional probe trials, we presented the rats with discriminations between Odor A and Odor D, and between Odor B and Odor C. According to our notion of relational representation, normal animals encode all the odor stimuli presented both within and across trials using an organized scheme that would support comparisons among odors not previously experienced together. Conversely, we postulated that the representation of rats with hippocampal system damage would not support recognition of the separate elements within each compound. To test these predictions, we intermixed within a series of trials on two different instruction problems occasional probe trials composed of a mispaired rewarded odor from one problem and the nonrewarded odor from the other. Both normal rats and rats with fornix lesions continued to perform well on the trials composed of the same odor pairings used on instruction trials. Normal rats also performed accurately on the probe trials, but in striking contrast, rats with fornix lesions performed at chance levels on the probe trials when they were introduced, as if presented with novel stimuli (Figure 7.20).

A further analysis focusing on the response latencies (or reaction times) of animals performing the simultaneous discrimination provided additional evidence that the nature of learned odor representations was abnormal in rats with hippocampal system damage; this analysis also provided insight into how they succeeded in learning some simultaneous discrimination problems. We determined that each rat with a fornix lesion had a quantitatively shorter average re-

DISTRIBUTION OF SCORES

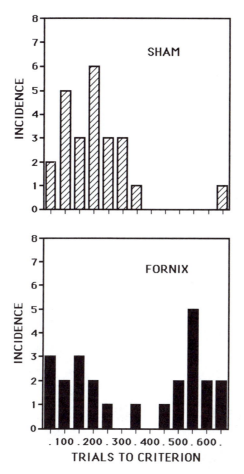

Figure 7.19. Distribution of learning scores among the series of successive odor discrimination problems.

sponse latency than each normal rat, even though all rats performed consistently at high accuracy and showed the speed-accuracy tradeoff typical of reaction time measures. Furthermore, the distribution of reaction times was abnormal in rats with fornix lesions (Figure 7.21). Each normal rat had a bimodal distribution of response latencies, and each of the two modes was associated with one of the positions where the rewarded odor was presented and response executed. This pattern of reaction times suggests that the rat consistently approached and sampled one odor port first, then either performed a nose poke there or approached and sampled the other odor port. In contrast, rats with fornix lesions had a unimodal distribution of response latencies, and the pattern of their response laten-

ODOR DISCRIMINATION - PROBE TESTS

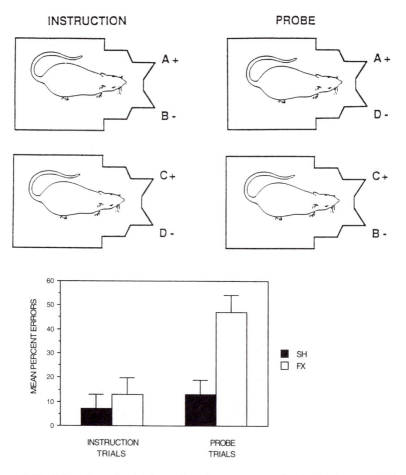

Figure 7.20. Mispair probe trials and performance on the first 50 presentations. (Reproduced, with permission, from Eichenbaum, Cohen, Otto, & Wible, 1992; Copyright Oxford University Press.)

cies was the same regardless of odor and response positions. It would seem that rats with hippocampal system damage sample the entire stimulus compound at once, requiring less time to complete the trial. On just those problems where different left-right combinations of the odors were distinguishable, they suc-ceeded in learning an individual association for each odor compound and the appropriate response. Indeed this account of representational strategies suggests that their performance was inflexible on our probe tests because novel mispair-ings of odors were perceived as unfamiliar odor compounds.

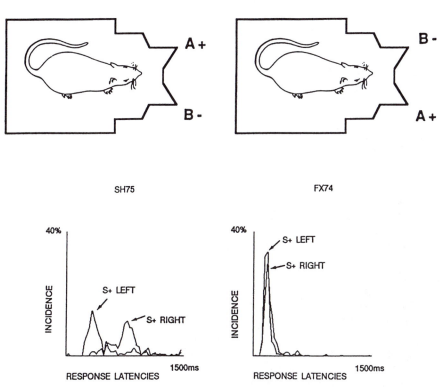

Figure 7.21. Top: The two arrangements of the stimuli in instruction trials. Bottom: Distribution of response latencies on these trials for one normal control rat (SH75) and one rat with a fornix transection (FX74). (Reproduced, with permission, from Eichenbaum, Mathews, & Cohen, 1989; Copyright American Psychological Association.)

Inferential Memory Expression of Stimulus-Stimulus Associations

Eichenbaum and colleagues have investigated more directly the question of whether rats can make inferential judgments from memories about odors (see Bunsey & Eichenbaum, 1996). They developed an odor-guided version of the paired-associate task for rodents and extended the learning requirement to include multiple stimulus-stimulus associations with overlapping stimulus elements. In this task, animals were initially trained to associate pairs of odor stimuli with one another (e.g., A-B; Figure 7.22). Then they were trained on a second set of paired associates, but this time each association involved an element that overlapped with one of those in the previous pairings (e.g., B-C). Subsequently they were given two probe tests to determine whether they had learned the arbi-

PAIRED ASSOCIATE LEARNING:
ASSOCIATIVE TRANSITIVITY AND SYMMETRY

Paired Associates:	A - B	B - C
Associative Transitivity:	A - C	
Symmetry:	C - B	

Figure 7.22. Schematic representation of the pairs of odor cues used on specific tests of paired associates.

trary associations and could use them flexibly to make inferences from memory. In the critical test for *associative transitivity,* subjects were asked to recognize the appropriate relations between indirectly associated elements (e.g., A-C). In the test for *symmetry,* subjects were asked to recognize appropriate pairings in the reverse order of that used in training (e.g., C-B).

Exploiting rodents' natural foraging strategies that employ olfactory cues, animals were trained with stimuli that consisted of distinctive odors added to a mixture of ground rat chow and sand through which they dug to obtain buried cereal rewards (Figure 7.23). On each paired-associate trial, one of two sample odors initially presented was followed by two choice odors, each assigned as the "associate" of one of the samples and baited only when preceded by that sample. Intact rats learned paired associates rapidly, and hippocampal damage did not affect acquisition rate on either of the two training sets, consistent with recent reports on stimulus-stimulus association learning in rats and monkeys (Murray et al., 1993; Saunders & Weiskrantz, 1989). Intact rats also showed strong transitivity across the sets, reflected in a preference for items indirectly associated with the presented sample (Figure 7.24). By contrast, rats with selective hippocampal lesions were severely impaired, showing no evidence of transitivity. In the symmetry test, intact rats again showed the appropriate preference in the direction of the symmetrical association. By contrast, rats with hippocampal lesions again were severely impaired, showing no significant capacity for symmetry.

Natural Paired-Associate Learning

In an effort to extend the range of our study of hippocampal involvement in paired associate learning, Bunsey and Eichenbaum (1995) assessed the role of the hippocampal region in a type of social olfactory learning and memory, the social transmission of food preferences (Strupp & Levitsky, 1984; Galef & Wigmore, 1983). Social transmission of food preferences involves alterations in food choice patterns consequent on experience with a conspecific that has recently eaten a particular food. When an "observer" rat encounters another ("demonstrator") rat that has recently eaten a distinctively scented food, the probability that the observer will later select that same food over other foods increases (Figure 7.25, top; Galef & Wigmore, 1983; Strupp & Levitsky, 1984). This form of social learning is

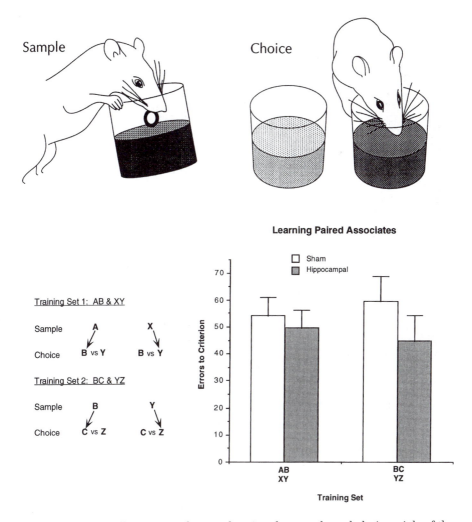

Figure 7.23. Top: Illustration of rat performing the sample and choice trials of the paired associate task. Bottom: Odors presented in the sample and choice trials in each training set (left) and performance of rats in learning each set. (Reproduced, with permission, from Bunsey & Eichenbaum, 1996; Copyright Macmillan Magazines Ltd.)

interpreted within the heuristic that a food recently consumed by a conspecific is safe, and thus transmitting this information is adaptive in rat social groups.

In a series of studies prior to the Bunsey and Eichenbaum work, Galef and colleagues (1988) had shown that the mechanism underlying this learning involves an association between two odors present in the observer rat's breath: the odor of the recently eaten food and an odorous constituent of rat's breath, carbon disulfide. It is of particular importance that exposing the observer to the distinctive food odor alone, or to carbon disulfide alone, has no effect on later food

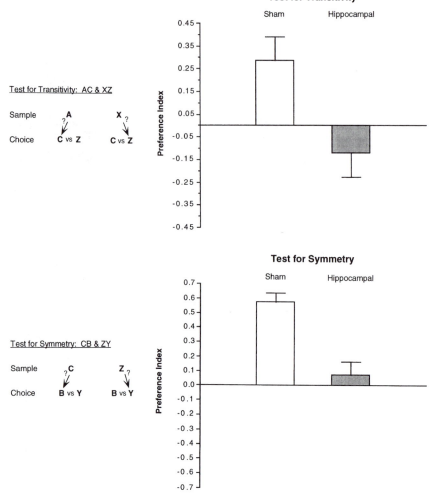

Figure 7.24. Odors presented on the probe tests for transitivity and symmetry (left) and performance of rats on each test. The preference index was calculated as the ratio of the difference in times spent (transitivity) or choice (symmetry) in digging between the two cups and that for the sum on the same measure for the two cups. (Reproduced, with permission, from Bunsey & Eichenbaum, 1996; Copyright Macmillan Magazines Ltd.)

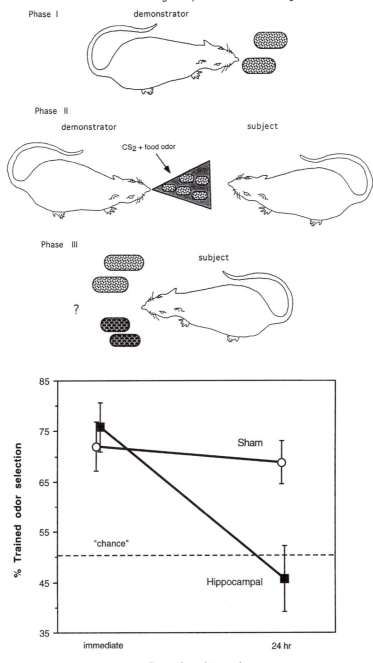

Figure 7.25. Top: Protocol for the social transmission of food preferences task. Bottom: Performance of intact rats (open circles) and rats with selective hippocampal lesions (filled squares) in immediate and one-day retention tests. (Reproduced, with permission, from Bunsey & Eichenbaum, 1995; Copyright John Wiley & Sons, Inc.)

preference. Thus the shift in food choice cannot be attributed to mere familiarity with the food odor. By contrast, exposure to the scented food mixed with carbon disulfide, even without the social context in which this association is usually experienced, increased later consumption of food with the same odor. The clear conclusion from these studies is that the formation of a specific stimulus-stimulus association, in the absence of any primary reinforcement, is both necessary and sufficient to support the shift in food selection.

Memory for the social transmission of food preference is decidedly nonspatial and hence would not be expected to depend on hippocampal function according to the view that the hippocampus evolved as part of a specialized spatial memory system. However, social transmission of food preferences involves the formation of a specific stimulus-stimulus association in a single training episode, plus expression of the memory in a situation different from the learning event, both consistent with the general relational properties of declarative memory.

Following on a previous observation that this type of learning is dependent on the hippocampal region (Winocur, 1990), the role of the hippocampus itself was investigated in this task, assessing both immediate memory and delayed (1-day) memory for social exposure to the odor of a novel food (Bunsey & Eichenbaum, 1995). Normal rats subsequently showed a strong selection preference for the trained food odor in both tests (Figure 7.25, bottom). By contrast, rats with damage selective to the hippocampus itself showed intact short-term memory, but their performance fell to chance within 24 hr. These findings, similar to the pattern of sparing and impairment in human amnesics, indicate that the hippocampus is not required for perceptual or motivational components of learning or the ability to express the learned choice preferences. But the hippocampus itself is required for long-term memory of the association when it must be expressed outside repetition of the learning context. In addition, Winocur's (1990) study showed hippocampal damage produced within a day of training, but not after 5 days, resulted in a retrograde loss of memory for the odor-odor association.

The combined results across all these odor memory experiments provide compelling evidence that some forms of stimulus-stimulus representations can be acquired independently of the hippocampus itself in animals, as indeed is the case in human amnesic patients as well (Moscovitch, 1994; Musen & Squire, 1993). How this might be accomplished will be discussed at length below. Nevertheless, only a hippocampally mediated representation can support the flexible expression of associations among items within a larger organization. This organization applies across many situations, including cognitive maps of spatial organizations, temporal organizations of spatial contexts visited, organizations of items in the "foreground" and "background" within a context, and organizations of items involved in conditional relations. The involvement of the hippocampus in organizing multiple stimulus representations is broad, but limited to organizations based on relations among perceptually independent items. According to our relational account, the organization of elements within a compound stimulus, such as a face or a complex scene, is specifically not included—that kind of processing is completed by already-existing cortical processors (such as the fusiform gyrus, in the case of faces) that send their already fully parsed outputs to the hippocampal system. And indeed, as will be discussed below, learning to distinguish complex stimuli by forming such configural cues sometimes offers a way animals with hippocampal damage succeed in learning (see chapter 9). Combined, these observations provide a bridge to current characterizations of declarative memory being accessible by many routes of expression, including literally one's verbal declarations about the contents of prior experiences. In this way the relational account permits us to see the fundamental processes of declarative memory that are common across species.

The Role of the Hippocampus Itself

The research on rodent memory has not consistently confounded examinations of the role of the hippocampus itself with those of the parahippocampal region, as happened in the research on monkeys. Thus most of what we know from studies on the rodent hippocampus is directly relevant to the function of the hippocampus per se. Early analyses by Olton and colleagues (1978, 1982) indicated that disconnection of the hippocampus either from its subcortical connections by fornix transection, or from its cortical connections by ablating the entorhinal cortex, resulted in severe impairment in spatial working memory. Also, any combination of unilateral and bilateral disconnections that eliminated transfer of information between these two pathways had the same devastating effects. Our own studies comparing these kinds of disconnections indicate that the capacity for nonspatial inferential memory expression is also dependent on both of its main input and output pathways (see chapter 9). These findings indicate that these kinds of memory are critically dependent on the circuitry within the hippocampus itself.

Nevertheless, in the rodent research, there has been considerable debate about which cytoarchitecturally distinct cell fields should be included within the designation *hippocampus.* In particular Jarrard (1986, 1993) has argued that the appropriate unit is restricted to Ammon's horn plus the dentate gyrus. Furthermore, he has pioneered techniques for the use of neurotoxic microinjections to produce entirely selective damage to this or other subdivisions of the hippocampus. Based on a series of elegant experiments using these lesions in rats performing a variety of the tasks described above, Jarrard concluded that damage limited to Ammon's horn plus the dentate gyrus results in a selective impairment in spatial learning and memory.

However, anatomical considerations based on the connectivity data, as well as a thorough analysis of Jarrard's own elegant experiments on subdivisions of the hippocampal formation, indicate that the subiculum should be combined with Ammon's horn and the dentate gyrus as a functional unit. Furthermore, that functional unit, when damaged, produces an impairment of both spatial and nonspatial learning.

Jarrard compared the effects of selective and combined lesions of Ammon's horn plus the dentate gyrus on both spatial and nonspatial radial arm maze performance (Figure 7.26; Jarrard, 1986). On spatial reference memory (learning to avoid consistently unbaited maze arms), lesions of Ammon's horn plus dentate gyrus, as well as those of the subiculum, each produced partial deficits compared to that following the combined ablation of both structures. On the working-memory variants of the task (learning to visit baited arms once) guided by either spa-

RADIAL MAZE

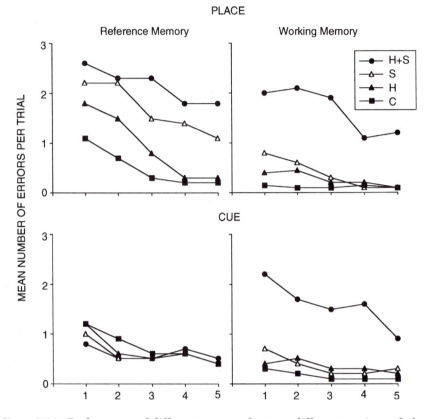

Figure 7.26. Performance of different groups of rats on different versions of place and cue guided memory in the radial maze. H+S = hippocampus plus subiculum; S = subiculum alone; H = hippocampus alone; C = normal controls. (Reproduced, with permission, from Eichenbaum, Otto, & Cohen, 1994; Copyright Cambridge University Press.)

tial or nonspatial cues, the same comparison is even more striking. Lesions restricted to Ammon's horn, dentate gyrus, or subiculum each resulted in minimal impairments, but the combination lesion including all elements of the hippocampus produced a severe impairment, as large as the deficit in spatial reference memory. Precisely the same findings were reported in a similar study using the Morris water maze (Morris et al., 1990), indicating that a severe and persistent deficit only follows complete ablation of the hippocampal formation. Thus selective neurotoxic lesions of Ammon's horn, dentate gyrus, or subiculum produce partial and equivalent effects, compared to those of the combination lesion that includes the entire hippocampus, in multiple forms of spatial learning. Jarrard has also found that ablation of the perirhinal and entorhinal areas (see Jarrard, 1986), a lesion that disconnects all hippocampal areas and removes nearly the entire parahippocampal region, produces radial maze deficits similar in pattern and magnitude to those of complete ablation of the hippocampal formation. In the same study he also showed that transection of the fornix, which disconnects all parts of the hippocampal formation from subcortical areas, produces the same pattern and magnitude of impairments.

Finally, Jarrard and his colleagues found that selective neurotoxic damage restricted to the hippocampus also is adequate to produce impairment in contextual fear conditioning (Selden et al., 1991) and in DRL (Sinden et al., 1986), two other tasks that lack a demand for cognitive mapping. Another study showed that neurotoxic damage limited to the hippocampus was adequate to produce a deficit in context-dependent retrieval of a conditioned response (Honey & Good, 1993). Our own efforts to examine the same anatomical issues have revealed that selective neurotoxic lesions of Ammon's horn, dentate gyrus, or subiculum produced little impairment in long-term memory in our natural odor paired-associate task, but combined damage removing all subdivisions of the hippocampus resulted in severe impairment (Bunsey & Eichenbaum, 1996). The required damage is even less extensive in our other paired-associate task: Selective neurotoxic ablations of Ammon's horn plus dentate gyrus were sufficient to completely eliminate inferential memory expression (Bunsey & Eichenbaum, 1996). Combining all of these data, the analysis of different lesions reveals that the functional domain of the hippocampus includes spatial (cognitive) mapping, working and reference memory, and conditional or context-dependent learning.

The Rodent Model of Amnesia Associated with Hippocampal Damage: Where Do We Stand?

Evaluating the rodent model of amnesia based on the same phenomenological features of human memory impairment with which we evaluated the primate model (in the previous chapter), we see that the rodent model fares well. The memory deficit following hippocampal damage is global. Severe deficits have been observed in a wide variety of both spatial and nonspatial tasks and working and reference memory tasks. Rats with hippocampal damage have intact short-term memory, with a long-term memory impairment that appears delay-dependent. There is, in addition, a retrograde loss of memory that appears to be graded. Finally, the mixture of data on virtually every learning and memory paradigm in which rats with hippocampal damage have been tested provides a testament to the notion that in rats, as well as humans and monkeys, there are types of memory representation that occur independently of hippocampal function. A precise characterization of the features of hippocampus-dependent and hippocampus-independent memory in rodents, as in humans, will need to continue to be clarified and elaborated. However, there appears a compelling case that hippocampal processing supports relational representation and representational flexibility, in common among humans, primates, and rodents. This common account provides a framework for continued progress in understanding the hippocampal memory system.

8

The Representation of Experience in Hippocampal Neuronal Activity

The foregoing analysis of the effects of damage to the hippocampal region suggest its fundamental role is in mediating the representation of relationships among items in memory to allow for flexible memory expression. What kind of neural representation would support this function? On a conceptual level, the form of such a representation might be constituted as a large network of associations in which the items in memory are nodal points, and the connectives among them reflect the relevant relationships. Hippocampal processing might mediate making the connections or permit "surfing" through the network to identify indirect as well as direct relations among the items. The latter would seem to support inferential judgments characteristic of flexible memory expression.

Can such a scheme be confirmed and elaborated by observations on the elements of the hippocampus, that is, in the firing patterns of single hippocampal neurons? While any conclusions about the nature of firing patterns in the hippocampus is still quite preliminary, there is an emerging body of data consistent with the scheme just proposed. A wealth of evidence indicates that hippocampal neurons encode a broad variety of information, including all modalities of perceptual input as well as behavioral actions, and cognitive operations. In addition, hippocampal neurons seem especially tuned to relevant conjunctions or relations among items, rather than single percepts or events. Moreover, hippocampal neural activity is particularly sensitive to modifications with experience so that alterations in the meaning of items or their relationships result in major changes in cellular firing patterns. The substance of these general observations, and their interpretation within the framework of a memory network introduced above, is the focus of this chapter.

Early Observations on the Firing Patterns of
Hippocampal Neurons

Following on the advent of technologies for recording the extracellular spike activity in behaving animals, several investigators began to explore the activity patterns of the large pyramidal cells in the hippocampus of rats and rabbits. The electrophysiological techniques allowed these investigators to make the recordings in waking and behaving subjects, providing the opportunity to correlate firing patterns with stimulus events and motor patterns during a broad variety of behaviors, including learning. The expectancies of investigators in these explorations were marked by caution. James Ranck, Jr., as he pioneered the earliest recording of hippocampal neurons in behaving animals, worried that cells in a brain structure that was positioned so far removed from sensory input and motor output would have firing activity significant only as part of a large network; he suspected that neural firing patterns in response to external stimuli or behavioral output would be uninterpretable. But this clearly turned out not to be the case. Quite the opposite: Hippocampal neuronal activity is well correlated with a very broad variety of stimuli and behavioral events, with the activity of cells "mirroring" virtually all the combinations of stimulus and behavioral events in any situation. Thus identifying the scope and nature of information processing by hippocampal neurons has proved a formidable challenge, not because of a paucity of responses, but because of the variety of responses observed, their complexity, and their plasticity in response to change.

In Ranck's (1973) landmark paper, he described a large number of behavioral correlates of hippocampal neurons. His categorization included cells that fired in association with specific orienting behaviors, approach movements, or cessation of movement, and with consummatory behaviors or the mismatch of expected consummatory events. At the same time, John O'Keefe was also recording from hippocampal cells in rats exploring open fields. But he came to a different conclusion: Rather than neuronal activity reflecting ongoing behaviors, he and his colleague, Dostrovsky, came to the remarkable and historic conclusion that hippocampal cells fired in association with the locations the animal occupied, more than with ongoing behavioral events (O'Keefe & Dostrovsky, 1971). Ranck (1973) noted the possibility that virtually all of his findings might be characterized in terms of the spatial specificity of firing patterns and later provided evidence that this might be the case (Best & Ranck, 1982).

Dating back to the time of Ranck's and O'Keefe's observations on freely moving animals, several investigators began following a different approach to correlating hippocampal neural activity with specific stimuli and behaviors evoked during learning performance. Olds and colleagues (1971; Segal & Olds, 1972; Segal et al., 1972) showed that hippocampal cells exhibit very short latency activation (less than 20 ms) to conditioned auditory stimuli that signal the availability of a reward or punishment. Shortly following, Berger and colleagues (1976; Berger & Thompson, 1978) studied the firing patterns of multiple units in the hippocampus of rabbits during classical eye blink conditioning. In this task rabbits are restrained and presented with pairings of a tone and air puffs, so that a tone conditioned stimulus (CS) precedes and lasts until presentation of an air puff unconditioned stimulus (US) that causes an unconditioned eye blink. Rabbits gradually learn to elicit conditioned blink responses (CRs) during the CS period prior to the US presentation. In these studies hippocampal neurons do not fire associated with presentation of either the CS or US when they are given unpaired. However, they begin to fire early in training, prior to the appearance of CRs. Initially hippocampal cells fire associated with the air-puff-elicited eye blink, and later begin to fire during the CS period prior to presentation of the US. In subsequent systematic studies Berger and colleagues (1983; Berger & Thompson, 1978) showed that these responses were generated by a large proportion of single pyramidal cells that fired only during conditioning at particular phases of the task, either during the CS period, the US period, or both. A few cells fired showed clear-cut tone-evoked responses.

These disparate findings suggest that hippocampal neurons can "adapt" to many situations, that is, shape their activity to reflect the important stimuli, behaviors, and contingencies across a variety of situations. Succeeding observations on hippocampal neurons have pursued both the spatial coding properties and the learning-correlate themes. Each of these will be reviewed here, with the aim of identifying the common fundamental coding properties of hippocampal neurons.

What Are Place Cells?
Do They Compose a "Cognitive Map"?

Shortly after O'Keefe and Dostrovsky's (1971) original report (see Figure 8.1), the existence of location-specific neural activity in hippocampal neurons was confirmed in systematic studies by O'Keefe (1976; O'Keefe & Conway, 1978) and others (Best & Ranck, 1982; Hill & Best, 1981; Hill, 1978; Olton, Branch, & Best, 1978; Miller & Best, 1980). Among the basic properties of hippocampal place cells are the following. Place cells are pyramidal neurons of the CA1 and CA3 fields of the hippocampus proper (i.e., Ammon's horn; Fox & Ranck, 1975). They fire at high rates when the animal is in a particular location in the environment, so that different place cells have distinct "place fields." Most current studies of place cells involve computerized tracking of the animal's position continuously in space and automated means of determining the firing rate of the neuron associated with a matrix of locations (Figure 8.2). These studies typically show that many hippocampal cells have spatially specific activity, and that the locus associated with increased firing is determined by available spatial cues.

The probability of firing of place cells is highly variable, in that sometimes the rate exceeds 100/s on a pass through the part of the environment generally associated with maximal activity, that is, the so-called place field. Yet, on other passes, the cell may not fire at all, so that the average firing rate within the place field is typically about 10/s. Place cells characteristically have very low (less than 1/s) firing rates outside the place field, which has made it difficult to assess how many hippocampal cells have a place field in any particular environment. In studies that consider all cells with a nonzero spontaneous firing rate in the behaving animal, estimates range from about half (Muller, 1996; Shen et al., 1997) to nearly 100% of the cells having a place field (e.g., Tanila et al., 1997b). However, in a careful study where cells were initially isolated under barbiturate anesthesia (when the spontaneous activity of hippocampal principal cells is high),

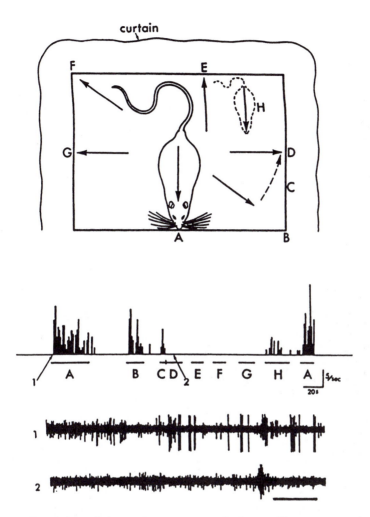

Figure 8.1. Examples of the earliest reports of place cells. An example from O'Keefe and Dostrovsky (1971) that fired only when the rat was in position A and facing as shown. Histogram indicates firing rates at all locations; 1 & 2 show raw firing patterns during the periods marked above. (Reproduced, with permission, from O'Keefe & Dostrovsky, 1971; Copyright Elsevier Science.)

Thompson and Best (1989) showed that nearly two thirds of hippocampal cells do not fire at all in some environments. Of the cells with identifiable spontaneous activity, most had a place field in at least one environment, but the proportion of cells that had a place field in any particular environment was less than a third. In addition, virtually all experiments described some proportion of the cells that have more than one place field. Finally, once established, place fields can be very stable and have been observed to show the same spatial firing pattern for months (Thompson & Best, 1990).

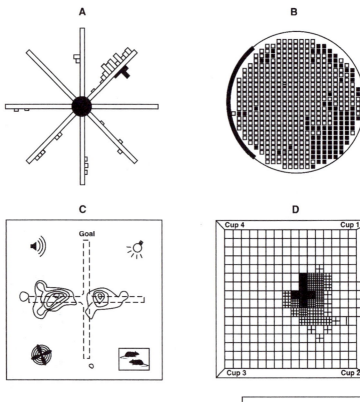

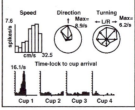

Figure 8.2. Examples of different ways to analyze place cells. A. Radial maze with firing rates plotted as histograms of firing rate at sequential positions on the arms. White bars indicate outward bound movement; black bars indicate inward bound movement. This cell fires primarily in one arm on outward bound traversals. (Reproduced, with permission, from McNaughton, Chen, & Markus, 1991; Copyright MIT Press.) B. Circular open field surrounded by a cylindrical wall with a cue card (black) covering part of the wall. Dark pixels indicate loci of high firing rate. (Reproduced, with permission, from Muller & Kubie, 1987; Copyright Society for Neuroscience.) C. Plus maze place discrimination with food at goal location defined by a set of distal cues. Between trials the cues are rotated together in 90 degree increments. Contour plots of firing rate indicate two place fields of this cell. (Reproduced, with permission, from O'Keefe & Speakman, 1987; Copyright Springer-Verlag). D. Square open field, surrounded by slanting walls, with cul-de-sac on one wall. The rat performs a radial-maze-like task, where it travels

In their initial report O'Keefe and Dostrovsky (1971) realized immediately the potential significance of this neural correlate and suggested that the hippocampus might subserve the creation and utilization of cognitive maps that animals use to navigate their environment, just as Tolman (1948) proposed in his efforts to characterize maze-learning capacities in animals. In support of this view, O'Keefe (1979) later reviewed the existing findings on hippocampal place cells, focusing on the number and types of stimulus features in the environment that were encoded by place cells. He concluded that "a place cell is a cell which constructs the notion of a place in the environment by connecting together several multisensory inputs each of which can be perceived when the animal is in a particular part of the environment" (p. 425). In a study that supported this characterization, O'Keefe and Conway (1978) recorded the activity of hippocampal principal cells in rats performing a place discrimination on an elevated T maze. The maze was enclosed within a plain, square black curtain and was surrounded by a set of four controlled cues (a light, a buzzer, a fan, a white card), each of which was located against one of the curtain walls. Between test trials the maze and the controlled cues were rotated 90 degrees in either direction from that on the previous trial, so that the location of the reward was predicted by only the spatial relations among the maze and the controlled cues and not by any other uncontrolled stimuli. Between recording sessions individual cues or subsets of the cues were rearranged or deleted to examine which stimuli determined the existence and location of spatial selective activity, called the *place field.*

Among the seven cells for which several of these probe trials could be conducted, five maintained the same place field when any two of the four controlled cues were removed, and the other two had place fields that depended on one or two of the cues. When all of the controlled cues were removed, six of eight tested cells lost their place fields, and two retained it. These findings supported the conclusion (a) that location-specific firing in hippocampal neurons is generated by the global configuration of the distant salient stimuli, and (b) that any substantial subset of those cues is sufficient to support spatially specific activity.

Both of these notions were supported by other experimental evidence generated shortly after O'Keefe's initial studies. The idea that place cells are normally controlled by global spatial relations among distal cues was supported by Miller and Best's (1980) finding that partial disconnections of the hippocampus altered place fields, so that location-specific firing became controlled by local cues on particular maze arms instead of distal spatial cues. The notion that any subset of

---

Figure 8.2. Continued.
back and forth between the center of the apparatus and each of the corners to receive water rewards at cups. Areas associated with high firing rate are indicated by dense stippling. Inset: Top: Other factors that influence the firing rate of the cell when the rat is in the place field. Bottom: Firing time-locked to the initiation of traversals to each of the cup locations. (Reproduced, with permission, from Wiener, Paul, & Eichenbaum, 1989; Copyright Society for Neuroscience.)

cues was sufficient for location-related activity was supported by Hill and Best's (1981) demonstration that some place cells in blind and deaf rats maintained the spatial firing, although the majority of cells in these rats followed local cues.

Also, support for the view that hippocampal cellular activity reflects the overall shape or topology of the environment came from two later studies. Muller and Kubie (1987) showed that when the apparatus and cue card were expanded proportionally and the shape was maintained, about a third of place cells "scaled up" in size but had the same shape and location place fields (Figure 8.3). By contrast when the shape of the apparatus was changed from cylindrical to square, or vice versa, without changing the size or types of cues, most place fields were lost or changed unpredictably. Additional recent support comes from a study by Cressant et al. (1997) showing that objects located asymmetrically within the cylinder or scattered around the edge of the cylinder wall can control place fields, but a cluster of objects in the center of the cylinder does not. This pattern of findings suggests that the objects gained control only when they provided non-ambiguous topological cues.

The view that hippocampal cells encode global spatial relations among salient distal stimuli is now widely accepted and indeed is a critical feature of O'Keefe and Nadel's (1978) cognitive mapping hypothesis. The concept of hippocampal spatial representation that has emerged from these findings, illustrated in Figure 8.4, is that the hippocampus contains a maplike representation of space. At a conceptual level, the map constitutes a coordinate grid, instantiated by intrinsic

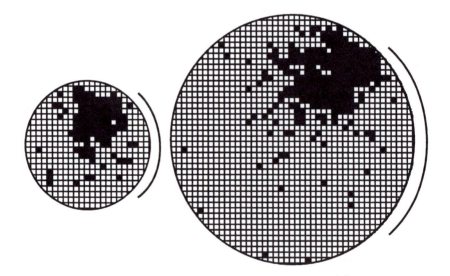

Figure 8.3. Left: Plotting of place field (darker pixels) from a hippocampal neuron of a rat foraging for food on a circular open field surrounded by a blank cylinder with a cue card (black curve) on one part of the wall. Right: Note enlargement and same position of the place field in a larger version of the apparatus. (Reproduced, with permission, from Muller & Kubie, 1987; Copyright Society for Neuroscience.)

Cognitive mapping

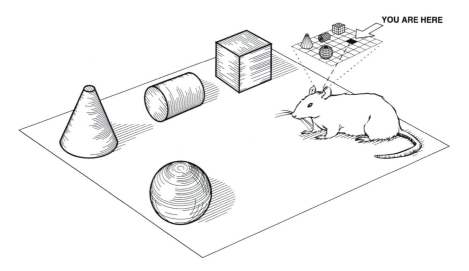

Figure 8.4. A schematic example of how an environment is mapped in the hippo-campus according to the cognitive mapping hypothesis. (Reproduced, with permission, from Eichenbaum, Dudchenko, Wood, Shapiro, & Tanila, 1999; Copyright Cell Press.)

connections among hippocampal neurons. During investigation of a novel environment, representations of the relevant environmental stimuli are associated with appropriate spatial coordinate points. The resulting map is Cartesian in that it provides metric representations of distances and angles between the relevant stimuli. At the physiological level, a place cell reflects the occurrence of the rat at a particular coordinate position within the map. Thus implicit in this model is the assumption that place fields can be considered "pointers" within a unified map, so that either every cell contains information about all of the cues or cells representing subsets of the cues are all linked and bound by the global coordinate framework. O'Keefe and Nadel's central notion, then, is that the hippocampus constructs a facsimile of the environment, including the salient environmental cues. The notion of a hippocampal representation providing a complete two-dimensional map of the environment has been modified in its details but remains fundamentally intact in Muller's (1996) concept of a hippocampal "graph" and McNaughton and colleagues (1996) notion of spatial "reference frames."

The Spatial Code Involves Representations of Specific Spatial Relations, Not a Unified Map of the Environment

The view that each hippocampal cell acts as a "pointer" in a unified map of space has been called into question by recent examinations of the cues that place cells encode. A central and critical aspect of the cognitive map model is that place cells are determined by the overall topology of all salient environmental cues. Operationally this is observed by each cell's activity being unaffected by the removal of any particular cue, so long as sufficient stimuli remain to retain the overall topology. Furthermore, the topological relations among place cell representations are fundamentally coherent; that is, they are bound to one another in the framework that represents a space. One might expect such a spatially systematic representation to be instantiated within a spatial organization of place representations in the hippocampus. Yet neither of these expectations turns out to be the case, and instead hippocampal spatial firing reflects distinct subsets of the attended-to environmental cues. One line of evidence inconsistent with the view that global topography is always predominant comes from Muller and Kubie's (1987) "expansion" experiment described above. In this study, place fields were initially mapped for animals exploring the cylinder apparatus, and then again after the animal explored a topologically identical but larger version of the same apparatus. Some of the cells retained the same overall spatial pattern of firing, and the size of their place fields scaled somewhat with the expanded environment. However, over half the cells lost or changed their place fields following this manipulation, indicating that something other than global topology controlled the majority of hippocampal neurons.

Other data directly indicate that the spatial firing patterns of many hippocampal neurons are controlled by specific subsets of the cues. O'Keefe and Burgess (1996) used a systematic set of environmental shape manipulations to show more strikingly that the location and shape of place fields are determined by the rat's distance from one or a few of the cues. They employed an apparatus composed of four gray walls arranged to form different topologies of a rectangular apparatus, either a small or a large square, and other rectangles with different aspect ratios. The major finding was that the firing rate as well as locus and shape of the place field of most of the cells varied systematically with the distance from a particular subset of the walls. Place fields very close to a corner of the apparatus were the same in all four chambers. Place fields near one wall were stretched when one or more walls were moved away from their center, so that some place fields even split into two firing maxima. None of the place cells were controlled by the distance from a single wall, in that none had a stripelike firing maximum along a wall. On the other hand, none of them were controlled by the proportionate distances among all four of the walls. Rather each cell's spatial activity appeared to be under the control of two or three walls, and some place fields were influenced by static room cues as well as by the moving walls. Consistent with the majority of Muller and Kubie's cells, because none of the cells had the same field in the two rectangles and another in the two squares, it did not appear that overall topology was the major influence.

In another study that explicitly addressed the issue of which cues determine place fields, Hetherington and Shapiro (1997) employed a square recording chamber where three of the four walls were differentiated by a distinct rectangular cue card. They found that place fields were more prevalent close to the chamber walls than expected by chance, contrary to some previous studies using less richly endowed environments (e.g., Muller et al., 1987). In addition they found that the removal of a single cue card altered the spatial specificity and firing rates of hippocampal place cells systematically (Figure 8.5). Removal of a card decreased spatial specificity reversibly regardless of what cue was removed. In addition, removal of a card near the place field decreased the firing rate and place field size. Conversely, removal of a card distant from the place field increased place cell firing rate and place field size. These findings are entirely consistent with O'Keefe and Burgess' data and indicate that a critical aspect of spatial firing is the distance from single proximal cues.

In addition, other studies have shown that when a particularly salient cue is moved repeatedly and randomly within the environment, some of the cells redistribute their spatial firing patterns solely relative to that cue (Gothard et al., 1996a, 1996b). In one experiment rats were trained within a large open-field enclosure to shuttle between a mobile starting box and a goal location identified in relation to a pair of landmarks that were also variously located. Subsequently the rat could return to the start box, which in the meanwhile had been moved to

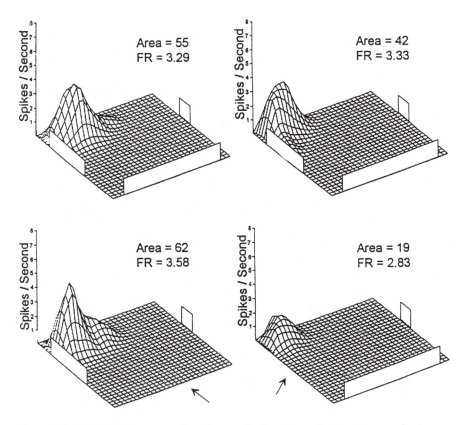

Figure 8.5. Firing rate maps of a place cell showing effects of removal of cues (small rectangles at the sides of the plotting area). On the top are baseline trials taken before each cue removal shown below (arrows). (Reproduced, with permission, from Hetherington & Shapiro, 1997; Copyright American Psychological Association.)

a new location, to obtain an additional reward. The authors found three main types of place cells: 45% fired when the rat was at one or more locations relative to the static environmental cues; 10% fired related to the rat's location relative to the landmark-defined goal site, usually only during the approach or departure, or when the rat was at the goal site; and 45% fired related to the box, again with selective or maximal firing as the rat approached and entered or left the box or as the rat occupied the box. In a subsequent experiment, the same pattern of findings was obtained in rats shuttling along a linear track between a movable start-end box and goal site. In this apparatus, many place cells fired when the animal was in the box or at a particular point near the departure or arrival. The other place cells fired when the rat was at a particular distance from the goal. Thus the anchor of the spatial representation of these cells switched between the two ends of the track, depending on which was closest. Under these conditions the majority of the activated hippocampal cells did not exhibit location-specific activity referenced to fixed environmental cues. Instead their activity could be characterized as "spatial" only to the extent that they fired at specific distances from a particular stimulus or goal.

To explain these findings Gothard and colleagues proposed the hippocampus can invoke multiple spatial "reference frames," distinct spatial maps tied to different anchors within the same environment. But such a view would leave it to other brain structures to accommodate environments that contain movable targets within a fixed overall topology. Furthermore, the notion of such a limited reference frame suggests that the hippocampus devotes its full network to tracking the animal's distance between a single starting point or target in ongoing experience. Such a narrow view is inconsistent with neuropsychological studies showing the hippocampus is not required for approaching or returning to visible goals. In our view, the data are alternatively, and more simply, explained as hippocampal representations of particular, highly relevant subsets of the cues within the environment, independent of the global topology.

Recently, Shapiro, Tanila, and colleagues (Shapiro et al., 1997; Tanila et al., 1997a) also characterized the responses of hippocampal place cells to alterations of the cues within a familiar environment. The design of these studies was similar to that of O'Keefe and Conway's (1978) experiment in that the apparatus consisted of a multiple-arm maze enclosed within a plain, square curtained environment containing several controlled cues (Figure 8.6). The apparatus consisted of a plus-shaped radial maze with the controlled cues composed of four "distal" cues, distinct objects hung on the center of each wall, and four "local" cues, overlays on each maze arm that contained distinctive visual, tactile, and olfactory cues. Initially rats were extensively trained to run to the ends of maze arms in order to receive rewarding hypothalamic stimulation, during which all eight cues were in a standard configuration. In subsequent recording sessions, trials with cues in the standard configuration were alternated with several types of probe trials in which subsets of the cues or individual cues were rearranged or deleted.

Systematic manipulations showed that different hippocampal place cells encoded individual local and distal cues, relationships between cues within a stimulus set, and relations between the local and distal cues. Thus the place fields of some cells were fully controlled by as little as a single cue within a very complex environment, and most cells were controlled by different subsets of the con-

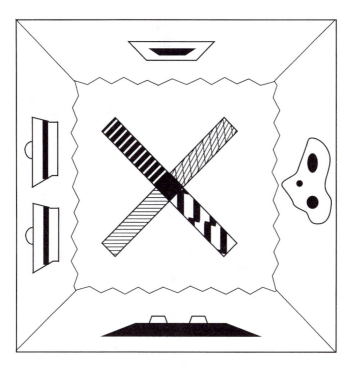

Figure 8.6. Radial maze apparatus used to assess effects of manipulations of sets of distal and local cues. Distal cues are composed as an object on each wall of the surrounding curtains. Local cues are composed as a surface covering on each arm that is unique in its visual, tactile, and olfactory cues. (Reproduced, with permission, from Tanila, Sipila, Shapiro, & Eichenbaum, 1997; Copyright Society for Neuroscience.)

trolled cues. One type of manipulation, called a *double rotation,* involved rotating the distal cues 90 degrees in one direction and the local cues 90 degrees in the opposite direction. Different cells responded to this manipulation in one of four general ways (see examples in Figure 8.7). The largest single set of place fields rotated with the distal cues, but a substantial proportion of place fields rotated with the local cues. Yet other place fields remained constant, indicating they were under the control of unidentified static room cues. In addition many of the cells changed their spatial firing pattern either by loss or gain of a place field or by a change in spatial firing pattern that was inconsistent with the cue rotations. When the subset of cues controlling a cell was spatially scrambled, some of the cells followed a single cue.

By examining small ensembles of these cells recorded simultaneously it was determined that different cells were controlled by distinct subsets of the cues at the same time (Tanila et al., 1997c). Thus some ensembles were fully "concordant" (that is, involved place cells that all responded to the double rotation in the same way), and indeed the overall concordance within an ensemble was 79%. However, fully concordant ensembles represented the minority of cases, so

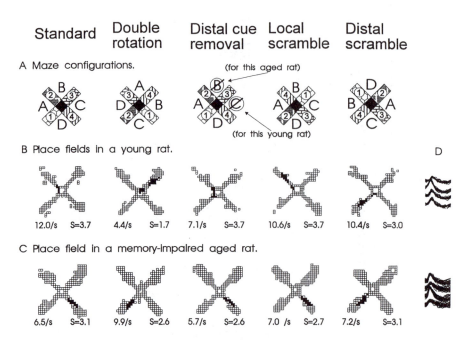

Figure 8.7. Responses of cells in a young and in an aged rat to manipulations of the cues. A: Cue configurations. A-D indicate positions of distal cues; 1-4 indicate positions of local cues. B & C: Spatial firing patterns of place cells. Dark pixels indicate high firing rates. D: Overlapping waveforms of the cells as recorded by four sites on a tetrode. (Reproduced, with permission, from Tanila, Sapila, Shapiro, & Eichenbaum, 1997; Copyright Society for Neuroscience.)

that in only 37% of the ensembles did all the cells respond identically. In the majority of cases some cells responded differently than others. A particularly striking example of discordance is provided in Figure 8.8. Here the place fields of Cells 2 and 3 followed the distal cues. However, Cell 1 had three place fields in the standard condition, and one of these rotated with the distal cues and one with the local cues, and the third disappeared altogether. Cell 4 had a very large field in the standard environment, which "split" into two fields that rotated in opposite directions during the double rotation.

That differently controlled cells can fire on the very same trial was demonstrated by an analysis of a few cells that had overlapping place fields in one of the environments, and the place fields responded differently to the double rotation showing they were under the control of different cues. For example, the ensemble whose activity is depicted in Figure 8.9 had two cells with overlapping place fields when the rat was in the standard environment. A trial-by-trial analysis showed that the overlapping spatial activity occurred on identical standard trials. However, after the double rotation, one field rotated with the distal cues and the other field changed location, showing these place fields were independently controlled by different cues. This experiment shows that these cells encoded different subsets of the cues at the same time, and that the differential encodings

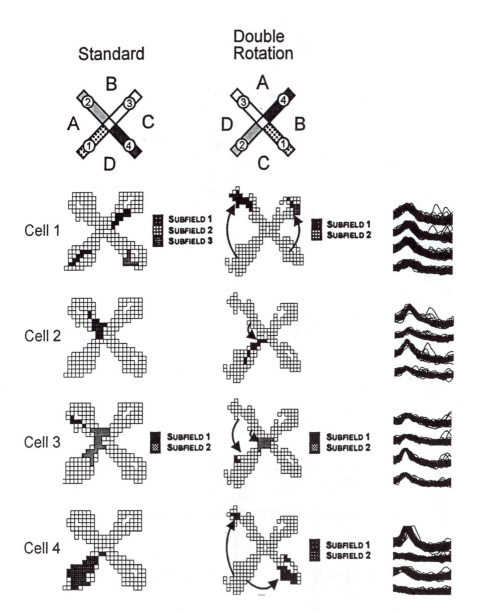

Figure 8.8. Responses of 4 simultaneously recorded cells to the double rotation manipulation. (Reproduced, with permission, from Tanila, Shapiro, & Eichenbaum, 1997; Copyright John Wiley & Sons, Inc.)

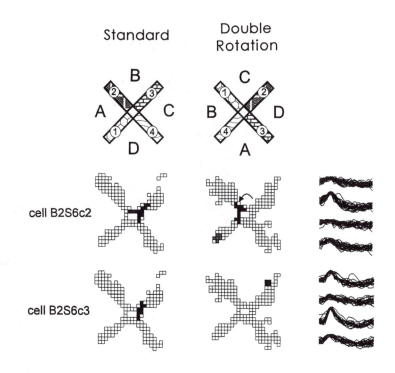

Standard

Double
Rotation

cell B2S6c2

cell B2S6c3

**B2S6 c2-c3
STANDARD CONFIGURATION
single trials**

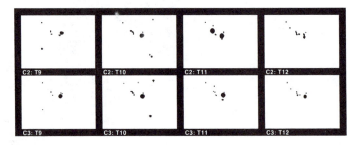

Figure 8.9. Responses of two simultaneously recorded cells (c2 and c3) to the double rotation. Top: Overall changes in place fields. Bottom: Plotting of firing on four sequential trials (T9-T12) in which both cells fired as the rat moved through the maze. Note completely overlapping firing of both cells during some parts of the trials.

were not due to shifts between two different "reference frames," each used by all cells (Gothard et al., 1996a, 1996b). Furthermore, other data from the Tanila et al. (1997b) "double-rotation" experiment show how representing the environment in independent codings of stimulus subsets can support the recognition of variants of the same environment. After animals were initially exposed to the double-rotation version of the cues, they were subsequently exposed repeatedly to both the standard and the double-rotation versions. Over the course of blocks of both types of sessions, the place cell representations redistributed, so that about two thirds of the cells acquired new representations, whereas all other cells converged on representation of the distal cues, local cues, and fixed cues, each with 10–15% of the population representation (Figure 8.10). Thus, after extensive experience with both representations, the hippocampal network captured both the large number of differences in cue relations and the different types of constant cue relations that were common to both environments. The full network representation could, in principle, be extended to incorporate and relate many variations of related environments or, by analogy, many other types of events.

These findings are also consistent with above-described examples of differential coding of distinct cues in the same environment (Gothard et al., 1996a, 1996b; Hetherington & Shapiro, 1997; O'Keefe & Conway, 1978; O'Keefe & Speakman, 1987; O'Keefe & Burgess, 1996), and with divergent responses of place cells to environmental manipulations (e.g., Muller et al., 1987). Other recent studies em-

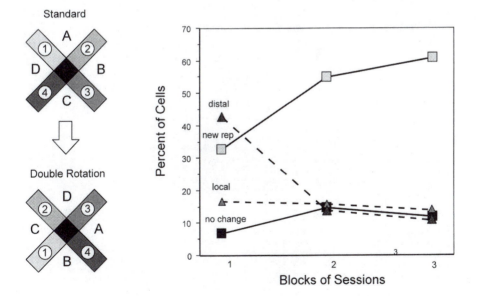

Figure 8.10. Distribution of subsets of cells controlled by different cues during the course of repeated exposures to two variants of the same environment.

phasize the variety of ways hippocampal cells encode subsets of the environmental cues. For example, in one study Markus et al. (1995) first trained rats to forage for food provided at random locations on an open field and then restricted the distribution of the food rewards to four locations. This change, which did not affect any of the salient environmental cues, resulted in changes in some of the place cells, but not others, so that even within groups of cells recorded at the same time, a distribution of altered and retained spatial representations was observed (Figure 8.11). These findings, combined with the others cited above, provide considerable evidence that individual cells within the hippocampal population encode spatial relations among particular environment cues, and not the global environmental topology.

The Hippocampus Encodes Actions and Experiences in Spatial Context

Do hippocampal place cells encode only the location of the animal? Even in his earliest description of place cells O'Keefe reported that the spatial activity of hippocampal neurons was influenced by more than just the location of the animal in the environment. Indeed the preliminary study by O'Keefe and Dostrovsky (1971) emphasized that all the place cells fired only when the rat was facing a particular direction. O'Keefe's (1976) subsequent full analysis reported a variety of variables in addition to location that determined place cell firing rate, including orientation, how long the rat was in the place field, and the elicitation of particular behaviors such as eating or grooming. In addition he recognized a subset of place cells that fired only when the rat was engaged in exploratory sniffing. Motion- and behavior-related correlates were the focus of Ranck's (1973) analysis of hippocampal firing properties, in which he described cells that fired primarily as a rat was involved in orientation, approach to particular objects or goals, consummatory movements, or cessation of movement. In addition, several more recent studies have shown that spatial firing patterns of hippocampal neurons are strongly affected by a variety of nonspatial, experiential factors by which the animal comes to view identical environments as different "situations." Examples of these nonspatial influences on spatial firing patterns follow.

Movement and Place Cells: Coding Actions in Space

Perhaps the most compelling evidence that movement-related variables strongly influence place cell firing comes from a study where rats were immobilized by restraint (Foster et al., 1989). In this study rats either stood still within or outside the defined place field or were held there while restrained by wrapping them in a towel. The cells showed clear increases in firing even while the animal was still within the field, but this firing ceased under the restraint condition, suggesting to the authors that preparedness for movement was a necessary component of the spatial representation. An alternative accounting of these findings, discussed in greater detail below, is that the restraint condition constituted a situation perceived by the rat as substantially different from when it was freestanding, even

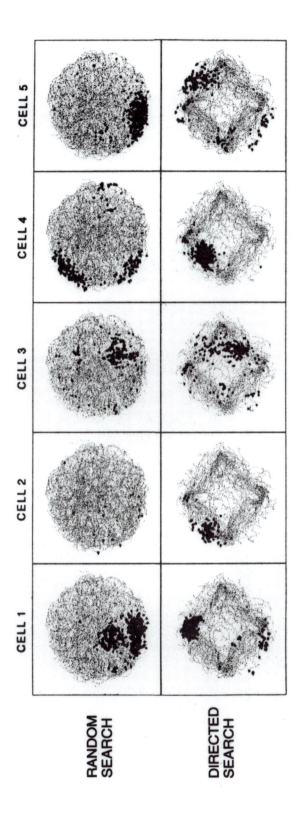

Figure 8.11. Place fields of 5 simultaneously recorded cells in rats first performing the random foraging task, then sequentially approaching four consistently rewarded locations in the same open field. Small dots indicate locations of the rat without spike activity, whereas larger dots indicate locations when the cell fired. Note that cell 1 changed its place field dramatically, cell 2 only fired in the second task, cell 3 had a very similar firing pattern in both tests, and cells 4 & 5 had both the same firing pattern in one area during both tasks, plus an additional area of firing in one task. (Reproduced, with permission, from Markus, Qin, Leonard, Skaggs, McNaughton, & Barnes, 1995; Copyright Society for Neuroscience.)

within the same environment, and that such a major (albeit nonspatial) alteration resulted in a distinct representation within each of the examined cells. As will be seen below, situational changes considerably more subtle than whole-body restraint can dramatically change hippocampal spatial firing patterns.

Regardless of the correct interpretation of this experiment, other studies have demonstrated that place cell firing is strongly influenced by an animal's movement patterns within the place field. One line of studies has emphasized the importance of vestibular activation associated with movement. Thus Hill and Best (1981) showed that vestibular disruption by rapid rotation of the animal altered place fields observed in a subsequent retest, and this finding has been confirmed by more systematic studies showing that rotation of the apparatus or disorientation outside the apparatus causes either rotational shifts in place fields or unpredictable changes in spatial firing patterns (Knierim et al., 1995; Sharp et al., 1995; Wiener et al., 1995). These findings have contributed to the view that self-motion is an important parameter of hippocampal representation (McNaughton et al., 1996).

Another line of evidence regarding movement-related information is the observation that the firing rate of hippocampal cells within the place field is strongly modulated by movement direction and speed. McNaughton et al. (1983) observed that the majority of place cells in rats running on a radial maze fired almost entirely when the animal was running outward or returning inward on the maze arms, and the firing rate was somewhat higher when the rat was running with greater speed (Figure 8.2A). In addition, Wiener et al. (1989) trained rats on a similar task, although within a square-shaped open field. Rats were required to begin each trial at the center of the open field and then could approach any of the four corners to obtain a reward. Subsequently they had to return to the center and then approach a different corner to obtain another reward, and so on. Similar to the findings of McNaughton et al., the majority of place cells fired differentially according to the direction the rat was moving (Figure 8.2D). In addition, most place cells were also tuned for the speed of movement, and in many of these cells there was an optimal movement speed so that the cell fired at lower rates for both slower and faster movements through the place field. Also, the majority of the place cells fired differentially depending on the angle of turns the rat made on its approach to the corner. Most cells preferred an angle close to straight ahead, but some cells were specifically tuned to particular left or right turning directions. The finding of "directional tuning" of place cells in these experiments stands in contrast to the observation of Muller et al. (1987) that place cells are not directional as rats perform their foraging task in the open cylinder. One possibility was that place cell directionality is attributable to limitations in the locations that could be occupied by the rat in the radial maze. However, this notion can be rejected because in the Wiener et al. (1989) task, there was no restriction on movement, yet most place fields were directional (see also Markus et al., 1995). The differences in observation of directionality are not due to the sampling of different cells. In a systematic examination, Muller et al. (1994) replicated the finding of poor directional tuning of place cells recorded in rats performing the random foraging task, and strong directionality of some of the same place cells recorded in rats performing the radial arm maze task.

Another potential explanation is that the nature and number of cues are considerably different in the foraging task and the radial maze task, so that in the cylinder task there is a single salient cue card and in the radial maze task there are many distal room cues. Markus et al. (1995) addressed this issue by training rats to perform the random foraging task in sparse or enriched cue conditions and with the food pellets distributed randomly on the open field or only at specific repeated locations. They found that the number and complexity of visual cues had no effect on the directionality of place cells. By contrast, and consistent with the previously described findings, place cells were generally nondirectional when rats performed the random foraging task but directional when rats approached a small number of repeated reward locations. These findings showed that, even in the identical apparatus, place cells were directional or nondirectional, depending on the movement patterns of the rats related to distributions of significant locations. Furthermore, in the Wiener et al. (1989) study, maximal activity of the cells was usually best observed by time-locking firing to the onset or end of movements toward the reward sites. These authors suggested that movement-modulated spatial firing was best described as reflecting specific actions in space, wherein the network of place cells encodes distinct segments of specific movement patterns.

These findings are further elaborated as somewhat distinct from the conventional characterization of place cells as localized with respect to static cues in the environment. The hippocampal unit activity associated with approaching specific targets or goals was first described by Ranck (1973), although he acknowledged these observations were confounded with consistent spatial locations of those targets. O'Keefe (1976) correspondingly acknowledged that some place cells fire specifically on the approach to a particular location. Eichenbaum et al. (1987) and Wiener et al. (1989) also described approach correlates of hippocampal cells in rats performing an odor discrimination task in the same apparatus in which they had performed a radial maze task. These "approach cells" fired well time-locked to the arrival at the stimulus-sampling area, but the spatial distribution of firing was diffuse compared to that of typical place cells. In addition, some cells fired at a particular phase of approach movements to multiple targets. The finding of goal-related firing challenges the notion of a place cell but confirms the influence of the significance of locations as determinants of hippocampal place cell activity (Breese et al., 1989; Kobayahi et al., 1997; Gothard et al., 1996a,b; but see Speakman & O'Keefe, 1990).

Hippocampal Spatial Representations are Highly Dependent on Experience

There are several findings in the place cell literature indicating that the spatial representations of hippocampal neurons are not simply reflections of the configuration of cues that define the environment. Rather, spatial firing patterns and the organization of the spatial codings are subject to considerable influence of experience with the environmental stimuli.

The effect of experience appears in two forms. One effect of experience involves a stabilization of spatial firing following substantial experience with an environment. Thus, once an animal is familiar with a particular environment, place cell firing does not critically depend upon the very sensory inputs that otherwise seem to control the cell's activity. Strong evidence supporting this conclusion comes from experiments that used the cylindrical open-field apparatus described above (Muller et al., 1987). In this apparatus the location of a place field was fully controlled by the angular position of the cue card (Figure 8.2B; Muller & Kubie, 1987). Initially the animal was exposed to this apparatus repeatedly, and place cell activity was determined. Subsequently, removal of the orienting cue card did not disrupt the firing pattern of most of the place cells, although some place fields rotated to new angular positions. Furthermore, after the initial place field determination, if all illumination was removed so that the rat could no longer see the card, the place fields continued to appear in the same places (Quirk et al., 1990), although spatial specificity might be degraded in the dark (Markus et al., 1994). The possibility that the rat could have identified the position of the cue card without lights could be discounted because the field did change when the rat began the trial in a darkened apparatus. Moreover, after substantial experience in beginning trials in the darkened apparatus, place fields observed in the dark persisted even after the lights were turned back on. Thus the same cells had different place fields within the identical apparatus, depending on whether they had begun the trial in the light or in the dark. Another study suggests, however, that extensive experience with both the lighted and the dark apparatus can bring the representations into correspondence (Markus et al., 1994).

A related study that included a relevant behavioral assessment was O'Keefe and Speakman's (1987) examination of place fields in rats performing a place discrimination in a cross maze. As in the earlier O'Keefe and Conway (1978) study, the environment consisted of blank curtains and a set of controlled cues located around the maze, and these cues and the maze were rotated together between trials to ensure behavioral performance was independent of any other cues. Many of the hippocampal cells had place fields that were predicted by the controlled cues, although others were predicted by the static room cues or combinations of the controlled and static cues. A major finding of this study was that the cells maintained their place fields when all of the controlled cues were removed while the rat was maintained in one of the arms. For example, the cell shown in Figure 8.2C had the same place fields when all the cues were removed. However, the place fields were not maintained if the cues were removed while the rat was off the maze and could not have known their previous spatial arrangement. Sometimes the shape and radial location of the place field were maintained but the arm on which the field was located changed. However, in these cases the location of the place field change was associated with the arm the rat selected while seeking to obtain the reward. Thus a reasonable inference is that the place field was determined by the orientation of the maze remembered by the rat.

The other major influence of experience involves substantial evidence that manipulations indicating a change in the test "situation," but not involving a change in any of the spatial cues, can dramatically alter place cell firing. An impressive demonstration of this phenomenon comes from an experiment that used the cylindrical open-field apparatus (Muller et al., 1987). In this apparatus the location of a place field is fully controlled by the angular position of the cue

card (Muller & Kubie, 1987). If the cue card is rotated in small (45-degree) increments, the place fields shift in correspondence with the cue. However, if the card
is rotated by 180 degrees, the place fields change unpredictably. Furthermore,
when the cue is subsequently rotated in 45-degree increments to its original positions, the new spatial firing characteristics prevail, showing prior experience can
strongly influence the coding of the identical cues (Rotenberg & Muller, 1997).

Additional evidence that experience can be more important than specific sensory cues came from a study where rats were initially exposed to the conventional version of the cylinder apparatus for several recording sessions, then presented with the same cylinder except that the color of the cue card was changed
to white instead of black (the color of the remainder of the wall was gray in both
situations; Bostock et al., 1991). Most cells persisted in having their original place
field, although the angular orientation shifted in some. However, after multiple
exposures to both versions of the apparatus, the typical finding was that the original place field persisted in the black-cue-card cylinder, but the place field
abruptly shifted to a new place field or no place field in the white-cue-card cylinder. As in the other study described above, the place field was not critically dependent on the available cues so much as on a combination of those cues and
recent experience with them. There was no behavioral assessment in this study.
However, one possible explanation of the findings is that the rat initially ignored
the change in cue card color but, after multiple exposures to both environments,
realized there were two versions of the apparatus and recoded the cues in the
newer version.

Yet other studies using the cylinder apparatus have shown that the addition
of a second cue card located at 180 degrees opposite to the initial card did not
change the place fields of most cells, showing that the addition of a potentially
confounding orientation cue did not disrupt a well-established place field (Sharp
et al., 1990). However, changing the location of reward placements from random
to repeated in four locations altered most place fields profoundly, showing that
consistent predominant spatial cues are not sufficient to control spatial firing
when the significance of loci and consequent patterns of exploration are changed
(Figure 8.11; Markus et al., 1995; see also Kobayashi et al., 1997). Also, a recent
experiment by Tanila (1999) using a two-chamber apparatus has shown that
when a rat leaves one apparatus and voluntarily enters another apparatus that
involves an identical set of spatial cues, all the place cells produce new encodings. However, Skaggs and McNaughton (1998), using a very similar task design,
found that many of the place cells in each of their experimental subjects changed
representation in the new but identical apparatus, whereas the remainder of simultaneously recorded cells maintained the same representation in both environments.

The combined findings from all of these experiments show that experience
can have two different and profound effects on spatial firing patterns of hippocampal cells. After substantial experience with a stable set of environmental
cues, removal of any or all of those cues has remarkably little effect on a place
cell's firing pattern. Conversely, subtle alterations in the environmental cues or
any other salient aspect of the test situation can result in substantial or complete
recoding of the spatial firing patterns. These general findings indicate that place

cells encode much more than the constellation of spatial cues and indicate instead that spatial coding reflects the unique situation in which the animal "thinks" it is.

The findings described to this point challenge the notion that place cells represent the topology of the environment as determined by the convergent coding of all the attended-to environmental cues. Each place cell represents only a subset of cues, and the most important cues tend to be proximal to the location of the place field. Place fields are not organized within an orderly representation related to the spatial topography but are clustered, as are the complex stimulus codings found in cortical areas. Moreover, the spatial codings are influenced more by where the animal "thinks it is" than by the sensory stimuli themselves. Thus place cells encode both something less than the full spatial topology, and they encode considerably more than the sensory cues that define the space. In any comprehensive conception of hippocampal spatial representation we need to incorporate the coding of actions and experiences within the spatial context. We will return to this point after considering yet other firing properties of hippocampal neurons.

The Hippocampus Encodes Nonspatial Stimuli and Events

As noted above, even the earliest studies on hippocampal activity in animals exploring open fields included some cells that appeared to have nonspatial firing correlates. For example, in their original paper on place cells, O'Keefe and Dostrovsky (1971) reported that the majority of cells fired in association with arousal or with specific behaviors. In O'Keefe's (1976) full analysis he described a subset of place cells that fired in association with sniffing a particular object, albeit always at a particular place, and some units labeled "other" that fired when the rat sniffed regardless of location. Ranck (1973) first called neurons with this characteristic "mismatch cells" because they fired most as the rat sniffed at a location where a removed object was expected by the rat. O'Keefe (1976) called the neurons that fired during sniffing at a particular place "misplace cells," and they represented about 20% of his place cells.

Consistent with these early findings, several investigators who have intentionally looked for event-related neural activity have demonstrated firing patterns of hippocampal neurons related to nonspatial stimuli and events. In most of these studies, as in the earliest place field studies, the relevant stimuli and behaviors were confounded with spatial location in that each event is associated with the animal's presence in one place. Nevertheless, these studies show that nonspatial stimuli and events can be a necessary component of cellular activation, and a recent study provides compelling evidence of nonspatial firing patterns that occur independent of the animal's spatial location (Wood et al., 1999). Our review of these studies is organized by the type of task examined and, correspondingly, the types of nonspatial stimuli and behaviors associated with hippocampal neural activity. Our intent in providing this brief summary is to show the diversity of stimuli and behavioral events reflected in hippocampal neural activity.

Classical Conditioning

Berger and Thompson's (1976) findings, described at the outset of this chapter, were striking in that they found hippocampal neurons that fired in association with the development of a conditioned eye blink, even when the animal was restrained throughout the training session (Figure 8.12). McEchron and Disterhoft (1997) recently examined the activity of single hippocampal pyramidal cells in rabbits during "trace" eye blink conditioning. This task is a variant of classical conditioning where the CS is brief followed by a gap before the US presentation, and learning of this task variant, unlike the conventional version of the task,

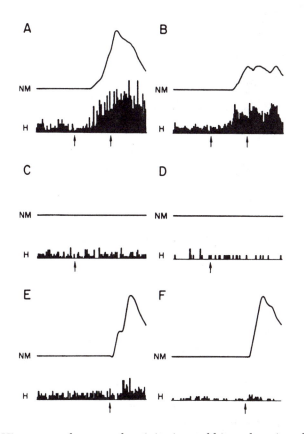

Figure 8.12. Hippocampal neuronal activity in a rabbit undergoing classical eye-blink conditioning. In each panel the upper trace shows the movements of the nictitating membrane (NM; inner eyelid) and the lower trace shows neuronal firing rates. A & B show the activity of two different cells after conditioning—note close neural "model" of the eyeblink (arrows indicate onsets of tone and airpuff, respectively). Other panels show activity associated with no learning after presentations of a tone alone (arrows in C & D) or airpuff alone (arrows in E & F). (Reproduced, with permission, from Berger, Rinaldi, Weisz, & Thompson, 1983; Copyright American Physiological Society.)

depends critically upon the hippocampus. The authors found that single hippo-campal cells exhibited large learning-related responses to the CS or US prior to the emergence of conditioned eye blinks. These responses were maximal when CRs first occurred, diminished somewhat in magnitude at asymptotic perfor-mance, and decreased activity with overtraining.

Sensory Discrimination Learning

Studies by Eichenbaum and colleagues (1987; Wiener et al., 1989) have focused on hippocampal neural activity during stimulus sampling in rats performing learned olfactory discriminations, as well as other tasks (e.g., Otto & Eichenbaum, 1992a; Figure 8.13). In two different versions of odor discrimination tasks, a sub-set of approximately 20% of the putative pyramidal cells fired while the animal

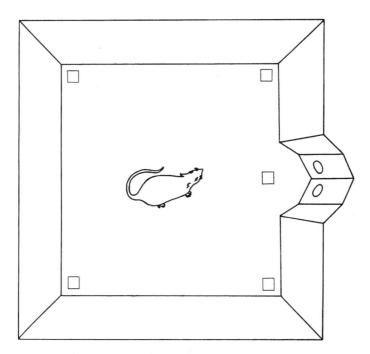

Figure 8.13. Apparatus used to characterize hippocampal neuronal activity in rats performing both a spatial memory test and an olfactory discrimination. Dur-ing the spatial task, the rat had to move to the center of the arena, and then could approach any of the corners to obtain a water reward. Subsequently it had to return to the center and then approach a different cup, etc., similar to the de-mands of the radial arm maze task. During the olfactory discrimination task, the rat had to enter the cul-de-sac (right) where it was presented with an odor from each of the odor ports. A correct response resulted in delivery of a water reward to the cup located just outside the cul-de-sac. (Reproduced, with permission, from Wiener, Paul, & Eichenbaum, 1989; Copyright Society for Neuroscience.)

sniffed odor cues and prepared to execute an appropriate behavioral response. These cells typically began to fire rapidly as the animal sampled the odor stimuli and ceased firing abruptly as the response was completed, even though the animal's position was identical to that during the sampling period (Figure 8.14). Thus the responses observed in these cells could have depended on the animal's location, but location per se was not sufficient to activate the neurons and therefore was a poor predictor of firing. Furthermore, the responses of these cells, like those of place cells described above, were highly dependent on experience. Within the identical environment, cells that fired associated with odor stimulus sampling during performance of the odor discrimination task became typical place cells when the animal subsequently performed a spatial memory task (Figure 8.15).

Many of these cells fired during the sampling of all odors, but some showed striking specificities. One task was the simultaneous olfactory discrimination, described above, where pairs of rewarded and nonrewarded odors were presented closely juxtaposed. In this task some cells' activity was selective to a particular spatial configuration of odors (Figure 8.16A; Wiener et al., 1989). Another task was a successive olfactory discrimination where several rewarded and nonrewarded odor cues were presented singly across trials. In this task some cells' activity was selective to sequences of rewarded and nonrewarded cues (Figure 8.16B; Eichenbaum et al., 1987). Thus individual neurons encoded conjunctions or relations among the odors, either in the form of left-right positional relations or in the form of sequential relations across time.

Notably in all these tasks other individual hippocampal cells exhibited striking responses associated with various behaviors including approach to the stimulus port or the reward. Indeed, the activity of the population of hippocampal cells could be characterized as a set of neurons firing selectively at each phase of the task. Finally, it is also notable that the same cells that had place fields when the animal was performing a spatial task in the same apparatus had equally robust but completely independent event-related firing as the animal performed the odor discrimination task.

Focusing on other types of discriminative cues, Wible et al. (1986) recorded from hippocampal cells as animals discriminated left and right, and black and white, goal boxes in a Y maze. Animals performed two tasks with the identical stimuli. In a visual cue discrimination task the animals had to choose the black or white goal arm consistently regardless of left or right arm positions. Conversely, in a place discrimination task the animals had to choose the left or right arm consistently regardless of the arm color. In both tasks individual cells fired associated with the color or position, or both, and some fired differentially depending on which task the rat was performing, and on interactions between task and goal color and position. Thus, as in the odor discrimination task described above, hippocampal cells encoded all of the contingencies, including spatial and nonspatial components of the task and their interactions. In a similar experiment, Sakurai (1996) recorded the activity of hippocampal neurons in rats performing successive discrimination tasks cued by visual or auditory cues, or combinations of visual and auditory stimuli. In each task the rat initially was presented with the discriminative cue for 2 s, then was allowed to make a go or no-go response.

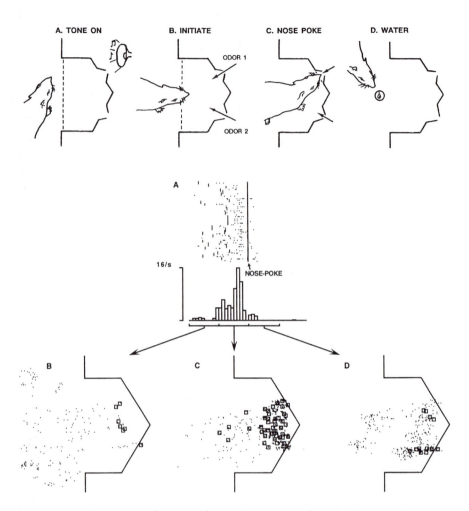

Figure 8.14. Hippocampal neuronal activity associated with odor sampling in a rat performing an odor discrimination task. Top: A-D. Successive phases of a training trial. A. The tone signals availability of the odor. B. The rat initiates a trial by breaking a photobeam at the entrance of a cul-de-sac. C. After odors are presented at each of two ports (arrows), the rat nose-pokes to indicate its choice. D. After a correct choice, the rat obtains a water reward. Bottom: Firing pattern of one hippocampal cell. A. Raster display and summary histogram of firing pattern time-locked to the nose-poke response. B-D. Spatial pattern of firing over indicated 1 sec time bins accumulated over all trials. Small dots indicate the positions of the rat's head sampled every 50 ms, and squares indicate spike activity. (Reproduced, with permission, from Wiener, Paul, & Eichenbaum, 1989; Copyright Society for Neuroscience.)

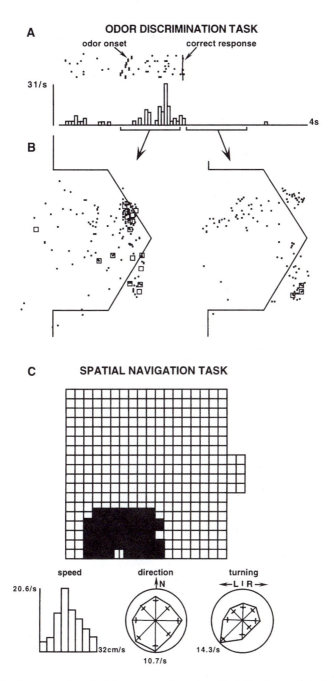

Figure 8.15. An example of a hippocampal neuron that fired associated with odor sampling during the olfactory discrimination task (A & B; see description of Fig. 8.14), and had a place field and other spatial firing characteristics as the rat performed the spatial working memory task (C; see description of Fig 8.2D). (Reproduced, with permission, from Eichenbaum & Cohen, 1988; Copyright Elsevier Science.)

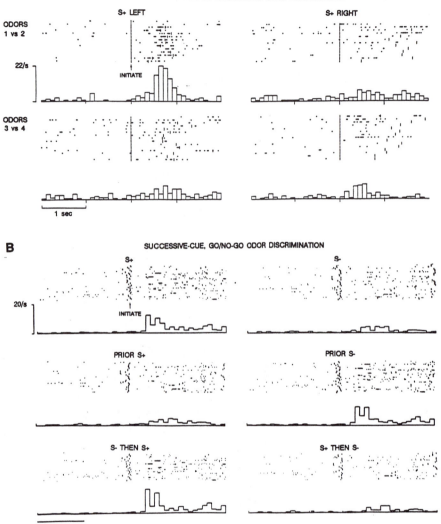

Figure 8.16. Highly selective hippocampal neuronal activity in rats performing two different kinds of olfactory discrimination tasks. A. In this task the rat was required to choose between two odors presented simultaneously in each of two different left-right positions. This cell fired only when the rewarded odor (S+) was on the left in a discrimination between odors 1 & 2, and not associated with either left-right configuration of odors 3 & 4. B. In this task the rat was required to prolong a nose poke when the S+ odor was presented and not when the S– was presented; these odors were presented singly and successively on different trials in random order. This cell fired more on S+ than S–. trials, when the odor on the previous trials had been an S– rather than an S+, and most associated with S– then S+ sequences and least associated with S+ than S– sequences. (Reproduced, with permission, from Eichenbaum, Cohen, Otto, & Wible, 1992; Copright Oxford University Press.)

Very large proportions of the cells were differentially activated by different cues, or combinations of cues, on all the tasks. In addition cross-correlated activity between pairs of cells was similar across the tasks.

Delayed Matching and Nonmatching to Sample

Because of evidence implicating a critical role for the hippocampal region in recognition memory (Mishkin, 1982; Gaffan, 1974), several studies have also characterized firing patterns in animals performing delayed-matching and non-matching-to-sample tasks that test recognition memory (for review see Olton, 1989). In these tasks, the animal is presented with a sequence of stimuli, and the requirement is to remember the initial "sample" stimulus during a delay period and then demonstrate the recognition of the stimulus by a subsequent choice. There are several variants of the task, including different types of stimuli, different response contingencies for matching and nonmatching, and different protocols where sample and choice stimuli are presented in discrete trials or in a continuous series.

Otto and Eichenbaum (1992a) used a continuous nonmatching-to-sample task where one of several odors was presented on each trial, and each was associated with reward only if it differed from (was a nonmatch with) the odor presented on the previous trial. In this task some hippocampal cells fired only on nonmatch trials, that is, on trials where the odor differed from that presented on the previous trial, and a few cells fired only on match trials where the odor was repeated. The activity of these cells did not differentiate among the odors, so that they fired in association with the match or nonmatch relationship between successively presented odors regardless of the particular odors involved. Notably, as in the studies on odor discrimination, there were also many cells that fired in association with odor sampling across all trials and with virtually all other identifiable behavioral events.

Sakurai (1990, 1994, 1996) studied hippocampal neuronal activity in rats performing a similar continuous delayed-nonmatching-to-sample task cued by auditory stimuli. The findings were very similar to those from the Otto and Eichenbaum (1992a) study. Cells fired during several phases of the task. Furthermore, some fired selectively in association with the nonmatch contingency, typically during the appropriate response. However, the activity of these cells could be dissociated from the motor response per se, because the same cells did not fire when the animal incorrectly made the same response on match trials (Otto & Eichenbaum, 1992a). In a comparison between this delayed nonmatching to sample task and the auditory discrimination task described above, Sakurai (1994) found that substantially more cells were engaged in the same way in the delayed-nonmatching-to-sample task than in the discrimination task.

Wible et al. (1986) used a discrete trials visual delayed nonmatch-to-sample task, using the same Y-maze apparatus employed in their discrimination tasks described above. In this task the animal was forced in the sample phase to enter either the black or the white goal box to obtain an initial reward. During the delay period the left-right position of the boxes was changed randomly; then the rat had to enter the box of the nonmatching color to obtain another reward. The activity of some cells was strongly related to one of the two box colors, the left-right position of the box, the sample or choice phase of the task, and combinations of these variables. Compared to the results on discrimination learning in the same apparatus, many more cells were engaged by the stimuli and events in the delayed-nonmatch-to-sample task.

Deadwyler and colleagues (1996; Hampson et al., 1993) studied the firing properties of single hippocampal neurons and neuronal ensembles in rats performing delayed matching and nonmatching to sample in a discrete trials version of the task where the cues were left and right positions of two response bars. On each trial one bar was extended into the apparatus and pressed by the animal to obtain an initial reward. During the delay period the bar was withdrawn and the animal had to nose-poke at a port on the opposite side of the apparatus. Finally both bars were extended into the apparatus, and the animal could press the matching or nonmatching bar to obtain a second reward. In the analysis of single hippocampal cells (Hampson et al., 1993), many of the neurons fired during the sample or match responses or upon the delivery of the reward, or combinations of these events. In each animal the activity of some neurons was associated with the position of the lever being pressed, regardless of whether this occurred during the sample or nonmatch trial phase. Conversely, other cells fired associated with the trial phase, independent of the lever position. Yet other cells fired associated with conjunctions of lever position and trial phase (e.g., left-match), or with multiple events that compose a specific type of trial (e.g., right-sample then left-nonmatch). So, hippocampal neuronal activity represented both the relevant aspects of space and the relevant nonspatial features of the task.

The characterization of the activity of ensembles of cells recorded at 10 locations in the hippocampus focused on a canonical discriminant analysis that could extract patterns of covariances among the cells associated with different task events (Deadwyler et al., 1996). Canonical "roots" determined by this analysis accounted for 85% of the overall variance in ensemble activity. The major roots corresponded to encoding of the sample versus choice phase of the task regardless of bar position, encoding of the spatial position of the lever independent of task phase, encoding of left versus right error responses, and encoding of the sample position during the sample and choice phase. The encoding of lever position may be regarded as a spatial mapping. However, the coding of task phase cut across locations where the rat was positioned, and the coding of the sample position lingered into the choice phase when the rat was at the opposite bar on correct trials. Thus, while all the correlates of these cells can be considered "spatial" in various ways, a considerable amount of the variance in ensemble activity was not associated strictly with the animal's location but rather with the encoding of task-relevant spatial information.

In addition, in a recent compilation of these findings, Hampson et al. (1999) took advantage of the fact that their microelectrode array allowed for determination of precise locations of the cells with different types of codings. They collapsed the data across several animals and, to their surprise, found a set of regular anatomical patterns. The cells that encoded lever position were segregated, such that alternating 0.6–0.8 mm cross-sectional segments of the hippocampus contained clusters of "left" or "right" lever position codings. Also, cells that represented the two trial phases were also segregated, this time in alternating 0.2–0.4

mm cross-sectional clusters of "sample" and "nonmatch" codings. These two topographies were interleaved, such that each position cluster contained clusters for both trial phases. This functional organization resembles the common finding of functional "columns" in many areas of the cerebral cortex (see chapter 4), and suggests that the combination of spatial and nonspatial representations relevant to this memory task may be interleaved within a structural organization of the hippocampus (Eichenbaum, 1999b).

Firing Patterns of Hippocampal Region Neurons in Monkeys and Humans

Analyses of the firing properties of hippocampal neurons have been extended to studies on the primate hippocampal region. In general the evidence for pure place-specific activity is poor, although sensory evoked neural activity is often gated or modulated by egocentric or allocentric spatial variables. Rolls and colleagues (1989) characterized the activity of hippocampal neurons in monkeys performing a task where subjects had to recognize a particular visual pattern stimulus presented in a particular part of a visual display. They found that under 10% of the cells had "spatial fields" in that the cells had visually evoked responses that were dependent on some positions on the display (Figure 8.17). Some of these cells had greater responses the first time a stimulus was seen than on subsequent presentations. In a later study Feigenbaum and Rolls (1991) determined that for the largest fraction of cells evoking these visual responses the source of the spatial modulation was the local frame of reference (the display), although a few cellular responses depended on the animal's egocentric position or on the absolute position of the stimulus in the room. Ono and colleagues (1993) reported similar spatially dependent visual and other responses of hippocampal neurons in monkeys that performed a visual discrimination while being moved about in a large testing room. Nearly half of the neurons recorded fired in some way associated with the task events. In about a third of the cells activity was not controlled by the animal's location, and 14% had task-related activity that was modulated by the monkey's place in the room. More recently, O'Mara et al. (1994) reported that another population of hippocampal neurons fired in association with whole-body motion through space. Some seemed responsive to vestibular stimuli associated with movement, and others depended on a view of a part of the test room for the response.

In humans visually evoked responses of hippocampal neurons have also been observed (Halgren et al., 1978), and a substantial fraction of these cells fired on the sight of a particular word or face stimulus or during execution of task-relevant key press responses (Heit et al., 1988, 1990). In a more recent study, Fried et al. (1997) characterized the responses of hippocampal neurons in human subjects performing a recognition memory task with face and visual object cues. Again a substantial number of cells responded to the stimuli, and individual cells had activity that differentiated faces from objects, or distinguished facial gender or expression, or new versus familiar faces and objects. The largest fraction of cells differentiated combinations of these features. Some of the cells had a specific pattern of responsiveness across all of these parameters.

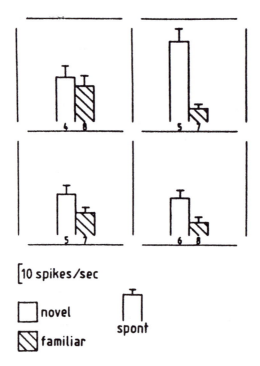

Figure 8.17. Hippocampal neuron of a monkey performing a recognition test for visual stimuli presented in different parts of a video screen. This cell fired maximally during presentation of a novel stimulus presented in the upper right quadrant of the screen. (Reproduced, with permission, from Rolls, Miyashita, Cahusac, Kesner, Niki, Feigenbaum, & Bach, 1989; Copyright Society for Neuroscience.)

Studies Specifically Designed to Distinguish Spatial and Nonspatial Firing Patterns of Hippocampal Neurons

Some studies have been directly aimed at dissociating spatial and nonspatial firing patterns of hippocampal neurons, by requiring animals to perform the same tasks using identical cues located at different locations in the environment. For example, the Wible et al. (1986) study showed that some hippocampal cells fired differentially according to the location of two goal boxes, whereas other cells only differentiated the color of the same goal boxes.

In a similar study, we found that hippocampal cells exhibit equally robust and prevalent nonspatial and spatial firing patterns in rats performing Olton and Feustle's (1981) nonspatial working-memory task. In this test rats explore a radial maze composed of distinctive maze arms presented in different locations (Figure 8.18, top row). The apparatus consisted of a radial maze with four movable arms, each of which was covered by a distinct set of visual and tactile cues (e.g., sandpaper, wire mesh). The rat began the first trial from the central platform and could approach the end of any of the arms to obtain a reward. After returning to the center, the rat was confined briefly while the spatial arrangement of the arms

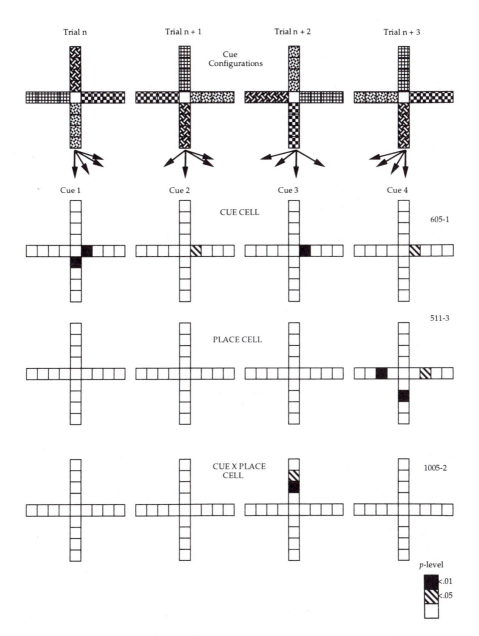

Figure 8.18. Hippocampal neural activity in rats performing a non-spatial radial arm maze task. The top row illustrates example configurations of cues, overlays on maze arms made of different materials. The other rows show examples of firing pattens that arise resulting from an analysis that combines neural activity associated with each cue in each of four possible spatial positions. The "Place cell" fires associated with the beginning of multiple rightward pointing arms. The "Cue cell" fires associated with cue 4 in multiple spatial positions. The "Place X Cue cell" fires only associated with cue 3 in the upward pointing position. (Reproduced, with permission, from Young, Otto, Fox, & Eichenbaum, 1997; Copyright Society for Neuroscience.)

was scrambled according to a predetermined random sequence. On the next trial to obtain another reward the rat had to enter an arm that differed in its cue properties regardless of spatial location. On subsequent trials the arms were again scrambled after each arm entry until the rat had entered all four distinct arms. Thus, unlike in Olton's conventional spatial working-memory task, the cues were nonspatial and the reinforcement contingency required the animal to ignore their spatial positions. Our analyses focused on the firing associated with each distinct arm cue when it was in each of the four positions.

We characterized neurons whose activity varied significantly only with the spatial position of the arms as place cells and neurons whose activity varied significantly only with the distinct arm cues as "cue cells" (Figure 8.18). The major finding was that place and cue cells showed equally robust activity differences and were equally prominent among the cell population. Some neurons were near-perfect place cells, in that they fired when the rat was in the same location in nearly all of the arms. Conversely, other cells could be characterized as "cue" cells, in that they fired when the rat was in the arm associated with one cue regardless of the location of that arm. Other cells were "conjunction cells" in that they fired robustly only in the arm with a particular cue and only when it was in a particular location (Figure 8.18). In the overall distribution of statistically significant cellular responses, approximately equivalent fractions of the cells were place or cue cells, and others fired in association with relative (radial) distance along an arm regardless of the cue or place. In both cue and place cells radial distance was typically a cofactor. For place cells, the differentiation of radial distance was interpreted as greater specification of the place field. For the cue cells, the differentiation was interpreted as greater specification of the part of the cue represented by the cell. Notably, the largest fraction of cells fired in association with conjunctions of the cues and places, usually with a relative distance component as well.

The results of the Wible et al. (1986) and Young et al. (1995) studies were interpreted as demonstrations of the existence of cue-specific hippocampal neural activity independent of spatial location. However, another possible interpretation is that the animal perceived each of the maze arms as a distinct environment, like rooms in a house, except that their locations could change within the overall environment. By this view, some cells, identified as place cells, used as their spatial reference frame the overall environment. Other cells, identified as cue cells, also typically had location-specific activity, but the reference frame was the particular maze arm characterized by its cues. This interpretation cannot be rejected by these or any other experiments where the "nonspatial cues" can be considered environments themselves.

A further study, however, involved punctate olfactory cues that were moved systematically among locations within a static environment and provided unambiguous evidence of place-independent nonspatial hippocampal activity (Wood et al., 1999). In that study rats were trained to perform an odor-guided delayed-nonmatch-to-sample task at multiple locations on a large open field (Figure 8.19). The stimuli were plastic cups that contained playground sand scented with one of nine common odors (e.g., coffee, cinnamon). On each trial one cup was placed randomly at any of nine locations on the open field. Whenever the odor differed from that on the previous trial (i.e., was a nonmatch) a Fruit Loop was buried in

Continuous Nonmatching to Sample

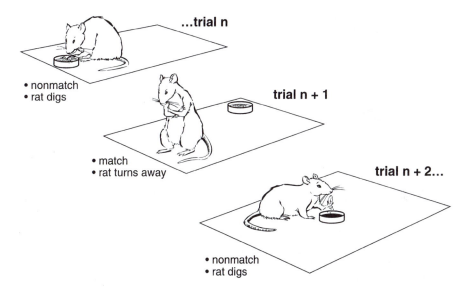

Figure 8.19. Delayed nonmatching to sample test where the location of trials varies randomly. On those trials when the odor is different from that presented on the preceding trial (i.e., a nonmatch) the rat can dig in the scented food cup for a buried reward. On those trials when the odor is the same as that on the preceding trial (i.e., a match), there is no reward and the rat turns away. (Reproduced, with permission, from Wood, Dudchenko, & Eichenbaum, 1999; Copyright Macmillan Magazines Ltd.)

the sand, and the rat would dig for the reward. Whenever the odor was the same as that on the previous trial (i.e., was a match) no Fruit Loop was buried and the rat would turn away. The firing rate of hippocampal cells was assessed during the approach to the cups, focusing on the last second of the approach during which the animal arrived at the cup and generated its response. Firing rates were statistically compared across the set of odors, the set of locations, and match-nonmatch conditions.

About two thirds of hippocampal cells were activated in association with one or more of these variables during the task (Figures 8.20, 8.21). About one third of the active cells' firing was not differentiated by the location of the cup, and about one third of the active cells demonstrated some spatial component of firing. Some of the nonspatial cells were activated during the approach to any of the odor cups at any of the nine locations. Other cells fired differentially across the odor set, or between match and nonmatch conditions, or in some combination of these variables and the approach. Only a small proportion of the location-selective cells fired in association only with the position of the cup. For the majority, the activity was conjointly associated with the cup position, odor, match-nonmatch,

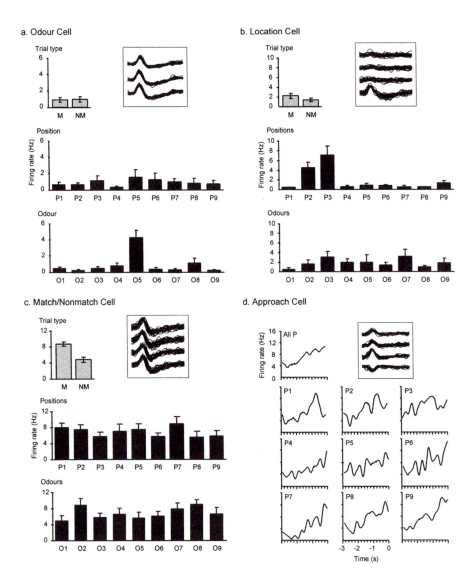

Figure 8.20. Examples of different cell types on the delayed nonmatch to sample task. A. A cell that fires associated with trials when odor 5 (O5) was presented but not when other odors were presented. The activity of this cell did not distinguish the locations where the trials were performed or the match/nonmatch status of the odor. B. This cell fired when trials were performed at adjacent locations P2-P3, but not when the trial was performed at other locations. The activity of this cell did not distinguish between different odors or their match/nonmatch status. C. This cell fired more on match than on nonmatch trials, but its activity did not distinguish the odors or locations where trials were performed. D. This cell increased firing as the animal approached and sampled odors at all locations. (Reproduced, with permission, from Wood, Dudchenko, & Eichenbaum, Copyright Macmillan Magazines Ltd.)

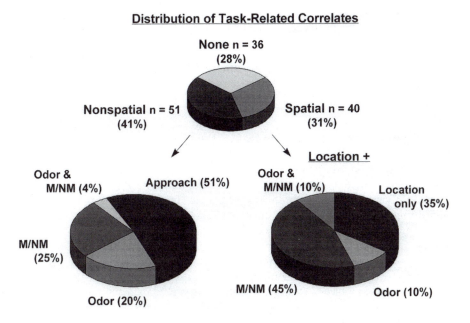

Figure 8.21. Proportions of hippocampal cells that showed statistically signifi-cant changes in activity associated with spatial and nonspatial features of the delayed nonmatching to sample task.

or approach. These results show that the activity of fully half of the activated cells was completely independent of location, and most of the location-specific cells were not purely spatial. In addition, while some cells encoded specific odors or places, the activity of most cells was associated with one of the many potential conjunctions of odors, places, approach movements, and match-non-match events. These data indicate that, as in the Gothard et al. (1996a, 1996b) experiments described above, when important stimuli move unpredictably within an environment, a segment of the hippocampal population encodes the regularities of these stimuli without coding the global topography. Any compre-hensive accounting of hippocampal representation must incorporate the coding of nonspatial stimuli and events that occur independent of their spatial location. We will now consider this issue, as well as others left unresolved to this point.

The Hippocampus Mediates a "Memory Space"

The findings described above are far-ranging, in part because of the broad scope of the behavioral paradigms in which hippocampal neural activity has been stud-ied, and in part because of differences in the focus of these experiments on dis-tinct aspects of behavior. Here we will begin with a general summary of the main findings on the stimuli and behavioral events that are reflected by hippocampal cellular activity. Then we will attempt to bring into correspondence the spatial and nonspatial neural firing patterns of hippocampal neurons by a proposal for how new information becomes encoded within a "memory space."

A Summary of Findings on Hippocampal Neural Firing Patterns

1. Cells with location-specific firing (place cells) exist, but these spatial firing patterns do not reflect a straightforward encoding of the global topology of all the attended-to environmental cues. Instead, substantial evidence now indicates that individual place cells encode only subsets of the attended-to cues. These representations include information about the relevant spatial relations among particular subsets of the cues, as perceived from a particular location relative to those cues. Furthermore, these representations are not initially driven by those cues, and ultimately they come under the control of the animal's judgment and memory about the spatial cues, as well as by the relevant sensory information. These representations, like those in the higher level cortical areas that provide input into the hippocampus, are clustered among neighboring cells.

2. Spatial firing patterns of hippocampal neurons reflect much more than the animal's location per se. These representations include substantial information about nonspatial stimuli and ongoing behavior, reflected in three ways. First, sometimes nonlocation variables influence the magnitude of the spatial firing. For example, the speed of running often influences firing rate in the place field. Second, a particular nonspatial stimulus or behavior can fully determine spatial firing. For example, even in the identical location, some cells fire only if the rat is actively sampling an odor cue. Thus, in many cases, ongoing behavioral actions are at least as important as the location of the animal. Third, nonlocation variables can qualitatively alter the spatial pattern of place cell activity. For example, changing the distribution of rewards in the environment dramatically alters the spatial firing patterns of some place cells.

3. Hippocampal cells encode nonspatial stimuli and behaviors. These nonspatial firing correlates are as robust and as prevalent as spatial firing patterns and, in a task where distinctive events are distributed around the environment, sometimes occur completely independent of the place where they happen. The nonspatial firing properties of hippocampal neurons, like those of spatial firing patterns, emphasize conjunctions or relations among task elements and include a very broad range of stimuli and behaviors.

Constructing Spatial "Maps" from the Bottom Up

The findings summarized above indicate that hippocampal place cells encode small portions of space or, more specifically, the spatial relations among subsets of the environmental cues. How can one build a representation of the environment that would support the important spatial navigation functions of the hippocampus? Suppose the environment as a whole is not represented explicitly by a "map" in the hippocampus. Rather, spatial memory could be mediated as the by-product of a large set of overlapping representations of spatial relations among specific subsets of the environmental stimuli. Within this view, individual hippocampal cells encode relative distances between small sets of cues, as well as the distance from the subject to those cues. Furthermore, each cell encodes only a subset of the available cues, and different cells encode overlapping combinations of those cues. The "map" of space, then, is constituted as a large collection of cue conjunctions that overlap so as to constrain the spatial relations among all the cues, and to provide a framework for moving among the cues.

A simplified version of this model is illustrated in Figure 8.22. In this illustration, each cell is conceived of as encoding only two cues in terms of their spatial separation and the distance of the animal from each of them. Furthermore, different cells encode overlapping pairs of cues, so that an organization of the cues emerges within the hippocampal population. To the extent that these overlapping codings constrain the overall population code, the network hippocampal representation crudely approximates the relative topography among all the codings. In this example, the topography of the network representation of Stimuli A–E is constrained to form an *L* shape, like the topography of the actual stimuli. Furthermore, this model can be envisioned as sufficient to support "navigation" among the cues in the sense that it can begin with any particular cue and know how to proceed to any other one by generating the entire set of representations. In the example, one can conceive of activation of each pairwise coding as also exciting adjacent codings that share overlapping elements. We will call this conception the *memory space model* because it describes a network of associative connections among related stimuli. The model is "spatial" only in the sense that the specific representations are based on spatial relations. However, the links between representational elements are based on associative strengths, not on metric distance or angle representations.

Relational coding of space

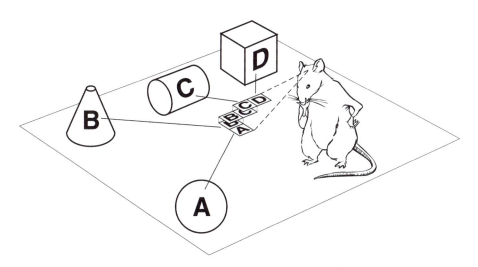

Figure 8.22. A schematic model of how an environment might be encoded by the activity of hippocampal neurons. (Reproduced, with permission, from Eichenbaum, Dudchenko, Wood, Shapiro, & Tanila, 1999; Copyright Cell Press.)

Building Actions and Experiences Into the "Memory Space"

The above considerations show how spatial representations might be built from the "bottom up" as a linked collection of overlapping representations for conjunctions of the environmental stimuli. But this model does not account for evidence showing that spatial representations also incorporate actions and experiences within space. To incorporate these data, we might imagine how the spatial codings are built from actions and experiences within the spatial context. Considerations of the development of spatial representations suggest that the codings of spatial relations per se emerge only secondarily from more preliminary, and much more specific, codings of behavioral episodes, and that the representation of episodes by the hippocampus involves a network of cells each of which encodes temporally defined segments of behavioral experience.

To envision how this kind of episodic coding occurs, and how it eventually generates spatial representations, one must take a novel perspective on characterizing place cell activity. The current convention is to describe place cell firing as fundamentally a location-specific activation, sometimes with secondary influences such as the speed and direction of movement and, rarely, other factors. Take, for example, our data from rats performing the spatial working-memory task in a large arena (Wiener et al., 1989). Many of the cells could conventionally be described as place cells having a place field in a particular portion of the arena, and their activity is typically modulated by several movement parameters so that the cells fire maximally when the rat is moving at a particular speed, in a particular direction, and when the rat is turning at one particular angle. One cell from this study, whose firing patterns are depicted in Figure 8.2D, was conventionally described as a cell with a place field near the center of the arena, and its activity is modulated by several movement parameters: It fires maximally when the rat is moving at a moderate speed, when the rat is moving "north," and when the rat is turning slightly to the right. Alternatively, however, virtually all of the activity of this cell can be characterized more simply as depicted in the lower right panel. The cell fires as the rat initiates its approach to Cup 1. We found that most cells recorded as rats performed this task could similarly be described by a complex combination of place and second-order spatial variables or could be at least as well described by when they fired during movements toward or in return from the reward cups (Wiener et al., 1989; e.g., see also Figure 8.16 bottom). Furthermore, the population of hippocampal neurons contains cells that fire at virtually every point in the trajectory to and from each of the cups (Figure 8.23, left). So one could describe the network representation of the task as a set of place fields broadly distributed around the arena, and indeed this is the conventional characterization of such data. Or one could describe the same data set as a network of neurons, each of which encodes one fragment of the approach and return from each reward cup. Indeed, studies by Wilson and McNaughton (1993) and McHugh et al. (1996) have focused on characterizing spatial firing as reflecting sequential activations along a particular movement trajectory.

Now let us expand the same kind of characterization to hippocampal cellular activity in rats performing the odor-discrimination and nonmatching-to-sample tasks described above, with the additional insight into how "secondary" nonspa-

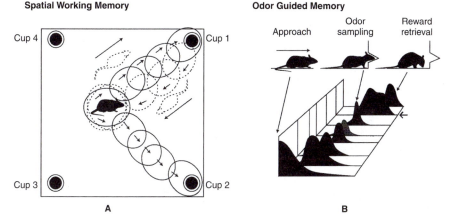

Figure 8.23. Temporal organization of hippocampal neuronal activity. A. Schematic illustration of firing patterns of a set of cells as the rat performs a spatial memory test. Different cells fire at each successive moment as the rat approaches each cup and returns. Note that each cell has a place field and directional firing preference associated with a particular segment of a particular outward-bound or inward bound episode. B. Schematic illustration of firing patterns of a set of cells as the rat performs an odor discrimination task. Different cells fire at each successive moment as the rat approaches the odor ports, samples the odors, and retrieves the reward, and other behaviors. Some cells fire on all trials, others fire only if a particular odor is presented (different stippling patterns). Some cells fire across successive trial events (see small arrow at right). (Reproduced, with permission, from Eichenbaum, Dudchenko, Wood, Shapiro, & Tanila, 1999; Copyright Cell Press.)

tial firing properties are accommodated by hippocampal spatial activity (Eichenbaum et al., 1987; Wiener et al., 1989; Otto & Eichenbaum, 1992a). As animals perform each of these tasks, individual cells activate at virtually every instant of the task, defined as time-locked neural activity to identifiable stimulus and behavioral events. As illustrated in Figure 8.24, for example, individual cells in animals performing the odor-guided nonmatch-to-sample task fired at different times in association with the approach to the odor-sampling port, during the odor-sampling period, and during the discriminative response and reward period. Thus, overall hippocampal activity in this situation, like that in the spatial task described above, can be described as a network of cells that encode each fragment of the events that characterize the discrimination trial (see Figure 8.23, right).

In addition, in both spatial and odor tasks, some of the hippocampal cells showed considerable specificity for particular locations of approach or odors sampled, whereas other cells fired on every trial for different directions of movement and different types of odor trials. This observation leads to an additional characterization of how hippocampal cells are "tuned" to brief segments of the

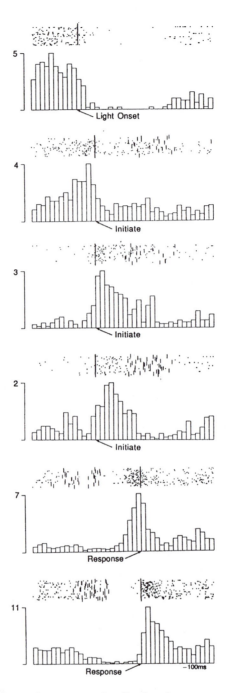

Figure 8.24. Examples of hippocampal cells that fire associated with sequential events as a rat performs an odor guided memory task. The activity of different cells is best time-locked to a "light onset" that signals availability of the odor, or to when the rat initiates the trial, or to when the rat makes the discriminative response. (Reproduced, with permission, from Otto & Eichenbaum, 1992; Copyright John Wiley & Sons, Inc.)

behavioral episode. Let us first consider the cells that show the greatest specificity for particular conjunctions or relations among stimuli or events. Prominent examples include conjunctions or relations between the places and actions that occur in those places, or between sequences of odors. A similar characterization can be offered to describe the data from the odor-guided delayed-nonmatch-to-sample task where the trials were performed at different locations on an open field (Wood et al., 1999). Some cells only associated with particular conjunctions of events, places, or both, and virtually every possible conjunction was represented. These most selective cells might be thought of as reflecting ever more rare variations of events.

Now let us consider the cells that fired consistently on different types of trials in spatial and odor tasks. Indeed many of these cells fired in association with locations or events that were common across all the different types of trials within a task (Figure 8.20). In the spatial task, some cells fired whenever the animal's path crossed a particular place, regardless of what cup was being approached or left behind. In the odor tasks, some cells fired during a particular common behavioral event (e.g., during the approach movement regardless of spatial location), and others fired on all match or nonmatch trials. In the task where an odor test was performed at multiple locations, some cells fired on all trials at a particular location regardless of the current odor or type of trial. These cells might be thought of as "nodal points," intersections among the codings for a variety of events that have in common at some time being in a particular place or executing some particular behavior. Of course, the full range of cells extends continuously from the most common nodal point cells to the most highly specific cells. From this perspective "pure" place cells (ones that are location-specific and have no other quality) are one of the more common nodal correlates, whereas the highly combinatorial cells observed in the Wood et al. (1999) study represent events that occurred only a few times in a session.

There are then three central aspects of this novel characterization of the firing properties of hippocampal neurons in these tasks. First, cellular activity can be described as a sequence of temporally and spatially defined events that constitute each trial. Second, some cells showed a very high degree of specialization, such as the approach to a particular odor at a particular place only when it was on a nonmatch trial. Third, other cells are activated on different kinds of trials, and the activity of some reflects the common places animals pass through and behavioral actions they take on all such trials. One hypothesis that may account for these three aspects of the firing patterns is that when the animal enters a novel situation the activity of the hippocampal neural network reflects specific ongoing behavioral episodes. As more and more experiences are accumulated within that overall situation, common locations, stimuli, and actions are reflected in enhanced firing by cells that initially are active during the relevant parts of episodes. Eventually the hippocampal network encodes the organization of related events, including both the frequent elements common across many similar events and rare conjunctions of elements that define infrequent episodes in the task. This view of hippocampal representation puts the hippocampus squarely central to episodic memory, and also assigns its purpose in identifying and organizing events into a general memory organization that relates events to one another.

One line of evidence consistent with this view is that location-specific activity is consistently observed in only a fraction of the cells when a rat is first exposed to a novel environment. Many hippocampal cells instead develop consistent spatial firing patterns only after longer exposure times ranging from 10 min to 1 hr (Wilson & McNaughton, 1993; Tanila et al., 1997c; see also Bostock et al., 1991; Hill, 1978). Perhaps this is a measure of the number of behavior episodes that must occur before spatial nodal points, observed as consistent place fields, emerge.

The Global Role of Hippocampal Neural Representations

How might such hippocampal episodic codings and organizational processing serve the global declarative memory function of the hippocampus? The present considerations provide support for a working hypothesis about a common organization of spatial and nonspatial memories in the hippocampus. According to this view, individual hippocampal neurons encode all manner of conjunctions and relations among combinations of perceptually independent cues. The domain of relations captured within hippocampal codings is broad; indeed it may involve virtually any conceivable dimension by which stimuli can be related. Furthermore, hippocampal representations include behavioral actions as well as stimuli and internal stimuli (e.g., hunger, fear) as well as exteroceptive stimuli.

In addition, hippocampal representations "overlap" in that different codings share subsets of the overall set of relevant cues. This creates a framework that extends the set of stimuli and actions represented in the network, and it constrains the nature of the network organization by the accommodation of multiple relations in a single framework. In our characterization of the encoding of the topological layout of an environment, specific subsets of the cues are encoded in terms of the crude distances between items and the distance of the rat from those items when they are perceived. When many such representations among the hippocampal neuronal population overlap, the overall organization is constrained to a framework that approximates the actual spatial topology of the environment (Figure 8.22). Imagine that precisely the same kind of hippocampal representation supports nonspatial learning dependent on the hippocampus.

Particularly good examples of this learning that involves overlapping representations of nonspatial stimulus items come from recent studies of transitivity in paired-associate and serial-order learning in rats. In the Bunsey and Eichenbaum (1996) study described in chapter 7, intact rats were trained on a set of overlapping odor associations and demonstrated the capacity to infer relations among indirectly related items. For example, after they had learned that Stimulus A was associated with Stimulus B, and B was associated with C, they could infer that A was associated with C. This task directly demonstrates that rats can represent overlapping stimulus associations, and that these associations become linked to support inferential judgments. Furthermore, the capacity to build the overlapping associations into a network representation that supports inferential judgments depends on the hippocampus. In the next chapter we will describe an experiment in which intact rats learned a more elaborate set of overlapping associations among odors (Dusek & Eichenbaum, 1997). In this study, rats learned to select Odor A over Odor B, Odor B over Odor C, C over D, and D over E. Subsequently intact rats demonstrated they had acquired a set of overlapping representations of these relationships and could express them inferentially, specifically by making the correct judgment about the relationship between Odor B and Odor D. Furthermore, as in the Bunsey and Eichenbaum study, hippocampal damage selectively abolished the inferential capacity, showing that the development of a network of overlapping representations was dependent on hippocampal function. In our conceptual model of the "memory space" for this task, distinct sets of hippocampal neurons might encode each pairwise trained cue relationship (Figure 8.25). Because of the structure of the learning task, these codings would necessarily provide a set of overlapping representations. Assuming that the representations that contain shared items are each activated by presentation of any stimulus pair that contains one of its elements, it would be expected that a sufficient amount of the entire representation of the odor series would be activated to support the inferential choice among nonadjacent items.

Within this overall conceptual framework, three guiding principles can account for both spatial and nonspatial memory dependent on the hippocampus: (a) Discrete subsets of cues and actions are encoded by hippocampal cells in terms of appropriate relations among the items; (b) the contents of these representations overlap to generate a higher order framework or "memory space"; and (c) animals can conceptually "navigate" this memory space by stepping across learned associations to make indirect novel associations or other inferential judgments among items in the memory space. In this view, the key properties of spatial memory performance are particularly powerful examples of a memory space

Transitive Inference in Serial Ordering
A>B>C>D>E

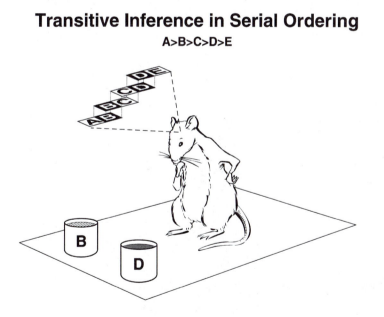

Figure 8.25. A schematic model of how stimuli in the transitive inference task might be encoded by the activity of hippocampal neurons. (Reproduced, with permisison, from Eichenbaum, Dudchenko, Wood, Shapiro, & Tanila, 1999; Copyright Cell Press.)

in operation. For example, the capabilities for taking "shortcuts" and "round-about routes," types of spatial inference outlined by Tolman as defining properties of a cognitive map, can be accomplished within such a memory space without performing metric calculations of exact distances or angles. Rather, they are reflections of inferential memory expression within a constrained framework of associations.

These considerations serve to show how the spatial and nonspatial firing properties of hippocampal neurons might be reconciled. Furthermore, the "memory space" model offers insights into how the hippocampus serves its global role in declarative memory, by mediating the establishment of a relational representation among items in memory. Finally, this model shows how such a relational representation can mediate the capacity for flexible, inferential expression of memory. How this specific role of hippocampal representation fits within the larger system of brain structures of the declarative memory system will be considered next.

9

The Hippocampal Memory System

To this point in the book, discussion of the functional role of the hippocampal system in memory has referred either to the entire set of medial temporal lobe structures removed in H.M.'s surgery, or to just the hippocampus itself. When discussing the *domain* of memory processing in amnesia, we have considered evidence from patients and from animals with damage to the anatomically and functionally related structures of the medial temporal lobe, on the grounds that they are all components of a coherent system. We have also considered the role of the hippocampus itself, as distinct from other medial temporal lobe structures, based particularly on the work on animal models of amnesia (see chapters 6 and 7). This chapter addresses the issue of just which structures should be considered part of the *hippocampal memory system,* describes its inputs in some detail, then explores how the components of the system interact, and, finally, considers the distinct contributions made by the separate components of this system.

Note that this chapter will present information about the anatomical organization and connections of this system in considerable detail, at a level of specificity that, for the moment, exceeds our knowledge about the functional significance of these features. Readers primarily interested in the functional properties of the hippocampal memory system may find the front portion of this chapter heavy going and may therefore wish to skip to the latter portion. However, we believe that neurobiologically informed modeling of the hippocampal memory system will require knowledge of these details, and thus we offer such information here.

Anatomical Characterization of the Hippocampal Memory System

There is no universal agreement on what constitutes the "hippocampal memory system," requiring that we justify the specific brain structures that will be included here as components of that system. The term *hippocampal region* was first used to describe the set of medial temporal lobe structures removed in the patient H.M., including most of the hippocampus proper (Ammon's horn), the dentate gyrus, the subicular complex, the amygdala, and parts of several cortical areas, including the entorhinal, perirhinal, and piriform cortices (Scoville & Milner, 1957; Corkin et al., 1997). Comparisons of H.M.'s memory performance with that of patients who have had more restricted medial temporal lobe removals suggested that the degree of damage to the hippocampus per se determined the severity of amnesia. Recent successes in developing animal models of amnesia have provided new ways of exploring this issue. Results from such work were discussed at length in chapters 6 and 7. Briefly, it is now clear that restricted amygdala lesions do not contribute to the memory impairment, although, as will become clear in chapter 12, the amygdala has a critical role to play in emotional memory. The cortical areas surrounding the hippocampus are more important than had been previously understood; selective damage to these areas alone produces as great a deficit in certain task performances (but not others) as does removal of the entire medial temporal lobe. Finally, the hippocampus itself plays a role in memory that appears to be different from that of the surrounding cortex.

Based on the findings from humans, primates, and rodents, we conclude that the critical structures in the memory system of the medial temporal lobe include the hippocampus proper (Ammon's horn), the dentate gyrus, the subicular complex, and neighboring cortical areas, including the entorhinal, perirhinal, and parahippocampal areas. Adopting the terminology suggested by Witter and colleagues (1989), this collection of structures will be consolidated into two functional components: the *hippocampus* and the *parahippocampal region*. Importantly, each of these major components performs its function via intimate interactions with widespread areas of the cerebral cortex. Thus the *hippocampal memory system* must be considered as including *three* major components: the hippocampus, the parahippocampal region, and the cerebral cortex.

Included in the term *hippocampus* are the following cytoarchitecturally distinct areas: Ammon's horn, the dentate gyrus, the subiculum, and the fornix. Within the parahippocampal region are included the entorhinal, perirhinal, and parahippocampal cortices. Note that the *parahippocampal cortex,* which is a discrete area in the primate cortex, should not be confused with the *parahippocampal region,* which includes this specific cortical area plus entorhinal and perirhinal cortex. Also note that these anatomical terms come from studies on primates. In rats, studies by Burwell and colleagues (1995) have identified the homologous areas for all three subdivisions of the parahippocampal region. The perirhinal and entorhinal areas have the identical names in monkeys and rats, but the area homologous to parahippocampal cortex in the monkey is called *postrhinal cortex* in the rat.

Figure 9.1 provides a general schematic diagram of the flow of information among the three major components of this system (Squire & Zola-Morgan, 1991).

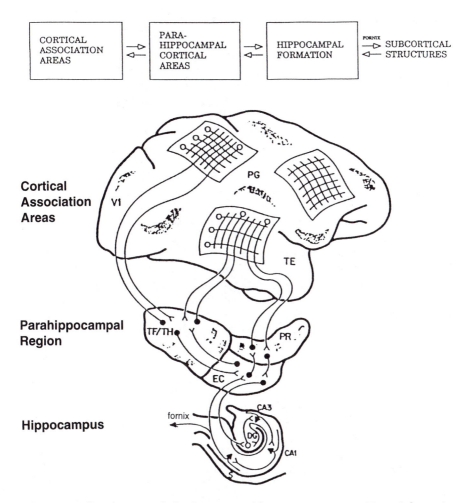

| CORTICAL ASSOCIATION AREAS | ⇄ | PARA-HIPPOCAMPAL CORTICAL AREAS | ⇄ | HIPPOCAMPAL FORMATION | FORNIX ⇄ | SUBCORTICAL STRUCTURES |

Figure 9.1. Illustrations of the hippocampal memory system. Top: Schematic view of main areas and connections. Bottom: More realistic views of the same areas and connections. V1 = primary visual cortex; PG posterior parietal cortex; TE = inferotemporal cortex; PR = perirhinal cortex; EC = entorhinal cortex; S = subiculum. (Reproduced, with permission, from Squire & Zola-Morgan, 1991; Copyright American Association for the Advancement of Science.)

This summary shows the basic anatomical connections between the neocortical areas that provide specific perceptual and motor information to the relevant medial temporal lobe areas; the parahippocampal region, which serves as a convergence center for neocortical inputs and mediates two-way communication between cortical association areas and the hippocampus; and the hippocampus itself (Deacon et al., 1983; Van Hoesen et al., 1972; Amaral & Witter, 1989). Before discussing in greater detail the connectivity of these areas, some additional justification is offered for this particular anatomical segregation of the major functional components of the hippocampal memory system.

Subdivisions of the Hippocampus

The subdivisions of the hippocampus are well defined and largely comparable in the monkey and rat (Rosene & Van Hoesen, 1987; Amaral & Witter, 1989). Because of unidirectional connectivity among the dentate gyrus, CA3, and CA1 regions of Ammon's horn, there is general consensus that these areas operate as a functionally integrated circuit (Figure 9.2). Including the subiculum along with these subdivisions of the hippocampus does not receive universal agreement (see Eichenbaum et al., 1994), but it is supported by both neuropsychological and anatomical findings. The most relevant neuropsychological evidence comes from the elegant experiments by Jarrard and colleagues in which selective neurotoxic lesions were made in particular subdivisions of the hippocampal formation (see Jarrard, 1986, 1993). Results from these studies are consistent in indicating that ablation of any of these components can produce severe memory impairment.

Jarrard has interpreted his findings as indicating a preferential role for Ammon's horn and the dentate gyrus in spatial learning. This conclusion was based largely on the finding that damage to Ammon's horn and the dentate gyrus are sufficient to produce spatial memory deficits and that subicular damage must be included to produce a deficit in nonspatial memory. More recent work, however, using the sensitive Morris water maze task indicates that, even for spatial learning, a severe deficit is found only after combined damage to the subiculum as

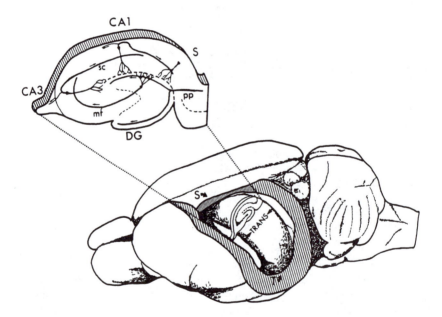

Figure 9.2. Position of the hippocampus in the rat brain and enlargement of a transverse slice through it, showing the main subdivisions and trisynaptic pathway. DG = dentate gyrus; mf = mossy fibers; sc = Schaffer collaterals; pp = perforant path; S = subiculum. (Reproduced, with permission, from Amaral & Witter, 1989; Copyright Oxford University Press.)

well as to Ammon's horn and the dentate gyrus (Morris et al., 1990). Based on the current state of the findings, it appears that the most restricted hippocampal system lesion that produces maximal impairment in any task must include the combination of the three structures comprising the hippocampal formation. With regard to anatomical evidence, Amaral and Witter (1989) and Witter (1989) viewed the subiculum as the final stage of intrinsic processing in the connectional "loops" between the parahippocampal and hippocampal areas (Figure 9.3). Their reviews of hippocampal pathways placed the subiculum as the fourth and final stage of serial hippocampal processing through the so-called trisynaptic circuit and drew close parallels between the parahippocampal connections with Ammon's horn and with the subiculum.

In addition, it is important to consider at the outset a designation for the fornix, the major fiber bundle that connects all subdivisions of the hippocampal formation with the septum and other subcortical areas. A complete transection of the fornix disrupts cholinergic and GABAergic function as well as electrical activity and induces morphological reorganization in the hippocampus (e.g., Lahtinen et al., 1993). Thus, a fornix transection produces significant disruption of information processing and output of the hippocampus; hence, it would be expected to have the same functional consequences as damage to the hippocampus itself. Notably, a fornix transection does not disconnect the parahippocampal region from the neocortex. Accordingly, a fornix transection may not disrupt functions that can be carried out by the parahippocampal region independent of processing by the hippocampus and hence would not be expected to produce the full-blown amnesia seen following more complete hippocampal system damage. Combining these behavioral and anatomical observations, the fornix will be considered along with Ammon's horn, the dentate gyrus, and the subiculum as a functional unit within the hippocampus.

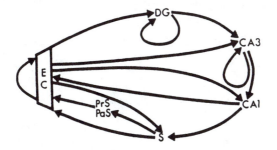

Figure 9.3. Schematic representation of the major pathways through subdivisions of the hippocampus, including the several known "loops" between these areas. The "traditional" trisynaptic circuit is the single outer "loop" proceeding successively from entorhinal cortex (EC), to the dentate gyrus (DG), to CA3, to CA1, to the subiculum (S) and then back to entorhinal cortex. PrS = Presubiculum; PaS = parasubiculum. (Reproduced, with permission, from Amaral & Witter, 1989; Copyright Oxford University Press.)

Subdivisions of the Parahippocampal Region

All three cortical areas included within the parahippocampal region are well defined in the monkey and in the rat (Figures 9.4, 9.5; Amaral et al., 1987; Burwell et al., 1995; Burwell & Amaral, 1998a, 1998b; Witter et al., 1989; Deacon et al., 1983; Van Hoesen, 1982). In both species, the entorhinal cortex has been characterized as a cytoarchitecturally distinct area surrounding the hippocampus and contributing the major cortical afferents to the hippocampus. It is a heterogeneous area composed of several subdivisions with topographically contiguous and often overlapping projections into the hippocampus (see Amaral & Witter, 1989).

The perirhinal cortex, composed of Brodmann's Areas 35 and 36 bordering the rhinal sulcus, is also distinguishable in both the rat and monkey (Suzuki, 1996a, 1996b; Burwell et al., 1995). The parahippocampal cortex in the monkey is clearly distinguished as the combination of von Bonin and Bailey's areas TH and TF lying posterior to the perirhinal cortex. In addition, studies by Burwell

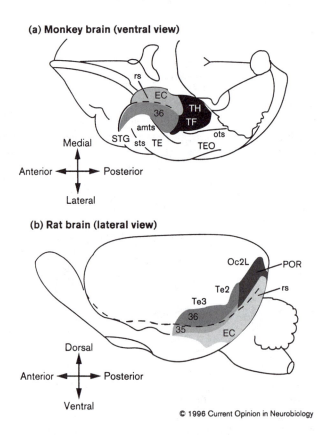

Figure 9.4. Illustrations of the parahippocampal region, as viewed from the ventral surface of the brain in the monkey, and from the lateral surface in the rat. (Reproduced, with permission, from Suzuki, 1996; Copyright Elsevier Science.)

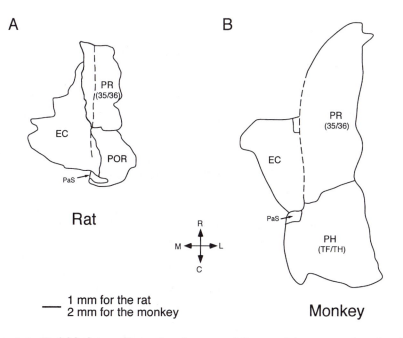

Figure 9.5. Unfolded two-dimensional maps of the parahippocampal region in the monkey and rat. (Reproduced, with permission, from Burwell, Witter, & Amaral, 1995; Copyright John Wiley & Sons, Inc.)

and colleagues (1995; Burwell & Amaral, 1998a, 1998b) have provided compelling evidence that the same area exists in rats, and the connectional correspondences have led them to confirm Deacon et al.'s (1983) proposal that the "postrhinal" cortex, the area that forms the caudal continuation of the rhinal sulcus, is homologous to the primate parahippocampal cortex.

In addition to these cytoarchitectural distinctions, the subdivisions of the parahippocampal region are distinguished from each other by several connectional differences. For example, in the monkey, the perirhinal area receives the greater portion of its inputs from higher-order visual areas, whereas the parahippocampal cortex receives the greater portion of its input from the parietal and cingulate cortices (Suzuki & Amaral, 1994a, 1994b). A similar topography of inputs distinguishes the perirhinal and postrhinal areas of the rat (Deacon et al., 1983; Burwell et al., 1995). The dominance of visual inputs to the perirhinal area is substantially greater in monkeys than in rats, whereas the modality specific inputs are more evenly balanced in rats. However, this difference is largely attributable to the dominance of the total cortical area devoted to visual processing in monkeys.

Despite the various differences in the cytoarchitecture of the entorhinal, perirhinal, and parahippocampal cortices, each of these areas can be characterized as receiving input from multiple neocortical association areas and thus comprises an important convergence site for neocortical input to the hippocampus (Squire et al., 1989; Witter et al., 1989; Deacon et al., 1983; Burwell et al., 1995). The input connections arise in virtually all the higher-order association areas, including several parts of the prefrontal cortex, parietal cortex, and temporal cortex in both monkeys and rats, as will be described below. A major similarity of the perirhinal and parahippocampal (postrhinal) areas is that both heavily project to parts of the entorhinal cortex. These areas connect with subdivisions of the hippocampus and also have major projections back to the same neocortical areas that provided the major inputs. Thus, while the precise pattern of cortical and hippocampal connections differs among these structures, there are significant commonalities in their connections, and neuropsychological data have yet to reveal any functional distinctions. Accordingly, these areas will be discussed collectively as a functional unit, at the risk of overshadowing potentially important functional distinctions that may yet be discovered.

The Flow of Information Within the Hippocampal Memory System

A schematic diagram summarizing the organization of the pathways within the hippocampal memory system is given in Figure 9.6; an earlier version of this summary is provided in Eichenbaum and Buckingham (1992). The nomenclature of this system varies across different species, but the weight of the evidence indicates that the pathways are essentially the same in rats, cats, and primates. This outline will focus on the generic aspects of pathway organization, and Figure 9.6 should serve to clarify these organizational principles, allowing readers to view the skeleton of hippocampal organization and, to the extent that it is helpful, ignore the vagaries of anatomical nomenclature. Several comprehensive reviews of these pathways are available (Amaral & Witter, 1989, 1995; Witter, 1989; Witter et al., 1989; Rosene & Van Hoesen, 1987; Burwell et al., 1995; Suzuki, 1996a).

The Origins of Cortical Inputs to the Hippocampus

Only highly preprocessed sensory information reaches the medial temporal lobe structures, but these inputs come from virtually all higher-order cortical processing areas. Sensory information that enters the primary cortical areas subsequently passes through multiple secondary and tertiary stages of unimodal sensory processing, as discussed in chapter 4. Thus, the cortical afferents to the parahippocampal region are composed of multiple successive stages of cortical processing including, at the lowest levels, the primary thalamocortical projection from the specific sensoria. At the highest levels are so-called association areas that, in the posterior half of the neocortex, receive multimodal sensory inputs and, in the anterior half of the neocortex, receive multiple sensory, motor, and limbic inputs. The outputs of these areas project to the parahippocampal region in rats (Figure 9.7) and monkeys (Figure 9.8).

The neocortical structures that project to the parahippocampal region are the temporal, parietal, prefrontal, and cingulate areas, each of which is involved with high-level multimodal processing rather than primary sensory processing, plus the piriform cortex. The functioning of some of these areas was discussed in chapter 4, and a brief summary of the firing properties of the cells in a few of the

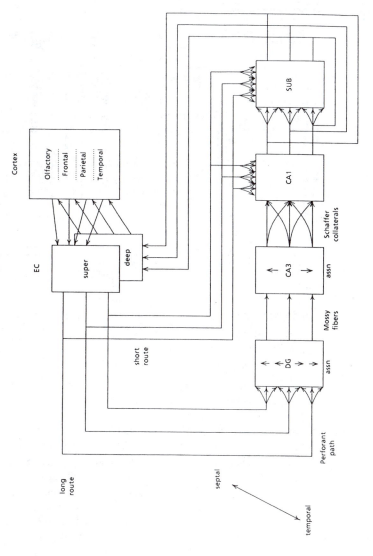

Figure 9.6. Schematic diagram of pathways through the hippocampus. (Reproduced, with permission, from Eichenbaum & Buckingham, 1992; Copyright MIT Press.)

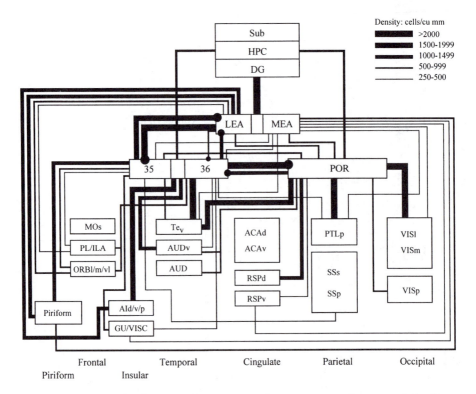

Figure 9.7. Schematic diagram of connections between cortical areas and the hippocampus in rats. (Reproduced, with permission, from Burwell & Amaral, 1998; Copyright John Wiley & Sons, Inc.)

better studied of these areas will be sketched here so that we can highlight the classes of signals that impinge on the hippocampal formation.

Inferior Temporal Cortex   Perhaps the most thoroughly studied cortical area afferent to the hippocampus is the inferotemporal (IT) cortex, the highest order visual object processor in primates. Ablation of the inferotemporal cortex results in deficits in visually guided learning without impairment in visual fields, acuity, or threshold. The behavioral physiology of inferotemporal cortex is consistent with the data from ablation studies. The receptive fields of inferotemporal neurons are large and sometimes bilateral; they always include the fovea. IT neurons are maximally driven by complex visual patterns, and the response properties of these cells are dependent on attentional mechanisms and reward association. Many IT neurons are preferentially responsive to a particular pattern, often one that is of obvious significance to the animal, including a subset that respond selectively to faces. The responses of IT neurons are relatively invariant across changes in stimulus size, orientation, and contrast. IT neurons recorded as monkeys perform memory tasks respond differently to the same stimuli when they appear as stimuli to be remembered, or when they are novel versus familiar, and

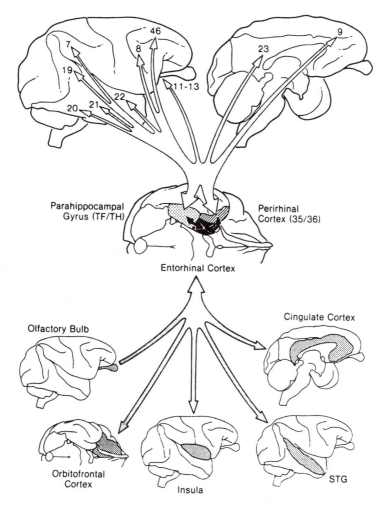

Figure 9.8. Illustration of major cortical areas that compose the afferent sources and efferent targets of information to and from the parahippocampal region in monkeys.

some cells maintain firing during the memory delay periods during performance of short-term memory tasks. Finally, there appears to be no topographical arrangement of the trigger features or receptive fields of cells in the temporal association area, although "clusters" of neighboring neurons have similar trigger features and receptive field properties.

Posterior Parietal Cortex   The posterior parietal area receives input from visual as well as somesthetic areas and can be subdivided into multimodal and primarily visual areas. Damage to this cortical area results in impairment in tactile discrimination and neglect of contralateral sensory stimulation across sensory modalities (see Mountcastle et al., 1975). Considerable recent work on the physiology of posterior parietal cortex has characterized several subdivisions of this area (for review see Andersen, 1989). Cells in the most rostral subdivision, Area 7b, are primarily somatosensory (plus sometimes visual) with large receptive fields, but these cells also fire during manual reaching or manipulation (Mountcastle et al., 1975). Of particular interest is Area 7a, the subdivision just caudal to Area 7b, where most cells are visually driven. These cells have very large, often bilateral, receptive fields that may or may not include the fovea, and visual field size and neuronal responsiveness are highly dependent on attentional factors; cells respond best when the stimulus is the target of an eye or hand movement (Mountcastle et al. 1975, 1981; Lynch et al., 1977; Robinson et al., 1978; Motter & Mountcastle, 1981). These cells prefer moving stimuli and are relatively insensitive to movement speed but prefer stimuli moving in the radial dimension, that is, inward or outward from the point of fixation. They show little preference for stimulus form or color. Their responsiveness to a stimulus in the same retinotopic position changes dramatically depending on the angle of gaze, so that these cells are best characterized as encoding the position of a visual target in head-centered space (Andersen et al., 1985). Combined, these data indicate that the posterior parietal area is specialized for egocentric spatial analyses including localization and visual and manual acquisition of targets in space.

Prefrontal Cortex   The prefrontal cortex has long been viewed as less a sensory processing zone than a sensory-motor-limbic integration area involved in the highest order cognitive functions including motor programming, vicarious trial and error, and memory (for reviews see Fuster, 1980, 1995; Goldman-Rakic, 1988). Neurons in prefrontal cortex are responsive to visual and other stimuli. They have very large visual receptive fields, and their response varies little in relation to the color, size, intensity, or position of spots of light but can change dramatically in relation to the significance of the stimulus or whether the stimulus is a target for reward-related movement. Most recording experiments with the prefrontal cortex have focused on unit activity associated with the presentation of stimuli and completion of manual or eye movement responses in short-term memory tasks sensitive to prefrontal damage: delayed-response, delayed-alternation, and delayed-visual-matching tasks (see chapter 14). A large proportion of neurons in both dorsolateral and orbital prefrontal cortex and in premotor cortex fire in relation to the onset of cues or responses. The neurons that fire during cue presentation can become tuned to the color, pattern, or position of visual stimuli and may fire differentially according to the trial phase (sample versus choice) or significance of the cue. Some prefrontal neurons fire during the delay period when the monkey must remember the cue. Other neurons fire at the time of, or in preparation for, a particular behavioral response.

Olfactory Bulb and Piriform Cortex   Both the olfactory bulb and the piriform cortex project directly to the lateral entorhinal area in all species, as well as to perirhinal cortex in rats. The organization and parameters of sensory responses in the olfactory system are poorly understood (Wilson & Leon, 1988; for review see Scott, 1986). In addition, few studies have examined the response properties of piriform cortex in waking animals. One study that compared odor responses in the olfactory bulb, piriform cortex, and orbitofrontal projection zone of the piriform cortex found that progressively higher-order areas had greater odor selectivity (Tanabe et al., 1975). In both monkeys (Rolls et al., 1989) and rats (Schoenbaum & Eichenbaum, 1995a), neurons in the piriform and olfactory orbitofrontal cortex demonstrate coarse tuning to odors and their responses that reflect the learned significance of odors.

Summary   Despite the variety of functionally distinct cortical areas that send afferents to the hippocampal formation, there are some strikingly similar general qualities in their behavioral physiology (Eichenbaum & Buckingham, 1990):

1. None of these hippocampal input sources are topographically organized with respect to simple sensory dimensions, in contrast to the neocortical primary sensory areas. Correspondingly, the neurons within each of these areas are broadly tuned; that is, they respond to many stimuli and/or have large receptive fields.

2. In all of these areas neuronal activity is dependent on attentional variables and/or the behavioral significance of cues, and cells in each area fire during the period when responses are withheld pending instructions.

3. In each of the cortical inputs to the hippocampal area there are signs of functional distinctions among subregions although, at this time, a full characterization of the functional dimensions has not been made (Andersen, 1989; Rosenkilde, 1979; Baylis & Rolls, 1987; Scott, 1986). Correspondingly, some of these areas receive similar sensory input, but each area handles information in a distinctive way. For example, inferotemporal, parietal, and prefrontal areas each receive heavy inputs from the same secondary visual areas, but they seem to encode that information to different functional ends. A combination of the lesion and neurophysiological data indicates that the function of inferotemporal cortex is to identify the stimulus rather than to analyze particular sensory qualities (size, color, location, etc.). Cells both in parietal and prefrontal cortex have mixed multisensory or motorlike components, and a combination of the lesion and recording data indicates that both areas are involved in aspects of spatial localization. In both areas sensory responses are not solely controlled by the physical properties of the stimulus; responses depend critically upon the significance of the cue. Motor responses are preparatory and less related to the specific muscle contractions than to the result of the action to be performed. But these areas differ in that some posterior parietal cells seem to encode head-centered spatial position, and prefrontal neurons fire in relation to active or intended hand or eye movements to specific targets in space independent of body orientation. Together with the lesion data, these findings indicate that these cortical zones are characterized by the specificity of their function, more than by that of sensory modality.

4. Although much of the comparative work remains to be done, the existing evidence suggests that homologous areas serve similar functions across species (cf. Eichenbaum et al., 1983a; Kesner & DiMattia, 1984).

This review indicates that the inputs to the hippocampal region involve the broadest possible variety of highly preprocessed, functionally specific information. It may not be too simplistic to conclude that the items processed within the hippocampal region are individual percepts of all sorts, including all kinds of sensory percepts as well as their functional significance, and behavioral plans and actions.

The Organization of Cortical Inputs to the Parahippocampal Region

The cortical inputs to the parahippocampal region demonstrate a systematic organization, but one that is unlike the punctate topographies that characterize the primary sensory and motor thalamocortical pathways. Instead, these projections involve large and overlapping zones of projection, an organization of "topographical gradients" (see Figure 9.6). Individual cortical association and olfactory areas project differentially along the parahippocampal region. Generally, more rostral cortical inputs, the ones from olfactory and frontal areas, terminate within rostral and ventral parts of the perirhinal and lateral entorhinal cortex, whereas more caudal cortical inputs, the ones from parietal and temporal areas, terminate in more caudal and dorsal parts of the perirhinal, parahippocampal (postrhinal), and lateral entorhinal cortex (Deacon et al., 1983; Room & Groenewegen, 1986; Burwell et al., 1995; Burwell & Amaral, 1998a; Suzuki & Amaral, 1994a). In monkeys, the overwhelming input to perirhinal cortex is from visual association areas, whereas in rats there is a more even distribution of inputs from all the ventral temporal association areas. Olfactory inputs to all areas of the parahippocampal region are more prominent in rats than monkeys. These differences largely reflect species differences in the distribution of cortical specializations, for example, differences across species in the amount of cortical area devoted to vision (Burwell et al., 1995).

The perirhinal and parahippocampal (postrhinal) areas, in turn, project heavily onto entorhinal cortex, providing about two thirds of their cortical input (Van Hoeson & Pandya, 1975; Witter et al., 1986; Kosel et al., 1982; Kohler, 1986) and contribute to the inputs to the hippocampus itself. The anterior corticolimbic association areas in the prefrontal, insular, retrosplenial, and cingulate cortices also project into the entorhinal cortex proper with overlapping but distinguishable projection areas in the rostral and lateral parts of the entorhinal area. Medial entorhinal cortex receives most of its cortical inputs from piriform and parahippocampal (postrhinal) cortex, but also minor inputs from retrosplenial, posterior parietal, and visual cortical areas.

Parahippocampal Inputs to the Hippocampus and Internal Pathways of the Hippocampus

There are two main routes by which the parahippocampal areas project into the hippocampal formation (Hjorth & Simonsen, 1972); these will be characterized here as the "long" and "short" routes, each of which end in Area CA1 and the subiculum after multisynaptic or direct connections, respectively (see Figure 9.6). The "long route" is the well-known trisynaptic circuit, which begins with the perforant path, composed of axons of the entorhinal cortex that penetrate the hippocampal fissure to invade the dentate gyrus (DG). The alternative, frequently overlooked "short route" is a parallel set of entorhinal outputs projecting directly into the output cells of CA1 and the subiculum.

The Trisynaptic Circuit (Long Route)   The perforant path originates in superficial cells of the entorhinal and perirhinal cortices, and the projection into the dentate gyrus involves two well-organized but coarse gradients. In the lateromedial (caudorostral in primates) dimension, axons of entorhinal cells reach corresponding septotemporal positions in the DG and CA3. The other dimension is based on cytoarchitectural definitions: Areas 28L, 28I, and 28M correspond to lateral, intermediate, and medial components of the entorhinal cortex, terms not to be confused with the above-described lateromedial dimension. These subdivisions project to different levels of the molecular layer of granule cells in the DG and on the apical dendrites of pyramidal cells in CA3, with Area 28L projecting to the outer third of the dendritic tree and Areas 28I and 28M projecting to the middle third of that layer. Also, more lateral parts of the entorhinal area project to DG cells nearer CA3 pyramids (the suprapyramidal blade), and more medial parts of the entorhinal area project to the granule cells below the CA3 pyramidal cell layer (infrapyramidal blade).

Granule cells, via the mossy fibers, project to the proximal dendrites of CA3 cells in Ammon's horn. This projection is topographically restricted, with granule cells projecting exclusively to CA3 cells in the same septotemporal level. In addition, the outputs of granule cells may reach different cell populations within CA3. Claiborne et al. (1986) showed that the infrapyramidal granule cells project preferentially to the more proximal CA3 cells, whereas the suprapyramidal granule cells project to CA3 cells near the CA3/CA1 border. Next, the CA3 pyramids give rise to a large number of collateral outputs: First, some of these axons terminate on other CA3 cells throughout the septotemporal axis; second, the CA3 pyramidal cells give rise to the earliest extrahippocampal projection, to the lateral septal nucleus; and third, CA3 pyramids also give rise to the Schaffer collateral system that provides the major long-route input to the pyramids of CA1, terminating along both the apical and the basal dendrites of these cells along most of the septotemporal axis. These projections are well organized within a septotemporal level; cells near the DG give rise to few associational fibers and project to CA1 cells nearest the subiculum, whereas CA3 pyramids farther from the DG give rise to most of the associational system and project to neighboring CA1 pyramids. CA1 pyramids project broadly onto the dendritic tree of columns of cells in the subiculum (Swanson & Cowan, 1977; Tamamaki et al., 1987).

Direct Parahippocampal-Ammon's Horn Projections (Short Route)   Both the subiculum and CA1 are the recipients of direct input from the parahippocampal cortex. The cells in entorhinal cortex just deep to those originating the perforant path project superficially to dendrites in CA1 and the subiculum (Witter et al., 1986, 1988). The organization of these inputs is essentially the same as that of the entorhinal-dentate inputs, although the CA1 termination field may be more widespread. These inputs also have a transverse organization by which 28M projects preferentially to the CA3 end of CA1, and 28L projects preferentially to the near-subiculum end of CA1. The entorhinal-subicular projections follow the same regional topographical organization as those characterizing the input to DG:

lateral-to-medial entorhinal areas project upon septal-to-temporal parts of the subiculum.

Hippocampal Efferents and the Return Circuit to Cortical Systems

The subiculum gives rise to the major subcortical and cortical efferent systems of the hippocampal formation. The subcortical projection is through the fornix and into the ventral striatum and mammillary bodies (Swanson & Cowan, 1977; Groenewegen et al., 1987). The cortical efferents, involving efferents of both CA1 and the subiculum, project primarily to deep layers of the entorhinal cortex, completing the parahippocampal-hippocampal loops. These projections follow the same topographic arrangement as the input connections: a topographic gradient of projections from septotemporal hippocampal areas projecting to lateromedial sites in entorhinal cortex.

The return circuit to the nonhippocampal cortex involves the deep pyramidal cells of entorhinal and perirhinal cortex projecting to the same cortical areas from which inputs originated (Van Hoesen & Pandya, 1975; Wyss, 1981). In addition, part of the prefrontal cortex receives a direct projection from the CA1 (Swanson, 1981; Ferino et al., 1987). Thus the cortical recipients of parahippocampal output include the polymodal association areas of the orbitofrontal, insular, and temporal areas, and the unimodal higher cortical areas in the piriform cortex and neocortex. The organization of these projections follows that of the input organization: More rostral parts of the parahippocampal gyrus project to rostral cortical areas, and more caudal parahippocampal areas to more caudal cortical sites.

Functional Distinctions Between the Parahippocampal Region and the Hippocampus

There is now substantial evidence that the major components of the hippocampal memory system contribute differentially to overall memory functions of the system. The nature of information coding and memory representation in the cerebral cortex has been discussed in chapter 4, and other findings on its role as the final repository of memories will be discussed further in the next chapter. Here evidence will be presented indicating two sequential functions corresponding to the parahippocampal region and the hippocampus (for a fuller description, see our account in Eichenbaum et al., 1994). First, it will be argued that the parahippocampal region by itself mediates the representation of isolated items and can hold these representations in a memory "buffer" for periods of at least several minutes. This "intermediate-term memory" function bridges the gap between the very brief period of immediate (or short-term) memory and the potentially permanent (or long-term) memory store. Second, it will be argued that during this intermediate period, the hippocampus itself mediates comparing and relating these individual representations to other memory representations, creating or modifying the overall memory organization according to the relevant relations between the items and the structure of any already-established memory organization that involves those items. The combination of these two processing functions comprises *declarative memory* as it has been characterized in previous chapters.

Although these two processing functions are seen as supported independently, they normally function interactively, with relational memory processing operating on new items being held in the intermediate-term store. The intermediate storage function is accomplished at the earlier stage of parahippocampal processing, which contains a full set of input and output connections with neocortical areas. Even without a functional hippocampus, one might expect that the parahippocampal region is able to support intermediate-term memory for individual items. By contrast, the hippocampus itself interacts with the neocortex only via the parahippocampal region, so one might expect that damage to the parahippocampal region would eliminate any relational processing contribution of the hippocampus. Thus the intermediate-term storage of single items does not require the relational memory-processing function, but relational memory processing depends on the intermediate-term store. This sequential stage model is entirely consistent with the known anatomy of the system described above.

Further supporting evidence comes from observations concerning the behavioral physiology of the parahippocampal region and the hippocampus. Consistent with the functional distinction proposed above, neural activity within the parahippocampal region reflects encoding of individual items and intermediate-term storage for specific items, whereas activity in the hippocampal formation is strongly associated primarily with relations among those items (see chapter 8). Much of the evidence on the effects of damage to these areas, as well as on the firing properties of cells in the hippocampus, has already been presented in previous chapters (see chapters 6–8).

In the following sections of this chapter other relevant findings will be presented, offering specific comparisons between the parahippocampal region and hippocampus. The memory functions assigned to these two regions are seen as parallel to two general distinctions of hippocampus-dependent memory that emerged in considering the function of this memory system in different species, particularly as differentially emphasized in experiments on monkeys and rats (Eichenbaum et al., 1992a, 1994). That is, there is a *temporal distinction* by which the hippocampal region has been shown to be critical in very rapid acquisition of information and in persistence of memory representations bridging the gap between short-term and long-term memory. Capacities for rapid acquisition and intermediate-term memory persistence are evident in a broad range of human memory tasks and are particularly prominent in studies on object recognition in monkeys, as will be described below. Second, there is a *representational distinction* by which the hippocampal region is involved in aspects of memory organization and expression that mediate the fundamental properties of declarative memory in humans and that are particularly evident in studies on spatial learning in rats, as will be discussed below.

The following section will summarize some recent explorations of these temporal and representational distinctions of hippocampal memory function. The role of the parahippocampal and hippocampal components of the hippocampal system has been explored with two strategies: neuropsychological studies that determine the effects of damage to different structures within the hippocampal memory system on performance of various memory tasks, and electrophysiologi-

cal studies that characterize the firing properties of neurons in different components of the hippocampal memory system of animals performing the same tasks.
Particular emphasis will be placed on a set of studies of the superb olfactory
learning and memory abilities of rats. These studies compare the effects of selective ablation of the parahippocampal region versus transection of the fornix, the
latter providing a means of causing selective dysfunction of the hippocampus
while minimizing damage to parahippocampal fibers. In addition, electrophysiological studies in both rats and monkeys will be described that focus on comparing the firing properties of neurons in the parahippocampal region to those in
the CA1 area of the hippocampus.

The Parahippocampal Region and Intermediate-Term Memory

The temporal properties of declarative memory have been studied extensively
with the simple recognition memory test known as *delayed nonmatch to sample*
(DNMS). This task, originally designed for monkeys (Gaffan, 1974; Mishkin &
Delacour, 1975), was described in chapter 6. Reiterating briefly here, animals are
presented with a novel "sample" object and rewarded for displacing it. Then,
after a variable memory delay, they are presented with two objects, one identical
to the sample and the other a novel one. In this choice phase, monkeys are rewarded for selecting the novel, nonmatching object. This rule is easily learned
because monkeys are naturally attracted to novelty. The DNMS task is ideal for
measuring the persistence of memory representations for single, isolated stimuli.
Indeed, to the extent that memory performance can be related specifically to variations in the length of the memory delay, it would seem that this task selectively
assesses the temporal distinction of hippocampal memory processing.

For rats, a variant of the DNMS task, called *continuous delayed nonmatch-to-
sample* (cDNM), was developed. This task employs odor cues and involves a
stimulus presentation protocol suitable for characterizing neural firing patterns
to single memory stimuli as well as behavioral responses in accordance with the
nonmatch memory contingency (Otto & Eichenbaum, 1992a, 1992b). On each
trial, one of a large set of odors was presented with the contingency that a response to the odor was rewarded only if that odor was different from (that is, a
nonmatch with) the immediately preceding one (Figure 9.9). Rats were trained
initially with a very brief interval between odor presentations. Subsequently, the
interstimulus interval was manipulated to vary the retention delay, allowing an
assessment of the persistence of memory as in the earlier studies on monkeys.

Neuropsychological Studies

In an initial experiment, Otto and Eichenbaum (1992b) compared the effects of
selective ablation of the parahippocampal region and a fornix transection that
selectively disrupted hippocampal function. Normal rats acquired the task within
approximately 150 trials; neither of the lesion groups was impaired on acquisition (Figure 9.10). Subsequent testing of memory across various delays showed
that intact rats performed at a level of 90% or better at the shortest delay, with

Continuous Delayed Non-Match to Sample (cDNM)

$$A^+ - B^+ - B^- - B^- - C^+ - C^- - D^+ - A^+ - A^- - E^+ - F^+ -$$

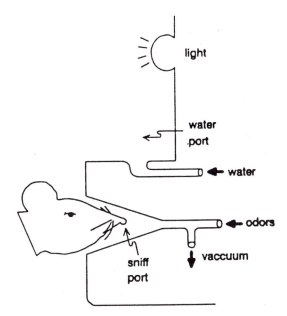

Figure 9.9. The continuous delayed non-match to sample (cDNM) task. Top: An example sequence of odors identified as letters. Those designated as "plus" are non-matches and rewarded; those designated as "minus" are matches and non-rewarded. Bottom: Illustration of the apparatus. Upon a light signal, the rat initiates a trial by performing a nose poke into the sniff port. This results in turning off the vacuum and onset of the odor. On nonmatch trials the rat can then poke its nose into the water port to receive a reward.

performance gradually declining as the retention interval was increased. Rats with damage to the parahippocampal region also showed good retention at the shortest delay, but their performance declined abnormally rapidly across delays, showing a severe deficit within 1 min. By contrast, rats with fornix lesions performed identically to normal rats across delays, showing intact performance at the short delay and the normal gradual memory decay as a function of increasing delay. These findings indicated that neither the parahippocampal region nor the hippocampus is critical for perception of the odor cues, for acquisition of the nonmatch rule, or for short-term retention of odors. However, the parahippocampal region was shown to be critical for mediating a memory representation that persists beyond immediate memory in rats, as it is in monkeys. Furthermore, we may infer from these results that through its direct, reciprocal connections with the cortex, the parahippocampal region is sufficient to mediate the persistence of

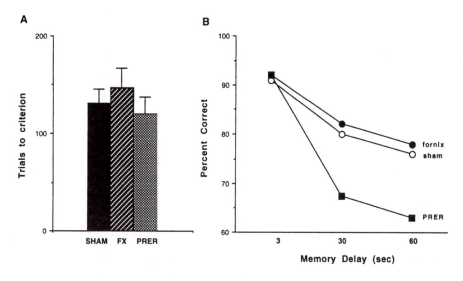

Figure 9.10. Performance on the cDNM task by control rats with SHAM surgeries, rats with fornix transections (FX) and rats with lesions of the perirhinal and entorhinal cortex (PRER). A. Initial training on the task with short memory delays. B. Performance with different delays.

single-item memories independent of hippocampal processing. These findings on the differential roles of the parahippocampal region and hippocampus in rats are entirely consistent with the data from several studies on monkeys, described in chapter 6. Monkeys with damage limited to the hippocampus itself or with fornix transection show no deficit or a modest deficit on object-cued DNMS; but monkeys with substantial damage to the parahippocampal region show a severe delay-dependent deficit on this task.

Electrophysiological Studies

Using the odor-guided cDNM task in electrophysiological studies of rats, Eichenbaum and colleagues have examined the response properties of neurons in the parahippocampal region (Young et al., 1995) and in the hippocampus (Otto & Eichenbaum, 1992a). In the studies of the parahippocampal region (Young et al., 1995), the firing patterns of cells were examined during both the period when rats were sampling the odor cues (in order to assess the extent to which odors were selectively encoded) and during the memory delay (in order to determine the capacity of these areas for maintaining an odor memory representation) (Figure 9.11). The analyses of delay related activity focused on the end of the delay period, immediately preceding the initiation of the subsequent odor presentation. At this time, the overt behavior of the animal is consistent across trials—it is approaching the stimulus port, in the absence of an odor cue—allowing one to determine if neural activity varies as a function of the memory for the identity of the preceding sample cue just before the recognition judgment must be made.

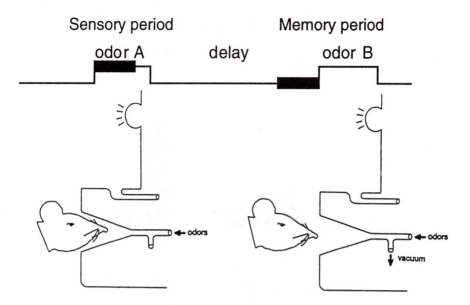

Figure 9.11. Illustration of critical data analysis periods in the CDNM task.

A substantial proportion of cells in each of the subdivisions of the parahippo-campal region and subiculum fired during the odor-sampling or delay periods. Many cells encoded the identity of the odor cues during the odor-sampling pe-riod (Figure 9.12). Some of these cells fired selectively or differentially to odors at odor onset and ceased firing when odor sampling was concluded, much as one would expect of a sensory neuron (Figure 9.12, bottom). Other cells showed strik-ing odor-specific activity at the end of the memory delay period, indicating some form of intermediate-term storage that was still available just before the choice phase of the trials regardless of the length of the delay (Figure 9.13, top). Some of these cells fired during odor sampling and then throughout the delay period, such as in the example shown in Figure 9.13, bottom. Indeed, substantial num-bers of cells in each of the subdivisions of the parahippocampal region demon-strated selective or differential firing patterns at the end of the delay period, as can be seen in Figure 9.14.

Other cells that showed odor-selective activity at the end of the memory delay fired transiently during the sample phase, then ceased firing during the delay, but recovered odor-selective activity just as the animal was initiating the choice phase (Figure 9.15). It is not clear how these cells maintained a subthreshold selective representation during most of the delay; apparently, in the rat at least, a stimulus-specific parahippocampal memory representation can be regenerated at just the time when it is needed to perform the recognition response.

Finally, another set of cells showed selective activity that reflected the match and nonmatch qualities of the odor cues during the choice phase (Figure 9.16). Some of these cells, called *match suppression cells,* fired at a higher rate when the rat was sampling a repeated (matching) odor, and this differential response was largest for the most preferred odor for that cell. Other cells, called *match*

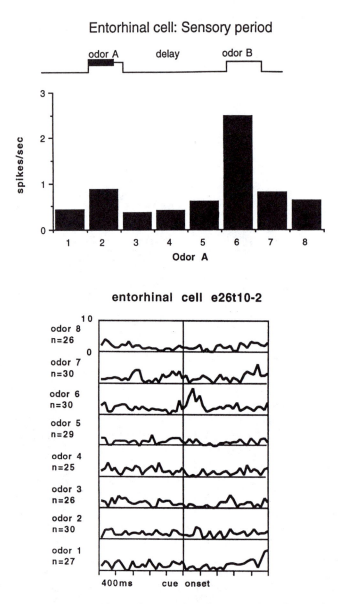

Figure 9.12. Analyses of cells in the entorhinal cortex that show odor selective responses in the sensory period of the cDNM task. Top: Comparison of firing rates during the sensory period. Bottom: Pattern of firing associated with different sample odors before and after odor onset.

Entorhinal cell: Memory Period

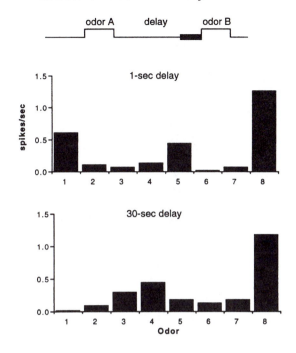

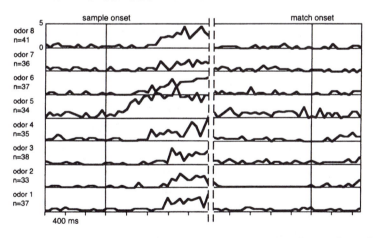

entorhinal cell e26t 11-1

Figure 9.13. Analyses of cells in the entorhinal cortex that show odor selective responses in the memory period of the cDNM task. Top: Comparison of firing rates during the memory period in short and long delay trials. Bottom: Pattern of firing associated with different sample odors before and after odor onset, and before and after match odor onset. There is a gap between these periods (dashed lines) because the actual memory delay varied somewhat in length corresponding to when the rat initiated the match phase. (Reproduced, with permission, from Young, Otto, Fox, & Eichenbaum, 1997; Copyright Society for Neuroscience.)

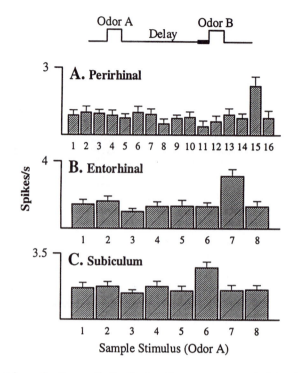

Figure 9.14. Odor selective activity during the memory period in different parts of the parahippocampal region and subiculum. (Reproduced, with permission, from Young, Otto, Fox, & Eichenbaum, 1997; Copyright Society for Neuroscience.)

enhancement cells, fired at a higher rate when the rat was sampling a different odor than the one on the previous trial (i.e., a nonmatch), and this differential response was largest for the most preferred odor for that cell.

Taken together, neurons in the parahippocampal region have all the properties required to support recognition performance. They encode specific odors, hold these representations (either by maintaining their activity or by regenerating activity) during an extended delay period during which an intact parahippocampal region is required, and detect match versus nonmatch qualities of the presented choice odors.

In the studies of hippocampus itself, CA1 pyramidal neurons of rats were recorded in animals performing the same cDNM task (Otto & Eichenbaum, 1992a). A large proportion of hippocampal cells could be activated in association with virtually every identifiable behavioral event in the task. A substantial subset of CA1 cells was selectively active during the odor stimulus sampling period, and the activity of some of these hippocampal cells reflected the "match" or "nonmatch" relationship critical to performance in this task (Figure 9.17). By contrast with the cells in the parahippocampal region, however, no hippocampal cells fired in association with the sampling of a particular odor or with particular com-

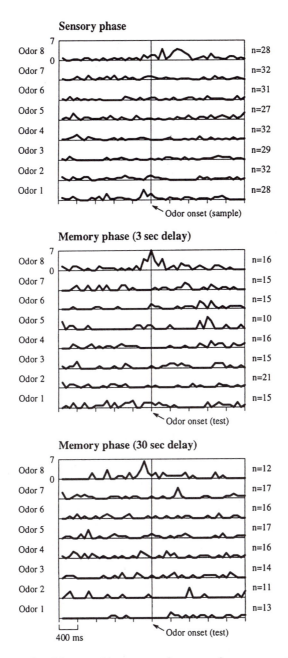

Figure 9.15. Example of the parahippocampal neuron that regenerated odor selective activity just prior to and during presentation of the choice cue during the cDNM task. (Reproduced, with permission, from Young, Otto, Fox, & Eichenbaum, 1997; Copyright Society for Neuroscience.)

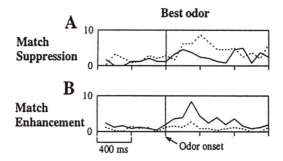

Figure 9.16. Examples of parahippocampal neurons that show (A) suppression of the response during the choice period to a matching stimulus (filled line) compared to the same odor presented as a nonmatch stimulus (dashed line), or (B) enhancement of the response during the choice period to a nonmatching stimulus compared to the same odor as a matching stimulus. (Reproduced, with permission, from Young, Otto, Fox, & Eichenbaum, 1997; Copyright Society for Neuroscience.)

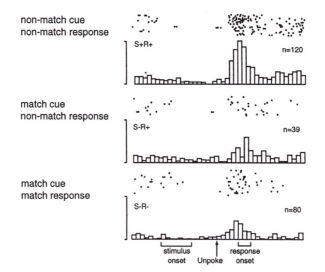

Figure 9.17. Example of a hippocampal neuron that showed enhanced responses on all non-match trials, as compared to match trials on which either type of behavioral response was performed. Neural activity was time-locked to the "unpoke", when the rat withdrew its nose from the sniff port. (Reproduced, with permission, from Otto & Eichenbaum, 1992; Copyright John Wiley & Sons, Inc.)

binations of odors that composed specific matching comparisons. Rather, hippocampal cellular activity reflected all comparisons with the same outcome. This finding is entirely consistent with the results of the lesion studies. It appears that the hippocampus itself is *not* involved in the encoding and storage of representations for *specific items* in this task. Instead, here the hippocampus encodes abstract relations among cues, as it does in many other test situations. Thus, for example, the match-mismatch relationship reflected in the activity of hippocampal cells in animals performing the cDNM task can be viewed as analogous to the spatial relations among cues reflected in the firing patterns of hippocampal place cells when rats explore open fields (O'Keefe, 1979; see chapter 7). Indeed, across a broad range of tasks, hippocampal cells encode all manner of relations among salient stimuli as well as behavioral actions (Deadwyler et al., 1995; Eichenbaum, 1993, 1996; see Eichenbaum & Cohen, 1988). In the cDNM task, *relational* cells in the hippocampus may mediate memory for match and nonmatch trial outcomes, even though this information contributes little directly to performance on this simple recognition task. Consistent with the data from the lesion work, the parahippocampal region, but not the hippocampus, maintains specific and persistent representations sufficient to support recognition performance.

Findings from recording studies of monkeys are entirely consistent with the above observations of hippocampal system activity in rats. Brown and colleagues (1987) first compared the firing properties of neurons in the cortical areas surrounding the hippocampus versus the hippocampus itself in monkeys performing a delayed-matching task guided by complex visual pattern cues. The cortical cells showed stimulus-specific decrements in response (match suppression) when the choice stimulus was a repetition of the sample, but no such responses were observed in the hippocampus itself. In subsequent studies, Brown and colleagues (Brown, 1996; Brown & Xiang, 1998; Riches et al., 1991; Fahy et al., 1993; Xiang & Brown, 1998) confirmed that a large percentage of cells in these cortical areas demonstrated match suppression responses. They showed evidence for three different types of recognition-related decremental responses in those cells (Figure 9.18). Some cells, called *novelty neurons,* fired only on the first presentation of a novel visual pattern and did not recover for at least 24 hr. Other cells, called *familiarity neurons,* did not decrement on the choice phase of the first trial in which the stimulus appeared but showed reduced responses on all subsequent presentations. Yet other cells, called *recency neurons,* showed match suppression only in the choice phase of each trial when a particular stimulus appeared but recovered fully when the same cue was presented as a sample in a subsequent trial. Brown has argued that all of these recognition-related firing patterns coexist and may serve different roles in visual recognition. Importantly, no stimulus-specific match suppression responses were observed in the hippocampus in any of his studies.

In similar studies on the rat, Zhu et al. (1995a) observed familiarity- and recency-related responses to visual stimuli in cortical areas of rats. They reported both incremental and decremental responses, with a greater incidence of decremental responses to stimulus repetition in several cortical areas than in the hippocampus, and more incremental responses in the hippocampus, although Brown & Xiang (1998) attributed the later observation to spatial attributes of the stimulus presentations. Using fos-activation as a marker for neuronal activation,

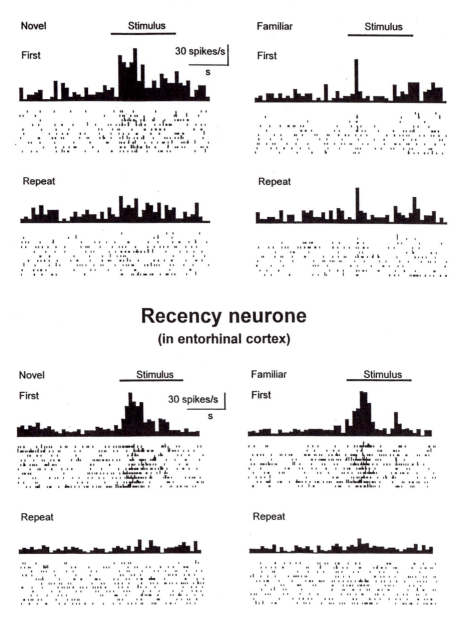

Figure 9.18. Examples of parahippocampal neurons that show suppressed responses to repeated visual stimuli in the monkey. The "novelty" neuron responds only on the very first presentation of a stimulus on a test day. The "recency" neuron responds each time the stimulus is presented as the sample cue, but not as the match. (Reproduced, with permission, from Xiang & Brown, 1998; Copyright Elsevier Science.)

stimulus repetition produced marked changes in cortical areas but little change in the hippocampus (Zhu et al., 1995b, 1997).

Other recent studies have provided evidence of intermediate-term memory processing by the parahippocampal region in monkeys performing a more complex delayed-matching-to-sample task. Miller, Desimone, and their colleagues (1991b, 1993; Miller & Desimone, 1994; Li et al., 1993; Desimone, 1996) trained monkeys to perform a variant of delayed matching to sample, where a pattern cue was presented as the "sample," and followed by several choice stimuli, the monkey had to respond only to the matching choice stimulus. In these studies, cells in the perirhinal cortex of monkeys showed selective responses to the visual cues. Some cells fired persistently during the initial part of the delay but ceased firing when the first choice item was presented. In a version of the task where each choice stimulus was presented only once per trial, the predominant observation was "match suppression," where many cells fired less to the matching choice item. In another version of the task, where incorrect (nonmatching) choice items were presented repeatedly, forcing the animal to attend to the designated sample cue, a substantial number of "match enhancement" cells were also observed.

Suzuki et al. (1997) employed the same task to study the firing properties of neurons in the entorhinal cortex of monkeys. They found a fraction of entorhinal cells that fired selectively to specific visual cues (Figure 9.19). In addition, unlike perirhinal cells in the monkey but like cells throughout the parahippocampal region in the rat, neurons in the entorhinal cortex fired throughout each of the delay periods between the sample stimulus and each of the choice items (Figure 9.20). Finally, entorhinal neuronal activity also reflected the match and nonmatch qualities of the choice stimulus, by showing match suppression and match enhancement responses (Figure 9.21).

Finally, recent evidence from brain-imaging studies in humans also suggests a prominent role for the parahippocampal region in maintaining memory representations. In this study Fernandez et al. (1999) found bilateral sustained activation of the entorhinal cortex selectively during intentional memorizing of words. Furthermore, the level of activation was correlated with subsequent retention performance.

The Role of the Hippocampus and Parahippocampal Region in Relational Memory

The above results indicate that the parahippocampal region plays a more critical role in simple recognition memory than does the hippocampus itself. Indeed, some have suggested that the parahippocampal region plays a more critical role than the hippocampus for a broad range of memory tasks, at least as tested in monkeys (Murray, 1996; Murray et al., 1993). However, as seen in chapters 5 and 7, studies of memory in humans and rats indicate that the hippocampus itself does play a critical role in some types of memory. The role of the hippocampus is seen most clearly in tasks that emphasize the representational properties of declarative memory rather than the temporal properties. It turns out that the

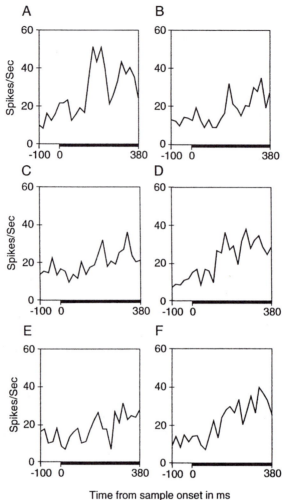

Figure 9.19. Differential responses of a monkey entorhinal neuron across different visual stimuli (A-F). (Reproduced, with permission, from Suzuki, Miller, & Desimone, 1997; Copyright American Physiological Society.)

heavy reliance of primate work on the DNMS task has led to emphasis in that literature on the temporal characteristics of the hippocampal memory system and has therefore focused attention on the role of the parahippocampal region, which has the ability to maintain a persistent intermediate-term memory representation. Work on amnesia in humans and rats, by contrast, has explored a variety of tasks that call upon the special representational characteristics of the hippocampal memory system, namely, the ability to perform relational memory processing, which depends critically on the hippocampus itself. In order to clarify this point, we will turn now to one further set of results in which the ability to learn the

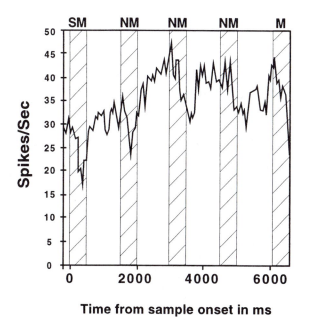

Figure 9.20. Sustained activity of a monkey entorhinal neuron during the delay periods after the sample (SM) and each nonmatching (NM) stimulus, up to the match (M). (Reproduced, with permission, from Suzuki, Miller, & Desimone, 1997; Copyright American Physiological Society.)

relations among items is challenged in rats with selective damage either to the parahippocampal region or to hippocampus (following transection of the fornix).

Among the evidence presented in chapter 7 for the role of the hippocampus in relational representation was the finding that learning and expression of pairwise associations in rats was critically dependent on the hippocampus (Bunsey & Eichenbaum, 1996). A more ambitious test of the role of the hippocampus was provided by Dusek and Eichenbaum (1997), who studied the capacity for learning and remembering large and structured odor memory organizations and the ability for representational flexibility. They developed a task that required animals to learn an orderly hierarchy of odor representations and then tested their ability to make transitive inference judgments. The task was based on a test Piaget (1928) pioneered to assess human cognitive development. In tests of this type in human children, subjects are initially presented with a set of *premises,* such as "The blue rod is longer than the red rod" and "The red rod is longer than the green rod." Then the children are asked whether they can make an inference that the blue rod is longer than the green rod. The capacity for inferential judgment in this test is interpreted as prima facie evidence of the representation of orderly relations; moreover, it is the kind of relational representation structure that we attribute to the hippocampal memory system.

In the study by Dusek and Eichenbaum (1997), rats were first trained on a series of two-item odor discriminations, called *premise pairs,* that collectively

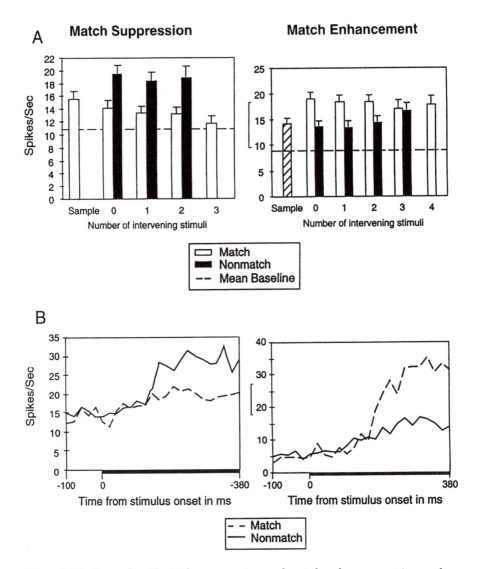

Figure 9.21. Examples of match suppression and match enhancement in monkey entorhinal neurons. A. Comparisons of firing rates for the same stimulus as match and nonmatch across memory delays. B. Firing pattern after stimulus onset. (Reproduced, with permission, from Suzuki, Miller, & Desimone, 1997; Copyright American Physiological Society.)

included five different odors (e.g., A+ vs. B−, B+ vs. C−, C+ vs. D−, D+ vs. E−, where + or − refers to which item is rewarded; see Figures 9.22, 9.23A). Animals were initially trained on the series of premise pairs using a trial-blocking method that introduced the pairs and their correct responses gradually. Ultimately, however, they were presented with premise pairs in random order. Learning could occur by representing each of the discriminations individually, or they could instead be represented within an orderly hierarchy that includes all five items. To examine which of the representations was actually employed by the animals, they were given probe tests derived from pairs of nonadjacent elements (in the case shown in Figure 9.22, the probes would test B vs. D and A vs. E). When presented with the probe pair B versus D, two nonadjacent and nonend elements, consistently choosing B provides unambiguous evidence for transitive inference. Note that correctly choosing A when presented with the probe pair A versus E could be entirely guided by the independent reinforcement histories of these elements individually, because choices of A during premise training were always rewarded and choices of E were never rewarded. Thus the combination of the probe tests B versus D and A versus E provided a powerful assessment of capaci-

Premise Pair Training

A > B

B > C

C > D

D > E

Ordered Representation

A > B > C > D > E

Probe Tests

B vs D   : test of transitivity

A vs E   : non-transitive novel pairing

Figure 9.22. Training and test items for the transitive inference task. (Reproduced, with permission, from Dusek & Eichenbaum, 1997; Copyright National Academy of Sciences, U.S.A.)

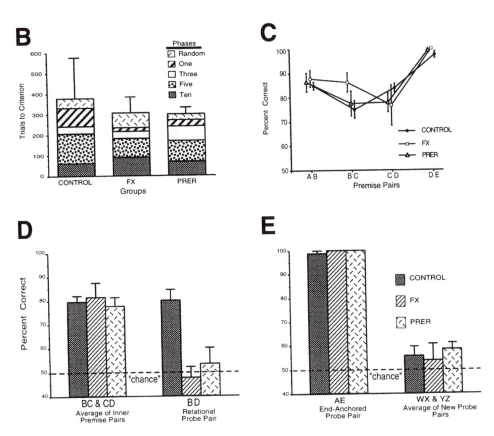

Figure 9.23. The transitive inference task. A. Illustration of a rat and the odor stimuli presented on a trial. B. Performance across phases of training on premise pairs. C. Performance on randomly presented premise pairs. D. Average performance on inner premise pairs, and on the transitive inference test (BD). E. Performance on the control probe AE and on new discriminations. FX = fornix transection; PRER = perirhinal and entorinal cortex lesion. (Reproduced, with permission, from Dusek & Eichenbaum, 1997; Copyright National Academy of Sciences, U.S.A.)

ties for making novel judgments guided by inferential expression of the orderly organization or by reward history of the individual elements, respectively.

After achieving solid performance on the premise pairs, probe trials containing the critical B versus D problem and the control A versus E problem were presented intermingled with repetitions of the premise pairs. On these probe trials, animals were rewarded for the "correct" (transitive) selection, in order to avoid dissuading them from making transitive choices and maintain performance on the probe trials. In order to minimize new learning of the B versus D problem, probes were presented only twice per test session and were widely spaced among repetitions of premise pairs. In addition, to test for possible contamination by new learning of the B versus D problem, all animals were subsequently tested for their ability to learn about new odor cues presented in the probe test format.

The performance of normal rats was compared to that of rats with fornix transection, preventing the normal operation of the hippocampus, and rats with ablation of perirhinal and entorhinal cortices. Both normal rats and rats with fornix transections or parahippocampal ablation achieved criterion performance on each training phase very rapidly (Figure 9.23B). In addition, all rats readily reached criterion with randomly presented premise pairs in an equivalent number of trials. In probe testing, all rats continued to perform well on the premise pairs during the test sessions (Figure 9.23C). All groups demonstrated a serial position curve, so that performance was best on pairs that included one of the end items. On the critical B versus D probe test, normal subjects demonstrated robust transitive inference. Their performance on B versus D trials significantly exceeded chance level and was not different from their performance on premise pairs that included items B and D (the B vs. C and C vs. D pairs; see Figure 9.23D). In striking contrast, the rats with either type of hippocampal damage performed no better than chance on the BD probe: Their performance on the B versus D problem was much lower than that on the premise pairs that included B and D, and much worse than the performance of normal animals on this test of transitivity.

A further analysis of transitivity examined performance on the very first presentation of the B versus D pair, which may be considered a "pure" test of inferential responding uncontaminated by food reinforcements given on repeated probe trials. Of the normal subjects, 88% chose correctly on the first B versus D probe, whereas only 50% of the rats with either type of hippocampal damage were successful on the initial B versus D judgment. Thus, by several measures, the data strongly indicate that rats with hippocampal damage have no capacity for transitive inference, despite their having learned each of the premise problems as well as normal subjects.

Analyses of performance on other types of probe trials demonstrated the selectivity of the deficit in transitive inference in rats with either type of hippocampal damage. All rats performed extremely well on the A versus E trials, which can be solved without a transitive judgment (Figure 9.23E), with no group differences in performance on this problem. Conversely, all groups showed minimal evidence of learning during presentations of the new odor pairs (WX and YZ), again with no group differences in performance on these problems. The contrast between robust performance on B versus D problems and poor performance for new odor pairs in normal rats strongly indicates that their judgments on the B versus

D pairs reflected inferential capacity. The striking inability of animals with either type of hippocampal damage to show this inferential capacity on the B versus D probe trials, despite normal performance on the premise pairs, suggests that they had learned the premise pairs in a way that did not involve the orderly relations among the odor cues.

These results are important for our considerations of anatomical distinctions within the hippocampal region. In this challenging test of relational memory, transection of the fornix and ablation of the parahippocampal region produced equivalent full-blown impairments. This pattern of findings strongly implicates the common structure compromised by these disconnections—the hippocampus itself—as playing the critical role in the representational properties of declarative memory.

Differential Activation of the Parahippocampal Region and Hippocampus

Three recent studies, one in rats and two in humans, provide further evidence consistent with the notion that the parahippocampal region and hippocampus are differentially activated in different types of memory processing. One study involved an extension of Brown and colleagues' (Zhu et al., 1995a, b, 1997) examination of c-fos activation in the hippocampal region (Wan et al., 1999). In this study they presented rats with computer images of novel and familiar object stimuli and compared responses to changes in the familiarity of particular stimuli or the familiarity of stimulus arrangements. To initiate each trial the rat placed its nose into an observing hole that stabilized the position of its eyes. Then two images were presented in the extreme left and right visual fields; because the visual circuitry of the rat involves a nearly complete hemispheric crossing of the most lateral parts of the visual fields, these images would be expected to drive neurons primarily in the contralateral hemisphere. In each case a familiar image was presented to one visual field and a novel image was presented to the other; the key variable in this study was the nature of the images. For some animals the images involved pictures of single objects, whereas in other animals the images involved novel and familiar spatial arrangements of the same three objects. When the images involved single stimuli, the perirhinal cortex showed greater c-fos activation in the perirhinal cortex on the side that viewed novel as compared to familiar pictures. No differential activation was observed for single stimuli in the hippocampus. By contrast, when the images involved arrangements of multiple stimuli, hippocampal subdivisions (as well as the postrhinal cortex) showed greater c-fos activation for novel as compared to familiar stimulus arrangements. In this condition, no differential activation was observed in the perirhinal cortex in this condition.

One recent study on humans involved recording field potentials from multiple sites in the medial temporal lobe (Fernandez et al., 1999). In this study a list of words was presented while recording from both the parahippocampal region and hippocampus; subsequently the subjects were tested for recall of the words. Memory related responses were evoked by words in both areas, although at different latencies after word presentation. In the parahippocampal, there was an

evoked field potential at about 300 ms after word-presentation, with a larger response for words that were subsequently recalled compared to studied words
that were not recalled. In the hippocampus, a word-evoked field potential was
observed at about 500 ms, and this response was also larger for successfully recalled words. Thus, while this study did not address the issue of the nature of
representations in these areas, it did separate memory processing into distinct
temporal domains differentially associated with the parahippocampal region and
hippocampus.

The other recent study in humans directly addressed the issue of different
kinds of memory processing in these two areas. This study used fMRI to examine
brain activation associated with the presentation of novel pictures in two memory conditions (Gabrieli et al., 1997). In one condition subjects were presented
with a series of novel pictures of indoor and outdoor scenes or line drawings. In
this condition, the parahippocampal region was activated but the hippocampus
itself was not, similar to previous findings by Stern et al. (1996). In the other
condition, prior to scanning, subjects were presented with and asked to remember a set of line drawings of common objects and animals, or the names of these
items. Then, during scanning, the subjects were presented with the names of the
drawings they had seen, or with the drawings of the items whose names they had
previously seen, respectively. In this condition, a subdivision of the hippocampus (the subiculum) was activated when the items were accurately remembered,
whereas no activation was observed in the parahippocampal region. This study
provided evidence in human subjects of a dissociation of memory-processing
functions in the hippocampal region.

Furthermore, the evidence from both of these studies can be viewed within
the framework outlined here based on single neuron recordings and neuropsychological experiments in animals. In both rats and humans, the parahippocampal region is activated during the perception and encoding of novel pictures. This
could reflect the activity of neurons in the parahippocampal region associated
with recognition of specific single items, as observed in rats and monkeys. These
activation findings complement the observations of selective deficits in recognition memory for single items in rats and monkeys with parahippocampal damage.
Furthermore, in rats the hippocampus itself is activated when memory processing involves the identification of novel arrangements of multiple items. In humans the hippocampus is activated when memory processing involves the identification of a word from a picture and vice versa. Both of these types of processing
are likely to invoke the processing of relationships between items in memory,
consistent with the role of the hippocampus in relational processing identified
in neuropsychological studies described above.

A Model of Processing Within the Hippocampal
Memory System

The findings discussed above speak to the roles of the parahippocampal region
and the hippocampus in realizing the temporal and representational properties,
respectively, of hippocampus-dependent memory processing. But how do these
components provide their separate functionalities within the hippocampal mem-

ory system, and how do they interact to produce declarative memory? In order to address this question, this chapter concludes with a model for successive stages of memory processing within the entire hippocampal memory system.

Prior to processing by the hippocampal system, neocortical areas create specific perceptual representations that can be sustained briefly within those processing areas. Such memory traces are able to support perceptual matchings between current and stored representations, and can support performance in short-term recognition, consistent with the observed sparing of working memory even in severe amnesia.

At the first stage of processing within the medial temporal lobe, perceptual codings from the neocortical processors reach the parahippocampal region, where functionally distinct representations of the to-be-remembered events converge prior to processing in the hippocampal formation itself. In the parahippocampal region, specific information is encoded, and neural activity representing that information is sustained, persisting through considerable interference and intervening processing. Furthermore, the parahippocampal region is capable of processing the matchings between current representations and the contents of the intermediate-term store. This processing appears to be sufficient to support DNMS performance in the absence of normal function of the hippocampus (see Murray & Bussey, 1999, for a related perspective).

At the final stage of hippocampal system processing, the hippocampus enters the picture, *not* to maintain a memory representation of single sensory cues, but to process comparisons among the various current stimuli and between current stimuli and representations of previous stimuli, presumably those maintained at earlier levels of this system. Hippocampal processing appears to be quite different from the perceptual matching taking place in cortical areas. Thus, hippocampal processing relies on cortical inputs (Miller & Best, 1980) and presumably will exert its effects by modifying those inputs or by making connections among those cortical areas (e.g., Squire, Cohen, & Nadel, 1984; Halgren, 1984; Sakai et al., 1994). In recognition memory, the hippocampus processes comparisons between current and previous stimuli as well as rich episodic and contextual information that goes beyond the strict perceptual properties on which cortical matchings are based; this may in some cases make a distinctive contribution to intermediate-term memory. Moreover, when the requirements of the task go beyond what can be accomplished by sensory matching processes, requiring comparisons among experiences with items and the flexible expression of memories, the entire hippocampal system contributes critically to a distinctly new capacity for declarative memory representation.

Putting together the results of the studies presented here, a preliminary picture of the processes that mediate declarative memory emerges. It appears that the parahippocampal region contributes to declarative memory by "buffering" specific representations that can be accessed and manipulated by the hippocampus. Then the hippocampus represents the critical relations among the items held by the parahippocampal region and indeed has access to the much larger organization of item representations in cortical association areas via the parahippocampal region. We presume the full relational memory organization comes about through multiple iterations of cortical input to the parahippocampal region and temporary storage there. This might be followed by hippocampus-mediated relational processing that adds to or restructures interconnections among the parahip-pocampal and the cortical representations. Over extended time periods, new experiences that bear on the established organization reactivate established repre-sentations as well as add new ones, and these are processed together by this hippocampal circuit to weave the new information into the established relational network. Precisely because this network is so extensive and systematically inter-connected, access to items via novel routes and in novel experiences is not only possible but also occurs continuously as we express memories to guide almost every aspect of daily life. These interactions, by feeding back and forth, can go on for a significant period and may be reinstated repeatedly by experiences that bear partial similarity to the learning event. This repetitive processing could con-tribute to the *consolidation* of memories over very long periods. The larger issue of memory consolidation itself will be considered in the next chapter.

10

Memory Consolidation

Thus far, the characterization of the functional role played by the hippocampal system in memory has focused on the *kind* of memory it supports and the nature of memory *representation* generated by hippocampal processing. This chapter considers what role the hippocampal system plays in the storage, maintenance, and consolidation of memory during the time after learning. The immediately preceding chapter discussed the interaction of the hippocampus proper with related medial temporal lobe regions in supporting declarative memory and relational memory processing. Here we show how the interaction of the hippocampal system and neocortical storage sites gives rise to memory consolidation.

Memory consolidation is the name given to the hypothetical process(es) by which new memories transition from an initially labile state to become permanently fixed in long-term storage. The notion of consolidation was first proposed formally by Müller and Pilzecker (1900), to account for the decrement in human memory performance caused by the presentation of other material shortly after exposure to the to-be-remembered items. They suggested that this memory phenomenon reflected the disruption, by the intervening material, of physiological activity that fixes associations established during learning. Until those associations were "fixed," or *consolidated,* memory would be susceptible to disruption. The connection between these experiments and the observation of retrograde amnesia following brain trauma—impairment of memories acquired prior to the trauma—was made shortly thereafter (see Polster et al., 1991; Lechner et al., 1999). Burnham (1903) proposed that consolidation involves a time-consuming "process of organization" of newly obtained memories through some combination of physical reorganization and psychological processes of repetition and association. Accordingly, he proposed that retrograde amnesia was a consequence of interrupted organizational processing, which must normally occur for

344

a considerable period of time after learning. Other, more physiologically based, conceptions followed. In particular, the notion that the physical reorganization involved networks of neurons interacting for long periods was captured prominently in Hebb's (1949) notion of reverberating activity by cell assemblies (see chapter 2).

Two Lines of Evidence Concerning Memory Consolidation

There are two major lines of evidence from neuropsychological studies of amnesia that have been offered in support of the notion of consolidation (see Squire, Cohen, & Nadel, 1984). One line of evidence concerns the course of forgetting in anterograde amnesia. The other line of evidence comes from studies of retrograde amnesia and, more specifically, of the differential susceptibility to retrograde amnesia of memories acquired at different times prior to the brain injury.

Forgetting in Anterograde Amnesia

As reviewed in previous chapters, a typical finding after damage to the medial temporal lobe is delay-dependent memory impairment for new materials. Human patients and animals with damage to medial temporal lobe structures typically have intact short-term memory, showing fully normal abilities in recall and recognition over a period of seconds after learning. However, they show a delay-dependent memory deficit, exhibiting impairment in the retention of information in the long term. For example, the patient H.M. can acquire and remember a series of numbers, letters, or words sufficiently to demonstrate immediate memory that is equivalent to that of normal subjects, but memory performance over longer delays is abnormally poor compared to that of normal subjects. Likewise, monkeys and rats with damage to the hippocampal system perform well in delayed nonmatching to sample (DNMS) for various types of stimuli, as long as the retention interval is limited to a few seconds, and they show intact performance in acquiring discrimination tasks and in short-term retention of this learning, but impairment in performance on delayed retention tests. These findings suggest that, even when initial acquisition is intact, declarative memory in animals and humans with damage to the hippocampal system is labile and cannot fully consolidate into a permanent form.

Temporally Limited Retrograde Amnesia

The other evidence for memory consolidation comes from the phenomenology of retrograde amnesia. Ribot (1882) is generally credited with providing the first thorough analysis of human retrograde amnesia, and with establishing the central observation that the extent to which memory is lost is inversely related to the recency of the event. That is, retrograde amnesia is temporally graded, with the impairment more severe for recently acquired memories than for memories acquired in the more remote past. As a result, there is better memory for remote events than for more recent events, a pattern of performance that, of course, is opposite to the typical pattern of normal forgetting. This striking phenomenon is known as *Ribot's law*. The consensual interpretation of this phenomenon is that recent memories are disproportionately vulnerable to disruption, consistent with the notion that memories remain in a labile state for some period of time. A more extended treatment of retrograde amnesia is provided below. First, however, we take a moment to clarify two different senses of the term *consolidation*, or two different conceptualizations of consolidation.

Two Distinct Stages of Memory Consolidation

The term *consolidation* has been used in two ways in the memory literature (e.g., see Dudai, 1996). These two conceptions differ both in the presumed mechanisms that mediate consolidation and in the time scale of the relevant events.

Cellular Events That Mediate Rapid Processes in Memory Consolidation

One approach to consolidation treats it as a cascade of molecular and microstructural events by which short-term synaptic modifications lead to permanent changes in connectivity between neurons. These events are intended to capture the transition of memories from a short-term store to long-term memory, on a time scale of seconds and minutes. These events can in principle occur in any brain structure that participates in memory. Molecular events that mediate the formation of permanent structural changes associated with memory have been studied in a broad variety of mammalian brain structures that participate in memory, as outlined in chapter 3.

The details of this work are beyond the scope of the present book. However, a few general points should be made here. First, studies on this conceptualization of consolidation focus on local network neural activity (i.e., on highly integrated "cell assemblies") and on intracellular events that initiate nuclear transcription mechanisms for protein synthesis. Many older studies examined the timing and mechanisms for these mechanisms by exploring the effects of strong electrical disturbances, such as electroconvulsive shock, and of drug treatments that block protein synthesis on memory for recently acquired information. Both of these manipulations produce a temporally graded retrograde amnesia. These findings were disputed by studies claiming to show that disrupted memories could be recovered by "reminder" treatments (for review see Polster et al., 1991), but such reminders could easily have constituted further training experiences rather than events restoring unrelated blocked memories.

More recent studies on the molecular mechanisms of long-term potentiation have renewed the focus on protein synthesis as required for permanent physiological and microstructural alterations consequent both on LTP and on learning (see chapter 3). These studies have identified specific proteins (e.g., CREB), the increased synthesis of which is seen as a candidate for critical events in the formation of LTP and of permanent memory. Such cellular events begin immediately with the learning experience but continue to unfold during the minutes and hours after learning. Treatments that disrupt the activity of cell assemblies and the molecular cascade leading to new protein synthesis are effective only within this relatively brief period, suggesting the time scale that characterizes this sense or this conception of memory consolidation.

Brain Systems That Mediate Slow Processes in Memory Consolidation

The mechanism for the other conception of memory consolidation involves events above the level of cellular physiology; this kind of consolidation occurs at the brain systems level. The time scale of events involved in systems-level phenomena of consolidation is several-fold greater than that of the cellular consolidation mechanisms. It appears that this kind of consolidation requires hours, days, months, or years, depending on the nature of the memory tested and the species tested. It will be argued that this consolidation never ends completely, for reasons that are of considerable theoretical importance.

The notion of consolidation at the brain systems level, operating at this long time scale, is tied to the temporally graded retrograde amnesias discussed earlier, in which the susceptibility of recent memories to disruption extends over years. Below, we will discuss the neural processing that underlies this phenomenon, addressing along the way various fundamental issues about consolidation. How long does this kind of consolidation go on? Precisely which brain structures are critical to mediate consolidation? Where are the memories stored after consolidation is complete? Are all kinds of memories subject to consolidation? How is the delay-dependent forgetting in anterograde amnesia related to this consolidation mechanism? Studies on both human amnesia and animal models of amnesia address different aspects of these issues and provide an increasingly clear picture of the role of hippocampal involvement, and of hippocampal-neocortical interaction, in consolidation.

Outlining the properties of this long-time-scale consolidation process is the focus of the remainder of this chapter. First, the literature on human retrograde amnesia will be reviewed, including the methods used to test for retrograde amnesia in human subjects, the findings of temporally graded retrograde amnesia, and the identification of critical brain structures. Next, there will be a review of attempts to model retrograde amnesia in animals, again focusing on the testing methods, the findings of temporally graded memory loss, and the critical brain structures. In addition, other relevant physiological findings will be reviewed. Finally, conceptualizations of the information processing and circuitry critical to mechanisms of consolidation will be considered, with the aim of combining the earlier-discussed observations on the nature of memory representation in cortical and hippocampal areas with the phenomenology of consolidation.

Retrograde Memory Loss in Human Amnesia

While a broad variety of cerebral insults can result in retrograde amnesia, the main focus of studies on the long-term process of consolidation has been studies of amnesia following hippocampal system damage. The conceptual linkage between the hippocampus and consolidation began with the earliest observations on the patient H.M. Scoville and Milner's (1957) report on H.M. focused on his disorder as a particularly good example of Ribot's law. They characterized his amnesia as a severe and selective impairment in "recent memory" in the face of spared remote memory capacities. Indeed, the dissociation in H.M. between impaired recent memories and intact remote memories was most striking. So far as could be ascertained by interviews with H.M. and his family, the retrograde memory loss dated back 2 years prior to the surgery, with more remote memory seeming intact. More recent evaluations confirm that H.M.'s remote memory impairment is indeed temporally limited.

However, an extensive battery of tests of memory for public and personal events also extend the period of impairment back to 11 years prior to the surgery (Corkin, Cohen, & Sagar, 1983; Corkin, 1984; Sagar, Cohen, Corkin, & Growdon, 1985; see chapter 5). These studies used several strategies to assess H.M.'s memory for material he was presumed to have acquired across the decades prior to his surgery. Some of these tests evaluated his memory for public events, including naming of tunes, verbal recognition of events, or identification of faces that became famous in a particular decade. For example, a test of recognition for famous events includes a series of questions about particularly important public events from the 1940s through the 1970s. H.M., whose surgery was performed in 1953, performed within the normal range of scores for questions about events that occurred in the 1940s, was borderline for events from the 1950s, and was clearly impaired on events from the 1960s onward. A test for recognition of public scenes was included, in which pictures depicting important scenes from the 1940s to the 1980s were selected so that the famous event could not be deduced from the picture alone. Subjects were asked if they had seen the picture before and could identify the event, and then further questions were asked about details of the event depicted. H.M.'s content scores were deficient in all decades except the 1940s. A method used to probe H.M.'s memory for personal events involved a test originally designed to access remote autobiographical memories. In this test, subjects were given concrete nouns and asked to relate them to some personally experienced event from any period in their life, and to describe when the event occurred. In addition, to assess the consistency of these memories, the test was readministered on another day. Normal subjects provided memories from throughout their life span, including especially the most recent time period. By contrast, the memories that H.M. retrieved to these cues all dated back to the age of 16 (i.e., 1942) or younger. Thus, he had no memories of the end of World War II or of his high school graduation (1947), or of any other events onward. These data provided the strongest evidence that his retrograde amnesia extends back 11 years prior to his surgery. Note, however, that because this time frame corresponds with the onset of H.M.'s seizure disorder (which ultimately precipitated the surgery he received), there is the possibility that at least some of the loss of memories might be a result of compromised hippocampal function during the period prior to his surgery (i.e., there might be a contribution here by a partial anterograde amnesia).

Subsequent studies on retrograde amnesia have provided confirmation of the phenomenon of temporally graded loss, in cases where the deficit is unambiguously a retrograde amnesia. For example, one line of studies with patients receiving electroconvulsive therapy (ECT) for severe depression, examined memory for television programs that were shown in a single viewing season (Squire et al., 1975; Squire & Cohen, 1979). These patients were found to have a (temporary) retrograde amnesia extending back 1–3 years before the treatments. Other studies have shown temporally graded retrograde amnesia dating 10–20 years back from an anoxic or ischemic event (reviewed in Squire & Alvarez., 1995).

In addition, a recent study of temporally graded retrograde amnesia associated with damage to the hippocampal region has tied the severity of retrograde amnesia to the amount of damage to this area (Rempel-Clower et al., 1996). This study involved four patients who had become amnesic without other cognitive impairment following specific brain insult and who had, for unrelated reasons, subsequently died and come to autopsy involving histological analysis of the brain damage. Two patients (R.B. and G.D.) developed moderately severe anterograde amnesia following a transient ischemic event. Both patients had a selective loss of cells in the CA1 field of the hippocampus and had a very limited retrograde amnesia, extending only 1–2 years. Two other patients (L.M. and W.H.) had more severe anterograde amnesia and more extensive retrograde amnesia extending back 15–25 years. The histopathological examination of these patients showed cell loss throughout the hippocampus and to some extent in entorhinal cortex as well. These studies further confirm that damage limited to the hippocampal region can result in temporally limited retrograde amnesia, and that the extent of the temporal gradient of retrograde amnesia might be associated with the anatomical extent of damage within the hippocampal region.

In a review of the literature on retrograde amnesia, Nadel and Moscovitch (1997) suggested that retrograde amnesia for spatial knowledge should be flat, consistent with the proposal that the hippocampus is a critical locus for the construction and retrieval of cognitive maps (O'Keefe & Nadel, 1978). Recently, Teng and Squire (1999) tested this view by examining the retrograde spatial memory capacities of a patient with extensive damage to the medial temporal lobe. They discovered that the patient had lived in a neighborhood in California during the 1930s and 1940s but had moved away and subsequently returned only occasionally. The patient's spatial memory for this period was evaluated by comparing his ability to construct routes between different locations in the community, using archival maps of the areas from the relevant period. In addition, the patient's ability to plot alternative roundabout routes was examined, using tests where he was asked how to navigate among places when the major route between them was blocked. These authors also measured the patient's accuracy in pointing in the direction of major landmarks from an imagined position in the neighborhood. On all these tests, the patient scored as well as or better than a group of age-matched control subjects who had lived in the same area during the target period, and who had also subsequently moved away. By contrast, and unlike the control subjects, the patient failed completely in solving the same navigational problems based on knowledge about one's current neighborhood. Thus, for this patient, the pattern of retrograde amnesia for spatial knowledge matched that of temporally graded nonspatial memory observed in previous studies in many amnesic patients.

Not all forms of retrograde amnesia are temporally graded, however. Thus, there are retrograde amnesias associated with a variety of etiologies in which gradients are flat, extending back to the earliest childhood memories (reviewed in Squire & Alvarez, 1995; Nadel & Moscovitch, 1997; Warrington, 1996). In addition, some have argued that some retrograde amnesias show a pattern of memory loss characterized less by the age of the memories than by their nature. Warrington (1996) presented data from four patients with retrograde amnesia showing impairments in the ability to recall or recognize faces of people who had become famous in the news media dating back several decades. Some of these patients showed flat gradients of retrograde amnesia dating for all periods of their life span. Nadel and Moscovitch's (1997) review of a large number of cases of retrograde amnesia concluded that retrograde amnesia following medial temporal lobe damage affects memory for personal episodes more severely than semantic memory, and that this deficit in autobiographical memory extends back many years and, in many cases, the entire life span. Squire and Alvarez (1995) argued, however, that flat gradients of retrograde amnesia, and particularly those involving autobiographical memory, occur only in cases where there is damage or suspected damage beyond the medial temporal lobe. They noted that cases of amnesia associated with Korsakoff's syndrome, closed-head injuries, seizure disorders, and certain other etiologies often include damage or cell loss in prefrontal cortex. This is important because damage to the prefrontal area is associated with disorders of "source memory," the ability to recall where and when information was acquired (Shimamura et al., 1990; Janowsky et al., 1989). Such an inability to identify the circumstances surrounding new learning might be expected to lead to a selective impairment in memory for personal experiences. In that case, the content selectivity of retrograde amnesia discussed by Nadel and Moscovitch (1997) would *not* be related to hippocampal function.

Animal Models of Retrograde Amnesia

The relatively recent development of experimental protocols for studying retrograde amnesia in animals has been a major advance in understanding the role of brain structures in memory consolidation. The use of animals allows an increased resolution of both the anatomical structures under study and the control over the learning experience prior to brain insult. Such prospective experiments can equalize the nature and extent of acquired information and can precisely control when learning takes place before brain damage. There have now been several prospective studies of retrograde amnesia, using different species and different learning and memory protocols. The majority of these studies support the notion that damage to medial temporal structures results in a temporally graded retrograde amnesia. Nevertheless this finding is not universal, and the severity and gradient of retrograde amnesia vary across studies with the species, types of tests, and locus of brain damage.

Zola-Morgan and Squire (1990) trained monkeys on a series of visual object discriminations at different times prior to ablation of the hippocampus and of some of the surrounding cortex. Animals were trained on 100 object discrimination problems, segregated into four 20-problem sets presented at 16, 12, 8, 4, or 2 weeks prior to the surgery. Each set of problems consisted of two problems per day, with each problem presented on 14 consecutive trials, thus requiring a total of 10 days. Performance was typically very good in learning, averaging 88% correct on the last trial of all the problems. Two weeks after the surgery, memory was assessed for all 100 problems, with random order presentation of a single trial of each problem over 2 days of testing. Normal monkeys performed best at problems that had been learned in the 4 weeks just prior to the (sham) surgery, with significantly poorer performance on problems that had been learned earlier, thus showing the typical forgetting curve (Figure 10.1). Monkeys with hippocampal damage showed the opposite pattern, however. They were significantly impaired—and indeed performed poorest—on problems presented at the shortest interval prior to surgery. These monkeys were not impaired on problems presented 8–16 weeks before surgery. Accordingly, these findings document the existence of temporally graded retrograde amnesia, and hence the presumption of a consolidation deficit, in animals with damage limited to medial temporal lobe structures.

Several studies using rats and rabbits have also demonstrated temporally graded retrograde amnesia following damage to the hippocampal region. In the study most similar to the work on monkeys, Wiig et al. (1996) trained rats on a series of five object discrimination problems at different times prior to transection of the fornix or ablation of the perirhinal cortex, or both lesions. Each problem was presented across five to seven daily training sessions, until the rat reached a performance criterion of 13 correct out of 16 successive trials. New problems were presented at 1-week intervals until all five problems were learned. On average, animals required 91 trials to learn the first object discrimination and 31–74 trials to learn the succeeding problems. In postoperative testing, 8 trials

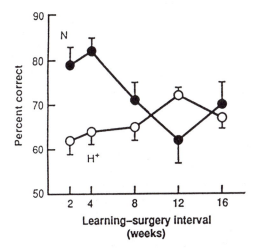

Figure 10.1. Performance of normal (N) monkeys and that of monkeys with removal of the hippocampus plus some surrounding cortex (H+) on retention of 100 object discrimination problems learned at different times prior to surgery. (Reproduced, with permission, from Zola-Morgan & Squire, 1990; Copyright American Association for the Advancement of Science.)

were presented each day for two of the problems until the animals reacquired the complete set of problems. Retention performance was assessed as the percentage of correct responses in the first 16 postoperative trials on each problem. As shown in Figure 10.2, rats with either fornix transections or perirhinal damage were clearly impaired on problems that had been learned 1–4 weeks prior to surgery; no deficit was observed on the problem learned 6 weeks prior to surgery. There was no deficit on the problem learned 8 weeks prior to surgery in the rats with fornix transections, but there was a deficit in animals with lesions of the perirhinal cortex, suggesting increased long-term forgetting or a modest reacquisition impairment after damage at that locus.

Another study on retrograde amnesia in rats involved the social transmission of food preferences described in chapter 7. In this study by Winocur (1990), pairs of rats were housed together for 2 days; then one of the rats was fed rat chow mixed with either cinnamon or cocoa. Subsequent training involved reexposure of the fed rat to its cagemate for a 30-min period. Then, either immediately, or after intervals varying between 2 and 10 days, rats were given lesions of the dorsal hippocampus, or a sham surgery, and were allowed to recover for 10 days. Thus the retention interval varied between 10 and 20 days. Memory for the social learning of the food odor was tested by measuring the consumption of cinnamon-versus cocoa-flavored chow in a preference test. Normal rats showed a striking preference for the trained odor that lasted at full strength for 15 days, with some subsequent forgetting on the 20-day test (Figure 10.3). Rats with hippocampal lesions were severely impaired when the interval between training and surgery was minimal, showing no significant preference for the odor trained closest to the time of surgery. They showed some retention when the surgery was delayed to 2 days after training and showed full recovery at longer training-to-surgery intervals. As in the experiment on monkeys described above, and as in human amnesia, the performance pattern after hippocampal damage was opposite to that seen in normal controls. Thus, whereas normal animals showed progressively poorer performance at progressively longer retention intervals, rats with hippocampal lesions performed better for learning that occurred at a more remote time. Winocur and Moscovitch (1999) have recently extended these findings, showing that, unlike hippocampal lesions, damage to the prefrontal cortex results in an extensive and flat gradient of retrograde amnesia.

Other evidence for temporally graded retrograde amnesia in rats comes from studies of contextual fear conditioning. In these studies, as in the one just described, animals were trained at different intervals prior to surgery. Then, all subjects were tested at a fixed interval postoperatively. Kim and Fanselow (1992) placed rats in a conditioning chamber and presented a series of 15 tone-shock pairings in a single session. Dorsal hippocampal lesions were performed at 1–28 days after this training. Testing for conditioned fear associated with the shock was conducted separately for the context (the training chamber) and for the tone. To test for contextual fear, rats were placed back in the training chamber and freezing was measured for several minutes. To test for conditioned fear to the tone, animals were placed in a different chamber and freezing during re-presentation of the tone was measured. As shown in Figure 10.4, normal rats exhibited substantial freezing across all retention intervals, indicating virtually no forgetting of the conditioned fear for both the context and the tone. By contrast, rats

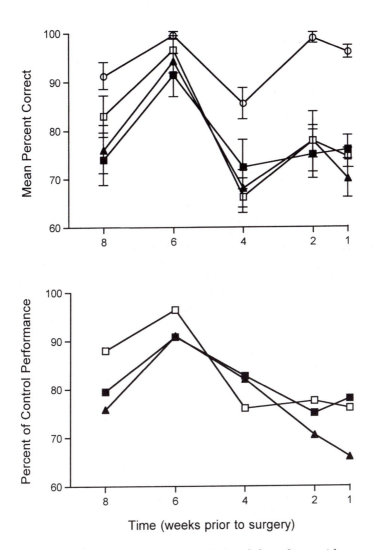

Figure 10.2. Performance of normal rats (circles) and that of rats with transection of the fornix (open squares), lesions of the perirhinal cortex (filled squares), or both surgeries (triangles) on retention of object discrimination problems learned at different times prior to surgery. The same data are plotted as (A) percent correct on each retention test, and (B) as a percent of average normal control subject performance. (Reproduced, with permission, from Wiig, Cooper, & Bear, 1996; Copyright Cold Spring Harbor Laboratory Press.)

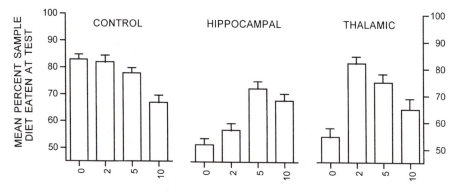

NUMBER OF DAYS BETWEEN ACQUISITION AND SURGERY

Figure 10.3. Performance of normal control rats and rats with lesions of the hippocampus or medial thalamus on retention of the social transmission of food preference trained at different times prior to the surgery. (Reproduced, with permission, from Winocur, 1990; Copyright Elsevier Science.)

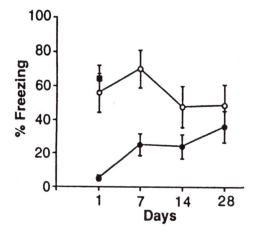

Figure 10.4. Performance of normal control rats (open circles) and rats with hippocampal lesions (closed circles) on retention of contextual fear conditioning trained at different times prior to the surgery. (Reproduced, with permission, from Kim & Fanselow, 1992; Copyright American Association for the Advancement of Science.)

with hippocampal lesions showed impairment in contextual fear conditioning in a temporally graded way: They were severely impaired when the interval between training and surgery was 1 day, showing virtually no freezing in the familiar chamber; they showed some retention when the surgery occurred a week after training; and they demonstrated full retention when the surgery occurred a month after training. In addition, the retrograde amnesia was material-specific in that rats with hippocampal damage showed fully normal retention of conditioned fear for the tone at all retention intervals (see also Young et al., 1994).

A temporally graded retrograde amnesia has also been observed in rabbits trained on hippocampus-dependent trace (classical) conditioning (Kim et al., 1995). Rabbits were trained using standard classical eyelid conditioning procedures for 100-trial-per-day sessions. On each trial, a 250-ms tone CS was followed by a 500-ms trace interval and then an air puff US. Daily training continued until the rabbit elicited eye blinks during the CS or trace interval on 8 out of 10 consecutive trials, requiring on average three to four training sessions. The rabbits then received hippocampal lesions, either 1 day or 1 month later. After a 7-day recovery period, all animals were tested for retention during retraining. As shown in Figure 10.5, normal rabbits showed complete savings of the conditioned eyeblink at both retention intervals. By contrast, rabbits given hippocampal lesions 1 day after training were severely impaired, exhibiting no retention of conditioning, and indeed were unable to acquire the task postoperatively. Nevertheless, when the surgery occurred 1 month after conditioning, rabbits were intact, showing as much savings as did control rabbits at both retention intervals.

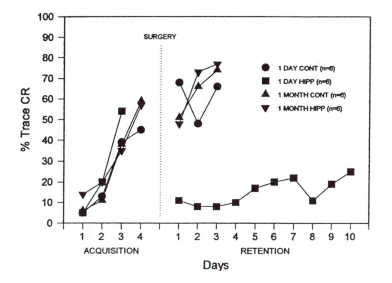

Figure 10.5. Performance of normal control rabbits (CONT) and rabbits with hippocampal lesions (HIPP) on preoperative acquisition and on postoperative retention of trace eyeblink conditioning performed at different times prior to the surgery. (Reproduced, with permission, from Kim, Clark, & Thompson, 1995; Copyright American Psychological Association.)

Temporally graded retrograde amnesia has also been observed in mice and rats on spatial discrimination problems. In one study, Cho et al. (1993) trained mice on a set of two-choice spatial discrimination problems using a radial maze. For each problem, the mouse was rewarded for selecting one of two adjacent maze arms, so that the same apparatus was used for multiple problems. Each problem was presented for 16 trials per day for 3–5 days, until the animals reached a performance criterion of 13 correct choices in a session. Training on successive problems was separated by 10 days. On the following day, animals were given ibotenic acid lesions of the entorhinal cortex, then allowed to recover for 10 days. Subsequent retention testing involved 16 trials on each problem presented concurrently on multiple problems. Control mice exhibited striking savings on problems presented 3 days prior to surgery, with significant forgetting at longer retention intervals (Figure 10.6). Mice with entorhinal lesions were severely impaired when the surgery had occurred 3 days after presentation of the problem, showing almost no retention at that interval, while some retention was observed when the surgery occurred 2 weeks after presentation of a problem, and normal retention was obtained for problems presented 4–8 weeks prior to surgery. Notably, as with other studies presented above, the patterns of performance

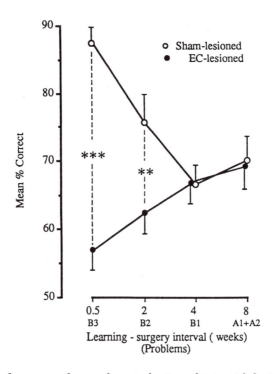

Figure 10.6. Performance of normal control rats and rats with lesions of the entorhinal cortex (EC) on maze problems learned at different times prior to the surgery. (Reproduced, with permission, from Cho, Beracochea, & Jaffard, 1993; Copyright Society for Neuroscience.)

across retention intervals were opposite for normal mice versus those with entorhinal lesions.

A similar study using rats, run subsequently (Cho & Kesner, 1996), replicated
the main findings with entorhinal lesions, showing a severe retention deficit
when the training-to-surgery interval was a few days, with better performance for
more remotely acquired spatial discriminations and indeed normal performance
for the longest interval (Figure 10.7). In addition, this study also examined the
performance of animals given lesions of the parietal cortex at varying intervals
after spatial discrimination training. In contrast to the pattern of findings on entorhinal lesions, rats with parietal lesions, though impaired, showed no sign of a
temporal gradient. These data are consistent with the notion that the hippocampal region, but not parietal cortex, plays a role in the consolidation process (see
also Cho et al., 1995).

Before leaving this section, however, it should be noted that not all findings
from animal models support the existence of temporally graded retrograde amnesia after hippocampal system damage. For example, Salmon et al. (1996) trained
monkeys on visual discriminations using a protocol that differed somewhat from
the one in the Zola-Morgan & Squire (1990) study, and they found a flat retrograde impairment that extended 32 weeks before the surgery. Also, Gaffan (1993)
found an extended (6.5-month) flat retrograde gradient for memory of visual discriminations in monkeys with fornix lesions, but the training protocol for recent

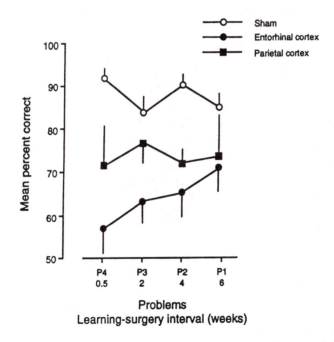

Figure 10.7. Performance of normal control rats (Sham) and rats with lesions of
the entorhinal cortex or parietal cortex on retention of maze problems learned at
different times prior to surgery. (Reproduced, with permission, from Cho &
Kesner, 1996; Copyright American Psychological Association.)

and remotely exposed materials was not fully equivalent (see Squire & Alvarez, 1995). In addition, Bolhuis et al. (1994) found a flat retrograde amnesia gradient for retention of water maze learning extending 14 weeks before the surgery. However, their control subjects showed only rather modest memory performance on this task at the longer retention intervals. Nadel and Moscovitch (1997) reviewed these findings and other mixed findings on the gradients of retrograde amnesia. Their analysis included several preliminary reports, whose data are also mixed. For example, Vnek, Gleason, Kromer, and Rothblat (1995) demonstrated a temporally graded amnesia for object discrimination in rats with hippocampal lesions, showing a deficit when training preceded surgery by 27 days and no deficit in retention at 56 days. By contrast several preliminary studies conducted by Sutherland and colleagues reported flat gradients on different tasks. These studies differ in the type of lesion and training, leaving open the critical parameters that determine the extent of the retrograde gradient in animals, as in humans. Notwithstanding the mixed results, the large number of successful demonstrations of temporally graded amnesia in animal models adds to the conclusions from studies of human amnesia. At least some components of the hippocampal system play a critical role in consolidation of memory during the time after learning at least some types of information.

Models of Cortical-Hippocampal Interactions in Memory Consolidation

There have been many theoretical proposals about the mechanisms of long-term consolidation. It is generally held that the final repository of long-term memories is neocortex, and that hippocampal processing somehow facilitates, organizes, or otherwise mediates the creation of permanent memory representations in specific neocortical sites. Studies by Winocur and Moscovitch (1999) and Cho and Kesner (1996), discussed above, contrasted the graded retrograde amnesic gradient following hippocampal region damage versus non-graded retrograde amnesia following neocortical damage. In addition, a recent study that measured metabolic activity in mice performing a previously learned spatial task, showed that shortly after learning hippocampal areas were engaged associated with retention performance, whereas long after learning cortical areas, and not hippocampal areas, were predominantly activated (Bontempi et al., 1999). Collectively, these findings provide strong confirmation of involvement of hippocampal structures for a time-limited period, and later permanent critical involvement of cortical areas. The question to be addressed here is: What is the nature of the interaction of the hippocampal system with neocortical processors that permits memory storage and consolidation to occur?

An early view was that the hippocampus is a component of an arousal system that signals the cerebral cortex to "chunk" information into semantic wholes that represent a binding of newly learned associations (Wickelgren, 1979). Other views have suggested that the hippocampus links distinct cortical memory representations, by storing an "index" or pointers of those cortical locations (Teyler & Discenna, 1986), or by maintaining coherence in activity within the connections between the cortical areas that maintain distinct representations (Squire, Cohen, & Nadel, 1984).

Marr (1971) postulated that the hippocampus rapidly develops a simplified representation of new information and acts as a temporary memory store during a prolonged consolidation period. He argued that the hippocampus serves as a temporary repository of memories about events that occurred during a period of approximately 1 day. Within that period, events could be recalled in the hippocampus by presenting partial events, and then evoking the full representation. Marr suggested that the cortical association areas use these hippocampal representations to build new associations among concepts. Briefly, Marr's model consisted of three populations of neurons, one representing the cortical input to the hippocampal formation, another representing entorhinal cortex, and one representing the hippocampus proper. The model contained a crude topographic organization of cortical fibers projecting to entorhinal cortex, and subsequent transformations in the entorhinal cortex allowed each unique cortical input pattern to be stored and to evoke a unique output pattern in the hippocampus. Intrahippocampal collaterals were included to support pattern completion, the ability of a portion of a previously stored input pattern to evoke the entire pattern in the hippocampus. Marr's model served mainly to show that an associative network could accomplish the required memory functions that might support pattern completion. But two aspects of his model are key features of later models: a rapidly developed, simplified representation of new events in the hippocampus, and a slowly evolving, more elaborated representation in the cortex.

Although he did not cite Marr's model, Halgren (1984) proposed a conceptual model of consolidation with similar characteristics (Figure 10.8). In his view, the medial temporal region stores a "gross" trace, one that does not contain all the items and relations of an experience but does contain many of the novel juxtapositions of familiar objects or thoughts that made the event unique. The hippocampal representation contributes to subsequent recall by interacting with the cortex over time to reconstruct the elements of the experience and to modify the overall semantic representation that will be remembered.

More recently, a number of computational models have appeared that implement various aspects of the above-mentioned ideas of Marr (1971), Teyler and Discenna (1986), and Squire, Cohen, and Nadel (1984) and extend them in interesting ways (McNaughton & Morris, 1987; Treves & Rolls, 1994; McClelland et al., 1995; Alvarez & Squire, 1994; Squire & Alvarez, 1995). Two recent views that will be considered here in detail focus on how the hippocampus could mediate a slow consolidation process.

Alvarez and Squire (1994) offered a simple network model that highlighted several basic distinctions in the operating characteristics of the cerebral cortex and the hippocampus. They argued that the cerebral cortex was capable of storing an immense amount of information, but that cortical representations change slowly and incrementally. By contrast, the hippocampus had a limited storage capacity but recorded information rapidly through changing of synaptic weights using rapid LTP mechanisms. Their focus was to show how these properties, instantiated within a simple neural network simulation, could demonstrate key properties of consolidation.

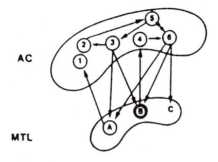

AC   INPUT

MTL

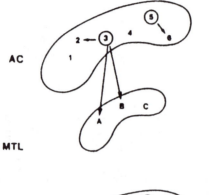

AC   CUE

MTL

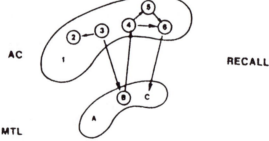

AC   RECALL

MTL

Figure 10.8. Halgren's (1984) model of cortical-hippocampal interactions in consolidation. (Reproduced, with permission, from Halgren, 1984; Copyright Guilford Press.)

The schematic diagram shown in Figure 10.9 illustrates this model. The simulation contained two distinct cortical areas and a medial temporal lobe region. Each neural unit in these areas was connected to every other unit in other areas, and the connection strengths could be modified by a use-dependent competitive learning rule. The rate of change in connections between the MTL and cortex was designed to be rapid, but short-lasting, whereas the changes in connections between the two cortical areas were slow, but long-lasting. When new informa-

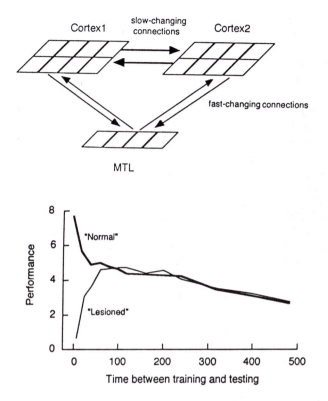

Figure 10.9. Alvarez and Squire's (1994) model of cortical-hippocampal interactions in consolidation. Top: Conceptualization of the model. Eight units in two cortical areas and four in the medial temporal lobe (MTL) have different rates of change in connectivity. Bottom: Performance of the intact model and the model with an MTL "lesion" on the capacity to excite units in one cortical area from the other in retention of associations acquired at different times prior to the "surgery." (Reproduced, with permission, from Alvarez & Squire, 1994; Copyright National Academy of Sciences, U.S.A.)

tion was presented to the network that set up activations in each of the cortical areas, the MTL connections changed substantially and rapidly to represent the conjointly active units in the cortical areas, although very little permanent change had occurred in the cortical representations or their connection between them. Subsequently, when the MTL area was randomly activated, to simulate a subsequent consolidation event, the originally activated cortical input areas were reactivated, incrementally enhancing their connections.

Memory performance of the model was assessed in terms of how well activation of one of the cortical representations could reinstate the associated representation in the other cortical area (Figure 10.9). The intact network showed strong performance in activating the associated representation shortly after learning and showed some forgetting over time. By contrast, if the MTL was removed shortly after learning, memory performance was very poor, and the longer the period the MTL was left intact after learning, the stronger was the consequent memory performances. Accordingly, the model seemed to simulate the essential characteristics of memory consolidation.

McClelland and colleagues (1995) developed a more elaborate and larger scale model, taking these ideas somewhat further. In their model, cortical representations involved systematic organizations of related items in parallel, multidimensional hierarchies (see Figure 10.10). They envisioned the operation of the cortex as identifying stimulus characteristics and sorting items into categories and subcategories within the large-scale organization. They noted that elaborate parallel distributed networks can readily be trained on such sorting operations for a large set of items. However, once a set of hierarchical organizations is established and stabilized, it is difficult to smoothly add new items. This is not because a network cannot be altered to include the new item by repetitive training, but because such novel training causes changes in an already-established network, resulting, in turn, in catastrophic interference among the already-existing items (see McCloskey & Cohen, 1989). New training alters a network to identify the new item, but such learning results in network modifications that interfere with the previously developed ability to correctly identify the old information (Figure 10.11).

McClelland et al.'s (1995) solution to the problem of catastrophic interference was to add a new, small network—a "hippocampus"—that could very rapidly acquire a representation of a new item and then have this small network slowly

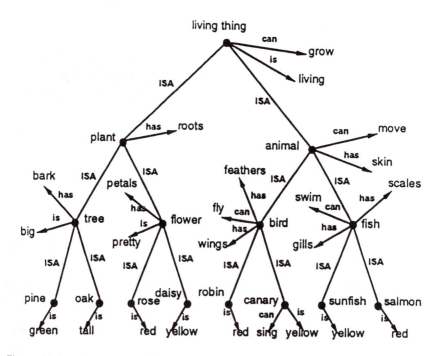

Figure 10.10. A semantic network used to train network models of the organization of propositional knowledge about living things. (Reproduced, with permission, from Rumelhart & Todd, 1993; Copyright MIT Press.)

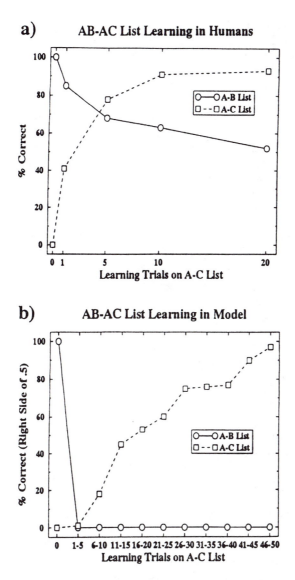

Figure 10.11. Performance of human subjects (a) and a computational model (b) on learning in the AB-AC list paradigm. In this paradigm subjects initially learn to associate arbitrarily selected pairings of words (A and B), then learn new associates for the first items (A and C). a: Human subjects show modest interference at the outset of learning the AC list, but recover quickly. (Reproduced, with permission, from McClelland, McNaughton, & O'Reilly, 1995; Copyright American Psychological Association.) b: The computer model suffers catastrophic interference on the AB list. (Reproduced, with permission, from McCloskey & Cohen, 1989; Copyright Academic Press.)

and gradually "train" the large network. As a result, as in the Alvarez and Squire (1994) simulation, the synaptic weights in the hippocampal network changed rapidly, and that network sent its representation repetitively to the large—"cortical"—network. The cortical network modifications were slow and incremental. Also, in addition to the occasional input from the hippocampus, the cortical model was repetitively exposed to the old materials it was built to represent, thereby resulting in an "interleaved learning" regimen that intermixed repetitions of old and new representations. Repetitions of old representations were seen as the kind of reinstatements or reactivations described in hippocampus by Wilson and McNaughton (1994) and Skaggs and McNaughton (1998), as discussed above (see also Nádasdy et al., 1999). This was key to the ability of the overall cortical network to be modified so as to incorporate new information without suffering from catastrophic interference (Figure 10.12).

Eventually, this process of interleaving produced an asymptotic state of the overall cortical representation, at which point it no longer benefited from hippocampal activations and thus no longer depended upon the hippocampus. In this fashion, the model exhibited the critical features of consolidation. The duration of consolidation required would be expected to be indeterminate, depending on the nature and extent of new information to be obtained, as well as on any other new learning that must be incorporated during the course of consolidation of already-stored information. Thus, consolidation should be conceived as a lifelong evolution of cortical networks, one that only asymptotically approaches a state where more interleaving does not alter the network substantially. In this way, we can come to understand at least some of the mixed results regarding the duration and nature of temporal gradients in retrograde amnesia.

The Nature of Hippocampal Representation and Consolidation

How might information processing by the hippocampus support the reorganization of cortical information during a prolonged consolidation period? A further consideration of the nature of hippocampal representations discussed in chapter 8, combined with our knowledge about cortical-hippocampal circuitry (chapter 9), offers potential insights about the cortical-hippocampal interplay proposed to underlie memory consolidation. In the model of the hippocampal "memory space" developed in chapter 8, the hippocampus was envisioned to represent learning episodes as a series of discrete events, each encoded within the activity of a single cell. Within the hippocampal memory space, some cells were characterized as encoding highly specific conjunctions of stimuli and actions that composed unique events that occurred in only one or a few learning episodes. Other cells were envisioned as encoding sequences of successive events, potentially linking multiple events as larger segments within particular episodes. Yet other cells were envisioned as encoding "nodal" events, features of experience that were common across different episodes; these might mediate our capacity to link an ongoing event to previous episodes that shared the nodal event.

In an extension of this model Eichenbaum et al. (1999) suggested that the sequence and nodal codings could subserve the linking and interleaving processes

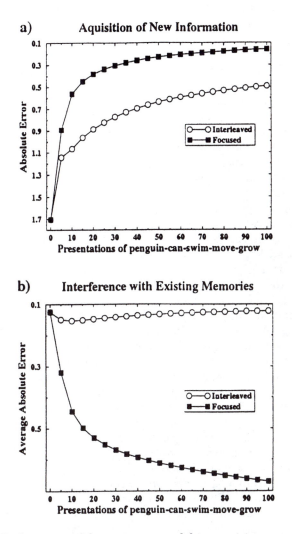

Figure 10.12. Performance of the computer model in acquiring new propositional information (a), and on the pre-existing information (b) about the knowledge structure outlined in Figure 10.10. Performance is compared between when the training on the new information was focused or interleaved with repetitions of the old information. (Reproduced, with permission, from McClelland, McNaughton, & O'Reilly, 1995; Copyright American Psychological Association.)

of consolidation proposed by Alvarez and Squire (1994) and McClelland et al. (1995). According to this scheme, representations of discrete events and sequences of events within the hippocampus are conceived to occur within one or a few learning trials. Furthermore, "nodal" representations are conceived as developing in parallel with the variations in experience that occur across related learning episodes. Because of the very high level of interconnectivity of hippocampal pyramidal cells relative to that in all the cortical areas, the initial development of these sequence and nodal representations is envisioned as primarily within the hippocampus shortly after learning. Subsequent cortical memory consolidation involves the creation of the sequence and nodal properties within cortical cells, mediated through connections with the hippocampus, in two sequential stages.

Within this framework, the first stage of consolidation involves interactions between the hippocampus and the parahippocampal region. Parahippocampal neurons receive direct inputs from many cortical areas, and so they would be expected to encode the configurations of stimuli to compose event representations based on simultaneity of these inputs alone. However, for some period immediately after learning, associations between the complex event representations within the parahippocampal region may depend upon the connections to and from the hippocampal cells that have encoded particular sequences or nodal events. At the same time, the feedback from the hippocampus to the parahippocampal cortex is envisioned to mediate the development of sequence and nodal representations within the parahippocampal region. This may occur by the hippocampus providing an indirect pathway that drives the coactivation of parahippocampal neurons, enhancing the connections within their intracortical network and producing sequence and nodal cell properties in parahippocampal neurons. Because parahippocampal neurons have an unusual capacity for prolonged firings following discrete events (Young et al., 1997; Suzuki et al., 1997), cells in this region may rapidly support the coding of event sequences through the interactions with the hippocampus. When sequence and nodal properties have been acquired by parahippocampal cells, the memory can be considered to have consolidated there, in the sense that the memory abilities conferred by these cells would no longer require hippocampal feedback.

The second stage of consolidation involves a similar interplay between the cortical association areas and the parahippocampal region. Initially cortical associations are viewed to depend on the parahippocampal region to supply linkages between their representations. In addition, by simultaneously driving cells in cortical areas and activating their intracortical connections, these linkages would be expected to mediate the ultimate development of context and nodal properties in the cortical association areas. When this is accomplished the entire hippocampal circuit would no longer be necessary for the existence of event, sequence, and nodal representations. Consistent with the proposal that consolidation occurs in stages involving first a consolidation within the parahippocampal region and then later in the cortex, human amnesics with damage extending into the parahippocampal region have a more extended retrograde amnesia than those with selective hippocampal damage (Rempel-Clower et al., 1996).

The key aspects of this model involve the unusual associational structure of hippocampal anatomy that makes it the earliest site for arbitrary associations that underlie event, sequence, and nodal properties. At the earliest stages of parahippocampal or neocortical processing, the range of associations and the speed of their formation may be much more limited. But they can mediate substantial development and reorganization of a memory space through the connections within the hippocampus initially. In this way the repeated invocation of hippocampal representations onto the cortex serves to reorganize cortical representations accommodating new information and new associations within the overall knowledge structure encoded there.

Exactly when these critical interactions between the cortex and the hippocampus occur is unknown. They could occur during repetitions of the learning experience, or during rehearsal after learning. It has also been suggested that these interactions may occur "off-line," for example, during sleep. There are now a few observations providing evidence of recurrent off-line firing patterns in hippocampal neurons. Pavlides and Winson (1989) first observed that hippocampal place cells that had been active during exploration fire at an elevated rate during subsequent slow-wave sleep. Building on this observation, Wilson and McNaughton (1994) and Skaggs and McNaughton (1996) showed that place cells that had shown overlapping location-specific activity during exploration showed elevated coactivity during subsequent sleep, and that the sequential ordering of firing in coactive cell pairs tended to replicate the preferential firing order observed during the previous exploration. Buzsaki and colleagues (1992; Buzsaki & Chrobak, 1995) have suggested that coactivities encoded during wakefulness might be consolidated by brief bouts of synchronized firing that are characteristic of slow-wave sleep. Nádasdy et al. (1999) found that indeed temporal patterns of hippocampal spike activity that occur when rats engage in wheel-running are repeated in "compressed" bouts of hippocampal activity during subsequent sleep. It is too soon to tell whether these particular phenomena provide the mechanism for long-term consolidation, but they are plausible candidates and provide some confidence to search for others.

Regardless of when it occurs, this integrative processing, involving the interleaving of new representations among the existing structure, can be seen to benefit the cortical memory organization for a very prolonged period (McClelland et al., 1995). Indeed, contrary to recent suggestions (Nadel & Moscovitch, 1997), memory reorganization is seen as a process that continues throughout life. From this view, the "completion" of consolidation is seen as a state at which integration of a new memory is asymptotic, that is, a state in which yet new experiences do not alter the relevant parts of the overall memory organization. When this state is achieved, removal of the hippocampus would not be expected to affect the operation of the cortical network. For some types of memory this might be achieved rather readily, within days or weeks (Winocur, 1990; Kim & Fanselow, 1992; Zola-Morgan & Squire, 1990). Other memory experiences might benefit by integration with earlier-formed memories over months or years (Corkin, 1984). Thus the duration of consolidation is viewed as dependent on the nature of the learned material in terms of how many appropriate linkages across experience will benefit subsequent retrieval. To the extent that these are few and repeated frequently, consolidation will be completed readily. To the extent that memory for unique episodes benefits by linkage with many related episodes and facts or continues to be reshaped by new experience, consolidation could go on for a lifetime.

PART III

SPECIALIZED MEMORY SYSTEMS
OF THE BRAIN

The hippocampal memory system mediates so much of what we call "everyday" memory, and the impairment in amnesia so profoundly impairs memory for the details of daily life, that having arrived at this point in the book one must wonder what is left to discuss. What other kinds of memory are there? Moreover, whatever they are, what relative importance could they have? Are memories that are *not* accessible to conscious recollection, or that are *not* about facts and events, of any practical importance? The answer is an unequivocal yes!

To conceive of how important nonconscious memories are to us, consider having to bring to consciousness every learned behavior you wish to perform or to consciously recollect all the facts and events you've learned whenever you wish to do something. Imagine having to consciously recollect how to walk, talk, read, and write in order to be able to perform any of those acts. Consider having to consciously recollect your history with every person you have met in order to identify her or him as friend or foe, teacher or student, mother or child. From this perspective, it is clear that we rely heavily in our lives upon other kinds of memory—the habits, dispositions, and skills that, as we shall see, shape and guide our interactions with the world. Now we will survey the other memory systems of the brain and characterize some of their learning and performance capacities.

In chapter 11, further motivation is offered for considering multiple memory systems by outlining some of the critical experiments that have demonstrated most directly the existence of multiple memory systems and that have provided clues about how to characterize their functional roles. These experiments are based on double and, in some cases, triple dissociations, in which different performances are selectively disrupted by distinct brain lesions. Ex-

369

amples will come both from work on animal models of amnesia and from the clinical literature on human amnesia. Subsequent chapters will review the anatomical pathways and functional components of some of the best studied of the other (i.e., nonhippocampal) memory systems. Chapter 12 reviews the evidence for a distinct system for mediating emotional memory. It turns out that there are multiple emotional memory systems that involve overlapping elements but distinct functional pathways. Chapter 13 presents evidence for distinct memory systems that mediate the acquisition of habits and skills, examples of procedural memories. There are multiple habit/skill (procedural) systems in the brain, as it turns out, and they can operate in parallel or interactively. Finally, in chapter 14, we review the evidence for a distinct set of cortical structures that mediate working memory. The prefrontal cortex plays a particularly prominent role in this system but operates within a network of cortical structures.

11

Dissociating Multiple Memory Systems in the Brain

Many studies have been presented in this book showing a dissociation between types of memory performance after hippocampal damage, with some memory performances being impaired and others spared. Such demonstrations have proven critical in proposals that there are multiple memory systems in the brain and in permitting characterization of the nature of the hippocampal system's role in memory. For example, damage to the hippocampal region in several species results in a selective impairment in delayed retention in nonmatch-to-sample and in other recognition tasks. By contrast, damage to various other brain regions, including even the amygdala, does *not* result in an impairment in performance on this task. The conclusion to be drawn is that the hippocampal region is critical to a certain type of memory necessary for DNMS performance, and that the amygdala is not. Even more powerful has been the opposite sort of finding, namely, that hippocampal damage does *not* impair performance on certain other memory tasks. The finding that acquisition and expression of skilled performance is preserved in H.M. and other patients with hippocampal system damage led directly to the proliferation of various multiple-memory-system theories of memory. The conclusion was that the type of memory necessary for skill learning and repetition priming is *not* the type of memory mediated by the hippocampal system; instead, the type of memory that supports skill learning and priming must be mediated by other systems in the brain.

Note that the above are examples of "single dissociation" logic: Damage to one brain structure, but not other structures, results in impairment on certain memory tasks but not other memory tasks. In the neuropsychological literature, it has long been held that the strongest evidence for the existence of independent systems is derived from "double dissociation," in which damage to Brain Structure A, but not Structure B, results in impairment on Task X, but not Task Y, while damage

371

to Brain Structure B and not Structure A results in impairment on Task Y and not Task X. This is a more stringent criterion to meet, but it is important because there are alternative accounts of any given single dissociation based on issues of task difficulty or lesion size (e.g., the task impaired after a given lesion is just more difficult than the tasks not impaired after that lesion, or the lesion that fails to produce impairment in a given task turns out to be too small to produce impairment on any task). To illustrate, let's return to the example of DNMS performance following damage to hippocampus versus amygdala. It would be more powerful to be able to demonstrate that the particular amygdala damage that is ineffective in affecting performance on the DNMS task is nonetheless effective in disrupting some other type of performance by the same animals. Zola-Morgan et al. (1989b) have provided just such a result. They showed that hippocampal region damage, but not amygdala damage, resulted in impairment on DNMS, whereas amygdala damage, but not hippocampal region damage, resulted in impairment on emotional responses to threatening objects in the same monkeys. This pattern of findings demonstrates that each brain area is critical to some type of behavior. The same strategy of double dissociation has now been applied successfully in dissociating functions of different brain areas in different types of memory performance. We turn now to some of the more telling double (and triple) dissociations and consider their implications for understanding the brain's various memory systems.

An Anatomical Framework for Parallel Memory Systems in the Brain

The studies to be described in the remainder of this chapter are examples of research from several laboratories guided by the view that distinct types of memory processing are mediated by distinct functional systems of the brain. A general, anatomically based framework for some of the major memory systems has emerged from this research. A preliminary outline will be presented here to provide a framework for discussing the hypotheses and results of the dissociation experiments that follow. In subsequent chapters, we will provide greater detail on the anatomical circuits of each pathway.

A sketch of some of the most prominent memory pathways currently under investigation was provided in Figure 2.6 (for a similar outline see Suzuki, 1997). In this scheme, the origin of each of the memory systems is the vast expanse of the cerebral cortex, focusing in particular on the highest stages of the several distinct sensory and motor processing hierarchies, the cortical association areas. As discussed in chapter 4, each of these areas is responsible for both processing and memory of particular, functionally defined domains of information. Some examples of the distinct role played by parts of the cerebral cortex will appear in a few of the dissociation experiments described below. In addition, the specific role of the prefrontal cortex in working memory is reserved for discussion in chapter 14.

The cerebral cortex, then, provides major inputs to each of three main pathways of processing related to distinct memory functions. One pathway, already discussed in detail in preceding chapters, is to the hippocampus via the parahippocampal region. As we have seen, this pathway supports the relational organization of cortical representations and representational flexibility in declarative memory expression. Accordingly, the main output of hippocampal and parahippocampal processing is back to the cortical areas, the sites of storage and consolidation of long-term declarative memories. The other two main pathways highlighted here involve cortical inputs to specific subcortical targets as critical nodal points in processing leading to direct output effectors.

One of these systems involves the amygdala as a nodal stage in the association of exteroceptive sensory inputs to emotional outputs effected via the hypothalamic-pituitary axis and autonomic nervous system, as well as emotional influences over widespread brain areas. The putative involvement of this pathway in such processing functions has led many to consider this system specialized for "emotional memory." We consider this hypothesis here and, in considerably more detail, in chapter 12.

The other system involves the neostriatum as a nodal stage in the association of sensory and motor cortical information with voluntary response via the brain stem motor system. The putative involvement of this pathway in associating cortical representations to specific behavioral responses has led many to consider this system specialized for "habit memory" or skill memory, an example of procedural memory. This hypothesis is considered below and, in considerably more detail, in chapter 13.

The outline of these systems is not intended as a comprehensive listing of memory systems. Other pathways supporting different aspects of memory are considered in subsequent chapters of this book. However, the systems noted above are the focus of the experiments described in this chapter. And they provide some of the most striking examples of the success of the double-dissociation approach in demonstrating and defining distinct memory systems.

We turn now, finally, to some of the critical multiple-dissociation experiments. The first two studies involve "triple dissociations" of memory functions in rats. Each of these studies found three different patterns of sparing and impairment of memory following damage to three different brain structures. However, the two studies involve somewhat different brain areas and, correspondingly, somewhat different types of memory. Following these, we will summarize three studies that involve double dissociations of memory functions in humans with specific types of brain damage. Taken together, the findings suggest a similar set of memory functions supported by homologous brain areas in animals and humans.

Distinct Memory Functions and Brain Areas Supporting Radial Maze Performance

One of the most striking dissociations among memory functions supported by separate brain structures comes from a study by McDonald and White (1993). This study involved multiple experiments in which separate groups of rats were trained on three different versions of the spatial radial maze task. Each version of the task used the same maze, the same general spatial cues and approach responses, and the same food rewards. But the stimulus and reward contingencies of each task differed, each focusing on a different kind of memory-processing demand. For each task, performance was compared across three separate groups of rats operated to disrupt the hippocampal system, the amygdala, or the neostriatum. In addition, different methods of brain damage were compared. Hippocampal system disruption was accomplished by a fornix transection or by neurotoxic lesion of the hippocampus. Damage to the amygdala and the neostriatum was accomplished by electrolytic or neurotoxic lesions of the lateral nucleus of the amygdala or dorsal part of the neostriatum, where cortical sensory inputs arrive in these structures.

One test was the conventional spatial-working-memory version of the radial maze task (Figure 11.1A). In this version of the task, an eight-arm maze was placed in the midst of a variety of extramaze stimuli in the testing room, providing animals with the opportunity to encode the spatial relations among these stimuli as spatial cues. On every daily trial, a food reward was placed at the end of each of the eight maze arms, and the animal was released from the center and was allowed to retrieve the rewards. Optimal performance would entail entering each arm only once, and subsequently avoiding already-visited arms in favor of the remaining unvisited arms. The central memory demand of this task was characterized as a "win-shift" rule; such a rule emphasizes memory for each particular daily episode with specific maze arms. Also, the task requires "flexible" use of memory by using the approach into previously rewarded locations to guide the selection of other new arms to visit (see chapter 7). Accordingly, it was expected that performance on this task would require the hippocampal system.

Normal animals learned the task readily, improving from nearly chance performance (four errors out of their first eight arm choices) on the initial training trial to an average of fewer than half an error by the end of training (Figure 11.2A). Consistent with expectations, damage to the hippocampal system resulted in an impairment on this version of the radial maze task. Compared to normal animals, rats with fornix transections made more errors by entering previously visited maze arms. Even after extended training, fornix-damaged rats continued to make substantially more errors than controls. By contrast, lateral amygdala and dorsal neostriatum lesions had no effect on task performance. Indeed, the group of animals with lateral amygdala lesions performed at least as well as did controls.

The second test involved a variant of the same radial maze task Figure 11.1B). In this version, the maze was again surrounded by a curtain, and lamps were used to cue particular maze arms. On the first trial of each daily training session, four arbitrarily selected arms were illuminated and baited with food, whereas the other four arms were dark and had no food. After the first time a lit arm was entered, that arm was rebaited, so that the animal could return to the arm for a second reward. Subsequently the lamp in that particular arm was turned off, and no more food was provided at that arm. Thus, here the task was characterized by a "win-stay" rule in which animals could approach any lit arm at any time and could even reexecute the approach to a particular arm for reward one time in each daily trial. This version of the task minimized the availability of spatial cues and indeed associated rewards with different sets of locations across days. Also, it did not require flexible expression of memory or response flexibility under conditions substantially different than original learning. Thus, performance was not expected to rely upon the hippocampal system. Instead, this task would seem

Trial N   **N+1**   **N+2...**

A. win-shift

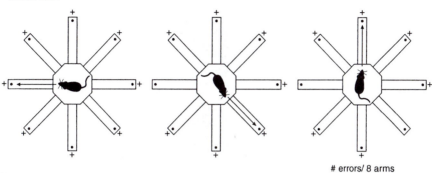

errors/ 8 arms

B. Win-stay

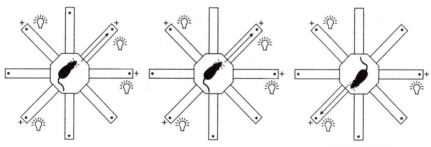

time in each arm

C. conditioned place preference

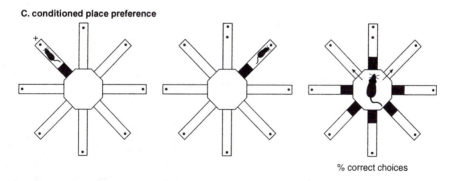

% correct choices

Figure 11.1. Illustrations of example trials in different variants of the radial arm maze task. For each, the measure of performance is indicated below the N+2 trial. + = rewarded arm.

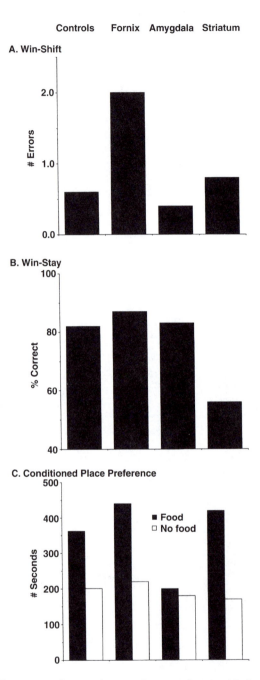

Figure 11.2. Performance of normal control rats and rats with lesions in the indicated structure on each of the radial arm maze tasks illustrated in Figure 11.1. (Reproduced, with permission, from McDonald & White, 1993; Copyright American Psychological Association.)

to require memory processes associated with learning consistent stimulus-response contingencies, or simple response habits, which, for reasons to be made clearer below, were expected to rely on the neostriatal system.

Results showed that normal control subjects learned the appropriate behavioral responses to the lit arms gradually over several training sessions. In the first few sessions they selected lit arms on only 50% of the trials (Figure 11.2B), but by the end of 24 sessions, they performed at about 80% correct. Consistent with expectations, animals with dorsal neostriatal damage were impaired, barely exceeding chance performance even with extended training. By contrast, animals with fornix transections succeeded in learning and even outperformed the control subjects in learning rate. Animals with lateral amygdala lesions were unimpaired, learning the task at a normal rate.

The third test involved yet another variant of the radial maze task in which animals were separately conditioned to be attracted to one maze arm and habituated to another arm (Figure 11.1C). In this version, the maze was surrounded by a curtain to diminish the salience of spatial cues. Six of the maze arms were blocked off to make them inaccessible, and one of the remaining two arms was illuminated by proximal lamps, whereas the other was only dimly illuminated. After a preliminary session in which rats could explore both available arms, conditioning proceeded with daily exposures to one of the two arms. For each rat, either the lit or the dark arm was associated with food by confining the animal in that arm for 30 min with a large amount of food on four separate trials. On another four trials, the same animal was confined for the same period of time to the other arm, but with no food. Thus, in half of the rats, the lit arm was associated with food availability and the dark arm was not; for the other half of the rats the opposite association was conditioned. In a final test session, no food was placed on the maze, and access to both the lit and the dark arm was allowed. The amount of time spent in each arm in a 20-min session was recorded to measure the preference for each of the two arms. This version of the radial maze task emphasized the strong and separate associations between food reward or absence of reward with a particular maze arm defined by a salient nonspatial cue. This task minimized the availability of spatial relations among stimuli. Also, because the same lit and dark arms used during training were re-presented in testing, the task did not require flexible expression of memory under conditions substantially different than original conditioning. Thus it was not expected that the hippocampal system would be critical to learning. Instead, learning would seem to depend on memory processes associated with emotional conditioning, which, for reasons that will become apparent below, was expected to depend upon the amygdala.

Normal animals showed a strong preference for the arm associated with food, typically spending 50–100% more time in the maze arm in which they had been fed than in the arm where no food had previously been provided (Figure 11.2C). Consistent with expectations, rats with lateral amygdala damage showed no conditioned preference for the cue arm associated with food. By contrast, rats with fornix transections or dorsal neostriatal lesions showed robust conditioned cue preferences; despite their lesions, they performed at least as well as intact animals.

In a follow-up study, the effects of selective neurotoxic lesions of the same three brain structures were examined, to exclude the possibility that the behavioral deficits in any of the tasks were due to damage of fibers that passed through those brain structures. The results of this study confirmed all of the findings described above, showing that selective ablation of the hippocampus disturbs win-shift spatial learning, that selective ablation of the dorsal neostriatum disturbs win-stay habit learning, and that selective ablation of the lateral amygdala disturbs conditioned preference or emotional conditioning.

Multiple Parallel Memory Systems

The same critical stimuli, rewards, and approach responses were part of all tasks, yet different patterns of sparing and loss of memory function were obtained on each task depending on the locus of brain damage. Thus none of the specific deficits following any of the lesions could be attributed to a general impairment in sensory, motor, or motivational functions. The choice of tests was critical to demonstrating the dissociations seen in this study. Many tasks, and especially real-world tasks, are likely solved by multiple alternative processing strategies that rely upon distinct memory systems, either separately or jointly. If any of the three tasks used here could have been solved by more than one of the three pathways under study, even if solved in different ways, then no deficit would have been observed on that task after any single site of brain damage. These observations provide strong evidence that each of the studied brain structures is a key nodal point in the processing system for a different form of memory.

Many other tasks do not permit such clear dissociations. A good example would be a simple spatial discrimination (e.g., learning to choose the left arm in a T maze). This problem could be solved in at least three different ways that would be expected to rely on one or another of the systems discussed here. The problem could be solved by representing the spatial relations among room cues and learning to go to a particular place where the reward was given. Such a relational memory-dependent strategy would likely be mediated by the hippocampal system. Alternatively, the task could be solved by learning to make a left body turn at the choice point, a strategy involving simple S-R or habit learning, likely to be mediated by the neostriatal system. Finally, the task could be solved by acquiring an attraction to or bias toward the goal arm that is consistently associated with food reward, a strategy that could be supported by emotional conditioning, likely to be mediated by the amygdala. These different systems, operating in parallel, would provide for multiple ways of handling the task, making it unlikely that damage to any particular one of the systems described could prevent learning. This is much more the typical case, making the triple dissociation discussed above all the more impressive and illuminating.

Even in situations where multiple routes for learning are available through the availability of multiple memory systems operating in parallel, it may be possible to discern the separate roles of these parallel systems through differences in the rate of acquisition of learned performance. Consider a study by Kemble and Beckman (1970), in which rats were trained to approach a goal box at the end of a runway. The initial learning of the approach response was impaired in rats with amygdala damage, but these animals subsequently improved to the same extent as normal rats. An explanation of this pattern of findings is that the amygdala system supported rapid acquisition of an attraction to the goal box, leading to the initial increase in running speed only in intact animals. The neostriatal system also supports increases in running speed associated with learning the approach response to the goal box, but this type of learning may involve a more gradual acquisition rate. Thus the eventual success of animals with amygdala damage can be interpreted as being due to the neostriatal system's eventually supporting learned performance.

In another study discussed much earlier in this book (chapter 2), Packard and McGaugh (1996) showed that initial successful performance in simple T-maze learning involves acquisition of a "place" strategy mediated by a hippocampal representation. With additional training, a "response" strategy dominates, and this strategy is mediated by the neostriatum. Most important to the present point, when the neostriatum was inactivated after substantial training, animals did not choose randomly. Rather, they reverted to the place strategy that had guided performance early in training. Thus, by the end of training, both the hippocampal and the neostriatal systems contained representations that could mediate choice performance. But the two systems differed in the rapidity of acquisition of their representations and in the dominance of one representation (the neostriatal one) when both representations are available.

Additional evidence of the operation of multiple parallel memory systems comes from the finding of enhanced learning rate in one of McDonald and White's experiments, in which animals with fornix lesions learned the win-stay problem more quickly than normal rats. This superficial facilitation of learning after hippocampal damage has been observed in several studies that involved simple stimulus-response or stimulus-reward contingencies (e.g., Eichenbaum et al., 1986a, 1989; Stevens & Cowey, 1972; Tonkiss et al., 1990; Walker et al., 1970). Such an enhancement of learning after hippocampal damage suggests that normally processing within the hippocampal system interferes with learning that can be accomplished by another system, so that removing the interference speeds learning mediated by the other system. In the case of the win-shift task, the hippocampus may be representing where rewards have been received or may be processing the sequence of recent trials with different lit arms and outcomes. Such processing is not required for mediation by the neostriatal system and may indeed slow its operation. Combined with the other findings described above, these observations support the notion that the distinct memory systems considered thus far operate in parallel.

Another Triple Dissociation of Memory Systems

Returning now to the insights about multiple memory systems provided by multiple dissociation findings, Kesner and colleagues (1993) provided another demonstration of a triple dissociation among memory systems in rats. This study used some of the same basic tasks and investigated some of the same brain areas as above. In this study, learning and memory performance were examined on three tasks in animals with experimental damage to the hippocampal system, the neostriatum, or the higher order visual cortex. The hippocampal system damage was made with electrolytic lesions of the entire hippocampus. The neostriatum was damaged with electrolytic lesions of the caudate nucleus. The visual cortex lesion was made by aspirating the extrastriate visual area. For each of the three tasks, the animals were trained, then operated, and then retrained and tested with different memory retention intervals. Each task involved presentation of a sample item that had to be remembered for short or longer delay periods, then a recognition test that required comparison of the sample item with another similar item.

In the first task, rats were trained on a variant of the spatial-working-memory task using a radial maze surrounded by a rich environment of room stimuli (Figure 11.3A). In the sample phase of this task, access to one of eight maze arms

Sample   **Choice**

A. spatial location

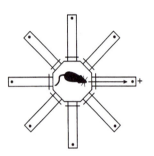   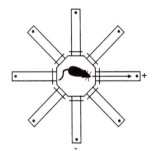

A. response

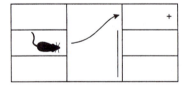   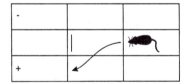

A. response

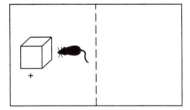   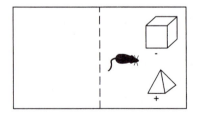

Figure 11.3. Illustrations of example trials in different tasks used to dissociate different forms of memory. (Reproduced, with permission, from Kesner, Bolland, & Dakis, 1993; Copyright Springer-Verlag.)

was allowed, and the animal obtained food by running to the end of the maze arm. Then, after a delay period in which the rat was contained in the center of the maze, a choice was offered between the sample arm and another arbitrarily selected arm on the right or left of the sample. The correct choice was to reenter the sample arm. Following the (sham) surgery, normal animals relearned the task readily (Figure 11.4A), with the standard delay-dependent decrement in performance as the memory delay was increased (Figure 11.5, top). Animals with neostriatal or visual cortex damage also readily reacquired the task and showed a similar pattern of memory decline in the delay phase. By contrast, rats with hippocampal damage were severely impaired in relearning and performed at near-chance levels at all delays.

In the second task, rats were trained on a novel response memory test. The apparatus involved a maze composed of six response arms arranged as illustrated in Figure 11.3B. At the outset of each trial, closed doors at the end of each arm prevented movements within the maze, and the animal would begin the sample phase of each trial contained within the middle arm on either end of the maze. Then the door to that arm would be opened, together with the door allowing access to either the left or the right arm on the opposite side of the maze. Thus the animal could obtain an initial reward by exiting the start arm and entering a goal arm on either its left or its right. Then the rat was placed in the middle arm opposite where it had started the sample phase. After a proscribed delay, the door to that arm, plus doors of both the left and the right arms on the opposite side, would be opened, and a reward was located in the goal arm corresponding to the same left or right turn performed on the sample phase. Thus, to obtain the second reward, the rat had to make the same left or right body turn even though it was not approaching the same place as previously rewarded. Normal rats reacquired this task rapidly (Figure 11.4B), with the standard delay-dependent decline in performance with increasing delay (Figure 11.5 middle). Animals with hippocampal or extrastriate visual cortex lesions also performed well both in reacquisition and delayed retention. However, animals with neostriatal damage were severely impaired in reacquisition of the task and performed poorly at all delays. Notably, some of the same animals were subsequently shown to perform well on a simple left-right discrimination, so the deficit in response recognition seen in rats with neostriatal damage cannot be attributed to an inability to discriminate body turns.

In the third task, rats were trained on a visual object recognition memory task using a DNMS procedure (Figure 11.3C). In the sample phase of each trial, rats were allowed to approach and displace an object and retrieve a reward hidden underneath. Subsequently, a partition in the apparatus was removed, allowing the rat access to two objects, one identical to the sample plus a novel object. The rats could obtain a second reward by displacing the novel object. Normal animals reacquired this task rapidly (Figure 11.4C) and showed the standard delay-dependent phenomena (Figure 11.5, bottom). Animals with hippocampal or neostriatal damage also performed well on this task. But rats with damage to extrastriate visual cortex were impaired in reacquisition of the task and performed poorly at all delays. Notably, all the rats with extrastriate visual cortex lesions subsequently performed well on a simple visual object discrimination task, so the deficit in DNMS cannot be attributed to a visual perceptual impairment.

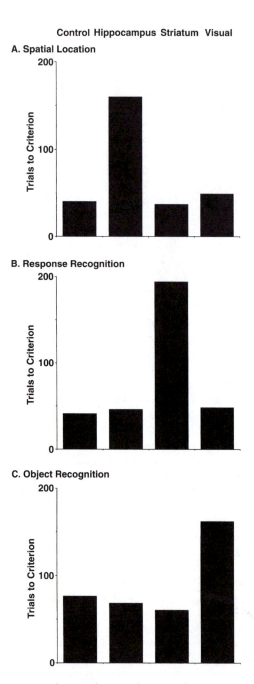

Figure 11.4. Performance of normal control rats and rats with lesions in the indicated structures in acquiring each of the tasks illustrated in Figure 11.3.

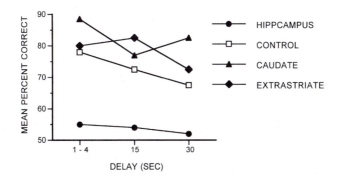

SPATIAL LOCATION RECOGNITION MEMORY

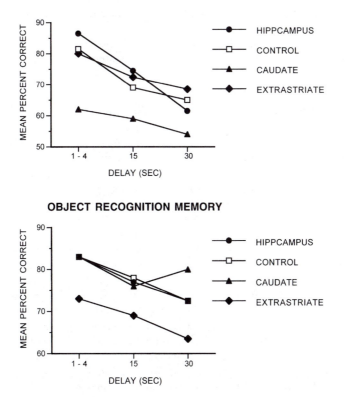

RESPONSE RECOGNITION MEMORY

OBJECT RECOGNITION MEMORY

Figure 11.5. Performance of normal control subjects and rats with lesions to the indicated structures across different memory delays. (Data taken from Kesner, Bolland, & Dakis, 1993; Copyright Springer-Verlag.)

Even though the testing apparatus differed across the three tasks, they were all two-choice recognition memory tasks and all required subjects to generate differential choices to obtain food rewards. Thus, the selective effects of the different brain lesions on specific tasks could not be attributed to any general deficit in perception, motor capacities, or motivation. Instead, Kesner and colleagues interpreted these findings as supporting the view that distinct brain systems mediate parallel memory processing functions dedicated to different informational attributes. They argued that the hippocampal system mediated recognition or working memory for spatial attributes that characterize arms in the radial maze; the neostriatum mediated recognition or working memory for behavioral response attributes that characterized the response memory test; and extrastriate visual cortex mediated recognition or working memory for visual perceptual attributes that characterized the object memory test. These findings confirm and extend the notion that there are parallel memory systems that mediate different forms of memory representation. Interestingly, this occurs even though there is apparently much in common in the operating properties of the different systems, particularly the properties that support short term recognition or working memory. But those operating mechanisms are applied distinctly to different kinds of information handled by the functionally distinct systems.

Double Dissociation of Memory Systems in Humans

A number of studies on human patients have also demonstrated double dissociations that serve (a) to extend the initial dissociation in amnesia between impaired explicit remembering of facts and events and intact acquisition and expression of skilled performance, and (b) to reveal significant similarities in the memory dissociation across species. Here we summarize the findings of three recent studies that have compared different patient populations on a variety of learning and memory paradigms. Despite some potentially important differences across studies in the etiologies of the disorders represented in these patients, there are strong similarities across studies in the overall pattern of findings. In each study, the learning and memory capacities of amnesic patients with damage to the medial temporal lobe was compared with those of "nonamnesic" patients, that is, humans with brain pathologies not producing the classic amnesic syndrome discussed in chapter 5. Also, in each study, the performance of these patient groups was compared on standard tests of declarative memory for the learning materials used in each of the tests. Taken together, these several double dissociations in human patients with various memory disorders provides especially compelling evidence for the existence of multiple parallel memory systems in the brain.

Declarative Memory and Emotional Memory

Bechara and colleagues (1995) studied three patients with selective damage to the hippocampus or amygdala. One patient suffered from Urbach-Wiethe disease, a disorder resulting in selective bilateral calcification of the tissue of the amygdala, sparing the adjacent hippocampus. Another patient experienced multiple cardiac arrests and associated transient hypoxia and ischemia that resulted in selective bilateral hippocampal atrophy, sparing the neighboring amygdala. The third patient suffered herpes simplex encephalitis resulting in bilateral damage to both the amygdala and the hippocampus.

This study focused on a form of autonomic conditioning involving an association between a neutral stimulus and a loud sound. The conditioning stimulus (CS+) was either a monochrome color slide or a pure tone. Subjects were initially habituated to the CS+ as well as to several like stimuli (different colors or tones) that would be presented as CS− stimuli. Subsequently, during conditioning, the CSs were presented in random order for 2 s each. Each presentation of the CS+ was terminated with the unconditioned stimulus (US), a loud boat horn that was sounded briefly. Autonomic responses to these stimuli were measured as skin conductance changes through electrodermal recordings.

Normal control subjects showed skin conductance changes to the US and robust conditioning to the CS+, with smaller responses to the CS− stimuli (Figures 11.6 and 11.7). The patient with selective amygdala damage showed normal unconditioned responses to the US, but failed to develop conditioned responses to the CS+ stimuli. By contrast, the patient with selective hippocampal damage showed robust skin conductance changes to the US and normal conditioning to the CS+ stimuli. This patient also showed responsiveness to the CS− stimuli, but clearly differentiated these from the CS+ stimuli. The subject with combined amygdala and hippocampal damage failed to condition, even though he responded to the US.

After the conditioning sessions, the subjects were debriefed with several questions about the stimuli and their relationships. Control subjects and the patient with selective amygdala damage answered most of these questions correctly, but both patients with hippocampal damage were severely impaired in recollecting the task events (Figure 11.7). These findings demonstrate a clear double dissociation, with a form of emotional conditioning disrupted by amygdala damage and declarative memory for the learning situation impaired by hippocampal damage. The finding that these different forms of memory for the identical stimuli and associations are differentially affected by localized brain damage further supports the notion of multiple memory systems.

Habit/Skill Learning and Declarative Memory

Knowlton and colleagues (1996) studied patients in the early stages of Parkinson's disease, associated with degeneration of neurons in the substantia nigra resulting in a major loss of input to the neostriatum, and amnesic patients with damage to the medial temporal lobe or to associated regions of the diencephalon.

Subjects were trained in a probabilistic classification-learning task formatted as a weather prediction game. The task involved predicting one of two outcomes (rain or shine) based on cues from a set of cards (Figure 11.8, top). On each trial, one to three cards from a deck of four was presented. Each card was associated with the sunshine outcome only probabilistically, either 75%, 57%, 43%, or 25% of the time, and the outcome with multiple cards was associated with the con-

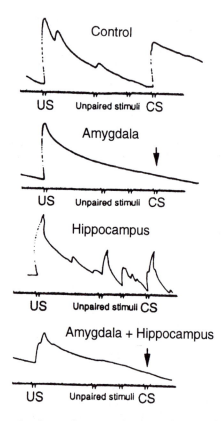

Figure 11.6. Samples of polygraph traces showing skin conductance responses to the unconditioned stimulus (US), unpaired stimuli, and conditioned stimulus in a normal control subject and patients with confirmed damage to indicated structures. Note the absence of responses to the CS in subjects with amygdala damage (arrows). The subject with hippocampal damage tends to produce the response to the unpaired stimuli as well as to the CS. (Reproduced, with permission, from Bechara, Tranel, Damasio, Adolphs, Rockland, & Damasio, 1995; Copyright American Association for the Advancement of Science.)

joint probabilities of the cards presented in any of 14 configurations. After presentation of the cards for each trial, the subject was forced to choose between rain and shine and was then given feedback as to the outcome. The probabilistic nature of the task made it somewhat counterproductive for subjects to attempt to recall specific previous trials, because repetition of any particular configuration of the cues could lead to different outcomes. Instead, the most useful information to be learned concerned the probability associated with particular cues and combinations of cues, acquired gradually across trials much as habits or skills are acquired.

Over a block of 50 trials, normal subjects gradually improved from pure guess-

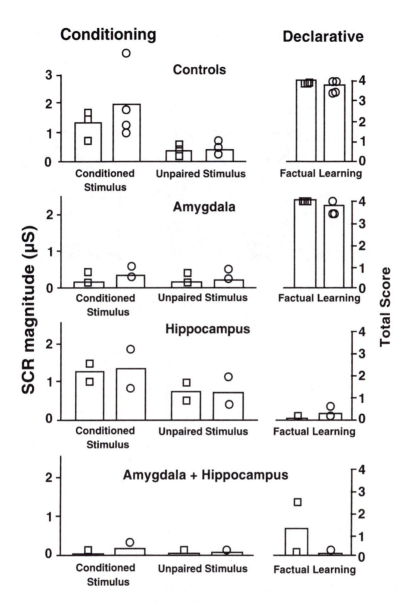

Figure 11.7. Overall performance patterns on conditioning and on declarative memory about the conditioning task in normal controls and patients with lesions in the indicated structures. Symbols indicate individual subject scores for controls, and scores on two versions of the tests (visual and auditory) in patients. (Reproduced, with permission, from Bechara, Tranel, Damasio, Adolphs, Rockland, & Damasio, 1995; Copyright American Association for the Advancement of Science.)

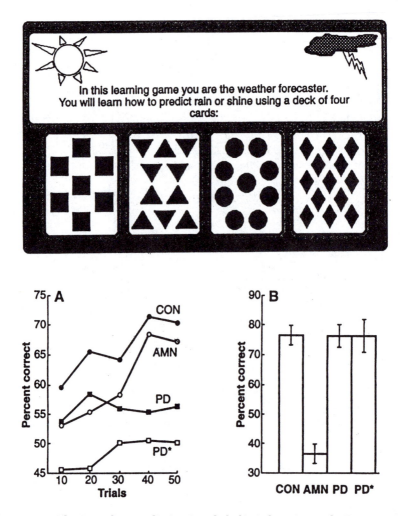

Figure 11.8. The "weather prediction" probabalistic learning task. Top: An example of the computer screen seen by subjects, with all four cards shown. Bottom: Performance of normal control subjects (CON), a group of amnesic subjects (AMN), and patients with mild (PD) or severe (PD*) symptoms of Parkinson's Disease on the weather prediction task (left) and on a test of declarative memory for the test materials (right). (Reproduced, with permission, from Knowlton, Mangels, & Squire, 1996; Copyright American Association for the Advancement of Science.)

ing (50% correct) to about 70% correct, a level consistent with the optimal probability of accuracy in this task (Figure 11.9, bottom). However, the patients with
Parkinson's disease failed to show significant learning, and the failure was particularly evident in those patients with more severe Parkinsonian symptoms. By
contrast, amnesic patients were successful in learning the task, achieving levels
of accuracy not different from those of controls by the end of the 50-trial block.

Subsequent to training on the weather prediction task, these subjects were
debriefed with a set of multiple-choice questions about the types of stimulus
materials and nature of the task. Normal subjects and those with Parkinson's disease performed very well in recalling the task events (Figure 11.8). But the amnesic subjects were severely impaired, performing near the chance level of 25%
correct. These findings demonstrate a clear double dissociation, with habit or
skill learning disrupted by neostriatal damage and declarative memory for the
learning events impaired by hippocampal or diencephalic damage, providing further evidence for the view that different forms of memory are represented for the
identical learning materials within parallel brain systems.

Visual Priming and Declarative Memory

The final double dissociation to be considered here involved a case study of a
patient (M.S.) with a large lesion in the right visual cortex resulting from surgical
unilateral removal of the occipital lobe for treatment of epilepsy (Figure 11.9;
Gabrieli et al., 1995a). The performance of this patient was compared with that
of two amnesic patients, one with Korsakoff's disease and one with epilepsy with
associated medial temporal lobe dysfunction. An additional control group was
comprised of patients with focal cortical damage.

All subjects were tested both directly (explicitly) and indirectly (implicitly)
for previously studied verbal materials. Subjects initially read aloud 24 words
presented individually, with each word presented twice in the study phase. They
were then tested in two ways. The indirect (implicit) memory test was a test of
perceptual priming. This involved a perceptual identification task in which
briefly presented words had to be identified. The words were initially presented
for only 16.7 ms, and subsequently for increasing multiples of that interval, until
the word was correctly identified. Half of the test items were words that had been
read in the study phase, and half were novel words. The measure of "priming"
was the extent to which shorter exposure durations were needed to identify previously studied versus novel words. The direct (explicit) test was a subsequently
administered recognition memory test to determine how many of the words presented during study were explicitly recollected.

Normal control subjects, subjects with focal brain damage outside the right
visual cortex, and amnesic subjects all showed perceptual priming (i.e., the advantage for previously studied items in their perceptual identification performance; Figure 11.10, top). Priming for the amnesic patients was normal, despite
their impairment compared to the other groups in recognition memory for the
words. However, the patient with right occipital damage showed no visual priming, despite normal performance in recognition memory for the same words (Figure 11.10, middle).

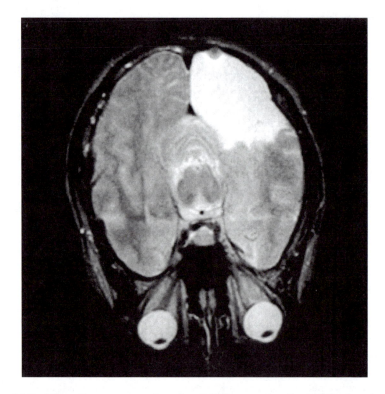

Figure 11.9. Magnetic resonance imaging (MRI) scan of patient M.S. showing loss of brain tissue in the right occipital area (white area imaged on left side). (Reproduced, with permission, from Gabrieli, Fleischman, Keane, Reminger, & Morrell, 1995; Copyright Blackwell Publishers.)

In a second experiment, patient M.S. was also tested on word stem completion for another assessment of priming. Here, the study words were presented during study either visually or auditorily. Then, at test, subjects were presented with three-letter stems of the study words and of other (nonstudied) words visually, and they were asked to complete the stems with the first word that came to mind. Control subjects and the amnesic patients showed substantial word stem priming, with higher completion rates for studied words over nonstudied words, for words that had initially been studied visually, with less priming for words that had initially been studied auditorily (Figure 11.10, bottom). By contrast, patient M.S. showed the same low level of priming for words initially studied either visually or auditorily. M.S.'s failure to show the normal priming advantage for items presented in the same (visual) form at study and test demonstrates that damage to the right occipital area resulted in a selective deficit in the (visual) modality-specific aspect of perceptual priming. This deficit in visual form priming following right occipital damage converges with findings from functional neuroimaging studies, in which visual priming in normal subjects is associated with activation of this right occipital area, as we saw in chapter 5. Gabrieli et al.'s (1995a) demon-

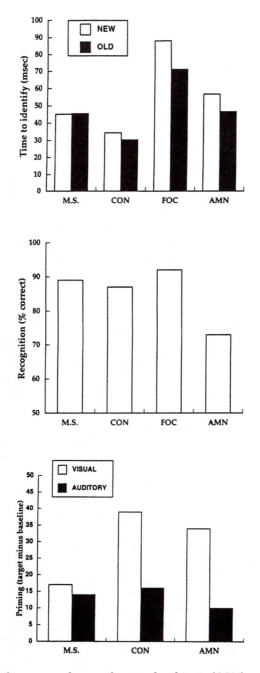

Figure 11.10. Performance of normal control subjects (CON), patient M.S., patients with other focal cortical lesions (FOC), and amnesic patients (AMN). Top:
Time to identify new and old words in the verbal priming test. Middle: Accuracy
in recognizing the study words in a test of explicit memory. Bottom: Priming
scores in a test of word completion for material presented in different modalities.
(Reproduced, with permission, from Gabrieli, Fleischman, Keane, Reminger, &
Morrell, 1995; Copyright Blackwell Publishers.)

stration of a double dissociation of memory functions for the identical learning materials provides yet further evidence for multiple, parallel memory representations mediated by distinct brain areas.

A Similar Set of Functional Dissociations in Animals and Humans

Combining the results of all of the studies presented in this chapter, we can designate some critical nodal points for memory processing and observe similarities in these functional assignments across species. These various multiple dissociations show repeatedly that the hippocampal region mediates memory for flexible expression of spatial locations in rats (McDonald & White, 1993; Kesner et al., 1993) and of facts and events in humans (Bechara et al., 1995; Knowlton et al., 1996; Gabrieli et al., 1995a). The similarity of hippocampal memory function across species has been discussed extensively in previous chapters and is only reinforced here.

These dissociation studies, taken together, show additionally that the amygdala is critical to emotional learning, as reflected in the acquisition of cue preferences in rats (McDonald & White, 1993) and conditioned autonomic responses in humans (Bechara et al., 1995). Furthermore, these present studies have provided compelling evidence that the neostriatum plays a critical role in the learning of habitual behavioral responses as reflected in stimulus approach learning and body turn recognition in rats (McDonald & White, 1993; Kesner et al., 1993), and in probabilistic cue response associations in humans (Knowlton et al., 1996). Finally, these findings inform us that areas of the visual cortex mediate forms of visual recognition as reflected in object recognition in rats (Kesner et al., 1993) and visual priming in humans (Gabrieli et al., 1995a). Across all these experiments, a salient theme is that these different forms of memory, even for the identical learning materials, are mediated largely independently and in parallel.

Note that although we speak here of particular nodal brain loci that are critical to particular forms of memory, the interconnectedness of these critical structures and the sharing of pathways in which they perform processing functions in the service of different forms of memory (see Figure 2.6) prevents us from thinking of these brain areas as "black boxes" that contain and perform different types of memory. Specific brain structures, including (but not restricted to) the hippocampal system, the amygdala, the neostriatum, and parts of the visual cortex, are key centers for processing in just one of the many streams of the flow of cortical information outward to other brain systems. Because these particular structures are both central "bottlenecks" for particular pathways, and because each is part of only one of the main functional pathways, these structures become loci of critical and selective processing of that type of memory. Thus one should be wary of viewing the hippocampal system as "the" center for relational or declarative memory. Rather it is only one (albeit a crucial) part of that memory system. And perhaps it is the only part that is not shared within the pathways of other memory systems. A similar characterization can be made for the amygdala and for the neostriatum.

Finally, the experiments reviewed here serve to introduce some of the memory systems that will be the focus of further discussion in the remaining chapters of this book. These chapters will elaborate the anatomical pathways of these memory systems and will expand on our understanding of the operating characteristics of the type of memory they mediate. There are yet other memory systems to be discussed at the close of this book. It must be emphasized that the systems discussed here are only the best studied examples of the multiple memory systems of the brain.

12

Emotional Memory and Memory Modulation

Emotion and memory mix quite well. Indeed, a major message of this chapter is that emotion and memory influence each other at multiple levels. At one level, emotion constitutes a major category of behavioral "output" and, as such, constitutes a venue for the expression of memories. Ordinarily we think first of memory expression via conscious recollection and "objective," verbal reflection on the accessed memory. At the same time, though, the consequences of memory often involve emotional expression by a broad range of behaviors, from the inflection of our speech, to flushing of the face, or sweating in the palms of our hands, for example. At another level, we know our memories are colored by their emotional impact. The items we remember after emotional experiences with them are scary or comforting or have any of a wide range of emotional features that seem as much a part of the item as its objective perceptual features. At yet another level, memories surrounding emotional experiences are often better remembered or remembered especially vividly. Something about the emotions themselves, or about the heightened arousal that accompanies emotional experiences, can enhance the memory for the objective (nonemotional) features of the facts and events that are perceived during an emotional experience.

In this chapter we will first review our understanding of the brain pathways that mediate emotional experience and expression. We will describe early behavioral and anatomical studies that identified brain areas, especially areas in the temporal lobe, that are involved in the appreciation of emotional cues and in the expression of emotional behaviors.

Second, we will introduce the current notion that some aspects of emotional memories involve a dedicated circuit of the brain that operates in parallel with other memory systems. In particular, it has been proposed that there is a specific memory system that mediates the learning and expression of emotional responses to stimuli of learned significance even in the absence of conscious memory for the events of the learning experience. Via this system, it is proposed, sometimes we can feel nervous, or happy, or scared at an image that evokes memory even before, or independent of, our ability to declare the source of such feelings. This kind of learning is mediated by plasticity in components of the known pathways for emotional expression introduced above. We will initially consider the evidence for a specific system for the acquisition of conditioned fear, and then we will extend the review to consider whether the same brain system mediates the acquisition and expression of a broad range of affective associations.

Third, we will consider two more general interactions between emotion and memory, both of which involve the modulation of memory by emotional experiences. These influences operate either indirectly, by influencing a broad range of perceptual and motivational systems that provide the contents of new memories, or directly, by influencing the memory storage process itself in some way. Both are probably the case, and we will consider this level of interaction between emotion and memory. One of these modulatory influences is generated by the arousing nature of emotional experiences—such experiences increase our attention to particularly salient events and can consequently increase the processing of memories for events as they occur during the experiences. Another modulatory influence involves increments in memory processing that occur even after the learning experience itself is completed. Thus emotional and arousing influences, or treatments that mimic the effects of emotional and arousing influences, which are applied even after learning is over, can enhance the later expression of memories for that learning. This modulatory influence is believed to operate on aspects of memory consolidation per se. Importantly these two related aspects of emotional modulation are quite distinct from the notion of a dedicated system for emotional memories. Unlike the dedicated-system concept, these modulatory influences can be expected to affect memory in a general way, that is, to affect all kinds of memory and all the memory systems outlined in chapter 11.

Anatomical Pathways for Emotional Experience

The first theoretical proposal of a brain system for emotion was provided by Papez (1937). He postulated that sensory experiences took distinct pathways for "thought" and "feelings." The stream of thought, he proposed, involved channeling the sensory inputs from the thalamus to the wide expanse of the cerebral cortex on the lateral surface of the brain. The stream of feeling, he argued, followed a different path from the thalamus to the medial cortical areas known as the *limbic lobe* plus the neighboring hypothalamus. Based on gross anatomical evidence available at that time, Papez speculated on the existence of a specific brain circuit for emotion. This involved at its core a circular set of connections between the cingulate cortex, a major cortical division of the limbic lobe, to the hippocampal region, the temporal component of the limbic lobe, to the mammillary bodies within the hypothalamus, to the anterior nuclei of the thalamus, which projected to the cingulate cortex, and so on around the circuit. Sensory inputs from the posterior parts of the thalamus arrived in this circuit via either of two routes: to the cingulate cortex from the lateral cortical areas that mediate the "stream of thought" or into the hypothalamus directly from the posterior thalamus. Indeed, Papez viewed the interactions between cortical and hypothalamic inputs as mediating the integration between cortical and subcortical processing of emotions. Outputs of this circuit then were reflected by the cingulate cortex back to the stream of thought and via the hypothalamus to bodily (autonomic) responses.

At around the same time other evidence indicated a critical role for additional temporal lobe areas in emotion. In 1939 Kluver and Bucy described a syndrome of affective disorder following removal of the temporal lobe in monkeys. This disorder was characterized by "psychic blindness," which was reflected mainly in a blunting of the emotional reactions usually associated with fear of novel objects. Part of this disorder involved an impairment in object recognition, a disorder known as *agnosia*. This part of the disorder is now associated with damage to the temporal cortex (see chapter 4). Another part of the disorder, and the focus of this chapter, was the "taming" of these normally aggressive animals, as well as other abnormalities of social behavior. This part of the disorder has been attributed to the amygdala.

These distinct components of an emotional system in the brain were integrated into a more elaborate theoretical structure by MacLean (1949). He combined the observations of Papez and those of Kluver and Bucy with clinical observations on emotional disorders and electrophysiological evidence of visceral sensory inputs to the hippocampus and other parts of the Papez circuit, arguing for the existence of a distinct "visceral brain." Using the full breadth of evidence from these various sources, MacLean (1952) expanded further on Papez's notion of distinct informational processing streams and on the anatomical components of the emotional system. He introduced the term *limbic system* as the anatomical designation of the emotional circuit and included within it the full Papez circuit plus the amygdala, septum, and prefrontal cortex (Figure 12.1). MacLean distinguished the functional domain of this system in mediating emotional experience from the role of lower brain stem structures in mediating instinctive behavioral stereotypes, and from the role of the higher cortical areas in mediating cognitive functions.

There have subsequently been many elaborations on and modifications to the notion of the limbic system. The evidence expanded the critical connectional pathways both forward toward the frontal lobe and backward toward the midbrain, so that Nauta (1971) proposed we view this system as a continuum of structures throughout the neuraxis. The strong connections of classic limbic structures have today become so intertwined with other brain systems that today the term *limbic* itself is somewhat outmoded. This and other evidence brought into question whether the specific components of the limbic system were correctly identified, and indeed whether one can circumscribe a distinct system for emotion (for a discussion see LeDoux, 1996). Nevertheless, more recent research has identified specific pathways associated with the old limbic system as critical elements in emotional output. We will consider these next.

Pathways for Emotional Expression

Recent research has brought the focus on emotional memory to pathways through the amygdala. This is justly deserved because this structure lies in a central posi-

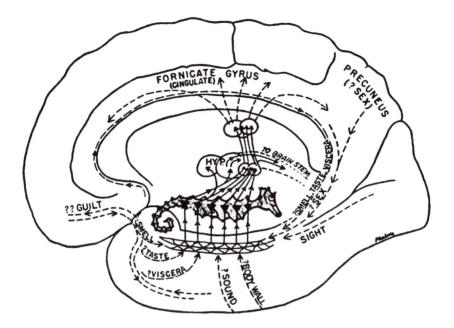

Figure 12.1. Schematic diagram of the limbic system as conceived by McLean. The hippocampus is illustrated as a "seahorse" (hippocampus is Greek for seahorse). Hyp = hypothalamus.

tion between cortical information processing, limbic circuitry, and hypothalamic outputs to brain-stem-mediated response mechanisms. Thus we will provide here a brief summary of the organization of the amygdala, including its main inputs, intrinsic connections, and outputs (Figure 12.2). The amygdala lies in the anterior medial temporal lobe, just rostral to the hippocampus and surrounded by the parahippocampal cortical region. This area involves a complex of many highly interconnected nuclei. The most prominent compartments are the cortical-like group including the lateral nucleus and basolateral complex of subnuclei, and the central and medial group of nuclei and their extensions (Amaral et al., 1992; Price et al., 1987; Swanson & Petrovich, 1998). As it turns out, this division roughly corresponds to the major input and output sides of amygdala processing. Thus sensory inputs from the thalamus and cortex project mainly to the lateral and basolateral nuclei, whereas cortical and subcortical amygdala outputs originate mainly in the central and medial nuclei.

Several studies have shown that the amygdala receives widespread sensory inputs from the thalamus and cerebral cortex (Turner & Herkenham, 1991; LeDoux et al., 1985, 1990a, 1990b; Price et al., 1987). These are derived largely from gustatory, thoracic-abdominal (vagus nerve inputs), and auditory thalamic nuclei, but not the main somatosensory or visual thalamic nuclei. Cortical inputs are derived through the olfactory bulb and piriform cortex, plus higher order sensory inputs from all modalities via the entire cortex surrounding the rhinal sulcus (insular and perirhinal cortex). LeDoux and colleagues have intensively studied

Pathways of the amygdala

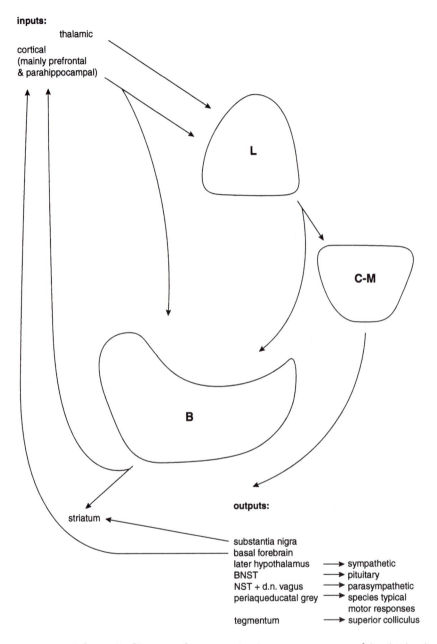

Figure 12.2. Schematic diagram of some major inputs, outputs, and intrinsic circuitry of the amygdala. L = lateral nucleus; CM = centromedial nucleus; B = basal (or basolateral) nucleus. BNST = bed nucleus of the stria terminalis; NST = nucleus of the solitary tract.

auditory inputs and argued the main locus of input involves a convergence of thalamic and cortical projections to the lateral nucleus. In addition the medial prefrontal cortex and hippocampal regions, specifically the subiculum and entorhinal cortex, send substantial inputs to the lateral nucleus. Some inputs, however, arrive in other amygdala nuclei. In particular, some of the olfactory inputs arrive mainly in the cortical nuclei, and the internal organ inputs arrive mainly in the central nuclei.

The intrinsic connectivity of amygdaloid nuclei is complex and is characterized mainly by a distribution of connections from the lateral nucleus to the basal nuclear complex and central nucleus, which are also interconnected. Thus whatever segregation of inputs may have been preserved at the input stage is likely converged within the amygdala. Indirect outputs from the amygdala to the cortex are largely derived from several nuclei to components of the thalamus, in particular the mediodorsal nucleus. The basal nuclear complex sends direct outputs to several cortical areas, including the perirhinal, entorhinal, and prefrontal areas. In addition, the amygdala projects heavily to multiple basal forebrain areas, including the bed nucleus of the stria terminalis, substantia innominata, horizontal limb of the diagonal band, and basal nucleus of Meynert. These projections then secondarily influence widespread cortical areas. Also, the basal amygdaloid nuclei project to components of the substantia nigra and striatum, and to the subiculum. Other main subcortical targets of amygdala output are directed mainly from the central and medial nuclei to the substantia nigra, lateral hypothalamus, and several brain stem motor, autonomic (vagus nerve), and endocrine effector areas. These provide a broad array of response modalities that are generated after amygdala stimulation and are observed in the syndrome of behaviors associated with emotional output (see Figure 12.3; Davis, 1992b; LeDoux, 1991; Gallagher & Holland, 1994).

These anatomical data tell us that the amygdala is the recipient of multimodal information from both lower order visceral and other specific thalamic inputs plus higher order sensory information, and that the intrinsic connectivity of the amygdala combines these inputs. This conclusion, based on anatomical data, is supported by physiological studies showing that single neurons in the rat, cat, and monkey amygdala respond to complex multimodal, affectively significant stimuli (O'Keefe & Bouma, 1969; Nishijo et al., 1988a, 1988b; Schütze et al., 1987; for review see LeDoux, 1989). The amygdala orchestrates an enormous range of influences on behavior. These include influences back onto the thalamic and cortical areas that provided sensory input, direct influences on other systems important for different forms of memory (specifically the striatum and hippocampal regions), and direct outputs to the autonomic, endocrine, and motor systems that generate bodily forms of emotional expression.

The Amygdala and Emotional Expression

Following on the initial findings of the "blunting" of affect in monkeys with damage to the temporal lobe, including the amygdala, several studies have shown that selective amygdala damage results in a syndrome characterized by decreases in responsivity to affective stimuli (for a review see Kling & Brothers, 1992). After amygdalotomy, monkeys fail to respond differentially to a wide range of painful shock intensities and are poor at temperature discrimination (Chin et al., 1976). These animals also fail to show normal orienting responses, including changes in heart rate and respiration, and have a diminished discrimination of galvanic skin response, the change in skin resistance associated with sweating (Bagshaw & Pribram, 1968). Monkeys with amygdala damage also demonstrate diminished selectivity in feeding, diminished sensitivity to food deprivation, and depressed shifts in operant behavior normally associated with changes in food reward magnitude or type of food reward (Schwartzbaum, 1960a, 1960b, 1961). Parallel impairments in responsiveness to food reward alterations have been observed in rats with amygdala damage (Henke, 1973; Becker et al., 1984).

A study on the amnesic patient H.M., whose surgical damage included removal of the amygdala bilaterally, provides confirmation of the blunting of affective responsiveness in humans with amygdala damage and offers some further insights into the nature of this disorder. In the clinical setting, H.M. was known to endure without complaint painful conditions, including hemorrhoids, and did not produce a normal galvanic skin response to electrical stimulation. He also was noted rarely to mention being hungry even when meals were delayed but ate in a normal manner when given a meal. These observations were followed up in a systematic study of H.M.'s responsiveness to pain and hunger (Hebben et al., 1985). In this study psychophysical evaluations of responses to thermal stimulation were compared in H.M. and other amnesic patients. H.M. showed moderately diminished discriminability of painful stimulation. More prominent was his failure to identify any of the stimuli as "painful" no matter how intense they were. The comparison amnesic patients did not show loss of pain discriminability and were as likely as normal subjects to label the stimuli painful, so it does not appear that H.M.'s impairment in pain perception was secondary to his memory deficit.

A further experiment aimed at characterizing H.M.'s appreciation of hunger involved an assessment of his reaction to eating multiple dinners. Initially H.M. was asked to rate his hunger on a scale of 0 to 100, with 0 identified as "famished" and 100 identified as "too full to eat another bite." Just before dinner, H.M. rated his hunger level as 50. He was served a full meal and again rated his hunger level as 50. After a 5-min rest period filled with conversation, by prearrangement he was served another full dinner. As expected H.M. did not remember eating dinner and ate the second meal at his usual slow steady pace. He stopped short of completing the meal, leaving his salad and cake. He remarked that he couldn't decide which to eat and, upon prompting, simply decided to eat the cake. Following this he also rated his hunger level at 50. When probed further why he had not fully completed the second meal, H.M. would only say he was "finished" but would not characterize himself as "full." Subsequently he rated his hunger level at 75, when he had forgotten what he had eaten. In a separate set of ratings taken before and after regular meals, both amnesic patients and normal controls consistently rated themselves as less hungry and thirsty after meals, but H.M. showed small and inconsistent changes in his hunger rating (Figure 12.3). These findings were interpreted as demonstrating that, while there was evidence of modest decrease in sensitivity, the major effect of his surgery was diminished accessibility of information about his internal states.

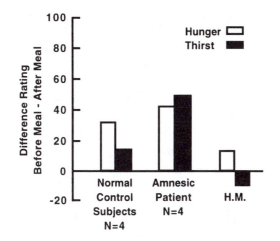

Figure 12.3. Differences in before- and after-meal ratings of hunger in normal control subjects, amnesic patients, and the patient H.M. (Reproduced, with permission, from Hebben, Corkin, Eichenbaum, & Shedlack, 1985; Copyright American Psychological Association.)

Because this impairment was not observed in other amnesic patients without involvement of the amygdala, H.M.'s deficit was attributed to amygdala damage per se.

More recent studies of the role of the human amygdala in the perception of affective stimuli have focused on responses to faces. Several studies have now shown that bilateral damage to the amygdala results in a deficit in the ability to recognize emotion in human faces (Adophs et al., 1994, 1995; Young et al., 1995; Hamann et al., 1996; Calder et al., 1996). These studies assessed the recognition of various facial expressions in human subjects with unilateral or bilateral removal of the amygdala and one subject (S.M.) with a rare disorder known as Urbach-Wiethe disease associated with calcification of the amygdala sparing the neighboring cortex and hippocampus (Figure 12.4). In general there was a diminished capacity of the appreciation and labeling of facial expressions, without other general deficits in language, memory, or perception. Furthermore, S.M. showed a selective impairment in the recognition of fearful expressions and related expressions such as surprise and anger. S.M. also showed a diminished capacity for recognizing similarities among different emotions that normal subjects typically demonstrate. S.M. was able to recognize familiar faces, even ones not seen in a considerable time. This dissociation contrasted with a selective deficit in face recognition sparing appreciation of emotional expressions in patients with temporal cortical damage. S.M. did perceive fearful faces as expressing emotion but refused to characterize the expression as fearful, leading the investigators to conclude she could perceive the facial expression but that it did not activate responses associated with fear.

These findings are consistent with electrophysiological data showing that neurons in the amygdala respond to faces in both monkeys (Leonard et al., 1985) and humans (Heit et al., 1988). In addition, a recent brain-imaging study using fMRI

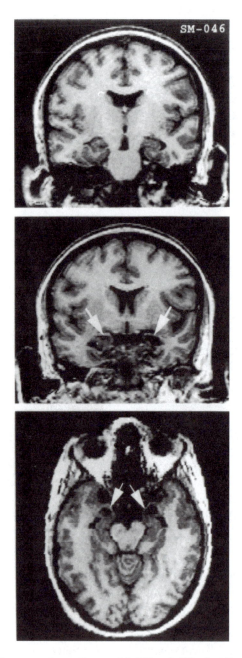

Figure 12.4. MRI images of a patient with Urbach-Wiethe disease. Arrows indicate loci where the amygdala would normally be found. (Reproduced, with permission, from Adolphs, Tranel, Damasio, & Damasio, 1995; Copyright Society for Neuroscience.)

showed that the amygdala is preferentially active in response to viewing fearful versus neutral faces, although some responses to facial expressions other than neutral expressions were also observed (Breiter et al., 1996). These data bring into focus the importance of the amygdala as a "performance system" for the analysis of affective information and for the expression of emotional output.

Evidence for a Dedicated Emotional Memory System

Is memory for emotions just a part of declarative memory? Or is there a distinct memory system for emotional memories? Or does emotion just enhance memory processing? In the following sections we will argue that all of the above are true. Certainly we do consciously recall emotional experiences, so these clearly can be a part of declarative memory. There is also substantial emerging evidence that some aspects or some types of emotional memory are accomplished by a distinct system, parallel to that for declarative memory; this is the subject of this section (see also LeDoux, 1989). In addition, emotion can indeed enhance all kinds of memory and can do so in multiple ways, and these mechanisms will be addressed later.

In a classic case study of amnesia, Cleparede (1911/1951; see chapter 2) pricked the hand of an unsuspecting patient with Korsakoff's disease. Subsequently, she refused to shake Cleparde's hand, although she could not recall the painful incident. Later, Damasio and colleagues (1989) described intact affective learning in their amnesic patient, Boswell. Even though he could not learn to recognize the hospital staff, he consistently claimed he liked those with whom he had had repeated positive encounters over those with whom he had had negative encounters. In a more formal study, Johnson and colleagues (1985) presented amnesics with pictures and biographical descriptions of two individuals, one characterized positively and the other negatively. Normal subjects preferred the positively described individual and based this on their recall of the biographical information. Amnesics could not recall the individual or descriptions but showed a strong preference for the "good guy." These and other case studies (see Tobias et al., 1992) show that memory for emotional aspects of experiences can indeed be dissociated from declarative memory for the same experiences in amnesic patients.

Additional findings from normal humans provide yet another line of evidence that affective memory can occur independently of declarative memory. Perhaps most prominent among the well-studied examples is the "mere exposure" effect of Zajonc (1980). In several studies Zajonc and his colleagues found that exposure to stimuli that were not memorable, or that simply were not explicitly remembered, nevertheless produced a preference for the familiar items. In some of these studies, the stimuli were even presented subliminally, so that their presentation did not reach consciousness. Nevertheless, subjects subsequently showed a preference for the experienced stimuli. Thus an emotional system could perceive and somehow store information that was not adequate to arouse the declarative memory system. The mere exposure effect has since been extended to many behavioral paradigms (see Tobias et al., 1992; LeDoux, 1996).

A Brain System for the Expression of Emotional Memories

What neural system mediates the capacity to form emotional memories independent of declarative memory? Several laboratories have studied different emotional memory paradigms and described somewhat different circuits and emotional learning mechanisms. In this section we will review some prominent examples of circuit analyses of emotional memory within the outlined brain system for emotional expression. It is important to note at the outset that accumulating compelling evidence about the memory functions of a brain system that is intimately involved in the perception and expression of emotions is bound to be difficult. The central challenges involve the need for clear-cut dissociations between aspects of memory and aspects of performance of emotional processing, as well as the need for specification of where in the system the critical plasticity events occur. These issues will be addressed in the following review and are further discussed in chapter 15.

Perhaps the best studied example of emotional memory involves the brain system that mediates Pavlovian fear conditioning (LeDoux, 1989, 1992, 1996; Davis, 1992a, 1992b, 1994, 1998). The work of LeDoux, Davis, and their colleagues has focused on the specific elements of the pathways through the amygdala that support the learning of a particular fear response to a simple auditory stimulus. The critical elements of the relevant pathway include auditory sensory inputs via the inferior colliculus to two different circuits through the thalamus (Figure 12.5). One of these circuits involves collicular inputs to three areas of the thalamus that are not the source of auditory input to the cortex: the medial division of the medial geniculate, the suprageniculate nucleus, and the posterior intralaminar nucleus (LeDoux et al., 1990b). These auditory thalamic areas then project directly to the lateral amygdaloid nucleus. The other circuit involves collicular inputs to the ventral division of the medial geniculate, which projects to the primary auditory area of temporal cortex (e.g., Romanski & LeDoux, 1993; Deacon et al., 1983). This cortical area in turn projects to secondary temporal areas and the perirhinal cortex. These secondary auditory cortical areas are the source of cortical inputs to the amygdala, particularly the lateral and basolateral nuclei of this structure. Those areas of the amygdala project into the central nucleus, which is the source of outputs to subcortical areas controlling a broad range of fear-related behaviors, including the autonomic and motor responses outlined above.

LeDoux and colleagues have focused on the input side of these circuits. Their studies have examined the neuropsychology and neurophysiology of these structures in animals during the course of a simple tone-cued fear-conditioning task. Rats are initially habituated to an operant chamber, then presented with multiple pairings of a 10-s pure tone terminating with a brief electric shock through the floor of the cage. Subsequently conditioned fear was assessed by measuring the autonomic response as reflected in changes to the tone only in arterial pressure, motor responses as reflected in a stereotypical crouching or freezing behavior when the tone is presented, and suppression of drinking sweetened water (LeDoux et al., 1990a). Unconditioned responses to the tone were evaluated by presenting other animals with unpaired tones and shocks.

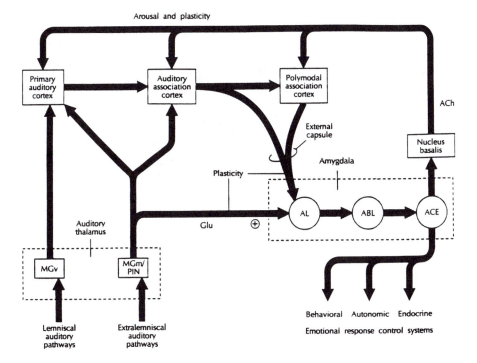

Figure 12.5. Schematic diagram of a brain system for emotional information processing and memory. MGv = ventral division of the medial geniculate; MGm = medial division of the medial geniculate; PIN = posterior intralaminar nucleus; AL = lateral nucleus of the amygdala; ABL = basolateral nucleus of the amygdala; ACE = central nucleus of the amygdala; glu = glutamate; ACh = acetylcholine. (Reproduced, with permission, from LeDoux, 1992; Copyright Elsevier Science.)

The initial experiments were aimed at identifying the critical input pathway to the amygdala. Animals with selective lesions in the lateral amygdala showed dramatically reduced conditioned responses to the tone, in the measures of both autonomic and motor responses (Figure 12.6, top). Unconditioned responses (consequent on unpaired presentations) were not affected by this damage. Also, animals with damage to the adjacent striatum performed normally. Subsequent efforts focused on identifying which of the two prominent auditory input pathways to the lateral amygdala was critical (Romanski & LeDoux, 1992a, 1992b). Broad destruction of all auditory areas of the thalamus eliminated conditioned responses. However, selective ablation of either of the two prominent direct inputs to the lateral amygdala was individually ineffective. Thus lesions of the medial division of the medial geniculate (including all three nuclei that project directly to the lateral amygdala) or of the entire auditory cortex that projects to the amygdala did not reduce either the autonomic or the freezing response (Figure 12.6, bottom). However, elimination of both of these inputs produced the full effect seen after lateral amygdala lesions. Thus, for this simple type of condition-

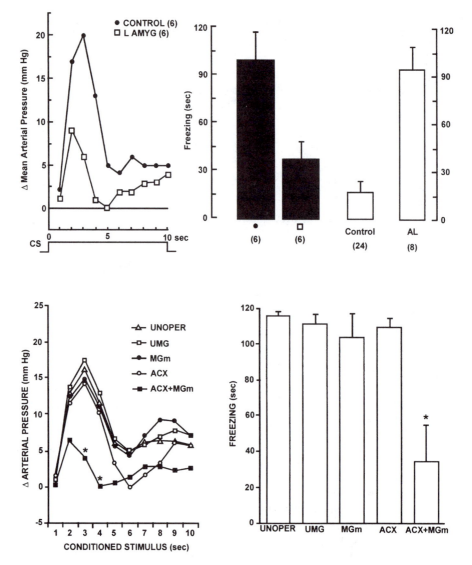

Figure 12.6. Performance of normal control rats and rats with lesions of the lateral amygdala, auditory cortex, or medial geniculate nucleus on the expression of conditioned fear. Top: Left panel: Time course of changes in arterial blood pressure following onset of the conditioned stimulus. Right panel: Freezing and cessation of drinking during onset of the conditioned stimulus. Bottom: Comparison of the effects of separate and combined cortical and thalamic lesions. L Amyg = AL = lateral amygdala; UNOPER = controls; UMG = unilateral lesions; MGm = medial segment of the medial geniculate nucleus; ACx = auditory cortex. (Reproduced, with permission, from LeDoux, Cicchetti, Xagoris, & Romanski, 1990; Copyright Society for Neuroscience. Reproduced, with permission, from Romanski & LeDoux, 1992; Copyright Society for Neuroscience.)

ing, either the direct thalamic or the thalamocortical input pathway is sufficient to mediate conditioning.

Additional studies were aimed at another component of fear conditioning observed in these studies. After conditioning, when rats are replaced in the conditioning chamber, they begin to freeze even before the tone-conditioning stimulus is presented. Thus they condition both to the tone and to the environmental context in which tones and shock have been paired. This contextual fear conditioning is selective to the environment in which conditioning occurs. Furthermore, contextual fear conditioning can be dissociated from conditioning to the tone by presenting conditioned tones in a different environment. Trained animals do not freeze prior to tone presentation in the different environment but do freeze when the tone is presented. Moreover, Phillips and LeDoux (1992) showed that contextual fear conditioning is mediated by a different pathway than tone-cued fear conditioning. They trained animals on the standard version of the task, then assessed freezing both immediately after the rats were placed in the conditioning chamber and in response to the tone. Amygdala lesions blocked conditioned freezing to both the context and the tone. By contrast, damage to the hippocampus selectively blocked contextual fear conditioning, sparing the conditioned response to the tone (Figure 12.7). Thus, if we combine these data with the known

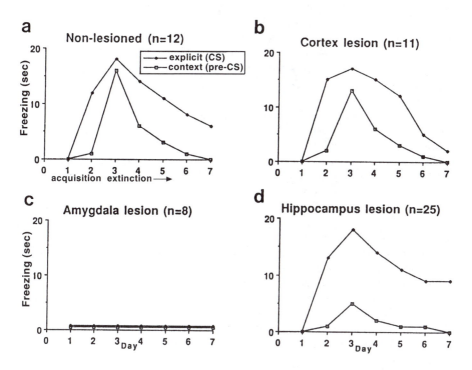

Figure 12.7. Course of conditioning and extinction to the explicit CS (tone) and context (the pre-CS period) following lesions to the indicated structures. (Reproduced, with permission, from Phillips & LeDoux, 1992; Copyright American Psychological Association.)

anatomy of these brain structures, the full set of circuits mediating fear conditioning in this task involves a set of parallel and serial pathways to the amygdala (Figure 12.6). The most direct pathway is from areas within the auditory thalamus. A secondary path through an auditory thalamocortical circuit can also mediate tone-cued conditioning. Contextual fear conditioning involves a yet more indirect pathway by which mulitmodal information arrives in the hippocampus and is sent to the amygdala via the subiculum.

Additional studies by LeDoux and colleagues have elucidated the physiology of the neurons in the direct thalamic and thalamocortical auditory pathways to the amygdala. Cells in both the medial geniculate nuclei that project directly to the amygdala and in the thalamic nucleus that projects to the cortex demonstrate a variety of auditory responses (Bordi & LeDoux, 1992, 1994a, 1994b). Overall finer auditory tuning was observed in the ventral medial geniculate than in areas that project directly to the amygdala. However, cells in the ventral nucleus responded only to auditory stimuli, whereas neurons in the medial geniculate nuclei that project to the amygdala also responded to foot shock stimulation. Furthermore, some amygdala-projecting cells that responded to somatosensory stimulation but not auditory stimulation showed potentiated responses to simultaneous presentation of both stimuli. In the amygdala, cells in the lateral nucleus were also auditory-responsive to both broadband stimuli at both short (12–25 ms) and long (60–150 ms) latencies. Some cells had clear tuning curves, whereas others had a broad spectrum of responsiveness. Some showed very rapid habituation. In general these cells had longer response latencies and broader tuning functions than cells in the ventral area of the medial geniculate. Cells in the lateral amygdala could also be driven by electrical stimulation of the medial geniculate, and their responses were typically shorter than those in the basolateral amygdala (Clugnet et al., 1990).

In addition, LeDoux and colleagues have now provided several lines of evidence suggesting that direct medial geniculate-lateral amygdala inputs exhibit learning-related plasticity. Tetanic stimulation of the medial geniculate produces LTP in synaptic responses recorded in the lateral amygdala (Clugnet & LeDoux, 1990). Furthermore, LTP produced in this pathway enhances auditory evoked responses in the lateral amygdala (Rogan & LeDoux, 1995). Correspondingly, fear conditioning also results in enhanced auditory evoked responses in the lateral amygdala (Figure 3.13; Rogan et al., 1997). At the level of neuronal activity, fear conditioning selectively enhances the short latency auditory responses of lateral amygdala neurons (Figure 12.8). In addition, some cells that were not responsive to tones prior to training showed postconditioning short-latency responses. Also, some pairs of cells recorded simultaneously showed postconditioning increases in cross-correlated activity. In a more recent study, activation of the amygdala was also observed early in fear conditioning in human subjects (LaBar et al., 1998). Combined, these lines of data provide evidence consistent with the notion that fear conditioning is mediated by increased synaptic efficacy of the thalamo-amygdala projections.

Davis and colleagues (1992a, 1992b, 1993, 1999) have investigated a different form of fear conditioning and have provided an extensive line of evidence that runs in parallel with LeDoux and colleagues' findings. This group has employed a fear-conditioning paradigm known as *fear-potentiated startle.* In this task ani-

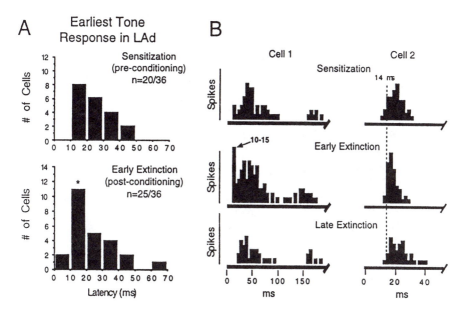

Figure 12.8. Decreased neural response latencies in the lateral amygdala following fear conditioning. A. Note increase in the number of cells showing short latency responses to the CS from prior to training to early in extinction. B. The same decreases in response latencies observed in two example individual cells. (Reproduced, with permission, from Quirk, Repa, & LeDoux, 1995; Copyright Cell Press.)

mals are initially exposed to pairings of a light or a tone with foot shock. Subsequently, their reflexive startle response to a loud noise is considerably augmented in the presence of the conditioned light or tone CS (Figure 12.9). Potentiated acoustic startle does not occur after unpaired presentations of the light or tone and shock and is thus as valid a measure of fear conditioning as those employed in the previously described studies. The brain pathway for fear-potentiated startle contains many of the same elements of the amygdala circuit studied by LeDoux and colleagues, as they intersect with the acoustic reflex pathway (Figure 12.10).

Davis and colleagues have independently demonstrated the importance of the amygdala in fear conditioning, showing that lesions of the lateral or basal amygdala or the central amygdala nucleus prevent conditioning and abolish expression of previously learned acoustic startle responses (Figure 12.11). Correspondingly, they found that electrical stimulation of the amygdala enhances acoustic startle, and the latency of onset of the influence of amygdala stimulation on brain stem motor neurons is very short.

Furthermore, Davis and his colleagues have shown that NMDA-dependent plasticity in the amygdala is critical for the development of fear conditioning, but not for the expression of already-learned fear responses. Thus application of the NMDA receptor blocker AP5 prior to training prevents conditioning, but similar treatment after conditioning or prior to testing has no effect on later expres-

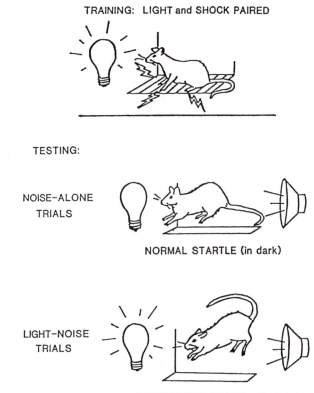

Figure 12.9. Potentiation of the acoustic startle response. (Reproduced, with permission, from Davis, 1992; Copyright John Wiley & Sons, Inc.)

sion of potentiated acoustic startle. To further address the possibility that NMDA receptors are directly involved in the expression of conditioned fear, Gerwitz and Davis (1997) first conditioned rats to fear a primary CS and then subsequently trained them to fear a secondary stimulus paired with the primary CS. AP5 infused into the amygdala during the final second-order conditioning stage actually enhanced the fear expression to the previously conditioned primary CS while preventing the second-order conditioning. This finding strongly supports the conclusion that NMDA receptors are differentially involved in the plasticity of startle but not in the performance of potentiated startle.

Similar results have also been obtained in another fear-conditioning task that involved inhibition of approach to a location previously associated with shock (Kim et al., 1991). Low doses of AP5 had no effect on initial learning but blocked subsequent retention (Figure 12.12). By contrast to the effects of AP5, injection of the AMPA receptor antagonist CNQX into the amygdala blocked the expression of fear-potentiated startle. This pattern of data is entirely consistent with

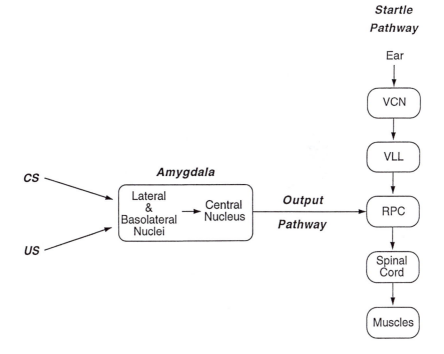

Figure 12.10. Pathways that mediate the potentiation of the acoustic startle response. (Reproduced, with permission, from Davis, Campeau, Kim, & Falls, 1992; Copyright John Wiley & Sons, Inc.)

our understanding of the differential roles of NMDA and non-NMDA receptors in the establishment of synaptic plasticity and in its expression, and it provided evidence parallel to that of LeDoux and colleagues supporting the notion that synaptic plasticity in the amygdala is critical to fear memory.

Davis and colleagues have also extended our understanding of the specific input and output pathways of fear conditioning. They have found that ablation of the auditory thalamus blocks tone-cued fear-potentiated startle, sparing visually cued potentiated startle. However, ablation of the perirhinal cortex eliminates previous conditioning in either modality, suggesting the cortical pathway through this area is normally predominant. Like LeDoux and colleagues, Davis (1993) has shown that tone-cued conditioning can be supported by the direct thalamic path as well.

Other studies of Davis and colleagues (1993, 1999) have focused on identifying the critical output circuitry for fear-potentiated startle. These studies have shown that the pathway from the amygdala via the ventral amygdalofugal pathway to caudal brain stem regions to the nucleus reticularis pontis oralis constitutes the critical circuit for expression of potentiated startle (Figure 12.13).

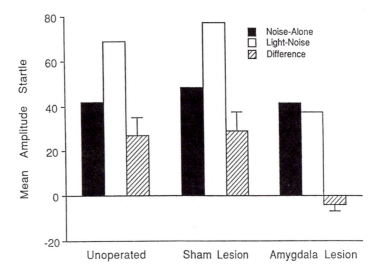

Figure 12.11. Performance of normal control rats and rats with amygdala lesions in potentiation of the acoustic startle response. Note potentiation of startle after light noise pairing in controls, but not in rats with amygdala damage. (Reproduced, with permission, from Sananes & Davis, 1992; Copyright American Psychological Association.)

Is This a General System for Stimulus-Reinforcer Associations?

The notion that the amygdala is central to associating rewards, as well as fear, with stimuli has been traced to Weiskrantz's (1956) early observations on monkeys with amygdala lesions: "The effect of amygdalectomy, it is suggested, is to make it difficult for reinforcing stimuli, whether positive or negative, to become established and recognized as such" (p. 390). Many amygdala neurons respond differentially to rewarded stimuli (Rolls, 1992; Ono & Nishijo, 1992). Neurophysiological data showing strongly held reward-related responses, and their relation to unlearned reinforcing stimuli, have supported the view that the amygdala maintains neural representations of stimulus-reward associations (Rolls, 1992; Muramoto et al., 1993). Thus the notion that the amygdala plays a critical role in mediating stimulus-reward associations is widely held (Kesner, 1992; McDonald & White, 1993; Gaffan 1992).

Yet, in studies on learning after damage to the amygdala, this notion has proven difficult to establish unambiguously in experimental analyses (Everitt & Robbins, 1992; Gallagher & Chiba, 1996; Gaffan, 1992). Thus the findings across a broad variety of learning tasks have indicated that amygdala lesions sometimes result in impairments in simple stimulus-reward learning tasks and sometimes do not (Jones & Mishkin, 1972; Cahill & McGaugh, 1990; Gaffan & Harrison, 1987; Gaffan et al., 1988; Murray & Gaffan, 1994; Everitt et al., 1989; Holland & Gallagher, 1993a, 1993b). Some studies have specifically contrasted the importance of the amygdala in appetitive and aversive learning. For example, Cahill and Mc-

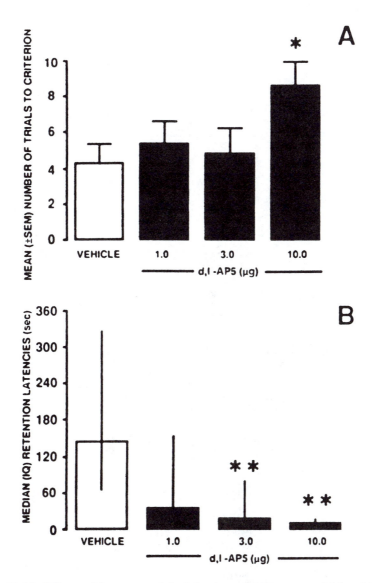

Figure 12.12. Effects of intra-amygdala injection of AP5 on acquisition (A) and later retention (B) of potentiated acoustic startle. Only the highest dose affected acquisition, whereas a lower dose blocked retention. (Reproduced, with permission, from McGaugh, Introini-Collison, Cahill, Kim, & Liang, 1992; Copyright John Wiley & Sons, Inc.)

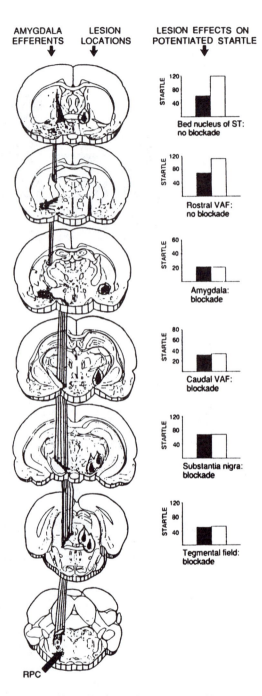

Figure 12.13. Summary of the effects of damage to different stages of amygdala efferents on fear potentiated startle. Blockade occurs at any stage of the efferent pathway. (Reproduced, with permission, from Davis, 1992; Copyright John Wiley & Sons, Inc.)

Gaugh (1990) trained rats with neurotoxic amygdala lesions on acquisition of a Y-maze task for a water reward, then gave the animals a foot shock while drinking and observed subsequent retardation in the latency to drink. Amygdala lesions had no effect on the appetitive component of the task but considerably reduced training on the aversive component (Figure 12.14). While this dissociation could reflect a distinction in different motivational influences, Cahill and McGaugh suggested the different results may only reflect differences in the levels of arousal produced by the different reinforcers.

McDonald and White (1993) suggested that the mixture of results may be explained by distinguishing cases where learning can be mediated by the establishment of stimulus-response associations even in the absence of normal stimulus-reward associations. Thus, in most simple conditioning and discrimination tasks, animals are rewarded for producing a specific behavior, for example, a choice and approach toward a particular stimulus. In such cases, they argued, the reinforcer increased the likelihood of that response mediated by brain systems that do not involve the amygdala. In particular, in their study of different forms of radial maze learning discussed in the preceding chapter, animals with amygdala lesions normally acquired consistent approach responses to illuminated maze arms when specifically rewarded for such approach behaviors. By contrast, when the training involved simply feeding animals in an illuminated maze arm, with no requirement for an approach behavior, amygdala lesions blocked a subsequent conditioned place preference. This distinction was made particularly compelling by a demonstration that neostriatal lesions had the opposite pattern of effects, blocking the learning of approach responses, but not affecting the conditioned place preference.

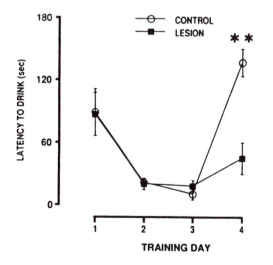

Figure 12.14. Performance of normal control rats and rats with amygdala lesions on learning to approach a drinking spout, then avoiding it after pairing with footshock on day 3. (Reproduced, with permission, from McGaugh, Introini-Collison, Cahill, Kim, & Liang, 1992; Copyright John Wiley & Sons, Inc.)

Another behavioral paradigm that distinguished stimulus-reward from stimulus-response associations is second-order conditioning, a procedure in which animals are trained to associate a stimulus with reward, and then to use that stimulus as a reinforcer for subsequent conditioning. In one such task, thirsty rats were trained to associate a visual stimulus with their approach to a dispenser where they received water (Everitt & Robbins, 1992). Subsequently they were trained to discriminate between two levers, one followed by the visual stimulus and an empty water dispenser, as a secondary-order reinforcer; the other lever was inactive. Normal animals pressed both bars somewhat, and pressed much more the bar associated with the second-order reinforcer (Figure 12.15, top). Amygdala lesions reduced responding on the lever associated with the second-order reinforcer without affecting bar pressing on the alternate bar. This pattern of results is consistent with McDonald and White's proposal that response learning is intact, but animals with amygdala lesions do not differentially associate a specific bar with its acquired reinforcing properties. Similar results were obtained using second-order conditioning to a sexual reinforcer. Initially male rats are allowed to interact sexually with an estrous female in the presence of a visual stimulus (a light). Subsequently the male rats could be trained to bar-press in the presence of the light. Normal animals bar-pressed at high rates for this second-order reinforcer, and amygdala lesions reduced responding to the second-order reinforcer (Figure 12.15, bottom).

The same pattern of results has been obtained in experiments on monkeys. Amygdala lesions have no effect on traditional forms of simple discrimination learning. However, impairments have been observed in the acquisition of preferences of novel foods (Gaffan, 1994a) and when the animals must change responses to shifting reward contingencies (Jones & Mishkin, 1972). In addition, Gaffan and Harrison (1987) showed that amygdala lesions interfered with the acquisition of a visual discrimination associated with a secondary auditory reinforcer. In this task, intact monkeys were initially trained on visual discriminations in which the food reward was given along with an auditory stimulus. Following amygdalectomy they were trained on new discrimination problems in which responses to one stimulus were followed by the second-order auditory reinforcer, and food reward was given only upon completion of the task. Bilateral amygdalectomy severely retarded learning (Figure 12.16). In addition, disconnection of the amygdala from auditory input had the same effect, but disconnection of the amygdala from visual association cortex had no effect on this type of learning. These results confirm the findings on second-order conditioning in rats and support the view that the effect of amygdalectomy is to block the association between the primary reinforcer (food) and the secondary reinforcer (auditory cue), but not the associations between the visual stimuli and the secondary reinforcer.

Additional evidence of the notion that the amygdala mediates stimulus-reward associations comes from tasks where animals must remember the magnitude of reward over a delay period. For example, Kesner et al. (1989) presented rats with either one or seven pieces of food in different arms of a radial maze. After a delay period the rats could obtain an additional reward by choosing the arm with the larger reward. Lesions of the basolateral nucleus had no effect on

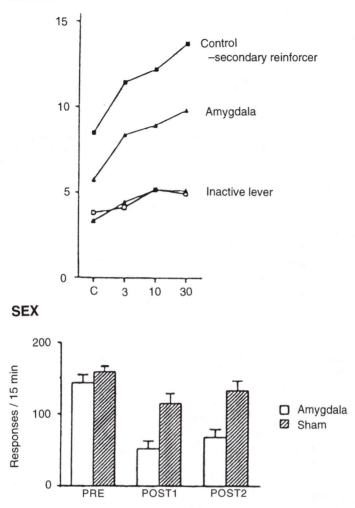

Figure 12.15. Effects of excitotoxic amygdala lesions on responses for secondary reinforcers. Top: Increased bar press responding to doses (µg) of d-amphetamine. Bottom: Bar pressing during a preoperative and two post operative sessions. (Reproduced, with permission, from Everitt & Robbins, 1992; Copyright John Wiley & Sons, Inc.)

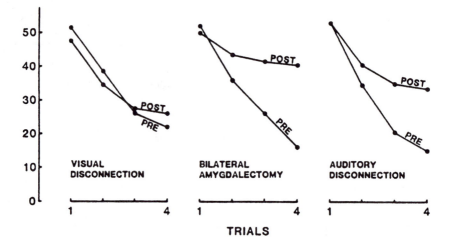

Figure 12.16. Effects of amygdala lesions on acquisition of a discrimination for a secondary reinforcer in monkeys. Scores are compared over the first four trials on different discrimination problems presented pre- or post-operatively. (Reproduced, with permission, from Gaffan & Harrison, 1987; Copyright Society for Neuroscience.)

performance in this task, but lesions of the central nucleus produced a severe, delay-dependent deficit in memory for reward magnitude (Figure 12.17).

A remaining issue concerns whether there are distinct pathways within or through the amygdala that support different types of stimulus-reinforcer learning. On the one hand, anatomical evidence indicates that the main sensory inputs to the amygdala arrive via the lateral and, to some extent the basolateral nuclei, and that the main outputs are from the central nucleus. This suggests that damage to either set of nuclei would necessarily have similar effects on learning. However, there have been several reports that lesions within these amygdala nuclei have dissociable effects on performance on different tasks. For example, in contrast to the findings of Kesner et al. (1989) just described, Peinado-Manzano (1989) reported that lesions of the lateral amygdala nucleus, but not the central nucleus, disrupted memory for a visual association with reward magnitude. Also, Hatfield et al. (1992) reported that basolateral nucleus damage, but not central nucleus lesions, blocked an odor-potentiated taste aversion. More recently Kilcross et al. (1997) reported that central nucleus lesions blocked a classically conditioned fear response but did not prevent discrimination between two bars, one of which was associated with the fear-producing stimulus. Conversely, basolateral nucleus lesions had the opposite pattern of effects. Vazdarjanova and McGaugh (1998) shocked rats in one arm of a three-arm maze, and found that basolateral nucleus lesions eliminated conditioned freezing when the rat was in the arm associated with shock. But the animals with basolateral amygdala lesions still learned to avoid the arm where they previously had been shocked—their latencies to enter the arm associated with shock were elevated and they spent less time in that arm than a nonshocked group of animals with the same lesions. However, the animals with basolateral lesions did not show as robust discrimination between the arms

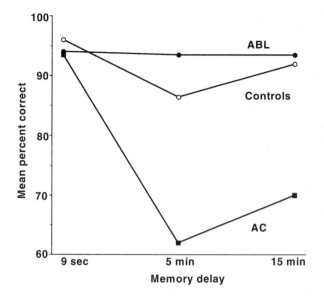

Figure 12.17. Performance of normal control rats and rats with lesions of the basolateral amygdala (ABL) or central nucleus of the amygdala (AC) on memory for reward magnitude. (Reproduced, with permission, from Kenser, 1992; Copyright John Wiley & Sons, Inc.)

as normal rats. The interpretation of these results with regard to whether they truly reflect distinct affective learning systems has been brought into question (Nader & LeDoux, 1997; Fanselow & LeDoux, 1999). Nevertheless, it is tempting to speculate on the possibility that the minor inputs to all the amygdala nuclei, combined with the divergent output pathways, might support different forms of affective learning and memory (see Gallagher & Chiba, 1996).

A Brain System for Arousal and Attention that Modulates Learning and Memory

In addition to its functions within a specific brain system for emotional learning, it has become increasingly clear that the amygdala is also a nodal structure in the modulation of memory processes by diverse pathways (Gallagher & Holland, 1994; Gallagher & Chiba, 1996; McGaugh et al., 1992, 1996). Within the general framework of modulatory influences, there are two proposals about how emotional experiences can affect memory processing. One proposal is that the amygdala, and particularly the central nucleus, plays a critical role in arousal and attention during ongoing learning experiences (Kapp et al., 1990, 1992). The other proposal is that the amygdala modulates the consolidation of recently acquired memories via arousal-activated hormonal influences that pervade all memory systems of the brain (McGaugh, 1996). These two proposals will be discussed in turn.

The influence of emotional arousal on attention during learning may be mediated by a collection of ascending systems in the pontine, mesencephalic, and basal forebrain areas that receive inputs from the central amygdala nucleus. These areas project to the striatum and the superior colliculus, which are associated with orienting behaviors, and to widespread areas of the cerebral cortex in a pathway associated with increased vigilance and attention (Figure 12.18). The former subcortical targets may initiate orienting and attentional processes directly, whereas the cortical influence may reflect arousal. Kapp and colleagues (1990, 1992) have provided substantial data showing that there is rapid differential conditioning of neurons in the central amygdala nucleus associated with fear conditioning (Figure 12.19), and correspondingly that lesions of this area block the particular form of conditioned heart rate responses. In addition to its influence over unconditioned and conditioned reflexive responses, Kapp and colleagues have argued that amygdala activation results in a generalized arousal of cortical processing mechanisms. They have shown that stimulation of the central nucleus elicits low-voltage fast activity associated with an aroused state in the cortex, and that activity in the central nucleus during heart rate conditioning naturally precedes episodes of neocortical fast activity.

Consistent with these observations, Gallagher and colleagues (1990) found that rats with central nucleus lesions were deficient in acquiring conditioned orienting responses. Initially rats were trained to approach a food cup in response to a light stimulus, then they were presented with a tone stimulus paired with the light. Rats with central nucleus lesions were unaffected in learning conditioned

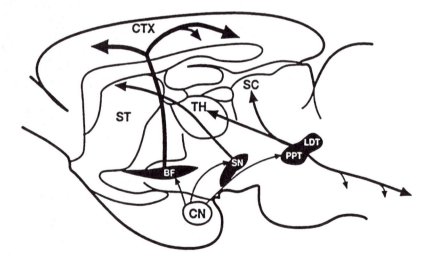

Figure 12.18. A schematic diagram of pathways that might mediate control of attention by the amygdala. CN = central amygdala nucleus; CTX = cortex; ST = striatum; TH = thalamus; SC = superior colliculus; BF = basal forebrain; SN = substantia nigra; PPT = pedunculopontine nucleus; LDT = lateral dorsal tegmental nucleus. (Reproduced, with permission, from Gallagher & Holland, 1994; Copyright National Academy of Sciences, U.S.A.)

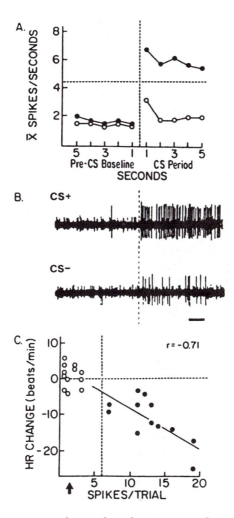

Figure 12.19. Firing patterns of central nucleus neurons during training in conditioned bradycardia. A. Averaged responses of 13 neurons prior to and during CS+ (filled circles) and CS– (open circles) presentations. B. Examples of responses to the stimuli. C. Correlation between heart rate (HR) changes and the firing of the neuron whose activity is depicted in B. (Reproduced, with permission, from Kapp, Whalen, Supple, & Pascoe, 1991; Copyright John Wiley & Sons, Inc.)

approach responses to visual and auditory stimuli and even acquired a second-order conditioned approach response to the tone at the normal rate in this task. In this study the investigators also observed orienting responses the animals made to the conditioning stimuli, responses that consisted of rearing on the hind legs and orientation to the light source. In striking contrast to no effect of the amygdala lesions on conditioned approach responses, conditioned orienting responses that normal animals made to the visual CS were abolished (Figure 12.20).

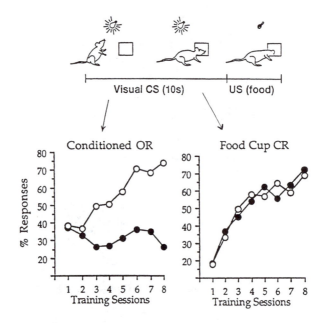

Figure 12.20. Conditioned orienting paradigm (top) and performance of the conditioned orienting response (OR) and conditioned responses (CR) to the food cup in intact rats (open circles) and rats with central nucleus lesions (filled circles). (Reproduced, with permission, from Gallagher & Holland, 1994; Copyright National Academy of Sciences, U.S.A.)

Further evidence of a critical role for the amygdala in attentional processes was obtained in studies on the modulation of attention by changes in stimulus expectancies. In these studies Holland and Gallagher (1993a, 1993b) found that manipulations that result in increases in attention by normal rats were blocked by central nucleus lesions, but manipulations that caused decreases in attention were unaffected. These studies employed procedures for measuring classically conditioned behavioral responses to tones and lights, and for altering attention to these cues. One procedure involved the "blocking" paradigm, in which pretraining with one stimulus retarded conditioning to a subsequently added stimulus. The reduction in conditioning to the added cue has been attributed to poor attention paid to a stimulus that carries no added information. In this study some animals first experienced pairings of a light and food and subsequently developed conditioned expectancy responses to the light (Figure 12.21). Subsequently all animals were given pairings of a light-plus-tone and food and were then tested for conditioned responses to the tone alone. Blocking was observed as a diminished response to the tone by the animals pretrained with the light alone and food. Another procedure that had the opposite effect was "unblocking." This paradigm was identical to the blocking paradigm, except that during the light-plus-tone phase, the amount of associated food was changed. This change in the level of food associated with the added tone cue does have new informational value

Group	Training procedure	Phase 1	Phase 2	Test
Control	High US, phase 2 only		Light/tone → US_H	Tone
Blocking	High US, phases 1 and 2	Light → US_H	Light/tone → US_H	Tone
Blocking	Low US, phases 1 and 2	Light → US_L	Light/tone → US_L	Tone
Unblocking	High US shifted to low US	Light → US_H	Light/tone → US_L	Tone

US_H, high-value US; US_L, low-value US; →, cued paired with US.

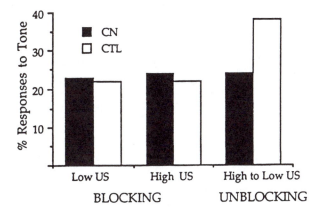

Figure 12.21. Blocking and unblocking. Top: Experimental design. Bottom: Performance of normal control rats (CTL) and rats with central nucleus lesions (CN) on different experimental protocols. (Reproduced, with permission, from Gallagher & Holland, 1994; Copyright National Academy of Sciences, U.S.A.)

and results normally in strong conditioning to the tone. Central nucleus lesions had no effect on blocking but prevented unblocking (Figure 12.21).

Another study exploited the observation that rats normally increase attention to a cue after an alteration in its predictive relationships. In this study (Holland & Gallagher, 1993b) rats were initially presented with light and tone combinations, followed by a food reward on half the trials (Figure 12.22). In a second phase of training some animals continued with the same procedure, whereas in other rats, during the unreinforced trials the light was presented alone. This procedure increases attention to the light stimulus as reflected in a subsequently increased conditioning rate to light and food pairings. However, this effect of increased attention was prevented in animals with central amygdala lesions. Indeed these animals conditioned less well to the light after presentations of light alone, suggesting greater habituation or some other effect counter to increased attention (Gallagher & Holland, 1994). Combining their results with those of other studies, Gallagher and Holland argued that a major influence of the amygdala in learning is to increase attention to predictive stimuli.

Training condition	Phase 1 (consistent light–tone relationship)	Phase 2 (experimental change in light–tone relationship)	Phase 3 (test of learning to light)
Consistent	L → T → food; L → T	L → T → food; L → T	L → food
Inconsistent	L → T → food; L → T	L → T → food; L	L → food

Half of the trials in phases 1 and 2 are reinforced with food; the other half are nonreinforced trials. In phase 3 the trials are always reinforced with food. L, light; T, tone.

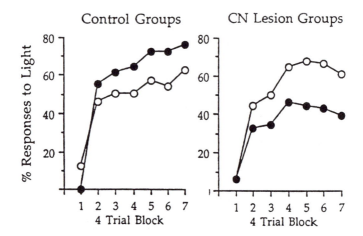

Figure 12.22. Incrementing attention to stimuli by changing the predictive relationships between two cues. Top: Experimental design. (Reproduced, with permission, from Holland & Gallagher, 1993; Copyright American Psychological Association.) Bottom: Performance during Phase 3 in groups with consistent prior experience (open circles) and inconsistent prior experience (filled circles). (Reproduced, with permission, from Gallagher & Holland, 1994; Copyright National Academy of Sciences, U.S.A.)

Influencing Memory by Hormonal Activation Associated with Emotional Arousal

An additional distinct line of current research implicates the amygdala as a critical nodal point in the modulation of all types of memory through emotional arousal. This work indicates that affectively charged experiences that activate stress hormone production begin a cascade of neurochemical and neural events that influence the amount of memory consolidation broadly within the brain's memory systems. According to this view of emotional influences on memory, the amygdala is a main target of stress hormone activation, its activation is modulated by other neurohormonal systems, and its targets of influence include the hippocampal and neostriatal memory systems introduced above.

Stressful events that activate the sympathetic nervous system and pituitary-adrenal axis result in the release of epinephrine and glucocorticoids by the adrenal glands. These hormones have a variety of effects associated with the "flight-or-fight" response, including increased heart rate and blood pressure, diversion of blood flow to the brain and muscles, and mobilization of energy stores. There is now a wealth of evidence that another effect of this activation is to improve memory storage for experiences surrounding stress activation, and that the amygdala is critical to this influence on memory.

Investigations on the facilitation of memory by adrenal hormone activation in animals has largely focused on the step-through inhibitory avoidance task and posttraining injections of drugs. In this task rats are initially placed in a small, well-illuminated chamber that is attached to a larger, dimly lit area. When a door separating these chambers opens, the rat typically steps through to the larger compartment, where the floor is subsequently electrified. After a brief period of foot shocks the animal is allowed to escape back to the small chamber. In later tests of memory for this aversive experience, the animal is again placed in the small chamber, and its latency to step-through is measured. Thus the effect of training is to inhibit subsequent entry into the aversive compartment.

Many of the studies of memory modulation involve the systemic injection or brain infusion of drugs after the initial learning, with the common result that subsequent memory performance is altered. The effect on performance typically depends on administration of the drug within minutes after training; there is no effect if drug adminstration is postponed for an hour or more. The posttraining administration procedure eliminates the possibility that the drugs are altering perception, arousal, or motor performance during the learning experience. Conversely, this methodology, combined with the time dependency of the efficacy of the drug administration, provides strong evidence that the neurochemical events involved influence the after-learning consolidation of memories.

There is now extensive evidence that administration of epinephrine or adrenal glucocorticoids improves memory for inhibitory avoidance, and that these effects are mediated by the amygdala. In an elegant systematic series of studies, Mc-Gaugh and colleagues (1992, 1996) have provided a framework for the pathway by which these effects are exerted (Figure 12.23). According to their scheme, glucocorticoids released during stressful events, or administered by injection, can enter the blood-brain barrier and influence steroid receptors in the brain directly. Epinephrine does not enter the blood-brain barrier easily, however, and so it is likely that its effects are exerted via peripheral stimulation. This conclusion is supported by experiments showing that a β-adrenergic antagonist that does not pass the blood-brain barrier blocks the memory-enhancing effects of epinephrine administration. The suspected target of peripheral epinephrine is β-adrenergic receptors on vagus nerve afferents that project to the nucleus of the solitary tract. This nucleus in turn projects into the amygdala, where its afferents release norepinephrine (NE). Supporting this view of the circuitry are studies showing that inactivation of the nucleus of the solitary tract by a local anesthetic blocks the effect of peripheral administration of epinephrine. In addition, other evidence shows that the foot shock results in the release of NE within the amygdala (Figure 12.24). Furthermore, NE infused directly into the amygdala posttraining enhances memory storage, and amygdala lesions or an NE antagonist infused into the amygdala blocks memory enhancement by peripheral epinephrine administration.

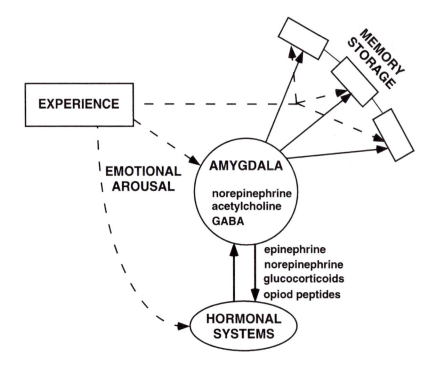

Figure 12.23. Schematic diagram of relationships between the amygdala and other systems, showing how the amygdala is influenced by hormonal systems and experience and can modulate memory storage in several memory systems.

The effects of glucocorticoids on memory are remarkably similar to those of epinephrine. Peripheral treatment with glucocorticoids enhances memory, and this effect is blocked by lesions of the stria terminalis. The effect of glucocorticoids appears to be mediated selectively by the basolateral nucleus of the amygdala; a glucocorticoid receptor agonist infused into that nucleus, but not the central amygdala nucleus, enhances memory; and lesions of the basolateral nucleus, but not the central nucleus, block the memory-enhancing effects of glucocorticoids (Figure 12.25). Basolateral amygdala activation by glucocorticoids involves NE release, as shown by blockade of the effects of glucocorticoids by local infusion of a β-adrenergic antagonist. These responses of the amygdala are modulated by multiple other neurochemical systems. In particular local infusions of agonists and antagonists of GABA and opioids have demonstrated that these substances inhibit the release of NE in the amygdala and influence memory performance accordingly. In addition, other findings implicate a muscarinic cholinergic mechanism at a later synapse within the amygdala, providing yet another modulatory influence over this system.

Although most of the research on memory modulation involves the inhibitory avoidance task, consistent effects are observed on discrimination-learning and maze-learning tasks. In particular, one study has shown that these influences extend specifically to the types of memory mediated by the hippocampus and neo-

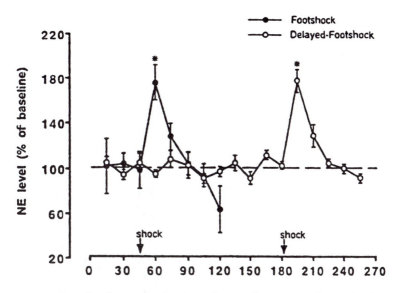

Figure 12.24. Footshock results in the release of norepinephrine (NE) in the amygdala. (Reproduced, with permission, from Galvez, Mesches, & McGaugh, 1996; Copyright Academic Press.)

striatum. In this study Packard and colleagues (1994) trained rats on two different versions of the Morris water maze task. In one, learning was cued by a visible marker at the escape site (Figure 12.26), and in the other, the platform was hidden (Figure 12.27). In previous studies the same team had shown that learning of the cued-platform task depends on the neostriatum and learning the hidden-platform task depends on the hippocampus (Packard & McGaugh, 1992). Animals were implanted bilaterally with cannuli in the caudate nucleus, dorsal hippocampus, or amygdala and, after recovery, trained in a single session on one of the tasks. Posttraining intrahippocampal infusions of d-amphetamine, which is an NE agonist, enhanced later retention on the spatial task, whereas intracaudate infusions had no effect (Figure 12.27). Conversely, posttraining intracaudate infusions of d-amphetamine enhanced later retention on the cued task, whereas intrahippocampal infusions had no effect (Figure 12.26). Posttraining intra-amygdala infusions of d-amphetamine enhanced retention on both tasks. A follow-up study was conducted to examine whether the effect of amygdala infusions involved an influence on hippocampal and neostriatal mechanisms or whether the enhancement was the result of a direct involvement of the amygdala in performance. Animals were trained on the two versions of the task, then given posttraining injections of d-amphetamine into the amygdala, as in the first study. Then, prior to the retention testing, the amygdala was inactivated to eliminate the possibility that it was exerting a direct effect on retention performance. These inactivations did not block the enhancement effect, consistent with the view that the intra-amygdala infusions had exerted their effects via projections to the hippocampus and amygdala.

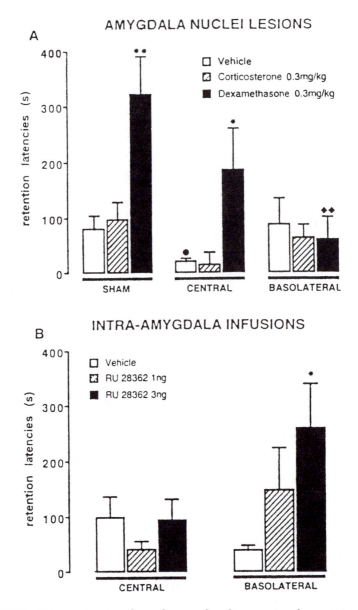

Figure 12.25. Latency to step through to a chamber previously associated with shock. A. Rats with sham lesions of amygdala nuclei treated with systemic injections immediately after training. Basolateral lesions block the memory enhancing effect of dexamethasone. B. The effects of intra-amygdala infusions of a glucocorticoid agonist. Only injections into the basolateral nucleus are effective. (Reproduced, with permission, from Roozendaal & McGaugh, 1996; Copyright Academic Press.)

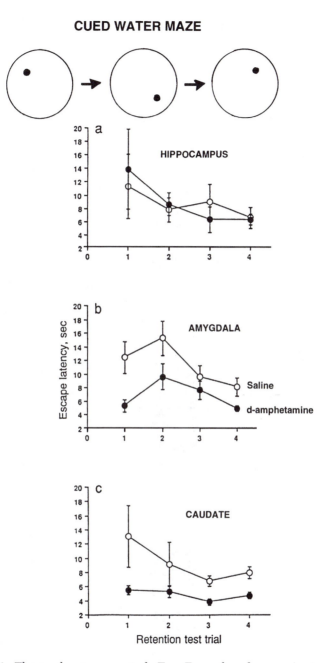

Figure 12.26. The cued water maze task. Top: Examples of successive trials where the positions of a visible platform are varied. Bottom: Effects of post-training injections into each of the indicated structures on retention performance. (Reproduced, with permission, from Packard, Cahill, & McGaugh, 1994; Copyright National Academy of Sciences, U.S.A.)

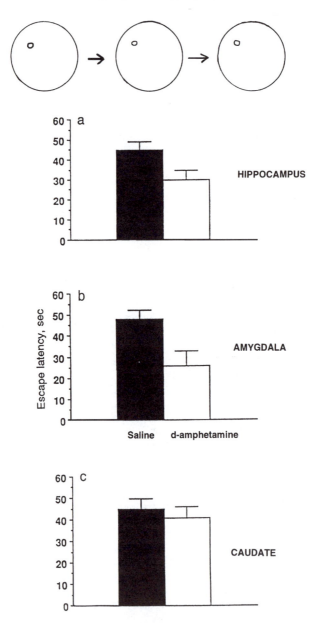

Figure 12.27. The spatial water maze task. Top: Examples of successive trials where the position of a submerged platform is not varied. Bottom: Effects of post-training injections into each of the indicated structures on retention performance. (Reproduced, with permission, from Packard, Cahill, & McGaugh, 1994; Copyright National Academy of Sciences, U.S.A.)

Emotion and the Role of the Amygdala in
Enhancing Memory in Humans

Additional evidence that emotional arousal can affect different forms of memory, and that this effect is mediated by the amygdala, comes from studies in human subjects. In a series of experiments, Cahill and colleagues (1994, 1995, 1996; Cahill & McGaugh, 1998) have examined the influence of emotional content on declarative memory. Their test involves presentation of a series of slides and a narrative that tell a story about a mother and son involved in a traumatic accident or tell a control story with neutral emotional content. The story has three parts. In the beginning and end parts the emotional and neutral stories are quite similar and are low in emotional content. In the middle section of the emotional story, the boy is critically injured and the events are depicted graphically; in the neutral

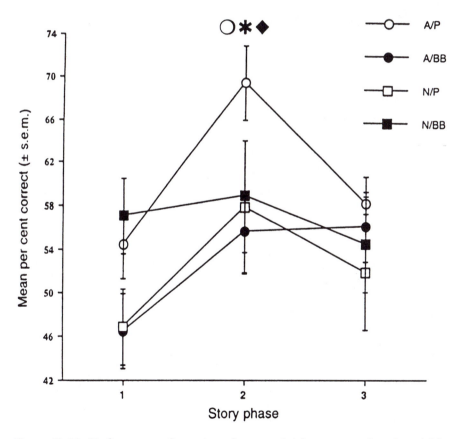

Figure 12.28. Performance of consistently neutral (phases 1 & 3) and variable (phase 2) components of the story. A/P = arousal story/placebo treatment; A/BB arousal story/beta-blocker; N/P = neutral story/placebo treatment; N/BB neutral story/beta-blocker. (Reproduced, with permission, from Cahill, Prins, Weber, & McGaugh, 1994; Copyright Macmillan Magazines Ltd.)

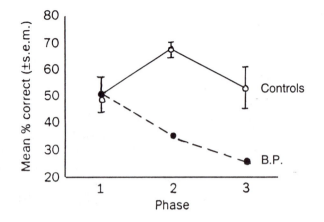

Figure 12.29. Performance of normal control subjects and patient B.P. on neutral (phases 1 & 3) and arousal (phase 2) phases of the emotional story. (Reproduced, with permission, from Cahill, Babinsky, Markowitsch, & McGaugh, 1995; Copyright Macmillan Magazines Ltd.)

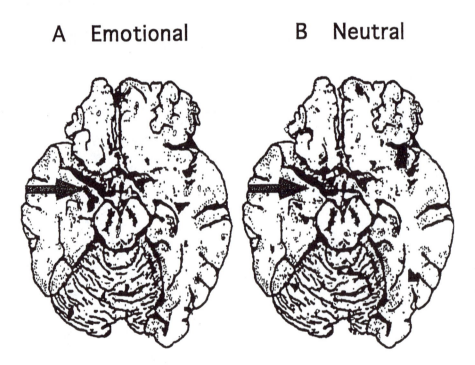

Figure 12.30. PET scans showing activations of the right amygdala (arrow on left) during presentations of emotional story component but not neutral component. (Reproduced, with permission, from Cahill, Haier, Fallons, Alkire, Tang, Keator, Wu, & McGaugh, 1996; Copyright National Academy of Sciences, U.S.A.)

story, no accident occurs. In subsequent delayed memory testing, normal subjects show enhanced recall for the emotional component of the story, as compared to the parallel section of the neutral story (Figure 12.28). By contrast, subjects given a β-adrenergic antagonist showed no facilitation of declarative memory for the emotional component of the story, even though they rated that component of the story as strongly emotional and their memory performance on other parts of the story was fully normal. Performance on the neutral story was not affected by the β-adrenergic antagonist, showing that there was no general effect of the drug on story memory. A subsequent study has now shown that an adrenergic agonist further enhances memory for the emotional component of the story.

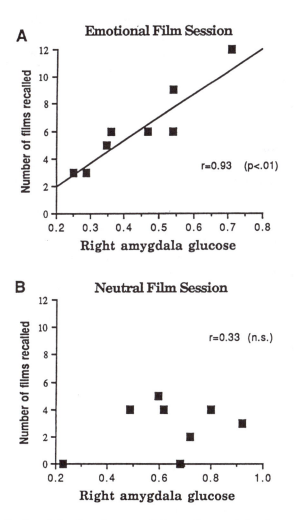

Figure 12.31. Scatterplots showing correlation of amygdala glucose utilization with recall of the emotional story phase but not that for the neutral story phase. (Reproduced, with permission, from Cahill, Haier, Fallons, Alkire, Tang, Keator, Wu, & McGaugh, 1996; Copyright National Academy of Sciences, U.S.A.)

The amygdala has been strongly implicated in the enhancement of memory for emotional events in humans. A patient with Urbach-Wiethe disease, a disorder that results in selective bilateral amygdala damage, was tested in the emotional story paradigm. This patient failed to show the normal enhancement of memory for the emotional part of the story (Figure 12.29). The patient performed as well as controls on the initial neutral segment of the story and rated the emotional material as affectively strong. In a complementary brain-imaging study on normal human subjects, the amygdala was activated during the viewing of emotional material, and this activation was related to enhanced memory for that material. In different PET scanning sessions subjects viewed film clips that were strong or neutral in emotional content. The amount of PET activation in the right amygdala was greater for the emotional than the neutral stories, and memory for this material was greater than that for the neutral stories (Figure 12.30). Furthermore, the amount of amygdala activation was correlated with performance in a delayed test of memory for the material in the emotional films but not in the neutral films (Figure 12.31).

Multiple Emotional Memory Systems that Involve the Amygdala

Combining the findings across all the studies presented in this chapter, it is apparent that there are multiple influences of emotion on memory, and the nodal point in all these influences is the amygdala. It seems most likely this confluence of emotional memory systems within the amygdala is more a consequence of the convergent inputs and divergent outputs of this area of the brain. Thus, on the basis of the evidence presented here, it seems reasonable to suggest there are multiple emotional memory systems that involve the amygdala (see also Fanselow & LeDoux, 1999). One of these systems, or one set of systems, involves specific pathways for the attachment of perceptions to emotions, and to emotional output effectors. Another set of systems involves more general influences of emotional arousal on memory. One of these influences is mediated by a neural pathway that increases memory processing during ongoing learning, whereas another influence involves a hormonal pathway for postlearning modulation of consolidation processes. These multiple aspects of emotional memory, and different types of emotional memory, are not incompatible. Instead, they could work largely in concert, both mediating acquisition of emotional responses and modulating memory for associated information processed by other systems.

13

Habits, Skills, and Procedural Memory

Although we usually think of motor performance or response output as distinct from memory and take pains in empirical studies to manipulate and assess memory independently of performance (and vice versa), it is clear that motor performance and memory are intimately connected. Motor performance is the voluntary output pathway of the brain—the primary means of behavioral expression. The current state of our repertoire of behavioral output or motor performance is surely a function of memory (i.e., of what we've learned). From typing the manuscript for this book, to driving a car, to running downfield and catching a thrown football, to the various actions we perform in everyday life, our motor performances reflect the operation of various *motor programs* that we have learned over the course of our lifetime. And these programs are continually modified by experience, tuned by repeated practice. One of the more remarkable behavioral phenomena is the continued increase in motor skill with practice, as seen, for example, in the systematic speed-up of performance across trials in various motor tasks ranging from typing (Grudin & Larochell, 1982) to cigar rolling (Welford, 1968). This speed-up continues indefinitely, for as long as practice continues, with the performance function following a power law—a phenomenon observed so reliably that it's called the *power law of practice* (Snoddy, 1926).

What are the circuits and properties of this kind of memory? What might it share with, and how is it distinct from, declarative memory? These are the issues of this present chapter. To anticipate, as was the case for the relationship between emotion and memory, there are multiple aspects of motor performance and correspondingly distinct pathways and mechanisms by which memory impacts and shapes motor performance.

From the perspective of the study of motor systems, a number of investigators have separated motor memory into two general types (e.g., Hallet et al., 1996).

One type involves adaptations (i.e., sensorimotor adjustments of reflexes), such as changing the force exerted to compensate for a new load, or conditioned reflexes that involve novel motor responses to a new sensory contingency. The other type involves sequence learning, the acquisition and refinement of long action sequences in response to highly complex stimuli, such as the learning seen in the complicated learned repertoires necessary to play a well-practiced tune on the piano.

Several examples of motor learning systems have been well studied, embodying one or another of these two general types of motor memory, and will be considered here. The current review cannot be fully comprehensive but will instead outline the essential properties of some of these systems. Our focus is on the distinct pathways critical to the acquisition of habits—that aspect of motor skill learning that refers to acquired, stereotyped, and unconscious behavioral repertoires. Understand that motor skill learning itself is just one aspect or example of procedural memory—involving the tuning and modification of, in this case, motor-system-specific systems. We turn now to a brief overview of the anatomy of the brain systems that contribute to habit (or motor skill) learning, and then we consider the roles of particular key structures within these systems.

Overview of Motor System Anatomy
Relevant to Habit Learning

The anatomy of motor systems that mediate habit learning is complex and so cannot be covered exhaustively here. This review will focus on a number of pathways that have been associated with different aspects of the acquisition of habits (see Kandel et al., 1991, for a more comprehensive treatment of the pathways). At the top level of these various circuits is primary motor cortex (although it is now well understood that this cortical area does not so much execute movement as direct the force and flow of contractions executed at the spinal level). An additional critical structure is the premotor cortex, which plays a central role in the preparation for movement and in the coordination of bilateral movements and motor sequencing (Wise, 1996a). These motor cortical areas work in close concert with two major subcortical structures: the striatum and the cerebellum (Figure 13.1). Each of these subcortical structures forms the nodal point in a major circuit "loop" that begins with downward projections from the cortex and ends in a thalamic route back to the cortex. However, there are important differences between these two pathways in the specific loci of the sources of cortical input and output, and in the brain stem and spinal cord connections.

The Striatal Subsystem

The striatum (or neostriatum) is the combination of the anatomically distinct caudate nucleus and putamen. It is a key input component of the basal ganglia, which also includes the globus pallidus, subthalamic nucleus, and substantia nigra. Although the focus here is on the striatum, where most of the recording and lesion studies have been centered, it should be kept in mind that this nucleus

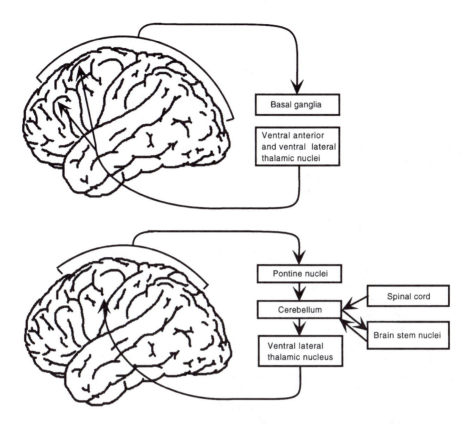

Figure 13.1. Two major motor system pathways. A. Connections from virtually every cortical area are sent to the basal ganglia. The major output of this subsystem is through the thalamus back to the frontal cortex. B. Connections from frontal and parietal cortical areas reach the pontine nuclei and cerebellum, which interacts directly with the spinal cord and brainstem motor and sensory nuclei. This system also has outputs via the thalamus back to parts of the frontal cortex. (Reproduced, with permission, from Kandel, Schwartz, & Jessell, 1991; Copyright The McGraw-Hill Companies.)

is just one part of the basal ganglia system. The striatum receives its cortical inputs from the entire cerebral cortex, and these projections are capable of activity-dependent changes in responsiveness (Calabresi et al., 1996). These projections are topographically organized into divergent and reconvergent projections into modules within the striatum that could sort and associate somatotopic and motor representations (Graybiel et al., 1994). The striatum projects mainly to the globus pallidus, which interacts with the subthalamic nucleus. Outputs of this circuit project mainly to the ventral anterior and ventrolateral nuclei in the thalamus. The projections from these thalamic areas target both the premotor and motor cortex and the prefrontal association cortex. Notably, there are minimal projections of this circuit to the brain stem motor nuclei and none to the spinal motor apparatus.

The anatomical connectivity of the striatum indicates that it is not involved directly in controlling motor output. Instead, the connections to premotor and prefrontal cortex suggest that the corticostriatal loop contributes to higher motor functions, including, many believe, the planning and execution of complex motor sequences (Houk et al., 1995; Graybiel et al., 1994; Alexander et al., 1986). When considered together with the anatomical connections between ventral striatum and the limbic system, combined with behavioral evidence of interactions between the ventral striatum and amygdala-mediated reward mechanisms, the suggestion has arisen that the striatum may be involved more generally in the planning and execution of goal-oriented behavior (for recent reviews see Cador et al., 1989; White, 1997; Graybiel, 1995; Schultz et al., 1995; Kimura, 1995; Mink, 1996; Lawrence et al., 1998).

The Cerebellar Subsystem

The cerebellum is a distinctive structure, remarkable particularly for the regularities of its internal circuitry. It has several distinct subdivisions, associated with different sensory and motor functions. The cerebellum receives cortical input from a much more restricted cortical area than the striatum, including only the strictly sensorimotor areas projecting via the pontine nuclei into the lateral part of the cerebellar cortex. Like the striatal system, the cerebellum has a thalamic output route to the cerebral cortex, although the cortical target is also more restricted than that of the striatum, limited to motor and premotor cortex (although a recent study has reported efferents from the dentate nucleus of the cerebellum to the prefrontal cortex; Middleton & Strick, 1994). In addition, the cerebellum receives somatic sensory inputs directly from the spinal cord and has major bidirectional connections with brain stem nuclei associated with spinal cord functions. Based on these connections, and on behavioral and electrophysiological data to be discussed later in this chapter, the cerebellum is believed to more directly contribute to the execution of movements, and to the acquisition of habits in the form of learned reflexes and body adjustments to changing environmental inputs.

Having sketched briefly some of the properties of the striatal and cerebellar systems, the subsequent sections lay out what is known from studies of humans and animals about the role these systems play in habit learning.

The Striatal Habit System: Animal Studies

In chapters 2 and 11, the striatal habit system was introduced via experiments that dissociated this system from the hippocampal and amygdala memory systems. Those experiments provided evidence indicating a role for the striatum in the acquisition of specific stimulus-response associations, as contrasted with declarative memory and emotional memory functions of the hippocampal and amygdala systems, respectively. Here we elaborate on the role of the striatum in habit acquisition, considering further the nature and scope of learning mediated by this system. Recent reviews on this topic have been offered by Graybiel (1995), White (1997), and Wise (1996b).

Evidence for a critical role of the striatum in learning and memory dates back at least to the mid-1960s (Phillips & Carr, 1987; Oberg & Divac, 1979; White, 1997). Following damage or electrical stimulation to this area in animals, deficits were observed in spatial-delayed-response performance, simple avoidance learning, and other simple forms of differential conditioning or appetitively motivated sensory discrimination. One study showed a particularly striking dissociation of regions within the striatum in their effects on inhibition of approach behavior conditioned by different cues (Viaud & White, 1989). In this study, thirsty rats with lesions of the posteroventral or ventrolateral regions of the striatum were trained to approach a water spout over several days. Subsequently, they were given foot shocks in the same chamber in the presence of a conditioning cue, which was either a light or an odor. The animals were tested later for their latency to approach the water spout when the conditioning cue was present versus when it was absent. Animals with lesions of the posteroventral striatum failed to show discriminative avoidance of the light cue but showed good avoidance of the olfactory cue (Figure 13.2). Conversely, animals with ventrolateral striatal lesions failed to show discriminative avoidance of the olfactory cue but showed good avoidance of the light cue.

It was clear from the early studies, taken together, that the scope of striatal involvement is not limited to a particular sensory or motivational modality, or to a particular type of response output. The early work emphasized two aspects of striatal memory function. One of these was its involvement in "sensorimotor integration," including higher-order perceptual and mnemonic guidance of various forms of learned behavior. The other aspect, based on studies showing that electrical stimulation of the striatum immediately after learning disrupted subsequent retention performance, was involvement in memory consolidation for habits (see White, 1997). These will be described more below. However, note that the early studies preceded the emergence of ideas about multiple memory systems in the brain and so were not designed to explore the special properties of this memory system as distinct from others.

The studies by Packard and McDonald and their colleagues (Packard & McGaugh, 1996; McDonald & White, 1993) outlined above indicate that the striatum is essential for learning that involves acquisition of a consistent approach response to a specific stimulus. How broadly does this characterization apply to the larger body of data on lesions of the striatum in animals? Let's consider some of that larger literature. In addition to an earlier study dissociating hippocampal and striatal involvement in radial maze learning (Packard et al., 1989), other studies by the same investigators have provided parallel data on versions of the aversively motivated water maze task. For example, in one study by Packard and McGaugh (1992), rats with fornix transection or lesions of the striatum were trained on two variants of the water maze task that used the same stimuli but involved different stimulus-response demands. In both tasks, the animals were always presented with two rubber balls distinguished by different visual patterns as the learning cues. One of the cues was attached to a stable submerged platform on which the animals could climb in order to escape swimming, and the other cue was anchored to a thin pedestal that could not be mounted. In the "place-learning" task variant, the escape platform was always located in the same place in the maze, but the visual pattern on the cue above it varied randomly (Figure

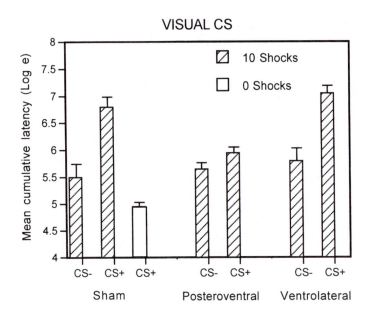

Figure 13.2. Performance (latency to approach a water spout) of normal control rats (sham) and rats with damage to different parts of the striatum in conditioning tasks that involve visual or olfactory conditioned stimuli. CS+ conditioning cue present; CS− conditioning cue absent. (Reproduced, with permission, from Viaud & White, 1989; Copyright Elsevier Science.)

13.3, top); here, the animal had to ignore the visual pattern and swim consistently to a particular location defined by extramaze stimuli. In the "visual discrimination" task variant, the positions of the cues varied, but the cue with a particular visual pattern was always mounted to the escape platform (Figure 13.4, top); here, the animal had to ignore the locations of previous escapes and consistently approach a particular visual pattern.

The results of this study indicated a clear double dissociation of hippocampal and striatal memory functions. Animals with fornix transection failed to acquire the place-learning variant of the task (Figure 13.3, bottom), performing hardly

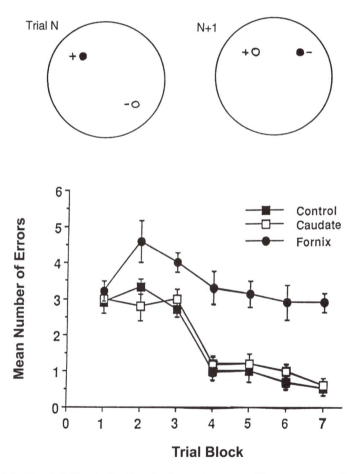

Figure 13.3. Spatial discrimination in the water maze. The same two stimuli described in Figure 13.3 were employed, but the escape platform was always in the same location regardless of which stimulus was nearby. (Reproduced, with permission, from Packard & McGaugh, 1992; Copyright American Psychological Association.)

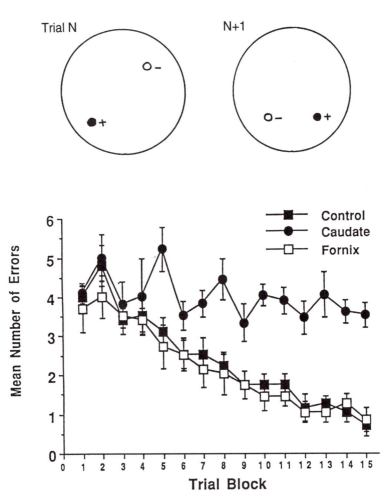

Figure 13.4. Visual discrimination in the water maze. The stimuli varied in location, and the escape platform was always identified by one particular visual cue (+) and not the other (–). (Reproduced, with permission, from Packard & McGaugh, 1992; Copyright American Psychological Association.)

better than chance (four correct choices out of each block of eight trials) over several training sessions. By contrast, rats with lesions of the striatum succeeded in learning to approach the correct location of the escape platform by the fourth training block, just as did normal rats. The results were precisely the opposite on the visual discrimination task variant: Animals with striatal lesions performed at chance levels over many training blocks, whereas rats with fornix transections, like normal rats, gradually acquired the pattern discrimination over the course of training (Figure 13.4, bottom).

In another study, by McDonald and White (1994), rats with fornix transection or striatal lesions were trained on the visible platform version of the water maze task, in which, from multiple starting points, they were to approach a platform that was visible above the surface of the water. Subsequently, the visible platform was replaced with a submerged platform in the same location for a single block of trials. Then, training continued with repetitions of multiple trial blocks with the visible platform and a single trial block with the submerged platform. Finally, the visible platform was moved to a new location, and the rats were tested in a single block of trials.

All rats quickly learned to swim to the visible platform. On the first test with the submerged platform after initial training, escape latencies were elevated for all groups. On subsequent trials with the submerged platform, normal rats and rats with caudate lesions quickly learned to approach the correct escape location with shorter latencies, approximating the performance level they had achieved with the visible platform. By contrast, rats with fornix lesions failed to improve on the submerged platform trials, consistent with their well-described deficits in place learning in the water maze. When the visible platform was moved to a new location, rats with fornix lesions swam directly to the visible platform despite its novel location, showing that their initial learning had been guided completely by the approach to the visible cue (Figure 13.5). In this condition, the performance of normal rats was also guided by the prominent visual cue. By contrast, rats with lesions of the striatum did not swim immediately to the visible platform but instead swam directly to its previous location and only subsequently to the visible platform at its new site. This finding indicates that the initial successful performance in striatally lesioned rats was guided primarily by learning the location of escape. Normal rats demonstrated they were capable of either learning strategy, whereas rats with fornix lesions were guided primarily by the visual cues. This pattern of results is entirely consistent with the earlier-described comparisons of hippocampal and striatal lesions. Furthermore, these data parallel those from the T-maze "place-versus-response" learning study of Packard and McGaugh (1996). They reveal that in water maze learning, too, even when initial learning performance is equivalent among animals with distinct brain damage, the representational strategies may differ qualitatively as revealed in subsequent probe tests (see also Whishaw et al., 1987).

These double dissociations of striatal and hippocampal functions followed on earlier studies showing a special role for the striatum in "egocentric" localization. Potegal (1972) first hypothesized that the striatum was involved in this kind of spatial learning, mediating navigation in space in terms of the direction and distance of items from the viewpoint of the observer. Potegal argued that such a view explains why animals with striatal damage perform poorly in delayed spatial response tasks, which require memory for an egocentrially defined location in space. Similarly, such a view would explain why rats with striatal lesions cannot learn left or right turns in the T-maze experiment or, in the previously described study by Kesner et al. (1993), why rats with striatal lesions failed to remember body-oriented turn directions. Additional evidence cited by Potegal (1972) included findings of impairment in rats with striatal lesions in learning to select the arm that was at a particular orientation (e.g., 30 degrees to the right) as it exited a start arm in a radial maze. Cook and Kesner's (1988) study distin-

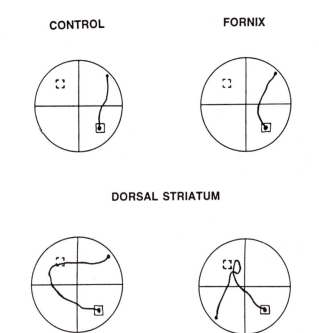

Figure 13.5. Examples of swim paths on the first trial (normal control and fornix lesioned rats) and first two trials (striatal lesioned rat) in which the escape platform was moved from its original location (dotted square) to a new locus and made visible (filled circle in square). (Reproduced, with permission, from McDonald & White, 1994; Copyright Academic Press.)

guished the striatum's role in egocentric as opposed to allocentric localization. In one experiment, a group of rats was trained on the standard eight-arm radial maze task, in which they were required to remember each of the arms they had visited based on their allocentric location in the room. The same rats were also trained in a different maze on a variant of the task in which they began each trial on an arbitrarily selected arm and were required to subsequently select an egocentrically defined adjacent arm. Rats with striatal lesions performed well on the standard radial maze (allocentric) task, but they could not learn the adjacent arm (egocentric) task (Figure 13.6). In a second experiment, rats were trained on two tasks in different radial mazes. In a place-learning (allocentric) task, only one arm of an eight-arm maze was consistently baited, and the rat began each trial from any of the remaining arms chosen at random. In a right-left discrimination (egocentric) task, the animal began each trial in the central area of the maze, and two randomly chosen adjacent arms were indicated for a choice. The rat had to choose only the left (or, for other rats, the right) of the two arms regardless of its absolute location. Here, too, rats with striatal lesions performed well on the place-learning task but did not learn the right-left discrimination task (Figure 13.6).

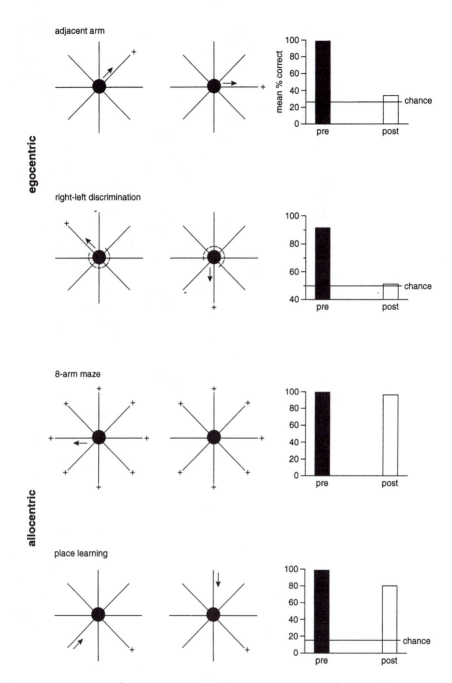

Figure 13.6. Pre- and post-operative performance of rats with striatal lesions on egocentric and allocentric spatial tasks. For each task two successive example trials are illustrated. + = rewarded arm; − = nonrewarded arm; arrow indicates beginning of run on a trial.

In other work, rats with striatal lesions were impaired in learning a three-arm radial maze (i.e., symmetrical Y maze) task in which rewards were contingent on a particular (e.g., left) turn, regardless of the arm used as the start arm (Mitchell & Hall, 1988b), and in learning a conventional Y-maze spatial discrimination task (Mitchell & Hall, 1988a). By contrast, they were unimpaired or even superior to normal rats in learning mazes where the goal arm was identified by distinctive visual cues (Mitchell & Hall, 1988a, 1988b).

Further detailed analyses have shown that the striatum is critical to generating responses in egocentric space (Carli et al., 1985, 1989; Brasted et al., 1997). These experiments required rats to perform a nose poke into a hole in a wall and then accurately identify the locus of an illuminated location to the right or left of the starting position (Figure 13.7). Unilateral lesions or depletion of dopamine in the striatum resulted in deficits in responding to lights presented on the contralateral side regardless of their absolute location. The lesions resulted in a systematic contralateral bias toward the nearest of alternative responses. Furthermore, re-gardless of the side of the target, the lesions increased the time required to with-draw from the starting nose poke but not the time to complete the second nose poke at the target location. The lengthening of the latency to initiate a response, observed wherever the target was presented, suggested that the impairment was a deficit in initiation of contralateral acts rather than in their completion. A control experiment was very illuminating, involving a variant of the task in which rats were not required to make a lateralized response but were simply required to respond to the same location behind the starting point regardless of where the target was presented. Rats with unilateral striatal lesions were intact on this task even when the stimuli were presented in the contralateral target locations, show-ing their deficit could be attributed to the lateralized response initiation and not inattention to the target cue.

Taken collectively, the extant animal literature suggests that the deficit follow-ing striatal damage is, or includes, an impairment in generating behavioral re-sponses to important environmental stimuli. The deficit extends to both ap-proach and avoidance responses and to both egocentric spatial and nonspatial stimuli. Even this characterization is not sufficiently comprehensive to explain the full range of impairments, however, such as those observed in reference mem-ory choices on the radial maze task (Columbo et al., 1989), disruption of motoric sequences in grooming behavior (Berridge & Whishaw, 1992; see also Aldridge et al., 1993) and in navigation during water maze learning (Whishaw et al., 1987). Thus it is likely that the deficits in egocentric localization and stimulus-response learning in animals with striatal damage reflect only a subset of the forms of behavioral sequence acquisition mediated by the striatum. Data obtained from other, converging, methods help to further articulate the nature of the striatum's contribution.

The Striatal Habit System: Human Studies

In chapter 11, findings were presented that patients with Parkinson's disease, with striatal dysfunction, showed impaired probabilistic learning in a weather prediction task (Knowlton et al., 1996). As we will see, this deficit is just one

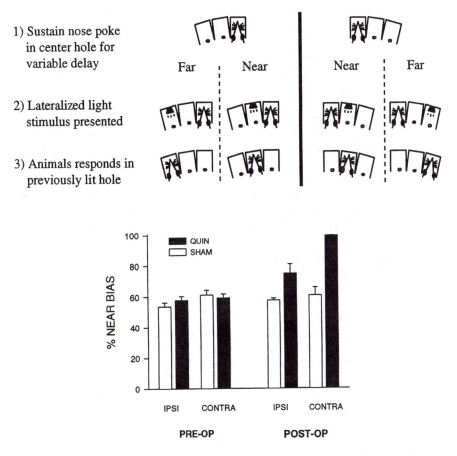

Figure 13.7. Task that required rats to perform light-cue guided nose pokes to near and far positions. Top: They had to initially sustain a nose poke in the center hole. Then a light briefly flashed to signal a near or far location to the left or right. Subsequently the rat withdraws its nose from the initial locus and pokes into the signaled hole. Bottom: Performance of normal control rats (SHAM) with rats with unilateral lesions of the striatum made by quinolinic acid injection (QUIN) to presentations of cues on the ipsilateral (IPSI) and contralateral (CONTRA) side of the lesion. Performance was tested before (PRE-OP) and after (POST-OP) the lesions were made. (Reproduced, with permission, from Brasted, Humby, Dunnett, & Robbins, 1997; Copyright Society for Neuroscience.)

aspect of the deficit in habit learning in patients with striatal damage. Indeed, the deficit in probabilistic learning is among a number of findings in the clinical literature that raise questions about the scope of learning and memory impairments following striatal damage—more specifically, about whether deficits are limited to habit or motor skill learning or whether, instead, they extend to all domains of skill learning. The Knowlton et al. result can be seen as entirely consistent with the findings in animals with striatal damage indicating an impairment in learning to generate one particular response among many to a complex stimulus, except that here patients were impaired in learning to generate a variety of specific responses to the appropriate sets of complex stimuli. This section considers other findings from the clinical literature, permitting us to explore how well this correspondence between the animal and human clinical literatures holds up.

Patients who have been studied in order to examine the role of the striatum in learning and memory come mainly from two etiologies: Parkinson's disease and Huntington's disease. Both disorders lead to profound motor deficits. In Parkinson's disease, patients suffer from tremor, rigidity, and akinesia (inability to move) following substantial cell death in the substantia nigra and the resultant depletion of dopamine in the striatum. Huntington's disease is characterized by primary degeneration of the striatum, and these patients exhibit irregularities in their movement patterns (athetosis and chorea). In addition to the motor deficits, some patients with Parkinson's disease also suffer from depression or dementia, and patients with Huntington's disease always progressively develop dementia. Furthermore, drug treatments administered to these patients, such as l-dopa for Parkinson's disease, have cognitive consequences. Thus, work with such patients aimed at characterizing the role of the striatum in memory is somewhat more complicated than the animal work (for a recent review see Lawrence et al., 1998).

Notwithstanding the constraints on clinical studies of striatal function, deficits have been demonstrated in patients with Parkinson's disease or Huntington's disease on several skill-learning tasks, including rotary pursuit, serial reaction time (see below), mirror reading, and the Tower of Hanoi puzzle (for reviews see Gabrieli, 1995; Salmon & Butters, 1995). A study by Gabrieli (1995) will be considered at some length here to illustrate the nature of the deficits seen after striatal damage. Patients with Huntington's disease received training on two motor-skill-learning tasks: rotary pursuit and mirror tracing. Rotary pursuit required subjects to maintain contact of a handheld stylus with a target metal disk revolving on a turntable. Normal subjects showed robust learning over repeated practice sessions on this often-studied task, increasing the amount of time they maintained contact with the target. However, patients with Huntington's disease showed virtually no learning (Figure 13.8). To control for the possible effects on learning of differences in baseline motor performance due to the motor deficits associated with Huntington's disease, Gabrieli manipulated the speed of the turntable rotation to equate the patients' initial performance to that of control subjects. Equating initial levels did not reduce the learning deficit; indeed, even when initial performance was adjusted to be better than that of normal subjects, the patients with Huntington's disease still failed to show learning.

Mirror tracing required subjects to use a handheld stylus to trace the pattern of a six-pointed star viewed only from its mirror image, reversing the normal view of the star, their hand, and the moving stylus. Normal subjects showed robust learning across trials, increasing the time per trial spent on target while tracing. Patients with Huntington's disease showed a normal rate of improvement even when they began at a poorer level of performance (Figure 13.9).

This dissociation in performance on two different motor skill tasks in Huntington's disease—impaired learning of rotary pursuit and intact learning of mirror tracing—indicates the selectivity of the striatum's role within this domain of

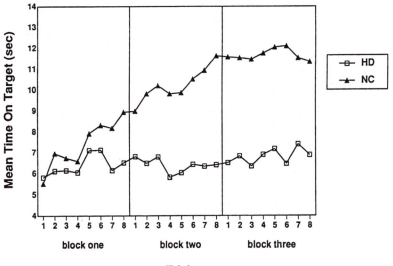

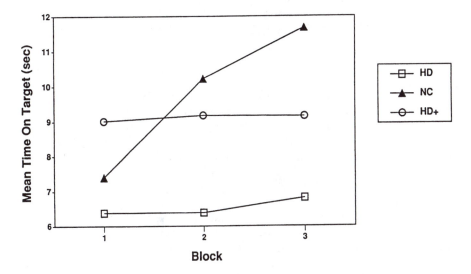

Figure 13.8. Performance of normal control subjects (NC) and patients with Huntington's disease (HD) on the rotary pursuit task (top). The learning rate of HD patients was not improved when their initial performance was equalized with that of normal subjects by making the task easier. (Reproduced, with permission, from Houk, Davis, & Beiser, 1995; Copyright MIT Press.)

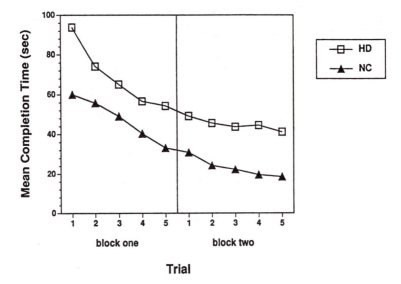

Figure 13.9. Performance of normal control subjects (NC) and patients with Huntington's disease (HD) across blocks of training trials on the mirror drawing task. (Reproduced, with permission, from Houk, Davis, & Beiser, 1995; Copyright MIT Press.)

learning and memory. Gabrieli suggested that the striatum's contribution can be seen in tasks requiring acquisition of a perceptual motor sequence and, more specifically, tasks in which the response output is driven by the sequence and/ or timing of the input, as required in the rotary pursuit task. By contrast, the striatum is not involved for an alteration in perceptual motor mapping, as emphasized in mirror tracing. Other observations of intact mirror reading in patients with Parkinson's disease but impaired mirror reading in patients with Huntington's disease make this interpretation more complicated (Martone et al., 1984; Huberman et al., 1994), however. On the other hand, parallel deficits in patients with Huntington's disease and patients with Parkinson's disease have been observed on implicit learning in the serial reaction time motor-sequencing task. In this task, one of a number of different locations on a computer screen is flashed on each trial, and the subject is to press the button corresponding to that location. Unbeknownst to the subject, the locations are flashed in a particular repeating order (e.g., a 12-item fixed sequence in which each of the four locations is flashed three times). Implicit learning of the sequence is shown on two performance measures: Subjects' average reaction time to respond to a given item gradually becomes faster for the repeating sequence across blocks, and reaction time slows substantially in a transfer test when subjects are switched to a block in which stimuli are presented in random order. Several reports have indicated deficits in learning on this task in patients with Parkinson's disease or Huntington's disease (Willingham and Koroshetz, 1993; Ferraro et al., 1993; Pascual-Leone et al., 1993), but such a deficit has not always been seen on both of the above measures of sequence learning and isn't always seen in patients with striatal damage (see Selco, Cohen, Stebbins, & Goetz, submitted). Finally, there are parallel deficits in patients with Parkinson's disease and patients with Huntington's disease in working memory. Despite ambiguity about some of the results, there is considerable evidence to suggest that tasks requiring memory for and sequencing of responses tap into the selective functions of the human striatum.

Functional neuroimaging studies have provided another way to explore the role of the striatum in learning and memory in humans, with results paralleling closely the neuropsychological results articulated above. Increases in striatal activation have been seen in association with learning of finger movement sequences (Seitz et al., 1990; Seitz & Roland, 1992) and with learning in the sequential reaction time task (Grafton et al., 1995). More recently, activation has been documented in striatum in the more perceptual and cognitively based skill-learning tasks used in current neuropsychological studies of striatal function, including probabilistic classification in the weather prediction task (Poldrack et al, 1999), category learning (Rao et al., 1997), and mirror reading (Poldrack et al. 1998). Taken together, these results indicate that the role of the striatum in habit or skill learning extends beyond the motor domain, encompassing a variety of performances that all involve multiple input or response options and that all show gradual, incremental learning across trials. The number of neuropsychological and functional imaging studies of striatal function is growing very rapidly, offering promise of clarifying the precise nature of the striatum's contribution to human learning and memory.

In characterizing the memory functions of the striatum in humans, it is important to note that all of the learning tasks described above as being impaired following striatal damage and/or as eliciting striatal activation in normal subjects are ones on which amnesic patients show intact learning (see chapter 5). This reminds us that the kind of memory supported by the striatum is thus dissociable from hippocampus-dependent declarative memory. Finally, to remind us that habit learning is just one example of procedural memory, note that rotary pursuit dissociates from word priming, with only rotary pursuit associated with striatal functioning, even though both of them are hippocampus-independent: Whereas rotary pursuit performance is impaired following striatal damage in Huntington's disease and activates the striatum in normal subjects, as was discussed above, word priming is impaired after cortical damage in Alzheimer's disease (Heindel et al., 1989) and activates extrastriate cortical areas in normal subjects (Buckner et al., 1998; Squire et al., 1992; see chapter 4).

Learning-Related Neural Activity in the Striatum

Recent neurophysiological studies have provided converging evidence for the involvement of the striatum in programming stimulus-response sequences. An early recording study by Rolls and colleagues (1979) examined the activity of striatal neurons in monkeys performing a visual discrimination task and during "clinical" testing for responses to various stimuli and during naturally evoked behaviors. Over half of the recorded cells had identifiable task-related firing patterns, with some purely sensory and others purely motor correlates, or more complex responses to stimuli or during specific behaviors in the "clinical" testing. In addition, a substantial number of cells fired in association with specific task-relevant behaviors in the visual discrimination task, and some fired in anticipation of arm projection movements associated with task performance. More recent studies have confirmed the existence of striatal neurons that anticipate movements, and have suggested that striatal activity might be associated with the relation between behavioral contexts and responses (for a review see Mink, 1996). Work by Schultz and colleagues (1995) revealed striatal neural activity associated with the expectation of predictable environmental events in monkeys performing conditional responses. In one experiment, such activity was found using a variant of the delayed-response task where delayed go and no-go responses were conditioned by visual stimuli (Apicella et al., 1992). Neuronal activity sustained during the delay period reflected anticipation of either the active arm movement or withholding that movement (Figure 13.10). Other cells anticipated the expected reward following the correct response. Such reward-related responses were more prevalent in the ventral striatal areas, consistent with strong inputs from the amygdala to that area of the striatum (Everitt & Robbins, 1992). A variety of cellular responses have been seen, including task-(context)-dependent anticipatory activity and activity related to the expectation and reception of reward (Figure 13.11). These findings led Schultz et al. (1995) to suggest that the striatum uses knowledge about the behavioral context to plan behavioral responses.

Other studies, focusing on striatal interneurons that are tonically active, have led to a similar conclusion. Studies by Graybiel and Kimura (1995; Graybiel et al., 1994; Kimura, 1995) identified a substantial population of tonically active neurons in the striatum that became responsive to an auditory cue only when the cue acquired predictive value for subsequent delivery of a reward (Aosaki et al.,

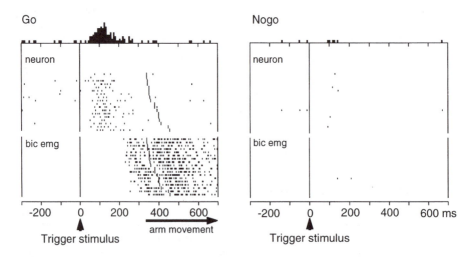

Figure 13.10. Responses of a striatal neuron when one trigger stimulus generates a reaching movement (left) and not when another stimulus signals no movement (right). bic emg = bicepts electromyographic activity. (Reproduced, with permission, from Houk, Davis, & Beiser, 1995; Copyright MIT Press.)

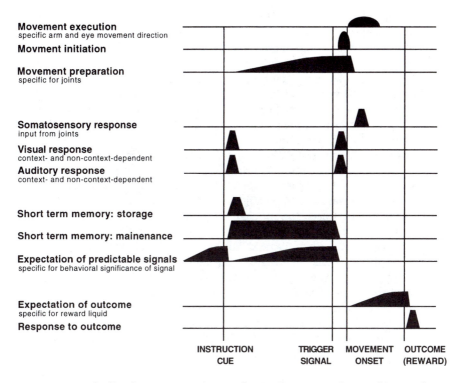

Movement execution
specific arm and eye movement direction

Movment initiation

Movement preparation
specific for joints

Somatosensory response
input from joints

Visual response
context- and non-context-dependent

Auditory response
context- and non-context-dependent

Short term memory: storage

Short term memory: mainenance

Expectation of predictable signals
specific for behavioral significance of signal

Expectation of outcome
specific for reward liquid

Response to outcome

| INSTRUCTION | TRIGGER | MOVEMENT | OUTCOME |
| CUE | SIGNAL | ONSET | (REWARD) |

Figure 13.11. Idealized response patterns of striatal neurons observed in monkeys performing sensory motor performance. (Reproduced, with permission, from Houk, Davis, & Beiser, 1995; Copyright MIT Press.)

1994). These cells did not respond to primary rewards but did establish cued responses in expectation of a reward and maintained those conditioned responses for weeks. The conditioned responses were entirely dependent on dopamine inputs from the substantia nigra. Selective depletion of dopamine cells in the substantia nigra resulted in a reduction of the cued responses of tonically active striatal neurons, to the same level as observed prior to conditioning. Subsequent systemic administration of a dopamine receptor agonist reinstated conditioned responses of these striatal cells. Based on these findings, Graybiel and Kimura emphasized the role of limbic reward-related inputs via the substantia nigra in mediating the establishment of context-dependent striatal activity participating in the selection and execution of learned behavioral repertoires.

A recent study has directly related alterations in neural activity patterns in the striatum to the acquisition of a conditional turning response (Jog et al., 1999). In this study rats were trained to turn left in a T-maze when signaled by one tone and to turn right when signaled by a different tone. At the beginning of training about half of the striatal cells recorded had activity related to the relevant task events, and the predominant type of response reflected the left or right turning behavior. As the animals' performance improved, the fraction of striatal cells with task-related activity increased to over 90%, but the number of cells that fired associated with turning behaviors was strikingly reduced. By contrast, a very large fraction of the cells were active selectively as the rat began a trial or as it approached one or both of the goal sites at the end of the choice arms. These acquired firing patterns persisted with extensive overtraining. Taken together, these observations suggest a reorganization of neural ensemble activity in the striatum associated with this form of habit learning. The authors interpreted the pattern of changes as a restructuring of the neural ensemble from emphasis on the turning responses to development of an action template for triggering the trial procedures as a behavioral unit.

In addition to these observations on simple and conditional motor responses, there are data indicating a prominent role for the striatum during spatial sequencing behavior. Kermadi and Joseph (1995) trained monkeys to fixate a central location and encode a sequence of spatial target illuminations, then visually orient to and subsequently reach toward each target (Figure 13.12, top). Many striatal neurons responded to the visual instruction stimuli during central fixation or during the saccade or arm movement. Furthermore, the responses of a substantial proportion of these cells were highly dependent on the sequential order of the targets, responding only to a particular visual cue if it was in a particular position in the three-item sequence (Figure 13.12, bottom). Kermadi and Joseph noted that none of the cells showed sustained activity after the target instructions; rather, the cells fired in anticipation of each item in the sequence, consistent with the view that the striatum participates with other structures in the anticipation of sequential behaviors to be performed.

Summarizing the Role of Striatum in Habit Learning

The neurophysiological, anatomical, and behavioral data converge well, leading to the suggestion that the striatum plays a critical role in habit learning on a variety of tasks that require resolution of competition among multiple input or response options, particularly tasks involving the learning of response sequences. The necessary circuitry exists in the striatum for cortical sensory input and direct motor outputs to mediate the association of (simple and highly complex) stimuli with specific behavioral outputs. Furthermore, there are clear striatal pathways for, and well-documented influences of, reward signals capable of gating the associations of stimuli and responses. The striatum represents a broad variety of cues, motor responses, and rewards, although in the spatial domain its role is limited to the egocentric domain of knowledge. There are both direct output pathways for control of voluntary behavior and feedback pathways to the cerebral cortex, particularly the prefrontal cortex, that could mediate complex sequencing and planning. Whether the system works to resolve competition among competing input or response options, or to permit manipulation of or shifting among representations of these input-response options, or, finally, to learn and execute the desired input-output mappings is not clear. But the data are clear in implicating this structure as a key element in a pathway for sequence learning and other aspects of habit learning involving the acquisition of stereotyped and unconscious behavioral repertoires. This skill-learning pathway is independent of the earlier-described circuits for declarative memory and for emotional memory.

The Cerebellum and Motor Learning: Animal Studies

A brain structure long associated with motor learning is the cerebellum, whose contribution has been highlighted since the pioneering theoretical work of Marr (1969) and Albus (1971; see *Learning and Memory* 3:6 & 3:7; *Trends in the Cognitive Sciences* 2:9). Experimental investigations into the role of the cerebellum in motor learning have focused on its highly organized circuitry and emphasized its mechanisms for reflex adaptations (for review see Ebner et al., 1996). This circuitry involves both the cerebellar cortex and underlying deep nuclei. The principal cells of the cerebellar cortex are the Purkinje cells, which send entirely inhibitory inputs to the deep nuclei. These cells receive two excitatory inputs, from the mossy fibers and the climbing fibers. The mossy fibers constitute the major afferent input. They originate from several brain stem nuclei that represent the spinocerebellar inputs, and they influence Purkinje cells indirectly through clusters of cerebellar granule cells that lie beneath. The granule cells originate the parallel fibers, the set of axons that run several millimeters along the long axis of the cerebellar folia. The parallel fibers make their excitatory connections onto the dendrites of a row of Purkinje cells, all oriented perpendicularly to the parallel fibers. There is considerable convergence of sensory inputs both at the level of the granule cells and onto Purkinkje cells. The other excitatory input, the climbing fibers, originates in the inferior olivary nucleus of the medulla. These axons rise within the cerebellar cortex and wrap around the Purkinje cell soma and dendrites, making numerous excitatory synaptic contacts. Each Purkinje cell receives input from only one climbing fiber, but these inputs have a powerful influence over the Purkinje cells, resulting in an all-or-none influence over the activity of Purkinje cells. Furthermore, coactivity of mossy and climbing fibers results in a long-term depression (LTD) of the mossy fiber synapse that is thought to play a central role in mediating the cerebellum contribution to motor learning. The cerebellum receives input from, and forms topographic representations of, the entire body surface. In addition inputs from the vestibular, visual, and auditory areas are conveyed through other deep nuclei. The main outputs of the cerebellum to spinal motor mechanisms are through the red nucleus and reticular formation, in addition to the upward-going outputs to the premotor and motor cortex.

Considerable study of cerebellar mechanisms has been devoted to examination of how this circuitry mediates adjustments to changes in load during movement, particularly during reflex movement (Gilbert & Thach, 1977). The particular reflex movement for which cerebellar involvement has been studied most extensively involves the vestibulo-ocular reflex (VOR), a reflex for keeping images stable on the retina during head movements by generating eye movements that are equal in magnitude but in the opposite direction. Adaptations in this reflex occur when distortions in visual input (such as are produced by prisms) cause the reflex to be maladaptive. Ito (1982) first proposed that mechanisms of LTD within

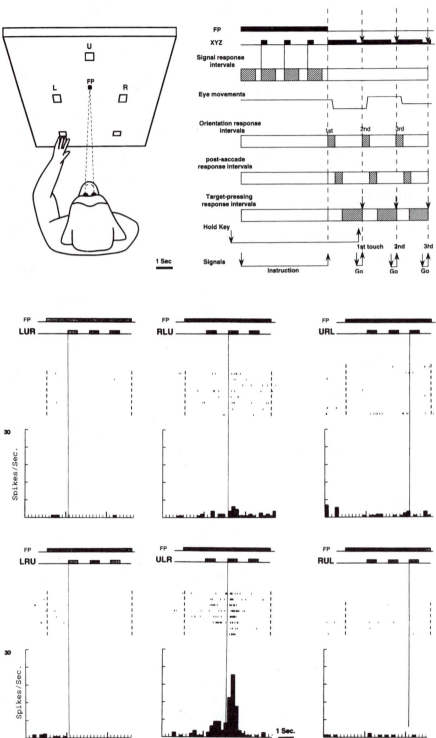

A

U

L   FP   R

1 Sec

B

FP

XYZ

Signal response
intervals

Eye movements

Orientation response
intervals   1st   2nd   3rd

post-saccade
response intervals

Target-pressing
response intervals

Hold Key   1st touch   2nd   3rd

Signals   Instruction   Go   Go   Go

FP

LUR

30

Spikes/Sec.

FP

RLU

FP

URL

FP

LRU

FP

ULR

30

Spikes/Sec.

1 Sec.

FP

RUL

RF0274.

the cerebellum could mediate this form of adaptation. Other work, such as that of Lisberger (1988), has outlined the circuitry for the VOR in detail.

Certain aspects of cerebellar circuitry have been linked by researchers to reflex adaptations, including particularly the interactions between mossy and climbing fibers. In the VOR, learning is thought to involve the combination of "contextual" inputs from the mossy fibers together with "teaching" inputs or "error signals" from the climbing fibers. The contextual input is the head turn, which results in weak inputs from the mossy fibers to the Purkinje cells. The alteration in image motion sends strong inputs to the Purkinje cells via the climbing fibers, resulting in LTD that adjusts the mossy fiber input.

In addition to work on the VOR, considerable recent attention has focused on eye blink conditioning. In this example of classical conditioning, a tone is paired repeatedly with an air puff to the eye until conditioned eye blinks eventually occur to the tone. Here, too, learning is thought to involve the combination of contextual inputs and teaching inputs or error signals. The contextual input in eye blink conditioning is the tone, which, when followed by the strong teaching input from the air puff, results in adaptation of the mossy fiber input and strengthening of control by the tone. Whether and how this circuitry mediates these and other learned reflex adaptations is still a matter of considerable controversy, however, and a full resolution remains to be worked out in the details of the circuitry of the cerebellum (see Raymond et al., 1996; Mauk, 1997). This will be discussed in more detail below.

The putative role of the cerebellum in learning extends beyond reflex modulation and classical conditioning, encompassing several aspects of voluntary learning. In the remainder of this chapter we will provide a summary of the case for its critical role in classical eyelid conditioning, and then a brief review of studies indicating a role in more complex forms of habit or skill learning.

Classical Conditioning of the Eye Blink Reflex

The model receiving the most intensive study currently is probably the conditioned eye blink reflex (see chapters in Bloedel et al., 1996; Woodruff-Pak, 1997). That the cerebellum mediates the storage of memory for a conditioned reflex has been advocated most forcefully by Thompson and colleagues in their work on eye blink conditioning in rabbits (e.g., Thompson & Kim, 1996), and their view has received considerable experimental support (Steinmetz, 1996; Mauk, 1997; Mauk et al. 1998). In this paradigm, immobilized rabbits are presented with a tone or light as the conditioning stimulus (CS). In classic *delay conditioning*, this

---

Figure 13.12. Top: Eye and arm movement sequencing task. The animal begins the trial by fixating its eyes at the fixation point (FP). This results in a sequence of brief illuminations of targets at right (R), left (L), and upward (U) positions in a particular order that is reproduced in eye and arm movements. Bottom: Example of a striatal neuron that fired upon presentation of the L cue, only when in the ULR sequence. (Reproduced, with permission, from Kermadi & Joseph, 1995; Copyright American Physiological Society.)

stimulus lasts 250–1000 ms and coterminates with an air puff or mild electrical shock to the eyelid (unconditioned stimulus or US) that produces the unconditioned (reflexive) eye blink (UCR). After several pairings of the CS and US, the eye blink begins to be elicited prior to the US. With more training, this conditioned response (CR) occurs somewhat earlier, and its timing becomes optimized so as to be maximal at the US onset, showing that not only is a CR acquired but also a timing of the CR is established.

Tying this learning to cerebellum, it has been shown that permanent lesions or reversible inactivation of the interpositus nucleus of the cerebellum results in impairments in the acquisition and retention of classically conditioned eye blink reflexes (Clark et al., 1992; Krupa et al., 1993). Inhibition of protein synthesis in the interpositus nucleus prevents establishment of the conditioned reflex (Bracha & Bloedel, 1996). In addition, cerebellar cortical lesions disrupt the timing of conditioned eye blink responses (Perrett et al., 1993). There is considerable controversy over whether any component of cerebellar circuitry is absolutely essential to CR storage that is not also critical for performance of the eye blink, based on evidence showing that conditioning eventually succeeds with extended training (Welsh & Harvey, 1989; Harvey et al., 1993; Harvey & Welsh, 1996). The resolution of this controversy seems to lie in the complicated nature of the circuitry of the cerebellum, allowing for several alternative routes of information flow, and hence several possible sites for the critical CS-US association (Mauk, 1997; Steinmetz, 1996; Bracha & Bloedel, 1996). A brief consideration, presented below, of the cerebellar and brain stem circuitry mediating eye blink conditioning reveals why this is the case and offers a deeper understanding of how complex the circuitry of even a simple conditioned reflex can be.

The circuit proposed by Thompson and Kim (1996) includes a central set of elements by which the CS input is sent via the pontine nuclei to the interpositus as well as to the cortex of the cerebellum. The US input is relayed by the trigeminal nucleus and inferior oliva to the same cerebellar sites where the essential plasticity occurs. Outputs for the CR are then mediated by projections from the interpositus to the red nucleus, which projects to the accessory abducens motor nucleus, which also executes the UR via direct inputs from the trigeminal nucleus.

The evidence for involvement of these structures in different aspects of eye blink conditioning is substantial. Studies by Steinmetz and colleagues (see Steinmetz, 1996) using stimulation and recording techniques within the cerebellar circuit have shown that stimulation of the auditory pathway via the pontine nucleus can substitute for the tone CS in establishing the conditioned response. Similarly, the US pathway has been traced through the trigeminal nucleus to a circumscribed area in the dorsal accessory inferior olive, by showing that lesions of this area prevent the UR and stimulation of this area substitutes for the US.

Additional compelling data come from studies using reversible inactivations of particular areas during training (Thompson & Krupa, 1994; Thompson & Kim, 1996). These studies showed that muscimol inactivation of the motor nuclei that is essential for production of the CR and UR prevented the elicitation of behavior during training. However, in trials immediately following removal of the inactivation, CRs appeared in full form, showing that the essential circuit for UR production is not critical for learning per se. A similar pattern of results was obtained with inactivation of the fibers leaving the interpositus or their target in the red nucleus, showing that the final pathway for CR production is also not required to establish the memory trace. By contrast, inactivation of the anterior interpositus nucleus and overlying cortex by muscimol, lidocaine, or cooling did not affect UR production, yet resulted in failure of CR development during inactivation and the absence of savings in learning after removal of the inactivation (Figure 13.13; Krupa et al., 1993).

These results point to a small area of the anterior interpositus nucleus and overlying cerebellar cortex as the essential locus of plasticity. It is in this area, of course, where the interactions occur between the mossy and climbing fibers resulting in LTD, and where the connections with the relevant outputs exist. Consistent with a view that this plasticity is essential, mice with gene knockouts

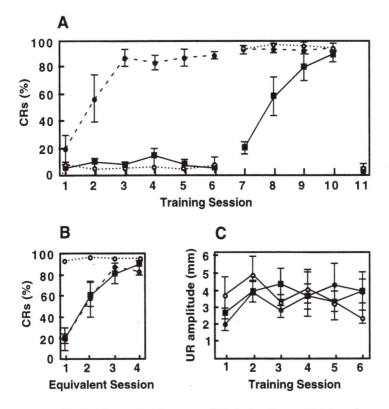

Figure 13.13. Effects of muscimol on conditioned reflexes (CRs) and unconditioned reflexes (URs). A. All groups received injections prior to training on sessions 1–6, not on sessions 7–10, and all groups received muscimol on session 11; circles = saline; squares = cerebellum; triangles = red nucleus. B. Comparing sessions 1–4 of the saline group with sessions 7–10 of the cerebellum and red nucleus groups. C. Effects of muscimol on URs. (Reproduced, with permission, from Lavond, Kim, & Thompson, 1993; Copyright Annual Reviews. Reproduced, with permission, from Krupa, Thompson, & Thompson, 1993; Copyright American Association for the Advancement of Science.)

resulting in deficient cerebellar LTD were impaired in eye blink conditioning (Thompson & Kim, 1996).

Recording studies have also been helpful, shedding light on the nature of the neural coding in the cerebellar cortex and interpositus nucleus that mediates the conditioning. During the course of training, neurons in both areas developed increased firing to the CS. During subsequent extinction trials, during which the US was withheld while the CS was presented repeatedly, the CR gradually disappeared while interpositus cells ceased firing. By contrast the neural code remained in the activity of the cerebellar cortex long after extinction (Steinmetz, 1996; Figure 13.14).

There must be sufficient redundancy in the circuit to mediate the critical association at sites in both the cerebellar cortex and interpositus nucleus in order to accommodate the empirical findings, a redundancy that is contained in Thompson's model circuit. However, as Brach and Bloedel (1996) argued, the full set of connections that could participate in eye blink conditioning is larger than that (Figure 13.15). They offered a "multiple-pathway" alternative model that is distinguished from the Thompson model in several ways. First, the model includes a role for cerebral cortex, which through thalamic and other circuits can mediate expression of the CR and the UR. Second, the multiple-pathway model includes bidirectional connectivity of many of the elements, raising the possibility of a large number of interactions that can mediate and modulate conditioning. Third, there are several pathways for output to the effectors and therefore many parallel sites that could mediate the learned reflex. The truly complicated nature of the details of this circuitry leave one wondering why any particular component of the circuit would have a significant influence. Yet, a wealth of data indicates that the interpositus is such a significant player in conditioning despite the multiple pathways. At the same time, there is clear-cut evidence of a functional role for several other components of the input and output components of the system.

An example of the larger circuit that participates in eye blink conditioning involves the hippocampus (Disterhoft et al., 1996). While the hippocampus is not required for the standard *delay-conditioning* paradigm, nonetheless neurons within the hippocampus develop increased activity associated with the appearance and timing of the CR (Figure 13.16). In addition, the hippocampus *is* required for a variant of the paradigm called *trace conditioning*. In this task, the CS involves a brief 100-ms tone followed by a silent 500-ms "trace" interval punctuated by the US. Rabbits develop CRs in this form of eye blink conditioning, and hippocampal neurons also are active associated with the CS and US (Figure 13.17). This variant of eye blink conditioning is sensitive to damage to the hippocampus. Thus, even though this form of learning does not fit the typical definitions of declarative or hippocampus-dependent memory, it is an example where the hippocampus is part of a larger circuit including the cerebellum in producing a form of reflex adaptation.

Contribution of the Cerebellum to Other Examples of Habit Learning

Thus far, the role of the cerebellum in learning has been considered in a restricted set of paradigms. To what other learning situations or types of learning

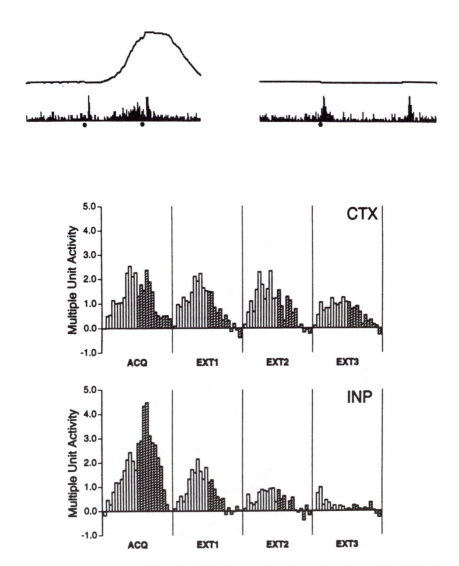

Figure 13.14. Top: Examples of eye blink responses (top of each panel) and single neuron activity in cerebellar cortex (bottom of each panel). Discharge to both the CS and US (dots) on paired trials (left) and after extinction (right). Bottom: Multiunit activity in the cerebellar cortex (CTX) and interpositus nucleus (INP) during the last day of acquisition (ACQ) and stages of extinction (EXT); clear bars are data from between CS and US onset; stippled bars after US onset. (Reproduced, with permission, from Steinmetz, 1996; Copyright MIT Press.)

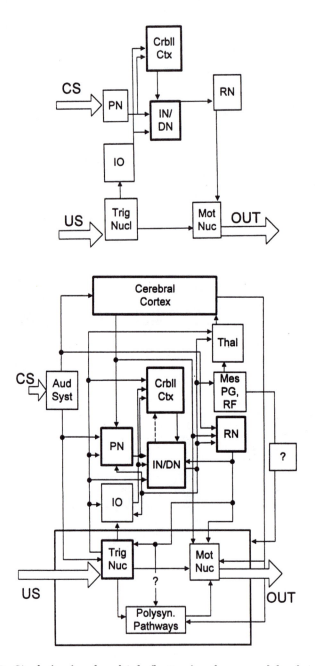

Figure 13.15. Single (top) and multiple (bottom) pathway models of circuitry supporting the conditioned eye blink reflex. (Reproduced, with permission, from Bracha & Bloedel, 1996; Copyright MIT Press.)

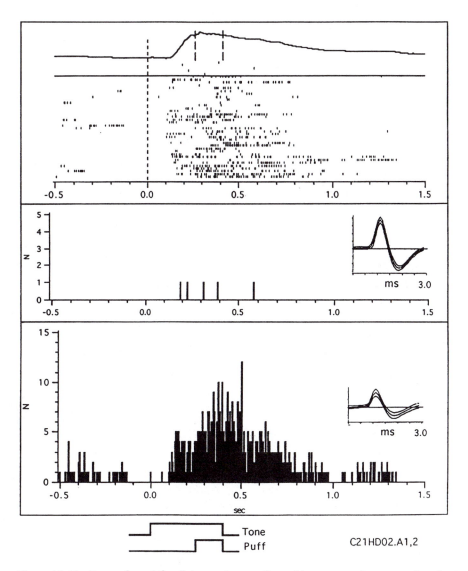

Figure 13.16. Examples of the firing patterns of two hippocampal neurons in rabbits performing the delay version of classical eyelid conditioning. In the top panel, the rasters of the two cells (separated by a horizontal line) are shown below the depiction of the eyelid response. In the lower panels are histograms of the firing pattern for the two cells. (Reproduced, with permission, from Bloedel, Ebner, & Wise, 1996; Copyright MIT Press.)

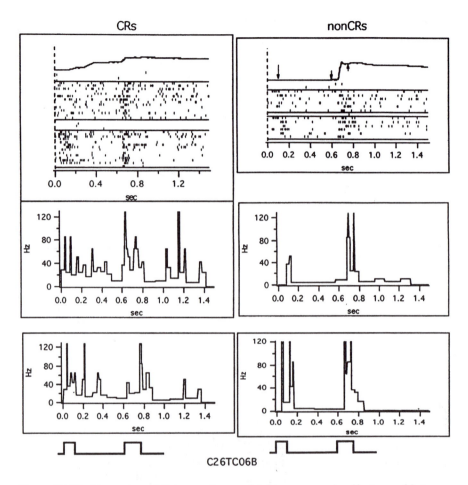

Figure 13.17. Examples of firing patterns of 5 hippocampal cells in a rabbit performing the trace version of classical eyelid conditioning. Upper panels show rasters for each cell when the CR is produced or not. Lower panels show histograms for two of the cells. (Reproduced, with permission, from Bloedel, Ebner, & Wise, 1996; Copyright MIT Press.)

does the cerebellum extend? Unlike striatal lesions, cerebellar damage, in general, is without a detrimental effect on instrumental learning across a broad variety of maze-learning, avoidance, and lever-pressing tasks (for a listing see Harvey & Welsh, 1996). For example, the same lesions that block classical eyelid conditioning have no effect on discriminative aversive avoidance learning in rabbits (Steinmetz et al., 1991). An initial exception was found in a study by Steinmetz et al. (1993), in which rats were trained on a signaled-bar-press task that was either appetitive or aversive. For both versions, a tone was presented for a fixed period. In the appetitive version, rats were trained to press the bar only during tones to obtain a food reward. In the aversive version, they were trained to press the bar to avoid a shock. Rats with lesions of the interpositus and dentate nuclei failed to acquire the aversive conditioning but were intact in appetitive conditioning. These results suggest a broader role for the cerebellum in aversive learning, at least in a situation in which a classical contingency is initially operative.

A broadening of the scope of cerebellar plasticity comes compellingly from studies in which rats were given "acrobatic" training by challenging them to acquire complex motor skills necessary to traverse a series of obstacles, involving moving over barriers and balancing on teeter-totters and tightropes (Figure 13.18, top). Rats with such training developed an increased volume of the parallel fiber layer in the cerebellar cortex and an increased number of synapses onto Purkinje cells without an increase in synaptic density (Black et al., 1990; Kleim et al., 1996, 1998; Figure 13.18, bottom). Control rats that had exercised in a running wheel without acrobatic training (i.e., that had extensive activity without the requirement to acquire new motor skills) did not develop these characteristics of synaptogenesis; instead, the activity controls demonstrated increased blood vessel density in the cerebellum.

The Cerebellum and Learning: Human Studies

Studies on humans have shown that the scope of the cerebellum's role in habit or motor skill learning extends still further, in classical conditioning and in several other forms of motor adaptation. Patients with cerebellar damage are impaired in the acquisition of classically conditioned eye blink responses and show other abnormalities of conditioned responses (Topka et al., 1993; Woodruff-Pak et al., 1996; see Hallet et al., 1996; Woodruff-Pak, 1997). In addition, patients with cerebellar damage are impaired in adaptation to lateral displacement of vision produced by prism glasses. When normal subjects first wear the prism glasses, their pointing to targets is typically off in a systematic way, but they gradually adapt and begin pointing correctly. When the glasses are subsequently removed, normal subjects' pointing is offset in the opposite direction and readapts to the normal matching. By contrast, patients with cerebellar damage show impaired adaptation (Figure 13.19; Hallett et al., 1996). Patients with cerebellar damage are also impaired in skill-learning tasks, including mirror tracing (Sanes, 1990), and in the serial reaction time test described above (Pascual-Leone et al,, 1993). Such patients have also been shown to be impaired at planning a sequence of actions in a problem-solving task (Grafman et al., 1992).

Functional imaging studies have documented decreases in cerebellar activation in association with learning of finger movement sequences (Friston et al., 1992; Jenkins et al., 1994), with learning in the sequential reaction time task (Hazeltine et al., 1997), and with learning in drawing or tracking tasks (Seitz et al., 1994; Flament et al., 1996).

In one view, virtually all skill-learning tasks require motor adaptations, in which case the cerebellum plays its role in the execution of skill learning (i.e., in the production of the learned responses) rather than (the learning of) movement sequences (Hallet et al., 1996). Alternatively, Pascual-Leone et al., (1993) have employed the same results to suggest that the cerebellum plays a critical role in

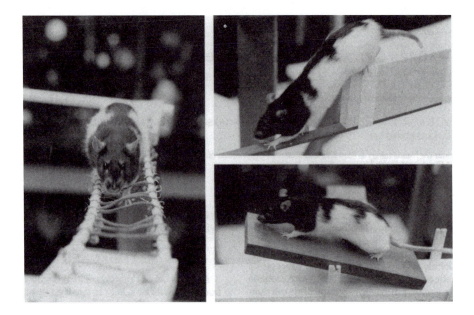

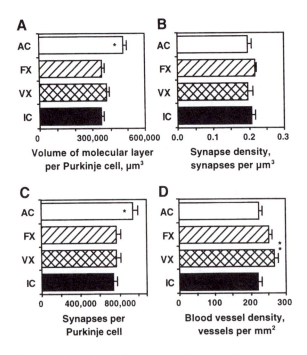

Figure 13.18. Top: Acrobatic training events. Bottom: Neuroanatomical measures in the cerebellum. AC = acrobatic training; FX = forced exercise (treadmill); VX = voluntary exercise (running wheel); IC = inactive controls. (Reproduced, with permission, from Black, Isaacs, Anderson, Alcantara, & Greenough, 1990; Copyright W.T. Greenough.)

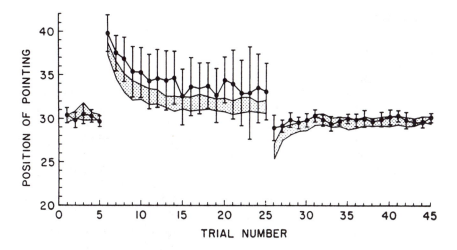

Figure 13.19. Performance of normal subjects (shaded area) and patients with cerebellar lesions (filled circles) with prism glasses that shifted vision to the right. (Reproduced, with permission, from Weiner, Hallett, & Funkerstien, 1983; Copyright Lippincott Williams & Wilkins.)

temporal sequencing itself. This conclusion follows from their work with the serial reaction time task, in which cerebellar patients showed a sequence-learning impairment not only in their reaction time performance but also in their explicit remembering (declarative knowledge) of repeating sequences.

Other work on cerebellum in humans has explored its possible role beyond the motor domain. Patients with cerebellar damage have been reported to show normal visual priming on the picture fragment completion task, as well as normal acquisition of mirror reading and the Tower of Hanoi puzzle (see Salmon & Butters, 1995). Yet functional imaging studies have found cerebellar activation in various nonmotor tasks. Cerebellar activation was seen in the deep nuclei during sensory discrimination (Gao et al., 1996), in the lateral cortex during an attentional task without movement (Allen et al., 1997), and in cortex during verb generation (Raichle et al., 1994). In the verb generation task, subjects are presented with nouns (e.g., *ball*) and are to generate an appropriate verb (e.g., *throw*) for each one. Compared to a control condition in which subjects were just to repeat the nouns aloud, generating verbs to the same nouns resulted in activation of cerebellar cortex along with activation of dorsal frontal cortex. There are now a number of reports of cerebellar activation associated with frontal cortex activation in various tasks requiring search or selection among multiple response options or representations (see Fiez, 1996). This participation of cerebellum in nonmotor tasks, while initially surprising, is consistent with anatomical findings of cerebellar outputs to higher cortical areas (Middleton & Strick, 1994). Moreover, the participation of such noncerebellar structures as the hippocampus in humans (Clark & Squire, 1998) as well as animals in the trace variant of the cerebellum-dependent eye-blink-conditioning task, further implicates the interaction of higher systems with essential cerebellar function.

Motor Cortical Areas

The motor and premotor cortical areas are involved in all the circuits for motor learning, so it is likely that these areas participate in some important ways in virtually all types of adaptation and skill acquisition. This is confirmed in various ways in studies of humans and of animals. Functional imaging studies have shown activation of the motor (and somatosensory) cortical areas during various examples of skill learning (see Salmon & Butters, 1995), such as learning finger movement sequences (Seitz et al., 1990; Schlaug et al., 1994; Grafton et al., 1995; Karni et al., 1995) and visuomotor tracking in the rotary pursuit task (Grafton et al., 1992, 1994). Several studies in animals have reported evidence of expansion of the motor cortex representation or of synaptogenesis in motor cortex associated with learning (see Donoghue, 1995; see chapter 4). An increased number of synapses per neuron in motor cortex was found in rats that had learned complex motor skills in the "acrobat" task (Black et al., 1990; Kleim et al., 1996), and training-induced physiological changes in the cortical representation of reaching movements were found in the motor cortex of monkeys (Nudo et al., 1996). These results make strong contact with the Karni et al. (1995) functional imaging study in humans, in which changes were found in the distribution (the spatial extent) of activation in motor cortex associated with learning of specific finger movement sequences.

Other studies in animals have shown other learning-dependent effects in motor cortex. Pioneering studies by Woody (1986) showed that cells in primary motor cortex demonstrated conditioning-dependent changes in activity and threshold in the eye-blink-conditioning task. Considerable attention has focused on the development of LTP and other cellular changes underlying alterations in excitability and in functional mappings of motor cortical cells as a function of learning (Woody, 1996; Donoghue et al., 1996; Asanuma & Keller, 1991; Kimura at al., 1994).

Finally, the premotor areas may play a special role in conditional motor learning. This type of learning involves the acquisition of different motor responses to distinct stimulus conditions. Lesions of the dorsal premotor cortex in monkeys result in severe impairments in conditional motor learning tasks but do not affect discrimination learning that involves only a single go/no-go response (Petrides, 1986, 1987; see also Passingham, 1993). Importantly, the other region especially important for conditional motor learning is the thalamic relay that brings striatal input to the frontal cortex (Canavan et al., 1989). Parallel findings from neurophysiological studies confirm an important role for the premotor area in conditional motor learning (Wise, 1996a). These studies involve recordings from single neurons in the premotor cortex of monkeys performing reaching or visual saccade tasks where distinct visual cues are associated with arbitrary arm or eye movement responses (Figure 13.20). The principal result of these studies is the appearance of visually evoked neural activity at the time when the correct conditional behavioral responses occur. These neurons did not respond to familiar and overlearned stimuli that signaled identical arm or eye movements. Many of these cells that developed responses during initial learning disappeared shortly after. These data suggest the premotor cortex may be involved in the initial correct selection of responses associated with novel stimulus contingencies.

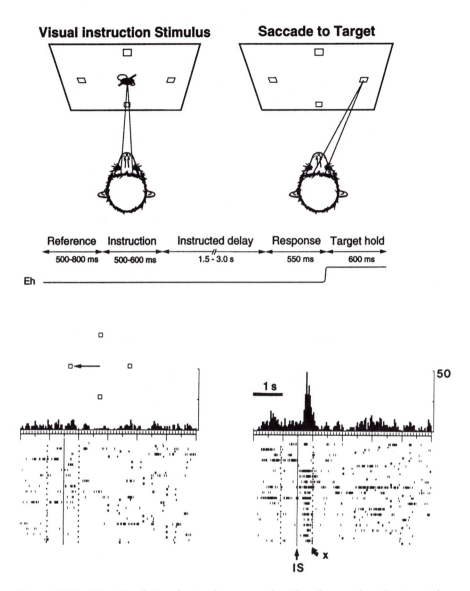

Figure 13.20. Top: Conditional visual-motor task. After the monkey fixates at the center of the screen, an instruction stimulus is presented, followed by a delay, then the monkey shifts its gaze to the assigned target locus. Eh = horizontal eye movement. Bottom: Responses of a neuron in the supplementary motor area on trials when the instruction stimulus signalled a leftward eye movement. Left: familiar stimulus; Right: novel stimulus. (Reproduced, with permission, from Wise, 1996; Copyright MIT Press.)

Different Forms of Procedural Learning in
Multiple Motor Systems?

The observations considered here indicate that forms of motor learning are mediated by a complex circuitry involving the motor cortical areas and two main subcortical loops, one through the striatum and another through the cerebellum. While we are still at a relatively early stage of understanding the brain circuits that mediate even the simpler forms of motor learning, some distinctions are beginning to emerge. The motor cortex and surrounding premotor and somatosensory areas are involved in many (all?) forms of motor learning. The striatum and associated basal ganglia structures play a critical role in habit learning, and particularly in the acquisition of skills that require resolution of competition among multiple input or response options, particularly in tasks involving the learning of response sequences. This role becomes important in more "cognitive" tasks where temporal sequencing of information is involved. The cerebellum is critical to a variety of reflex adaptations that are played out in simple, direct form in conditioning situations or are fundamental parts of more complicated sequencing tasks. Whether the roles of the striatum and cerebellum in temporal sequencing are fundamentally the same or are really quite different is unclear at this time. While the findings considered above have allowed for dissociations in the functional roles of these systems in different kinds of habit memory or skill learning, it is also clear that there are several points of intersection among them, as well as overlap in the contributions of these systems with the cortex, hippocampus, and amygdala across a broad range of learning situations.

14

Working Memory and the Prefrontal Cortex

The final general kind of memory considered here is working memory. The current concept of working memory is an elaboration of the earlier distinction *short-term memory*, the capacity to hold items briefly in consciousness and then repeat or identify them. The elaboration of short-term memory into working memory involves the important addition of mental "work" (that is, cognitive processing) and its combination with "memory." So working memory is much more than a short-term store. It typically involves some form of recognition and comprehension of the stimulus materials, thus invoking long-term retrieval of, for example a word meaning or object recognition. In addition to storing the presented stimulus information, working memory often involves some cognitive manipulation, such as a matching to recent items or an ordering or some other type of reasoning. Consider the task of counting backward by 7s from 100. One has to recognize the numerical symbols (7 and 100) and comprehend their mathematical values. Then one has to perform the initial subtraction and store the new value (93). Then one recalls the 7 again while holding the 93, performs another subtraction, and stores the new value (86), and so on. We do tasks that demand working memory for almost all of our conscious time, from running through our morning routine to preparing for bed.

Working memory can be characterized as a form of declarative memory, because this sort of processing goes on in consciousness, involves relational and inferential judgments, and is accessible to explicit forms of expression. The consideration of the short-term mechanisms of working memory here is a distinct departure from all discussion of long-term memory that has been the focus of this book so far. While many early notions held that short-term memory is the gateway to the long-term store (for any kind of long-term memory), there is evidence

471

that working memory can be fully dissociated from long-term memory. As described in detail in chapter 5, amnesic patients with damage to the hippocampal system have no difficulty holding information in consciousness. And they typically have no difficulty performing a variety of tasks that, like mental arithmetic, require considerable cognitive "work." Conversely patients with other types of brain damage have selective deficits in working memory. The first well-recognized patient with such a disorder was a man known as K.F., who had a lesion in the left temporo-parietal area (Shallice & Warrington, 1970). His long-term memory for semantic content was intact, but he had no capacity to hold in memory a string of words or digits. Below, we will discuss other cases of selective disorders of working memory. These findings have led many to consider working memory a distinct memory system, and now accumulating evidence that will be the focus of discussion below has provided a preliminary framework for the brain system that mediates this form of memory.

Cognitive and Brain System(s) for Working Memory

Baddeley and Hitch (1974; Baddeley, 1986, 1992, 1996) first realized the importance of distinguishing the cognitive and storage processes in short-term memory and replaced the concept of a unitary short-term memory with a multiple component conception of working memory. This multiple component model was inspired by findings from experiments in which they found an unexpected low degree of interference in the capacity for storing lists of visual pattern or word items when people performed cognitive tasks simultaneously. So, in their model of working memory, they proposed the existence of a set of specialized subsystems (recurrent loops), which mediate the storage process, and a distinct "central executive," which controls the subsystems and performs the mental "work" of controlling the slave subsystems and forming strategies. Corresponding to the materials involved in their studies, the model involved two distinct subsystems, a "visuospatial sketch pad" that could maintain nonverbal images and a "phonological loop" that mediated speech perception and subvocal rehearsal of verbal materials (Figure 14.1). These should be considered just examples of the full range of specialized subsystems available to the central executive.

Because this kind of conceptual model of working memory involves multiple types of cognitive processing combined with a range of stored material, it will come as no surprise that working memory relies on a widespread network of brain structures. Indeed there is considerable evidence that the brain network for working memory is large and, corresponding to the Baddeley and Hitch model, can be subdivided into a central executive with multiple subsystems. Considerable evidence points to the prefrontal cortex as the locus of the central executive, and to a variety of other cortical areas as the mediators of subsystem processes.

The assignment of the central executive function to the prefrontal cortex is supported by substantial anatomical data. The phenomenal expansion of the prefrontal area in primates and especially humans is impressively associated with the evolution of cognitive capacities (Figure 14.2). The prefrontal cortex in humans is a diverse area, composed of several cytoarchitecturally distinct subdivisions. In monkeys there is considerable consensus on correspondences with iden-

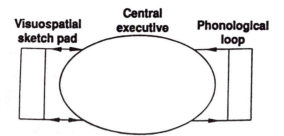

Figure 14.1. The Baddeley-Hitch model of working memory in humans. (Reproduced, with permission, from Baddeley, 1992; Copyright American Association for the Advancement of Science.)

tified areas in the human prefrontal cortex (Petrides & Pandya, 1994). Although several anatomical areas have been characterized based on morphological appearance, most of the functional evidence has been related to four general regions: the medial, dorsolateral, lateral, and orbital areas. Most of the attention with regard to working-memory functions in monkeys and humans has focused on the dorsolateral and ventrolateral areas, and these areas are partially distinct in their connectional patterns with more posterior parts of the cerebral cortex. Each of the subdivisions receives input from a diverse set of rostral and caudal cortical areas, and each has a distinctive input pattern (Pandya & Yeterian, 1996; Barbas & Pandya, 1989; Barbas, 1995). In addition, prefrontal areas are characterized by considerable associative connections with other prefrontal areas.

Nevertheless, despite this diversity and associativity with the prefrontal cortex, a few generalities have emerged with regard to distinctions among prefrontal areas and their inputs from posterior cortical areas (Figure 14.3). Thus, in general, the dorsolateral prefrontal area receives inputs mainly from medially and dorsolaterally located cortical areas that preferentially represent somatosensory and visuospatial information. Conversely, in general, the lateral prefrontal areas receive inputs mainly from ventrolateral and ventromedial cortical areas that represent auditory and visual pattern information. In particular, the differentiation of "dorsal stream" visuospatial input to the dorsolateral prefrontal area and "ventral stream" visual pattern input to the lateral prefrontal area has received considerable attention in studies on distinct working-memory systems (Ungerleider, 1995; Owen, 1997; Jonides & Smith, 1997; Goldman-Rakic, 1996a).

In rats there is also clear connectional evidence for correspondences with some prefrontal regions in primates. However, the number of these areas is limited. And in particular, there is little evidence for the existence of rodent homologies to the dorsal and lateral convexity subdivisions of the prefrontal cortex prominent in views on working memory in primates and humans. Nevertheless, there is evidence that the medial and orbital areas in the rodent prefrontal cortex serve some of the general functions of working memory observed in primates, as will be discussed below.

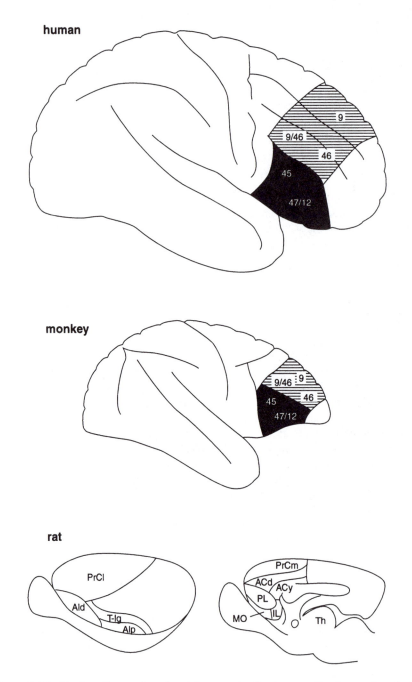

Figure 14.2. Designations of prefrontal areas in the human (top), monkey (middle), and rat (bottom; lateral and medial views). In the human and monkey, the designations are Brodman's areas. In the rat the designations are: AI = agranular insular; PrC = premotor; AC = anterior cingulate; PL = prelimbic; IL = infralimbic; MO = medial orbital; d = dorsal; l = lateral; m = medial. (Reproduced, with permission, from Owen, 1997; Copyright Blackwell Science. Reproduced, with permission, from Kolb, 1984; Copyright Elsevier Science.)

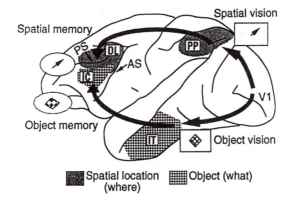

Figure 14.3. Schematic diagram of pathways from visual areas to components of the prefrontal cortex. PP = posterior parietal cortex; IT = inferotemporal cortex; DL = dorsolateral prefrontal cortex; IC = inferior convexity of prefrontal cortex; V1 = primary visual cortex. (Reproduced, with permission, from Wilson, Ó Scalaidhe, & Goldman-Rakic, 1993; Copyright American Association for the Advancement of Science.)

The Neuropsychology of Prefrontal Memory Function in Humans

Deficits in short-term or working memory can arise from a variety of disorders, including those attributed to damage to several brain areas (e.g., see Vallar & Shallice, 1990). Nevertheless, the greatest attention in behavioral studies has been accorded the prefrontal cortex, befitting its role as the putative "central executive" of working-memory systems. However, prefrontal cortex function is a large issue, not limited to or even considered by some as primarily an issue of memory processing (e.g., Roberts et al., 1996). Rather, the role of the prefrontal cortex in human memory is differently viewed as only a part of its role in multiple higher cognitive functions, including personality, affect, motor control, language, and problem solving (Luria, 1966; McCarthy & Warrington, 1990; Shallice, 1988).

In general, neuropsychological studies suggest that deficits in memory are secondary to attentional and problem-solving deficits. For example, one of the best studied and most profound impairments following prefrontal damage in humans is a deficit in the Wisconsin Card Sorting Task. In this test subjects are initially presented with four target items, playing cards each with a repeating pattern design that involves a unique combination of pattern color, shape, and number. Subsequently, they are given a deck of similar cards and must sort the cards onto the target cards according to a criterion (color, shape, or number) the experimenter selects. The subject is given feedback with every choice and must search for the correct sorting criterion. When the subject is sorting correctly, the experimenter shifts to a new criterion without warning, and the subject must discover the new criterion.

This task contains an obvious working-memory component, in that subjects must keep in mind the currently judged sorting criterion, dispense with it, and then select and maintain a new one. Patients with frontal lobe lesions are severely impaired on this task (Figure 5.2; Milner, 1963). However, the observed impairment in these patients is not that they forget the current sorting criterion. On the contrary, prefrontal patients have no difficulty learning the initial sorting criterion. Moreover, their disorder is that they subsequently *perseverate*, that is, continue to use a sorting criterion that is no longer operative. This pattern of findings is not consistent with the notion that the prefrontal cortex is specifically involved in the memory aspect of the task. A more recent study by Owen et al. (1993) examined whether the perseverative deficit was attributable more to the patients' inability to switch away from the previously relevant dimension, or to their inability to take on a new one. Owen and colleagues explored this question using a computer-controlled task that required subjects to learn visual discriminations among compound visual patterns. As in the Wisconsin task, the subjects had to discover which dimension of the compound pattern was relevant. Subsequently they systematically shifted the relevant dimension and did so by substituting a new component dimension in one of two ways. Either they substituted the new relevant component for the previously relevant component, which did not allow the subjects to perseverate. Or they substituted the new relevant component for the previously ignored component. The result was that patients with prefrontal damage were impaired only when they could perseverate, and they shifted normally when they could adopt a new relevant dimension without the formerly relevant dimension present. Other studies explicitly designed to assess problem-solving ability have also demonstrated that prefrontal patients are severely impaired whenever the overall goal of the task involves planning and choosing among subgoals and strategies. For example, Shallice (1982) examined the performance of patients with prefrontal damage on variants of the Tower of London task, which requires subjects to move beads around on a series of pegs, using the least number of moves to reach a prescribed final configuration (Figure 14.4). He found that these patients could not solve even versions of the task with relatively few subgoals.

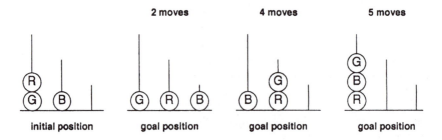

Figure 14.4. Illustration of the Tower of London task. The test begins with three colored beads in positions shown at left. The task is to use the least number of moves to achieve a designated final configuration, examples of which are shown in the other panels. (Reproduced, with permission, from Jonides & Smith, 1997; Copyright Psychology Press.)

A final example involves an effort by Owen et al. (1996) to dissociate strategy and memory components of short-term memory tasks in frontal and temporal lobe patients. The test involved computer-controlled spatial and nonspatial working-memory tasks in which subjects were required to identify goal stimuli among a series of items and then not repeat selection of those items in subsequent choices. Normal control subjects developed a successful self-ordered repetitive search strategy that involved sampling the items in a strict ordering on each trial and returning to the last point in the sequence after each correct identification of a goal item. Patients with frontal or temporal damage were impaired on the task, but the pattern of their impairments differed. Frontal patients failed to develop the successful search strategy even in the least difficult versions of the task. By contrast, patients with large temporal lobe lesions or unilateral amygdala and hippocampus damage performed poorly only on the most difficult levels of the task, and their deficit was not related to use of an inefficient search strategy. Based on this pattern of findings, Owen et al. concluded that the prefrontal contribution to working memory is in the mediation of problem-solving strategies and not in memory per se.

This does not mean that patients with prefrontal damage perform perfectly well on standard memory tasks (for review see Shimamura, 1995). They do well at some, but not others. They perform normally in recall of stories or nonverbal diagrams. And they learn verbal paired associates as well as normal control subjects. These findings stand in marked contrast to the typically poor performance of amnesic subjects on the same paired-associate learning tasks (Figure 14.5). By contrast, frontal patients perform poorly on other variants of memory tasks. For example, by contrast to their success in initial verbal paired-associate learning, they are inordinately sensitive to proactive interference in learning paired associates composed of different pairings of the same target words (Figure 14.6). Frontal patients also perform poorly in "metamemory," that is, self-assessments of whether they feel they could recognize verbal memory items they cannot recall; yet they perform just as well as normal subjects in their accuracy of recall of the same word items. Similarly, frontal patients do poorly in recalling the situation in which they learned correctly recalled materials. This deficit in "source memory" has been viewed as reflecting a deficit in memory for the context of learned items.

Another, potentially related, area of memory impairment in patients with prefrontal damage is a difficulty in remembering the temporal order of recent events (Milner et al., 1990; Kesner, 1992). In one study patients were presented with a long series of cards in rapid succession, each card bearing two line drawings. Some cards also contained question marks, requiring the subject to indicate which of the two items had appeared more recently (Figure 14.7). In some cases both items had appeared earlier, but at different times in the sequence. In other cases one item had appeared before and the other item was new. Frontal patients could recognize the earlier-appearing items but could not identify their order. Temporal patients could identify the ordering of old items but showed impairments in recognizing new items. Similarly, Shimamura and colleagues (1990) presented subjects with a list of 15 words and subsequently asked them to reconstruct the order in which the words appeared. Frontal patients showed poor correlations between their ordering and the presented order but performed relatively

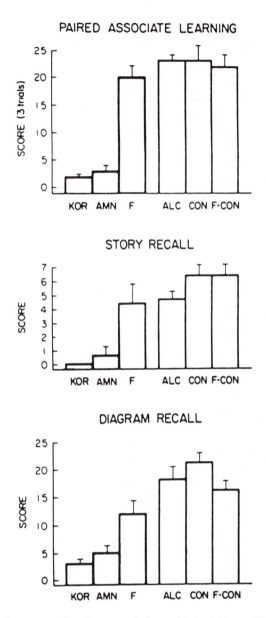

Figure 14.5. Performance of patients with frontal lobe lesions (F), Korsakoff's patients (KOR), and amnesic patients (AMN), as well as controls on standard memory tasks. (Reproduced, with permission, from Shimamura, 1995; Copyright MIT Press.)

AB-AC Paired-Associate Learning

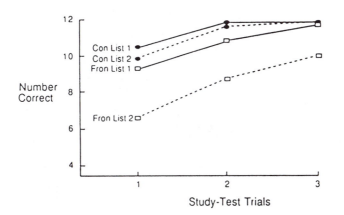

Figure 14.6. Performance of frontal lobe patients (Fron) and controls (Con) in learning an initial list of paired associates (AB), and then a second list that included the same initial items with new associates (AC). (Reproduced, with permission, from Shimamura, 1995; Copyright MIT Press.)

well in recall and recognition of other presented words (Figure 14.8). Frontal patients also performed poorly in remembering items in a self-ordering task (Milner & Petrides, 1984). This pattern of deficits led Shimamura (1995) to suggest that the fundamental deficit in humans with prefrontal damage is an inability to inhibit irrelevant information (see also Schnider & Ptak, 1999). Such a deficit could account straightforwardly for their difficulties on the Wisconsin Card Sorting and other tasks that require switching attentional set and could underlie the impairments in source and metamemory, as well as problem solving and temporal ordering, to the extent that performance on such tasks requires inhibiting irrelevant cognitive strategies (see Schacter, 1987, for a related view).

Neuropsychology of the Prefrontal Cortex in Monkeys

Deficits in short-term memory following damage to the prefrontal cortex have been highlighted since the pioneering studies of Jacobsen and his colleagues (1935; see Rosenkilde, 1979; Fuster, 1985). These studies focused on the delayed-response task, a variant of the "shell game" in which monkeys view a reward being hidden under one of two plaques, then, after a memory delay, must choose the location of the reward (Figure 14.9). The specific demand on short-term memory was emphasized in an experiment where poor performance after prefrontal lesions was observed in delayed response, but not in a visual pattern discrimination task using the same stimuli. Furthermore, Goldman et al. (1971) have shown that the deficit following damage to the dorsolateral prefrontal cortex is observed only when there is both a spatial and a memory component of the task. In addi-

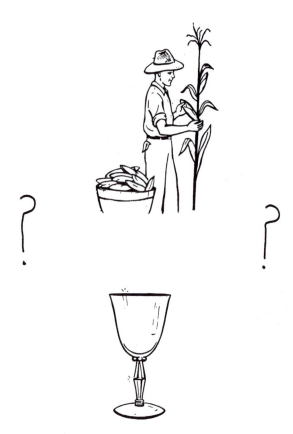

Figure 14.7. An example item from the recency discrimination test. (Reproduced, with permission, from Milner & Petrides, 1984; Copyright Elsevier Science.)

tion, a variety of other deficits in short-term memory, and sometimes in nonspatial learning, are observed after damage to different areas with the prefrontal cortex in monkeys (see Rosenkilde, 1979, for a review). Most prominent among these are selective deficits associated with damage to three of the key areas of prefrontal cortex. Damage to the dorsolateral area produces a severe deficit in spatial delayed response and in the related spatial delayed-alternation task, where food is hidden in the left and right locations on alternate trials. No deficits are observed on object alternation, discrimination or delayed nonmatch to sample, or a variety of other tasks with no spatial memory requirement. By contrast, damage to the lateral prefrontal cortex does not result in severe deficits in spatial delayed response or delayed alternation but does produce severe impairments in object alternation and delayed nonmatch to sample. Damage to the orbital prefrontal area produces deficits in olfactory, taste, visual, and auditory discriminations and especially in discrimination reversal learning; orbital lesions also result in emotional disorders (Barbas, 1995; Rolls, 1996). These data are consistent with the above-described heterogeneity of prefrontal connections, and with the pro-

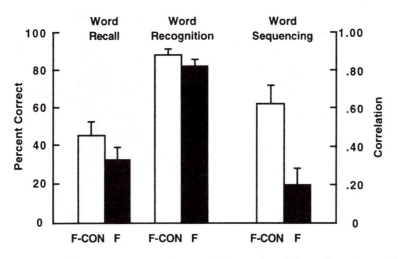

Figure 14.8. Performance of frontal control (F-CON) and frontal patients (F) in recalling and recognizing words, and in reconstructing their order of presentation. (Reproduced, with permission, from Shimamura, 1995; Copyright MIT Press.)

posal that areas of the prefrontal cortex may be distinct in the modality of information they process in memory.

More recent studies on the neuropsychology of prefrontal function in monkeys have expanded on these early findings, suggesting a broader role for the prefrontal cortex in cognition as observed in humans. For example, in a recent study by Dias et al. (1996) monkeys with lateral or orbital prefrontal lesions were trained on a variant of the attentional set-switching tasks described above. In this experiment animals learned to discriminate compound visual stimuli each composed of a polygon and a curved line (Figure 14.10). In the preliminary discrimination they had to attend to one dimension (e.g., the polygon) and ignore the other (the line). Then they learned other discrimination problems, first one involving an intradimensional shift (discrimination between new polygons, ignoring new lines), then one involving an extradimensional shift (discrimination between new lines, ignoring the new polygons), and finally a reversal of the last problem. Neither lesion affected performance on the intradimensional shift problem. Monkeys with lateral lesions were impaired on the extradimensional shift problem, but not on its reversal. Monkeys with orbital prefrontal lesions showed the opposite pattern: They were unimpaired on the extradimensional shift but impaired on its reversal. These results are consistent. They indicate selective impairments after different prefrontal lesions not within the same visual modality but associated with different cognitive demands. The lateral prefrontal region seems to be essential for switching the relevant visual perceptual dimension, whereas the orbital prefrontal area seems to be critical for reversing the affective association for the same stimuli.

Another recent study examined the capacity of monkeys with dorsolateral prefrontal lesions in working memory for temporal order. The key test for self-

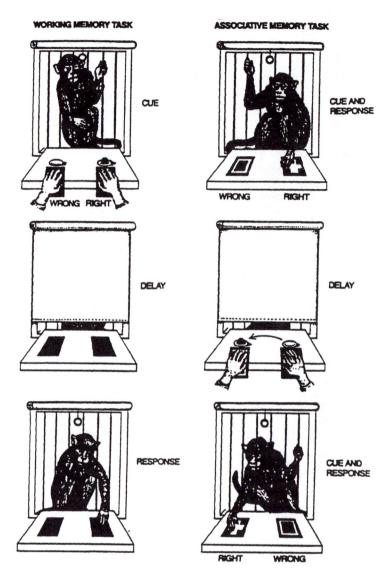

WORKING MEMORY TASK

ASSOCIATIVE MEMORY TASK

Figure 14.9. Sequence of steps (top to bottom) in two memory tasks.

ordering involved presentations of three distinct objects on three successive trials each day. On the first trial all the objects were baited, and any could be selected to obtain a reward. After a 10-s delay the same objects were again presented with their positions randomized, and the initially selected item was not rebaited, so that the subject was required to choose one of the remaining objects to obtain a second reward. On the third trial, the objects were again randomly rearranged, and the monkey had to select the remaining object. In a series of tests, Petrides (1995b) showed that monkeys with dorsolateral prefrontal lesions were impaired

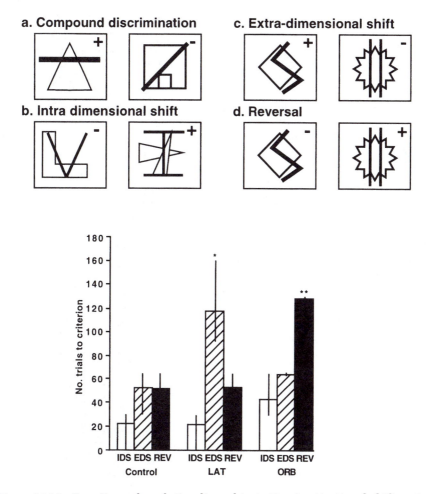

Figure 14.10. Top: Examples of stimuli used in testing in attentional shift proto-col. The large polygon is the relevant dimension in all but the extradimensional shift and reversal conditions. + = rewarded stimulus; − = nonrewarded stimulus. Bottom: Performance of monkeys with lateral (lat) or orbital (orb) prefrontal lesions on intradimensional shift (IDS), extradimensional shift (EDS), and reversal (REV) conditions. (Reproduced, with permission, from Dias, Robbins & Roberts, 1996; Copyright Macmillan Magazines Ltd.)

on this self-ordering task. They did no better when the same stimuli were presented one at a time during the first two trials, that is, when the stimuli were externally ordered. However, the same monkeys performed well on delayed object alternation (as observed following dorsolateral lesions in the above-described studies), and a variant of the task showed that the central difference involved in the ordering task and delayed alternation was the number of stimuli that had to be remembered. In one more test, the same monkeys could readily learn to appropriately select objects presented repeatedly in the same order, that is, in a task not requiring the monitoring of order in working memory. These findings demonstrate a strong parallel with the studies showing temporal ordering deficits in human patients with prefrontal damage and suggest a common mechanism in strategic processing functions of the prefrontal area in humans and monkeys.

Neuropsychological Studies in Rodents

Finally, yet other neuropsychological studies have provided parallel evidence of functionally heterogeneous areas in the prefrontal cortex of rats, suggesting these mechanisms of prefrontal function are common in mammalian evolution. Kolb (1984, 1990) surveyed the anatomical and behavioral evidence on rodent prefrontal areas, and concluded there are substantial similarities between rats and monkeys in the connectional patterns between the medial prefrontal area and spatial cortical areas, and between the orbital prefrontal area and subcortical limbic structures. The findings from neuropsychological investigations also suggest substantial similarities across species in the functions of these areas. Damage to the medial prefrontal area in rats results in deficits in spatial alternation, spatial working memory on the radial maze task, and impairments in the Morris water maze. These data indicate the rodent medial prefrontal area is involved in spatial memory performance similar to dorsolateral prefrontal involvement in spatial functions in monkeys. Notably the poor performance in the water maze has been attributed to poor navigational strategies rather than memory per se, consistent with the findings of Owen et al. (1996) from studies on human spatial working memory. A recent study by Granon and Poucet (1995) showed that rats with medial prefrontal lesions normally acquired the water maze when trained from a single starting point, a variant of the task in which animals with hippocampal damage are impaired (Eichenbaum et al., 1990). Furthermore, they accommodated successfully to finding the escape platform from a second location. However, they were impaired when the number of starting positions exceeded two, a finding reminiscent of Petrides's findings on object working memory in monkeys just discussed.

Also consistent with the findings on monkeys and humans, damage to the prefrontal cortex results in impairments in attentional switching and temporal ordering. Olton et al. (1988) trained rats to time each of two stimuli either independently or simultaneously by varying their bar-pressing rate in anticipation of rewards delivered at different fixed intervals after each stimulus. Lesions of the prefrontal cortex severely disrupted performance on this task, consistent with an impairment in dividing or switching attention between two processing events. Hippocampal lesions do not impair performance on this divided-attention task. In contrast, hippocampal lesions produce amnesia in a variant of the timing task where a gap is inserted in the timing procedure, whereas prefrontal lesions did not affect memory in the gap procedure. Thus, as in the previously described studies in monkeys, prefrontal damage results in a deficit in "executive" function, not memory, and hippocampal lesions result in the opposite pattern.

In addition, Kesner (1992) performed a series of experiments demonstrating that medial prefrontal lesions result in deficits in temporal ordering in rats. In the experiments most similar in design to those used with monkeys, rats were trained to enter arms on a radial maze to obtain rewards. On each order-training trial, they were first allowed to visit each of four arms in a predetermined sequence for that day. Then they were given one of two types of memory tests. In the test for order they were presented with a choice of the first and second, or the second and third, or the third and fourth presented arms, with the contingency that another reward could be obtained in the arm that was presented earlier that day. Alternatively, they were presented with one of the arms that had been visited that day and another arm that was not presented in that trial. Animals were trained on the task preoperatively and retested after medial prefrontal lesions. They performed well on both tests preoperatively, but very poorly on the order test after surgery. They performed well when tested on recognition of the first arm presented on each day but were impaired on subsequently presented arms. Thus, like monkeys with dorsolateral lesions, rats with medial prefrontal lesions are more severely impaired on order memory than on recognition. Unlike the monkeys in Petrides's (1995b) study, the rats with medial prefrontal lesions remained impaired on order memory even when the same ordering was presented each day. However, the dissociation between order and recognition memory was more striking: These animals were completely unimpaired in recognizing repeatedly presented arms. Kolb (1984) documented several reports of medial prefrontal damage resulting in disruption of species-specific behavioral patterns, including food hoarding, nest building, and maternal and sexual behavior. Kolb interpreted these findings as reflecting a general deficit in the temporal organization of behavioral sequences.

There are also several studies that have demonstrated similarities in behavioral abnormalities in emotion and response inhibition after orbital prefrontal lesions in rats and monkeys (Kolb, 1984, 1990). Some studies have uncovered specific dissociations of function in medial and orbital lesions in rats. Perhaps the most striking example comes from a double dissociation of the effects of selective prefrontal lesions on performance in spatial delayed alternation and olfactory discrimination (Eichenbaum et al., 1983a). Preoperatively, all animals were trained on spatial delayed alternation in a standard Y maze, and on two go/no-go odor discrimination problems. Postoperatively, all animals were retrained on those tasks plus one more odor discrimination problem. Rats with medial prefrontal lesions were severely impaired on spatial delayed alternation, similar to the results of several earlier studies, and were not impaired in retention or acquisition of odor discriminations (Figure 14.11). Rats with orbital prefrontal lesions showed the opposite pattern of effects. They were not impaired in reacquisition of the spatial delayed alternation but were severely impaired in both retention and acquisition of odor discriminations. Subsequent analyses focused on the nature of the impairments in both tasks. These analyses focused on perseverative tendencies in both tasks. In the spatial alternation task, perseverative errors were measured as repetitive responses made during correction trials given following selection of the incorrect arm. This analysis showed that rats with medial prefrontal lesions made substantially more perseverative errors in the spatial alternation task than controls or rats with orbital prefrontal lesions. The analysis of perseveration in the odor discrimination task involved a replication of the previously described experiment, but with the addition of a symmetrical reward contingency by which animals were rewarded for correct go and no-go responses.

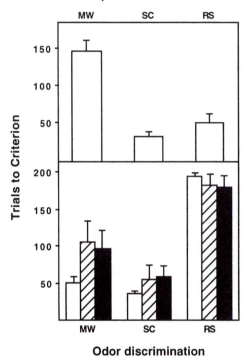

Spatial Alternation

Odor discrimination

Figure 14.11. Performance of sham-operated control rats (SC) and rats with le-sions of the medial prefrontal cortex (MW) or orbital prefrontal cortex (RS) on spatial delayed alternation and on three odor discrimination problems. (Repro-duced, with permission, from Eichenbaum, Clegg, & Feeley, 1983; Copyright Aca-demic Press.)

Under these conditions intact rats show relatively little overall bias toward go or no-go responses. Rats with orbital prefrontal lesions were again severely im-paired, but the deficit was not attributable to a shift in their response bias. In addition, rats with orbital lesions showed an increased level of repetitive re-sponses for both the go and no-go response types, showing their impairment was associated with a general tendency to perseverate the last rewarded response. This pattern of findings shows that the different deficits associated with medial and orbital lesions can be characterized as modality-specific perseveration.

The scope of the deficit in odor-guided learning following damage to the or-bital prefrontal cortex in rodents has recently been extended by demonstrations of impairments in acquisition and performance of delayed nonmatch to sample and conditional discrimination learning. In an odor-guided delayed-nonmatch-to-sample task described in detail in chapter 9. Unlike hippocampal and parahip-pocampal cortical lesions, damage to the orbital prefrontal cortex results in a deficit in acquisition of the task even with brief memory delays, combined with no subsequent deficit in forgetting at extended delays. Rats with orbital prefrontal lesions were impaired, however, when the pool of repeating odor cues was reduced, that is, under conditions of increased inter-item interference. This pattern of results indicates once more that the effects of prefrontal and hippocampal lesions on performance on working-memory tasks are quite different, and that the effects of prefrontal lesions are less attributable to a memory deficit per se, than to an impairment in strategic functions subject to interference.

Winocur (1992) reached a similar conclusion based on his studies that compare the effects of medial prefrontal and hippocampal lesions. Animals were tested on a delayed-matching-to-sample task that required them to respond differentially to sample and choice lights that were of the same or different brightness. Normal rats performed the task very well, and their accuracy declined only slightly as the memory delay was increased. Rats with prefrontal lesions were impaired in matching even at the shortest delay, and their accuracy declined over longer delays at the same rate as that of controls. By contrast, rats with hippocampal lesions performed normally at the shortest memory delay, whereas their performance across delays declined abnormally rapidly. These results suggested that the prefrontal cortex was essential to the working-memory requirement for briefly remembering and matching the stimuli, whereas the hippocampus was essential to the maintenance of the stimulus representation.

Finally, Whishaw et al. (1992) reported a severe impairment in conditional odor-tactile discrimination following orbital prefrontal lesions in rats. In this study rats were trained on a set of four discriminations between compound stimuli. The correct choice for each problem was a particular combination of two stimulus elements, although each element was individually rewarded equally often (Figure 14.12). The findings in this study parallel the findings from Shimamura and colleagues (Shimamura, 1995) showing that under conditions of high interference, animals and humans are impaired in learning stimulus-stimulus associations.

Neurophysiological Studies on Coding Properties of Prefrontal Neurons in Monkeys Performing Working-Memory Tasks

In the early 1970s two laboratories first described activity in prefrontal neurons that encoded events in working memory. Kubota and Niki (1971) reported the existence of neurons that fired only during the delay period in monkeys performing a delayed-alternation task, whereas Fuster and Alexander (1971) described similar activity of neurons in monkeys performing the delayed-response task. The results of both studies were remarkably similar, in that cells were found that encoded each of the relevant task events (Figure 14.13). Some fired in association with presentation of the left or right cue in both the sample and choice periods, and subsequent work has shown that prefrontal neurons show considerable selectivity for visual and spatial properties of memory cues across a variety of working-memory tasks (reviewed in Funahashi & Kubota, 1994; Fuster, 1995), as well as selectivity for sensory stimuli or for eye or arm movements (Tanila et al., 1992). Moreover, many prefrontal neurons also continued to fire throughout the ensuing delay period, whereas other cells increased their activity only at the end of the sample period and ceased firing at the outset of the choice period. The

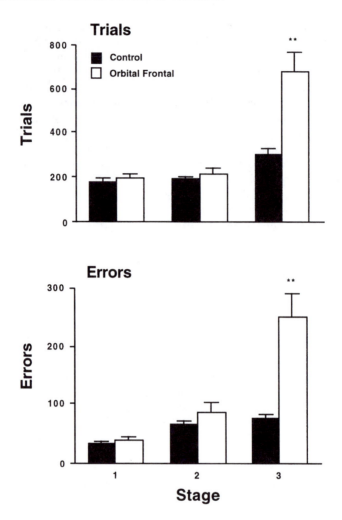

Figure 14.12. Performance of rats with orbitofrontal lesions on three stages of learning a configural discrimination. Stages 1 and 2 involve selecting a string with a particular odor cue. Stage 3 involves selecting the correct combination of a strong size and odor from four compounds made of two odors and two strong sizes. (Reproduced, with permission, from Whishaw, Tomie, & Kolb, 1992; Copyright American Psychological Association.)

latter delay cells fired only when the cue was meaningful: They were activated only when bait was provided indicating the stimulus was a cue to be remembered (Figure 14.14). The delay cells, numbering half the recorded neurons in the prefrontal cortex, have received the most attention because they provided the first evidence of neuronal activity specifically involved in storing a short-term memory.

Recent studies have focused on the delay cells, using a oculomotor version of the delayed-response task (Figure 14.15; Funahashi et al., 1989, 1993a, 1993b;

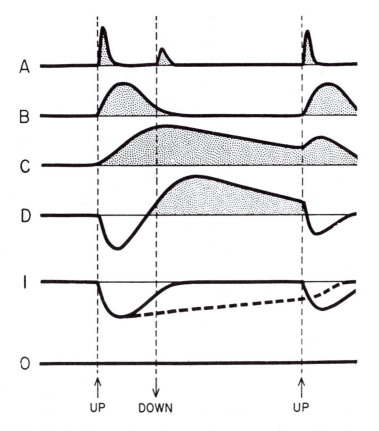

Figure 14.13. Idealized examples of neuronal responses observed in the prefrontal cortex of monkeys performing a delayed response task. Arrows mark movements of a screen that allows the monkey to view the sample, then the choice. (Reproduced, with permission, from Milner & Petrides, 1984; Copyright Elsevier Science.)

Goldman-Rakic et al., 1990; Goldman-Rakic, 1995). In this paradigm monkeys are trained to fixate a central spot on a display, and to maintain fixation while a target at one of eight locations is briefly illuminated. Following a delay period when the target must be remembered, the monkey then moved its eye to the location of the former target to obtain a reward. In this variation of the delayed-response task, the prefrontal cortex is critical to memory, and this paradigm allowed a dissection of the topography of spatial memory in this cortical area. In a key experiment, monkeys were trained to perform the task and then given small unilateral lesions of the dorsolateral prefrontal cortex. Subsequently their performance was measured for each of the eight target locations, both in the memory task and in a simple saccade task where the target stimulus was on at the time of eye movement, eliminating the need for spatial memory. The lesions had no effect on eye movements in the saccade task but resulted in poor delay-dependent performance within a spatially restricted region during the memory task. Further-

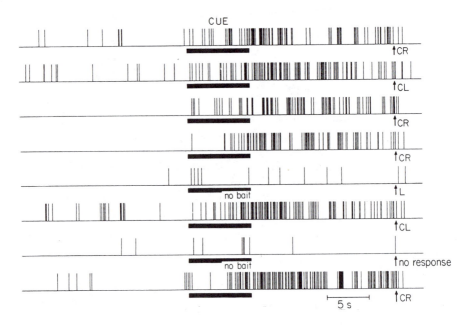

Figure 14.14. Activity patterns of a prefrontal cell in example trials. This cell fires during the delay only when the presence of the bait indicates the need to remember the location. (Reproduced, with permission, from Milner & Petrides, 1984; Copyright Elsevier Science.)

more, the deficit was restricted to a portion of the contralateral visual field and the magnitude of error in eye movements was minimal at short delays and greater at longer delays (Figure 14.16). These data provided the first evidence of a mnemonic scotoma, a "blindness" in memory for a specific region of visual space.

Correspondingly, recordings made of prefrontal neurons in intact monkeys performing this task revealed that the majority of delay cells fired selectively while the animal was remembering a stimulus presented in a particular part of visual space (Figure 14.17). The average area of space where excitatory activity was observed was about 45 degrees, and most cells preferred the contralateral part of space, consistent with the findings in the lesion study. In addition, some cells showed distinct inhibitory activity for the direction opposite the preferred direction, suggesting a network mechanism for sharpening the spatial memory signal (Goldman-Rakic, 1995). These delay cells fired only on trials when a correct saccade was produced, indicating their activity reflected the maintenance of the spatial memory. Furthermore, subsequent analyses showed that most of these cells were maintaining the memory of the target location, rather than firing in anticipation of the incipient response. To test this question directly Funahashi et al. (1993b) trained monkeys in both the standard version of the task and an "antisaccade" version of the task where the monkey was required to move its eyes to the opposite location from where the spatial target had been illuminated. About 80% of the delay cells with directional activity fired during memory for a particular target stimulus location regardless of the direction of the subsequent response.

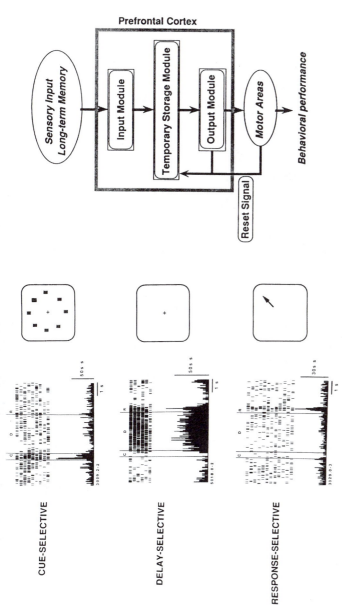

Figure 14.15. The occulomotor delayed response task. Left: Successive trial stages, and examples of prefrontal cells that fire selectively during each trial period, shown top to bottom. The cue is an illuminated spot at one of 8 positions (the circled one in this case); during the delay the cue is not illuminated; during the response period the monkey saccades to the locus of the previous cue. Right: Goldman-Rakic and colleagues' model of prefrontal functions in working memory. (Reproduced, with permission, from Goldman-Rakic, 1995; Copyright Cell Press. Reproduced, with permission, from Funahashi & Kubota, 1994; Copyright Elsevier Science.)

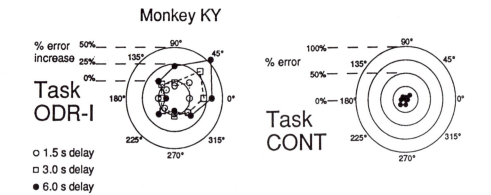

Figure 14.16. Performance of a monkey with a localized prefrontal lesion on the oculomotor delayed response (ODR) task and on a control (CONT) test where the cue is left on. Note increase in error only in a part of the visual field and only at long delays. (Reproduced, with permission, from Funahashi, Bruce, & Goldman-Rakic, 1993; Copyright Society for Neuroscience.)

For example, the cells shown in Figure 14.18 fired during the delay period following presentation of a target on the right side but not on the left during the standard version of the oculomotor delayed-response task, and it fired for the same target location when the required response was an anti-saccade, even when the incorrect saccade response was made. The remaining 30% of the directional delay cells fired in association with the incipient direction of the saccade, indicating the prefrontal cortex also contains information about the intended response. Cells whose activity predicts preparatory motor responses are much more prevalent in the nearby premotor area (Pellegrino & Wise, 1993) and in the posterior parietal cortex (Gnadt & Anderson, 1988).

Another elegant experiment that dissociated prefrontal cellular activity associated with the memory of the cue from preparatory motor activity was a study by Quintana and Fuster (1992) in which monkeys were trained on a delayed-response task with multiple color and spatial contingencies (Figure 14.19, top). During the sample phase a central colored target panel was illuminated briefly. After the subsequent delay period right and left choice panels were illuminated with colors or white light. The contingencies were complex: For yellow and blue samples, the choice stimuli were always white. The contingency was that a yellow sample signaled a correct right choice response, whereas the blue sample signaled a left response. When a red or green sample was presented, on some trials the choice was red and green and the monkey was required to select the same-colored choice regardless of its location. However, on other choice trials following a red or green sample, white choice lights were presented, and a red-to-left and green-to-right contingency prevailed. The combination of these contingencies allowed a separation of cellular activity during the delay associated with the stimulus color versus the planned response. Consistent with the above described data Quintana and Fuster found cells that reflected both types of coding. Some cells showed activity tightly linked to the cue, and their firing rate declined

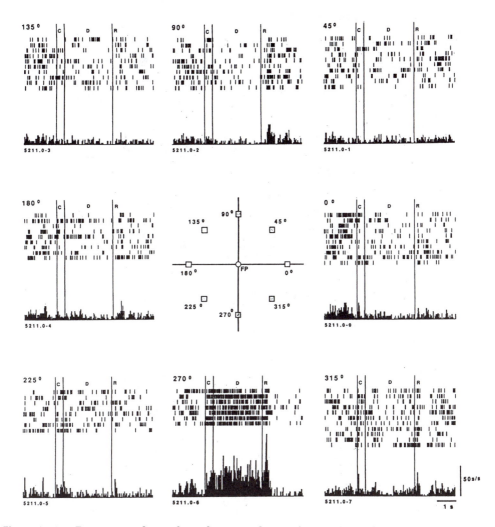

Figure 14.17. Responses of a prefrontal neuron during the cue (C), delay (D), and response (R) periods of the ODR task when the cue was presented at different loci. Note selective response when the cue was at 270 degrees, and signs of inhibited activity when the cue was presented at 90 degrees. (Reproduced, with permission, from Funahashi, Bruce, & Goldman-Rakic, 1989; Copyright American Physiological Society.)

during the memory period. Other cells increased firing rate during the delay, and the rate of firing was related to the predictability of the location of the response direction (Figure 14.19, bottom).

In addition to cue specificity, a study by Watanabe (1996) has shown that some prefrontal cells can encode an anticipated reward. In his variant of the delayed-spatial-response task, the sample cues involved either the presentation of different types of rewards (e.g., raisin, apple, cabbage) at right and left loca-

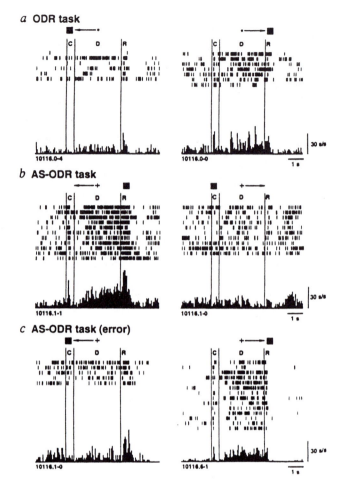

Figure 14.18. Responses of a prefrontal neuron during performance of the conventional and antisaccade (AS) versions of ODR. This cell fired associated with rightward stimulus regardless of whether the response was to the right (a), left (b), or an incorrect rightward response when it should have been left (c). (Reproduced, with permission, from Funahashi, Chafee, & Goldman-Rakic, 1993; Copyright Macmillan Magazines Ltd.)

tions or colored panel lights that were consistently associated with a subsequent reward type. After the memory delay the animal was required to select the correct choice panel location, without the cues present, to obtain the predicted reward. A substantial proportion of prefrontal neurons encoded the spatial location of the sample cue during the delay. In addition, half of the cells active during the delay showed different activity associated with the type of reward. The activity of some of these delay cells reflected both the spatial position and the type of reward, but other cells fired only in association with the reward. Furthermore, the reward-related activity patterns were the same when the reward itself was the cue, or if

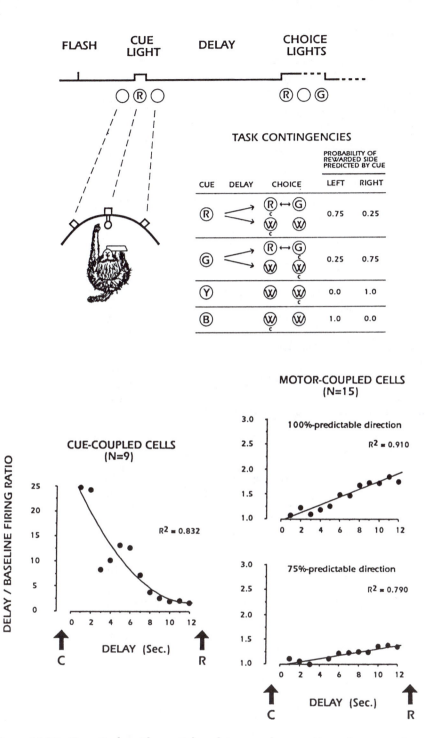

Figure 14.19. Top: Task with spatial and temporal separation of cues and responses. R, G, W refer to cue colors. Bottom: Composite responses of cue- and motor-coupled cell types. (Reproduced, with permission, from Quintana & Fuster, 1992; Copyright Lippincott Williams & Wilkins.)

the type of reward was only signaled by its arbitrary color associate. The example shown in Figure 14.20 (left) showed the greatest levels of delay activity for a cabbage reward or its associated color stimulus, and the response pattern was the same regardless of sample cue location. The example shown in Figure 14.20 (right) encoded both the spatial location of the sample and the reward type.

Funahashi and Kubota (1994) proposed that the combination of functional cell types observed in these studies is sufficient to mediate working memory. In their model (see Figure 14.15), the main three stages of processing of the central executive in spatial delayed response are an input module that encodes the stimulus qualities, a temporary storage model that holds specific information about the to-be-remembered item, and an output module that plans the response. Cells reflect-

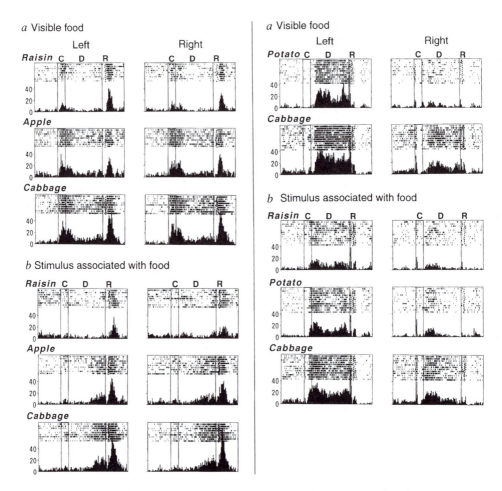

Figure 14.20. Examples of cells that fired differentially associated with presentation of specific foods or with cues that signalled the subsequent presentation of the same food. (Reproduced, with permission, from Watanabe, 1996; Copyright Macmillan Magazines Ltd.)

ing each of these stages are prevalent in the above-described studies. In addition, cells that fire after saccadic responses in monkeys performing the oculomotor task could provide a required "reset" signal to refresh the temporary store. Reinforcing the view that the prefrontal cortex contains a specialized temporary store, Miller and colleagues (1996) compared the capacity of prefrontal and temporal neurons in maintaining selective visual codings during the delay in monkeys performing a matching-to-sample task. A greater fraction of temporal cells showed selective responses to visual features, but the delay-related activity of these cells ceased abruptly when intervening stimuli were presented. Prefrontal cells that encoded specific visual features were not as prevalent, but these cells maintained stimulus specific activity throughout a memory delay filled with intervening stimuli.

A central current question about delay activity in the prefrontal cortex regards whether there is regional specialization of memory storage functions. Particularly striking evidence in favor of this view came from a study by Wilson et al. (1993) in which monkeys were trained on two variants of the delayed-response task. One version was the standard oculomotor spatial-delayed-response task, although only right and left target locations were employed. The other version was a visual-pattern-delayed-response task where one of two elaborate visual stimuli was presented at the central fixation point, and then after the delay the monkey was required to make a left or right saccade depending on which pattern was the sample cue. Neurons in the lateral prefrontal area (Figure 14.21A) were particularly responsive in the pattern-delayed-response task, so that over three quarters of the delay cells differentially fired in association with one visual cue. The example shown in Figure 14.21B fired differentially between the two visual cues on pattern-delayed-response trials but lacked responsiveness on spatial-delayed-response trials. Some of these cells showed highly selective delay responses, such as cells that fired selectively in association with one of two faces, but did not differentiate two other visual patterns. The opposite result was obtained for cells in the dorsolateral prefrontal cortex, so that most delay cells fired selectively in the spatial task and not in the pattern task (see example in Figure 14.21C). These results are consistent with anatomical distinctions in connectivity to posterior cortical regions, and with the differential distribution of sensory responses in the prefrontal cortex (Ó Scalaidhe et al., 1999; Tanila et al., 1993). The combination of these findings has been interpreted as strong support for the notion that there exist distinct working-memory areas in the prefrontal cortex, one in the dorsolateral prefrontal area supporting spatial working memory and another in the lateral area supporting visual pattern working memory (Goldman-Rakic, 1996b). Further evidence for specialization of functions within the prefrontal cortex of monkeys comes from studies showing convergence of taste and olfactory information in the orbitofrontal area and neural responses that reflect stimulus-reward associations (Rolls, 1996).

Activation of the Prefrontal Cortex in Humans Performing Working-Memory Tasks

The emergence of brain imaging techniques has allowed investigators to examine the areas of cortex activated during working-memory performance in human sub-

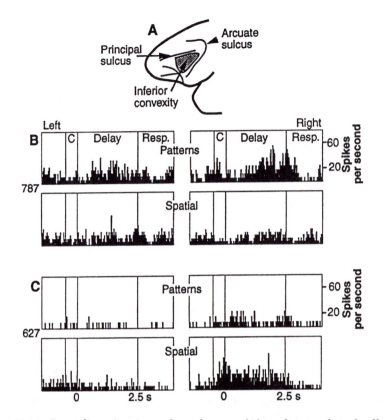

Figure 14.21. Recording sites in prefrontal cortex (A), and examples of cells that showed selective activity in the visual pattern (B) or spatial (C) ODR task. (Reproduced, with permission, from Wilson, Ó Scalaidhe, & Goldman-Rakic, 1993; Copyright American Association for the Advancement of Science.)

jects (for reviews see Buckner et al., 1999; Jonides & Smith, 1997; Cabeza & Nyberg, 1997; Owen, 1997; Smith & Jonides, 1994; Petrides, 1994). Among the first of these studies, Jonides et al. (1993) characterized areas of the human brain activated during a variant of the spatial-delayed-response task. In this task subjects fixated a central point on a computer monitor and were presented with three dots as target sample stimuli. Following a 3-s delay period, a circle marked one location on the screen where one of the targets had appeared, or another location. Thus subjects had to remember a set of target locations and later identify a choice item as one of the set. The control task was similar, except that the three dots were presented only during the end of the delay, then during the choice period when one of them was circled, so that responses were guided by perception, not memory. The brain areas prominently activated by PET included all the components of the working-memory circuit outlined in monkeys, but all on the right side of the human brain. These included the dorsolateral prefrontal cortex and the posterior parietal area, plus parts of the occipital and premotor areas. Confirming these findings, a closeby area of dorsolateral prefrontal cortex was activated in an fMRI study when subjects were required to identify repetitions of stimuli among a series of items presented at various spatial locations (McCarthy et al., 1994).

In humans, of course, one can examine the very same verbal and visuospatial working-memory processes that were the focus of the Baddeley and Hitch (1974) model, and indeed there is evidence for the existence of distinct areas that mediate the visuospatial sketch pad and the phonological loop (Paulesu et al., 1993; reviewed in Cabeza & Nyberg, 1997; also see below). Tasks that require subjects to rehearse verbal material activate a part of the parietal cortex, whereas different parietal areas are activated during visuospatial processing. All tasks that require working memory activate prefrontal areas. In addition, parts of the prefrontal cortex are especially strongly activated when subjects are required to update verbal information (Salmon et al., 1996), consistent with the putative role of this area as the central executive.

There is considerable agreement that different posterior areas are activated during modality-specific working-memory processing. On the other hand, there is considerable controversy over whether different kinds of processing are specialized within the prefrontal cortex, and over the nature of parcellation. One study, directly modeled after the work on monkeys, and examining this issue involved the "three-back" task, designed to test working memory for spatial or verbal material (Smith et al., 1996). In both versions of the task, on a series of trials subjects fixated a central location and were presented with a series of letters at a peripheral site, with one letter presented each trial with blank presentations intervening (Figure 14.22). In the spatial memory condition, on each trial the subject had to identify whether the target on the current trial matched in location the item presented three trials back and had to ignore the identity of the letters. In the verbal memory condition, the subject had to conversely identify whether the current letter matched the identity of the letter presented three trials back, ignoring the location of presentations. Thus the stimulus presentations in both tasks were identical, but the memory demands differed according to a spatial or verbal rule. The findings indicated a clear dissociation of brain regions involved in the two tasks. In the spatial task there was more activation in the right hemisphere, which included both a posterior parietal and a prefrontal site of most prominent activation. Conversely, the verbal task activated primarily parietal and prefrontal areas in the left hemisphere. This dissociation is consistent with clinical observations of selective spatial and verbal working-memory deficits following damage to the right and left prefrontal cortex, respectively (see Jonides & Smith, 1997).

A separate set of PET studies modeled after experiments on self-ordering and conditional learning in monkeys examined whether these cognitive operations could be dissociated in human brain activations (Petrides et al., 1993a, 1993b). In one of these studies subjects performed either the self-ordering task described above or a conditional visual motor response task in which subjects had to point to a different design assigned to each of a set of distinct color stimuli. Consistent with his studies on monkeys with selective prefrontal lesions, Petrides (1987) found that a mid-dorsolateral part of the prefrontal cortex was selectively activated in the self-ordering task, whereas a premotor area was selectively activated in the conditional visuomotor task (see chapter 13). In another study Petrides

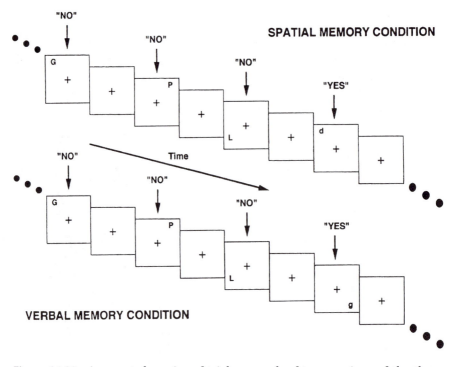

Figure 14.22. An example series of trials on each of two versions of the three-back task. (Reproduced, with permission, from Jonides & Smith, 1997; Copyright Psychology Press.)

(1993a) found that the same mid-dorsolateral area was selectively activated in a verbal self-ordering task, showing the generality of function of this area over nonverbal and verbal stimulus materials. There was some degree of hemispheric lateralization consistent with the Smith et al. study described above. In the nonverbal self-ordering task the right prefrontal area was differentially activated, whereas in the verbal task both hemispheres were equally activated.

In additional studies, Petrides and colleagues directly addressed potential distinctions between the dorsolateral and lateral areas of the human prefrontal cortex. These studies examined strategic retrieval from long-term memory for verbal and visuospatial materials. In the study on verbal strategic retrieval, Petrides et al. (1995) scanned subjects performing different verbal recall tasks. In one task subjects were required to recall a list of unrelated words, a task well acknowledged to depend on active retrieval mechanisms. To control specifically for strategic monitoring of the words that had been recalled, as opposed to the search in long-term memory per se, activation during word list retrieval was compared with that during a control condition in which subjects produced correct responses in a previously well-learned verbal paired-associate task. The latter task is much less demanding on active retrieval processes but involves the same degree of self-monitoring. They found that indeed the left dorsolateral area was equally activated in both tasks, but the lateral prefrontal area was more activated in the list retrieval task. In the study on visuospatial strategic retrieval, subjects were trained to touch each of a set of boxes displayed on a screen, touching each box as a nearby indicator light was illuminated. The sequence of indicated boxes was the same on each trial, so subjects reduced their reaction times over the course of training. This initially involved implicit learning, because the subjects could not generate the sequence explicitly. However, explicit training was then given by requiring subjects to touch each box in anticipation of the indicator. Following training in this condition the subjects were scanned in both conditions of the task. Activity in the right lateral prefrontal area was greater in the explicit condition than in the implicit condition, consistent with the interpretation that only the explicit sequencing required active retrieval of the stored sequence. The combination of all these findings led Petrides (1996) to propose that the prefrontal cortex is anatomically specialized, not according to different stimulus materials as Goldman-Rakic (1996b) argued, but according to the cognitive processing demands. Petrides argued that both verbal and nonverbal strategic ordering processes are reflected in selective activation of the dorsolateral prefrontal cortex, whereas strategic retrieval from long-term memory for both verbal and nonverbal materials selectively activates the lateral prefrontal cortical area. Notably, however, there are clear hemispheric differences in Petrides's findings on verbal and visuospatial materials, consistent with the proposal of Smith and Jonides (1994). On the other hand, there are also considerable data showing hemispheric differences in the prefrontal cortex based on cognitive demands associated with long-term memory encoding and retrieval processes, so that encoding in episodic memory for various materials is associated with enhanced activity in the left prefrontal cortex, whereas retrieval of various materials is associated with enhanced activity on the right side (Fletcher et al., 1997; Tulving et al., 1994a; Owen et al., 1996; Moscovitch et al., 1995).

A recent meta-analysis of a large number of studies using brain-imaging techniques to characterize prefrontal activation in working memory has generally sided with Petrides's view of parcellation by cognitive functions. In his analysis Owen (1997) found that spatial-working-memory tasks can activate either the dorsolateral or the lateral prefrontal region, so that the lateral region was activated when the task demanded retention of one or a few items, whereas the dorsolateral region was activated when the subject was required to constantly monitor and manipulate a series of ongoing spatial locations. A generally similar pattern was found across studies on visual working memory. Tasks that required subjects only to retain visual pattern information over a delay did not activate the dorsolateral area, whereas tasks that required constant monitoring and updating did. Overall Owen concluded that the dorsolateral region is activated when the demand for continuous monitoring is high, regardless of the materials to be remembered.

Two other recent studies have contributed to the view that different cognitive demands contribute to the distribution of activations during working-memory performance in humans. Cohen et al. (1997) used variants of the "n-back" task combined with rapid fMRI scans to compare regional activations as a function of differing demands for executive control in managing memory load versus maintenance over time. They trained subjects to match verbal stimuli to items presented previously under four different conditions. These included comparisons to items either one, two, or three items back, and a zero-back condition where a particular stimulus was identified whenever it was presented. Scans were made during and just after the stimulus presentation and repeatedly during the 10-s delay between trials. Areas in both the left prefrontal cortex and the posterior visual areas were activated, but the extent of activation differed under the controlled conditions. Prefrontal cortex activation was maximal under high-memory-load conditions, that is, in the two- and three-back tasks, and less so in the zero- and one-back tasks, and the level of activation was constant throughout the memory delay. Conversely, the visual areas were more activated late in the delay, when the memory demand was highest, regardless of load. In addition the amount of activation in Broca's area was affected by both factors, with the greatest activation for the highest load at the longest memory delay. These data are consistent with the notion that working-memory circuits are widespread in the cortex, and with the findings from earlier-described neuropsychological studies across species showing that the prefrontal cortex is more involved in strategic processing associated with the number of items in memory as opposed to storage of those items per se.

Another recent study compared posterior and prefrontal activations in humans performing a working memory task that required subjects to remember a face over a delay (Courtney et al., 1997). In this study fMRI activations were compared during presentations of face versus visual "noise" stimulation, and during the memory delay between stimulus presentations. Responses of posterior and prefrontal areas were characterized using multiple-regression analyses aimed at three components of the task, transient nonselective visual responses, transient selective responses to faces, and sustained responses over the memory delay. Posterior visual cortical areas showed primarily transient nonselective or selective visual responses, whereas prefrontal areas exhibited strong delay responses plus face selectivity. Furthermore, the extent to which these factors activated areas throughout the cortex was graded, with the most posterior area responsive only nonselectively and without delay, and the most rostral prefrontal areas most responsive to delay with face selectivity. These findings again are consistent with the notion of widespread networks for working memory, with graded contributions of processing functions throughout the network.

A Potential Resolution to the Controversy About Parcellation of Working-Memory Functions in the Prefrontal Cortex

There are such considerable differences between working-memory tasks used across species and in different laboratories that it is currently impossible to reach a conclusion about the nature of division of functions within the prefrontal cortex. There are consistencies in the data across techniques and species implicating prefrontal processing as more "strategic" than "memory," even though there are also considerable data showing extensive intermixing of executive and storage functions in working memory. While a final resolution of the functional mechanism of prefrontal cortex remains elusive, new studies on prefrontal neurons in monkeys performing novel learning and memory tests are providing insights that may supersede notions about division of function by modality or cognitive processing.

In one study Rao et al. (1997) trained monkeys on a variant of Miller's delayed-matching-to-sample task, in which subjects were shown a sample object stimulus at the central fixation point, then after a memory delay were shown that object plus another object choice at peripheral locations, then after another memory delay had to saccade to the location of the matching stimulus item (Figure 14.23, top). Thus the monkeys had to remember two aspects of the sample object. During the initial delay, they had to retain the object's featural properties, or the "what" quality of the stimulus. Then, in the second delay, they had to retain the location where the object was again presented, that is, its "where" quality. Neurons in the lateral prefrontal area responded to the "what" and the "where" qualities of objects. One example shown in Figure 14.23 (middle) fired more to one particular object during the initial "what" delay. The other example in this figure fired during the "where" delay more associated with location where the sample reappeared, regardless of which object was remembered. Yet other cells encoded both the "what" and "where" attributes. The first example shown in Figure 14.23 (bottom) fired in association with one object in the "what" delay and then switched its coding to represent one memory location in the "where" delay. The other example shown in this figure fired maximally in association with the combination of a particular object and a particular place it was presented. These data indicate that cells in the same area of the prefrontal cortex can represent both visual and spatial information when it is demanded by the task requirements.

The prefrontal cortex may be also especially suited to retrieving and utilizing representations of associations in memory. Rainer et al. (1999) recorded from neurons in the prefrontal cortex in monkeys trained on a task where they were initially presented with a sample visual stimulus and then, after a delay, had to identify an arbitrarily paired stimulus associate from multiple choices. During the sample stimulus presentation, and partially into the memory delay, the activity of prefrontal neurons was selective for the characteristics of the sample stimulus. However, toward the end of the delay, and prior to presentation of the choice stimuli, prefrontal neurons altered their activity associated with the characteristics of the appropriate stimulus associate. These findings suggest that prefrontal neurons may have access to long-term stored representations of visual as well as spatial associations.

Another experiment by Miller and his colleagues showed that neurons in the same lateral prefrontal area are fully capable of selective representation of the relevant what or where properties in accordance with task demands (Rainer et al., 1998). In this variant of the delayed-matching-to-sample task, monkeys were first cued as to which of three objects was the target. Initially the training involved trials in which only the target item was the sample and subjects were required to respond only when that item appeared in the same location on choice trials (Figure 14.24, top). Then the training involved "array trials," in which all three objects were shown with the target in one of three positions. In subsequent choice trials the monkey had to match the location in which the target had been presented as the sample to choice arrays, regardless of the locations of the other items. Many cells showed activity during the sample and delay associated with particular objects, regardless of position or whether they appeared in array or cue

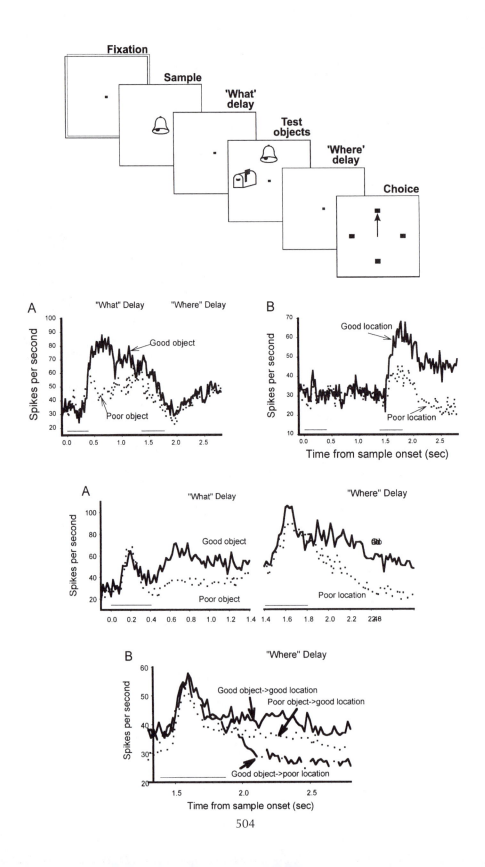

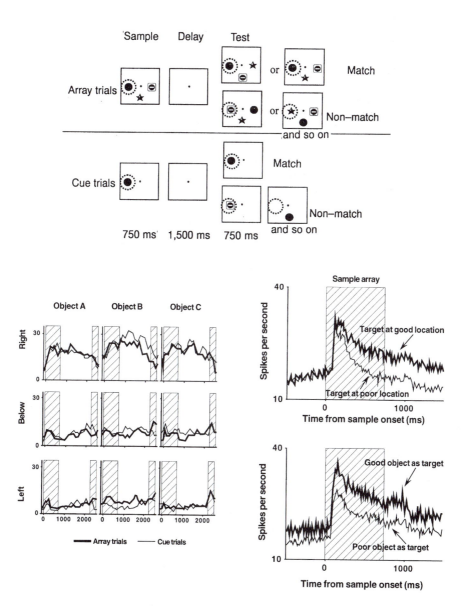

Figure 14.24. Tests of object location memory. Top: In array trials the monkey had to match an object in a particular location and ignore other objects. In cue trials, the monkey had to attend to only one object and its location. Bottom: Left: example of cells that encoded the relevant location on both array and cue trials. Right: Examples of equally rapid responses to both the relevant object and location information. (Reproduced, with permission, from Rainer, Asaad, & Miller, 1998; Copyright Macmillan Magazines Ltd.)

Figure 14.23. Top: Sequence of trial stages in the what and where task. Middle: Examples of object-tuned (A) and location-tuned (B) cells. Bottom: Examples of cells showing distinct object and location tuning (A) and a combination of object and location tuning (B). (Reproduced, with permission, from Rao, Rainer, & Miller, 1997; Copyright American Association for the Advancement of Science.)

trials, or a particular target regardless of position (Figure 14.24, bottom). These observations support the view that neurons within a prefrontal region can encode both visual and spatial information (see also Rainer et al., 1998), and that they can exclude information about irrelevant objects or locations according to demands for selective attention and memory. These findings are consistent with neuropsychological data described above showing deficits in attentional processing in patients and monkeys with prefrontal damage, and they highlight the notion that the role of prefrontal cortex in working memory has more to do with executive functions than with maintaining representations of particular stimuli or responses.

15

Multiple Memory Systems in the Brain: Where Do We Stand?

In this final chapter, we will consider some loose ends that suggest potential paradoxes in understanding memory systems. Then we will sum up by restating the main claims about memory systems of the brain.

Loose Ends: The Memory-Performance Distinction

This book began with two propositions: (a) that memory is a fundamental property of brain function, and its storage is an integral part of ongoing information processing, and (b) that memory is manifested in multiple functionally and anatomically distinct systems. Add to these the acknowledgment that the brain operates through the activity of distinct information-processing systems, and it should be no surprise that there would be multiple memory systems. To the extent that memory is indeed a property of information-processing, and that information processing functions are divided into distinct brain systems, it follows that memory systems should be distinguished by their functionalities and circuitries. This conclusion should be taken as the fundamental insight about memory systems arising from the present review.

The conclusion that memory and performance are inextricably linked creates some loose ends—perhaps even paradoxes—about why our "memories" seem so distinct from our acts of perception, motion, and thinking and other aspects of our "performance." And it raises some questions about how we can investigate memory independent of nonmemory information-processing functions. Vanderwolf and Cain (1994) characterized this apparent paradox as a discontinuity between psychological concepts about memory and neuroscientific evidence about synaptic mechanisms of plasticity in the brain's information-processing systems.

They argued that the predominant psychological conception of memory remains the "warehouse" metaphor in which memories are viewed as independent entities, separated from the brain's information-processing mechanisms (see chapter 1). This conception is sometimes viewed entirely as a metaphor. Nevertheless, many of its features are thoroughly embodied in common concepts about memory processing. For example, we strongly rely on notions of memory operations including "encoding," "storing," "transferring," and "retrieving," as if memories were objects that are handled and manipulated as entities distinct from perception, thinking, action, and other manipulations of information. Yet there is a vast body of neuroscientific knowledge outlined in this text that indicates that the features of memory are no more than a reflection of the plastic properties of those brain information-processing functions.

Is this a paradox? The present accounting should lay the issue to rest: Memory operations emerge from, and are therefore determined by, information-processing mechanisms of brain systems. The apparent paradox between the warehouse metaphor and our knowledge about mechanisms of brain information processing can be best understood by considering two separate "loose ends." One of these involves a special problem for the declarative memory system, and the other involves the converse issue for the procedural memory systems. A discussion of these two loose ends follows.

What Is the (Nonmemory) Information-Processing Function of the Cortical-Hippocampal Circuit?

We have argued here that memory is essentially a reflection of the plasticity of the brain's information-processing systems. And we have argued that cortical-hippocampal circuitry composes one of those memory systems. Therefore we are obliged to characterize what information-processing function is performed within the hippocampal circuit. At the same time, we should account for why this function appears so inextricably bound to memory itself. At the earliest stages of the hippocampal system, in the parahippocampal region, information processing may involve both the construction of complex "configural" representations and the maintenance of those representations for extended periods (see chapter 9). Thus damage to the parahippocampal region can result in deficits in the performance of complex, configural discriminations, and this high-order perceptual processing deficit may not be dissociable from the learning and memory of these stimuli (see Murray & Bussey, 1999). However, damage to the hippocampus itself does not result in any specific abnormality in perception, cognition, motor coordination, motivation, or any other aspect of *performance* on memory tasks. Conversely, the deficit involves only the capacity to *remember* what was learned during prior performances. Indeed, the dissociation of memory deficits from performance effects is precisely what is so attractive about the hippocampus as critical to *memory* per se. Yet, to the extent that the hippocampus participates only in memory, its role would seem to violate our proposition that memory is a property of the brain's information-processing—that is, *performance*—systems.

We envision two possible explanations for this apparent paradox. One possibility is that the hippocampal circuit is an exception to the rule, that is, that it's function is dedicated to memory. The other possibility is that the hippocampal circuit has an information-processing function, but that this function is so intimately tied to memory that this role cannot be independently distinguished by any nonmemory test. These two explanations are not so different from one another if one considers the special role the hippocampal circuit plays in information processing. Our review of the literatures on human and animal amnesia, and on the neurophysiology of the hippocampus, converges on an account in which the hippocampal circuit mediates the organization of cortical representations (see chapters 5–10). This organizational function is seen to be derived from the automatic episodic codings that are observed in the hippocampus and is seen to underlie the critical role the hippocampus plays in forms of memory expression that require relational processing. We contend that such a role is so basic to declarative memory that the hippocampal circuit seems to play a fully selective *memory* function.

Some insight into this role, and into why it is so inextricably bound to memory, comes from consideration of recent studies on the language capacities of the amnesic patient H.M. MacKay and colleagues (1998a, 1998b) have re-examined the transcripts and performance of H.M. in evaluations of his linguistic competence made by earlier studies. These re-examinations have focused on H.M.'s language comprehension in the analysis and interpretation of ambiguous sentences, such as "Hortense defended the man she loved with all of her heart." This sentence has two possible meanings: Either Hortense put up a defense with all of her heart, or she loved the man with all of her heart. In two different tests, H.M. detected 34–38% of the ambiguous sentences and could describe the ambiguity. By comparison, matched normal control subjects succeeded in identifying and describing the two meanings on 77–81% of the sentences (MacKay et al., 1998a). In addition, MacKay and colleagues (1998b) found that H.M.'s descriptions of these sentences were less clear and concise and were more repetitive than those of normal control subjects. Their interpretation of these findings was that this sort of ambiguity detection requires the formation of links between words and their episodic contexts, and that H.M. is impaired at the process of linking word concepts to represent new ideas in sentence production. Instead, they observed that H.M. exhibited an unusual strategy in detecting ambiguity. He often "free-associated" to one word or phrase after another until he evoked a sufficiently comprehensible different meaning. This accounting of H.M.'s language production was interpreted as an exception to his otherwise intact abilities in the verbal (and nonverbal) domain, and as supporting the view that some language functions and memory are inextricably intertwined.

These findings are reminiscent of the deficits in flexible and inferential memory expression following hippocampal damage in animals described in the chapters above. For example, in Dusek and Eichenbaum's (1997) study, rats with hippocampal disconnections could slowly acquire and retain the ability to make appropriate choices between adjacent items in a serial ordering (A > B, B > C, C > D, etc.; see also Bunsey & Eichenbaum, 1996). However, they could not subsequently make inferential choices between indirectly related items (B > D). This capacity requires the subject to recollect the relevant learning pairings and then generate the new links between them. Similar to H.M., rats with hippocampal disconnections could reproduce specifically trained responses, even in situations of ambiguity (B means one thing when presented with A and another thing when presented with C), but they failed to express their memory in situations where a novel linkage that relied on representations of previous episodes with familiar cues had to be made. Is this the "performance" function of the hippocampus? Such a function, employing representations of previous experiences to identify links to present experience, is precisely one of those kinds of information-processing mechanisms that can readily be seen as inextricably tied to memory, and in particular to declarative memory. Current research on neural firing patterns of hippocampal neurons is consistent with the notion that hippocampal circuitry indeed detects links between past and current episodes. This approach may in the future offer a fully mechanistic explanation of the nature of hippocampal information processing that underlies declarative memory.

Is It Really Possible to Distinguish "Memory" and "Performance" Within the Procedural Memory Systems?

To the extent that memory is a property of the brain's performance systems, how can we really dissociate and characterize the nature of the essential memory trace? This issue has most recently been brought to the forefront in comments by Cahill et al. (1999) that question the findings on the emotional memory system. The studies in question involve those of LeDoux, Fanselow, Davis, and their colleagues (see chapter 12) on fear conditioning. In particular, Cahill and colleagues call into question the conclusion that an essential plasticity occurs within the amygdala to mediate conditioned fear responses by raising doubts about three major lines of evidence that have been interpreted as supporting this conclusion. First, they questioned the interpretation of the finding that lesions of the amygdala block conditioned fear responses. Considerable evidence indicates that amygdala lesions interfere with the expression of *unconditioned* as well as conditioned fear responses (see chapter 12; see Maren, 1999), suggesting that the lesions affect performance functions of the amygdala and have no special role in blocking emotional memory. Second, Cahill et al. suggested a similar interpretation of the studies that use NMDA receptor blockers to prevent conditioned fear. These drugs may also interfere with the normal transmission and information-processing functions of the amygdala. Third, Cahill et al. suggested that evidence of changes in synaptic efficacy in the amygdala consequent on learning may simply reflect "upstream" plasticity in the sensory structures that send inputs to the amygdala. Each of these alternative interpretations is appropriate, and these confounds highlight the difficulty of identifying critical plasticity mechanisms within brain structures that are essential to performance functions involved in memory expression (see Fanselow & LeDoux, 1999). Future recording studies will have to show learning-related changes at critical sites independent of changes in their inputs. In addition, other future studies will tell whether the plasticity of this performance system can be fully dissociated from its performance per se. These will be difficult studies, but they are possible. The compelling evidence will have to include a way to block plasticity in these structures so that learning but not performance is affected. One approach, involving a complex design that demonstrated impairment of learning under NMDA receptor blockade at the same time as intact expression of a previously acquired response, provides strong evidence in the right direction (see Gewirtz & Davis, 1997—outlined above). In another study that provides this kind of evidence, Baily et al. (1999) examined the effects of infusion during learning of an mRNA synthesis inhibitor within the amygdala, a treatment that blocks the long-term maintenance phase of LTP. This treatment substantially attenuated subsequent retention of cued and contextual fear conditioning, without affecting freezing observed during the training session. The strategy employed in this study circumvents the nonselective role of NMDA receptors in the amygdala and shows that blockade of a later stage in the molecular cascade of LTP can result in a selective memory impairment.

Notably these issues have been circumvented in studies on the cerebellum and classical eyelid conditioning (Thompson & Kim, 1996). In these studies, it is possible to inactivate a part of the system that is not essential for expression of the unconditioned response and still prevent learning of conditioned responses. However, in this case, there may still be an as-yet-undetected information-processing function of that nucleus. Indeed, our fundamental insight suggests there must be an information-processing function of each structure whose plasticity is essential to learning. This view suggests a major lesson of neuroscientific efforts to localize the "engram." It is not to be identified by designating a locus where there is no function other than memory. Rather, the engram is to be understood in terms of plasticity of an information-processing function essential to that kind of memory.

Summing Up

The above considerations raised some issues that will have to be resolved for a full understanding of memory systems to be achieved. Nevertheless, recent decades have seen remarkable progress in demonstrating the existence of distinct memory systems in the brain and in characterizing their nature. Here we outline briefly some of the major conclusions of our review concerning the distinct properties of the different memory systems and some speculations about how they emerge.

1. The notion of multiple forms of memory is an old one that can be traced back at least 200 years. The story presented here is "old news" in that sense. However, the present account has focused on recent improvements in our understanding of multiple memory systems that have come from empirical science and particularly from empirical work in neuroscience. Indeed, the central claim of this book, that the features of different forms of memory arise from, and are determined by, the properties and the plasticity of the brain's information-processing systems, reflects an understanding that had to come from a neuroscientific approach.

2. Memory can be studied across a continuity of levels—from molecular to cellular to structural to brain-systems to behavioral. There may be many molecular and cellular bases of plasticity underlying the persistence of memory. In addition, it appears that the same pool of mechanisms may underlie plasticity in all the brain's memory systems, and these mechanisms support a short-term (minutes-to-hours) aspect of memory consolidation. However, these mechanisms

would seem to be independent of a longer term (days-to-years) consolidation process that occurs at the brain systems level. Most important, the major differences in memory systems emerge only at the structural, systems, and behavioral levels. The differences among memory systems could emerge only at the level where different functional systems divide, in line with our central claim about the inextricable link between memory systems and processing systems.

3. Notwithstanding the large number of distinct processing systems in the brain, memory systems are fundamentally differentiated into two general types: one that supports declarative memory and a collection of other systems that support procedural and emotional memory. The system that mediates declarative memory is "special," or seems so, and that is why we dedicated so much of this book (and why so much of the research in the field is likewise dedicated) to that system. The declarative system is special because it is the one that mediates "everyday memory"—our capacity to consciously recollect facts and past events, and to use our memories to plan and execute our actions. This kind of memory is the one that comes to mind when we think of "memory" as a distinct psychological capacity. However, this system is the most difficult to understand. This is likely because its functions are tied to, and in important ways support, the highest-order kinds of information processing: consciousness, planning, and problem solving. By contrast, the procedural memory systems are relatively "easier" to comprehend precisely because their functions are derived from information-processing systems that underlie better understood perceptual, motor, and emotional and attentional performance functions.

4. Despite the difficulty of uncovering and characterizing the features of declarative memory, we have made considerable progress in uncovering its pathways and its neurocognitive mechanisms. The main information-processing pathways of this system involve bidirectional connections between widespread association areas of the cerebral cortex and the parahippocampal region, and between the parahippocampal region and the hippocampus. This two-stage, bidirectional processing scheme constrains the functions of the hippocampal region to the service of cortical representations. That is, the hippocampal region must operate by extending the persistence of, organizing, and/or otherwise modifying cortical representations. That these modifications occur in two stages offers the possibility that the parahippocampal region and hippocampus can mediate different influences over cortical representations. The emerging consensus from work on animals and humans is that the parahippocampal region supports the ultimate convergence of information from functionally distinct cortical areas and can sustain an extended persistence of their representations. The additional stage of memory processing supported by the hippocampus is critical to the organization of cortical representations, so that experiences are encoded in terms of relevant temporal, spatial, and other relations among perceptually distinct cortical representations. The nature of the hippocampal-cortical representation may be based on an automatic encoding of (the relations among the constituent elements of) learning episodes; these codings critically involve the detection of common ("nodal") events and elements that tie episodes together, constituting a "memory space" by which present experiences can be linked to past episodes. Even in this memory system, memory is tied to processing, so that a full understanding of the workings of this system depends as much on clarifying the cortical information

domains and processing mechanisms upon which the hippocampal structures operate, as it does on understanding the mechanisms of the hippocampal structures themselves.

5. A full identification of procedural memory systems, and an understanding of their pathways and functional mechanisms, is also emerging. The major procedural memory systems involve (plasticities within the) circuitries that mediate emotion and motor control. These memory systems contain components and pathways that are parallel with, and are in part anatomically distinct from, the hippocampal memory system. It is clear that particular brain structures are involved exclusively in one or another system: The amygdala is part of only the emotional memory system, and the striatum and cerebellum are components of only the motor memory system. But these major procedural memory systems are far from simple. First, each involves partially distinct subsystems and corresponding subfunctions. For example, the emotional memory system involves subsystems for connecting arbitrary stimuli to emotional responses, and for employing emotional arousal to modulate attentional processes and plasticity throughout the brain. The motor memory system involves distinct subsystems that involve contributions by the striatum to higher motor coordination and contributions by the cerebellum to fine reflex coordination. And second, each procedural system involves pathways that link its functions to the other memory systems. The elaborated diagram of memory systems shown in Figure 15.1 illustrates the major pathways by which these memory systems are distinguished, as well as where they interconnect. This anatomical information is consistent with our success in dissociating the functions of different memory systems at particular anatomical sites and corresponding functional levels. At the same time, this information tells us that the systems must also work together closely.

6. The cerebral cortex is a central component of all the memory systems and performs distinct memory-processing functions through interactions within its own functionally distinct areas (Figure 15.1). The cortex is a major source of input of higher-order information to each of the memory systems and, at the same time, a major target of the influences of the memory systems. The cortex itself mediates working memory, through interactions between the prefrontal cortex and higher-order areas of the posterior cortex. For this type of memory, too, memory functions and processing functions are intimately linked. Hence, the nature and scope of working memory are determined by the information-processing mechanisms of the prefrontal cortex, although at this time these are only weakly understood.

From Conditioning to Conscious Recollection: A Final Point

Many of those who have written on multiple memory systems have considered the differences among types of memory a reflection of a continuum of complexities. But here we take the opposite stance. There is no continuity between conditioning and conscious recollection. In our view, above the level of synaptic and cellular mechanisms, where the functions of memory divide according to the brain's information-processing systems, the properties of various types of "condi-

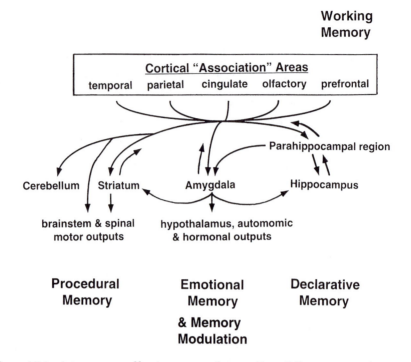

Figure 15.1. A taxonomy of brain systems that mediate different types of memory. This outline elaborates the tentative sketch provided in Figure 2.6, and provides a more complete and current conception of the flow of information in each pathway.

tioning" that are embodied in emotional and procedural memory have evolved separately from those of conscious recollection and the declarative memory representations that support it. A full understanding of brain's various types of memory, we believe, will require recognizing the discontinuities between them and gaining a richer conceptualization of the information-processing functions they have evolved to support.

References

Adam, G. (Ed.). 1971. *Biology of Memory*. New York: Plenum Press.

Adolphs, R., Tranel, D., Damasio, H., & Damasio, A. 1994. Impaired recognition of emotion in facial expressions following bilateral damage to the human amygdala. *Nature* 372: 669–672.

Adolphs, R., Tranel, D., Damasio, H., & Damasio, A. R. 1995. Fear and the human amygdala. *The Journal of Neuroscience* 15: 5879–5891.

Aggleton, J. P. (Ed.). 1992. *The Amygdala*. New York: Wiley-Liss.

Aggleton, J. P., Blint, H. S., & Rawlins, J. N. P. 1989. Effects of amygdaloid and amygdaloid-hippocampal lesions on object recognition and spatial working memory in rats. *Behavioral Neuroscience* 103: 962–974.

Aggleton, J. P., Hunt, P. R., & Rawlins, J. N. P. 1986. The effects of hippocampal lesions upon spatial and non-spatial tests of working memory. *Behavioral Brain Research* 19: 133–146.

Aggleton, J. P., & Mishkin, M. 1985. Mamillary-body lesions and visual recognition in monkeys. 1985. *Experimental Brain Research* 58: 190–197.

Aggleton, J. P., Nicol, R. M., Huston, A. E., & Fairbairn, A. F. 1988. The performance of amnesic subjects on tests of experimental amnesia in animals: Delayed matching-to-sample and concurrent learning. *Neuropsychologia* 26(2): 265–272.

Aguirre G. K., & D'Esposito, M. 1997. Environmental knowledge is subserved by separable dorsal/ventral neural areas. *The Journal of Neuroscience* 17: 2512–2518.

Aguirre, G. K., Detre, J. A., Alsop, D. C., & D'Esposito, M. 1996. The parahippocampus subserves topographic learning in man. *Cerebral Cortex* 16: 823–829.

Ahissar, E., Vaadia, E., Ahissar, M., Bergman, H., Arieli, A., & Abeles, M. 1992. Dependence of cortical plasticity on correlated activity of single neurons and on behavioral context. *Science* 257: 1412–1415.

Albus, J. S. 1971. A theory of cerebellar function. *Mathematical Biosciences* 10: 25–61.

Aldridge, J. W., Berridge, K. C., Herman, M., & Zimmer, L. 1993. Neuronal coding of serial order: Syntax of grooming in the neostriatum. *Psychological Science* 4: 391–395.

Alexander, G. E., Delong, M. R., & Strick, P. L. 1986. Parallel organization of functionally segregated circuits linking basal ganglia and cortex. *Annual Review of Neuroscience* 9: 357–381.

Allard, T., Clark, S. A., Jenkins, W. M., & Merzenich, M. M. 1991. Reorganization of somatosensory area 3b representations in adult owl monkeys after digital syndactyly. *Journal of Neurophysiology* 66: 1048–1058.

Allen, G., Buxton, R. B., Wong, E. C., & Courchesne, E. 1997. Attentional activation of the cerebellum independent of motor inolvement. *Science* 275: 1940–1943.

Allen, W. F. 1940. Effect of ablating the frontal lobes, hippocampi, and occipitoparieto-temporal (excepting pyriform areas) lobes on positive and negative olfactory conditioned reflexes. *American Journal of Physiology* 128: 754–771.

Allman, J., & Brothers, L. 1994. Faces, fear and the amygdala. *Nature* 372: 613–614.

Altman, J. R., Brunner, R. L., & Bayer, S. A. 1973. The hippocampus and behavioral maturation. *Behavioral Biology* 8: 557–596.

Alvarado, M. C., & Rudy, J. W. 1995. Rats with damage to the hippocampal formation are impaired on the transverse patterning problem but not on elemental discriminations. *Behavioral Neuroscience* 109: 204–211.

Alvarez, P., & Squire, L. R. 1994. Memory consolidation and the medial temporal lobe: A simple network model. *Proceedings of the National Academy of Sciences (United States of America)* 91: 7041–7045.

Alvarez, P., Zola-Morgan, S., & Squire, L. R. 1994. The animal model of human amnesia: Long-term memory impaired and short-term memory intact. *Proceedings of the National Academy of Sciences (United States of America)* 91: 5637–5641.

Alvarez, P., Zola-Morgan, S., & Squire, L. R. 1995. Damage limited to the hippocampal region produces long-lasting memory impairment in monkeys. *The Journal of Neuroscience* 15: 5 3796–3807.

Alvarez-Royo, P., Clower, R. P., Zola-Morgan, S., & Squire, L. R. 1991. Stereotaxic lesions of the hippocampus in monkeys: Determination of surgical coordinates and analysis of lesions using magnetic resonance imaging. *Journal of Neuroscience Methods* 38: 223–232.

Amaral, D. G., Insausti, R., & Cowan, W. M. 1987. The entorhinal cortex of the monkey: I. Cytoarchitechtonic organization. *Journal of Comparative Neurology* 264: 326–355.

Amaral, D. G., & Price, J. L. 1995. Hippocampal formation. In G. Paxinos (Ed.), *The Rat Nervous System* (2nd ed.). San Diego: Academic Press. Pp. 443–493.

Amaral, D. G., Price, J. L., Pitkanen, A., & Carmichael, S. T. 1992. Anatomical organization of the primate amygdaloid complex. In J. P. Aggleton (Ed.), *The Amygdala: Neurobological Aspects of Emotion, Memory and Mental Dysfunction.* London: Wiley-Liss, pp. 1–66.

Amaral, D. G., & Witter, M. P. 1989. The three-dimensional organization of the hippocampal formation: A review of anatomical data. *Neuroscience* 31: 571–591.

Amsel, A. 1993. Hippocampalfunction in the rat: cognitive mapping or vacarious trial and error? *Hippocampus* 3: 251–256.

Andersen, P., & Moser, E. I. 1995. Brain temperature and hippocampal function. *Hippocampus* 5: 491–498.

Andersen, P., & Trommald, M. 1995. Possible strategies for finding the substrate for learning-induced changes in the hippocampal cortex. *Journal of Neurobiology* 26: 396–402.

Andersen, R. A. 1989. Visual and eye movement functions of the posterior parietal cortex. *Annual Review of Neuroscience* 12: 377–403.

Andersen, R. A., Essick, G. K., & Siegel, R. M. 1985. Encoding of spatial location by posterior parietal neurons. *Science* 230: 456–458.

Aosaki, T., Brayiel, A. M., & Kimura, M. 1996. Effect of the nigrostriatal dopamine system in primates. *Critical Reviews in Neurobiology* 10: 317–356.

Aosaki, T., Tsubokawa, H., Ishida, A., Watanabe, K., Graybiel, A. M., & Kimura, M. 1994. Responses of tonically active neurons in the primate's striatum undergo systematic changes during behavioral sensorimotor conditioning. *The Journal of Neuroscience* 14: 3969–3984.

Apicella, P., Scarnati, E., Ljungber, T., & Schultz, W. 1992. Neuronal activity in monkey striatum related to the expectation of predictable environmental events. *Journal of Neurophysiology* 68: 945–960.

Armony, J. L., Servan-Schreiber, D., Cohen, J. D., & LeDoux, J. E. 1995. An anatomically constrained neural network model of fear conditioning. *Behavioral Neuroscience* 2: 246–257.

Artola, A., Brocher, S., & Singer, W. 1990. *Nature* 347: 69–72.

Asanuma, H., & Keller, A. 1991. Neurobiological basis of motor learning and memory. *Concepts in Neuroscience* 2: 1–30.

Bachevalier, J., & Meunier, M. 1996. Cerebral ischemia: Are the memory deficits asociated with hippocampal cell loss? *Hippocampus* 6: 553–560.

Bachevalier, J., Saunders, R. C., & Mishkin, M. 1985. Visual recognition in monkeys: Effects of transection of fornix. *Experimental Brain Research* 57: 547–553.

Baddeley, A. 1986. *Working Memory*. Oxford: Oxford University Press.

Baddeley, A. 1992. Working memory. *Science* 255: 556–559.

Baddeley, A. 1996. The fractionation of working memory. *Proceedings of the National Academy of Sciences* 93: 13468–13472.

Baddeley, A. D., & Hitch, G. 1974. In G. A. Bower (Ed.), *The Psychology of Learning and Motivation* (Vol. 8). New York: Academic, pp. 47–89.

Bagshaw, M. H., & Pribram, J. D. 1968. Effect of amgdalectomy on stimulus threshold of the monkey. *Experimental Neurology* 20: 197–202.

Bailey, D. J., Kim, J. J., Sun, W., Thompson, R. F., & Helmstetter, F. J. 1999. Acquisition of fear conditioning in rats requires the synthesis of mRNA in the amygdala. *Behavioral Neuroscience* 113: 276–282.

Baker, S. C., Frith, C. D., Frackowiak, R. S. J., & Dolan, R. J. 1996. Active representation of shape and location in man. *Cerebral Cortex* 6: 612–619.

Balsam, P. D., & Tomie, A. (Eds.). 1985. *Context and learning.* Hillsdale, NJ: Erlbaum.

Banich, M. T. 1997. *Neuropsychology: The Neural Basis of Mental Function.* Boston: Houghton Mifflin.

Bannerman, D. M., Good, M. A., Butcher, S. P., Ramsay, M., & Morris, R. G. M. 1995. Prior experience and N-methyl-D-aspartate receptor blockade dissociate components of spatial learning in the watermaze. *Nature* 378: 182–186.

Barbas, H. 1995. Anatomic basis of cognitive-emotional interactions in the primate prefrontal cortex. *Neuroscience and Biobehavioral Reviews* 19: 499–510.

Barbas, H., & Pandya, D. N. 1989. Architecture and intrinsic connections of the prefrontal cortex in the rhesus monkey. *The Journal of Comparative Neurology* 286: 353–375.

Barnes, C. A., Jung, M. W., McNaughton, B. L., Korol, D. L., Andreasson, K., & Worley, P. F. 1994. LTP saturation and spatial learning disruption: Effects of task variables and saturation levels. *The Journal of Neuroscience* 14: 5793–5806.

Barnes, C. A., McNaughton, B. L., Mizumori, S. J. Y., Leonard, B. W., & Lin, L-H. 1990. Comparison of spatial and temporal characteristics of neuronal activity in sequential stages of hippocampal processing. *Progress in Brain Research* 83: 287–300.

Barone, P., & Joseph, J. P. 1989. Prefrontal cortex and spatial sequencing in macaque monkeys. *Experimental Brain Research* 78: 447.

Barria, A., Muller, D., Derkach, V., Griffith, L. C., & Soderling, T. R. 1997. Regulatory phosphorylation of AMPA type glutamate receptors by CaM-KII during long-term potentiation. *Science* 276: 2042–2045.

Bartlett, F. C. 1932. *Remembering.* London: Cambridge University Press.

Baudry, M., & Davis, J. L. 1991. *Long Term Potentiation: A Debate of Current Issues.* Cambridge, MA: MIT Press.

Baudry, M., & Davis, J. L. (Eds.). 1994. *Long-term potentiation: Volume 2.* Cambridge, MA: MIT Press.

Baudry, M., & Davis, J. L. (Eds.). 1996. *Long-term potentiation: Volume 3.* Cambridge, MA: MIT Press.

Baylis, G. C., & Rolls, E. T. 1987. Responses of neurons in the inferior temporal cortex in short term and serial recognition memory tasks. *Experimental Brain Research* 65: 614–622.

Baylis, L. L., & Gaffan, D. 1991. Amygdalectomy and ventromedial prefrontal ablation produce similiar deficits in food choice and in simple object discrimination learning for an unseen reward. *Experimental Brain Research* 86: 617–622.

Bear, M. F. 1996. A synaptic basis for memory storage in the cerebral cortex. *Proceedings of the National Academy of Sciences (United States of America)* 93: 13453–13459.

Bear, M. F. 1997. How do memories leave their mark? *Nature* 385: 481–482.

Bear, M. F., Connors, B. W., & Paradiso, M. A. 1996. Synaptic mechanisms of memory. *Neuroscience: Exploring the Brain.* Baltimore: Williams & Wilkins.

Bear, M. F., Cooper, L. N., & Ebner, F. F. 1987. A physiological basis for a theory of synapse modification. *Science* 237: 42–47.

Bear, M. F., & Malenka, R. C. 1994. Synaptic plasticity: LTP and LTD. *Current Opinion in Neurobiology* 4: 389–399.

Beason-Held, L. L., Rosene, D. L., Killiany, R. J., & Moss, M. B. 1999. Hippocampal formation lesions produce memory impairment in the rhesus monkey. *Hippocampus* 9: 562–574.

Bechara, A., Tranel, D., Damasio, H., D., Adolphs, R., Rockland, C., & Damasio, A. R. 1995. Double dissociation of conditioning and declarative knowledge relative to the amygdala and hippocampus in humans. *Science* 269: 1115–1118.

Bechterev, V. M. 1907. *La psychologie objective* (Russian original). *General principles of human reflexology* (English translation).

Becker, H. C., Jarvis, M. F., Wagner, G. C., & Flaherty, C. F. 1984. Medial and lateral amygdalectomy differentially influences consummatory negative contrast. *Physiology and Behavior* 33: 707–712.

Bell, R. E., & Scoville, W. B. 1967. Significance of delay in the performance of monkeys with medial Temporal Lobe resections. *Experimental Brain Research* 4: 85–96.

Benowitz, L. I., & Routtenberg, A. 1987. A membrane phosphoprotein associated with neural development, axonal regeneration, phospholipid metabolism, and synaptic plasticity. *Trends in Neurosciences* 10: 527–532.

Berger, T. W. 1984. Long-term potentiation of hippocampal synaptic transmission affects rate of behavioral learning. *Science* 224: 627–630.

Berger, T. W., Alger, B. E., & Thompson, R. F. 1976. Neuronal substrates of classical conditioning in the hippocampus. *Science* 192: 483–485.

Berger, T. W., Clark, G. A., & Thompson, R. F. 1980. Learning dependant neuronal esponses recorded from limbic system brain structures during classical conditioning. *Physiological Psychology* 8(2): 155–167.

Berger, T. W., Rinaldi, P. C., Weisz, D. J., & Thompson, R. F. 1983. Single-unit analysis of different hippocampal cell types during classical conditioning of rabbit nictitating membrane response. *Journal of Neurophysiology* 50: 1197–1219.

Berger, T. W., & Thompson, R. F. 1978. Neuronal plasticity in the limbic system during classical conditioning of the rabbit nictitating membrane response: I. The hippocampus. *Brain Research* 145: 323–346.

Bergson, H. 1911/1950. *Matter and memory.* London: George Allen & Unwin Ltd.

Berman, D. E., Hazvi, S., Rosenblum, K., Seger, R., & Dudai, Y. 1998. Specific and differential activation of mitogen-activated protein kinase cascades by unfamiliar taste in the insular cortex of the behaving rat. *The Journal of Neuroscience* 18: 10037–10044.

Berman, R. F., Kesner, R. P., & Partlow, L. M. 1978. Passive avoidance impairment in rats following cycloheximide injection into the amygdala. *Brain Research* 158: 171–188.

Berridge, K. C., & Whishaw, I. Q. 1992. Cortex, striatum and cerebellum: Control of serial order in a grooming sequence. *Experimental Brain Research* 90: 275–290.

Best, P. J., & Ranck, J. B., Jr. 1982. Reliability of the relationship between hippocampal unit activity and sensory-behavioral events in the rat. *Experimental Neurology* 75: 652–664.

Bingman, V. P. 1992. The importance of comparative studies and ecological validity for understanding hippocampal structure and cognitive function. *Hippocampus* 2: 213–220.

Black, J. E., Isaacs, K. R., Anderson, B. J., Alcantara, A. A., & Greenough, W. T. 1990. Learning causes synaptogenesis, whereas motor activity causes angiogenesis, in cerebellar cortex of adult rats. *Proceedings of the National Academy of Sciences* 87: 5568–5572.

Blakemore, C. 1974. Developmental factors in the formation of feature-extracting neurons. In F. O. Schmitt & F. G. Worden (Eds.), *The Neurosciences: Third Study Program.* Cambridge, MA: MIT Press, pp. 105–113.

Bliss, T. V. P., & Collingridge, G. L. 1993. A synaptic model of memory: Long-term potentiation in the hippocampus. *Nature* 361: 31–39.

Bliss, T. V. P., & Gardner-Medwin, A. R. 1973. Long-lasting ptentiation of synaptic transmission in the dentate area of the unanaesthetized rabbit following stimulation of the perforant path. *Journal of Physiology (London)* 232: 357–374.

Bliss, T. V. P., & Lomo, T. 1973. Long-lasting potentiation of synaptic transmission in the dentate area of anesthetized rabbit following stimulation of the perforant path. *Journal Physiology (London)* 232: 331–356.

Bliss, T. V. P., & Lynch, M. A. 1988. Long term potentiation of synaptic transmission in the hippocampus: Properties and mechanisms. In *Long Term Potentiation: From Biophysics to Behavior.* New York: Liss, pp. 3–72.

Bliss, T. V. P., & Richter-Levin, G. 1993. Spatial learning and saturation of long-term potentiation. *Hippocampus* 3(2): 123–125.

Bloedel, J. R., Ebner, T. J., & Wise, S. P. 1996. The acquisition of motor behavior in vertebrates. Cambridge, MA: MIT Press.

Bolhuis, J. J., Stewart, C. A., & Forrest, E. M. 1994. Retrograde amnesia and memory reactivation in rats with ibotenate lesions to the hippocampus or subiculum. *Quarterly Journal of Experimental Psychology: Comparative and Physiological Psychology* 47B: 129–150.

Bolles, R. C. 1970. Species-specific defense reactions and avoidance learning. *Psychological Review* 77: 32–48.

Bontempi, B., Laurent-Demir, C., Destrade, C., & Jaffard, R. 1999. Time-dependent reorganization of brain circuitry underlying long-term memory storage. *Nature* 400: 671–674.

Bordi, F., & LeDoux, J. E. 1992. Sensory tuning beyond the sensory system: An initial analysis of auditory response properties of neurons in the lateral amygdaloid nucleus and overlying areas of the striatum. *The Journal of Neuroscience* 12: 2493–2503.

Bordi, F., & LeDoux, J. E. 1994a. Response properties of single units in areas of rat auditory thalamus that project to the amygdala: I. Acoustic discharge patterns and frequency receptive fields. *Experimental Brain Research* 98: 261–274.

Bordi, F., & LeDoux, J. E. 1994b. Response properties of single units in areas of rat auditory thalamus that project to the amygdala: II. Cells receiving convergent auditory and somatosensory inputs and cells antodromically activated by amgdala stimulation. *Experimental Brain Research* 98: 275–286.

Bostock, E., Muller, R. U., & Kubie, J. L. 1991. Experience-dependent modifications of hippocampal place cell firing. *Hippocampus* 1: 193–206.

Bourtchuladze, R., Frenguelli, B., Blendy, J., Cioffi, D., Schutz, G., & Silva, A. J. 1994. Deficient long-term memory in mice with a targeted mutation of the cAMP-responsive element-binding protein. *Cell* 79(1): 59–68.

Bracha, V., & Bloedel, J. R. 1996. The multiple-pathway model of circuits subserving the classical conditioning of withdrawal reflexes. In J. R. Bloedel, T. J. Ebner, & S. P. Wise (Eds.), *The Acquisition of Motor Behavior in Vertebrates*. Cambridge, MA: MIT Press, pp. 175–204.

Brasted, P. J., Humby, T., Dunnett, S. B., & Robbins, T. W. 1997. Unilateral lesions of the dorsal striatum in rats disrupt responding in egocentric space. *The Journal of Neuroscience* 17: 8919–8926.

Breese, C. R., Hampson, R. E., & Deadwyler, S. A. 1989. Hippocampal place cells: Stereotypy and plasticity. *The Journal of Neuroscience* 9: 1097–1111.

Breiter, H. C., Etcoff, N. L., Whalen, P. J., Kennedy, W. A., Rauch, S. L., Buckner, R. L., Strauss, M. M., Hyman, S. E., & Rosen, B. R. 1996. Response and habituation of the human amygdala during visual processing of facial expression. *Neuron* 17: 875–887.

Breland, K., & Breland, M. 1961. The misbehavior of organisms. *American Psychologist* 16: 681–684.

Breland, K., & Breland, M. 1996. *Animal Behavior*. New York: Macmillan.

Brewer, J. B., Zhao, Z., Desmond, J. E., Glover, G. H., & Gabrieli, J. D. E. 1998. Making memories: Brain activity that predicts how well visual experience will be remembered. *Science* 281: 1185–1188.

Brodmann, K. 1909. *Vergleichen de Lokalisationslehre der Grosshirnrinde in irhen Prinzipien dargestellt auf Grund des Zellenbaues*. Leipzig: Barth.

Brooks, D. N., & Baddeley, A. 1976. What can amnesic patients learn? *Neuropsychologia* 14: 111–122.

Brown, M. W. 1996. Neuronal responses and recognition memory. *Seminars in the Neurosciences* 8: 23–32.

Brown, M. W., Wilson, F. A. W., & Riches, I. P. 1987. Neuronal evidence that inferomedial temporal cortex is more important than hippocampus in certain processes underlying recognition memory. *Brain Research* 409: 158–162.

Brown, M. W., & Xiang J.-Z. 1998. Recognition memory: Neuronal substrates of the judgement of prior occurrence. *Progress in Neurobiology* 55: 149–189.

Brown, T. H., & Chattarji, S. 1994. Hebbian synaptic plasticity: Evolution of the contemporary concept. In E. Domany, J. L. Van Hemmen, & K. Schulten (Eds.), *Models of Neural Networks*. New York: Springer-Verlag.

Buckner, R. L., Goodman, J., Burock, M., Rotte, M., Koutstaal, W., Schacter, D., Rosen, B., & Dale A. M. 1998. Functional-anatomic correlates of object priming in humans revealed by rapid presentation event-related fMRI. *Neuron* 20: 285–296.

Buckner, R. L., Kelley, W. M., & Petersen, S. E. 1999. Frontal cortex contributes to human memory formation. *Nature Neuroscience* 2: 311–314.

Buckner, R. L., Petersen, S. E., Ojemann, J. G., Miezin, F. M., Squire, L. R., & Raichle, M. E. 1995. Functional anatomical studies of explicit and implicit memory retrieval tasks. *The Journal of Neuroscience* 15: 12–29.

Buckner, R. L., Strauss, M. M., Hyman, S. E., & Rosen, B. R. 1996. Response and habituation of the human amygdala during visual processing of facial expression. *Neuron* 17: 875–887.

Bunsey, M., & Eichenbaum, H. 1993. Paired associate learning in rats: Critical involvement of the parahippocampal region. *Behavioral Neuroscience* 107: 740–747.

Bunsey, M., & Eichenbaum, H. 1995. Selective damage to the hippocampal region blocks long term retention of a natural and nonspatial stimulus-stimulus association. *Hippocampus* 5: 546–556.

Bunsey, M., & Eichenbaum, H. 1996. Conservation of hippocampal memory function in rats and humans. *Nature* 379: 255–257.

Burnham, W. M. 1903. Retroactive amnesia: Illustrative cases and a tentative explanation. *American Journal of Psychology* 14: 382–396.

Burwell, R. D., & Amaral, D. G. 1998a. The cortical afferents of the perirhinal, postrhinal, and entorhinal cortices of the rat. *Journal of Comparative Neurology* 398: 179–205.

Burwell, R. D., & Amaral, D. G. 1998b. Perirhinal and postrhinal cortices of the rat: Interconnectivity and connections with the entorhinal cortex. *Journal of Comparative Neurology* 391: 293–321.

Burwell, R. D., Witter, M. P., & Amaral, D. G. 1995. Perirhinal and postrhinal cortices in the rat: A review of the neuroanatomical literature and comparison with findings from the monkey brain. *Hippocampus* 5: 390–408.

Bussey, T. J., Warburton, E. C., Aggleton, J. P., & Muir, J. L. 1998. Fornix lesions can facilitate acquisition of the transverse patterning task: A challenge for "configural" theories of hippocampal function. *The Journal of Neuroscience* 18: 1622–1631.

Butters, N., & Delis, D. C. 1995. Clinical assessment of memory disorders in amnesia and dementia. *Annual Review of Psychology* 46: 493–523.

Butters, N., Salmon, D. P., & Heindel, W. C. 1994. Specificity of the memory deficits associated with basal ganglia dysfunction. *Revue Neurologique (Paris)* 150: 580–587.

Buzsaki, G., & Chrobak, J. J. 1995. Temporal structure in spatially organized neuronal ensembles: A role for interneuronal networks. *Current Opinion in Neurobiology* 5: 504–510.

Buzsaki, G., Grastyan, E., Czopf, J., Kellenyi, L., & Prohaska, O. 1981. Changes in neuronal transmission in the rat hippocampus during behavior. *Brain Research* 225: 235–247.

Buzsaki, G., Haas, H. L., & Andersen, E. G. 1987. Long-term potentiation induced by physiologically relevant stimulus patterns. *Brain Research* 435: 331–333.

Buzsaki, G., Horvath, Z., Urioste, R., Hetke, J., & Wise, K. 1992. High frequency network oscillation in the hippocampus. *Science* 256: 1025–1027.

Byrne, J. H. 1997. *Learning & Memory*, Vol. 3, No. 6. Cold Spring Harbor, NY: Cold Spring Harbor Laboratory Press.

Byrne, W. L., et al. 1966. Memory transfer. *Science* 153: 658–659.

Cabeza, R., & Nyberg, L. 1997. Imaging cognition: An empirical review of PET studies with normal subjects. *Journal of Cognitive Neuroscience* 9(1): 1–26.

Cador, M., Robbins, T. W., & Everitt, B. J. 1989. Involvement of the amygdala in stimulus-reward associations: Interaction with the ventral striatum. *Neuroscience* 30(1): 77–86.

Cahill, L., Haier, R. J., Fallons, J., Alkire, M. T., Tang, C., Keator, D., Wu, J., & McGaugh, J. L. 1996. Amygdala activity at encoding correlated with long-term free recall of emotional information. *Proceedings of the National Academy of Sciences* 93: 8016–8021.

Cahill, L., & McGaugh, J. L. 1990. Amygdaloid complex lesions differentially affect retention of tasks using appetitive and aversive reinforcement. *Behavioral Neuroscience* 104: 523–543.

Cahill, L., & McGaugh, J. L. 1998. Mechanisms of emotional arousal and lasting declarative memory. *Trends in Neuroscience* 21: 273–313.

Cahill, L., Prins, B., Weber, M., & McGaugh, J. L. 1994. ß-Adrenergic activation and memory for emotional events. *Nature* 371: 702–704.

Cahill, L., Weinberger, N. M., Roozendaal, B., & McGaugh, J. L. 1999. Is the amygdala a locus of "conditioned fear"? Some questions and caveats. *Neuron* 23: 227–228.

Cahill, L. F., Babinksy, R., Markowitsch, H. J., & McGaugh, J. L. 1995. The amygdala and emotional memory. *Nature* 377: 6547.

Cain, D. P. 1997. LTP, NMDA, genes and learning. *Current Opinion in Neurobiology* 7: 235–242.

Cain, D. P., Hargreaves, E. L., Boon, F., & Dennison, Z. 1993. An examination of the relations between hippocampal long-term potentiation, kindling, afterdischarge, and place learning in the water maze. *Hippocampus* 3(2): 153–163.

Cain, D. P., Saucier, D., Hall, J., Hargreaves, E. L., & Boon, F. 1996. Detailed behavioral analysis of water maze acquisition under APV or CNQX: Contribution of Sensori-motor disturbances to drug induced acquisition deficits. *Behavioral Neuroscience* 110: 86–102.

Calabresi, P., Pisani A., Mercuri N. B., & Bernardi G. 1992. Long-term potentiation in the striatum is unmasked by removing the voltage-dependent magnesium block of NMDA receptor channels. *European Journal of Neuroscience* 1: 638–643.

Calabresi, P., Pisani, A., Mercuri, N. B., & Bernardi, G. 1996. The corticostriatal projection: from synaptic plasticity to dysfunctions of the basal ganglia. *Trends in Neurosciences* 19: 19–24.

Calder, A. J., Young, A. W., Rowland, D., Perrett, D. I., Hodges, J. R., & Etcoff, N. L. 1996. Facial emotion recognition after bilateral amygdala damage: Differentially severe impairment of fear. *Cognitive Neuropsychology* 13: 699–745.

Campeau, S., & Davis, M. 1995. Involvement of subcortical and cortical afferents to the lateral nucleus of the amygdala in fear conditioning measured with fear-potentiated startle in rats trained concurrently with auditory and visual conditioned stimuli. *The Journal of Neuroscience* 15: 2312–2327.

Canavan, A. G. M., Nixon, P. D., & Passingham, R. E. 1989. Motor learning in monkeys (*Macaca fasicularis*) with lesions in motor thalamus. *Experimental Brain Research* 77: 113–126.

Carli, M., Evenden, J. L., & Robbins, T. W. 1985. Depletion of unilateral striatal dopamine impairs initiation of contralateral actions and not sensory attention. *Nature* 313: 679–682.

Carli, M., Jones, G. H., & Robbins, T. W. 1989. Effects of unilateral dorsal and ventral striatal dopamine depletion on visual neglect in the rat: A neural and behavioral analysis. *Neuroscience* 29: 309–327.

Cassaday, H. J., & Rawlins, J. N. 1995. Fornix-fimbria section and working memory deficits in rats: Stimulus complexity and stimulus size. *Behavioral Neuroscience* 109(4): 594–606.

Castro, C. A., Silbert, L. H., McNaughton, B. L., & Barnes, C. A. 1990. Recovery of spatial learning deficits after decay of electrically induced synaptic enhancement in the hippocampus. *Nature* 342: 545–548.

Castro, C. A., Silbert, L. H., McNaughton, B. L., Barnes, C. A., Christie, B. R., Kerr, D. S., & Abraham, W. C. 1994. Flip side of synaptic plasticity: Long-term depression mechanisms in the hippocampus. *Hippocampus* 4: 127–135.

Castro-Alamancos, M. A., Donoghue, J. P., & Connors, B. W. 1995. Different forms of synaptic plasticity in somatosensory and motor areas of the neocortex. *The Journal of Neuroscience* 15: 5324–5333.

Cave, C. B., & Squire, L. R. 1992. Intact verbal and nonverbal short term memory following damage to the human hippoampus. *Hippocampus* 2: 151–163.

Chang, F.-L. F., & Greenough, W. T. 1984. Transient and enduring morphological correlates of synaptic activity and efficacy change in the rat hippocampal slice. *Brain Research* 309: 35–46.

Chapman, P. F., Kairiss, E. W., Kennan, C. L., & Brown, T. H. 1990. Long-term synaptic potentiation in the amygdala. *Synapse* 6: 271–278.

Chen, W. R., Lee, S., Kato, K., Spencer, D. D., Shepard, G. M., & Williamson, A. 1996. Long-term modifications of synaptic efficacy in the human inferior and middle temporal cortex. *Proceedings of the National Academy of Sciences (United States of America)* 93: 8011–8015.

Chiba, A. A., Bucci, D. J., Holland, P. C., & Gallagher, M. 1995. Basal forebrain cholinergic lesions disrupt increments but not decrements in conditioned stimulus processing. *The Journal of Neuroscience* 15: 7315–7322.

Chin, J. H., Pribram, K. H., Drake, K., & Greene, O., Jr. 1976. Disruption of temperature
discrimination during limbic forebrain stimulation in monkeys. *Neuropsychologia* 14: 293–310.

Cho, Y. H., Beracochea, D., & Jaffard, R. 1993. Extended temporal gradient for the
retrograde and anterograde amnesia produced by ibotenate entorhinal cortex lesions in mice. *The Journal of Neuroscience* 13: 1759–1766.

Cho, Y. H., Giese, K. P., Tanila, H., Silva, A. J., & Eichenbaum, H. 1998. Abnormal
hippocampal spatial representations in $\alpha CaMKII^{T286A}$ and $CREB^{\alpha A-}$ mice. *Science*
279: 867–869.

Cho, Y. H., & Kesner, R. P. 1996. Involvement of entorhinal cortex or parietal cortex in
long-term spatial discrimination memory in rats: Retrograde amnesia. *Behavioral
Neuroscience* 110: 436–442.

Cho, Y. H., Kesner, R. P., & Brodale, S. 1995. Retrograde and anterograde amnesia for
spatial discrimination in rats: Role of the hippocampus, entorhinal cortex, and
parietal cortex. *Psychobiology* 23: 185–194.

Christie, B. R., Kerr, D. S., & Abraham, W. C. 1994. Flip side of synaptic plasticity:
Long-term depression mechanisms in the hippocampus. *Hippocampus* 4: 127–
135.

Chun, M. M., & Phelps, E. A. 1999. Memory deficits for implicit contextual information in amnesic subjects with hippocampal damage. *Nature Neuroscience* 2: 844–
847.

Churchland, P. S., & Sejnowski, T. J. 1992. *The Computational Brain.* Cambridge, MA:
MIT Press.

Clairborne, B. J., Amaral, D. G., & Cowan, W. M. 1986. A light and electron microscope
analysis of the mossy fibers of the rat dentate gyrus. *Journal of Comparative Neurology* 246: 453–458.

Claparede, E. 1951. Recognition and "me"ness. In D. Rapaport (Ed.), Organization and
pathology of thought. New York: Columbia University Press. (Reprinted from *Archives de Psychologies* 1911: 11:79–90.) pp. 58–75.

Clare, R. E., Zhang, A. A., & Lavond, D. G. 1992. Reversible lesions of the cerebellar
interpositus nucleus during acquistion and retention of a classically conditioned
behavior. *Behavior Neuroscience* 106(6): 879–888.

Clark, R. E., & Squire, L. R. 1998. Classical conditioning and brain systems: The role
of awareness. *Science* 280: 77–81.

Clark, R. E., Lavond, D. G., & Zhang, A. A. 1992. Reversible lesions of the cerebellar
interpositus nucleus during acquisition and retention of a classically conditioned
behavior. *Behavioral Neuroscience* 106: 879–888.

Clark, S. A., Allard, T., Jenkins, W. M., & Merzenich, M. M. 1988. Receptive fields in
the body-surface map in adult auditory cortex defined by temporally correlated
inputs. *Nature Lond.* 332: 444–445.

Clugnet, M., & LeDoux, J. E. 1990. Synaptic plasticity in fear conditioning circuits:
Induction of LTP in the lateral nucleus of the amygdala by stimulation of the
medial geniculate body. *The Journal of Neuroscience* 10: 2818–2824.

Clugnet, M., LeDoux, J. E., & Morrison, S. F. 1990. Unit responses evoked in the amygdala and striatum by electrical stimulation of the medial geniculate body. *The
Journal of Neuroscience* 10: 1055–1061.

Cohen, J. D., Perlstein, W. M., Braver, T. S., Nystrom, L. E., Noll, D. C., Jonides, J., &
Smith, E. E. 1997. Temporal dynamics of brain activation during a working memory task. *Nature* 386: 604–607.

Cohen, N. J. 1981. *Neuropsychological evidence for a distinction between procedural
and declarative knowledge in human memory and amnesia.* Unpublished doc-
toral dissertation, University of California, San Diego.

Cohen, N. J. 1984. Preserved learning capacity in amnesia: Evidence for multiple memory systems. In N. Butters & L. R. Squire (Eds.), *The Neuropsychology of Memory*. New York: Guilford Press, pp. 83–103.

Cohen, N. J. 1985. Levels of analysis in memory research: The neuropsychological approach. In N. M. Weinberger, J. L. McGaugh, & G. Lynch (Eds.), *Memory Systems of the Brain*. New York: Guilford, pp. 419–432.

Cohen, N. J., & Eichenbaum, H. 1993. *Memory, Amnesia, and the Hippocampal System*. Cambridge, MA: MIT Press.

Cohen, N. J., Eichenbaum, H., Deacedo, B. S., & Corkin, S. 1985. Different memory systems underlying acquisition of procedural and declarative knowledge. In D. S. Olton, E. Gamzu, & S. Corkin (Eds.), *Memory Dysfunctions: An Integration of Animal and Human Research from Preclinical and Clinical Perspectives*. New York: New York Academy of Sciences, pp. 54–71.

Cohen, N. J., & Poldrack, R. A. & Eichenbaum, H. 1997. Memory for items and memory for relations in the procedural/declarative memory framework. *Memory* 5: 131–178.

Cohen, N. J., Ryan, J., Hunt, C., Romine, L., Wszalek, T., & Nash, C. 1999. Hippocampal system and declarative (relational) memory: Summarizing the data from functional neuroimaging studies. *Hippocampus*: 83–98.

Cohen, N. J., & Squire, L. R. 1980. Preserved learning and retention of a pattern-analyzing skill in amnesia: Dissociation of knowing how and knowing that. *Science* 210: 207–210.

Colley, P. A., & Routtenberg, A. 1993. Long-term potentiation as synaptic dialogue. *Brain Research Reviews* 18: 115–122.

Collingridge, G. L., & Bliss, T. V. P. 1987. NMDA receptors-their role in long-term potentiation. *Trends in Neurosciences* 10: 288–293.

Collins, P. 1998. *Trends in Cognitive Sciences*, Vol. 2, No. 9. New York: Elsevier Science Ltd.

Colombo, P. J., Hasker, P. D., & Volpe, B. T. 1989. Allocentric spatial and tactile memory impairments in rats with dorsal caudate lesions are affected by preoperative behavioral training. *Behavioral Neuroscience* 103: 1242–1250.

Constantine-Paton, M., & Law, M. I. 1978. Eye-specific termination bands in tecta of three-eyed frogs. *Science* 202: 639–641.

Constantine-Paton, M., & Law, M. I. 1982. The development of maps and stripes in the brain. *Scientific American* 247: 62–70.

Cook, D., & Kesner, R. P. 1988. Caudate nucleus and memory for egocentric localization. *Behavioral and Neural Biology* 49: 332–343.

Cordeau, J. P., & Mahut, H. 1964. Some long-term effects of temporal lobe resections on auditory and visual discrimination in monkeys. *Brain* 87: 177–188.

Corkin, S. 1965. Tactually-guided maze-learning in man: Effects of unilateral cortical excisions and bilateral hippocampal lesions. *Neuropsychologia* 3: 339–351.

Corkin, S. 1968. Acquisition of a motor skill after bilateral medial temporal lobe excision. *Neuropsychologia* 6: 225–265.

Corkin, S. 1984. Lasting consequences of bilateral medial temporal lobectomy: Clinical course and experimental findings in H.M. *Seminars in Neurology* 4: 249–259.

Corkin, S., Amaral, D. G., González, R. G., Johnson, K. A., & Hyman, B. T. 1997. H. M.'s medial temporal lobe lesion: Findings from magnetic resonance imaging. *The Journal of Neuroscience* 17: 3964–3979.

Corkin, S. H., Bagshaw, M. H., & Pribram, J. D. 1968. Effect of amygdalectomy on stimulus threshold of the monkey. *Experimental Neurology* 20: 197–202.

Corkin, S., Cohen, N. J., & Sagar, H. J. 1983. Memory for remote personal and public events after bilateral medial temporal lobectomy. *Society for Neuroscience Abstracts* 9: 28.

Correll, R. E., & Scoville, W. E. 1965. Effects of medial temporal lesions on visual discrimination performance. *Journal of Comparative and Physiological Psychology* 60: 175–181.

Correll, R. E., & Scoville, W. B. 1967. Significance of delay in the performance of monkeys with medial temporal lobe resections. *Experimental Brain Research* 4: 85–96.

Correll, R. E., & Scoville, W. B. 1970. Relationship of ITI to acquistion of serial visual discriminations following temporal rhinencephalic resection in monkeys. *Journal of Comparative and Physiological Psychology* 70: 464–469.

Courtney, S. M., Ungerleider, L. G., Kell, K., & Haxby, J. V. 1997. Transient and sustained activity in a distributed neural system for human working memory. *Nature* 386: 608–611.

Cressant, A., Muller, R. U., & Poucet, B. 1997. Failure of centrally placed objects to control the firing fields of hippocampal place cells. *The Journal of Neuroscience* 17: 2531–2542.

Cruikshank, S. J., & Weinberger, N. M. 1996. Receptive-field plasticity in the adult auditory cortex induced by hebbian covariance. *The Journal of Neuroscience* 16: 861–875.

Damasio, A. R. 1985. Prosopagnosia. *Trends in Neurosciences* 8: 132–135.

Damasio, A. R. 1989. Time-locked multiregional retroactivation: A systems-level proposal for the neural substrates of recall and recognition. *Cognition* 33: 25–62.

Damasio, A. R., Tranel, D., & Damasio, H. 1989. Amnesia caused by herpes simplex encephalitis, infarctions in basal forebrain, Alzheimer's disease and anoxia/ischemia. In F. Boller & J. Grafman (Eds.), *Handbook of Neuropsychology* (Vol. 3). Amsterdam: Elsevier.

Damasio, A. R., Tranel, D., & Damasio, H. 1990. Face agnosia and the neural substrates of memory. *Annual Review of Neuroscience* 13: 89–109.

Daum, I., Channon, S., & Canavan, A. 1989. Classical conditioning in patients with severe memory problems. *Journal of Neurosurgery and Psychiatry* 52: 47–51.

Daum, I., Channon, S., Polkey, C. E., & Gray, J. A. 1991. Classical conditioning after temporal lobe lesions in man: Impairment in conditional discrimination. *Behavioral Neuroscience* 105: 396–408.

Davidson, T. L., & Jarrard, L. E. 1989. Retention of concurrent conditional discriminations in rats with ibotenate lesions of hippocampus. *Psychobiology* 17: 49–60.

Davidson, T. L., McKernan, M. G., & Jarrard, L. E. 1993. Hippocampal lesions do not impair negative patterning: A challenge to configurational association theory. *Behavioral Neuroscience* 107: 227–234.

Davis, M. 1992a. The role of the amygdala in conditioned fear. In J. P. Aggleton (Ed.), *The Amygdala: Neurobiological Aspects of Emotion, Memory, and Mental Dysfunction.* New York: Wiley-Liss, pp. 255–305.

Davis, M. 1992b. The role of the amygdala in fear and anxiety. *Annual Review of Neuroscience* 15: 353–375.

Davis, M. 1994. The role of the amygdala in emotional learning. *International Review of Neurobiology* 36: 225–266.

Davis, M., Falls, W. A., Campeau, S., & Kim, M. 1993. Fear potentiated startle: A neural and pharmacological analysis. *Behavioural Brain Research* 58: 175–198.

Davis, M., Walker, D. L., & Lee Y. 1999. Neurophysiology and neuropharmacology of startle and its affective modulation. In M. E. Dawson, A. M. Schell, & A. H. Bohmelt (Eds.), *Startle Modification: Implications for Neuroscience, Cognitive Science, and Clinical Science.* Cambridge: Cambridge University Press, pp. 95–113.

Davis, S., Butcher, S. P., & Morris, R. G. M. 1992. The NMDA receptor antagonist D-2-amino-5-phosphonopentanoate (D-AP5) impairs spatial learning and LTP in vivo at intracerebral concentrations comparable to those that block LTP in vitro. *The Journal of Neuroscience* 12: 21–34.

Day, L. B., Weisend, M., Sutherland, R. J., & Schallert, T. 1999. The hippocampus is not necessary for a place response but may be necessary for pliancy. *Behavioral Neuroscience* 113: 914–924.

Deacon, T. W., Eichenbaum, H., Rosenberg, P., & Eckmann, K. W. 1983. Afferent connections of the perirhinal cortex in the rat. *Journal of Comparative Neurology* 220: 168–190.

Deadwyler, S. A., Bunn, T., & Hampson, E. 1995. Hippocampal ensemble activity during spatial delayed-nonmatch-to-sample performance in rats. *The Journal of Neuroscience* 16: 354–372.

Deadwyler, S. A., Bunn, T., & Hampson, R. E. 1996. Hippocampal ensemble activity during spatial delayed-nonmatch-to-sample performance in rats. *The Journal of Neuroscience* 16: 354–372.

Deadwyler, S. A., Hampson, R. E., Fisher, T. C., & Marlow, G. 1988. The functional significance of long-term potentiation: Relation to sensory processing by hippocampal circuits. In P. W. Landfield & S. A. Deadwyler (Eds.), *Long-Term Potentiation: From Biophysics to Behavior*. New York: Liss, pp. 499–534.

deCharms, R. C., & Merzenich, M. 1996. Primary cortical representation of sounds by the coordination of action-potential timing. *Nature* 381: 610–613.

Derrick, B. E., & Martinez, J. L., Jr. 1996. Associative, bidirectional modifications at the hippocampal mossy fibre-CA3 synapse. *Nature* 381: 429–434.

Desimone, R. 1992. The physiology of memory: Recordings of things past. *Science* 258: 245–246.

Desimone, R. 1996. Neural mechanisms for visual memory and their role in attention. *Proceedings of the National Academy of Sciences (United States of America)* 93: 13494–13499.

Desimone, R., Albright, T. D., Gross, C. G., & Bruce, C. 1984. Stimulus-selective properties of inferior temporal neurons in the macaque. *The Journal of Neuroscience* 4: 2051–2062.

Desimone, R., Miller, E. K., Chelazzi, L., & Lueschow, A. 1995. Multiple memory systems in the visual cortex. In M. S. Gazzaniga (Ed.), *The Cognitive Neurosciences*. Cambridge, MA: MIT Press, pp. 475–486.

Desmond, N. L., & Levy, W. B. 1988. Anatomy of associative long-term synaptic modification. In P. W. Landfield & S. A. Deadwyler (Eds.), *Long-Term Potentiation: From Biophysics to Behavior*. New York: Liss, pp. 265–305.

Devenport, L. D., Hale, R. L., & Stidham, J. A. 1988. Sampling behavior in the radial maze and operant chamber: Role of the hippocampus and prefrontal area. *Behavioral Neuroscience* 102: 489–498.

Devenport, L. D., & Holloway, F. A. 1980. The rat's resistance to superstition: Role of the hippocampus. *Journal of Comparative and Physiological Psychology* 94(4): 691–705.

Diamond, D. M., Dunwiddie, T. V., & Rose, G. M. 1988. Characteristics of hippocampal primed burst potentiation in vitro and in the awake rat. *The Journal of Neuroscience* 8: 4079–4088.

Diamond, D. M., & G. Rose. 1994. Does associative LTP underlie classical conditioning? *Psychobiology* 22: 263–269.

Diamond, M. E., Huang, W., & Ebner, F. 1994. Laminar comparison of somatosensory cortical plasticity. *Science* 265: 1885–1888.

Dias, R., Robbins, T. W., & Roberts, A. C. 1996. Dissociation in prefrontal cortex of affective and attentional shifts. *Nature* 380: 69–72.

Dickinson, A. 1980. *Contemporary Animal Learning Theory*. Cambridge: Cambridge University Press.

diPellegrino, G., & Wise, S. P. 1993. Visuospatial versus visuomotor activity in the premotor and prefrontal cortex of a primate. *The Journal of Neuroscience* 13: 1227–1243.

Disterhoft, J. F., Kronforst, M. A., Moyer, J. R., Thompson, L. T., Van der Zee, E. A., & Weiss, C. R. 1996. Hippocampal neuron changes during trace eyeblink conditioning in the rabbit. In J. R. Bloedel, T. J. Ebner, & S. P. Wise (Eds.), *The Acquisition of Motor Behavior in Vertebrates*. Cambridge, MA: MIT Press, pp. 143–174.

Divac, I., Gunilla, R., & Oberg, E. 1978. *The Neostriatum*. Oxford: Pergamon Press.

Donoghue, J. P. 1995. Plasticity of adult sensorimotor representations. *Current Opinion in Neurobiology* 5: 749–754.

Donoghue, J. P., Hess, G., & Sanes, J. N. 1996. Substrates and mechanisms for learning in motor cortex. In J. R. Bloedel, T. J. Ebner, & S. P. Wise (Eds.), *The Acquisition of Motor Behavior in Vertebrates*. Cambridge, MA: MIT Press, pp. 363–387.

Doré, F. Y., Thornton, J. A., White, N. M., & Murray, E. A. 1998. Selective hippocampal lesions yield nonspatial memory impairments in rhesus monkeys. *Hippocampus* 8: 323–329.

Douglas, R. J. 1967. The hippocampus and behavior. *Psychological Bulletin* 67: 416–442.

Douglas, R. J., & Pribram, K. H. 1966. Learning and limbic lesions. *Neuropsychologia* 4: 197–220.

Doyere, V., & Laroche, S. 1992. Linear relationship between the maintenance of long-term potentiation and retention of an associative memory. *Hippocampus* 2: 39–48.

Doyon, J., Owen, A. M., Petrides, M., Sziklas, V., & Evans, A. C. 1996. Functional anatomy of visuomotor skill learning in human subjects examined with positron emission tomography. *European Journal of Neuroscience* 8: 637–648.

Drachman, D. A., & Ommaya, A. K. 1964. Memory and the hippocampal complex. *Archives of Neurology* 10: 411–424.

Drewe, E. A. 1974. The effect of type and area of brain lesion on Wisconsin card sorting test performance. *Cortex* 10: 159–170.

Dudai, Y. 1996. Consolidation: fragility on the road to the engram. *Neuron* 17: 367–370.

Dusek, J. A., & Eichenbaum, H. 1997. The hippocampus and memory for orderly stimulus relations. *Proceedings of the National Academy of Science (United States of America)* 94: 7109–7114.

Dusek, J. A., & Eichenbaum, H. 1998. The hippocampus and transverse patterning guided by olfactory cues. *Behavioral Neuroscience* 112: 762–771.

Ebbinghaus, H. 1913. *Memory: A Contribution to Experimental Psychology*. New York: Dover. (Original work published 1885)

Ebner, T. J., Flament, D., & Shanbhag, S. 1996. The cerebellum's role in voluntary motor learning: clinical, electrophysiological, and imaging studies. In J. R. Bloedel, T. J. Ebner, & S. P. Wise (Eds.), *The Acquisition of Motor Behavior in Vertebrates*. Cambridge, MA: MIT Press, pp. 223–234.

Edeline, J. M., & Weinberger, N. M. 1993. Receptive-field plasticity in the auditory cortex during frequency discrimination training: Selective retuning independent of task difficulty. *Behavioral Neuroscience* 107: 82–103.

Eichenbaum, H. 1993. Amnesia, the hippocampus and episodic memory. *Hippocampus* 8: 197.

Eichenbaum, H. 1994. The hippocampal system and declarative memory in humans and animals: Experimental analysis and historical origins. In D. L. Schacter & E. Tulving (Eds.), *Memory Systems*. Cambridge, MA: MIT Press, pp. 147–202.

Eichenbaum, H. 1995. The LTP-memory connection. *Nature* 378: 131.

Eichenbaum, H. 1996. Is the rodent hippocampus just for "place"? *Current Opinion of Neurobiology* 6: 187–195.

Eichenbaum, H. 1997a. Declarative memory: Insights from cognitive neurobiology. *Annual Review of Psychology* 48: 547–572.

Eichenbaum, H. 1997b. Memory: Old questions, new perspectives. *Current Biology* 7: R53–R55.

Eichenbaum, H. 1998. Amnesia, the hippocampus and episodic memory. *Hippocampus* 8: 197.

Eichenbaum, H. 1999a. Conscious awareness, memory, and the hippocampus. *Nature Neuroscience* 2: 775–776.

Eichenbaum, H. 1999b. The topography of memory. *Nature* 402: 597–599.

Eichenbaum, H., & Buckingham, J. 1990. Studies on hippocampal processing: Experiment, theory and model. In M. Gabriel & J. Moore (Eds.), *Learning and Computational Neuroscience: Foundations of Adaptive Networks.* Cambridge, MA: MIT Press.

Eichenbaum, H., & Buckingham, J. 1992. Studies on hippocampal processing: Experiment, theory, and model. In M. Gabriel & J. Moore (Eds.), *Learning and Computational Neuroscience: Foundations of Adaptive Networks.* Cambridge, MA: MIT Press.

Eichenbaum, H., & Bunsey, M. 1995. On the binding of associations in memory: Clues from studies on the role of the hippocampal region in paired-associate learning. *Current Directions in Psychological Science* 4: 19–23.

Eichenbaum, H., Clegg, R. A., & Feeley, A. 1983a. A re-examination of functional subdivisions of the rodent prefrontal cortex. *Experimental Neurology* 79: 434–451.

Eichenbaum, H., & Cohen, N. J. 1988. Representation in the hippocampus: What do the neurons code? *Trends in Neurosciences* 11: 244–248.

Eichenbaum, H., Cohen, N. J., Otto, T., & Wible, C. G. 1992a. Memory representation in the hippocampus: Functional domain and functional organization. In L. R. Squire, G. Lynch, N. M. Weinberger, & J. L. McGaugh (Eds.), *Memory: Organization and Locus of Change.* Oxford: Oxford University Press, pp. 163–204.

Eichenbaum, H., Cohen, N. J., Otto, T., & Wible, C. G. 1992b. A snapshot without the album. *Brain Research Reviews* 16: 209–215.

Eichenbaum, H., Dudchenko, P., Wood, E., Shapiro, M., & Tanila, H. 1999. The hippocampus, memory, and place cells: Is it spatial memory or memory space? *Neuron* 23: 1–20.

Eichenbaum, H., Dusek, J., Young, B., & Bunsey, M. 1996. Neural mechanisms of declarative memory. *Quantitative Biology* 61: 197–206.

Eichenbaum, H., Fagan, A., & Cohen, N. 1986a. Normal olfactory discrimination learning set and facilitation of reversal learning after medial temporal damage in rats: Implications for an account of preserved learning abilities in amnesia. *Journal of Neurology* 6: 1876–1884.

Eichenbaum, H., Fagan, A., Mathews, P., & Cohen, N. J. 1988. Hippocampal system dysfunction and odor discrimination learning in rats: Impairment or facilitation depending on representational demands. *Behavioral Neuroscience* 102: 3531–3542.

Eichenbaum, H., Kuperstein, M., Fagan, A., & Nagode, J. 1986b. Cue-sampling and goal-approach correlates of hippocampal unit activity in rats performing an odor discrimination task. *The Journal of Neuroscience* 7: 716–732.

Eichenbaum, H., Kuperstein, M., Fagan, A., & Nagode, J. 1987. Cue-sampling and goal-approach correlates of hippocampal unit activity in rats performing an odor discrimination task. *The Journal of Neuroscience* 7: 716–732.

Eichenbaum, H., Mathews, P., & Cohen, N. J. 1989. Further studies of hippocampal representation during odor discrimination learning. *Behavioral Neuroscience* 103: 1207–1216.

Eichenbaum, H., Morton, T., Potter, H., & Corkin, S. 1983b. Selective olfactory deficits in case H.M. *Brain* 106: 459–472.

Eichenbaum, H., & Otto, T. 1993. LTP and memory: Can we enhance the connection? *Trends in Neurosciences* 16: 163–164.

Eichenbaum, H., Otto, T., & Cohen, N. J. 1992. The hippocampus—What does it do? *Behavioral and Neural Biology* 57: 2–36.

Eichenbaum, H., Otto, T., & Cohen, N. J. 1994. Two functional components of the hippocampal memory system. *Brain and Behavioral Sciences* 17: 449–518.

Eichenbaum, H., Stewart, C., & Morris, R. G. M. 1990. Hippocampal representation in spatial learning. *The Journal of Neuroscience* 10: 3531–3542.

Eifuku, S., Nishijo, H., Kita, T., & Ono, T. 1995. Neuronal activity in the primate hippocampal formation during a conditional association task based on the subject's location. *The Journal of Neuroscience* 15: 4952–4969.

Engert, F., & Bonhoeffer, T. 1999. Dendritic spine changes associated with hippocampal long term synaptic plasticity. *Nature* 399: 66–69.

Epstein, R., & Kanwisher, N. 1998. A cortical representation of the local visual environment. *Nature* 392: 598–601.

Erickson, C. A., & Desmione, R. 1999. Responses of macaque perirhinal neurons during and after visual stimulus association learning. *The Journal of Neuroscience* 19: 10404–10416.

Eskandar, E. N., Richmond, B. J., & Optican, L. M. 1992a. Role of inferior temporal neurons in visual memory: I. Temporal encoding of information about visual images, recalled images, and behavioral context. *Journal of Neurophysiology* 68: 1277–1295.

Eskandar, E. N., Richmond, B. J., & Optican, L. M. 1992b. Role of inferior temporal neurons in visual memory: II. Multiplying temporal waveforms related to vision and memory. *Journal of Neurophysiology* 68: 1296–1306.

Everitt, B. J., Cador, M., & Robbins, T. W. 1989. Interactions between the amygdala and ventral striatum in stimulus-reward associations: Studies using a second-order schedule of sexual reinforcement. *Neuroscience* 30: 63–75.

Everitt, B. J., Morris, K. A., O'Brien, A., & Robbins, T. W. 1991. The basolateral amygdala-ventral striatal system and conditioned place preference: Further evidence of limbic-striatal interactions underlying reward-related processes. *Neuroscience* 42: 1–18.

Everitt, B. J., & Robbins, T. W. 1992. Amygdala-ventral striatal interactions and reward-related processes. In J. P. Aggleton (Ed.), *The Amygdala: Neurobiological Aspects of Emotion, Memory, and Mental Dysfunction.* New York: Wiley-Liss, pp. 401–429.

Fahy, F. L., & Riches, I. P. 1987. Role of inferior temporal neurons in visual memory: I. Temporal encoding of information about visual images, recalled images, and behavioural context. *Journal of Neurophysiology* 68: 1277–1295.

Fahy, F. L. Riches, I. P., & Brown M. W. 1993. Neuronal activity related to visual recognition memory: Long-term memory and the encoding of recency and familiarity information in the primate anterior and medial inferior temporal and rhinal cortex. *Experimental Brain Research* 96: 457–472.

Falls, W. A., & Davis, M. 1995. Lesions of the central nucleus of the amygdala block conditioned excitation, but not conditioned inhibition of fear as measured with the fear-potentiated startle effect. *Behavioral Neuroscience* 109: 379–387.

Fanselow, M. S., & LeDoux, J. E. 1999. Why we think plasticity underlying Pavlovian fear conditioning occurs in the basolateral amygdala. *Neuron* 23: 229–232.

Farah, M. J. 1996. Is face recognition "special"? Evidence from neuropsychology. *Behavioural Brain Research* 76: 181–189.

Farah, M. J., Wilson, K. D., Drain, M., & Tanaka, J. N. 1998. What is "special" about face perception? *Psychological Review* 105: 482–498.

Feigenbaum, J. D., & Rolls, E. T. 1991. Allocentric and egocentric information processing in the hippocampal formation of the behaving primate. *Psychobiology* 19: 21–40.

Ferino, F., Thierry, A. M., & Glowinski, J. 1987. Anatomical and electrophysiological evidence for a direct projection from Ammon's horn to the medial prefrontal cortex in the rat. *Experimental Brain Research* 65: 421–426.

Fernández, G., Brewer, J. B., Zhao, Z., Glover, G. H., & Gabrieli, J. D. E. 1999. Level of sustained entorhinal activity at study correlates with subsequent cued-recall performance: A functional magnetic resonance imaging study with high acquisition rate. *Hippocampus* 9: 35–44.

Fernández, G., Effern, A., Grunwald, T., Pezer, N., Lehnertz, K., Dümpelmann, M., Van Roost, D., & Elger, C. E. 1999. Real-time tracking of memory formation in the human rhinal cotrex and hippocampus. *Science* 285: 1582–1585.

Ferraro, F. R., Balota, D. A., & Connor, L. T. 1993. Implicit memory and the formation of new associations in non-demented Parkinson's disease individuals and individuals with senile dementia of the Alzheimer type: A serial reaction time (SRT) investigation. *Brain and Cognition* 21: 163–180.

Ferrier, D. 1890. *The Croonian lectures on cerebral localisation.* London: Smith, Elder.

Ferry, B., Sandner, G., & DiScala, G. 1995. Neuroanatomical and functional specificity of the basolateral amygdaloid nucleus in taste-potentiated odor aversion. *Neurobiology of Learning and Memory* 64: 169–180.

Fiez, J. A. 1996. Cerebellar contributions to cognition. *Neuron* 16: 13–15.

Fifkova, E., & Van Harreveld, A. 1977. Long-lasting morphological changes in dendritic spines of dentate granular cells following stimulation of the entorhinal area. *Journal of Neurocytology* 6: 211–230.

Finkbeiner, S., Tavazoie, S. F., Maloratsky, A., Jacobs, K. M., Harris, K. M., & Greenber, M. E. 1997. CREB: A major mediator of neuronal neurotrophin responses. *Neuron* 19: 1031–1047.

Flament, D., Ellermann, J. M., Kim, S. G., Ugurbil, K., & Ebner, T. J. 1996. Functional magnetic resonance imaging of cerebellar activation during the learning of a visuomotor dissociation task. *Human Brain Mapping* 4: 210–226.

Fletcher, P. C., Frith, C. D., & Rugg, M. D. 1997. The functional neuroanatomy of episodic memory. *Trends in Neurosciences* 20: 213–218.

Flourens, P. 1824. *Recherces expérimentales sure les propriétés et les fonctions du systéme nerveux, dans les animaux vertébrés.* Paris: Chez Crevot.

Foster, T. C., Castro, C. A., & McNaughton, B. L. 1989. Spatial selectivity of rat hippocampal neurons: Dependence on preparedness for movement. *Science* 244: 1580–1582.

Fodor, J. A. 1984. *The Modularity of the Mind: An Essay on Faculty Psychology.* Cambridge, MA: MIT Press.

Foster, T. C., Christian, E. P., Hampson, R. E., Campbell, K. A., & Deadwyler, S. A. 1987. Sequential dependencies regulate sensory evoked responses of single units in the rat hippocampus. *Brain Research* 40: 86–96.

Fox, S. E., & Ranck, J. B., Jr. 1975. Localization and anatomical identification of theta and complex spike cells in dorsal hippocampal formation of rats. *Experimental Neurology* 49: 299–313.

Frank, D. A., & Greenberg, M. E. 1994. CREB: A mediator of long-term memory from mollusks to mammals. *Cell* 79: 5–8.

Fregnac, Y., Burke, J., Smith, D., & Friedlander, M. 1994. Temporal covariance of pre- and postsynaptic activity regulates functional connectivity in the visual cortex. *Journal of Neurophysiology* 71: 1403–1421.

Fregnac, Y., Shulz, D., Thorpe, S., & Bienenstock, E. 1992. Cellular analogs of visual cortical epigenesis: I. Plasticity of orientation selectivity. *The Journal of Neuroscience* 12: 1280–1300.

Frey, U., & Morris, R. G. M. 1997. Synaptic tagging and long-term potentiation. *Nature* 385: 533–536.

Frey, U., & Morris, R. G. M. 1998. Synaptic tagging: Implications for later maintenance of hippocampal long term potentiation. *Trends in Neuroscience* 21: 181–188.

Fried, I., MacDonald, K. A., & Wilson, C. L. 1997. Single neuron activity in human hippocampus and amygdala during recognition of faces and objects. *Neuron* 18: 753–765.

Friston, K. J., Frith, C. D., Passingham, R. E., Liddle, P. F., & Frackowiak, R. S. J. 1992. Motor practice and neurophysiological adaptation in the cerebellum: A positron emission tomography study. *Proceedings of the Royal Society London* 244: 241–246.

Fujita, I., Tanaka, K., Ito, M., & Cheng, K. 1992. Columns for visual features in monkey inferotemporal cortex. *Nature* 360: 343–346.

Funahashi, S., Bruce, C. J., & Goldman-Rakic, P. S. 1989. Mnemonic coding of visual space in the monkey's dorsolateral prefrontal cortex. *Journal of Neurophysiology* 61: 331–349.

Funahashi, S., Bruce, C. J., & Goldman-Rakic, P. S. 1990. Visuospatial coding in primate prefrontal neurons revealed by oculomotor paradigms. *Journal of Neurophysiology* 63: 814.

Funahashi, S., Bruce, C. J., & Goldman-Rakic, P. S. 1991. Neuronal activity related to saccadie eye movements in the monkey's dorsolateral prefrontal cortex. *Journal of Neurophysiology* 65(6): 1464–1483.

Funahashi, S., Bruce, C. J., & Goldman-Rakic, P. S. 1993a. Dorsolateral prefrontal lesions and oculomotor delayed-response performance: Evidence for mnemonic "scotomas." *The Journal of Neuroscience* 13(4): 1479–1497.

Funahashi, S., Chafee, M. V., & Goldman-Rakic, P. S. 1993b. Prefrontal neuronal activity in rhesus monkeys performing a delayed anti-saccade task. *Nature* 365: 753–756.

Funahashi, S., & Kubota, K. 1994. Working memory and prefrontal cortex. *Neuroscience Research* 21: 1–11.

Fuster, J. M. 1980. *The Prefrontal Cortex.* New York: Raven.

Fuster, J. M. 1984. Behavioral electrophysiology of the prefrontal cortex. *Trends in Neurosciences.* 7: 408–414.

Fuster, J. M. 1985. The prefrontal cortex and temporal integration. In E. G. Jones & A. Peters, *Cerebral Cortex* (Vol 4). New York: Plenum Press.

Fuster, J. M. 1990. Inferotemporal units in selective visual attention and short-term memory. *Journal of Neurophysiology* 64: 681–697.

Fuster, J. M. 1995. *Memory in the Cerebral Cortex: An Empirical Approach to Neural Networks in the Human and Nonhuman Primate.* Cambridge, MA: MIT Press.

Fuster, J. M., & Alexander, G. E. 1971. Neuron activity related to short-term memory. *Science* 173: 652–654.

Fuster, J. M., Bauer, R. H., & Jervey, J. P. 1982. Cellular discharge in the dorsolateral prefrontal cortex of the monkey in cognitive tasks. *Experimental Neurology* 77: 679–694.

Fuster, J. M., & Jervey, J. P. 1981. Inferotemporal neurons distinguish and retain behaviorally relevant features of visual stimuli. *Science* 212: 952–955.

Fuster, J. M., & Jervery, J. P. 1982. Neuronal firing in the inferotemporal cortex of the monkey in a visual memory task. *The Journal of Neuroscience* 2: 361–375.

Gabriel, M., Sparenborg, S., & Stolar, N. 1986. An executive function of the hippocampus: Pathway selection for thalamic neural significance code. In R. L. Isaacson & K. Pribram (Eds.), *The Hippocampus* (Vol. 3). New York: Plenum.

Gabrieli, J. 1995. Contribution of the basal ganglia to skill learning and working memory in humans. In J. C. Houk, J. L. Davis, & D. G. Beiser (Eds.), *Models of Information Processing in the Basal Ganglia.* Cambridge, MA: MIT Press, pp. 227–294.

Gabrieli, J. D., Cohen, N. J., & Corkin, S. 1988. The impaired learning of semantic knowledge following bilateral medial temporal-lobe resection. *Special Issue: Single-Case Studies in Amnesia: Theoretical Advances. Brain and Cognition* 7: 157–177.

Gabrieli, J. D., Fleischman, D. A., Keane, M. M., Reminger, S. L., & Morrell, F. 1995a. Double dissociation between memory systems underlying explicit and implicit memory in the human brain. *Psychological Science* 6: 76–82.

Gabrieli, J. D. E. 1998. Cognitive neuroscience of human memory. *Annual Review of Psychology* 49: 87–115.

Gabrieli J. D. E., Brewer, J. B., Desmond, J. E., Glover, G. H. 1997. Separate neural bases of two fundamental memory processes in the human medial temporal lobe. *Science* 276: 264–266.

Gabrieli, J. D. E., Carrillo, M. C., Cermak, L. S., McGlinchey-Berroth, R., Gluck, M. A., & Disterhoft, J. F. 1995b. Intact delay-eyeblink classical conditioning in amnesia. *Behavioral Neuroscience* 109: 819–27.

Gabrieli, J. D. E., Milberg, W., Keane, M., & Corkin, S. 1990. Intact priming of patterns despite impaired memory. *Neuropsychologia* 28: 417–427.

Gaffan, D. 1974. Recognition impaired and association intact in the memory of monkeys after transection of the fornix. *Journal of Comparative and Physiological Psychology* 86: 1100–1109.

Gaffan, D. 1985. Hippocampus: Memory, habit and voluntary movement. *Philosophical Transactions. The Royal Society of London. Series B: Biological Sciences*, 308: 87–99.

Gaffan, D. 1992. Amygdala and the memory of reward. In J. P. Aggleton (Ed.), *The Amygdala: Neurobiological Aspects of Emotion, Memory, and Mental Dysfunction*. New York: Wiley-Liss, pp. 471–483.

Gaffan, D. 1993. Additive effects of forgetting and fornix transection in the temporal gradient of retrograde amnesia. *Neuropsychologia* 31: 1055–1066.

Gaffan, D. 1994a. Dissociated effects of perirhinal cortex ablation, fornix transection and amygdalectomy: Evidence for multiple memory systems in the primate temporal lobe. *Experimental Brain Research* 99: 411–422.

Gaffan, D. 1994b. Scene-specific memory for objects: A model of episodic memory impairment in monkeys with fornix transection. *Journal of Cognitive Neuroscience* 6: 305–320.

Gaffan, D. 1996. Memory, action and the corpus striatum: Current developments in the memory-habit distinction. *Seminars in the Neurosciences* 8: 33–38.

Gaffan, D., & Harrison, S. 1987. Amygdalectomy and disconnection in visual learning for auditory secondary reinforcement by monkeys. *The Journal of Neuroscience* 7: 2285–2292.

Gaffan, D., & Harrison, S. 1988. Disconnection of the amygdala from visual association cortex impairs visual reward-association learning in monkeys. *The Journal of Neuroscience* 8: 3144–3150.

Gaffan, D., & Harrison, S. 1989. Place memory and scene memory: Effects of fornix transection in the monkey. *Experimental Brain Research* 74: 202–212.

Gaffan, D., Murray, E. A., & Fabre-Thorpe, M. 1993. Interaction of the Amygdala with the frontal lobe in reward memory. *European Journal of Neuroscience* 5: 968–975.

Gaffan, E. A., Gaffan, D., & Harrison, S. 1988. Disconnection of the amygdala from visual association cortex impairs reward-association learning in monkeys. *The Journal of Neuroscience* 8: 3144–3150.

Gaffman, D. 1993. Normal forgetting, impaired acquisition in memory for complex naturalistic scenes by fornix-transected monkeys. *Neuropsychologia* 31: 403–406.

Galef, B. G. 1990. An adaptionist perspective on social learning, social feeding, and social foraging in Norway rats. In D. A. Dewsbury (Ed.), *Contemporary Issues in Comparative Psychology*. Sunderland, MA: Sinauer, pp. 55–79.

Galef, B. G., Mason, J. R., Preti, G., & Bean, N. J. 1988. Carbon disulfide: A semiochemical mediating socially-induced diet choice in rats. *Physiology and Behavior* 42: 119–124.

Galef, B. G., & Wigmore, S. R. 1983. Transfer of information concerning distant foods: A laboratory investigation of the "information-centre" hypothesis. *Animal Behavior* 31: 748–758.

Gall, F. J. 1835. *The Influence of the Brain on the Form of the Head* (W. Lewis translation). Boston: Marsh, Capen & Lyon.

Gallagher, M., & Chiba, A. A. 1996. The amygdala and emotion. *Current Opinion in Neurobiology* 6: 221–227.

Gallagher, M., Graham, P. W., & Holland, P. C. 1990. The amygdala central nucleus and appetitive Pavlovian conditioning: Lesions impair one class of conditioned behavior. *The Journal of Neuroscience* 10: 1906–1911.

Gallagher, M., & Holland, P. C. 1992. Preserved configural learning and spatial learning impairment in rats with hippocampal damage. *Hippocampus* 2: 81–88.

Gallagher, M., & Holland, P. C. 1994. The amygdala complex: Multiple roles in associative learning and attention. *Proceedings of the National Academy of Sciences* 91: 1171–1776.

Galvez, R., Mesches, M. H., & McGaugh, J. L. 1996. Norepinephrine release in the amygdala in response to footshock stimulation. *Neurobiology of Learning and Memory* 66: 253–257.

Gao, J.-H., Parsons, L. M., Bower, J. M., Xiong, J., Li, J., & Fox, P. T. 1996. Cerebellum implicated in sensory acquisition and discrimination rather than motor control. *Science* 272: 545–547.

Garcia, J., & Ervin, F. R. 1968. Gustatory-visual and telereceptor-cutaneous conditioning—adaptation in internal and external milieus. *Communications in Behavioral Biology Part A* 1: 389–415.

Garcia, J., & Koelling, R. A. 1966. Relation of cue to consequence in avoidance learning. *Psychonomic Science* 4: 123–124.

Gazzaniga, M. S., Ivry, R. B., & Mangun, G. R. 1998. *Cognitive Neuroscience: The Biology of the Mind.* New York: Norton.

Geinisman, Y. 1993. Perforated axospinous synapses with multiple, completely partitioned transmission zones: Probable structural intermediates in synaptic plasticity. *Hippocampus* 3: 417–434.

Geinisman, Y., deToledo-Morrell, L., Morrell, F., Heller, R., Rossi, M., & Parshall, R. F. 1993. Structural synaptic correlate of long-term potentiation: Formation of axospinous synapses with multiple, completely partitioned transmission zones. *Hippocampus* 3: 435–445.

Gewirtz, J. C., & Davis, M. 1997. Second order fear conditioning prevented by blocking NMDA receptors in the amygdala. *Nature* 388: 471–474.

Giese, K. P., Fedorov, N. B., Filipkowski, R. K., & Silva, A. J. 1998. Autophosphorylation at threonine 286 of the α-calcium-calmodulin-kinase II is required for LTP and learning. *Science* 279: 870–873.

Gilbert, C. D. 1992. Horizontal integration and cortical dynamics. *Neuron* 9: 1–13.

Gilbert, C. D., Das, A., Ito, M., Kapadia, M., & Wetsheimer, G. 1996. Spatial integration and cortical dynamics. *Proceedings of the National Academy of Sciences (United States of America)* 93: 615–622.

Gilbert, C. D., & Wiesel, T. N. 1992. Receptive field dynamics in adult primary visual cortex. *Nature* 356: 150–152.

Gilbert, P. F. C., & Thach, W. T. 1977. Purkinje cell activity during motor learning. *Brain Research* 128: 309–328.

Glickman, S. E. 1961. Perseverative neural processes and consolidation of the memory trace. *Psychological Bulletin* 58: 218–233.

Glisky, E. L., Schacter, D. L., & Tulving, E. 1986. Learning and retention of computer-related vocabulary in memory-impaired patients: Method of vanishing cues. *Journal of Clinical and Experimental Neuropsychology* 8: 292–312.

Gluck, M. A., & Myers, C. E. 1997. Psychobiological models of hippocampal function in learning and memory. *Annual Review of Psychology* 48: 481–514.

Gnadt, J. W., & Andersen, R. A. 1988. Memory related motor planning activity in posterior parietal cortex of macaque. *Experimental Brain Research* 70: 216–220.

Gochin, P. M., Miller, E. K., Gross, C. G., & Gerstein, G. L. 1991. Functional interactions among neurons in inferior temporal cortex of the awake macaque. *Experimental Brain Research* 84: 505–516.

Goddard, G. V. 1964. Functions of the amygdala. *Psychological Bulletin* 62: 89–109.

Goldman, P. S., Rosvold, H. E., Vest, B., & Galkin, T. W. 1971. Analysis of the delayed-alteration deficit produced by dorsolateral prefrontal lesions in the rhesus monkey. *Journal of Comparative and Physiological Psychology* 77: 212–220.

Goldman-Rakic, P. S. 1988. Topography of cognition: Parallel distributed networks in primate association cortex. *Annual Review of Neuroscience* 11: 137–156.

Goldman-Rakic, P. S. 1995. Cellular basis of working memory. *Neuron* 14: 477–485.

Goldman-Rakic, P. S. 1996a. The prefrontal landscape: Implications of functional architecture for understanding human mentation and the central executive. *Philosophical Transactions. Royal Society of London. Series B. Biological Sciences* 351: 1445–1453.

Goldman-Rakic, P. S. 1996b. Regional and cellular fractionation of working memory. *Proceedings of the National Academy of Sciences* 93: 13473–13480.

Goldman-Rakic, P. 1997. Space and time in the mental universe. *Nature* 386: 559–560.

Goldman-Rakic, P. S., Funahashi, S., & Bruce, C. J. 1990. Neocortical memory circuits. *Cold Spring Harbor Symposia on Quantitative Biology* 55: 1025–1038.

Good, M., & Bannerman, D. 1997. Differential effects of ibotenic acid lesions of the hippocampus and blockade of N-methyl-D-aspartate receptor-dependent long-term potentiation on contextual processing in rats. *Behavioral Neuroscience* 111: 1171–1183.

Good, M., de Hoz, L., & Morris, R. G. M. 1998. Contingent versus incidental context processing during conditioning: Dissociation after excitotoxic hippocampal plus dentate gyrus lesions. *Hippocampus* 8: 147–159.

Good, M., & Honey, R. C. 1991. Conditioning and contextual retrieval in hippocampal rats. *Behavioral Neuroscience* 105: 499–509.

Gothard, K. M., Skaggs, W. E., Moore, K. M., & McNaughton, B. L. 1996a. Binding of hippocampal CA1 neural activity to multiple reference frames in a landmark-based navigation task. *The Journal of Neuroscience* 16: 823–835.

Gothard, K. M., Skaggs, W. E., & McNaughton, B. L. 1996b. Dynamics of mismatch correction in the hippocampal ensemble code for space: Interaction between path integration and environmental cues. *The Journal of Neuroscience* 16: 8027–8040.

Gould, J. L., & Marler, P. 1994. Learning by instinct. *Scientific American* 256: 74–85.

Grady, C. L., McIntosh, A. R., Horwitz, B., Maisog, J. M., Ungerleider, L. G., Mentis, M. J., Pietrini, P., Schapiro, M. B., & Haxby, J. V. 1995. Age-related reductions in human recognition memory due to impaired encoding. *Science* 269: 218–221.

Graf, P., Mandler, G., & Haden, P. E. 1982. Simulating amnesic symptoms in normals. *Science* 218: 1243–1244.

Graf, P., & Schacter, D. L. 1985. Implicit and explicit memory for new associations in normal and Amnesi subjects. *Journal of Experimental Psychology: Learning, Memory and Cognition* 11: 501–518.

Graf, P., Squire, L. R., & Mandler, G. 1984. The information that amnesic patients do not forget. *Journal of Experimental Psychology: Learning, Memory and Cognition* 10: 164–178.

Grafman, J., Litvan, I., Massaquoi, S., Stewart, M., et al. 1992. Cognitive planning deficit in patients with cerebellar atrophy. *Neurology* 42: 1493–1496.

Grafton, S. T., Hazeltine, E., & Ivry, R. 1995. Functional mapping of sequence learning in normal humans. *Journal of Cognitive Neuroscience* 7: 497–510.

Grafton, S. T., Mazziotta, J. C., Presty, S., Friston, K. J., et al. 1992. Functional anatomy of human procedural learning determined with regional cerebral blood flow and PET. *Journal of Neuroscience* 12: 2542–2548.

Grafton, S. T., Woods, R. P., & Tyszka, M. 1994. Functional imaging of procedural motor learning: Relating cerebral blood flow with individual subject performance. *Human Brain Mapping* 1: 221–234.

Granon, S., & Poucet, B. 1995. Medial prefrontal lesions in the rat and spatial navigation: Evidence for impaired planning. *Behavioral Neuroscience* 109: 474–484.

Grant, S. G. N., O'Dell, T. J., Karl, K. A., Soriano, P., & Kandel, E. R. 1992. Impaired long-term potentiation, spatial learning and hippocampal developement in FYN Mutant Mice. *Science* 258: 1903–1910.

Gray, J. A. 1982. *The Neuropsychology of Anxiety: An Enquiry into the Functions of the Septohippocampal System.* Oxford: Oxford University Press.

Gray, J. A., & McNaughton, N. 1983. Comparison between the behavioural effects of septal and hippocampal lesions: A review. *Neuroscience and Biobehavioral Reviews* 7: 119–188.

Gray, J. A., & Rawlins, J. N. P. 1986. Comparator and buffer memory: An attempt to integrate two models of hippocampal function. In R. L. Isaacson & K. H. Pribram (Eds.), *The Hippocampus, Volume 4.* New York: Plenum Press, pp. 159–201.

Graybiel, A. M. 1995. Building action repertoires: Memory and learning functions of the basal ganglia. *Current Opinion in Neurobiology* 5: 733–741.

Graybiel A. M., Aosaki, T., Flaherty, A. W., & Kimura, M. 1994. The basal ganglia and adaptive motor control. *Science* 265: 1826–1832.

Graybiel, A. M., & Kimura, M. 1995. Adaptive neural networks in the basal ganglia. In J. C. Houk, J. L. Davis, & D. G. Beiser (Eds.), *Models of Information Processing in the Basal Ganglia.* Cambridge, MA: MIT Press, pp. 103–116.

Green, E. J., & Greenough, W. T. 1986. Altered synaptic transmission in dentate gyrus of rats reared in complex environments: Evidence from hippocampal slices maintained in vitro. *Journal of Neurophysiology* 55: 739–750.

Green, E. J., McNaughton, B. L., & Barnes, C. A. 1990. Exploration-dependent modulation of evoked responses in fascia dentata: Dissociation of motor, EEG, and sensory factors and evidence for a synaptic efficacy change. *The Journal of Neuroscience* 10: 1455–1471.

Greenough, W. T., & Anderson, B. J. 1991. Cerebellar synaptic plasticity: Relation to learning versus neural activity. *Annals of the New York Academy of Sciences* 627: 231–247.

Greenstein, Y. J., Pavlides, C., & Winson, J. 1988. Long-term potentiation in the dentate gyrus is preferentially induced at theta rhythm periodicity. *Brain Research* 438: 331–334.

Groenewegen, H. J., E. Vermeulen-Van der Zee, te Kortschot, A., & Witter, M. P. 1987. Organization of the projections from the subiculum to the ventral stiatum in the rat: A study using anterograde transport of phaseolus vulgaris leucoagglutin. *Neuroscience* 23: 103–120.

Gross, C. G. 1973. Visual functions of inferotemporal cortex. In R. Jung (Ed.), *Handbook of Sensory Physiology* (Vol. 7/3B). Berlin: Springer, pp. 451–474.

Gross, C. G. 1978. Inferior temporal lesions do not impair discrimination of rotated patterns in monkeys. *Journal of Comparative and Physiological Psychology* 92: 1095–1109.

Gross, C. G. 1992. Representation of visual stimuli in inferior temporal cortex. *Philosophical Transactions. Royal Society of London. Series B. Biological Sciences* 335: 3–10.

Gross, C. G., Bender, D. B., & Gerstein, G. L. 1979. Activity of inferior temporal neurons in behaving monkeys. *Neuropsychologia* 17: 215–228.

Gross, C. G., Bender, D. B., & Miranda-Rocha, C. E. 1969. Visual receptive fields of neurons in inferotemporal cortex of the monkey. *Science* 166: 1303–1306.

Gross, C. G., Miranda-Rocha, C. E., & Bender, D. B. 1972. Visual properties of neurons in inferotemporal cortex of the macaque. *Journal of Neurophysiology* 35: 96–111.

Grudin, J. T., & Larochell, S. 1982. *Digraph Frequency Effects in Skilled Typing.* (Technical Report No. CHIP 110). San Diego: University of California, Center for Human Information Processing.

Guthrie, E. R. 1952. *The Psychology of Learning.* New York: Harper.

Haist, F., Musen, G., & Squire, L. R. 1991. Intact priming of words and nonwords in amnesia. *Psychobiology* 19: 275–285.

Halgren, E. 1984. Human hippocampal and amygdala recording and stimulation: Evidence for a neural model of recent memory. In L. R. Squire & N. Butters (Eds.), *The Neuropsychology of Memory*. New York: Guilford Press, pp. 165–182.

Halgren, E., Babb, T. L., & Crandal, P. H. 1978. Activity of human hippocampal formation and amygdala neurons during memory testing. *Electroencephalography and Clinical Neurophysiology* 45: 585–601.

Hallet, M., Pascual-Leone, A., & Topka, H. 1996. Adaptation and skill learning: Evidence for different neural substrates. In J. R. Bloedel, T. J. Ebner, & S. P. Wise (Eds.), *The Acquisition of Motor Behavior in Vertebrates*. Cambridge, MA: MIT Press, pp. 289–302.

Hamann, S. B., & Squire, L. R. 1995. On the acquisition of new declarative knowledge in amnesia. *Behavioral Neuroscience* 1009: 1027–1044.

Hamann, S. B., Stefanacci, L., Squire, L. R., Adolphs, R., Tranel, D., Damasio, H., & Damasio, A. 1996. Recognizing facial emotion. *Nature* 379: 497.

Hampson, R. E., Heyser, C. J., & Deadwyler, S. A. 1993. Hippocampal cell firing correlates of delayed-match-to-sample performance in the rat. *Behavioral Neuroscience* 107: 715–739.

Hampson, R. E., Rogers, G., Lynch, G., & Deadwyler, S. A. 1998. Facilitative effects of the ampakine CX516 on short-term memory in rats: Enhancement of delayed-nonmatch-to-sample performance. *The Journal of Neuroscience* 18(7): 2740–2747.

Hampson, R. E., Simeral, J. D., & Deadwyler, A. 1999. Distribution of spatial and non-spatial information in dorsal hippocampus. *Nature* 402: 610–614.

Han, J-S., Gallagher, M., & Holland, P. 1998. Hippocampal lesions enhance configural learning by reducing practive interference. *Hippocampus* 8: 138–146.

Hargreaves, E. L., Cain, D. P., & Vanderwolf, C. H. 1990. Learning and behavioral-long-term-potentiation: Importance of controlling for motor activity. *The Journal of Neuroscience* 10: 1472–1478.

Harris, K. M., Jensen, F., & Tsao, B. 1989. Ultrastructure, development, and plasticity of dendritic spine synapses in area CA1 of the rat hippocampus: Extending our vision with serial electron microscopy and three-dimensional analyses. In V. Chan-Palay, & C. Kohler (Eds.), *Neurology and Neurobiology. Vol. 52: The Hippocampus—New Vistas*. New York: Liss.

Harvey, J. A., & Welsh, J. P. 1996. Learning and performance: A critical review of the role of the cerebellum in instrumental and classical conditioning. In J. R. Bloedel, T. J. Ebner, & S. P. Wise (Eds.), *The Acquisition of Motor Behavior in Vertebrates*. Cambridge, MA: MIT Press, pp. 115–142.

Harvey, J. A., Welsh, J. P., Yeo, C. H., & Romano, A. G. 1993. Recoverable and nonrecoverable deficits in conditioned responses after cerebellar cortical lesions. *The Journal of Neuroscience* 13: 1624–1635.

Hasselmo, M. E., Rolls, E. T., & Baylis, G. C. 1989. The role of expression and identity in the face-selective responses of neurons in the temporal visual cortex of the monkey. *Behavioral Brain Research* 32: 203–218.

Hatfield, T., & Gallagher, M. 1995. Taste-potentiated odor conditioning: Impairment produced by infusion of an N-methyl-D-asparate antagonist into basolateral amygdala. *Behavioral Neuroscience* 109: 663–668.

Hatfield, T., Graham, P. W., & Gallagher, M. 1992. Taste-potentiated odor aversion learning: Role of the amygdaloid basolateral complex and central nucleus. *Behavioral Neuroscience* 106: 286–293.

Haxby, J., Ungerleider, L., Horwitz, B., Maisog, J., Ropoport, S., & Grady, C. 1996. Face encoding and recognition in the human brain. *Proceedings of the National Academy of Sciences* 93: 922–927.

Hayman, C. A., MacDonald, C. A., & Tulving, E. 1993. The role of repetition and associative inference in new semantic learning in amnesia: A case experiment. *Journal of Cognitive Neuroscience* 5: 375–389.

Hazeltine, E., Grafton, S. T., & Ivry, R. 1997. Attention and stimulus characteristics determine the locus of motor-sequence learning—A PET study. *Brain* 120: 123–140.

Head, H. 1920. *Studies in Neurology*. London: Oxford Medical Publications.

Hebb, D. O. 1949. *The Organization of Behavior*. New York: Wiley.

Hebben, N., Corkin, S., Eichenbaum, H., & Shedlack, K. 1985. Diminished ability to interpret and report internal states after bilateral medial temporal resection: Case H. M. *Behavioral Neuroscience* 99(6): 1031–1039.

Heindel, W. C., Salmon D. P., Shults, C. W., Walicke, P. A., & Butters, N. 1989. Neuropsychological evidence for multiple implicit memory systems: A comparison of Alzheimer's, Huntington's, and Parkinson's disease patients. *The Journal of Neuroscience* 9: 582–587.

Heit, G., Smith, M. E., & Halgren, E. 1988. Neural encoding of individual words and faces by the human hippocampus and amygdala. *Nature* 333: 773–775.

Heit, G., Smith, M. E., & Halgren, E. 1990. Neuronal activity in the human medial temporal lobe during recognition memory. *Brain* 113: 1093–1112.

Henke, P. G. 1973. Effects of reinforcement omission on rats with lesions in the amygdala. *Journal of Comparative and Physiological Psychology* 84: 187–193.

Henke, K., Buck, A., Weber, B., & Wieser, H. G. 1997. Human hippocampus establishes associations in memory. *Hippocampus* 7: 249–256.

Herrmann, D. J., & Chaffin, R. (Eds.). 1988. *Memory in Historical Perspective: The Literature Before Ebbinghaus*. New York: Springer-Verlag.

Hetherington, P. A., & Shapiro, M. L. 1997. Hippocampal place fields are altered by the removal of single visual cues in a distance-dependent manner. *Behavioral Neuroscience* 111: 20–34.

Hilgetag, C. C., O'Neil, M. A., & Young, M. P. 1996. Indeterminate organization of the visual system. *Science* 271: 776–777.

Hill, A. J. 1978. First occurrence of hippocampal spatial firing in a new environment. *Experimental Neurology* 62: 282–297.

Hill, A. J., & Best, P. J. 1981. Effects of deafness and blindness on the spatial correlates of hippocampal unit activity in the rat. *Experimental Neurology* 74: 204–217.

Hiroi, N. M., & White, E. L. 1991. The lateral nucleus of the amygdala mediates expression of the amphetamine conditioned place preference. *The Journal of Neuroscience* 11: 2107–2116.

Hirsh, R. 1974. The hippocampus and contextual retrieval of information from memory: A theory. *Behavioral Biology* 12: 421–444.

Hirsh, R. 1980. The hippocampus, conditional operations, and cognition. *Physiological Psychology* 8: 175–182.

Hirsh, R., Davis, R., & Holt, L. 1979. Fornico-thalamic fibers, motivational states and contextual retrieval. *Experimental Neurology* 65: 373–390.

Hjorth Simonsen, A. 1972. Projection of the lateral part of the entorhinal area to the hippocampus and facia dentata. *Journal of Comparative Neurology* 146: 219–232.

Holland, P. C. 1990. Forms of memory in Pavlovian conditioning. In J. L. McGaugh, N. M. Weinberger, & G. Lynch (Eds.), *Brain Organization and Memory: Cells, Systems, and Circuits*. New York: Oxford University Press, pp. 78–105.

Holland, P. C., & Bouton, M. E. 1999. Hippocampus and contect in classical conditioning. *Current Opinion in Neurobiology* 9: 195–202.

Holland, P. C., & Gallagher, M. 1993a. Amygdala central nucleus lesions disrupt increments, but not decrements, in conditioned stimulus processing. *Behavioral Neuroscience* 107: 246–253.

Holland, P. C., & Gallagher, M. 1993b. Effects of amygdala central nucleus lesions on blocking and unblocking. *Behavioral Neuroscience* 107: 235–245.

Holmes, E. J., & Gross, C. G. 1984a. Effects of inferior temporal lesions on discrimination of stimuli during orientation. *The Journal of Neuroscience* 4: 3063–3068.

Holmes, E. J., & Gross, C. G. 1984b. Stimulus equivalence after inferior temporal lesions in monkeys. *Behavioral Neuroscience* 98: 898–901.

Honey, R. C., & Good, M. A. 1993. Selective hippocampal lesions abolish the contextual specificity of latent inhibition and conditioning. *Behavioral Neuroscience* 107: 23–33.

Houk, J. C., Davis, J. L., & Beiser, D. G. (Eds.). 1995. *Models of Information Processing in the Basal Ganglia.* Cambridge, MA: MIT Press.

Hubel, D. H., & Wiesel, T. N. 1970. The period of susceptibility to the physiological effects of unilateral eye closure in kittens. *Journal of Physiology* 206: 419–436.

Huberman, M., Moscovitch, M., & Freedman, M. 1994. Comparison of patients and Alzheimer's and Parkinson's disease on different explicit and implicit tests of memory. *Neuropsychiatry, Neuropsychology, and Behavioral Neurology* 7: 185–193.

Huerta, P. T., & Lisman, J. E. 1995. Bidirectional synaptic plasticity induced by a single burst during cholinergic theta oscillation in CA1 in vitro. *Neuron* 15: 1053–1063.

Hull, C. L. 1943. *Principles of Behavior.* New York: Appleton-Century-Crofts.

Hull, C. L. 1952. *A Behavior System.* New Haven, CT: Yale University Press.

Isaacson, R. L., Douglas, R. J., & Moore, R. Y. 1961. The effect of radical hippocampal ablation on acquisition of avoidance response. *Journal of Comparative and Physiological Psychology* 54: 625–628.

Isaacson, R. L., & Wickelgren, W. O. 1962. Hippocampal ablation and passive avoidance. *Science* 138: 1104–1106.

Ito, M., Sakurai, M., & Tongroach, P. 1982. Climbing induced depression of both mossy fiber responsiveness and glutamate sensitivity of cerebellar purkinje cells. *Journal of Physiology (London)* 324: 113–134.

Iwai, E., Aihara, T., & Hikosaka, K. 1987. Inferotemporal neurons of the monkey responsive to auditory signal. *Brain Research* 410: 121–124.

Jacobsen, S. F., Wolfe, J. B., & Jackson, T. A. 1935. An experimental analysis of the frontal association areas in primates. *Journal of Nervous and Mental Disease* 82: 1–14.

Jagielo, J. A., Nonneman, A. J., Isaac, W. L., & Jackson-Smith, P. A. 1990. Hippocampal lesions impair rats' performance of a nonspatial matching to sample task. *Psychobiology* 18: 55–62.

James, W. 1918. *The Principles of Psychology.* New York: Holt. (Original work published 1890)

Janowsky, J. S., Shimamura, A. P., & Squire, L. R. 1989. Source memory impairment in patients with frontal lobe lesions. *Neuropsychologia* 27: 1043–1056.

Jarrard, L. E. 1986. Selective hippocampal lesions and behavior: Implications for current research and theorizing. In R. L. Isaacson & K. H. Pribram (Eds.), *The Hippocampus* (Vol. 4). New York: Plenum Press, pp. 93–126.

Jarrard, L. E. 1993. Review: On the role of the hippocampus in learning and memory in the rat. *Behavioral and Neural Biology* 60: 9–26.

Jarrard, L. E., & Davidson, T. L. 1991. On the hippocampus and learned conditional responding: Effects of aspiration versus ibotenate lesions. *Hippocampus* 1: 107–117.

Jarrard, L. E., & Lewis, T. C. 1967. Effects of hippocampal ablation and intertrial interval on acquisition. *Amerian Journal of Psychology* 80: 66–72.

Jeffery, K. J., & Morris, R. G. M. 1993. Cumulative long-term potentiation in the rat dentate gyrus correlates with, but does not modify, performance in the water maze. *Hippocampus* 3: 133–140.

Jenkins, I. H., Brooks, D. J., Nixon, P. D., Frackowiak, R. S. J., & Passingham, R. E. 1994. Motor sequence learning: A study with positron emission tomography. *The Journal of Neuroscience* 14: 3775–3790.

Jenkins, W. M., Merzenich, M. M., Ochs, M. T., Allard, T., & Guic-Robles, E. 1990. Functional reorganization of primary somatosensory cortex in adult owl monkeys after behaviorally controlled tactile stimulation. *Journal of Neurophysiology* 63: 82–104.

Jog, M. S., Kubota, Y., Connolly, C. I., Hillegaart, V., & Graybiel, A. M. 1999. Building neural representations of habits. *Science* 286: 1745–1749.

John, E. R. 1967. *Mechanisms of Memory.* New York: Academic Press.

John, E. R. 1972. Switchboard versus statistical theories of learning and memory. *Science* 177: 850–864.

Johnson, M. H., Kim, J. K., & Risse, G. 1985. Do alcoholic Korsakoff's syndrome patients acquire affective reactions? *Journal of Experimental Psychology: Learning, Memory, and Cognition* 11: 27–36.

Jones, B., & Mishkin, M. 1972. Limbic lesions and the problem of stimulus-reinforcement associations. *Experimental Neurology* 36: 362–377.

Jonides, J., & Smith, E. E. 1997. The architecture of working memory. In Michael D. Rugg (Ed.), *Cognitive Neuroscience.* Hove, East Sussex: Psychology Press, pp. 243–276.

Jonides, J., Smith, E. E., Koeppe, R. A., Awh, E., Minoshima, S., & Mintun, M. A. 1993. Spatial working memory in humans as revealed by PET. *Nature* 363: 623–625.

Joseph, J. P., & Barone, P. 1987. Prefrontal unit activity during a delayed oculomotor task in the monkey. *Experimental Brain Research* 67: 460.

Kaas, J. H. 1991. Plasticity of sensory and motor maps in adult mammals. *Annual Review of Neuroscience* 14: 137–167.

Kaas, J. H. 1995. The reorganization of sensory and motor maps in adult mammals. In M. S. Gazzaniga (Ed.), *The Cognitive Neurosciences.* Cambridge, MA: MIT Press, pp. 51–71.

Kaas, J. H., Krubitzer, L. A., Chino, Y. M., Lanston, A. L., Polley, E. H., & Blair, N. 1990. Reorganization of retinotopic cortical maps in adult mammals after lesion of the retina. *Science* 248: 229–231.

Kahana, M. J., Sekuler, R., Caplan, J. B., Kirschen, M., & Madsen, J. R. 1999. Human theta oscillations exhibit task dependence during virtual maze navigation. *Nature* 399: 781–784.

Kamin, L. J. 1968. Attention-like processes in classical conditioning. In M. R. Jones (Ed.), *Miami Symposium on the Prediction of Behavior: Aversive Stimulation.* Miami, FL: University of Miami Press, pp. 9–32.

Kamin, L. J. 1969. Predictability, surprise, attention, and conditioning. In B. Campbell & R. Church (Eds.), *Punishment and Aversive Behavior.* New York: Appleton-Century-Crofts, pp. 279–298.

Kandel, E. R., & O'Dell, T. 1992. Are adult learning mechanisms also used for development? *Science* 258: 243–245.

Kandel, E. R., & Schwartz, J. H. 1985. *Principles of Neural Science* (2nd ed.). New York: Elsevier.

Kandel, E. R., Schwartz, J. H., & Jessell, T. M. (Eds.). 1991. *Principles of Neural Science* (3rd ed.). Norwalk, CT: Appleton & Lange.

Kandel, E. R., Schwartz, J. H., & Jessell, T. M. 1995. Cellular mechanisms of learning and memory. In E. R. Kandel, J. H. Schwartz, & T. M. Jessell (Eds.), *Essentials of Neural Science and Behavior.* Norwalk, CT: Appleton & Lange.

Kanwisher, N., McDermott, J., & Chun, M. M. 1997. The fusiform face area: A module in human extrastriate cortex specialized for face perception. *The Journal of Neuroscience* 17: 4302–4311.

Kapp, B. S., Pascoe, J. P., & Bixler, M. A. 1984. The amygdala: A neuroanatomical systems approach to its contribution to aversive conditioning. In N. Butters & L. S. Squire (Eds.), *The Neuropsychology of Memory.* New York: Guilford, pp. 473–488.

Kapp, B. S., Whalen, P. J., Supple, W. F., & Pascoe, J. P. 1992. Amygdaloid contributions to conditioned arousal and sensory information processing. In J. Aggleton (Ed.), *The Amygdala: Neurobiological Aspects of Emotion, Memory, and Mental Dysfunction.* New York: Wiley-Liss, pp. 229–254.

Kapp, B. S., Wilson, A., Pascoe, J. P., Supple, W. F., & Whalen, P. J. 1990. A neuroanatomical systems analysis of conditioned bradycardia in the rabbit. In M. Gabriel & J. Moore (Eds.), *Neurocomputation and Learning: Foundations of Adaptive Networks.* New York: Bradford Books.

Kapur, N., Friston, K. J., Young, A., Frith, C. D., & Frackowiak, R. S. J. 1995. Activation of human hippocampal formation during memory for faces: A PET study. *Cortex* 31: 99–108.

Karni, A., Meyer, G., Jezzard, P., Adams, M. M., Turner, R., & Ungerleider, L. G. 1995. Functional MRI evidence for adult motor cortex plasticity during motor skill learning. *Nature* 377: 155–158.

Keith, J. R., & Rudy, J. W. 1990. Why NMDA-receptor-dependent long-term potentiation may not be a mechanism of learning and memory: Reappraisal of the NMDA-receptor blockade strategy. *Psychobiology* 18: 251–257.

Kelley, W. M., Miezen, F. M., McDermott, K. B., Buckner, R. L., Raichle, M. E., Cohen, N. J., Ollinger, J. M., Akbudak, E., Conturo, T. E., Snyder, A. Z., & Petersen, S. E. 1998. Hemispheric specialization in human dorsal frontal cortex and medial temporal lobe for verbal and nonverbal memory encoding. *Neuron* 20: 927–936.

Kelly, C. M., & Jacoby, L. L. 1990. The construction of subjective experience: Memory attributions. *Mind and Language* 5: 49–68.

Kemble, E. D., & Beckman, G. J. 1970. Runaway performance of rats following amygdaloid lesions. *Physiology and Behavior* 5: 45–47.

Kentros, C., Hargreaves, E., Hawkins, R. D., Kandel, E. R., Shapiro, M., & Muller, R. V. 1998. Abolition of long-term stability of new hippocampal place cell maps by NMDA receptor blockade. *Science* 280: 2121–2126.

Kermadi, I., & Joseph, J. P. 1995. Activity in the caudate nucleus of monkey during spatial sequencing. *Journal of Neurophysiology* 74: 911–933.

Kesner, R. P. 1990. Learning and memory in rats with an emphasis on the role of the hippocampal formation. In R. P. Kesner & D. S. Olton (Eds.), *Neurobiology of Comparative Cognition.* Mahwah, NJ: Erlbaum, pp. 179–204.

Kesner, R. P. 1992. Learning and memory in rats with an emphasis on the role of the amygdala. In J. P. Aggleton (Ed.), *The Amygdala: Neurobiological Aspects of Emotion, Memory, and Mental Dysfunction.* New York: Wiley-Liss, pp. 379–399.

Kesner, R. P., & Beers, D. R. 1988. Dissociation of data-based and expectancy-based memory following hippocampal lesions in rats. *Behavioral and Neural Biology* 50: 46–60.

Kesner, R. P., Bolland, B. L., & Dakis, M. 1993. Memory for spatial locations, motor responses, and objects: Triple dissociation among the hippocampus, caudate nucleus, and extrastriate visual cortex. *Experimental Brain Research* 93: 462–470.

Kesner, R. P., & DiMattia, B. V. 1984. Posterior parietal association cortex and hippocampus: Equivalency of mnemonic functions in animals and humans. In N. Butters & L. R. Squire (Eds.), *The Neuropsychology of Memory.* New York: Guilford Press.

Kesner, R. P., & Jackson-Smith, P. 1992. Neurobiology of an attribute model of memory: Role of prefrontal cortex. In I. Gormezano & E. A. Wasserman (Eds.), *Learning and Memory: The Behavioral and Biological Substrates.* Mahwah, NJ: Erlbaum, pp. 251–273.

Kesner, R. P., & Novak, J. M. 1982. Serial position curve in rats: Role of the dorsal hippocampus. *Science* 218: 173–175.

Kesner, R. P., Wasler, R. D., & Winzenried, G. 1989. Central but not basolateral amygdala mediates memory for positive affective experiences. *Behavioural Brain Research* 33: 189–195.

Killcross, S., Robbins, T. W., & Everitt, B. J. 1997. Different types of fear-conditioned behavior mediated by separate nuclei within amygdala. *Nature* 338: 377–380.

Kim, J. J., Clark, R. E., & Thompson, R. F. 1995. Hippocampectomy impairs the memory of recently, but not remotely, acquired trace eyeblink conditioned responses. *Behavioral Neuroscience* 109: 195–203.

Kim, J. J., DeCola, J. P., Landeira-Fernandez, J., & Fanselow, M. S. 1991. N-methyl-D-aspartate receptor antagonist APV blocks acquisition but not expression of fear conditioning. *Behavioral Neuroscience* 105: 126–133.

Kim, J. J., & Fanselow, M. S. 1992. Modality-specific retrograde amnesia of fear. *Science* 256: 675–677.

Kimble, D. P. 1963. The effects of bilateral hippocampal lesions in rats. *Journal of Comparative and Physiological Psychology* 56: 273–283.

Kimble, D. P. 1968. Hippocampus and internal inhibition. *Psychological Bulletin* 70: 285–295.

Kimble, D. P., & Kimble, R. J. 1969. The effect of hippocampal lesions on extinction and "hypothesis" behavior in rats. *Physiology and Behavior* 5: 735–738.

Kimble, D. P., & Pribram, K. 1963. Hippocampectomy and behavior sequences. *Science* 139: 824–825.

Kimura, A., Caria, M. A., Melis, F., & Asanuma, H. 1994 Long-term potentiation within the cat motor cortex. *Neuroreport* 5: 2372–2376.

Kimura, M. 1995. Role of basal ganglia in behavioral learning. *Neuroscience Research* 22: 353–358.

Kleim, J. A., Lussnig, E., Schwartz, E. R., Comery, T. A., & Greenough, W. T. 1996. Synaptogenesis and fos expression in the motor cortex of the adult rat following motor skill learning. *The Journal of Neuroscience* 16: 4529–4535.

Kleim, J. A., Swain, R. A., Armstrong, K. E., Napper, R. M. A., Jones, T. A., & Greenough, W. T. 1998. Selective synaptic plasticity within the cerebellar cortex following complex motor skill learning. *Neurobiology of Learning and Memory* 69: 274–289.

Kling, A. S., & Brothers, L. A. 1992. The amygdala and social behavior. In J. Aggleton (Ed.), *The Amygdala: Neurobiological Aspects of Emotion, Memory and Mental Dysfunction*. New York: Wiley-Liss, pp. 353–378.

Klintsova, A. V., & Greenough, W. T. 1999. Synaptic plasticity in cortical systems. *Current Opinion in Neurobiology* 9: 203–208.

Kluver, H., & Bucy, P. 1937. "Psychic blindness" and other symptoms following bilateral temporal lobectomy in rhesus monkeys. *American Journal of Physiology* 119: 352–353.

Kluver, H., & Bucy, P. C. 1939. Preliminary analysis of functions of the temporal lobes in monkeys. *Archives of Neurology and Psychiatry* 42: 979–1000.

Knierim, J. J., Kudrimoti, H. S., & McNaughton, B. L. 1995. Place cells, head direction cells, and the learning of landmark stability. *The Journal of Neuroscience* 15: 1648–1659.

Knowlton, B. J., Mangels, J. A., & Squire, L. R. 1996. A neostriatal habit learning system in humans. *Science* 273: 1399–1401.

Knowlton, B. J., Ramus, S., & Squire, L. R. 1992. Intact artificial grammar learning in amnesia. *Psychological Science* 3: 172–179.

Knowlton, B. J., & Squire, L. R. 1993. The learning of categories: Parallel brain systems for item memory and category knowledge. *Science* 262: 1747–1749.

Knowlton, B. J., Squire, L. R., & Gluck, M. A. 1994. Probabilistic classification in amnesia. *Learning and Memory* 1: 106–120.

Kobayahi, T., Nishijo, H., Fukuda, M., Bures, J., & Ono, T. 1997. Task-dependent representations in rat hippocampal place neurons. *Journal of Neurophysiology* 78: 597–613.

Koch, K. W., & Fuster, J. M. 1989. Unit activity in monkey parietal cortex related to haptic perception and temporary memory. *Experimental Brain Research* 76: 292–306.

Kogan, J. H., Frankland, P. W., Blendy, J. A., Coblentz, J., Marowitz, Z., Schutz, G., & Silva, A. J. 1997. Spaced training induces normal long term memory in CREB mutant mice. *Current Biology* 7: 1–11.

Kohler, C. 1986. Intrinsic connections of the retrohippocampal region in the rat brain: II. The medial entorhinal area. *Journal of Comparative Neurology* 246: 149–169.

Kohler, W. 1924. *The Mentality of Apes*. London: Routledge & Kegan Paul.

Kolb, B. 1984. Functions of the frontal cortex of the rat: A comparative review. *Brain Research Reviews* 320(1): 65–98.

Kolb, B. 1990. Prefrontal cortex. In B. Kolb & R. C. Tees (Eds.), *The Cerebral Cortex of the Rat*. Cambridge, MA: MIT Press, pp. 437–458.

Kolb, B., & Wishaw, I. (1996). *Fundamentals of Human Neuropsychology* (4th ed.). New York: Freeman.

Konishi, M. 1986. Centrally synthesized maps of sensory space. *Trends in Neuroscience* 9: 163–168.

Koriat, A., & Goldsmith, M. 1996. Memory metaphors and the real-life/laboratory controversy: Correspondence versus storehouse conceptions of memory. *Brain and Behavioral Sciences* 19: 167–228.

Korol, D. L., Abel, T. W., Church, L. T., Barnes, C. A., & McNaughton, B. L. 1993. Hippocampal synaptic enhancement and spatial learning in the Morris swim task. *Hippocampus* 3: 127–132.

Kosel, K. C., Van Hoesen, G. W., & Rosene, D. L. 1982. Nonhippocampal cortical projections from the entorhinal cortex in the rat and rhesus monkey. *Brain Research* 214: 201–213.

Krebs, J. R. 1990. Food storing in birds: Adaptive specialization in brain and behavior? *Philosophical Transactions. Royal Society of London. Series B. Biological Sciences* 329: 153–160.

Kreiter, A. K., & Singer, W. 1996. Stimulus-dependent synchronization of neuronal responses in the visual cortex of the awake macaque monkey. *The Journal of Neuroscience* 16: 2381–2396.

Krupa D. J., Thompson, J. K., & Thompsom, R. F. 1993. Localization of a memory trace in the mammalian brain. *Nature* 260: 989–991.

Kubota, K., & Niki, H. 1971. Prefrontal cortical unit activity and delayed alternation performance in monkeys. *Journal of Neurophysiology* 34: 337–347.

Kuperstein, M., Eichenbaum, H., & VanDeMark, T. 1986. Neural group properties in the rat hippocampus during the theta rhythm. *Experimental Brain Research* 61: 438–442.

LaBar, K. S., Gatenby, J. C., Gore, J. C., Ledoux, J. E., & Phelps, E. A. 1998. Human amygdala activation during conditioned fear acquisition and extinction: A mixed-trial fMRI study. *Neuron* 20: 937–945.

LaBar, K. S., LeDoux, J. E., Spencer, D. D., & Phelps, E. A. 1995. Impaired fear conditioning following unilateral temporal lobectomy in humans. *The Journal of Neuroscience* 15: 6846–6855.

Lahtinen, H., Miettinen, R., Ylinen, A., Halonen, T., & Riekkinen, P. J., Sr. 1993. Biochemical and morphological changes in the rat hippocampus following transection of the fimbria-fornix. *Brain Research Bulletin* 31: 311–318.

Lalonde, R. 1994. Cerebellar contributions to instrumental learning. *Neuroscience and Biobehavioral Reviews* 18: 161–170.

Larson, J., & Lynch, G. 1986. Induction of synaptic potentiation in hippocampus by patterned stimulation involves two events. *Science* 232: 985–988.

Larson, J., & Lynch, G. 1989. Theta pattern stimulation and the induction of LTP: The sequence in which synapses are stimulated determines the degree to which they potentiate. *Brain Research* 489: 49–58.

Larson, J., Wong, D., & Lynch, G. 1986. Patterned stimulation at the theta frequency is optimal for the induction of hippocampal long-term potentiation. *Brain Research* 368: 347–350.

Lashley, K. S. 1950. In search of the engram. *Symposia. Society for Experimental Biology* 4: 454–482.

Lashley, K. S. 1963. *Brain Mechanisms and Intelligence: A Quantitative Study of Injuries to the Brain.* New York: Dover. (Work originally published 1929)

Laurent, G. 1997. Olfactory processing: maps, time, and codes. *Current Opinion in Neurobiology* 7: 547–553.

Lavond, D. G., Kim, J. J., & Thompson, R. F. 1993. Mammalian brain substrates of aversive classical conditioning. *Annual Review of Psychology* 44: 317–342.

Lawrence, A. D., Sahakian, B. J., & Robbins, T. W. 1998. Cognitive functions and corticostriatal circuits: Insights from Huntington's disease. *Trends in Cognitive Science* 2: 379–388.

Lechner, H. A., Squire, L. R., & Byrne, J. H. 1999. 100 years of consolidation—Remembering Muller and Pilzecker. *Learning and Memory* 6: 77–87.

LeDoux, J. 1989. Cognitive-emotional interactions in the brain. *Cognition and Emotion* 3: 267–289.

LeDoux, J. 1996. *The Emotional Brain.* New York: Simon & Schuster.

LeDoux, J. E. 1991. Emotion and the limbic system concept. *Concepts in Neuroscience* 2: 169–199.

LeDoux, J. E. 1992. Brain mechanisms of emotion and emotional learning. *Current Opinion in Neurobiology* 2: 191–197.

LeDoux, J. E. 1994. Emotion, memory and the brain. *Scientific American* 270: 32–39.

LeDoux, J. E., Cicchetti, P., Xagoris, A., & Romanski, L. M. 1990a. The lateral amygdaloid nucleus: Sensory interface of the amygdala in fear conditioning. *The Journal of Neuroscience* 10: 1062–1069.

LeDoux, J. E., Farb, C., & Ruggiero, D. A. 1990b. Topographic organization of neurons in the acoustic thalamus that project to the amygdala. *The Journal of Neuroscience* 10: 1043–1054.

LeDoux, J., Ruggiero, D., Forest, R., Stornetta, R., & Reis, D. 1987. Topographic organization of convergent projections to the thalamus from the inferior colliculus and spinal cord in the rat. *Journal of Comparative Neurology* 264: 123–146.

LeDoux, J. E., Ruggiero, D. A., & Reis, D. J. 1985. Projections to the subcortical forebrain from anatomically defined regions of the medial geniculate body in the rat. *Journal of Comparative Neurology* 242: 182–213.

Lee, K. S., Schottler, F., Oliver, M., & Lynch, G. 1980. Brief bursts of high-frequency stimulation produce two types of structural change in rat hippocampus. *Journal of Neurophysiology* 44: 247–258.

Leonard, C. M., Rolls, E. T., Wilson, F. A. W., & Baylis, G. C. 1985. Neurons in the amygdala of the monkey with responses selective for faces. *Behavioural Brain Research* 15: 159–176.

Lepage, M., Habib, R., & Tulving, E. 1998. Hippocampal PET activations of memory encoding and retrieval: The HIPER model. *Hippocampus* 8: 313–322.

Leung, S. 1980. Behavior-dependent evoked potentials in the hippocampal CA1 region of the rat: I. Correlation with behavior and EEG. *Brain Research* 198: 95–117.

Levy, W. B., Jr., & Steward, O. 1979. Synapses as associative memory elements in the hippocampal formation. *Brain Research* 175: 233–245.

Li, L., Miller, E. K., & Desimone, R. 1993. The representation of stimulus familiarity in anterior inferior temporal cortex. *Journal of Neurophysiology* 69: 1918–1929.

Lisberger, S. G. 1988. The neural basis for motor learning in the vestibulo-ocular reflex in monkeys. *Trends in Neuroscience* 11: 147–152.

Lisberger, S. G. 1996. Learning and memory in the vestibuloocular reflex. In J. R. Bloedel, T. J. Ebner, & S. P. Wise (Eds.), *The Acquisition of Motor Behavior in Vertebrates.* Cambridge, MA: MIT Press. Pp. 7–28.

Lisman, J. E. 1989. A mechanism for the Hebb and anti-Hebb processes underlying learning and memory. *Proceedings, National Academy of Sciences (United States of America)* 86: 9574–9578.

Lisman, J. E. 1997. Bursts as a unit of neural information: Making unreliable synapses reliable. *Trends in Neurosciences* 20: 38–43.

Lisman, J., & Harris, K. M. 1993. Quantal analysis and synaptic anatomy: Integrating two views of hippocampal plasticity. *Trends in Neurosciences* 16: 141–147.

Lisman, J. E., Malenka, R. C., Nicoll, R. A., & Malinow, R. 1997. Learning mechanisms: The case for CaM-KII. *Science* 276: 2001–2002.

Lo, D. C. 1995. Neurotrophic factors and synaptic plasticity. *Neuron* 15: 979–981.

Lockhart, R. S., & Craik, F. I. M. 1990. Levels of processing: A retrospective commentary on a framework for memory research. *Canadian Journal of Psychology* 44: 87–112.

Logothetis, N. K., Pauls, J., & Poggio, T. 1995. Shape representation in the inferior temporal cortex of monkeys. *Current Biology* 5: 552–563.

Lorenz, K. 1965. *Evolution and Modification of Behavior.* Chicago: University of Chicago Press.

Luria, A. R. 1966. *Higher Cortical Functions in Man.* London: Tavistock.

Lyford, G. L., Gutnikov, S. A., Clark, A. M., & Rawlins, J. N. P. 1993. Determinants of non-spatial working memory deficits in rats given intraventricular infusions of the NMDA antagonist AP5. *Neuropsychologia* 31: 1079–1098.

Lynch, J. C., Mountcastle, V. B., Talbot, W. H., & Yin, T. C. T. 1977. Parietal lobe mechanisms of directed visual attention. *Journal of Neurophysiology* 40: 362–389.

MacKay, D. G., Stewart, R., & Burke, D. M. 1998a. H.M. revisited: Relations between language comprehension, memory and the hippocampal system. *Journal of Cognitive Neuroscience* 10: 377–394.

MacKay, D. G., Burke, D. M., & Stewart, R. 1998b. H.M.'s language production deficits: Implications for relations between memory, semantic binding, and the hippocampal system. *Journal of Memory and Language* 38: 28–69.

Mackintosh, N. J. 1983. *Conditioning and Associative Learning.* New York: Oxford University Press.

Mackintosh, N. J. 1994. Introduction. In N. J. Mackintosh (Ed.), *Animal Learning and Cognition.* San Diego: Academic Press, pp. 1–11.

MacLean, P. D. 1949. Psychosomic disease and the "visceral brain": Recent developments bearing on the Papez theory of Emotion. *Psychosomatic Medicine* 11: 338–353.

MacLean, P. D. 1952. Some psychiatric implications of physiological studies on frontotemporal portion of the limbic system (visceral brain). *Electroencephalography and Clinical Neurophysiology* 4: 407–418.

MacLean, P. D. 1970. The triune brain, emotion, and scientific bias. In Francis O. Schmidt (Ed.-in-Chief), *The Neurosciences: Second Study Program.* New York: Rockefeller University Press, pp. 336–349.

Madison, D. V., Malenka, R. C., & Nicoll, R. A. 1991. Mechanisms underlying long-term potentiation of synaptic transmission. *Annual Review of Neuroscience* 14: 379–397.

Maguire, E. A., Frackowiak, R. S. J., & Frith, C. D. 1997. Recalling routes around London: Activation of the right hippocampus in taxi drivers. *The Journal of Neuroscience* 17: 7103–7110.

Maguire, E. A., & Mummery, C. J. 1999. Differential modulation of a common memory retrieval network revealed by positron emission tomography. *Hippocampus* 9: 54–61.

Mahut, H. 1971. Spatial and object reversal learning in monkeys with partial temporal lobe ablations. *Neuropsychologia* 9: 409–424.

Mahut, H. 1972. A selective spatial deficit in monkeys after transection of the fornix. *Neuropsychologia* 10: 65–74.

Mahut, H., & Zola, S. M. 1973. A non-modality specific impairment in spatial learning after fornix lesions in monkeys. *Neuropsychologia* 11: 255–269.

Maine de Biran, F.-P.-G. 1929. *The Influence of Habit on the Faculty of Thinking.* Baltimore: Williams & Wilkins. (First published in 1804)

Malamut, B., Saunders, R. C., & Mishkin, M. 1984. Monkeys with combined amygdalo-hippocampal lesions succeed in object discrimination learning despite 24 hour intertrial intervals. *Behavioral Neuroscience* 98: 770–778.

Malenka, R. C. 1994. Synaptic plasticity in the hippocampus: LTP and LTD. *Cell* 78: 535–538.

Malenka, R. C., & Nicoll, R. A. 1997. Silent synapses speak up. *Neuron* 19: 473–476.

Maletic-Savatic, M., Malinow, R., & Svoboda, K. 1999. Rapid dendritic morphogenisis in CA1 hippocampal dendrites induced by synaptic activity. *Science* 283: 1923–1927.

Malinow, R. 1994. LTP: Desperately seeking resolution. *Science* 266: 1195–1196.

Maren, S. 1999. Neurotoxic basolateral amygdala lesions impair learning and memory but not the performance of conditional fear in rats.*The Journal of Neuroscience* 19: 8696–8703.

Markus, E. J., Barnes, C. A., McNaughton, B. L., Gladden, V. L., & Skaggs, W. E. 1994. Spatial information content and reliability of hippocampal CA1 neurons: Effects of visual input. *Hippocampus* 4: 410–421.

Markus, E. J., Qin, Y-L., Leonard, B., Skaggs, W. E., McNaughton, B. L., & Barnes, C. A. 1995. Interactions between location and task affect the spatial and directional firing of hippocampal neurons. *The Journal of Neuroscience* 15: 7079–7094.

Marr, D. A. (1969). A theory of cerebellar cortex. *Journal of Physiology (London)* 202: 437–470.

Marr, D. 1971. Simple memory: a theory for archicortex. *Philosophical Transactions of the Royal Society London, Series B* 262: 23–81.

Martin, A. 1999. Automatic activation of the medial temporal lobe during encoding: Lateralized influences of meaning and novelty. *Hippocampus* 9: 62–70.

Martin, A., Haxby, J. V., Lalonde, F. M., Wiggs, C. L., et al. 1995. Discrete cortical regions associated with knowledge of color and knowledge of action. *Science* 270: 102–105.

Martin, A., Wiggs, C. L., Ungerleider, L. G., & Haxby, J. V. 1996. Neural correlates of category-specific knowledge. *Nature* 379: 649–652.

Martin, A., Wiggs, C. L., & Weisberg, J. A. 1997. Modulation of human medial temporal lobe activity by form, meaning, and experience. *Hippocampus* 7: 587–593.

Martone, M., Butters, N., Payne, M., Becker, J., & Sax, D. 1984. Dissociations between skill learning and verbal recognition in amnesia and dementia. *Archives of Neurology* 41: 965–970.

Mauk, M. D. 1997. Roles of cerebellar cortex and nuclei in motor learning: Contradictions or clues. *Neuron* 18: 343–346.

Mauk, M. D., Garcia, K. S., Medina, J. F., & Steele, P. M. 1998. Does cerebellar LTD mediate motor learning? Toward a resolution without a smoking gun. *Neuron* 20: 359–362.

Mayford, M., Abel, T., & Kandel, E. R. 1995. Transgenic approaches to cognition. *Current Opinion in Neurobiology* 5: 141–148.

Mayford, M., Bach, M. E., Huang, Y. Y., Wang, L., Hawkins, R. D., & Kandel, E. R. 1996. Control of memory formation through regulated expression of a CaMKII transgene. *Science* 274: 1678–1683.

McCarthy, G., Blamire, A. M., Puce, A., Nobre, A. C., Bloch, G., Hyder, F., Goldman-Rakic, P., & Shulman, R. G. 1994. Functional magnetic resonance imaging of human prefrontal cortex activation during a spatial working memory task. *Proceedings of the National Academy of Sciences* 91: 8690–8694.

McCarthy, G., Puce, A., Gore, J. C., & Allison, T. 1997. Face-specific processing in the human fusiform gyrus. *Journal of Cognitive Neuroscience* 9: 605–610.

McCarthy, R. A., & Warrington, E. K. 1990. *Cognitive Neuropsychology: A Clinical Introduction.* San Diego: Academic Press.

McClelland, J. L., McNaughton, B. L., & O'Reilly, R. C. 1995. Why there are complimentary learning systems in the hippocampus and neocortex: Insights from the successes and failures of connectionist models of learning and memory. *Psychological Review* 102: 419–457.

McCloskey, M., & Cohen, N. J. 1989. Catastrophic interference in connectionist networks: The sequential learning problem. In G. H. Bower (Ed.), *The Psychology of Learning and Motivation.* New York: Academic Press.

McDonald, R. J., Murphy, R. A., Guarraci, F. A., Gortler, J. R., White, N. M., & Baker, A. G. 1997. Systematic comparison of the effects of hippocampal and fornix-fimbria lesions on acquisition of three configural discriminations. *Hippocampus* 7: 371–388.

McDonald, R. J., & White, N. M. 1993. A triple dissociation of memory systems: Hippocampus, amygdala, and dorsal striatum. *Behavioral Neuroscience* 107: 3–22.

McDonald, R. J., & White, N. M. 1994. Parallel information processing in the water maze: Evidence for independent memory systems involving dorsal striatum and hippocampus. *Behavioral and Neural Biology* 61: 260–270.

McEchron, M. D., & Disterhoft, J. F. 1997. Sequence of single neuron changes in CA1 hippocampus of rabbits during acquisition of trace eyeblink conditioned responses. *Journal of Neurophysiology* 78: 1030–1044.

McGaugh, J. L. 1966. Time dependent processes in memory storage. *Science* 153: 1351–1358.

McGaugh, J. L., Cahill, L., & Roozendaal, B. 1996. Involvement of the amygdala in memory storage: Interactions with other brain systems. *Proceedings of the National Academy of Sciences* 93: 13508–13514.

McGaugh, J. L., & Herz, M. J. 1972. *Memory Consolidation.* San Francisco: Albion.

McGaugh, J. L., Introini-Collison, I. B., Cahill, L., Kim, M., & Liang, K. C. 1992. Involvement of the amygdala in neuromodulatory influences on memory storage. In J. P. Aggleton (Ed.), *The Amygdala: Neurobiological Aspects of Emotion, Memory, and Mental Dysfunction.* New York: Wiley-Liss, pp. 431–452.

McGlinchey-Berroth, R., Carillo, M., Gabrieli, J. D. E., Brawn, C. M., & Disterhoft, J. F. 1997. Impaired trace eyeblink conditioning in bilateral medial temporal lobe amnesia. *Behavioral Neuroscience* 111: 873–890.

McHugh, T. J., Blum, K. I., Tsien, J. Z., Tonegawa, S., & Wilson, M. A. 1996. Impaired hippocampal representation of space in CA1-specifi NMDAR1 knockout mice. *Cell* 87: 1339–1349.

McNamara, R. K., Kirkby, R. D., dePape, G. E., Skelton, R. W., & Corcoran, M. E. 1993. Differential effects of kindling and kindled seizures on place learning in the Morris water maze. *Hippocampus* 3: 149–152.

McNaughton, B. L. 1989. Neuronal mechanisms for spatial computation and information storage. In L. Nadel & L. A. Cooper (Eds.), *Neural Connections, Mental Computation: Computational Models of Cognition and Perception.* Cambridge, MA: MIT Press, pp. 285–350.

McNaughton, B. L. 1993. The mechanism of expression of long-term enhancement of hippocampal synapses: Current issues and theoretical implications. *Annual Review of Physiology* 55: 375–396.

McNaughton, B. L., Barnes, C. A., Gerrard, J. L., Gothard, K., Jung, M. W., Knierim, J. J., Kudrimoti, H., Qin, Y., Skaggs, W. E., Suster, M., & Weaver, K. L. 1996. Deciphering the hippocampal polyglot: The hippocampus as a path integration system. *Journal of Experimental Biology* 199: 173–185.

McNaughton, B. L., Barnes, C. A., & O'Keefe, J. 1983. The contributions of position, direction, and velocity to single unit activity in the hippocampus of freely-moving rats. *Experimental Brain Research* 52: 41–49.

McNaughton, B. L., Barnes, C. A., Rado, G., Baldwin, J., & Rasmussen, M. 1986. Long-term enhancement of hippocampal synaptic transmission and the acquisition of spatial information. *The Journal of Neuroscience* 6: 563–571.

McNaughton, B. L., Chen, L. L., & Markus, E. J. 1991. Dead reckoning, landmark learning and the sense of direction: A neurophysiological and computational hypothesis. *Journal of Cognitive Neuroscience* 3: 190–202.

McNaughton, B. L., & Morris, R. G. 1987. Hippocampal synaptic enhancement and information storage within a distributed memory system. *Trends in Neurosciences* 10: 408–415.

Merigan, W. H., & Maunsell, J. H. R. 1993. How parallel are the primate visual pathways? *Annual Review of Neuroscience* 16: 369–402.

Merzenich, M. M., Recanzone, G. H., Jenkins, W. M., & Grajski, K. A. 1990. Adaptive mechanisms in cortical networks underlying cortical contributions to learning and nondeclarative memory. *Brain*. Cold Spring Harbor. *Cold Spring Harbor Symposium LV,* pp. 873–887.

Merzenich, M. M., & Sameshima, K. 1993. Cortical plasticity and memory. *Current Opinion in Neurobiology* 3: 187–196.

Metcalfe, J., Mencl, W. E., & Cottrell, G. W. 1994. Cognitive binding. In D. L. Schacter & E. Tulving (Eds.), *Memory Systems*. Cambridge, MA: MIT Press, pp. 369–394.

Meunier, M., Bachevalier, J., Mishkin, M., & Murray, E. A. 1993. Effects on visual recognition of combined and separate ablations of the entorhinal and perirhinal cortex in rhesus monkeys. *The Journal of Neuroscience* 13: 5418–5432.

Meunier, M., Hadfield, W., Bachevalier, J., & Murray, E. A. 1996. Effects of rhinal cortex lesions combined with hippocampectomy on visual recognition memory in rhesus monkeys. *Journal of Neurophysiology* 75: 1190–1205.

Middleton, F. A., & Strick. P. L. 1994. Anatomical evidence for cerebellar and basal ganglia involvement in higher cognitive function. *Science* 266: 458–461.

Mikami, A., & Kubota, K. 1980. Inferotemporal neuron activities and color discrimination with delay. *Brain Research* 182: 65–78.

Miller, E. K., & Desimone, R. 1994. Parallel neuronal mechanisms for short-term memory. *Science* 263: 520–522.

Miller, E. K., Erickson, C. A., & Desimone, R. 1996. Neural mechanisms of visual working memory in prefrontal cortex of the macaque. *The Journal of Neuroscience* 16: 5154–5167.

Miller, E. K., Gochin, P. M., & Gross, C. G. 1991a. Habituation-like decrease in the responses of neurons inferior temporal cortex of the macaque. *Visual Neuroscience* 7: 357–362.

Miller, E. K., Li, L., & Desimone, R. 1991b. A neural mechanism for working and recognition memory in inferior temporal cortex. *Science* 254: 1377–1379.

Miller, E. K., Li, L., & Desimone, R. 1993. Activity of neurons in anterior inferior temporal cortex during a short-term memory task. *The Journal of Neuroscience* 13: 1460–1478.

Miller, V. M., & Best, P. J. 1980. Spatial correlates of hippocampal unit activity are altered by lesions of the fornix and entorhinal cortex. *Brain Research* 194: 311–323.

Milner, B. 1962. Les troubles de la memoire accompagnant des lésions hippocampiques bilatérales. In P. Passant (Ed.), *Physiologie de Hippocampe*. Paris: C.N.R.S. Paris, pp. 257–272.

Milner, B. 1963. Effects of different brain lesions on card sorting. *Archives of Neurology* 9: 100–110.

Milner, B. 1971. Interhemispheric differences in the location of psychological processes in man. *British Medical Bulletin* 27: 272–277.

Milner, B. 1972. Disorders of learning and memory after temporal-lobe lesions in man. *Clinical Neurosurgery* 19: 421–446.

Milner, B. 1974. Hemispheric specialization: Scope and limits. *The Neurosciences: Third Study Program.* Cambridge, MA: MIT Press.

Milner, B., Corkin, S., & Teuber, H. L. 1968. Further analysis of the hippocampal amnesic syndrome: 14-year followup study of H.M. *Neuropsychologia* 6: 215–234.

Milner, B. M., McAndrews, P., & Leonard, G. 1990. Frontal lobes and memory for the temporal order of recent events. *Cold Spring Harbor Symposium on Quantitative Biology* 55: 987–994.

Milner, B., & Petrides, M. 1984. Behavioural effects of frontal-lobe lesions in man. *Trends in Neurosciences* 7: 403–407.

Mink, J. W. 1996. The basal ganglia: Focused selection and inhibition of competing motor programs. *Progress in Neurobiology* 50: 381–425.

Miserendino, M. J. D., Sananes, C. B., Melia, K. R., & Davis, M. 1990. Blocking of acquisition but not expression of conditioned fear potentiated startle by NMDA antagonists in the amygdala. *Nature* 345: 716–718.

Mishkin, M. 1978. Memory in monkeys severely impaired by combined but not by separate removal of amygdala and hippocampus. *Nature* 273: 297–298.

Mishkin, M. 1982. A memory system in the monkey. *Philosophical Transactions. Royal Society of London. Series B. Biological Sciences* 298: 85–95.

Mishkin, M., & Delacour, J. 1975. An analysis of short-term visual memory in the monkey. *Journal of Experimental Psychology: Animal Behavior Processes* 1: 326–334.

Mishkin, M., & Petri, H. L. 1984. Memories and habits: Some implications for the analysis of learning and retention. In N. Butters & L. R. Squire (Eds.), *Neuropsychology of Memory.* New York: Guilford, pp. 287–296.

Mishkin, M., Vargha-Khadem, F., & Gadian, D. G. 1998. Amnesia and the organization of the hippocampal system. *Hippocampus* 8: 212–216.

Mitchell, J. A., & Hall, G. 1988a. Caudate-putamen lesions in the rat may impair or potentiate maze learning depending upon availability of stimulus cues and relevance of response cues. *Quarterly Journal of Experimental Psychology* 40: 243–258.

Mitchell, J. A., & Hall, G. 1988b. Learning in rats with caudate-putamen lesions: Unimpaired classical conditioning and beneficial effects of redundant stimulus cues on instrumental and spatial learning deficits. *Behavioral Neuroscience* 10: 504–514.

Miyashita, Y. 1993. Inferior temporal cortex: Where visual perception meets memory. *Annual Review of Neuroscience* 16: 245–263.

Miyashita, Y., & Chang, H. S. 1988. Neuronal correlate of pictorial short-term memory in the primate temporal cortex. *Nature* 331: 68–70.

Mondadori, C., Weiskrantz, L., Buerki, H., Petschke, F., & Fagg, G. E. 1989. NMDA receptor antagonists can enhance or impair learning performance in animals. *Experimental Brain Research* 75: 449–456.

Montaldi, D., Mayes, A., Barnes, A., Pirie, H., Hadley, D. M., Patterson, J., & Wyper, D. J. 1998. Associative encoding of pictures activates the medial temporal lobes. *Human Brain Mapping* 6: 85–104.

Morris, R. G. M. 1981. Spatial localization does not require the presence of local cues. *Learning and Motivation* 12: 239–260.

Morris, R. G. M. 1984. Developments of a water-maze procedure for studying spatial learning in the rat. *Journal of Neuroscience Methods* 11: 47–60.

Morris, R. G. M. 1989. *Parallel Distributed Processing: Implications for Psychology and Neurobiology.* Oxford: Clarendon Press.

Morris, R. G. M., Anderson, E., Lynch, G. S., & Baudry, M. 1986. Selective impairment of learning and blockade of long term potentiation by a *N*-methyl-D-aspartate receptor antagonist, AP5. *Nature* 319: 774–776.

Morris, R. G. M., Davis, S., & Butcher, S. P. 1991. Hippocampal synaptic plasticity and N-methyl-D-aspartate receptors: A role in information storage? In M. Baudry & J. L. Davis (Eds.), *Long Term Potentiation: A Debate of Current Issues*. Cambridge, MA: MIT Press, pp. 267–300.

Morris, R. G. M., & Frey, U. 1997. Hippocampal synaptic plasticity: Role in spatial learning or the automatic recording of attended experience? *Philosophical Transactions. Royal Society of London*. 352: 1489–1503.

Morris, R. G. M., Garrud, P., Rawlins, J. P., & O'Keefe, J. 1982. Place navigation impaired in rats with hippocampal lesions. *Nature* 297: 681–683.

Morris, R. G. M., Schenk, F., Tweedie, F., & Jarrard, L. 1990. Ibotenate lesions of the hippocampus and/or subiculum: Dissociating components of allocentric spatial learning. *European Journal of Neuroscience* 2: 1016–1028.

Moscovitch, M. 1984. The sufficient conditions for demonstrating preserved memory in amnesia: A task analysis. In N. Butters & L. R. Squire (Eds.), *Neuropsychology of Memory*. New York: Guilford Press, pp. 104–114.

Moscovitch, M. 1994. Memory and working with memory: Evaluation of a Component process model and comparisons with other models. In D. L. Schacter & E. Tulving (Eds.), *Memory Systems*. Cambridge, MA: MIT Press. Pp. 269–310.

Moscovitch, M., Kapur, S., Kohler, D., & Houle, S. 1995. Distinct neural correlates of visual long-term memory for spatial location and object identity: A positron emission tomography study in humans. *Proceedings of the National Academy of Sciences (United States of America)* 92: 3721–3725.

Moscovitch, M., Winocur, G., & Behrmann, M. 1997. What is special about face recognition? Nineteen experiments on a person with visual object agnosia and dyslexia but normal face recognition. *Journal of Cognitive Neuroscience* 9: 555–604.

Moscovitch, M., Winocur, G., & McLachlan, D. 1986. Memory as assessed by recognition and reading time in normal and memory impaired people with Alzheimer's disease and other neurological disorders. *Journal of Experimental Psychology: General* 115: 331–347.

Moser, E. I., & Andersen, P. 1994. Conserved spatial learning in cooled rats in spite of slowing of dentate filed potentials. *Journal of Neuroscience* 14(7): 4458–4466.

Moser, E. I., Krobert, K. A., Moser, M-B., & Morris, R. G. M. 1998. Impaired spatial learning after saturation of long-term potentiation. *Science* 281: 2038–2042.

Moser, E. I., Mathiesen, I., & Andersen, P. 1993. Association between brain temperature and dentate field potentials in exploring and swimming rats. *Science* 259: 1324–1326.

Moser, E. I., Moser, M. B., & Andersen, P. 1994. Potentiation of dentate synapses initiated by exploratory learning in rats: Dissociation from brain temperature, motor activity, and arousal. *Learning and Memory* 1: 55–73.

Motter, B. C., & Mountcastle, V. B. 1981. The functional properties of light sensitive neurons of the posterior partiatal cortex studied in waking monkeys: Fovela sparing and opponent vector organization. *The Journal of Neuroscience* 1: 3–26.

Mountcastle, V. B., Andersen, R. A., & Motter, B. C. 1981. The influence of attentive fixation upon the excitability of light sensitive neurons of the posterior parietal cortex. *The Journal of Neuroscience* 1: 1213–1235.

Mountcastle, V. B., Lynch, J. C., & Georgopoulos, A. 1975. Posterior partial association cortex of the monkey: Command functions for operations within personal space. *Journal of Neurophysiology* 38: 871–908.

Müller, G. E., & Pilzecker, A. 1900. Experimentelle Beitrage zur Lehre vom Gedachtniss. *American Psychologist* 1: 1–288.

Muller, R. U. 1996. A quarter of a century of place cells. *Neuron* 17: 813–822.

Muller, R. U., Bostock, E., Taube, J. S., & Kubie, J. L. 1994. On the directional firing properties of hippocampal place cells. *The Journal of Neuroscience* 14: 7235–7251.

Muller, R. U., & Kubie, J. L. 1987. The effects of changes in the environment on the spatial firing of hippocampal complex-spike cells. *The Journal of Neuroscience* 7: 1951–1968.

Muller, R. U., Kubie, J. L., & Ranck, J. B., Jr. 1987. Spatial firing patterns of hippocampal complex spike cells in a fixed environment. *The Journal of Neuroscience* 7: 1935–1950.

Mumby, D. G., & Pinel, P. J. 1994. Rhinal cortex lesions and object recognition in rats. *Behavioral Neuroscience* 108: 11–18.

Mumby, D. G., Wood, E. R., & Pinel, J. P. 1992. Object recognition memory is only mildly impaired in rats with lesions of the hippocampus and amygdala. *Psychobiology* 20: 18–27.

Muramoto, K., Ono, T., Nishijo, H., & Fukuda, M. 1993. Rat amygdaloid neuron responses during auditory discrimination. *Neuroscience* 52: 621–636.

Murray, E. A. 1990. Representational memory in nonhuman primates. In R. P. Kesner & D. S. Olton (Eds.), *Neurobiology of Comparative Cognition*. Hillsdale: Erlbaum, pp. 127–155.

Murray, E. A. 1996. What have ablation studies told us about the neural substrates of stimulus memory? *Seminars in the Neurosciences* 8: 13–22.

Murray, E. A., & Bussey, T. J. 1999. Perceptual-mnemonic functions of the perirhinal cortex. *Trends in Cognitive Science* 3: 142–151.

Murray, E. A., Davidson, M., Gaffan, D., Olton, D. S., & Suomi, S. 1989. Effects of fornix transection and cingulate cortical ablation on spatial memory in rhesus monkeys. *Experimental Brain Research* 74: 173–186.

Murray, E. A., & Gaffan, D. 1994. Removal of the amygdala plus subjacent cortex disrupts the retention of both intramodal and crossmodal associative memories in monkeys. *Behavioral Neuroscience* 108: 494–500.

Murray, E. A., Gaffan, E. A., & Flint, R. W., Jr. 1996. Anterior rhinal cortex and amygdala: dissociation of their contributions to memory and food preference in rhesus monkeys. *Behavioral Neuroscience* 110: 30–42.

Murray, E. A., Gaffan, D., & Mishkin, M. 1993. Neural substrates of visual stimulus-stimulus association in rhesus monkeys. *The Journal of Neuroscience* 13: 4549–4561.

Murray, E. A., & Mishkin, M. 1984. Severe tactual as well as visual memory deficits follow combined removal of the amygdala and hippocampus in monkeys. *The Journal of Neuroscience* 4: 2565–2580.

Murray, E. A., & Mishkin, M. 1986. Visual recognition in monkeys following rhinal cortical ablations combined with either amygdalectomy or hippocampectomy. *The Journal of Neuroscience* 6: 1991–2003.

Murray, E. A., & Mishkin, M. 1998. Object recognition and location memory in monkeys with excitotoxic lesions of the amygdala and hippocampus. *The Journal of Neuroscience* 18: 6568–6582.

Murray, E. A., & Wise, S. P. 1996. Role of the hippocampus plus subjacent cortex but not amygdala in visuomotor conditional learning in monkeys. *Behavioral Neuroscience* 110: 1261–1270.

Musen, G., Shimamura, A. P., & Squire, L. R. 1990. Intact text-specific reading skill in amnesia. *Journal of Experimental Psychology: Learning, Memory and Cognition* 6: 1068–1076.

Musen, G., & Squire, L. R. 1991. Normal acquisition of novel verbal information in amnesia. *Journal of Experimental Psychology: Learning, Memory and Cognition* 17: 1095–1104.

Musen, G., & Squire, L. R. 1992. Nonverbal priming in amnesia. *Memory and Cognition* 20: 441–448.

Musen, G., & Squire, L. R. 1993. On implicit learning of novel associations by amnesic patients and normal subjects. *Neuropsychology* 7: 119–135.

Nádasdy, Z., Hirase, H., Czurkó, A., Csicsvari, J., & Buzsáki, G. 1999. Replay and time compression of recurring spike sequences in the hippocampus. *The Journal of Neuroscience* 19: 9497–9507.

Nadel, L. 1991. The hippocampus and space revisited. *Hippocampus* 1: 221–229.

Nadel, L. 1992. Multiple memory systems: What and why. *Journal of Cognitive Neuroscience* 4: 179–188.

Nadel, L., & Moscovitch, M. 1997. Memory consolidation, retrograde amnesia and the hippocampal complex. *Current Opinion in Neurobiology* 7: 217–227.

Nadel, L., & Willner, J. 1980. Context and conditioning: A place for space. *Physiological Psychology* 8: 218–228.

Nader, K., & LeDoux, J. E. 1997. Is it time to invoke multiple fear learning systems in the amygdala? *Trends in Cognitive Sciences* 1: 241–244.

Nakamura, K., Mikami, A., & Kubota, K. 1992. Activity of single neurons in the monkey amygdala during performance of a visual discrimination task. *Journal of Neurophysiology* 67: 1447–1463.

Nauta, W. J. H. 1971. The problem of the frontal lobe: A reinterpretation. *Journal of Psychiatric Research* 8: 167–187.

Neisser, U. 1967. *Cognitive Psychology*. New York: Appleton-Century-Crofts.

Nicoll, R. A., Kauer, J. A., & Malenka, R. C. 1988. The current excitement in long-term potentiation. *Neuron* 1: 87–103.

Nicoll, R. A., & Malenka, R. C. 1995. Contrasting properties of two forms of long-term potentiation in the hippocampus. *Nature* 377: 115–118.

Nishijo, H., Ono, T., & Nishino, H. 1988a. Single neuron responses in amygdala of alert monkey during complex sensory stimulation with affective significance. *The Journal of Neuroscience* 8: 3570–3583.

Nishijo, H., Ono, T., & Nishino, H. 1988b. Topographic distribution of modality-specific amygdalar neurons in alert monkey. *The Journal of Neuroscience* 8: 3556–3569.

Nissen, M. J., & Bullemer, P. 1987. Attentional requirements of learning: Evidence from performance measures. *Cognitive Psychology* 19: 1–32.

Nudo, R. J., Milliken, G. W., Jenkins, W. M., & Merzenich, M. M. 1996. Use-dependent alterations of movement representations in primary motor cortex of adult squirrel monkeys. *The Journal of Neuroscience* 16: 785–807.

Nyberg, L., Cabeza, R., & Tulving, E. 1996. PET studies of encoding and retrieval: The HERA model. *Psychonomic Bulletin and Review A* 3: 135–148.

Nyberg, L., McIntosh, A. R., Cabeza, R., Habib, R., Houle, S., & Tulving, E. 1996. General and specific brain regions involved in encoding and retrieval of events: What, where, and when. *Proceedings of the National Academy of Sciences (United States of America). B* 93: 11280–11285.

Oberg, R. G. E., & Divac, J. 1979. Cognitive functions of the neostriatum. In I. Divac & R. G. E. Oberg (Eds.), *The Neostriatum*. London: Pergamon, pp. 291–313.

O'Boyle, V. J., Jr., Murray, E. A., & Mishkin, M. 1995. Effects of excitotoxic amygdalohippocampal lesions on visual recognition in rhesus monkeys. *Society for Neuroscience Abstracts* 19: 438.

Ogden, J. A., & Corkin, S. 1991. Memories of H.M. In W. C. Abraham, M. Corballis, & K. G. White (Eds.), *Memory Mechanisms: A Tribute to G. V. Goddard*. Hillsdale, NJ: Erlbaum, pp. 195–215.

O'Keefe, J., & Bouma, H. 1969. Complex sensory properties of certain amygdala units in the freely moving cat. *Experimental Neurology* 23: 384–398.

O'Keefe, J., & Burgess, N. 1996. Geometric determinants of the place fields of hippocampal neurons. *Nature* 381: 425–428.

O'Keefe, J., & Conway, D. H. 1980. On the trail of the hippocampal engram. *Physiological Psychology* 8: 229–238.

O'Keefe, J., & Dostrovsky, J. 1971. The hippocampus as a spatial map. Preliminary evidence from unit activity in the freely-moving rat. *Brain Research* 34: 171–175.

O'Keefe, J. 1976. Place units in the hippocampus of the freely moving rat. *Experimental Neurology* 51: 78–109.

O'Keefe, J. 1979. A review of hippocampal place cells. *Progress in Neurobiology* 13: 419–439.

O'Keefe, J., & Conway, D. H. 1978. Hippocampal place units in the freely moving rat: Why they fire when they fire. *Experimental Brain Research* 31: 573–590.

O'Keefe, J., & Nadel, L. 1978. *The Hippocampus as a Cognitive Map.* New York: Oxford University Press.

O'Keefe, J., & Nadel, L. 1979. Precis of O'Keefe and Nadel's *The Hippocampus as a Cognitive Map. Behavioral and Brain Sciences* 2: 487–533.

O'Keefe, J., & Speakman, A. 1987. Single unit activity in the rat hippocampus during a spatial memory task. *Experimental Brain Research* 68: 1–27.

Olds, J., Disterhoft, J. F., Segal, M., Kornblith, C. L., & Hirsh, R. 1971. Learning centers of rat brain mapped by measuring latencies of conditioned unit responses. *Journal of Neurophysiology* 35: 202–219.

Olton, D. S. 1984. Comparative analyses of episodic memory. *Brain and Behavioral Sciences* 7: 250–251.

Olton, D. S. 1986. Hippocampal function and memory for temporal context. In R. L. Isaacson & K. H. Pribram (Eds.), *The Hippocampus* (Vol. 4). New York: Plenum Press.

Olton, D. S. 1989. Mnemonic functions of the hippocampus: single unit analyses in rats. In V. Chan-Palay (Ed.), *The Hippocampus—New Vistas.* New York: Alan R. Liss, pp. 411–424.

Olton, D. S., Becker, J. T., & Handlemann, G. E. 1979. Hippocampus, space, and memory. *Brain and Behavioral Sciences* 2: 313–365.

Olton, D. S., Branch, M., & Best, P. J. 1978. Spatial correlates hippocampal unit activity. *Experimental Neurology* 58: 387–409.

Olton, D. S., & Feustle, W. A. 1981. Hippocampal function required for nonspatial working memory. *Experimental Brain Research* 68: 1–27.

Olton, D. S., & Papas, B. C. 1979. Spatial memory and hippocampal function. *Neuropsychologia* 17: 669–682.

Olton, D. S., Walker, J. A., & Wolf, W. A. 1982. A disconnection analysis of hippocampal function. *Brain Research* 233: 241–253.

Olton, D. S., Wenk, G. L., Church, R. M., & Meck, W. H. 1988. Attention and the frontal cortex as examined by simultaneous temporal processing. *Neuropsychologia* 26: 307–318.

O'Mara, S. M., Rolls, E. T., Berthoz, A., & Kesner, R. P. 1994. Neurons responding to whole-body motion in the primate hippocampus. *The Journal of Neuroscience* 14: 6511–6523.

Ono, T., Nakamura, K., Nishijo, H., & Eifuku, S. 1993. Monkey hippocampal neurons related to spatial and non-spatial functions. *Journal of Neurophysiology* 70: 1516–1529.

Ono, T., & Nishijo, H. 1992. Neurophysiological basis of the Kluver-Bucy syndrome: responses of monkey amygdaloid neurons to biologically significant objects. In J. Aggleton (Ed.), *The Amygdala: Neurobiological Aspects of Emotion, Memory and Mental Dysfunction.* New York: Wiley-Liss, pp. 167–190.

Orbach, J., Milner, B., & Rasmussen, T. 1960. Learning and retention in monkeys after amygdala-hippocampus resection. *Archives of Neurology* 3: 230–251.

Osborne, B., & Black, A. H. 1978. A detailed analysis of behavior during the transition from acquiisition to extinction in rats with fornix lesions. *Behavioral Biology* 23: 271–290.

Ó Scalaidhe, S., Wilson, F. A. W., & Goldman-Rakic, P. 1999. Face-selective neurons during passive viewing and working memory performance in rhesus monkeys: Evidence for intrinsic specialization of neuronal coding. *Cerebral Cortex* 9: 459–475.

Otto, T., & Eichenbaum, H. 1992a. Complementary roles of orbital prefrontal cortex and the perirhinal-entorhinal cortices in an odor-guided delayed non-matching to sample task. *Behavioral Neuroscience* 106: 763–776.

Otto, T., & Eichenbaum, H. 1992b. Neuronal activity in the hippocampus during delayed non-match to sample performance in rats: Evidence for hippocampal processing in recognition memory. *Hippocampus* 2: 323–334.

Otto, T., Eichenbaum, H., Wiener, S., & Wible, C. 1991. Learning related patterns of CA1 spike trains parallel stimulation parameters optimal for inducing hippocampal long-term potentiation. *Hippocampus* 1: 181–192.

Owen, A. M. 1997. The functional organization of working memory processes within human lateral frontal cortex: The contribution of functional neuroimaging. *European Journal of Neuroscience* 9: 1329–1339.

Owen, A. M., Milner, B., Petrides, M., & Evans, A. C. 1996. Memory for object-features versus memory for object-location: A positron emission tomography study of encoding and retrieval processes. *Proceedings of the National Academy of Sciences (United States of America)*. 93: 9212–9217.

Owen, A. M., Morris, R. G., Sahakian, B. J., Polkey, C. E., & Robbins, T. W. 1996. Double dissociations of memory and executive functions in working memory tasks following frontal lobe excisions, temporal lobe excisions or amygdalo-hippocampectomy in man. *Brain* 119: 1597–1615.

Owen, A. M., Roberts, A. C., Hodges, J. R., Summers, B. A., Polkey, C. E., & Robbins, T. W. 1993. Contrasting mechanisms of impaired attentional set-shifting in patients with frontal lobe damage or Parkinson's disease. *Brain* 116: 1159–1175.

Owen, M. J., & Butler, S. R. 1981. Amnesia after transection of the fornix in monkeys: Long-term memory impaired, short-term memory intact. *Behavioral Brain Research* 3: 115–123.

Packard, M. G., Cahill, L., & McGaugh, J. L. 1994. Amygdala modulation of hippocampal-dependent and caudate nucleus-dependent memory processes. *Proceedings of the National Academy of Sciences (United States of America)*. 91: 8477–8481.

Packard, M. G., Hirsh, R., & White, N. M. 1989. Differential effects of fornix and caudate nucleus lesions on two radial maze tasks: Evidence for multiple memory systems. *The Journal of Neuroscience* 9: 1465–1472.

Packard, M. G., & McGaugh, J. L. 1992. Double dissociation of fornix and caudate nucleus lesions on acquistion of two water maze tasks: Further evidence for multiple memory systems. *Behavioral Neuroscience* 106: 439–446.

Packard, M. G., & McGaugh, J. L. 1996. Inactivation of hippocampus or caudate nucleus with lidocaine differentially affects expression of place and response learning. *Neurobiology of Learning and Memory* 65: 65–72.

Packard, M. G., & Teather, L. A. 1998. Amygdala modulation of multiple memory systems: hippocampus and caudate-putamen. *Neurobiology of Learning and Memory* 69: 163–203.

Palm, G. 1990. Cell assemblies as a guideline for brain research. *Concepts in Neuroscience* 1: 133–147.

Pandya, D. N., & Yeterian, E. H. 1996. Comparison of prefrontal architecture and connections. *Philosophical Transactions. Royal Society of London. Series B. Biological Sciences*. 351: 1423–1432.

Papez, J. W. 1937. A proposed mechanism of emotion. *Archives of Neurology and Psychiatry* 7: 217–224.

Parkin, A. J. 1987. *Memory and Amnesia*. Oxford, UK: Blackwell.

Pascalis, O., & Bachevalier, J. 1999. Neonatal aspiration lesions of the hippocampal formation impair visual recognition memory when assessed by paired-comparison task but not by delayed nonmatching-to-sample task. *Hippocampus* 9: 609–616.

Pascual-Leone, A., Grafman, J., Clark, K., Stewart, M., Massaquoi, S., Lou, J., & Hallett, M. 1993. Procedural learning in Parkinson's disease and cerebellar degeneration. *Annual Neurology* 34: 594–602.

Passingham, R. E. 1975. Delayed matching after selective prefrontal lesions in monkeys *(Macaca mulatta). Brain Research* 92: 89–102.

Passingham, R. E. 1993. *The Frontal Lobes and Voluntary Action.* Oxford: Oxford University Press.

Paulesu, E., Frith, C. D., & Frackowiak, R. S. J. 1993. The neural correlates of the verbal component of working memory. *Nature* 362: 342–345.

Paulsen, J. S., Butters, N., Salmon, D. P., Heindel, W. C., & Swenson, M. R. 1993. Prism adaptation in Alzheimer's and Huntington's disease. *Neuropsychology* 7: 73–81.

Pavlides, C., Greenstein, Y. J., Grudman, M., & Winson, J. 1988. Long-term potentiation in the dentate gyrus is induced preferentially on the positive phase of theta rhythm. *Brain Research* 439: 383–387.

Pavlides, C., & Winson, J. 1989. Influences of hippocampal place cell firing in the awake state on the activity of these cells during subsequent sleep episodes. *The Journal of Neuroscience* 9: 2907–2918.

Pavlov, I. P. 1927. *Conditioned Reflexes.* Oxford University Press.

Peinado-Manzano, M. A. 1988. Effects of bilateral lesions of the central and lateral amygdala on free operant successive discrimination. *Behavior and Brain Research* 29: 61–71.

Peinado-Manzano, M. A. 1989. Intervention of the lateral and central amygdala on the association of visual stimuli with different magnitudes of reinforcement. *Behavior and Brain Research* 32: 289–295.

Penick, S., & Solomon, P. R. 1991. Hippocampus, context, and conditioning. *Behavioral Neuroscience* 105: 611–617.

Perrett, D. I., Mistlin, A. J., & Chitty, A. J. 1987. Visual neurones responsive to faces. *Trends in Neurosciences* 10: 358–364.

Perrett, D. I., Rolls, E. T., & Caan, W. 1982. Visual neurones responsive to faces in the monkey temporal cortex. *Experimental Brain Research* 47: 329–342.

Perrett, S. P., Ruiz, B. P., & Mauk, M. D. 1993. Cerebellar cortex lesions disrupt learning-dependent timing of conditioned eyelid responses. *The Journal of Neuroscience* 13(4): 1708–1718.

Petrides, M. 1986. The effect of periarcuate lesions in the monkey on the performance of symmetrically and asymmetrically reinforced visual and auditory go, no-go tasks. *The Journal of Neuroscience* 6: 2054–2063.

Petrides, M. 1994. Frontal lobes and behavior. *Current Opinion in Neurobiology* 4: 207–211.

Petrides, M. 1995a. Functional organization of the human frontal cortex for mnemonic processing. *Annals of the New York Academy of Sciences* 769: 85–96.

Petrides, M. 1995b. Impairments on nonspatial self-ordered and externally ordered working memory tasks after lesions of the mid-dorsal part of the lateral frontal cortex in the monkey. *The Journal of Neuroscience* 15: 359–375.

Petrides, M. 1996. Specialized systems for the processing of mnemonic information within the primate frontal cortex. *Philosophical Transactions. Royal Society of London. Series B. Biological Sciences.* 351: 1455–1462.

Petrides, M., Alisiatos, B., & Evans, A. C. 1995. Functional activation of the human ventrolateral frontal cortex during mnemonic retrieval of verbal information. *Proceedings of the National Academy of Sciences (United States of America).* 92: 5803–5807.

Petrides, M., Alivisatos, B., Evans, A. C., & Meyer, E. 1993a. Dissociation of human mid-dorsolateral from posterior dorsolateral frontal cortex in memory processing. *Proceedings of the National Academy of Sciences (United States of America).* 90: 873–877.

Petrides, M., Alivisatos, B., Meyer, E., & Evans, A. C. 1993b. Functional activation of the human frontal cortex during the performance of verbal working memory tasks. *Proceedings of the National Academy of Sciences (United States of America).* 90: 878–882.

Petrides, M., & Pandya, D. N. 1994. Comparative architectonic analysis of the human and the macaque frontal cortex. In F. Boller & J. Grafman (Eds.), *Handbook of Neuropsychology* (Vol. 9). Amsterdam: Elsevier, pp. 17–58.

Pettet, M. W., & Gilbert, C. D. 1992. Dynamic changes in receptive-field size in cat primary visual cortex. *Proceedings of the National Academy of Sciences (United States of America).* 89: 8366–8370.

Phillips, A. G., & Carr, G. D. 1987. Cognition and the basal ganglia: a possible substrate for procedural knowledge. *Canadian Journal of Neurological Science* 14: 381–385.

Phillips, R. G., & LeDoux, J. E. 1992. Differential contribution of amygdala and hippocampus to cued and contextual fear conditioning. *Behavioral Neuroscience* 106: 274–285.

Piaget, J. 1928. *Judgement and Reasoning in the Child* (Trans., Marjorie Warden). New York: Harcourt, Brace, & World, Inc.

Pitkänen, A., Stefanacci, L., Farb, C. R., Go, G. G., LeDoux, J. E., & Amaral, D. G. 1995. Intrinsic connections of the rat amygdaloid complex: Projections originating in the lateral nucleus. *Journal of Comparative Neurology* 356: 288–310.

Poldrack, R. A., Desmond, J. E., Glover, G. H., & Gabrieli, J. D. E. 1998. The neural basis of visual skill learning: An fMRI study of mirror reading. *Cerebral Cortex* 8: 1–10.

Poldrack, R. A., Prabakharan, V., Seger, C., & Gabrieli, J. D. E. 1999. Striatal activation during cognitive skill learning. *Neuropsychology* 13: 564–574.

Polster, M. R., Nadel, L., & Schacter, D. L. 1991. Cognitive neuroscience analyses of memory: A historical perspective. *Journal of Cognitive Neuroscience* 3: 95–116.

Pons, T. P., Garraghty, P. E., Ommaya, A. K., Kaas, J. H., Taub, E., & Mishkin, M. 1991. Massive cortical reorganization after sensory deafferentation in adult macaques. *Science* 252: 1857–1860.

Potegal, M. 1972. The caudate nucleus egocentric localization system. *Acta Neurobiologiae Experimentalis* 32: 479–494.

Price, J. L., Carmichael, S. T., Carnes, K., Clugnet, M-C., Kuroda, M., & Ray, J. P. 1991. Olfactory input to the prefrontal cortex. In J. L. Davis & H. Eichenbaum (Eds.), *Olfaction: A Model System for Computational Neuroscience.* Cambridge, MA: MIT Press, pp. 101–120.

Price, J. L., Russchen, F. T., & Amaral, D. G. 1987. The limbic region: II. The amygdaloid complex. In A. Bjorkland, T. Hokfelt, & L. W. Swanson (Eds.), *Handbook of Chemical Neuroanatomy: Vol. 5. Integrated Systems of the CNS, Part I.* Amsterdam: Elsevier, pp. 279–381.

Quintana, J., & Fuster, J. M. 1992. Mnemonic and predictive functions of cortical neurons in a memory task. *NeuroReport* 3: 721–724.

Quirk, G. J., Muller, R. U., & Kubie, J. L. 1990. The firing of hippocampal place cells in the dark depends on the rat's recent experience. *The Journal of Neuroscience* 10: 2008–2017.

Quirk, G. J., Muller, R. U., Kubie, J. L., & Ranck, J. B., Jr. 1992. The positional firing properties of medial entorhinal neurons: Descriptions and comparison with hippocampal place cells. *The Journal of Neuroscience* 12: 1945–1963.

Quirk, G. J., Repa, C., & LeDoux, J. 1995. Fear conditioning enhances short-latency auditory responses of lateral amygdala neurons: Parallel recordings in the freely behaving rat. *Neuron* 15: 1029–1039.

Raffaele, K. C., & Olton, D. S. 1988. Hippocampal and amygdaloid involvement in working memory for non-spatial stimuli. *Behavioral Neuroscience* 102: 349–355.

Raichle, M. E., Fiez, J. A., Videen, T. O., MacLeod, A. K., Pardo, J. V., Fox, P. T., & Petersen, S. E. 1994. Practice-related changes in human brain functional anatomy during non-motor learning. *Cerebral Cortex* 4: 8–26.

Rainer, G., Asaad, W. F., & Miller, E. K. 1998. Selective representation of relevant information by neurons in the primate prefrontal cortex. *Nature* 393: 577–579.

Rainer, G., Rao, C., & Miller, E. K. 1999. Prospective coding for objects in the primate prefrontal cortex. *The Journal of Neuroscience* 19: 5493–5505.

Ramachandran, V. S., Rodgers-Ramachandran, D., & Stewart, M. 1992. Perceptual correlates of massive cortical reorganization. *Science* 258: 1159–1160.

Ranck, J. B., Jr. 1973. Studies on single neurons in dorsal hippocampal formation and septum in unrestrained rats. Part I. Behavioral correlates and firing repertoires. *Experimental Neurology* 41: 461–531.

Rao, S. M., Bobholz, J. A., Hammeke, T. A., Rosen, A. C., Woodley, S. J., Cunningham, J. M., Cox, R. W., Stein, E. A., & Binder, J. R. 1997. Functional MRI evidence for subcortical participation in conceptual reasoning skills. *Neuroreport* 8: 1987–1993.

Rao, S., Chenchal, R. G., & Miller, E. K. 1997. Integration of what and where in the primate prefrontal cortex. *Science* 276: 821–824.

Rapp, P. R., & Amaral, D. G. 1989. Evidence for task-dependent memory dysfunction in the aged monkey. *The Journal of Neuroscience* 9: 3568–3576.

Rawlins, J. N. P. 1985. Associations across time: The hippocampus as a temporary memory store. *Behavioral and Brain Sciences* 8: 479–496.

Rawlins, J. N. P., Lyford, G. L., Seferiades, A., Deacon, R. M. J., & Cassaday, H. J. 1993. Critical determinants of nonspatial working memory deficits in rats with conventional lesions of the hippocampus or fornix. *Behavioral Neuroscience* 107: 236–249.

Raymond, J. L., Lisberger, S. G., & Mauk, M. D. 1996. The cerebellum: A neuronal learning machine? *Science* 272: 1126–1131.

Recanzone, G. H., & Merzenich, M. M. 1991. Alterations of the functional organization of primary somatosensory cortex following intracortical microstimulation or behavioral training. In L. R. Squire, N. M. Weinberger, G. Lynch, & J. L. McGaugh (Eds.), *Memory: Organization and Locus of Change.* New York: Oxford University Press, pp. 217–238.

Recanzone, G. H., Merzenich, M. M., & Jenkins, W. M. 1992a. Frequency discrimination training engaging a restricted skin surface results in an emergence of a cutaneous response zone in cortical area 3a. *Journal of Neurophysiology* 67: 1057–1070.

Recanzone, G. H., Merzenich, M. M., Jenkins, W. M., Grajski, K. A., & Dinse, H. R. 1992b. Topographic reorganization of the hand representation in cortical area 3b of owl monkeys trained in a frequency-discrimination task. *Journal of Neurophysiology* 67: 1031–1056.

Recanzone, G. H., Merzenich, M. M., & Schreiner, C. E. 1992c. Changes in the distributed temporal response properties of SI cortical neurons reflect improvements in performance on a temporally based tactile discrimination task. *Journal of Neurophysiology* 67: 1071–1090.

Recanzone, G. H., Schreiner, C. E., & Merzenich, M. M. 1993. Plasticity in the frequency representation of primary auditory cortex following discrimination training in adult owl monkeys. *The Journal of Neuroscience* 13: 87–103.

Rempel-Clower, N. L., Zola, S. M., Squire, L. R., & Amaral, D. G. 1996. Three cases of enduring memory impairment following bilateral damage limited to the hippocampal formation. *The Journal of Neuroscience* 16: 5233–5255.

Rescorla, R. A. 1988a. Behavioral studies of Pavlovian conditioning. *Annual Review of Neuroscience* 11: 329–352.

Rescorla, R. A. 1988b. Pavlovian conditioning: It's not what you think it is. *American Psychologist* 43: 151–160.

Rescorla, R. A., & Holland, P. C. 1982. Behavioral studies of associative learning in animals. *Annual Review of Psychology* 33: 265–308.

Restle, F. 1957. Discrimination of cues in mazes: A revolution of the "place-vs.-response" question. *Psychological Review* 64: 217–228.

Ribot, R. 1882. *Diseases of Memory.* New York: Appleton.

Richardson-Klaven, A., & Bjork, R. A. 1988. Measures of memory. *Annual Review of Psychology* 39: 475–543.

Riches, I. P., Wilson, F. A. W., & Brown, M. W. 1991. The effects of visual stimulation and memory on neurons of the hippocampal formation and the neighboring parahippocampal gyrus and inferior temporal cortex of the primate. *The Journal of Neuroscience* 11: 1763–1779.

Ridley, R. M., & Baker, H. F. 1991. A critical evaluation of monkey models of amnesia and dementia. *Brain Research Reviews* 16: 15–37.

Ridley, R. M., Timothy, C. J., Maclean, C. J., & Baker, H. F. 1995. Conditional learning and memory impairments following neurotoxic lesion of the CA1 field of the hippocampus. *Neuroscience* 67: 263–275.

Roberts, A. C., Robbins, T. W., & Weiskrantz, L. (Eds.). 1996. Executive and cognitive functions of the prefrontal cortex. *Philosophical Transactions of the Royal Society of London B* (vol. 351). London: The Royal Society.

Robertson, D., & Irvine, D. R. F. 1989. Plasticity of frequency organization in auditory cortex of guinea pigs with partial unilateral deafness. *Journal of Comparative Neurology* 282: 456–471.

Robinson, D. L., Goldberg, M. E., & Stanton, G. B. 1978. Parietal association cortex in the primate: Sensory mechanisms and behavioural modulations. *Journal of Neurophysiology* 41: 910–932.

Rodman, H. R., Skelly, J. P., & Gross, C. G. 1991. Stimulus selectivity and state dependence of activity in inferior temporal cortex of infant monkeys. *Proceedings of the National Academy of Sciences (United States of America).* 88: 7572–7575.

Roe, A. W., Pallas, S. L., Hahm, J.-O., & Sur, M. 1990. A map of visual space induced in primary auditory cortex. *Science* 250: 818–820.

Rogan, M. T., & LeDoux, J. E. 1995. LTP is accompanied by commensurate enhancement of auditory-evoked responses in a fear conditioning circuit. *Neuron* 15: 127–136.

Rogan, M. T., Staubli, U. V., & LeDoux, J. E. 1997. Fear conditioning induces associative long-term potentiation in the amygdala. *Nature* 390: 604–607.

Rolls, E. T. 1992. Neurophysiology and functions of the primate amygdala. In J. P. Aggleton (Ed.), *The Amygdala: Neurobiological Aspects of Emotion, Memory and Mental Dysfunction.* New York: Wiley-Liss, pp. 143–165.

Rolls, E. T. 1996. The orbitofrontal cortex. *Philosophical Transactions. Royal Society of London. Series B. Biological Sciences* 351: 1433–1444.

Rolls, E. T., Baylis, G. C., Hasselmo, M. E., & Nalwa, V. 1989a. The effect of learning on the face selective responses of neurons in the cortex in the superior temporal sulcus of the monkey. *Experimental Brain Research* 76: 153–164.

Rolls, E. T., Miyashita, Y., Cahusac, P., Kesner, R. P., Niki, H. D., Feigenbaum, J. D., & Bach, L. 1989b. Hippocampal neurons in the monkey with activity related to the place where a stimulus is shown. *The Journal of Neuroscience* 9: 1835–1846.

Rolls, E. T., Thorpe, S. J., Maddison, S., Roper-Hall, A., Puerto, A., & Perret, D. 1979. Activity of neurones in the neostriatum and related structures in the alert animal. In I. Divac, R. Gunilla, & E. Öberg (Eds.), *The neostriatum.* Oxford: Pergamon Press, pp. 163–182.

Roman, F. S., Chaillan, F. A., & Sourmireau-Mourat, B. 1993. Long term potentiation in rat piriform cortex following discrimination learning. *Brain Research* 601: 265–272.

Roman, U. V., Staubli, F. U., & Lynch, G. 1987. Evidence for synaptic potentiation in a cortical network during learning. *Brain Research* 418: 221–226.

Romanski, L. M., & LeDoux, J. E. 1992a. Bilateral destruction of neocortical and peri-rhinal projection targets of the acoustic thalamus does not disrupt auditory fear conditioning. *Neuroscience Letters* 142: 228–232.

Romanski, L. M., & LeDoux, J. E. 1992b. Equipotentiality of thalamo-amygdala and thalamo-cortico-amygdala circuits in auditory fear conditioning. *The Journal of Neuroscience* 12: 4501–4509.

Romanski, L. M., & LeDoux, J. E. 1993. Information cascade from primary auditory cortex to the amygdala: corticocortical and corticoamygdaloid projections of temporal cortex in the rat. *Cerebral Cortex* 3: 515–532.

Room, P., & Groenewegen, H. J. 1986. Connections of the parahippocampal cortex in the cat: I. Cortical afferents. *Journal of Comparative Neurology* 251: 415–450.

Roozendaal, B., & McGaugh, J. L. 1996. Amygdaloid nuclei lesions differentially affect glucocorticoid-induced memory enhancement in an inhibitory avoidance task. *Neurobiology of Learning and Memory* 65: 1–8.

Rose, G. M., & Dunwiddie, T. V. 1986. Induction of hippocampal long-term potentiation using physiologically patterned stimulation. *Neuroscience Letters* 69: 244–248.

Rosen, J. B., Hitchcock, J. M., Miserendino, J. D., Falls, W. A., Campeau, S., & Davis, M. 1992. Lesions of the perirhinal cortex but not of the frontal, medial, prefrontal, visual, or insular cortex block fear-potentiated startle using a visual conditioned stimulus. *The Journal of Neuroscience* 12: 4624–4633.

Rosenblum, K., Berman, D. E., Hazvi, S., Lamprecht, R., & Dudai, Y. 1997. NMDA receptor and the tyrosine phosphorylation of its 2B subunit in taste learning in the rat insular cortex. *The Journal of Neuroscience* 17: 5129–5135.

Rosenblum, K., Meiri, N., & Dudai, Y. 1993. Taste memory: The role of protein synthesis in gustatory cortex. *Behavioral and Neural Biology* 59: 49–56.

Rosene, D. L., & Van Hoesen, G. W. 1987. The hippocampal formation of the primate brain: A review of some comparative aspects of cytoarchitecture and connections. In E. G. Jones & A. Peters (Eds.), *Cerebral Cortex* (Vol. 6). London: Plenum Press, pp. 345–456.

Rosenkilde, C. E. 1979. Functional heterogeneity of the prefrontal cortex in the monkey: A review. *Behavioral and Neural Biology* 25: 301–345.

Rotenberg, A., Mayford, M., Hawkins, R. D., Kandel, E. R., & Muller, R. U. 1996. Mice expressing activated CaMKII lack low frequency LTP and do not form stable place cells in the CA1 region of the hippocampus. *Cell* 87: 1351–1361.

Rotenberg, A., & Muller, R. U. 1997. Variable place-cell coupling to a continuously viewed stimulus: Evidence that the hippocampus acts as a perceptual system. *Philosophical Transactions of the Royal Society of London B* 352: 1505–1513.

Rothblat, L. A., & Kromer, L. F. 1991. Object recognition memory in the rat: The role of the hippocampus. *Behavioural Brain Research* 42: 25–32.

Rozin, P. 1976. The evolution of intelligence and access to the cognitive unconscious. *Progress in Psychobiology and Physiological Psychology* 6: 245–280.

Rozin, P., & Kalat, J. W. 1971. Specific hungers and poison avoidance as adaptive specializations of learning. *Psychological Review* 78: 459–486.

Rozin, P., & Kalat, J. W. 1972. Learning as a situation-specific adaptation. In: M. E. P. Seligman & J. Hager (Eds.), *Biological Boundaries of Learning*. New York: Appleton, pp. 66–97.

Rudell, A. P., Fox, S. E., & Ranck, J. B., Jr. 1980. Hippocampal excitability phase-locked to the theta rhythm in walking rats. *Experimental Neurology* 68: 87–96.

Rudy, J. W., & Sutherland, R. J. 1995. Configural association theory and the hippocampal formation: An appraisal and reconfiguration. *Hippocampus* 5: 375–389.

Rugg, M. D. (Ed.). 1997. *Cognitive Neuroscience*. Hove East Sussex, UK: Psychology Press.

Rupniak, N. M. J., & Gaffan, D. 1987. Monkey hippocampus and learning about spatially directed movements. *The Journal of Neuroscience* 7: 2331–2337.

Ruthrich, H., Matthies, H., & Ott, T. 1982. Long-term changes in synaptic excitability of hippocampal cell populations as a result of training. In C. A. Marsan & H. Matthies (Eds.), *International Brain Research Organization Monograph Series: Vol. 9. Neuronal Plasticity and Memory Formation.* New York: Raven Press, pp. 289–294.

Ryan, J. D., Althoff, R. R., Whitlow, S., & Cohen, N. J. (2000). Amnesia is a deficit in relational memory. *Psychological Science*, in press.

Sagar, H. H., Cohen, N. J., Corkin, S., & Growdon, J. M. 1985. Dissociations among processes in remote memory. In D. S. Olton, E. Gamzu, & S. Corkin (Eds.), *Memory Dysfunctions.* New York: NY Academy of Science, pp. 533–535.

Sakai, K., & Miyashita, Y. 1991. Neural organization for the long-term memory of paired associates. *Nature* 354: 152–155.

Sakai, K., Naya, Y., & Miyashita, Y. 1994. Neuronal tuning and associative mechanisms in form representation. *Learning and Memory* 1: 83–105.

Sakurai, Y. 1990. Hippocampal cells have behavioral correlates during performance of an auditory working memory task in the rat. *Behavioral Neuroscience* 104: 253–263.

Sakurai, Y. 1994. Involvement of auditory cortical and hippocampal neurons in auditory working memory and reference memory in the rat. *The Journal of Neuroscience* 14: 2606–2623.

Sakurai, Y. 1996. Hippocampal and neocortical cell assemblies encode memory processes for different types of stimuli in the rat. *The Journal of Neuroscience* 16: 2809–2818.

Salmon, D. P., & Butters, N. 1995. Neurobiology of skill and habit learning. *Current Opinion in Neurobiology* 5: 184–190.

Salmon, E., Van der Linden, M., Collette, F., Delfiore, G., Maquet, P., Degueldre, C., Luxen, A., & Franck, G. 1996. Regional brain activity during working memory tasks. *Brain* 119: 1617–1625.

Sananes, C. B., & Davis, M. 1992. N-methyl-D-aspartate lesions of the lateral and basolateral nuclei of the amygdala block fear-potentiated startle and shock sensitization of startle. *Behavioral Neuroscience* 106: 72–80.

Sanes, J. N., Suner, S., & Donoghue, J. P. 1990. Dynamic organization of primary motor cortex output to target muscles in adult rats: I. Long-term patterns of reorganization following motor or mixed nerve lesions. *Experimental Brain Research* 79: 479–491.

Sanes, J. R., & Lichtman, J. W. 1999. Can molecules explain long term potentiation. *Nature Neuroscience* 2: 597–604.

Sary, G., Vogels, R., & Orban, G. A. 1993. Cue-invariant shape selectivity of macaque inferior temporal neurons. *Science* 260: 995–997.

Saucier, D., & Cain, D. P. 1995. Spatial Lerarning without NMDA receptor-dependant long-term potentiation. *Nature* 378: 186–189.

Saunders, R. C., & Weiskrantz, L. 1989. The effects of fornix transection and combined fornix transection, mammillary body lesions and hippocampal ablations on object pair association memory in the rhesus monkey. *Behavioural Brain Research* 35: 85–94.

Schacter, D. L. 1985. Multiple forms of memory in humans and animals. In N. M. Weinberger, J. L. McGaugh, & G. Lynch (Eds.), *Memory Systems of the Brain.* New York: Guilford Press, pp. 351–380.

Schacter, D. L. 1987a. Implicit memory: History and current status. *Journal of Experimental Psychology: Learning, Memory, and Cognition* 13: 501–518.

Schacter, D. L. 1987b. Memory, amnesia, and frontal lobe dysfunction. *Psychobiology* 15: 21–36.

Schacter, D. L. 1989. Memory. In M. I. Posner (Ed.), *Foundations of Cognitive Science.* Cambridge, MA: MIT Press, pp. 683–726.

Schacter, D. L. 1990. Perceptual representation systems and implicit memory: Toward a resolution of the multiple memory systems debate. *Annals of the New York Academy of Sciences* 608: 543–571.

Schacter, D. L. 1992. Priming and multiple memory systems: Perceptual mechanisms of implicit memory. *Journal of Cognitive Neuroscience* 4: 232–243.

Schacter, D. L., & Buckner, R. L. 1998a. On the relations among priming, conscious recollection, and intentional retrieval: Evidence from neuroimaging research. *Neurobiology of Learning and Memory* 70: 284–303.

Schacter, D. L., & Buckner, R. L. 1998b. Priming and the brain. *Neuron* 20: 185–195.

Schacter, D. L., Buckner, R. L., Koutstaal, W., Dale, A. M., & Rosen, B. R. 1997. Late onset of anterior prefrontal activity during retrieval of veridical and illusory memories: A single trial fMRI study. *Neuroimage* 6: 259–269.

Schacter, D. L., Chiu, C.-Y. P., & Ochsner, K. N. 1993. Implicit memory: A selective review. *Annual Review of Neuroscience* 16: 159–182.

Schacter, D. L., Reiman, E., Uecker, A., Polster, M. R., Yun, L. S., & Cooper, L. A. 1995. Brain regions associated with retrieval of structurally coherent visual information. *Nature* 376: 587–590.

Schacter, D. L., & Tulving, E. 1982. Memory, amnesia, and the episodic/semantic distinction. In R. L. Isaacson & N. L. Spear (Eds.), *The Expression of Knowledge.* New York: Plenum Press, pp. 33–61.

Schacter, D. L., & Tulving, E. 1994. What are the memory systems of 1994? In D. L. Schacter & E. Tulving (Eds.), *Memory Systems.* Cambridge, MA: MIT Press, pp. 1–38.

Schacter, D. L., & Wagner, A. D. 1999. Medial temporal lobe activations in fMRI and PET studies of episodic encoding and retrieval. *Hippocampus* 9: 7–24.

Schlaug, G., Knorr, U., & Seitz, R. J. 1994. Inter-subject variability of cerebral activations in acquiring a motor skill: A study with positron emission tomography. *Experimental Brain Research* 98: 523–534.

Schmajuk, N. A. 1984. Psychological theories of hippocampal function. *Physiological Psychology* 12: 166–183.

Schmaltz, L. W., & Isaacson, R. L. 1967. Effect of bilateral hippocampal destruction on the acquisition and extinction of an operand response. *Physiology and Behavior* 2: 291–298.

Schnider, A., & Ptak, R. 1999. Spontaneous confabuators fail to suppress currently irrelevant memor traces. *Nature Neuroscience* 2: 677–681.

Schoenbaum, G., & Eichenbaum, H. 1995a. Information coding in the rodent prefrontal cortex: I. Single neuron activity in the orbitofrontal cortex compared with that in the piriform cortex. *Journal of Neurophysiology* 74: 733–750.

Schoenbaum, G., & Eichenbaum, H. 1995b. Information coding in the rodent prefrontal cortex. II. Ensemble activity in the orbitofrontal cortex. *Journal of Neurophysiology* 74: 751–762.

Schultz, W., Apicella, P., Romo, R., & Scarnati, E. 1995. Context-dependent activity in primate striatum reflecting past and future behavioral events. In J. C. Houk, J. L. Davis, & D. G. Beiser (Eds.), *Models of Information Processing in the Basal Ganglia.* Cambridge, MA: MIT Press. Pp. 11–28.

Schütze, I., Knuepfer, M. M., Eismann, A., Stumpf, H., & Stock, G. 1987. Sensory input to single neurons in the amygdala of the cat. *Experimental Neurology* 97: 499–515.

Schwaber, M. K., Garraghty, P. E., & Kaas, J. H. 1993. Neuroplasticity of the adult primate auditory cortex following cochlear hearing loss. *American Journal of Otolaryngology* 14: 252–258.

Schwartzbaum, J. S. 1960a. Changes in reinforcing properties of stimuli following ablation of the amygdaloid complex in monkeys. *Journal of Comparative and Physiological Psychology* 43: 388–395.

Schwartzbaum, J. S. 1960b. Response to changes in reinforcing conditions of bar-pressing after ablation of the amygdaloid complex in monkeys. *Psychological Reports* 6: 215–221.

Schwartzbaum, J. S. 1961. Some characteristic of 'amgdaloid hyperphagia' in monkeys. *American Journal of Psychology* 74: 252–259.

Scott, J. W. 1986. The olfactory bulb and central pathways. *Experientia* 42: 223–232.

Scoville, W. B., & Milner, B. 1957. Loss of recent memory after bilateral hippocampal lesions. *Journal of Neurology, Neurosurgery and Psychiatry* 20: 11–12.

Segal, M. 1978. A correlation between hippocampal responses to interhemispheric stimulation, hippocampal slow rhythmical activity and behavior. *Clinical Neurophysiology* 45: 409–411.

Segal, M., Disterhoft, J. D., & Olds, J. 1972. Hippocampal unit activity during classical aversive and appetitive conditioning. *Science* 175: 792–794.

Segal, M., & Olds, J. 1972. Behavior of units in hippocampal circuit of the rat during learning. *Journal of Neurophysiology* 35: 680–690.

Seitz, R. J., Canavan, A. G. M., Yaguez, L., Herzog, H., Tellmann, L., Knorr, U., Huang, Y. X., & Homberg, V. 1994. Successive roles of the cerebellum and premotor cortices in trajectorial learning. *Neuroreport* 5: 2541–2544.

Seitz, R. J., & Roland, P. E. 1992. Learning of sequential finger movements in man: A combined kinematic and positron emission tomography (PET) study. *European Journal of Neuroscience* 4: 154–165.

Seitz, R. J., Roland P. E., Bohm, C., Greitz, T., & Stone-Elander, S. 1990. Motor learning in man: A positron emission tomographic study. *Neuroreport* 1: 57–66.

Selden, N. R. W., Everitt, B. J., Jarrard, L. E., & Robbins, T. W. 1991. Complementary roles for the amygdala and hippocampus in aversive conditioning to explicit and contextual cues. *Neuroscience* 42: 335–350.

Seligman, M. E. P. 1970. On the generality of the laws of learning. *Psychological Review* 77: 406–418.

Sergent, J., Ohta, S., & Macdonald, B. 1992. Functional neuroanatomy of faces and object processing. *Brain* 115: 15–36.

Shallice, T. 1982. Specific impairments of planning. *Philosophical Transactions of the Royal Society of London, Part B* 298: 199–209.

Shallice, T. 1988. *From Neuropsychology to Mental Structure.* Cambridge: Cambridge University Press.

Shallice, T., & Warrington, E. K. 1970. Independent functioning of the verbal memory stores: A neuropsychological study. *Quarterly Journal of Experimental Psychology* 22: 261–273.

Shapiro, M. L., & O'Connor, C. 1992. N-methyl-D-aspartate receptor antagonist MK-801 and spatial memory representation: Working memory is impaired in an unfamiliar environment but not in a familiar environment. *Behavioral Neuroscience* 106: 604–612.

Shapiro, M. L., & Olton, D. S. 1994. Hippocampal function and interference. In D. L. Schacter & E. Tulving (Eds.), *Memory Systems.* Cambridge, MA: MIT Press, pp. 87–117.

Shapiro, M. L., Tanila, H., & Eichenbaum, H. 1997. Cues that hippocampal place cells encode: Dynamic and hierarchical representation of local and distal stimuli. *Hippocampus* 7: 624–642.

Sharp, P. E., Barnes, C. A., & McNaughton, B. L. 1987. Effects of aging on environmental modulation of hippocampal evoked responses. *Behavioral Neuroscience* 101: 170–178.

Sharp, P. E., Blair, H. T., Etkin, D., & Tzanetos, D. B. 1995. Influences of vestibular and visual motion information on the spatial firing patterns of hippocampal place cells. *The Journal of Neuroscience* 15: 173–189.

Sharp, P. E., Kubie, J. L., & Muller, R. U. 1990. Firing properties of hippocampal neurons in a visually symmetrical environment: Contributions of multiple sensory cues and mnemonic processes. *The Journal of Neuroscience* 10: 3093–3105.

Sharp, P. E., McNaughton, B. L., & Barnes, C. A. 1985. Enhancement of hippocampal field potentials in rats exposed to a novel, complex environment. *Brain Research* 339: 361–365.

Sharp, P. E., McNaughton, B. L., & Barnes, C. A. 1989. Exploration-dependent modulation of evoked responses in fascia dentata: Fundamental observations and time course. *Psychobiology* 17: 257–269.

Shaw, C., & Aggleton, J. P. 1993. The effects of fornix and medial prefrontal lesions on delayed nonmatching-to-sample by rats. *Behavioural Brain Research* 54: 91–102.

Shen, J., Barnes, C. A., McNaughton, B. L., Skaggs, W. E., & Weaver, K. L. 1997. The effect of aging on experience-dependent plasticity of hippocampal place cells. *The Journal of Neuroscience* 17: 6769–6782.

Shepherd, R. N., & Cooper, L. A. 1986. *Mental Images and Their Transformations.* Cambridge, MA: MIT Press.

Sherrington, C. S. 1906. *The Integrative Action of the Nervous System.* New Haven: Yale University Press.

Sherry, D. F., Jacobs, L. F., & Gaulin, S. J. C. 1992. Spatial memory and adaptive specialization of the hippocampus. *Trends in Neuroscience* 15: 298–303.

Sherry, D. F., & Schacter, D. L. 1987. The evolution of multiple memory systems. *Psychological Review* 94: 439–454.

Shettleworth, S. J. 1972. Constraints on learning. *Advanced Study of Behavior* 4: 1–68.

Shettleworth, S. J. 1993. Varieties of learning and memory in animals. *Journal of Experimental Psychology: Animal Behavior Processes* 19: 5–14.

Shimamura, A. P. 1986. Priming effects in amnesia: Evidence for a dissociable memory function. *Quarterly Journal of Experimental Psychology* 38A: 619–644.

Shimamura, A. P. 1995. Memory and frontal lobe function. In M. S. Gazzaniga (Ed.), *The Cognitive Neurosciences.* Cambridge, MA: MIT Press, pp. 803–813.

Shimamura, A. P., Janowsky, J. S., & Squire, L. R. 1990. Memory for the temporal order of events in patients with frontal lobe lesions and amnesic patients. *Neuropsychologia* 28: 803–813.

Silva, A. J., & Giese, K. P. 1998. Gene targeting: A novel window into the biology of learning and memory. In J. Martinez and R. Kesner (Eds.), *Neurobiology of Learning and Memory.* San Diego: Academic Press, pp. 89–142.

Silva, A. J., Kogan, J. H., Frankland, P. W., & Kida, S. 1998. CREB and Memory. *Annual Review of Neuroscience* 21: 127–148.

Silva, A. J., Paylor, R., Whener, J. M., & Tonegawa, S. 1992a. Impaired spatial learning in (-calcium-calmodulin kinase II mutant mice. *Science* 257: 206–211.

Silva, A. J., Smith, A. M., & Giese, K. P. 1997. Gene targeting and the biology of learning and memory. *Annual Review of Genetics* 31: 527–547.

Silva, A. J., Stevens, C. F., Tonegawa, S., & Wang, Y. 1992b. Deficient hippocampal long-term potentiation in α-calcium-calmodulin kinase II mutant mice. *Science* 257: 201–206.

Sinden, J. D., Rawlins, J. N. P., Gray, J. A., & Jarrard, L. E. 1986. Selective cytotoxic lesions of the hippocampal formation and DRL performance in rats. *Behavioral Neuroscience* 100: 320–329.

Singer, W. 1990. Search for coherence: A basic principle of cortical self-organization. *Concepts in Neuroscience* 1: 1–26.

Singer, W. 1995. Development and plasticity of cortical processing architectures. *Science* 270: 758–763.

Skaggs, W. E., & McNaughton, B. L. 1996. Replay of neuronal firing sequences in rat hippocampus during sleep following spatial experience. *Science* 271: 1870–1873.

Skaggs, W. E., & McNaughton, B. L. 1998. Spatial firing properties of hippocampal CA1 populations in an environment containing two visually identical regions. *Journal of Neuroscience* 18: 8455–8466.

Skelton, R. W., Scarth, A. S., Wilkie, D. M., Miller, J. J., & Phillips, A. G. 1987. Long-term increases in dentate granule cell responsivity accompany operant conditioning. *The Journal of Neuroscience* 7: 3081–3087.

Small, W. S. 1901. Experimental study of the mental processes of the rat II. *American Journal of Psychology* 12: 206–239.

Smith, E. E., & Jonides, J. 1994. Working memory in humans: Neuropsychological evidence. In M. Gazzaniga (Ed.), *The Cognitive Neurosciences*. Cambridge, MA: MIT Press, pp. 1009–1020.

Snoddy, G. S. 1926. Learning and stability. *Journal of Applied Psychology* 10: 1–36.

Sorra, K. E., & Harris, K. M. 1998. Stability in synapse number and size at 2 hr after long-term potentiation in hippocampal area CA1. *The Journal of Neuroscience* 18(2): 1–15.

Speakman, A., & O'Keefe, J. 1990. Hippocampal complex spike cells do not change their place fields if the goal is moved within a cue controlled environment. *European Journal of Neuroscience* 2: 544–555.

Spevack, A. A., & Pribram, K. H. 1973. Decisional analysis of the effects of limbic lesions on learning in monkeys. *Journal of Comparative and Physiological Psychology* 82: 211–226.

Spinelli, D. N., & Jensen, F. E. 1979. Plasticity: The mirror of experience. *Science* 203: 75–78.

Squire, L. R. 1987. *Memory and Brain*. New York: Oxford University Press.

Squire, L. 1992. Memory and the hippocampus: A synthesis from findings with rats, monkeys, and humans. *Psychological Review* 99: 195–231.

Squire, L. R., & Alvarez, P. 1995. Retrograde amnesia and memory consolidation: A neurobiological perspective. *Current Opinion in Neurobiology* 5: 169–177.

Squire, L. R., & Cohen, N. J. 1979. Memory and amnesia: resistance to disruption develops for years after learning. *Behavioral and Neural Biology* 35: 115–125.

Squire, L. R., & Cohen, N. J. 1984. Human memory and amnesia. In G. Lynch, J. L. McGaugh, & N. M. Weinberger (Eds.), *Neurobiology of Learning and Memory*. New York: Guilford Press, pp. 3–64.

Squire, L. R., Cohen, N. J., & Nadel, L. 1984. The medial temporal region and memory consolidation: A new hypothesis. In H. Weingartner & E. Parker (Eds.), *Memory Consolidation*. Hillsdale, NJ: Erlbaum.

Squire, L. R., Knowlton, B., & Musen, G. 1993. The structure and organization of memory. *Annual Review of Psychology* 44: 453–495.

Squire, L. R., & McKee, R. 1992. Influence of prior events on cognitive judgements in amnesia. *Journal of Experimental Psychology: Learning, Memory and Cognition* 18: 106–115.

Squire, L. R., Ojemann, J. G., Miezin, F. M., Petersen, S. E., Videen, T. O., & Raichle, M. E. 1992. Activation of the hippocampus in normal humans: A functional anatomical study of memory. *Proceedings of the National Academy of Sciences (United States of America)* 89: 1837–1841.

Squire, L. R., Shimamura, A. P., & Amaral, D. G. 1989. Memory and the hippocampus. In J. Byrne & W. O. Berry (Eds.), *Neural Models of Plasticity*. San Diego, CA: Academic Press.

Squire, L. R., Slater, P. C., & Chase, P. M. 1975. Retrograde amnesia: Temporal gradient in very long-term memory following electroconvulsive therapy. *Science* 187: 77–79.

Squire, L. R., & Zola, S. M. 1996. Ischemic brain damage and memory impairment: A commentary. *Hippocampus* 6: 546–552.

Squire, L. R., & Zola, S. M. 1998. Episodic memory, semantic memory and amnesia. *Hippocampus* 8: 205–211.

Squire, L. R., & Zola-Morgan, S. 1983. The neurology of memory: The case for corre-
spondence between the findings for human and nonhuman primates. In J. A.
Deutsch (Ed.), *The Physiological Basis of Memory*, 2nd ed. New York: Academic
Press, pp. 199–268.

Squire, L. R., & Zola-Morgan, S. 1991. The medial temporal lobe memory system. *Science* 253: 1380–1386.

Squire, L. R., Zola-Morgan, S., & Chen, K. 1988. Human amnesia and animal models
of amnesia: Performance of amnesic patients on tests designed for the monkey.
Behavioral Neuroscience 102: 210–221.

Staubli, U. 1992. A peculiar form of potentiation in mossy fiber synapses. In C. E.
Ribak, C. M. Gall, & I. Mody (Eds.), *The Dentate Gyrus and Its Role in Seizures
(Epilepsy Res. Suppl. 7)*. North Holland: Elsevier Science Publishers, B. V, pp.
151–157.

Staubli, U., Ivy, G., & Lynch, G. 1984. Hippocampal denervation causes rapid forgetting of olfactory information in rats. *Proceedings of the National Academy of Sciences* 81: 5885–5887.

Staubli, U., & Lynch, G. 1991. NMDA receptors and memory: Evidence from pharmacological and correlational studies. In A. P. Kozikowski (Ed.), *Neurobiology of the
NMDA Receptor: From Chemistry to the Clinic*. New York: VCH.

Staubli, U., Rogers, G., & Lynch, G. 1994. Facilitation of glutamate receptors enhances
memory. *Proceedings of the National Academy of Science USA* 91: 777–781.

Staubli, U., Thibault, O., DiLorenzo, M., & Lynch, G. 1989. Antagonism of NMDA
receptords impairs acquisition but not retention of olfactory memory. *Behavioral
Neuroscience* 103: 54–60.

Steele, R. J., & Morris, R. G. M. 1999. Delay dependent impairment in matching-to-
place task with chronic and intrahippocampal infusion of the NMDA-antagonist
D-AP5. *Hippocampus* 9: 118–136.

Steinmetz, J. E. 1996. The brain substrates of classical eyeblink conditioning in rabbits.
In J. R. Bloedel, T. J. Ebner, & S. P. Wise (Eds.), *The Acquisition of Motor Behavior
in Vertebrates*. Cambridge, MA: MIT Press, pp. 89–114.

Steinmetz, J. E., Logue, S. F., & Miller, D. P. 1993. Using signaled barpressing tasks to
study the neural substrates of appetitive and aversive learning in rats: Behavioral
manipulations and cerebellar lesions. *Behavioral Neuroscience* 107: 941–954.

Steinmetz, J. E., Sears, L. L., Gabriel, M., Kubota, Y., & Poremba, A. 1991. Cerebellar
interpositus nucleus lesions disrupt classical nictitating membrane conditioning
but not discriminative avoidance learning in rabbits. *Behavioural Brain Research*
45: 71–80.

Stern, C. E., Corkin, S., Gonzalez, R. G., Guimaraes, A. R., Baker, J. R., Jennings, P. J.,
Carr, C. A., Sugiura, R. M., Vedantham, V., & Rosen, B. R. 1996. The hippocampal
formation participates in novel picture encoding: Evidence from function magnetic resonance imaging. *Proceedings of the National Academy of Sciences* 93:
8660–8665.

Stevens, C. F. 1994. CREB and memory consolidation. *Neuron* 13(4): 769–770.

Stevens, C. F. 1996. Strengths and weaknesses in memory. *Nature* 381: 471–472.

Stevens, C. F. 1998. A million dollar question: Does LTP = memory. *Neuron* 20: 1–2.

Stevens, R., & Cowey, A. 1972. Enhanced alternation learning in hippocampectomized
rats by means of added light cues. *Brain Research* 46: 1–22.

Strupp, B. J., & Levitsky, D. A. 1984. Social transmission of food preferences in adult
hooded rats *(Rattus Norvegicus). Journal of Comparative and Physiological Psychology* 98: 257–266.

Sur, M., Pallas, S. L., & Roe, A. W. 1990. Cross-modal plasticity in cortical development: Differentiation and specification of sensory neocortex. *Trends Neuroscience* 13: 227–233.

Sutherland, R. J., Dringenberg, H. C., & Hoesing, J. M. 1993. Induction of long-term potentiation at perforant path dentate synapses does not affect place learning or memory. *Hippocampus* 3: 141–147.

Sutherland, R. J., Macdonald, R. J., Hill, C. R., & Rudy, J. W. 1989. Damage to the hippocampal formation in rats selectively impairs the ability to learn cue relationships. *Behavioral and Neural Biology* 52: 331–356.

Sutherland R. J., & Rudy, J. W. 1989. Configural association theory: The role of the hippocampal formation in learning, memory, and amnesia. *Psychobiology* 17: 129–144.

Suzuki, W. A. 1996a. The anatomy, physiology and functions of the perirhinal cortex. *Current Opinion in Neurobiology* 6: 179–186.

Suzuki, W. A. 1996b. Neuroanatomy of the monkey entorhinal, perirhinal, and parahippocampal cortices: Organization of Cortical inputs and interconnections with amygdala and striatum. *Neuroscience* 8: 3–12.

Suzuki, W. A., & Amaral, D. G. 1994a. Perirhinal and parahippocampal cortices of the macaque monkey: Cortical afferents. *Journal of Comparative Neurology* 350: 497–533.

Suzuki, W. A., & Amaral, D. G. 1994b. Topographic organization of the reciprocal connections between monkey entorhinal corex and the perirhinal and parahippocampal cortices. *The Journal of Neuroscience* 14: 1856–1877.

Suzuki, W. A., Miller, E. A., & Desimone, R. 1997. Object and place memory in the macaque entorhinal cortex. *Journal of Neurophysiology* 78: 1062–1081.

Suzuki, W. A., Zola-Morgan, S., Squire, L. R., & Amaral, D. G. 1993. Lesions of the perirhinal and parahippocampal cortices in the monkey produce long-lasting memory impairment in the visual and tactal modalities. *The Journal of Neuroscience* 13: 2430–2451.

Swann, H. G. 1934. The function of the brain in olfaction. *Journal of Comparative Neurology* 59: 175–201.

Swanson, L. W. 1981. A direct projection from Ammon's horn to prefrontal cortex in the rat. *Brain Research* 217: 150–154.

Swanson, L. W., & Cowan, W. M. 1977. An autoradiographic study of the organization of the efferent connections of the hippocampal formation of the rat. *Journal of Comparative Neurology* 172: 49–84.

Swanson, L. W., & Petrovich, G. D. 1998. What is the amygdala. *Trends in Neurosciences* 21: 315–365.

Tamamaki, N., Abe, K., & Nojyo, Y. 1987. Columnar organization in the subiculum formed by axon branches originating from single CA1 pyramidal neurons in the rat hippocampus. *Brain Research* 412: 156–160.

Tanabe, T., Iino, M., & Takagi, S. F. 1975. Discrimination of odors in olfactory bulb pyriform-amygdaloid areas, and orbitofrontal cortex of the monkey. *Journal of Neurophysiology* 38: 1284–1296.

Tanaka, K. 1993. Neuronal mechanisms of object recognition. *Science* 262: 685–688.

Tanaka, K., Saito, H. A., Fukada, Y., & Moriya, M. 1991. Coding visual images of objects in the inferotemporal cortex of the macaque monkey. *Journal of Neurophysiology* 66: 170–189.

Tanila, H. 1999. Hippocampal place cells can develop distinct representations of two visually identical environments. *Hippocampus* 9: 234–246.

Tanila, H., Carlson, S., Linnankoski, I., & Kajhila, H. 1993. Regional distribution of functions in dorsolateral prefrontal cortex of the monkey. *Behavioural Brain Research* 53: 63–71.

Tanila, H., Carlson, S., Linnankoski, I., Lindroos, F., & Kahila, H. 1992. Functional properties of dorsolateral prefrontal cortical neurons in awake monkey. *Behavioural Brain Research* 47: 169–180.

Tanila, H., Shapiro, M. L., & Eichenbaum, H. E. 1997a. Discordance of spatial representation in ensembles of hippocampal place cells. *Hippocampus* 7: 613–623.

Tanila, H., Shapiro, M., Gallagher, M., & Eichenbaum, H. 1997b. Brain aging: Impaired coding of novel environmental cues. *The Journal of Neuroscience* 17: 5167–5174.

Tanila, H., Sipila, P., Shapiro, M., & Eichenbaum, H. 1997c. Brain aging: Changes in the nature of information coding by the hippocampus. *The Journal of Neuroscience* 17: 5155–5166.

Taylor, R. 1992. Neuroscientists lay the groundwork for detente in the battle of learning and memory research. *Journal of NIH Research* 4: 58–64.

Teng, E., & Squire, L. R. 1999. Memory for places learned long ago is intact after hippocampal damage. *Nature* 400: 675–677.

Teyler, T. J., & Discenna, P. 1986. The hippocampal memory indexing theory. *Behavioral Neuroscience* 100: 147–154.

Thiels, E., Barrionuevo, G., & Berger, T. 1994. Excitatory stimulation during postsynaptic inhibition induces long-term depression in hippocampus in vivo. *Journal of Neurophysiology* 72: 3009–3016.

Thomas, G. J., & Gash, D. M. 1988. Differential effects of hippocampal ablations on dispositional and representational memory in the rat. *Behavioral Neuroscience* 102: 635–642.

Thompson, L. T., & Best, P. J. 1989. Place cells and silent cells in the hippocampus of freely-behaving rats. *The Journal of Neuroscience* 9: 2382–2390.

Thompson, L. T., & Best, P. J. 1990. Long-term stability of place-field activity of single units recorded from the dorsal hippocampus of freely behaving rats. *Brain Research* 509: 299–308.

Thompson, L. T., Van der Zee, E. A., & Weiss, C. 1996. Hippocampal neuron changes during trace eyeblink conditioning in the rabbit. In J. R. Bloedel, T. J. Ebner, & S. P. Wise (Eds.), *The Acquisition of Motor Behavior in Vertebrates*. Cambridge, MA: MIT Press, pp. 143–174.

Thompson, R. F., & Kim, J. J. 1996. Memory systems in the brain and localization of a memory. *Proceedings of the National Academy of Sciences (United States of America)* 93: 13438–13444.

Thompson, R. F., & Krupa, D. J. 1994. Organization of memory traces in the mammalian brain. *Annual Review of Neuroscience* 17: 519–549.

Thorndike, E. L. 1898. Animal intelligence: An experimental study of the associative processes in animals. *Psychological Monographs, 2*.

Thorndike, E. L. 1911. *Animal Intelligence: Experimental Studies*. New York: Macmillan.

Timberlake, W., & Lucas, G. A. 1989. Behavior systems and learning: From behavior to general principles. In S. B. Klein & R. B. Mowrer (Eds.), *Contemporary Learning Theories*. Hillsdale, NJ: Erlbaum, pp. 237–275.

Tinbergen, N. 1951. *The Study of Instinct*. London: Oxford University Press.

Tobias, B. A., Kihlstrom, J. F., & Schacter, D. L. 1992. Emotion and implicit memory. In S. Christianson (Ed.), *The Handbook of Emotion and Memory: Research and Theory*. Hillsdale, NJ: Erlbaum, pp. 67–92.

Tolman, E. C. 1951. *Purposive Behavior in Animals and Men*. Berkeley: University of California Press. (Work originally published 1932)

Tolman, E. C. 1948. Cognitive maps in rats and men. *Psychological Review* 55: 189–208.

Tolman, E. C. 1949. There is more than one kind of learning. *Psychological Review* 56: 144–155.

Tolman, E. C., & Honzik, C. H. 1930. "Insight" in rats. *University of California Publications in Psychology* 4: 215–232.

Tolman, E. C., Ritchie, B. F., & Kalish, D. 1946. Studies in spatial learning: II. Place learning versus response learning. *Journal of Experimental Psychology* 35: 221–229.

Tonkiss, J., Feldon, J., & Rawlins, J. N. 1990. Section of the descending columns of the fornix produces delay- and interference-dependent working memory deficits. *Behavioral Brain Research* 36: 113–126.

Tonkiss, J., Morris, R. G. M., & Rawlins, J. N. P. 1988. Intra-ventricular infusion of the NMDA antagonist AP5 impairs performance on a non-spatial operant DRL task in the rat. *Experimental Brain Research* 73: 181–188.

Topka, H., Valls-Sole, J., Massaquoi, S. G., & Hallett, M. 1993. Deficit in classical conditioning in patients with cerebellar degeneration. *Brain* 116: 961–969.

Treves, A., & Rolls, E. T. 1994. Computational analysis of the role of the hippocampus in memory. *Hippocampus* 4: 374–391.

Tsien, J. Z., Chen, D. F., Gerber, D., Tom, C., Mercer, E. H., Anderson, D. J., Mayford, M., Kandel, E. R., & Tonegawa, S. 1996a. Subregion- and cell type-restricted gene knockout in mouse brain. *Cell* 87: 1317–1326.

Tsien, J. Z., Huerta, P. T., & Tonegawa, S. 1996b. The essential role of hippocampal CA1 NMDA receptor-dependent synaptic plasticity in spatial memory. *Cell* 87: 1327–1338.

Tulving, E. 1972. Episodic and semantic memory. In E. Tulving & W. Donaldson (Eds.), *Organization of Memory.* New York: Academic Press, pp. 382–403.

Tulving, E. 1983. *Elements of Episodic Memory.* New York: Oxford University Press.

Tulving, E. 1984. Multiple learning and memory systems. In K. M. J. Lagerspetz & P. Niemi (Eds.), *Psychology in the 1990's.* Amsterdam: Elsevier, pp. 163–184.

Tulving, E. 1985. How many memory systems are there? *American Psychologist* 40: 385–398.

Tulving, E. 1993. What is episodic memory? *Current Directions in Psychological Science* 2: 67–70.

Tulving, E., Hayman, C. A. G., & McDonald, C. A. 1991. Long-lasting perceptual priming and semantic learning in amnesia: A case experiment. *Journal of Experimental Psychology: Learning, Memory and Cognition* 17: 595–617.

Tulving, E., Kapur, S., Craik, F. I. M., Moskovitch, M., & Houle, S. 1994a. Hemispheric encoding/retrieval asymmetry in episodic memory: Positron emission tomography findings. *Proceedings of the National Academy of Sciences USA* 91: 2016–2020.

Tulving, E., & Markowitsch, H. J. 1998. Episodic and declarative memory: Role of the hippocampus. *Hippocampus* 8: 198–204.

Tulving, E., Markowitsch, H. J., Kapur, S., Habib, R., & Houle, S. 1994b. Novelty encoding networks in the human brain: Positron emission tomography data. *NeuroReport* 5: 2525–2528.

Tulving, E., & Schacter, D. L. 1990. Priming and human memory systems. *Science* 247: 301–306.

Tulving, E., Schacter, D. L., McLachlin, D. R., & Moscovitch, M. 1988. Priming of semantic autobiographical knowledge: A case study of retrograde amnesia. *Brain and Cognition* 8: 3–20.

Tulving, E., Schacter, D. L., & Stark, H. A. 1982. Priming effects in word-fragment completion are independent of recognition memory. *Journal of Experimental Psychology: Learning, Memory and Cognition* 8: 336–342.

Turner, B. H., & Herkenham, M. 1991. Thalamoamygdaloid projections in the rat: A test of the amygdala's role in sensory processing. *Journal of Comparative Neurology* 313: 295–325.

Ungar, G., Desiderio, D. M., & Parr, W. 1972. Isolation, identification, and synthesis of a specific-behavior-inducing brain peptide. *Nature* 238: 198–202.

Ungerleider, L. G. 1995. Functional brain imaging studies of cortical mechanisms for memory. *Science* 270: 769–775.

Vaadia, E., Haalman, I., Abeles, M., Bergman, H., Prut, Y., Slovin, H., & Aertsen, A. 1995. Dynamics of neuronal interactions in monkey cortex in relation to behavioral events. *Nature* 373: 515–518.

Vallar, G., & Shallice, T. (Eds.). 1990. *Neuropsychological Impairments of Short-Term Memory*. Cambridge: Cambridge University Press.

Vanderwolf, C. H. 1969. Hippocampal electrical activity and voluntary movement in the rat. *Electroencephalography and Clinical Neurophysiology* 26: 407–418.

Vanderwolf, C. H., & Cain, D. P. 1994. The behavioral neurobiology of learning and memory: A conceptual reorientation. *Brain Research Reviews* 19: 264–297.

Van Essen, D. C., Anderson, C. H., & Felleman, D. J. 1992. Information processing in the primate visual system: An integrated systems perspective. *Science* 255: 419–423.

Van Essen, D. C., & Deyoe, E. A. 1995. Concurrent processing in the primate visual cortex. In M. S. Gazzaniga (Ed.), *The Cognitive Neurosciences*. Cambridge, MA: MIT Press, pp. 383–400.

Van Hoesen, G. W. 1982. The parahippocampal gyrus: New observations regarding its cortical connections in the monkey. *Trends in Neurosciences* 5: 345–350.

Van Hoesen, G. W., & Pandya, D. N. 1975. Some connections of the entorhinal (area 28) and perirhinal (area 35) cortices of the rhesus monkey: III. Efferent connections. *Brain Research* 95: 39–59.

Van Hoesen, G. W., Pandya, D. N., & Butters, N. 1972. Cortical afferents to the entorhinal cortex of the rhesus monkey. *Science* 175: 1471–1473.

Vargha-Khadem, F., Gadin, D. G., Watkins, K. E., Connelly, A., Van Paesschen, W., & Mishkin, M. 1997. Differential effects of early hippocampal pathology on episodic and semantic memory. *Science* 277: 376–380.

Vazdarjanova, A., & McGaugh, J. L. 1998. Basolateral amygdala is not critical for cognitive memory of contextual fear conditioning. *Proceedings of the National Academy of Sciences (United States of America)* 95: 15003–15007.

Viaud, M. D., & White, N. M. 1989. Dissociation of visual and olfactory conditioning in the neostriatum of rats. *Behavioral Brain Research* 32: 31–42.

Vinogradova, O. S. 1975. Functional organization of the limbic system in the process of registration of information: Facts and hypothesis. In R. L. Isaacson & K. H. Pribram (Eds.), *The Hippocampus*. New York: Plenum Press.

Vnek, N., Gleason, T. C., Kromer, L. F., & Rothblat, L. A. 1995. Entorhinal-hippocampal connections and object memory in the rat: Acquisition versus retention. *The Journal of Neuroscience* 15: 3193–3199.

Von Bonin, G., & Bailey, P. 1947. *The Neocortex of Maccaca mulatta*. Urbana, IL: University of Illinois Press.

Wagner, A. D., Schacter, D. L., Rotte, M., Koutstaal, W., Maril, A., Dale, A. M., Rosen, B. R., & Buckner, R. L. 1998. Building memories: Remembering and forgetting of verbal experiences as predicted by brain activity. *Science* 281: 1188–1191.

Walker, D. W., Means, L. W., & Issacson, R. I. 1970. The effects of hippocampal and cortical lesions on single alternation go/no go acquisition in rats. *Psychonomic Science* 21: 29–31.

Wallace, C. S., Hawrylak, N., & Greenough, W. T. 1990. Studies of structural modifications after long-term potentiation and kindling: Context for a molecular morphology. In M. L. Baudry & J. L. Davis (Eds.), *Long-Term Potentiation: A Debate of Current Issues*. Cambridge, MA: MIT Press.

Wan, H., Aggleton, J. P., & Malcolm, W. B. 1999. Different contributions of the hippocampus and perirhinal cortex to recognition memory. *The Journal of Neuroscience* 19: 1142–1148.

Wang, G., Tanaka, T., & Tanifuji, M. 1996. Optical imaging of functional organization in the monkey inferotemporal cortex. *Science* 272: 1665–1668.

Warrington, E. K. 1996. Studies of retrograde memory: A long-term view. *Proceedings of the National Academy of Sciences (United States of America)* 93: 13523–13526.

Warrington, E. K., & Weiskrantz, L. 1968. New method for testing long-term retention with special reference to amnesic patients. *Nature* 217: 972–974.

Warrington, E. K., & Weiskrantz, L. 1970. Amnesic syndrome: Consolidation or retrieval? *Nature* 228: 628–630.

Watanabe, M. 1996. Reward expectancy in primate prefrontal neurons. *Nature* 382: 629–632.

Weinberger, N. M. 1993. Learning-induced changes of auditory receptive fields. *Current Opinion in Neurobiology* 3: 570–577.

Weinberger, N. M. 1995a. Dynamic regulation of receptive fields and maps in the adult sensory cortex. *Annual Review of Neuroscience* 18: 129–158.

Weinberger, N. M. 1995b. Retuning the brain by fear conditioning. In M. S. Gazzaniga (Ed.), *The Cognitive Neurosciences*. Cambridge, MA: MIT Press, pp. 1071–1089.

Weinberger, N. M., Ashe, J. H., Metherate, R., McKenna, T. M., Diamond, D. M., & Bakin, J. 1990. Retuning auditory cortex by learning: A preliminary model of receptive field plasticity. *Concepts in Neuroscience* 1: 91–132.

Weinberger, N., Ashe, J., Metherate, R., McKenna, T., Diamond, D., Baking, J., Lennartz, R., & Cassady, J. 1990. Neural adaptive information processing: A preliminary model of receptive-field plasticity in auditory cortex during Pavlovian conditioning. In M. Gabriel & J. Moore (Eds.), *Learning and Computational Neuroscience: Foundations of Adaptive Networks*. Cambridge, MA: MIT Press, pp. 91–138.

Weinberger, N. M., Javid, R., & Lepan, B. 1993. Long-term retention of learning-induced receptive field plasticity in the auditory cortex. *Proceedings of the National Academy of Sciences (United States of America)* 90: 2394–2398.

Weiner, M. J., Hallett, M., & Funkenstein, H. H. 1983. Adaptation to lateral displacement of vision in patients with lesions of the central nervous system. *Neurology* 33: 766–772.

Weiskrantz, L. 1956. Behavioral changes associated with ablation of the amygdaloid complex in monkeys. *Journal of Comparative Physiology* 49: 381–391.

Weiskrantz, L., & Mondadori, C. 1991. MK-801 can facilitate passive avoidance memory when retention is not present in control animals, and can fail to facilitate when it is present. *Psychopharmacology* 105: 145–150.

Weiskrantz, L., & Warrington, E. K. 1979. Conditioning in amnesic patients. *Neuropsychologia* 17: 187–194.

Weisz, D., Clark, G. A., & Thompson, R. F. 1984. Increased responsivity of dentate granule cells during nictitating response conditioning in the rabbit. *Behavioural Brain Research* 12: 145–154.

Welford, A. T. 1968. *Fundamentals of Skill*. London: Methuen.

Welsh, J. P., & Harvey, J. A. 1989. Cerebellare lesions and the nictitating membrane response: Performance deficits of the conditioned and unconditioned response. *The Journal of Neuroscience* 9: 299–311.

Whishaw, I. Q., Cassel, J. C., & Jarrard, L. E. 1995. Rats with fimbria-fornix lesions display a place response in a swimming pool: A dissociation between getting there and knowing where. *The Journal of Neuroscience* 15: 5779–5788.

Whishaw, I. Q., Mittleman, G., Bunch, S. T., & Dunnett, S. B. 1987. Impairments in the acquisition, retention and selection of spatial navigation strategies after medial caudate-putamen lesions in rats. *Behavioural Brain Research* 24: 125–138.

Whishaw, I. Q., & Tomie, J. 1995. Rats with fimbria-fornix lesions can acquire and retain a visual-tactile transwitching (configural) task. *Behavioral Neuroscience* 109: 607–612.

Whishaw, I. Q., & Tomie, J. 1997. Perseveration on place reversals in spatial swimming pool tasks: Further evidence for place learning in hippocampal rats. *Hippocampus* 7: 361–370.

Whishaw, I. Q., Tomie, J., & Kolb, B. 1992. Ventrolateral prefrontal: Cortex lesions in rats impair the acquisition and retention of a tactile-olfactory configural task. *Behavioral Neuroscience* 106: 597–603.

White, N. M. 1997. Mnemonic functions of the basal ganglia. *Current Opinion in Neurobiology* 7: 164–172.

White, N. M., & Ouellet, M. 1997. Roles of movement and temporal factors in spatial learning. *Hippocampus* 7: 511–523.

Wible, C. G., Findling, R. L., Shapiro, M., Lang, E. J., Crane, S., & Olton, D. S. 1986. Mnemonic correlates of unit activity in the hippocampus. *Brain Research* 399: 97–110.

Wickelgren, W. A. 1979. Chunking and consolidation: A theoretical synthesis of semantic networks, configuring in conditioning, S-R versus cognitive learning, normal forgetting, the amnesic syndrome, and the hippocampal arousal system. *Psychological Review* 86: 44–60.

Wiener, S. I., Korshunov, V. A., Garcia, R., & Berthoz, A. 1995. Inertial, substratal and landmark cue control of hippocampal CA1 place cell activity. *European Journal of Neuroscience* 7: 2206–2219.

Wiener, S. I., Paul, C. A., & Eichenbaum, H. 1989. Spatial and behavioral correlates of hippocampal neuronal activity. *The Journal of Neuroscience* 9: 2737–2763.

Wiig, K. A., Cooper, L. N., & Bear, M. F. 1996. Temporally graded retrograde amnesia following separate and combined lesions of the perirhinal cortex and fornix in the rat. *Learning Memory* 3: 315–325.

Willingham, D. B., & Koroshetz, W. J. 1993. Evidence for dissociable motor skills in Huntington's disease patients. *Psychobiology* 21: 173–182.

Wilson, D. A., & Leon, M. 1988. Spatial patterns of olfactory bulb single-unit responses to learned olfactory cues in young rats. *Journal of Neurophysiology* 59: 1770–1782.

Wilson, F. A. W., Scalaidhe, S. P., & Goldman-Rakic, P. S. 1993. Dissociation of object and spatial processing domains in primate prefrontal cortex. *Science* 260: 1955–1958.

Wilson, M., & McNaughton, B. L. 1993. Dynamics of the hippocampal ensemble code for space. *Science* 261: 1055–1058.

Wilson, M. A., & McNaughton, B. L. 1994. Reactivation of hippocampal ensemble memories during sleep. *Science* 265: 676–679.

Winocur, G. 1985. The hippocampus and thalamus: Their roles in short and long-term memory and the effects of interference. *Behavioural Brain Research* 16: 135–152.

Winocur, G. 1990. Anterograde and retrograde amnesia in rats with dorsal hippocampal or dorsomedial thalamic lesions. *Behavioural Brain Research* 38: 145–154.

Winocur, G. 1992. A comparison of normal old rats and young adult rats with lesions to the hippocampus or prefrontal cortex on a test of matching-to-sample. *Neuropsychologia* 30: 769–781.

Winocur, G., & Moscovitch, M. 1999. Anterograde and retrograde amnesia after lesions to frontal cortex in rats. *The Journal of Neuroscience* 19: 9611–9617.

Winocur, G., & Olds, J. 1978. Effects of context manipulation on memory and reversal learning in rats with hippocampal lesions. *Journal of Comparative and Physiological Psychology* 92: 312–321.

Winocur, G., Rawlins, J. N. P., & Gray, J. A. 1987. The hippocampus and conditioning to contextual cues. *Behavioral Neuroscience* 101: 617–625.

Winson, J., & Dahl, D. 1986. Long-term potentiation in dentate gyrus: Induction by asynchronous volleys in separate afferents. *Science* 234: 985–988.

Wise, S. P. 1996a. Evolution of neuronal activity during conditional motor learning. In J. R. Bloedel, T. J. Ebner, & S. P. Wise (Eds.), *The Acquisition of Motor Behavior in Vertebrates.* Cambridge, MA: MIT Press, pp. 261–286.

Wise, S. P. 1996b. The role of the basal ganglia in procedural memory. *Neurosciences* 8: 39–46.

Wise, S. P., & Murray, E. A. 1999. Role of the hippocampal system in conditional motor learning: Mapping antecedents to action. *Hippocampus* 9: 101–117.

Witter, M. P. 1989. Connectivity of the rat hippocampus. In V. Chan-Palay & C. Kohler (Eds.), *The Hippocampus*. New York: Liss, pp. 53–69.

Witter, M. P., Griffioen, A. W., Jorritsma-Byham, B., & Krijnen, J. L. M. 1988. Entorhinal projections to the hippocampal CA1 region in the rat: An underestimated pathway. *Neuroscience Letters* 85: 193–198.

Witter, M. P., Groenewegen, J. J., Lopes da Silva, F. H., & Lohman, A. H. M. 1989. Functional organization of the extrinsic and intrinsic circuitry of the parahippocampal region. *Progress in Neurobiology* 33: 162–243.

Witter, M. P., Room, P., Groenewegen, H. J., & Lohman, A. H. M. 1986. Connections of the perihippocampal cortex in the cat: V. Intrinsic connections; Comments on input/output connections with the hippocampus. *Journal of Neurology* 252: 78–94.

Wood, E. R., Dudchenko, P. A., & Eichenbaum, H. 1999. The global record of memory in hippocampal neuronal activity. *Nature* 397: 613–616.

Woodruff-Pak, D. S. 1993. Eyeblink classical conditioning in H.M.: Delay and trace paradigms. *Behavioral Neuroscience* 107: 911–925.

Woodruff-Pak, D. S. 1997. Classical conditioning. *International Review of Neurobiology* 41: 341–366.

Woodruff-Pak, D. S., Papka, M., & Ivry, R. B. 1996. Cerebellar involvement in eyeblink classical conditioning in humans. *Neuropsychology* 10: 443–458.

Woody, C. D. 1986. Understanding the cellular basis of memory and learning. *Annual Review of Psychology* 37: 433–493.

Woody, C. D. 1996. Control of motor behavior acquisition by cortical activity potentiated by decreases in a potassium A-current that increase neural excitability. In J. R. Bloedel, T. J. Ebner, & S. P. Wise (Eds.), *The Acquisition of Motor Behavior in Vertebrates*. Cambridge, MA: MIT Press, pp. 205–222.

Wyss, J. M. 1981. An autoradiographic study of the efferent connections of the entorhinal cortex in the rat. *Journal of Comparative Neurology* 199: 495–512.

Xiang, J. Z., & Brown, M. W. 1998. Differential neuronal encoding of novelty, familiarity and recency in regions of the anterior temporal lobe. *Neuropharmarmacology* 37: 657–676.

Xu, L., Anwyl, R., & Rowan, M. J. 1998. Spatial exploration induces a persistent reversal of long-term potentiation in rat hippocampus. *Nature* 394: 891–894.

Yamane, S., Kaji, S., & Kawano, K. 1988. What facial features activate face neurons in the inferotemporal cortex of the monkey? *Experimental Brain Research* 73: 209–214.

Yee, B. K., & Rawlins, J. N. P. 1994. The effects of hippocampal formation ablation or fimbria-fornix section on performance of a nonspatial radial arm maze task by rats. *The Journal of Neuroscience* 14: 3766–3774.

Yerkes, R. M. 1916. The mental life of monkeys and apes. *Behavior Monographs, 3*.

Young, A. W., Aggleton, J. P., Hellawell, D. J., Johnson, M., Broks, P., & Hanley, J. R. 1995. Face processing impairments after amygdalotomy. *Brain* 118: 15–24.

Young, B. J., Otto, T., Fox, G. D., & Eichenbaum, H. 1997. Memory representation within the parahippocampal region. *The Journal of Neuroscience* 17: 5183–5195.

Young, M. P., & Yamane, S. 1992. Sparse population coding of faces in the inferotemporal cortex. *Science* 256: 1327–1331.

Young, S. L., Bohenek, D. L., & Fanselow, M. S. 1994. NMDA processes mediate anterograde amnesia of contextual fear conditioning induced by hippocampal damage: Immunization against amnesia by context preexposure. *Behavioral Neuroscience* 108: 19–29.

Zajonc, R. B. 1980. Feeling and thinking: Preferences need no inferences. *American Psychologist* 35: 547–563.

Zalutsky, R. A., & Nicoll, R. A. 1990. Comparison of two forms of long-term potentiation in single hippocampal neurons. *Science* 248: 1619–1624.

Zhou, Y., & Fuster, J. M. 1992. Unit discharge in monkey's parietal cortex during perception and mnemonic retention of tactile features. *Society for Neuroscience Abstracts* 18: 706.

Zhu, X. O., & Brown, M. W. 1995. Changes in neuronal activity related to the repetition and relative familiarity of visual stimuli in rhinal and adjacent cortex of the anaesthetised rat. *Brain Research* 689: 101–110.

Zhu, X. O., Brown, M. W., & Aggleton, J. P. 1995a. Neuronal signalling of information important to visual recognition memory in rat rhinal and neighbouring cortices. *The Journal of Neuroscience* 7: 753–765.

Zhu, X. O., Brown, M. W., McCabe, B. J., & Aggleton, J. P. 1995b. Effects of the novelty or familiarity of visual stimuli on the expression of the immediate early gene c-fos in rat brain. *Neuroscience* 69: 821–829.

Zhu, X. O., McCabe, B. J., Aggleton, J. P., & Brown, M. W. 1997. Differential activation of the hippocampus and perirhinal cortex by novel visual stimuli and a novel environment. *Neuroscience Letters* 229: 141–143.

Zola, S. M., & Mahut, H. 1973. Paradoxical facilitation of object reversal learning after transection of the fornix in monkeys. *Neuropsychologia* 11: 271–284.

Zola, S. M., Squire, L. R., Teng, E., Stefanacci, L., & Clark, R. E. (2000) Impaired recognition memory in monkeys after damage limited to the hippocampal region. *The Journal of Neuroscience* 20: 451–463.

Zola-Morgan, S. 1995. Localization of brain function: The legacy of Franz Joseph Gall (1758–1828). *Annual Review of Neuroscience* 18: 359–383.

Zola-Morgan, S., & Squire, L. R. 1984. Preserved learning in monkeys with medial temporal lesions: Sparing of motor and cognitive skills. *The Journal of Neuroscience* 4: 1072–1085.

Zola-Morgan, S., & Squire, L. R. 1985. Medial temporal lesions in monkeys impair memory on a variety of tasks sensitive to human amnesia. *Behavioral Neuroscience* 99: 22–34.

Zola-Morgan, S., & Squire, L. R. 1990. The primate hippocampal formation: Evidence for a time-limited role in memory storage. *Science* 250: 288–290.

Zola-Morgan, S., & Squire, L. R. 1992. The components of the medial temporal lobe memory system: In L. R. Squire & N. Butters (Eds.), *Neuropsychology of Memory* (2nd Ed.). New York: Guilford Press, pp. 325–335.

Zola-Morgan, S., Squire, L. R., Alvarez-Royo, P., & Clower, R. P. 1991. Independence of memory functions and emotional behavior: Separate contributions of the hippocampal formation and amygdala. *Hippocampus* 1: 207–220.

Zola-Morgan, S., Squire, L. R., & Amaral, D. G. 1989a. Lesions of the hippocampal formation but not lesions of the fornix or the mammillary nuclei produce long-lasting memory impairment in monkeys. *The Journal of Neuroscience* 9: 897–912.

Zola-Morgan, S., Squire, L. R., & Amaral, D. G. 1989b. Lesions of the amygdala that spare adjacent cortical regions do not impair memory or exacerbate the impairment following lesions of the hippocampal formation. *The Journal of Neuroscience* 9: 1922–1936.

Zola-Morgan, S., Squire, L. R., Amaral, D. G., & Suzuki, W. 1989c. Lesions of perirhinal and parahippocampal cortex that spare the amygdala and the hippocampal formation produce severe memory impairment. *The Journal of Neuroscience* 9: 4355–4370.

Zola-Morgan, S., Squire, L. R., Clower, R. P., & Rempel, N. L. 1993. Damage to the perirhinal cortex exacerbates memory impairment following lesions to the hippocampal formation. *The Journal of Neuroscience* 13: 251–265.

Zola-Morgan, S., Squire, L. R., & Ramus, S. J. 1994. Severity of memory impairment in monkeys as a function of locus and extent of damage within the medial temporal lobe memory system. *Hippocampus* 4: 483–495.

Zola-Morgan, S., Squire, L. R., Rempel, N. L., Clower, R. P., & Amaral, D. G. 1992. Enduring memory impairment in monkeys after ischemic damage to the hippocampus. *The Journal of Neuroscience* 12: 2582–2596.

Index